Index
to
Loudoun County, Virginia
Land Deed Books
3E-3M
1822-1826

Patrici

WILLOW BEND BOOKS
2006

WILLOW BEND BOOKS
AN IMPRINT OF HERITAGE BOOKS, INC.

Books, CDs, and more—Worldwide

For our listing of thousands of titles see our website
at
www.HeritageBooks.com

Published 2006 by
HERITAGE BOOKS, INC.
Publishing Division
65 East Main Street
Westminster, Maryland 21157-5026

International Standard Book Number: 978-0-7884-3559-0

Introduction

The following is an extended index to Loudoun County, Virginia Land Deed Books 3E-3M. In addition to providing the basic information of book:page number, parties involved, and type of document, I have also included the date of the document, the date recorded in court, a brief description of the item, including adjoining neighbors, and witnesses.

Microfilms of these records are currently available from the Library of Virginia Interlibrary Loan Service. Copies of the documents may be obtained from the Office of Clerk of Circuit Court County of Loudoun, Box 550, Leesburg, VA 20178-0550.

Abbreviations:
Admr - Administrator
A/L – Assignment of lease
AlexDC – Alexandria, District of Columbia
B/S – Bargain and sale
BaltMd – Baltimore, Maryland
beq. - bequeathed
BerkVa – Berkeley County, Virginia
BoS - Bill of sale
br/o – brother of
CamP – Cameron Parish in Loudoun
ChstrPa – Chester County, Pennsylvania
CoE - Certificate of examination [of wife]
CoI – certificate of importation [for slaves]
Commr - commissioner
cnvy/b – cnvy/b (to person now selling the land)
dau – daughter
DBk letter(s):numbers - deed book:page
delv. – examined and delivered to
dev. – devised to
div. – division (of estate of)
d/o - daughter of
DoE – Deed of Emancipation [for slaves]
Exor – Executor
Ffx – Fairfax County, Virginia
Fqr – Fauquier County, Virginia
FrdkMd – Frederick County, Maryland
FrdkVa – Frederick County, Virginia
Gent. – gentleman
h/o - husband of
HdnNJ – Hunterdon County, New Jersey
Hllb - Hillsborough
int. - interest

KingG – King George County, Virginia
L/L – Lease for life
L/R – Lease/release
Ldn – Loudoun County, Virginia
Lsbg - Leesburg
Mdbg – Middleburg
MontMd – Montgomery County, Maryland
[number]a = number of acres
PhilPa – Philadelphia County, Pa
PoA – Power of attorney
PrG – Prince George County, Maryland
PrWm – Prince William County, Virginia
prch/o – purchase(d) of
RichVa – Richmond County, Virginia
RtCt – returned to court and ordered to be recorded
S/L – Surrender of lease
s/o - son of
ShelP – Shelburne Parish in Loudoun
StafVa – Stafford County, Virginia
und. - und.
w/o - wife of
WashDC – Washington, D. C.
WashMd – Washington County, Maryland
wd/o – widow of
WstmVa – Westmoreland County, Virginia

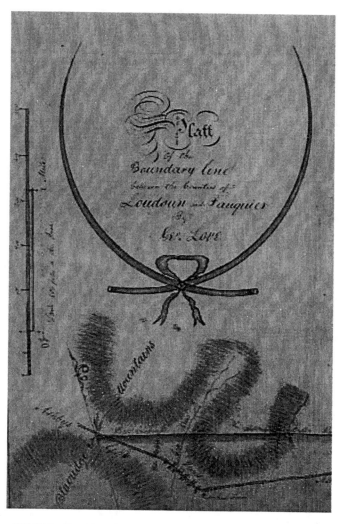

3M:328 - Portion of Loudoun and Fauquier Boundary Plat

Deed Books 3E-3M

3E:001   Date: 5 Nov 1821   RtCt: 11 Mar 1822
John H. CASSADAY to George W. HENRY. Trust for debt to
Sanford RAMEY and Saml. McPHERSON using negro man Isaac.
Wit: Isaac THOMAS, Saml. SMITH, Alex'r CORDELL. Delv. to S. J.
RAMEY per order 18 Feb 1823.

3E:002   Date: 1 Jan 1822   RtCt: 11 Mar 1822
Lewis ELLZEY of Ldn to Thomas GREGG of Ldn. B/S of 2a below
Gregg's Mill dam.

3E:004   Date: 12 Sep 1820   RtCt: 11 Mar 1822
David LOVETT of Ldn to John GOWER of Ldn. B/S of 10a (prch/o
Edmond J. LEE of Alexandria) adj John MOORE, John BOOTH Sr.
Wit: Noble S. BRADEN, John GEORGE, Aaron BOOTH. Delv. to
John SHOVER who has prch/o GOWER's heirs 4 Jun 1832.

3E:005   Date: 9 Mar 1822   RtCt: 11 Mar 1822
John HUTCHISON & wife Keren of Ldn to son Thomas
HUTCHISON of Ldn. Gift of 133a at fork of Bull Run. Wit: Charles
LEWIS, Thomas DARNE.

3E:007   Date: 9 Mar 1822   RtCt: 11 Mar 1822
Enoch HUTCHISON & wife Abigail of Ldn to Dean JAMES of Ldn.
B/S of int. in landed estate of William JAMES dec'd and widow's
dower. Wit: Thomas DARNE, Charles LEWIS, Lewis AMBLAR. Delv.
to JAMES 25 Aug 1823.

3E:008   Date: 1 Feb 1822   RtCt: 11 Mar 1822
Joseph HOUGH of Ldn to Thomas NICHOLS of Ldn. Trust for debt
to Abel JANNEY of Ldn using 6a (prch/o Thomas SANDS) where
HOUGH now lives. Wit: Asa ROGERS, James M. JANNEY, Nancy
C. JANNEY. Delv. to A. JANNEY 4 May 1824.

3E:010   Date: 8 Mar 1822   RtCt: 11 Mar 1822
Elias THRASHER of Ldn to Thomas J. MARLOW of Ldn. Trust for
debt to John S. MARLOW and Edward MARLOW of Ldn using
275a. Wit: Geo. MARLOW, E. G. HAMILTON, Thomas A. MOORE.

3E:011   Date: 10 Feb 1822   RtCt: 11 Mar 1822
Calvin THATCHER of Ldn to Mahlon PURSELL of Ldn. B/S of land
where THATCHER now lives that Richard THATCHER dec'd leased
for 3y. Wit: L. ELLZEY, Samuel PURSEL, Thomas GREGG, Edwin
PURSEL. Delv. to PURCELL 20 Dec 1823.

3E:013   Date: 22 Feb 1822   RtCt: 11 Mar 1822
Elias THRASHER of Ldn to William HILLEARY of FredMd. Trust for
debt to HILLEARY using 123a adj Peter HICKMAN, Adam SHOVER

...ö8a adj George SHAVER. Wit: Perry HILLEARY, John H. HILLEARY, Chas. B. McGILL.

3E:016 Date: 12 Feb 1822 RtCt: 11 Mar 1822
John TAYLOR of Ldn to Isaac NICHOLS Jr of Ldn. Trust for debt to Samuel & Isaac NICHOLS using 94a nr Fairfax Meeting House, adj William WRIGHT, John A. BINNS. Wit: James BRANDON, John COLLINS, William C. RAGAN. Delv. to Isaac NICHOLS Exors 10 Nov 1825.

3E:018 Date: 9 Mar 1822 RtCt: 11 Mar 1822
William H. LANE of Ffx to Benjamin BRIDGES of Ldn. B/S of int. in und. 'two sister's tract' (as heir of Hardage LANE dec'd). Wit: W. H. DORSEY, Henry G. SHELL, Newton KEEN, James HORSEMAN.

3E:019 Date: 28 Aug 1821 RtCt: 11 Mar 1822
John WILLIAMS & wife Lydia of Ldn to John MORROW of Ldn. B/S of ¼a Lot #51 in Wtfd. Wit: Abiel JENNERS, Saml. HOUGH Jr.

3E:021 Date: 10 Feb 1821 RtCt: 22 Aug 1821/11 Mar 1822
George B. WHITING of Ldn to Robert H. LITTLE of PrWm. Trust for benefit of Francis Henry WHITING (s/o of George B.) until age 21y using negro boy Marlow [or Marton] abt 14y old and farm animals until Francis H. WHITING becomes 21y old. (WHITING sold to Fuel PERRY of Ffx a negro boy Hampton {had been bequeathed to Francis H. with directions to bind negro to trade} for benefit of Francis H.) Wit: William HARRISON, Wm. McPHERSON.

3E:022 Date: 2 Mar 1822 RtCt: 12 Mar 1822
Thomas A. DENNIS & wife Lettice of Ldn to Townsend McVEIGH of Ldn. B/S of 91¼a where DENNIS now lives (Lot #1 allotted by John SINCLAIR Feb 1812). Wit: Abner GIBSON, William NOLAND. Delv. to McVEIGH 23 Jun 1822.

3E:025 Date: 2 Mar 1822 RtCt: 12 Mar 1822
Thomas A. DENNIS & wife Lettice of Ldn to William A. DENNIS of Ldn. B/S of 91¼a on Wancopin branch of Goose Creek. Wit: Samuel DENNIS, Absalom DENNIS, John RUSSELL, Abner GIBSON, Wm. NOLAND. Delv. to W. A. DENNIS 3 Apr 1822.

3E:027 Date: 1 Mar 1822 RtCt: 12 Mar 1822
William A. DENNIS & wife Kitty of Ldn to Thomas A. DENNIS of Ldn. B/S of land previously purchased jointly of George BALY. Wit: Samuel DENNIS, Absalom DENNIS, John RUSSELL, Abner GIBSON, William NOLAND.

3E:028 Date: 21 Feb 1822 RtCt: 12 Mar 1822
James T. RUST of Ldn to Townsend McVEIGH of Ldn. Trust for Mandly T. RUST as security on bond in executions by Noble BEVERIDGE, Saml. CARR using lot in Aldie. Wit: Hiram McVEIGH, H. B. LOWELL, Benj. SMITH. Delv. to McVEIGH 24 Jun 1822.

3E:030 Date: 20 Nov 1821 RtCt: 12 Mar 1822
George M. GRAYSON of Ldn to Benjamin GRAYSON. Trust to Ben.
GRAYSON (note of Nov 1819 to John H. BUTCHER with
GRAYSON as bail in suit) using crops, farm animals and items.
Delv. to Geo. M. GRAYSON 7 Sep 1829.

3E:032 Date: 14 Mar 1822 RtCt: 16 Mar 1822
Joseph H. WRIGHT & wife Mary of Ldn to Emanuel WALTMAN of
Ldn. B/S of 11a Lot #4 in plat for Ferd. FAIRFAX (cnvy/b John
WINNER and Jacob WALTMAN in Feb 1822) on E side of short hill
nr N end. Wit: Abiel JENNERS, Saml. HOUGH Jr. Delv. to
WALTMAN 24 May 1823.

3E:034 Date: 21 Mar 1822 RtCt: 21 Mar 1822
Joseph C. WRIGHT of Ldn to Abiel JENNERS of Ldn. B/S of 103a
and 31a (purchased by William WRIGHT dec'd f/o Joseph C. from
Moses CALDWELL in 1796 and the second prch/o Anthony
CONNARD in Jun 1811). Delv. to JENNERS 24 Jan 1823.

3E:035 Date: 15 Feb 1822 RtCt: 22 Mar 1822
John W. GRAYSON of Ldn to Benjamin GRAYSON. B/S for farm
animals, farm and household items. (John W. bound as security on
notes to Joseph JANNEY of Alexandria, Joshua B. OVERFIELD,
Lewis P. W. BALCH, John H. BUTCHER, Hugh SMITH.) Wit: Jno. L.
GILL, Benj. GRAYSON Jr., Geo. M. GRAYSON, Alex. C.
GRAYSON. Delv. to G. M. GRAYSON 7 Sep 1829.

3E:038 Date: 11 Mar 1821 RtCt: 12 Aug 1821/23 Mar 1822
Maria P. HARRISON of Ldn to James ALLEN of Ldn. B/S of 9a adj
ALLEN. Wit: Burr W. HARRISON, Henry T. HARRISON, Wm. W.
ELLZEY.

3E:039 Date: 1 Mar 1822 RtCt: 25 Mar 1822
John IDEN & wife Hannah of Ldn to H. B. POWELL of Ldn. Trust for
debt to Burr POWELL (Exor of Leven POWELL dec'd) using,
Stephen McGEATH ass'ee of W. H.HANDY using 125a on Goose
Creek adj Isaac GOCHNORER. Delv. pr order 24 Sep 1827.

3E:041 Date: 7 Mar 1822 RtCt: 25 Mar 1822
Burr POWELL & wife Catherine of Ldn to Benjamin MOFFETT of
Ldn. B/S of part of Lot #16 in Mdbg leaving other part held by
Nelson GREEN still liable for rents (Amos JOHNSON & wife Sarah
conveyed to Benjamin MOFFETT part of Lot #16 in Mdbg with
annual rents reserved to Burr POWELL). Wit: A. GIBSON, Burr
WEEKS, John KEENE, H. B. POWELL, Cuthbert POWELL. Delv. to
MOFFETT 11 Sep 1846.

3E:043 Date: 25 Mar 1822 RtCt: 25 Mar 1822
James SPEAKS of Ldn to Cephus HANKS. BoS for farm animals,
farm and household items. Wit: S. HOUGH Jr. Daniel GOODING.

3E:044   Date: 25 Mar 1822   RtCt: 25 Mar 1822
Gabriel MEGEATH & wife Martha of Ldn to Isaac NICHOLS and
James HOGUE of Ldn. Trust for debt to Samuel & Isaac NICHOLS
using 116a adj snigger's gap turnpike road. Wit: John McCORMICK,
James H. HAMILTON. Delv. to Saml. NICHOL's Exors. 10 Nov
1825.

3E:047   Date: 20 Mar 1822   RtCt: 25 Mar 1822
Conrad WERTS & wife Elizabeth of Ldn to David WIRE of Ldn. B/S
of 2a and Sanford RAMEY, Frederick COOPER. Wit; Samuel M.
EDWARDS, Robert BRADEN. Delv. to WIRE 24 May 1823.

3E:049   Date: 21 Mar 1822   RtCt: 25 Mar 1822
George REED of Ldn to David LOVETT of Ldn. Trust for debt to
Craven OSBURN using farm animals and household items. Wit:
Jane NEER, Lettie EDMONSON.

3E:051   Date: 26 Mar 1822   RtCt: 26 Mar 1822
Richard H. HENDERSON of Ldn to William NOLAND of Ldn.
Release of trust for Thomas SWANN and Robt. J. TAYLOR of
Alexandria as security to Farmers Bank.

3E:052   Date: 22 Sep 1821   RtCt: 27 Mar 1822
Wilson C. SELDON & wife Mary B. of Ldn to Barnett HOUGH of
Lsbg. B/S of 181a on Tuskarora held under lease by SELDON of
Geo. CARTER. Wit: Richard H. HENDERSON, Thomas A. MOORE,
Benjamin SHREVE, John McCORMICK, James H. HAMILTON.

3E:055   Date: __ Aug 1819   RtCt: 28 Mar 1822
Joseph CARR of Ldn to Thomas FRANCIS. Release of trust for debt
to Jacob LEWIS. Wit: Cuthbert POWELL.

3E:057   Date: 17 Aug 1821   RtCt: 28 Mar 1822
Harrison FITZHUGH & wife Ann Carr of Ffx to Deputy Francis M.
BECKWITH. Trust for debts to David OGDEN and William H. LANE
using lot and house in Lsbg former property of LANE. Wit: Rich'd
Henry LEE, Edw'd HAMMATT, Josiah L. DREAN.

3E:059   Date: 23 Apr 1821   RtCt: 29 Mar 1822
Lewis HUNT & wife Mary of Union to Josias M. CLARKE of Union.
B/S of ¼a Lot #4 in Union (cnvy/b Michael PLASTER). Wit: John
WEADON, Joseph MERCER, James SUTHERD, Wm.
BRONAUGH, Francis W. LUCKETT.

3E:060   Date: 11 Mar 1822   RtCt: 29 Mar 1822
Benjamin RUSSELL of Belmont Co Ohio to Samuel RUSSELL of
Ldn. B/S of 1/12th int. in 122a (from father Thomas RUSSELL dec'd).

3E:062   Date: 18 Mar 1822   RtCt: 29 Mar 1822
Neal RUSSELL of Ldn to Samuel RUSSELL of Ldn. B/S of 1/12th int.
in 122a (from father Thomas RUSSELL dec'd). Delv. pr order 29 Jul
1822.

3E:063 Date: 13 Dec 1821 RtCt: 29 Mar 1822
Jonathan CARTER & wife Elizabeth of Ldn to Gainer PIERCE. B/S of 87½a on N side of Goose Creek on old road from Snicker's Gap and nr Johnston's ford. Wit: Wm. BRONAUGH, Francis W. LUCKETT. Delv. to PIERCE 2 Jul 1822.

3E:065 Date: 13 Dec 1821 RtCt: 29 Mar 1822
Jonathan CARTER & wife Elizabeth of Ldn to Gainer PIERCE of Ohio. B/S of 26a on N side of Goose Creek on Snicker's Gap Turnpike Road. Wit: William BRONAUGH, Francis W. LUCKETT. Delv. to PIERCE 2 Jul 1822.

3E:067 Date: 14 Dec 1821 RtCt: 29 Mar 1822
Gainer PIERCE of Ohio to William J. BRONAUGH of Ldn. Trust for debt to Jonathan CARTER using 87½a on No side of Goose Creek. Delv. to CARTER 25 Jun 1824.

3E:069 Date: 27 Dec 1821 RtCt: 29 Mar 1822
John WEADON & wife Margaret of Ldn to Willis TRIPLETT of Ldn. B/S of ½a lot in Union adj __ DUNKIN, __ GALLEHER. Wit: Wm. BRONAUGH, Francis W. LUCKETT.

3E:070 Date: 28 Mar 1822 RtCt: 29 Mar 1822
Francis M. BECKWITH (trustee of Harrison FITZHUGH) to David OGDEN of Lsbg. B/S of house and lot in Lsbg. Delv. to OGDEN 16 Dec 1828.

3E:071 Date: 13 May 1820 RtCt: 11 Mar 1822
Samuel GREGG & wife Hannah of Ldn to Henry BROWN of Ldn. LS of 50a where William CARTER resides, adj John WRIGHT, Grace FOX, Patrick McINTIRE, school house lot. Wit: Jno. M. MONROE, Abraham SKILLMAN, John WRIGHT.

3E:073 Date: 27 Mar 1822 RtCt: 1 Apr 1822
John JANNEY & wife Susan of Ldn to Andrew OGDEN of Ldn. B/S of 97¾a (cnvy/b Aaron MILLER & wife Rachel). Wit: Abiel JENNERS, Samuel HOUGH Jr. Delv. to George SHAWEN pr order 11 Feb 1827.

3E:075 Date: 27 Nov 1821 RtCt: 1 Apr 1822
Charles Fenton MERCER of Aldie to James SWART and sons James Jr. and Manley SWART an infant of Ldn. B/S of 112a on Bull Run Mt and Barton's branch (prch/o James TORBERT & wife) adj Jonathan CARTER, Owen SULLIVAN, Matthew RUST. Delv. to Jos. SWART pr G. B. WHITING 12 Sep 1822

3E:078 Date: 27 Nov 1821 RtCt: 1 Apr 1822
Charles Fenton MERCER of Aldie to Burr POWELL. Trust for debt to James SWART using 30a. Mentions trust by MERCER to uncle of James TORBERT living in Pa. Delv. to Jas. SWART 10 Jun 1833.

3E:080 Date: 11 Feb 1822 RtCt: 1 Apr 1822
William NOLAND & wife Catharine of Aldie to James SWART and John SWART of Ldn. B/S of 166a adj Thomas ASBERRY, Jeremiah

FOSTER and 20a. Wit: Robert ARMISTEAD, Francis W. LUCKETT. Delv. to Jas. SWART 23 Apr 1833.

3E:082   Date: 18 May 1820   RtCt: 11 Mar 1822
Samuel GREGG of Ldn to James CRAIG of Ldn. Trust for safety of Henry BROWN (GREGG leased a lot to BROWN for 10y period, William WILKINSON a former proprietor threatens suit to regain property) using 113a. Wit: John M. MONROE, Abraham SKILLMAN, John WRIGHT. Delv. to Hugh ROGERS Admr of James CRAIG dec'd 29 Apr 1824.

3E:085   Date: 2 Apr 1822   RtCt: 2 Apr 1822
William GILMORE of Ldn to Joshua RILEY of Lsbg. Release of trust of Jan 1821 for debt to Samuel BUCK (DBk BBB:370). Wit: J. A. BINNS.

3E:086   Date: 25 Mar 1822   RtCt: 5 Apr 1822
John MINES of Ldn to William CHILTON of Ldn. B/S of 2a (prch/o late David LACEY) adj John McCORMICK.

3E:087   Date: 15 Apr 1822   RtCt: 5 Apr 1822
Elias HUGHES of Ldn to Thomas HUGHES of Ldn. B/S of 6a (purchased jointly of Abigale SANDS & Henry LONG in Nov 1811). Delv. pr order 28 Nov 1823.

3E:089   Date: 15 Apr 1822   RtCt: 5 Apr 1822
Thomas HUGHES of Ldn to Elias HUGHES of Ldn. B/S of 69a (purchased jointly of Giles CRAVEN in Sept 1810). Delv. to Elias HUGHES 4 Oct 1822.

3E:090   Date: 21 Mar 1822   RtCt: 5 Apr 1822.
Peter and James MOORE of Wtfd to Robert BRADEN of Wtfd. B/S of house & lot in Wtfd (from trust of Margaret HIXSON in March 1820 to MOORE) adj __ SMALWOOD, Richard CHILTON. Delv. to BRADEN 23 Sep 1825.

3E:092   Date: 5 Apr 1822   RtCt: 5 Apr 1822
William PAXSON & wife Jane of Ldn to John PAXSON of Ldn. B/S of 105a (part of tract prch/o heirs of William HIXSON dec'd) adj Jno. A. BINNS, Joseph JANNEY. Wit: Robert BRADEN, Samuel HOUGH Jr. Delv. to John PAXSON 2 Apr 1824.

3E:094   Date: 15 Feb 1822   RtCt: 8 Apr 1822
William TAYLOR now of Gurnsey Co OH to Francis STRIBLING of Ldn. Trust for Timothy TAYLOR as security using 1a (prch/o Thomas HUMPHREY). Wit: Jas. M. BELL, Wm. CLARKE.

3E:096   Date: 6 Apr 1822   RtCt: 6 Apr 1822
John MINES and John A. BINNS. Agreement – MINES sells BINNS 20a S of Lsbg adj James RUST with BINNS giving bonds to pay annual amt w/o int. and take immediate possession.

3E:097   Date: 26 Apr 1822   RtCt: 27 Apr 1822
James SIMPSON of Ldn to H. B. POWELL of Ldn. Trust for debt to
Noble BEVERIDGE and Aquilla GLASSCOCK using slaves Sam,
David, Isaac, Madison, Henry and Nancy.

3E:099   Date: 23 Apr 1822   RtCt: 26 Apr 1822
James RUST Jr. of Ldn to Joel OSBURN of Ldn. Trust for debt to
Morris OSBURN using 322a (cnvy/b Jos. CALDWELL Dec 1819) adj
__ MILHOLLIN, A. T. MASON.

3E:101   Date: 12 Jan 1822   RtCt: 14 Jan 1822
Eli McKNIGHT of Ldn to Thomas NICHOLS of Ldn. Trust for debt to
Abel JANNEY using 50a adj Issachar BROWN. Wit: David JAMES,
Timothy TAYLOR, James HILL. Delv. to JANNEY 4 May 1824.

3E:103   Date: 16 Mar 1822   RtCt: 8 Apr 1822
Thomas PHILLIPS to Peter SANDERS. Release of trust for John
SANDERS and George SANDERS of Apr 1816 of 119a.

3E:105   Date: 17 Jan 1822   RtCt: 8 Apr 1822
Geo. B. WHITING to Richard B. BUCKNER and Robt. BAYLY. Trust
for Ariss BUCKNER as endorser using int. in slaves Fanny & her
son John, Billy weaver, and George the smith, and tools and
household items. Wit: Murphey SHUMATE, Rich'd B. HOMER.

3E:106   Date: 1 Jan 1822   RtCt: 8 Apr 1822
William HANN & wife Mary of Ldn to John J. HARDING (President of
the board of Overseers of the Poor of Ldn - Aaron SANDERS,
James MOORE, Joseph DANIEL, James COCHRAN, Seth SMITH,
David LEWIS, George B. WHITING and John DULIN). B/S of 50a
adj Joseph BURSON, Peter HANN, John BURSON, Mathias HANN,
George MARKS. Wit: William BRONAUGH, Francis W. LUCKETT.

3E:108   Date: 1 Jan 1822   RtCt: 8 Apr 1822
William H. DORSEY & wife Judith of Ldn to John J. HARDING
(President of the board of Overseers of the Poor of Ldn - Aaron
SANDERS, James MOORE, Joseph DANIEL, James COCHRAN,
Seth SMITH, David LEWIS, George B. WHITING and John DULIN).
B/S of 154a adj Joseph BURSON, Jonathan BURSON. Wit: William
BRONAUGH, Francis W. LUCKETT. Delv. to Saml. M. EDWARDS
an overseer 15 Feb 1831.

3E:111   Date: __ 1822   RtCt: 8 Apr 1822
Bennett MARKS of Ldn to John C. BAZZIL of FredVa. B/S of 12a.

3E:112   Date: 27 Mar 1822   RtCt: 8 Apr 1822
John JANNEY & wife Susan of Ldn to Sanford RAMEY of Ldn. B/S
of 9a (prch/o Zorobable WELLS Apr 1817) adj RAMEY, Michael
COOPER. Wit: Abiel JENNERS, Saml. HOUGH Jr.

3E:114   Date: 15 Dec 1821   RtCt: 8 Apr 1822
John H. CASADA(Y) to Alexr. CORDELL and John E. PALMER of
Ldn. Trust for debts to Sanford RAMEY, John MYERS using 384a
adj Wm. WRIGHT, __ THOMPSON, __ JANNEY, __ MATHEWS,

Stephen DANIEL. Wit: Saml. E. HENDERSON, John CURTIS, George LEAMING   Delv. RAMEY pr order 18 Feb 1823.

3E:117   Date: 21 Mar 1822   RtCt: 9 Apr 1822
Thomas STEVENS & wife Ann H. of Ldn to Philip FRY of Ldn. B/S of 72a adj James McDANIEL, Catocton Creek. Wit: Robt. BRADEN, Abiel JENNERS. Delv. to J. G. KERNER h/o Cath'e KERNER under will of P. FRYE on __.

3E:119   Date: 10 Apr 1822   RtCt: 10 Apr 1822
John CRIDLER & wife Elizabeth of Ldn to John A. BINNS of Lsbg. Trust for debt to Jesse RICE using 1a and 1/6th of land is within new addition to Lsbg (prch/o John LITTLEJOHN, DBk WW:415). Wit: Presley CORDELL, Thomas SANDERS.

3E:120   Date: 13 Apr 1822   RtCt: 13 Apr 1822
John Alexander BINNS and Samuel M. EDWARDS to Henry STEVENS & wife Eleanor. Release of trust for debt to George KILGORE. Wit: Geo. RICHARDS, Ann B. RICHARDS. Delv. to STEVENS 12 Nov 1823.

3E:121   Date: 15 Apr 1822   RtCt: 16 Apr 1822
John JACKSON (Exor of John JACKSON dec'd) of Ldn to Benjamin SHREVE of Ldn. B/S of 197a (prch/o Peter R. BEVERLY & wife Lovely Aug 1811) adj Peter STONE, Charles CRIM, George SHOMAKER, Wm. BAKER. Delv. to SHREVE 7 Apr 1824.

3E:123   Date: 1 Aug 1821   RtCt: 17 Apr 1822
Richard HIRST & wife Elizabeth of Ldn to David SMITH and Daniel JAMES of Ldn. Trust for James BRADFIELD jointly bound with HIRST in debt for benefit of Thomas George and Thomas assignees of Geo. JANNEY and bound with Jesse HIRST as security for Richard using 60a (cnvy/b Thomas PRICE) on NW fork of Goose Creek. Delv. to Jesse HIRST 23 Mar 1825.

3E:126   Date: 17 Nov 1821   RtCt: 13 May 1822
Jacob HOUSER & wife Abigail, Adam MILLER & wife Elizabeth and Cephus HANKS of Ldn and Jeremiah HANKS & wife Catharine and Stiles HANKS & wife Ann of Muskingum Co Oh (heirs at large of Zedock HANKS dec'd) to Aaron MILLER of Ldn. B/S of 25a (cnvy/b Peter SAUNDERS to Abigail HOUSER in trust for heirs of John HANKS dec'd) on E side of Short Hill. Wit: Jacob SHIVELY, John WILLIAMSON, Robert BRADEN, Saml. HOUGH Jr. Delv. to MILLER 7 Mar 1823.

3E:130   Date: 24 Apr 1822   RtCt: 25 Apr 1822
Joseph STUMP of Ldn to John MANN of Ldn. B/S of 103a (allotted from land of Thomas STUMP dec'd) nr Potomac River adj __ WINNER. Wit: Aaron BOOTH, Samuel BRISCOE, Wm. COSST [COST], Jno. MOORE. Delv. to MANN 25 Feb 1825.

3E:131   Date: 23 Apr 1822   RtCt: 27 Apr 1822
Benjamin GRAYSON & wife Nancy of Ldn to Isaac NICHOLS and
James HOGUE of Ldn. Trust for debt to Isaac & Samuel NICHOLS
using 200a (where Thomas DRAKE dec'd formerly lived) on E side
of Beaverdam adj Wm. R. COMBS and 50a adj Abner HUMPHREY,
Rich'd O. GRAYSON. Wit: Notley C. WILLIAMS, John W.
GRAYSON. Delv. to Saml. NICHOLS 10 Nov 1825.

3E:135   Date: 15 Jan 1822   RtCt: 27 Apr 1822
John SHAFFER of Ldn to William JENNERS. Trust for debt to
Henson MARLOW using crops on farm of Daniel AXLINE and
Manuel AXLINE. Wit: M. JANNEY, Amos JANNEY, John HAWLING.

3E:137   Date: 10 Apr 1822   RtCt: 27 Apr 1822
William COOPER & wife Elenor. CoE for deed of Jan 1821. Wit:
Robt. McCRUM, John M. HART. Delv. to Alex'r COOPER Jr. 11 Nov
1822.

3E:138   Date: 17 Feb 1821   RtCt: 29 Apr 1822
Charles SINGER of Ldn to Benjamin JACKSON of Ldn. Trust for
debt to John MARKS using farm animals, farm and household items.
Wit: William JACOBS, Marks [Mark?] MATHIAS.

3E:139   Date: 29 Apr 1822   RtCt: 29 Apr 1822
Charles SMITH to French SIMPSON and David J. COE. Trust for
John SIMPSON as security for SMITH as guardian of his daughter
Ann for her part of estate of Menan COE dec'd using int. in 2a
allotted to Ann and sister Emely SMITH dec'd from Menan COE.
Wit: E. G. HAMILTON, Thomas A. MOORE.

3E:141   Date: 20 Apr 1822   RtCt: 29 Apr 1822
John WALKER of Ldn to Joshua PANCOST of Ldn. Trust for debt to
Jonathan EWERS using 13a (cnvy/b Edward CATING & wife
Martha) and 20a (from div. of father Benjamin WALKER dec'd). Wit:
Wm. P. EATON, Joseph HUMPHREY, Felix H. THORNTON.

3E:143   Date: 20 Dec 1820   RtCt: 1 May 1822
Aaron HOLLOWAY & wife Rachel of Ldn to Stephen WILSON of
Mont Md. B/S of 69a (prch/o said WILSON Dec 1814) on NW fork of
Goose Creek adj Benjamin DANIELS, Richard COPELAND, __
GREGG, S. DODD, John LOVE. Wit: Benjamin GRAYSON, Notley
C. WILLIAMS. Delv. pr order 1 Apr 1825.

3E:145   Date: 1 May 1822   RtCt: 1 May 1822
Sarah CURRY of Ldn to George RHODES of Ldn. B/S of und. 1/8th
of 64a of her father Isaac CURRY dec'd, adj RHODES, Chs. BINNS.
Delv. to RHODES 3 Sep 1836.

3E:147   Date: 16 Mar 1822   RtCt: 4 May 1822
John HEISKELL, John MILLER and Abiel JENNERS to Joseph
LEWIS Jr. of Ldn. Release of trust of Nov 1819 for debt to John
MILLER. Delv. to LEWIS 8 Nov 1822.

3E:149   Date: 27 Nov 1821   RtCt: 4 May 1822
Thomas BROWN of Ldn to Gourley REEDER of Ldn. Trust for debt
to William VICKERS using lot in Millsville where BROWN lives, farm
animals, household items. Delv. to VICKERS 12 Sep 1822.

3E:151   Date: 3 May 1822   RtCt: 4 May 1822
John C. HANDY of Ldn to Humphrey B. POWELL of Ldn. Trust for
debt to Noble BEVERIDGE using lot in Wtfd in occupancy of Isaac
P. THOMAS (prch/o John B. STEVENS).

3E:153   Date: 14 Mar 1822   RtCt: 4 May 1822
Joseph LEWIS of Ldn to John H. LEWIS of JeffVa. B/S of 140a adj
Jacob SHOEMAKER. Wit: Henry S. TURNER, James B. WAGER,
Carter BEVERLY. Delv. to J. H. LEWIS 8 Nov 1822.

3E:154   Date: 20 Mar 1822   RtCt: 4 May 1822
Benjamin JONSON of Ldn to David SHAWEN of Ldn. Trust for debt
to Charles G. EDWARDS using ¾a adj Isaac WILSON, Geo. W.
HENRY.

3E:156   Date: 10 Mar 1822   RtCt: 4 May 1822
George W. HENRY & wife Elizabeth of Ldn to Benjamin JONSON of
Ldn. B/S of ¾a (prch/o Charles G. EDWARDS) adj Asa MOORE, J.
WILLIAMS. Wit: Robert BRADEN, Saml HOUGH Jr.

3E:158   Date: 22 Sep 1821   RtCt: 6 May 1822
B. HOUGH to Dr. Wilson C. SELDEN. Release all right of action in
sale of Tuscarora Mill tract by SELDON to Rich. H. NEWTON & Co
by agreement of 15 Nov 1802 as SELDON conveyed to Benjamin
SHREVE 4a and water privileges. Wit: Rich'd H. HENDERSON,
Benjn. SHREVE, Thomas A. MOORE.

3E:159   Date: 10 May 1822   RtCt: 10 May 1822
Elias THRASHER & wife Sally of Ldn to John Stone MARLOW of
Ldn. Trust for debt to Thomas J. MARLOW using 123a and 88a
(prch/o George SAGER & wife Mary Elizabeth Apr 1806). Wit: Abiel
JENNERS, Robert BRADEN.

3E:162   Date: 10 May 1822   RtCt: 10 May 1822
Elias THRASHER & wife Sarah of Ldn to Thomas J. MARLOW of
Ldn. B/S of 45¼a (prch/o TANKERVILLE and Henry J. BENNETT
Feb 1796) adj __ CARNES, __ HICKMAN. Wit: Robert BRADEN,
Abiel JENNERS.

3E:164   Date: 10 May 1822   RtCt: 10 May 1822
Thomas J. MARLOW & wife Mary of Ldn to Elias THRASHER of
Ldn. B/S of 45¼a (prch/o TANKERVILLE and Henry J. BENNETT
Feb 1796) adj __ HICKMAN, __ CARNES. Wit: Abiel JENNERS,
Robert BRADEN.

3E:166   Date: 13 May 1822   RtCt: 13 May 1822
Roger CHEW, Timothy CARRINGTON and Wm. WOODFORD.
Bond on CHEW as constable.

3E:166   Date: 13 May 1822   RtCt: 13 May 1822
John BOYD, Nelson GREEN, John KEEN. Bond on BOYD as constable.

3E:167   Date: 11 Mar 1822   RtCt: 13 May 1822
Benjamin WALKER dec'd. Division – Part 1 - Lot #1 (51a) to widow Sophia WALKER, Lot #2 (21a) to Jas. & Mary WELSH, Lot #3 (32a) to Thos. & Sarah GORE, Lot #4 (20) to John WALKER, Lot #5 (25a) to Benjamin WALKER, Lot #6 (16a) to Wm. WALKER, Lot #7 (8a) to Garret WALKER, Lot #8 (15a) to Jos. WALKER. Gives plats and details. Part 2 – Lot #1 (10a) to William WALKER, Lot #2 (10a) to Joseph WALKER, Lot #3 (17a) to Garrett WALKER. Divisors: Wm. BRONAUGH, Barton EWERS, Jonah TAVENNER.

3E:173   Date: __ 1822   RtCt: 13 May 1822
James BOOTH dec'd. Division – court order dated 17 Feb 1822 – Lot #1 (5a) to John STEER & wife Elenor, Lot #2 (5a) to James SPENCER & wife Mary, Lot #3 (14a) to Fancy [Fanny?] BOOTH, Lot #4 (5a) to John DAY & wife Catherine, Lot #5 (5a) to John BOOTH, Lot #6 (6a) to Aaron BOOTH, Lot #7 (6a) to James BOOTH, Lot #8 (6a) to George SANDERS & wife Elizabeth, Lot #9 (6a) to Fanny BOOTH. Gives plat. Divisors: John GEORGE, John G. MARLOW.

3E:175   Date: 10 Dec 1819   RtCt: 13 May 1822
Thomas MINOR & wife Nancy & their children Daniel, Rebekah, Elizabeth, Spencer, Eskridge, Margaret, John and Nancy MINOR of Jefferson Co Ohio. DoE for negro woman Lettice (will of Rebekah MINOR dec'd of 14 Jan 1811 beq. to Thomas MINOR & wife Nancy and at death to their children use of negroes Stephen & Lettice). Wit: Michael COYLE, Stephen FORD. Delv. to Letty 5 Aug 1822.

3E:176   Date: 10 Jun 1813   RtCt: 14 Mar 182/3 May 1822
Thomas LESLIE & wife Nancy of Ldn to Joseph PURSELL of Ldn. B/S of 107a (cnvy/b Ferdinando FAIRFAX and Mrs. B. PAGE) adj __ GRUBB, __ NEAR, __ ABLES, __ JACOBS, __ SHADACRE. Wit: Saml. W. YOUNG, Robt. WHITE, S. A. JACKSON.

3E:178   Date: 9 Mar 1822   RtCt: 13 May 1822
John DUNKIN of Ldn to William DUNKIN. Trust for debt to Samuel & Isaac NICHOLS and Aaron BURSON using farm and household items. Wit: Thomas N. JONES.

3E:179   Date: 2 Apr 1822   RtCt: 13 May 1822
Joseph LAMBAG & wife Jane of Ldn to Francis SAUNDERS and Presley CORDELL of Ldn. Trust for debt to Adam HOUSHOLDER using und. 1/5th (as heir of Anthony LAMBAG dec'd) of lot in Lsbg occupied by Dr. George FIETCHER and small building sold to Joseph on lot belonging to estate of Henry GLASSGOW dec'd. Wit: William B. HARRISON and John McCORMICK. Delv. to HOUSEHOLDER 18 Feb 1825.

3E:181   Date: 1 Apr 1822   RtCt: 13 May 1822
Joseph GREGG of Ldn to Barton EWERS of Ldn. Trust for debt to
Swithen NICHOLS using 162a. Delv. to NICHOLS 25 May 1829.

3E:183   Date: 5 May 1812   RtCt: 13 May 1822
Burr POWELL & wife Catharine of Ldn to Noble BEVERIDGE of
Mdbg. LS of 12½a on Marshall St. in Mdbg. Wit: Francis W.
LUCKETT, A. GIBSON, Jesse McVEIGH, John UPP. Delv. pr
direction by BINNS 25 Jun 1833.

3E:184   Date: 18 Apr 1822   RtCt: 13 May 1822
Burr POWELL (as Exor of Leven POWELL dec'd) to Humphrey B.
POWELL. Trust for John McCAFFERY who gave all his property to
Shff due to debt now in trust to support his family, including a house
provided by Burr POWELL. Delv. to B. W. HARRISON pr order of
H. B. POWELL 4 Nov 1822.

3E:187   Date: 30 Apr 1822   RtCt: 13 May 1822
Edward MARLOW of Ldn to John STOUTSENBERGER of Ldn.
Trust for debt to John STOUTSENBERGER and Exors of Conrad
SHAVER using 98a formerly the prop. of Conrod SHAVER (cnvy/b
Earl of TANKERVILLE and Henry A. BENNETT in Apr 1783).

3E:188   Date: 1 Aug 1816   RtCt: 13 May 1822
Burr POWELL & wife Catherine of Ldn to Noble BEVERIDGE of
Ldn. B/S of Lot #34 in Mdbg adj BEVERIDGE. Wit: Francis W.
LUCKETT, A. GIBSON. Delv. by direction of BEVERIDGE 25 Jun
1833.

3E:190   Date: 13 Apr 1822   RtCt: 13 May 1822
Mahlon JANNEY & wife Rachel and Elizabeth, Ruth, John and
Amos JANNEY (ch/o Amos JANNEY dec'd) of Ldn to Philip
HEATER of Ldn. B/S of 161a (cnvy/b commrs. of John SAUNDERS
dec'd to Amos JANNEY dec'd) and 21a (Mahlon prch/o Anthony
CUNNARD). Wit: Robert BRADEN, Eben'r. GRUBB. Delv. to
HEATER 7 May 1825.

3E:192   Date: 11 May 1822   RtCt: 13 May 1822
Francis McKEMIE & wife Elizabeth of Ldn to George SMITH of Ldn.
B/S of 5a (formerly prop. of John McKEMIE) adj Isaac BALL. Wit:
Robt. BRADEN, Abiel JENNERS. Delv. pr order 22 Apr 1825.

3E:194   Date: 6 May 1822   RtCt: 13 May 1822
John BRADY & wife Sarah of Mdbg to Humphrey B. POWELL of
Ldn. Trust for debt to Noble BEVERIDGE using part of lot in Mdbg
cnvy/b Elizabeth BOYD. Wit: Francis W. LUCKETT, A. GIBSON.
Delv. to BEVERIDGE 5 Nov 1835.

3E:196   Date: 3 May 1814   RtCt: 13 Jun 1814/14 May 1822
Wm. P. BAYLY of StafVa, John BAYLY of Ldn and George BAYLY
of Fred Va to Burr POWELL of Ldn. PoA for settling with Thomas
FAIRFAX Esqr and others for value of land recovered by Joseph

SHEARMAN for tract cnvy/b Joseph WATSON to father Perce BAYLY . Wit: Lloyd NOLAND, Noble BEVERIDGE, A. GIBSON.

3E:197   Date: 13 Feb 1822   RtCt: 13 May 1822
George TURNER and Jesse McVEIGH & Geo. Washington McCARTY. Agreement to act as security for Geo. TURNER who m. Mary SIMPSON wd/o Henson SIMPSON dec'd about to apply to ct to be appointed Guardian to Wm., Elizabeth, Emily and John SIMPSON ch/o Henson. Each is due money from estate of Henson which is object of TURNER to recover by suit and money due to Mary from Isaac SIMPSON (Exor of Henson SIMPSON). Wit: James H. McVEIGH. Delv. to Jesse McVEIGH 12 Jun 1824.

3E:198   Date: 14 May 1822   RtCt: 14 May 1822
Burr POWELL to Richard H. HENDERSON. B/S of int. in deed executed by late Shff John HAMILTON to land cnvy/b Ann JAMES and Smith JAMES.

3E:199   Date: 11 Jan 1821   RtCt: 12 Apr 1822
Andrew MARTIN of Ldn to Humphrey B. POWELL of Ldn. Trust for debt to A. GIBSON using negro woman Noaroh, boy Daniel, girls Mary & Lett and household furniture and farm animals.

3E:200   Date: 14 May 1822   RtCt: 14 May 1822
Betsey REESE wd/o Silas REED dec'd of Ldn to Joseph HILLIARD of Ldn. B/S of land cnvy/b Silas in trust to Presley CORDELL in Jan 1821.

3E:201   Date: 14 May 1822   RtCt: 14 May 1822
Sheriff John HAMILTON to Burr POWELL. B/S of int. of insolvent debtors Ann JAMES & Smith JAMES in land of Jacob JAMES dec'd (h/o Ann and f/o Smith).

3E:203   Date: 14 Mar 1822   RtCt: 12 May 1822
Ely/Eli CARRINGTON of Ldn to William THRIFT of Ldn. Trust for debt to Peter SKINNER using lot (prch/o Thomas GHEEN) on old turnpike road below Aldie. Wit: William BEVERIDGE, Jas. T. RUST, Nathan SKINNER, Jr. Delv. to THRIFT 28 Sep 1831.

3E:204   Date: 12 Jan 1822   RtCt: 18 May 1822
John PAYNE & wife Rosanah of Georgetown D.C. to Fleet SMITH of Washington D.C. B/S of 2a (former property of Dr. John McCABE) adj William CHILTON, Dr. SELDON. Delv. to SMITH 15 Aug 1822.

3E:206   Date: 20 May 1822   RtCt: 20 May 1822
David SORBAUGH/SAURBAUGH of Ldn to L. P. W. BALCH of Ldn. Trust for debt to Jacob SMITH using farm animals.

3E:207   Date: 18 May 1822   RtCt: 20 May 1822
Samuel IDEN & wife Rebecca of Ldn to H. B. POWELL of Ldn. Trust for debt to Abner GIBSON lot in Mdbg on N side of Washington St with 2-story brick house and farm animals and items and household items. Wit: Leven LUCKETT, Francis W. LUCKETT.

3E:210 Date: 21 May 1822 RtCt: 21 May 1822
Henry PEERS of Lsbg to Colin AULD. Trust for debt to James
DUNLOP and Adam STEWART surviving partners of Colin Dunlop
and son & Co using lot in Lsbg on Market St.

3E:211 Date: 23 Mar 1822 RtCt: 21 May 1822
John MOUNT & wife Mary Ann of Ldn to David YOUNG of Ldn.
Trust for debt to Joshua PANCOAST using 102a (cnvy/b Andrew B.
McMILLEN). Wit: Wm. BRONAUGH, Francis W. LUCKETT. Delv. to
PANCOAST 17 Mar 1824.

3E:214 Date: 19 Feb 1822 RtCt: 21 May 1822
Nelson GREEN & wife Jane of Mdbg to Hugh ROGERS and
Hamilton ROGERS of Mdbg. Trust for debt to Elizabeth BOYD of
Mdbg using Lot #23 in Mdbg. Wit: Francis W. LUCKETT, A.
GIBSON. Delv. to Jesse McVEIGH Exor of Elizabeth BOYD 13 Oct
1823.

3E:217 Date: 21 May 1822 RtCt: 21 May 1822
Deputy Marshall F. M. BECKWITH to Henry PEERS. B/S of lot in
Lsbg adj tavern prop. of PEERS (from estate of William DOUGLASS
dec'd in trust for debt to James DUNLOP and Adam STEWART
surviving partners of Colin Dunlop and son & Co).

3E:218 Date: 21 May 1822 RtCt: 21 May 1822
John SHAW & wife Rebecca of Ldn to Colin AULD. Trust for debt to
James DUNLOP and Adam STEWART surviving partners of Colin
Dunlop and sons & Co. using lots in Lsbg lately belonging to estate
of William DOUGLAS. Wit: Presley CORDELL, Thomas SANDERS.
Delv. to AULD 9 Jul 1825.

3E:220 Date: 30 May 1822 RtCt: 21 May 1822
Giles HAMMAT & wife Alice B. and Edward HAMMAT & wife Sarah
of Ldn to Charles SHEPHERD of Ldn. B/S of house and lot in Lsbg
(cnvy/b John BENEDUM of John) occupied by Giles, adj reps. of
Peter BOSS. Wit: Jno. McCORMICK, Thomas SANDERS.

3E:223 Date: 22 May 1822 RtCt: 22 May 1822
Deputy Francis M. BECKWITH to Colin AULD. B/S of 755a and
691a and 'Greens Lot' (from estate of Wm. DOUGLAS dec'd). Delv.
to F. M. BECKWITH 24 Sep 1822.

3E:225 Date: 4 Jun 1822 RtCt: 10 Jun 1822
Frederick CRIDER dec'd. Dower to widow Margaret CRIDER –
given Lot #20 estate including from Lot #20 with 2 log dwelling
houses on Washington St in Mdbg and Lot #59 with large dwelling
house on Madison St in Mdbg and adj ½a tan yard lot (neighbors
are Lot #21 of Oliver DENHAM, Lot #14 of Nancy HARRISON).
Divisors: Burr POWELL, A. GIBSON, Edwin C. BROWN.

3E:226   Date: 21 May 1822   RtCt: 22 May 1822
Dpty Francis M. BECKWITH to John SHAW of Lsbg. B/S of lot on
Market St. in Lsbg adj James HAMILTON (from estate of William
DOUGLAS dec'd). Delv. to SHAW 9 Jan 1823.

3E:228   Date: 5 Jun 1822   RtCt: 5 Jun 1822
John SHAW to Fielding BROWN. Agreement to allow BROWN to
buy whenever he want a lot he currently leases.

3E:228   Date: 30 May 1822   RtCt: 5 Jun 1822
John SHAW of Lsbg to Simon SMALE of Lsbg. LS of lot on Market
St in Lsbg. Delv. to SMALE 6 Jul 1826.

3E:230   Date: 7 Jun 1822   RtCt: 6 Jun 1822
John A. BINNS & wife Mary M. of Ldn to Joshua RILEY of Ldn. B/S
of lot and house in Lsbg occupied by RILEY (prch/o Peter
BENEDUM, DBk ZZ:243) adj BINNS. Delv. to RILEY 24 Jan 1827.

3E:231   Date: 3 Jun 1822   RtCt: 8 Jun 1822
John VIOLETT of Ldn to Edward CARTER of Ldn. BoS for all crops
on farm on Goose Creek where VIOLETT resides

3E:232   Date: 28 May 1822   RtCt: 29 May 1822
John SHAW of Lsbg to Presley CORDELL of Lsbg. LS of lot on
Market St. in Lsbg. Delv. to CORDELL 26 Dec 1822.

3E:234   Date: 31 May 1822   RtCt: 31 May 1822
John SHAW of Lsbg to Fielding BROWN of Lsbg. LS of lot on Back
St in Lsbg.

3E:236   Date: 21 May 1822   RtCt: 28 May 1822
Edward KELLEY (insolvent debtor with judgment agst him by Asher
WATERMAN) of Ldn to Sheriff Burr POWELL. B/S of int. in 4000a in
Orangeburg Dist. of __ Co, SC (in name of John WAMPTON, John
RYMMS? and Edward KELLEY) and int. in 500a on Congaill?
Creek, Orangeburg Dist. of __ Co, SC and int. in 6000a on Eagle
Creek, Grant Co Ky (in name of Joseph KELLEY, Joseph FARROW
and Joseph HUTCHISON). Wit: Presley CORDELL, Thomas
SANDERS, Saml. HAMMETT. Delv. to A. G. WATERMAN on __.

3E:237   Date: 30 May 1822   RtCt: 31 May 1822
George SHEID & wife Rebeccah of Ldn to Christopher FRYE of Ldn.
B/S of lot on S side of Cornwall St in Lsbg (cnvy/b Samuel G.
HAMILTON in Mar 1821, DBk CCC:129) adj Thomas R. SANDERS.
Wit: Presley CORDELL, Thomas SANDERS.

3E:240   Date: 17 Nov 1821   RtCt: 31 May 1822
Robert BRADEN & wife Elizabeth of Ldn to Mary FOX of Ldn. B/S of
136a (prch/o Joseph BRADEN) adj Wm. SMITH, R. BRADEN, __
COOPER. Wit: Abiel JENNERS, Saml. HOUGH Jr. Delv. to Francis
L. PATTON atty 5/31/1946 [1846?].

3E:241   Date: 17 Nov 1821   RtCt: 31 May 1822
Mary FOX of Ldn to Robert BRADEN of Ldn. B/S of 103a adj Wm.
SMITH, Mary FOX, P. CORDELL, Saml. GREGG, Matthew BEANS.
Delv. to Francis L. PATTON atty 5/31/1946 [1846?].

3E:243   Date: 31 May 1822   RtCt: 31 May 1822
John SHAW of Lsbg to John SURGHNOR of Lsbg. LS of lot on
Market & Back Sts in Lsbg. Delv. to SURGHNOR 18 Aug 1823.

3E:245   Date: 25 May 1821   RtCt: 1 Jun 1822
Aaron SANDERS & wife Susannah of Ldn to George W. SHAWEN
and David SHAWEN of Ldn. B/S of 37a Lot #7 and ½ of 33½a Lot
#6 in div. of John A. BINNS dec'd (prch/o John A. BINNS by
SANDERS and Cornelious SHAWEN now dec'd f/o George W. &
David). Wit: Thomas SANDERS, John H. McCABE. Delv. to David
SHAWEN 25 Mar 1824.

3E:247   Date: 22 May 1822   RtCt: 1 Jun 1822
Eli H. HANDY of Ldn to Edward WILSON and James SINCLAIR of
Ldn. Trust for debt to Enoch FRANCIS using 147½a (Lot #1 in div.
of John HANDY dec'd). Wit: John FRANCIS, Lewis FRANCIS.

3E:249   Date: __ 1820   RtCt: 3 Jun 1822
John ROSE (Admr of George KILGORE dec'd) of Ldn to Henry
STEVENS of Ldn. Correction of description errors in B/S of 19 Apr
1819 of 23a including island in Broad Run and 9¾a adj William
SHEID. Delv. to STEVENS 12 Nov 1823.

3E:250   Date: 21 May 1822   RtCt: 4 Jun 1822
James SIMPSON of Ldn to John SIMPSON. Trust for William
NOLAND, David J. COE, John R. ADAMS, Benjamin HAGERMAN
and Frederick SIMPSON of Ldn as security in administration of
estate of Henson SIMPSON dec'd using all int., book accts, crops
on land where Rolly GREEN lives.

3E:251   Date: 5 Apr 1822   RtCt: 4 Jun 1822
James SIMPSON of Ldn to John SIMPSON of Ldn. Trust for John
R. ADAMS, French SIMPSON, David J. COE, William NOLAND and
Benjamin HAGERMAN of Ldn as security as Exor of Hanson
SIMPSON dec'd using Lot #46 and #47 in Aldie on Mercer St., part
of Lot #51 and slaves Sam, David, Harry, Nancey, Isaac and
Madison. Wit: Lewis M. SMITH, Thomas SMARR, Samuel
SIMPSON, Thos. ROBINSON, Edward JENKINS, D'd BEATTY.
Delv. to John SIMPSON 5 Apr 1825.

3E:253   Date: 25 Apr 1822   RtCt: 10 Jun 1822
Benjamin SINCLAIR & wife Prescilla of Scott Co Ky to Charles
THORNTON of Ldn. B/S of 40a and 8a. Wit: Job STEVENSON, Jno.
BRANHAM. Delv. to THORNTON 30 Oct 1822.

3E:256   Date: 27 May 1822   RtCt: 27 May 1822
James COCHRAN & wife Rachel of Ldn to William NICHOLS,
William PIGGOTT, Samuel HATCHER and Mahlon WATERS as

trustees for benefit of poor belonging to the Goose Creek Monthly Meeting. B/S of 3a on NW fork of Goose Creek (Benjamin BRADFIELD entitled from estate of Stephen WILSON dec'd and Rachel as an heir). Wit: John McCORMICK, Presley CORDELL. Delv. to Wm. NICHOLS 14 Apr 1832.

3E:258   Date: 3 May 1822   RtCt: 13 May 1822
Mary Ann KELLY (Admr of James M. KELLY) of Ldn to William WRIGHT of Ldn. Trust for possible debt to Edmund TYLER Admr of John TYLER dec'd of Ldn (in suit of Mary A. KELLY vs. Tunis TITUS) using int. in negroes Jack Nag Jack Joe and Jacob. Wit: Frederick COLEMAN, Thomas THORNTON, James BEAVERS.

3E:260   Date: 14 May 1822   RtCt: 13 May 1822
Mary Ann KELLY of Ldn to William THRIFT of Ldn. Trust for debt to James BEAVERS using int. in 4 negroes Jack Nag Jack Jacob and Joe. Wit: Frederick ROBINAUER?, Thomas THORNTON, Edmund J. TYLER.

3E:261   Date: 8 Jun 1822   RtCt: 8 Jun 1822
John DUNKIN of Ldn to Isaac BROWN of Ldn. Trust for debt to John PANCOAST, Thomas MURPHEY, John DUNKIN Jr. using 90¼a. Delv. to Thornton WALKER pr direction of Isaac BROWN 8 Oct 1831.

3E:262   Date: 24 May 1822   RtCt: 10 Jun 1822
William and Henry HARDEN of Ldn to Silas GARRETT of Ldn. Trust for debt to Stephen GARRETT using und. slaves in possession of mother Elizabeth HARDEN – man James, boy Auldridge, Roy, Anderson and Robbert, woman Ann, Maria, Eliza, Emelia and Mary Ann and Charity (died before 5y term was complete). Wit: H. SMITH, A. GIBSON, Towns'd McVEIGH, Asa ROGERS. Delv. to Stephen GARRETT 24 May 1823.

3E:264   Date: 25 Apr 1822   RtCt: 10 Jun 1822
Burr POWELL (acting Exor of Leven POWELL dec'd) to Thomas L. HUMPHREY only son and heir at law of Jacob HUMPHREY dec'd. B/S of 98a (deed executed with Jacob in Mar 1805) adj John BALDWIN, John WILLIAMS, John WILKINSON, John HATCHER. Wit: Stephen R. MOUNT, Jonah TAVENER, Burr WEEKS. Delv. to Thomas L. HUMPHREY 11 Nov 1823.

3E:266   Date: 2 Feb 1822   RtCt: 10 Jun 1822
Jacob LUKE & wife Sarah of FredVa to Walter LANGLEY of Ldn. B/S of 44a Lot #3 (dev. to Sarah by father William CLAYTON dec'd) adj Mrs. HUFFMAN, Israel CLAYTON and 51½a Lot #17.

3E:268   Date: 8 Jun 1822   RtCt: 10 Jun 1822
Susan P. B. HARDING of JeffVa to Sanford RAMEY of Ldn. B/S of 17a (as devisee of John A. BINNS dec'd) on Catocton Creek, adj James MOORE. Wit: John HUMPHREYS, Sanford J. RAMEY, David HUMPHREYS Jr. Delv. to RAMEY 13 Mar 1827.

3E:270   Date: __ 1822   RtCt: 10 Jun 1822
Yardly TAYLOR (as trustee for James COCHRAN in debt to
Stephen WILSON) of Ldn to Isaac & Samuel NICHOLS of Ldn. B/S
of 22a (inherited by Sarah COCHRAN d/o Jonathan BRADFIELD)
adj __ ZIMMERMAN, Thomas JANNEY, Goose Creek Meeting
House. Delv. to Wm. HOGUE 11 Jun 1827.

3E:272   Date: 16 Jan 1822   RtCt: 17 Jun 1822
Lewis ELLZEY of Ldn to Craven OSBURN of Ldn. Trust for Joshua
OSBURN as security for ELLZEY to Enoch FRANCES and David
WILLIAMSON using 300a adj Thomas GREGG, William HOUGH, __
HOWELL, heirs of Andrew READ, James McILHANEY. Wit: Henry
T. HARRISON, J. RUST, John M. HARRISON. Delv. to Joshua
OSBURN 16 May 1823.

3E:275   Date: 8 Jun 1822   RtCt: 10 Jun 1822
Elizabeth P. B. HARDING of JeffVa to Sanford RAMEY of Ldn. B/S
of 33½a (as devisee of Jno. A. BINNS dec'd). Wit: John
HUMPHREYS, Sanford J. RAMEY, David HUMPHREYS. Delv. to
RAMEY 13 Mar 1827.

3E:277   Date: 17 May 1822   RtCt: 10 Jun 1822
Henry PLASTER of Ldn to James PLASTER of Ldn. B/S of 115a on
NW side of Goose Creek adj James PATTERSON, John
PATTERSON. Delv. to Jas. PLASTER 22 Feb 1823.

3E:279   Date: 4 May 1822   RtCt: 10 Jun 1822
Thomas L. HUMPHREY & wife Sarah of Ldn to Sarah HUMPHREY
of Ldn. B/S of 43a adj John WILLIAMS, John WILKERSON, in
consideration of the dower Sarah is entitled to in lands cnvy/b Burr
POWELL Exor of L. POWELL to Thomas L. and money advanced to
Sarah for benefit of Thomas L. Wit: Stephen R. MOUNT, Jonah
TAVENNER, Burr WEEKS, William BRONAUGH, A. GIBSON. Delv.
to Sarah HUMPHREY 22 Mar 1823.

3E:281   Date: 10 Jun 1822   RtCt: 10 Jun 1822
William RUST of Ldn to Humphrey B. POWELL of Ldn. Trust for
debt to Charles S. CARTER of PrWm using lot known at 'Tecumseh'
laid off by Thomas NELSON Jr. in May 1822.

3E:282   Date: 3 Jun 1822   RtCt: 10 Jun 1822
Francis W. LUCKETT & wife Sarah Smith of Ldn to Isaac NICHOLS
Jr. of Ldn. Trust for debt to James HOGE using 177a on N side of
Goose Creek nr Burson's Mill. Wit: Wm. BRONAUGH, Benj.
GRAYSON. Delv. to HOGE 2 Sep 1823.

3E:285   Date: 10 Jun 1822   RtCt: 10 Jun 1822
Charles S. CARTER of PrWm to William RUST of Ldn. B/S of land in
PrWm and Ldn known as 'Tecumseh' surveyed by Thomas
NELSON Jr. of PrWm – Division #I (539a), Division #II (59a).

3E:287   Date: 8 Jun 1822   RtCt: 10 Jun 1822
Frederick BROOKS of PrWm to Humphrey B. POWELL of Ldn.
Trust for debt to Benjamin EDWARDS signed over to Hiram
McVEIGH using 25a on Hunger Run adj Matthew RUST and carding
machine now in use by BROOKS & Stephen BURSON.

3E:289   Date: 10 Jun 1822   RtCt: 10 Jun 1822
George LEE of Ldn to William LASABER/LAFABER of Ldn. B/S of
108a on Beaverdam adj Peter SMITH, William DAWSON. Delv. to
LAFAVER 9 Dec 1822.

3E:290   Date: 1 Nov 1821   RtCt: 10 Jun 1822
Samuel HOUGH Jr. & wife Jane of Ldn to Lydia HOUGH of Ldn. B/S
of lot in Wtfd adj Isaac WALKER, John JAMES and another lot adj
John F. SAPPINGTON, Lewis KLINE. Wit: Robert BRADEN, Abiel
JENNERS. Delv. to S. HOUGH Jr. 17 Dec 1822.

3E:293   Date: 21 May 1822   RtCt: 10 Jun 1822
Yeoman Isaac COWGILL & wife Mary of Ldn to wheelmaker Isaac
FRY. B/S of 1a in tract known as 'Rutterlands' (cnvy/b Nathaniel
CRAUFORD) adj __ WILKINSON. Wit: Benj. GRAYSON, John W.
GRAYSON. Delv. pr order 22 Mar 1823.

3E:294   Date: 27 Jan 1822   RtCt: 10 Jun 1822
John ERSKINE & wife Elizabeth to William GREGG. CoE for sale of
173a (deed rec'd DBk JJ:91). Wit: George DOVE and Giles
TURLEY of Rockingham Co.

3E:296   Date: 13 Dec 1813   RtCt: 10 Jun 1822
Ezekiel MOUNT & wife Sarah of Ldn to Daniel BROWN of Ldn. B/S
of 2a on N side of Goose Creek below new Snicker's Gap Turnpike
(part of tract where MOUNT lives). Wit: John SINCLAIR, James
MOUNT, Stephen R. MOUNT, Wm. BRONAUGH, Francis W.
LUCKETT.

3E:298   Date: 14 Mar 1822   RtCt: 11 Jun 1822
Joseph CARR of Ldn to Samuel C. HENDERSON of Ldn. LS of 1a
in Upperville on N side of Turnpike road adj John JAMES, John
GIBSON.

3E:300   Date: 21 May 1822   RtCt: 10 Jun 1822
William GREGG & wife Rebeccah of Ldn to John UMBAUGH of Ldn.
B/S of 173a (prch/o John ERSKINE) on road to Roaches Mill, adj
John STEER, __ ANSEL, __ DOUGLAS. Wit: Robert BRADEN,
Abiel JENNERS. Delv. to UMBAUGH 8 Feb 1848.

3E:302   Date: 2 May 1822   RtCt: 10 Jun 1822
Richard COCHRAN of Mdbg to Hiram McVEIGH of Mdbg. Trust for
debt to Noble BEVERIDGE using lot in Mdbg (cnvy/b Burr POWELL
in Dec 1813).

3E:304   Date: 17 Feb 1821   RtCt: 10 Jun 1822
John UPP of Mdbg to Humphrey B. POWELL of Ldn. Trust for
Richard COCHRAN and Nelson GREEN as security on debt to

Abner GIBSON of Mdbg and Bank of the Valley and others using tavern lot in Mdbg, int. in Lot #30 (from estate of Thomas CHINN dec'd) and 96a adj John WEATHERLY and lot in Franklin Co and negro man George, women Sylla and Let and farm and household items. Wit: A. GIBSON.

3E:308   Date: 29 Mar 1822   RtCt: 10 Jun 1822
Joseph B. MERSHON & wife Ann of Ldn to Samuel O'BANNION of Ffx. B/S of 93a (part of DESKIN and BLAND patent) on old Lsbg road adj. Joseph B. & Thomas B. MERSHON, T. W. LEE, __ ELLZAY. Wit: Charles LEWIS, Johnston CLEVELAND.

3E:310   Date: 2 May 1822   RtCt: 10 Jun 1822
John UPP of Ldn to Humphrey B. POWELL of Ldn. Trust for debt to Noble BEVERIDGE and Hiram McVEIGH using Lot #23 in Mdbg and int. in 84a adj Jane WEATHERLY allotted to his wife in div. of estate of Thomas CHINN Sr.

3E:312   Date: 17 May 1822   RtCt: 11 Jun1822
William NOLAND & wife Catharine of Ldn to Lewis BERKELEY of PrWm. B/S of 326½a adj Aldie adj Matthew ADAMS, __ SINCLAIR, __ RUST, __ HESKETT, __ FERGUSON, Misses LACEY, __ HOCKINGS and 18¼a on old Snicker's Gap road adj Thomas H. REILEY. Wit: A. GIBSON, Robert ARMISTEAD. Delv. to BERKLEY 28 Feb 1823.

3E:315   Date: 19 Jun 1822   RtCt: 22 Jun 1822
Carpenter John JOHNSON & wife Sarah of Union to Gent. John N. T. G. E. KEENE & wife Harriett of Mdbg. B/S of lot in Union cnvy/b Lewis HUNT to JOHNSON (paid by conveying int. of Harriet in real estate of father Reuben TRIPLETT dec'd with exception of lot in Union held jointly by TRIPLETT and Thornton WALKER). Wit: William BRONAUGH, Francis W. LUCKETT. Delv. to Jno. McDANIEL 11 Nov 1823.

3E:317   Date: 17 May 1822   RtCt: 11 Jun 1822
William NOLAND & wife Catharine of Aldie to Thomas R. MOTT of Lsbg and Burr POWELL of Mdbg. Trust for debt to Lewis BERKELEY of PrWm using 131a on Bull Run Mt. Wit: A. GIBSON, Robt. ARMISTEAD. Delv. to BERKELEY 28 Feb 1823.

3E:321   Date: 11 Jun 1822   RtCt: 11 Jun 1822
Peter BENEDUM of Ldn to John Gill WATT of Ldn. LS of 7a (part of land previously LS to by James HEREFORD of Ffx to Patrick CAVAN).

3E:323   Date: 8 May 1821   RtCt: 26 May 1821/12 Jun 1822
William CHILTON & wife Sarah H. of Ldn to John ROSE, Richard H. HENDERSON and Otho M. LINTHICUM of D.C. Trust for debt to Ninion MAGRUDER of D.C. with notes to Burr POWELL and Cuthbert POWELL using 610a (prch/o Geo. Fairfax LEE and 140a abt 1 mile W of Lsbg (prch/o Geo. RUST Jr.) adj George RHODES,

Jno. CARR, Ellis WILLIAMS, Jesse RICE, heirs of Isaac CURRY, John McCORMICK, __ KIMMINGS. Wit: Samuel MURRY, Presley CORDELL. Delv. to Thomas A. MOORE for Rich'd. H. HENDERSON 27 Aug 1823.

3E:327 Date: 2 May 1822 RtCt: 12 Jun 1822
Warner WASHINGTON of FredVa to Lawrence LEWIS of Ffx. Assignment of trust made by Mordecai THROCKMORTON & wife Sarah McCarty of Ldn to Warner W. THROCKMORTON of JeffVa in trust for debt to Warner WASHINGTON of FredVa.

3E:330 Date: 1 May 1822 RtCt: 12 Jun 1822
Mordecai THROCKMORTON & wife Sarah McCarty of Ldn to Warner W. THROCKMORTON of JeffVa in trust for debt to Warner WASHINGTON of FredVa using 500a (und. part of 660a and und. 400a). Wit: Benj. GRAYSON, N. C. WILLIAMS.

3E:333 Date: 14 Jan 1822 RtCt: 12 Jun 1822
Burr POWELL of Ldn to Nancy HARRISON of FredVa. LS of Lot #14 in Mdbg at intersection of Federal and Liberty Sts adj heirs of Dr. CHANNEL.

3E:335 Date: 24 May 1822 RtCt: 12 Jun 1822
Sheriff Burr POWELL to Sarah JONES. B/S of 85a on Ashby's Gap Turnpike and little river (with Sarah JONES satisfying debts from insolvency of John SINCLAIR in 1821 and John & wife Susan joining in the deed). Wit: Leven LUCKETT, A. GIBSON. Delv. to Alex'r LEE Exor of Sarah JONES 12 Dec 1829.

3E:338 Date: 28 Feb 1821 RtCt: 12 Mar 1821
Matthew ORRISON of Ldn to Charles DAWSON of Ldn. Trust for debt to Peter OATYER using farm animals, household items. Wit: Jacob MYR[E]S, Ezra MILLS. Delv. to OATYER 9 Jan 1826.

3E:340 Date: 15 Jun 1822 RtCt: 15 Jun1822
Edward KELLEY (insolvent debtor) to Sheriff Burr POWELL. B/S of land in schedule given 28 May last for judgments by Elijah RETECOR, Burr POWELL, Asher WATERMAN Exors.

3E:341 Date: 10 Jun 1822 RtCt: 15 Jun 1822
Ludwell LEE of Ldn to Levi WHALEY of Ldn. B/S of 15a on SW side of Turnpike road from Lsbg to Georgetown and Alexandria. Delv. to WHALEY 31 Jan 1823.

3E:342 Date: 13 Jun 1822 RtCt: 15 Jun 1822
Samuel GREGG to children Samuel GREGG Jr and Susanna GREGG. Gift of 51a adj William CAMBY (residue of tract cnvy/b Geo. TAVENER Jr.)

3E:344 Date: 16 Nov 1821 RtCt: 15 Jun 1822
Samuel MULLEN & wife Sarah of Ldn to John DRISH of Ldn. B/S of lot with log house on N addition of Lsbg on W side of King St (cnvy/b Ellis WILLIAMS in Nov 1818). Wit: L. P. W. BALCH, Benj.

JACKSON, John BEATY, John McCORMICK, Presley CORDELL.
Delv. to DRISH 28 Mar 1824.

3E:346   Date: 17 May 1822   RtCt: 17 Jun 1822
Charles MASTERSON to James McKENDRICK. BoS for horses.
Wit: John M. WILSON, Thos. H. MUSE, James SHAREMON?

3E:346   Date: 17 May 1822   RtCt: 17 Jun 1822
Philip JONES of Ldn to John SMARR of Ldn. BoS for negro boy
James abt 14y old of dark complexion, a slave for life, inherited from
my late father. Wit: Jno. A. BINNS, Wm. SMARR.

3E:347   Date: 27 Nov 1821   RtCt: 19 Jun 1822
Mary MARKS, Marcus HUMPHREY & wife Margaret, Bennet
MARKS, Thomas MARKS, James WARFORD & wife Elizabeth,
Mason MARKS, Elisha M. PEUGH & wife Mary, Abel MARKS, Lydia
MARKS, Matt MARKS and Samuel MARKS of Ldn (WARFORD
from Ky) to John GRAHAM of Ldn. B/S of 42a allotted to Marcus
HUMPHREY & wife Margaret from estate of Abel MARKS dec'd and
conveyed to Mary MARKS in trust for benefit of Margeret and
children. Delv. to GRAHAM 24 May 1824.

3E:349   Date: 19 Jun 1822   RtCt: 22 Jun 1822
John N. T. G. E. KEENE & wife Harriet to John JOHNSON of Union.
B/S of lot in Union with JOHNSON as tenant (from real estate of
Reuben TRIPLETT f/o Harriet, except her int. held jointly with
TRIPLETT and Thornton WALKER). Wit: William BRONAUGH,
Francis W. LUCKETT.

3E:351   Date: 19 Jun 1822   RtCt: 22 Jun 1822
John JOHNSON carpenter & wife Sarah of Union to Seth SMITH of
Union. Trust for debt to Samuel DUNKIN and John N. T. G. E.
KEENE using und. int. in real estate of Reuben TRIPLETT dec'd.
Wit: Wm. BRONAUGH, Francis W. LUCKETT. Delv. to Jas.
McDANIEL 11 Nov 1822 pr order.

3E:353   Date: 13 Jun 1822   RtCt: 22 Jun 1822
John WYNN & wife Susannah of Ldn to Daniel JANNEY of Ldn.
Trust for debt to William HOGE of Ldn using 109¼a on Beaverdam
nr Snicker's Gap Turnpike (cnvy/b Joseph HAINS in 1818). Wit:
William BRONAUGH, Notley C. WILLIAMS. Delv. to HOGUE 23 Mar
1824.

3E:356   Date: 13 Jun 1822   RtCt: 24 Jun 1822
Samuel GREGG & wife Hannah of Ldn to Joseph CANBY of Ldn.
Trust for debt to Sarah CANBY w/o William CANBY of Ldn using
61a on NW fork of Goose Creek adj __ NICHOLS, __ HOLMES.
Wit: William BRONAUGH, Notley C. WILLIAMS.

3E:359   Date: 13 Jun 1822   RtCt: 24 Jun 1822
John HOLMES to Samuel GREGG. Release of trust of Aug 1821 for
debt to Josiah GREGG.

3E:361   Date: 13 Jun 1822   RtCt: 24 Jun 1822
Lewis GRIGGSBY to Samuel GREGG. Release of trust of Jan 1816 for debt to John GREGG acting Exor of John GREGG Sr. dec'd.

3E:363   Date: 19 Jun 1822   RtCt: 25 Jun 1822
John N. T. G. E. KEENE & wife Harriot of Ldn to Thornton WALKER of Ldn. B/S of lot in Union adj heirs of Reuben TRIPLETT dec'd and und. int. of Harriot in ½ of lot of Reuben TRIPLETT dec'd. Wit: William BRONAUGH, Francis W. LUCKETT.

3E:365   Date: 26 Jun 1822   RtCt: 26 Jun 1822
John W. BERKELEY of Ffx to Robert MOFFETT of Ldn. B/S of 1/3 part of land that belonged to Nancy BREWER (Nancy BREWER dec'd originally Nancy MILHOLLAND acquired int. in estate of John MILHOLLAND dec'd for land in Ldn adj George RUST but MOFFETT had already purchased land from Patrick B. MILHOLLAND and John W. BERKELEY m. Elizabeth a ch/o Nancy BREWER and Elizabeth died leaving issue and int. to John W.) Delv. to MOFFETT 21 Feb 1823.

3E:366   Date: 25 Jun 1822   RtCt: 28 Jun 1822
Thornton WALKER & wife Frances and Willis TRIPLETT of Ldn to Richard H. HENDERSON of Ldn. Trust for debt to Frederick WAESCHE, MANDEVILLE and LANNOM, William B. BEND and John CREIGHTEN and WOFIELD and BOGUE using und. 1/8th int. in land of Reuben TRIPLETT dec'd f/o Willis & Frances and house & lot in Union lately belonging to John WEEDON as a tavern now property of Willis and house & lot of WALKER adj Union. Wit: John McCORMICK, Presley CORDELL.

3E:369   Date: 4 Jul 1822   RtCt: 4 Jul 1822
Peter BENEDUM of Ldn to Robert CAMPBELL of Ldn. A/L part of 1a originally leased by James HEREFORD dec'd to Patrick CAVAN dec'd and later sold by CAVAN, adj CAMPBELL. Delv. to CAMPBELL 27 Aug 1823.

3E:371   Date: 22 Sep 1821   RtCt: 3 May/6 Jul 1822
Wilson C. SELDON & wife Mary B. of Ldn to Benjamin SHREVE of Ldn. B/S of 4a adj Alexander LUTTRAIL, Mary FOSTER (cnvy/b Patrick McINTYRE in May 1810). Wit: Rich'd. H. HENDERSON, Thomas A. MOORE, B. HOUGH. Delv. to SHREVE 1 Feb 1823.

3E:373   Date: 22 Jun 1822   RtCt: 6 Jul 1822
William NOLAND & wife Catharine of Ldn to Daniel P. CONRAD of Ldn. B/S of ½a Lot #69 & #70 on Mercer St. in Aldie. Wit: Abner GIBSON, Leven LUCKETT. Delv. to G. RICKARD pr order 21 Sep 1835.

3E:375   Date: 7 Sep 1818   RtCt: 14 Jan/8 Jul 1822
James MOORE and James FARQUHAR of Ldn to David JANNEY of Ldn. B/S of 2a exclusive of race on Ball's run running through the

prop. of Mahlon JANNEY dec'd, below Lsbg Road. Wit: John WILLIAMS, John PIERPOINT, William JANNEY.

3E:377   Date: 29 Jun 1822   RtCt: 31 Jul 1822
Thomas RUSSELL & wife Mary of Ldn to David LOVETT and John A. MANN of Ldn. Trust for debt to James McILHANY using tract adj Mortimer McILHANEY, T. Milton McILHANEY, Michael ARNOLD, John JANNEY (part of 87a of William RUSSELL Sr. dec'd). Wit: Craven OSBURN, John WHITE.

3E:381   Date: 12 Jan 1822   RtCt: 31 Jul 1822
Alexander M. BRISCOE & wife Matilda of PrWm to Enos WILDMAN of Lsbg. B/S of 40a (und. int. in prop. of Israel LACEY dec'd) on Potomac. Wit: Presley CORDELL, Thomas SANDERS, S. BLINCOE. Delv. to WILDMAN 11 Jun 1828.

3E:384   Date: 1 Aug 1822   RtCt: 2 Aug 1822
Reuben SCHOOLEY to Thomas HEIR of Lsbg. B/S of lot in Lsbg adj Thomas HEATHERLY and another lot in Lsbg adj Bazil HALL, Reuben SCHOOLEY (cnvy/b John HAWLING in Feb 1817 and Jonathan FOUCH in Feb 1817).

3E:385   Date: 23 Feb 1822   RtCt: 3 Aug 1822
Samuel CHINN & wife Emmily of Ldn to Studly MIDDLETON & wife Maryann of Ldn. LS of 4a on S side of Goose Creek nr Dawson's Mill adj William CHILTON. Wit: Francis W. LUCKETT, A. GIBSON. Delv. pr order 23 Sep 1829.

3E:387   Date: 24 Jul 1822   RtCt: 7 Aug 1822
Benjamin MITCHELL Jr. & wife Martha of Ldn to Price JACOBS of Ldn. Trust for debt to Christopher FRY using 76a adj __ BRONAUGH. Wit: William BRONAUGH, Francis W. LUCKETT. Delv. to FRYE 2 Jul 1830.

3E:389   Date: 28 Feb 1822   RtCt: 10 Aug 1822
Abel PALMER of Ldn to John HATCHER and William R. COMBS of Ldn. Trust for debt to William C. PALMER using 100a. Wit: Towns'd McVEIGH, George MARKS, Geo. H. ALLDER, Stephen R. MOUNT. Delv. to W. C. PALMER 20 Jan 1830.

3E:391   Date: 6 Aug 1822   RtCt: 7 Aug 1822
Abiel JENNERS of Ldn. DoE for negro Thomas TURNER. Wit: L. P. W. BALCH, Chs. G. ESKRIDGE, Wm. JENNERS.

3E:392   Date: 22 Jun 1822   RtCt: 30 Jul 1822
William NOLAND & wife Catharine of Ldn to Gabriel GREEN of FredVa. B/S of ½a Lot #85 & #86 on Mercer St in Aldie and 2a on little river. Wit: Leven LUCKETT, A. GIBSON.

3E:394   Date: 10 Jun 1822   RtCt: 25 Jul 1822
Nelson GREEN & wife Jane of Mdbg to John O. DUVAL of Fqr. Trust for debt to Gabriel GREEN using brick house and lot where GREEN resides and wooden home on tanyard lot in Mdbg.

3E:396   Date: 9 Jun 1822   RtCt: 26 Jul 1822
Nelson GREEN of Mdbg to John O. DUVAL of Fqr. Trust for debt to
Fanny HARRISON of Mdbg using negro woman Clary & her 4
children Maria, George, Mary Ann and Lemmon, household items,
farm animals.

3E:398   Date: 19 Jul 1822   RtCt: 25 Jul 1822
Nelson GREEN & wife Jane of Mdbg to H. B. POWELL of Mdbg.
Trust for debt to Abner GIBSON using lot where they now live on
Madison St in Mdbg (cnvy/b Amos JOHNSON). Wit: Burr WEEKS,
James B. BISCOE, Francis W. LUCKETT, James ROGERS. Delv.
pr order 4 Feb 1823.

3E:400   Date: 18 Jul 1822   RtCt: 24 Jul 1822
Isaac BROWN Sr. & wife Sarah of Ldn to Mahlon BALDWIN of
Union. B/S of 1a in Union adj __ WEADON, __ BROWN, __
GALLAHER. Wit: Wm. DUNKIN, Jonathan W. BRADFIELD, William
BRONAUGH, Benjamin GRAYSON.

3E:402   Date: 22 Apr 1819   RtCt: 24 Jul 1822
William NOLAND & wife Catharine of Ldn to James LLOYD of Ldn.
B/S of ½a Lot #44 and #45 on Mercer St. in Aldie. Wit: Lewis M.
SMITH, James TURLEY Jr., Amos GULICK, Leven LUCKETT, Robt.
ARMSTEAD.

3E:404   Date: 24 Jul 1822   RtCt: 24 Jul 1822
Deputy Francis M. BECKWITH to Mason CHAMBLIN and John
CHAMBLIN of Ldn. B/S of 100a (auctioned off to Thomas WHITE
who directed it to the CHAMBLINs) in Scotland adj J. WALRAVEN,
Alexander HARRISON. Delv. pr order 11 May 1830.

3E:405   Date: 11 Feb 1822   RtCt: 23 Jul 1822
Walter LANGLEY of Ldn to William NOLAND of Ldn. Trust for debt
to George PELTER using 95a (cnvy/b PELTER).

3E:407   Date: 31 May 1822   RtCt: 22 Jul 1822
Thomas CLOWES & wife Ann of Ldn to Edward B. GRADY of Ldn.
Trust for debt to George S. MARKS using 204a adj John DUNKIN,
road leading to Drake's Mill, Matthias HANN, Benjamin JACKSON,
Thomas DRAKE, John MARKS. Wit: Notley C. WILLIAMS, John W.
GRAYSON. Delv. to MARKS 12 Oct 1827.

3E:410   Date: 28 Jun 1822   RtCt: 21 Jul 1822
Alexander McKIM of Richmond to James BOSHER and Henry L.
CARTER of Richmond. Trust for debt to Elisha BAKER of Richmond
(McKIM with Daniel HUTCHISON) using und. 1/7th int. in 330a on
Elklick Creek (from William H. McKIM who died underage, without
issue and intestate).

3E:413   Date: 13 Jul 1822   RtCt: 19 Jul 1822
Mason MARKS & wife __ to Charles TAYLOR. Trust for debt to
Jonathan JAMES using 30a (from div. of estate of Abel MARKS
dec'd). Wit: Fra's. STRIBLING, S. A. JACKSON, George PURSEL.

3E:416   Date: 16 Jul 1822   RtCt: 18 Jul 1822
Edward DULIN & wife Nancy of Ldn to Truman GORE of Ldn. B/S of
77a. Wit: Samuel CLAPHAM, Samuel DAWSON. Delv. to GORE 14
May 1824.

3E:418   Date: 16 Jul 1822   RtCt: 16 Jul 1822
John MANLEY & wife Sarah of Ldn to John S. MARLOW of Ldn. B/S
of int. in 96a (allotted to Sarah by father Thomas STUMP dec'd)
during natural life of MANLEY per agreement.

3E:419   Date: 30 Apr 1822   RtCt: 15 Jul 1822
Amos JANNEY (and Adam HOUSEHOLDER & wife Sarah late
JANNEY, Mahlon JANNEY & wife Rachel, John JANNEY, Elozabeth
JANNEY, Ruth JANNEY and Nathan JANNEY ch/o Amos JANNEY
dec'd) of Ldn to Benjamin GRUBB. B/S of 4a (from estate of Amos
JANNEY dec'd) adj Ruth JANNEY heirs of Mrs. Susannah
HOUSEHOLDER Delv. to GRUBB 3 Jan 1822. Wit: Robert
BRADEN, Ebenezer GRUBB.

3E:421   Date: 13 Jul 1822   RtCt: 13 Jul 1822
Walter ELGIN Sr. & wife Diadema of Ldn to Richard H.
HENDERSON, Jesse TIMMS and Samuel CARR of Ldn. Trust for
debt to George CARTER of Oatlands using 408a (cnvy/b CARTER).
Wit: Walter ELGIN Jr., Thomas A. MOORE. Delv. pr order 26 Aug
1830.

3E:424   Date: 12 Jul 1822   RtCt: 12 Jul 1822
George CARTER of Oatlands to Walter ELGIN Sr. of Ldn. B/S of
408a on N side of Goose Creek. Wit: Walter ELGIN Jr., Thomas A.
MOORE. Delv. pr order 26 Aug 1830.

3E:425   Date: 23 Mar 1822   RtCt: 2 Jul 1822
John VANHORN to Isaac GRIFFITH. Trust for debt to William M.
McCARTY using und. int. in slave Grace & her children Kit, Susan,
Joe, George and Jim (held by his mother and father during their
natural lives). Wit: Samuel HAMMETT, George HAMMAT, Daniel
GREENWALL.

3E:426   Date: 10 Jul 1822   RtCt: 10 Jul 1822
John MANLY to L. P. W. BALCH. Trust for debt to John S.
MARLOW using farm animals, household items, 1/3 of crops on land
where George WINNER lives adj remainder of his lease.

3E:428   Date: 13 Apr 1822   RtCt: 10 Jul 1822
Mahlon JANNEY & wife Rachel of Ldn to Amos JANNEY and Ruth
JANNEY of Ldn. B/S of land from div. of estate of father Amos
JANNEY dec'd, on E side of short hill. Wit: Robert BRADEN,
Ebenezer GRUBB.

3E:430   Date: 29 Jun 1822   RtCt: 8 Jul 1822
Frederick BROOKS of PrWm to Richard H. HENDERSON of Ldn.
Trust for debt to Elizabeth POTTER of Ldn using int. in 2a (tract of
Matthew RUST where BROOKS lives on unexpired lease).

3E:431   Date: 8 Jul 1822   RtCt: 8 Jul 1822
Charles TURNER of Ldn to Towns'd McVEIGH of Ldn. Trust for debt to George TURNER jointly bound for debt to Noble BEVERIDGE using farm animals and household items.

3E:433   Date: 16 Jun 1822   RtCt: 14 Aug 1822
Reuben SCHOOLEY of Ldn to Matthew MITCHELL of Lsbg. PoA for sale of 6a lot adj James RUST, Marton KITZMILLER and prop. adj (prch/o P. BENEDUM) occupied by Thomas AIR [HEIR?] at E end of town.

3E:434   Date: 10 May 1822   RtCt: 8 Jul 1822
Enos WILLIAMS dec'd. Division – Lot #7 (121a) and wood Lot #7 (10a) & negro woman Patty & Clary and boy Nathan to dower of widow Hannah, Lot # 1 (56a) and wood Lot #1 (16a) & negro boy John to Charles WILLIAMS, Lot #2 (90a) & negro boy Peter to Phineas WILLIAMS, Lot #3 (93a) & negro boy Presley to Israel WILLIAMS, Lot #4 (120a) & negro girl Izra to Benjamin HOUGH & wife Mary, Lot #5 (86a) & negro boy George to John WILLIAMS, Lot #6 (97a) and wood Lot #6 (16a) & negro boy Timothy to Sidney WILLIAMS. Gives plat and full details. Divisors: Robt. BRADEN, Chs. ELGIN, Abiel JENNERS.

3E:439   Date: __ 1820   RtCt: 8 Jul 1822
Thomas STUMP dec'd. Division – Lot #1 (103a) to Joseph STUMP, Lot #2 (97a) to Sarah MANLEY. Gives plat and details. Divisors: John MOOR, John GEORGE, Michael EVERHART.

3E:440   Date: 21 Jul 1821   RtCt: 19 Aug 1822
William FULKISON (insolvent debtor) of Ldn to Sheriff Burr POWELL. B/S of ½a in Upperville (debts to Joseph LLOYD, Edward DAWES and Margaret THOMPSON Exor of John THOMPSON dec'd.) Wit: John McCORMICK, Wm. M. McCARTY.

3E:441   Date: 24 Jun 1822   RtCt: 12 Aug 1822
Jacob HOWSER & wife Abigail of Ldn to John KALB, Jas. WHITE, John SAUNDERS, Aaron MILLER, Saml. KALB, James GREENLEESE, Richard TAVENER, Jacob HOWSER and Mortimer McILHANEY (trustees of Methodist Episcopal Church at Rahobeth) in Ldn. B/S of 1a on which Methodist meeting house is erected adj Wm. WOOLFORD. Wit: Robert BRADEN, Samuel HOUGH Jr. Delv. to Jno. KALB 21 May 1829.

3E:444   Date: 18 May 1822   RtCt: 13 Aug 1822
John COMPHER of Ldn to Jacob STOUSABERGER of Ldn. BoS for slave for life Henry of dark complexion aged 4y. Wit: Saml. M. JOHNSON, Henry SNUTS, Alfred A. ESKRIDGE, Benj. SHREVE.

3E:445   Date: 6 Mar 1822   RtCt: 12 Aug 1822
Leonard THOMAS to Philip SWANK and Adam SANBOWER. Trust for debt to John HICKMAN, Henry HICKMAN, John BOOTHE Jr.,

and Benj. MILES using int. in real estate of Peter HICKMAN Sr.
dec'd and household items and farm animals.

3E:447   Date: 31 Jul 1822   RtCt: 12 Aug 1822
Aaron BOOTH & wife Sarah of Ldn to George SANDERS of Ldn.
B/S of int. in land of father James BOOTHE dec'd. Wit: Robert
BRADEN, Saml. HOUGH Jr. Delv. to SANDERS 21 Mar 1823.

3E:449   Date: 28 Jul 1822   RtCt: 15 Aug 1822
Fanny ANDERSON to Gabrial GREEN. PoA to convey to Capt.
Samuel CHINN a negro girl Harriet. Wit: James McDANIEL, W.
HARRISON.

3E:450   Date: 20 Aug 1822   RtCt: 20 Aug 1822
Stacey HAINES of Ldn to James STONE of MontMd. B/S of 87a adj
HAINES, ferry road, __ HOGLAND, __ Newton. Wit: Presley
CORDELL, Henry TALBOTT, S. STERRET. Delv. to S. M.
EDWARDS commr for STONE's heirs 16 Aug 1832.

3E:451   Date: 31 Mar 1821   RtCt: 12 Aug 1822
Hanson MARLOW of Ldn to Edward MARLOW of Ldn. B/S of 98a
on E side of Ferry road adj Anthony AMONDS, Col. CLAPHAM.

3E:453   Date: 13 Mar 1822   RtCt: 12 Aug 1822
Moses KIMLER thru PoA from Hannah KIMLER and Israel KIMLER
to Daniel KIMLER. B/S of 1/10th int. in 75a where father John
KIMLER lived. Wit: Nathaniel POLEN, Walter ACERS, Daniel B.
PALMER, John POLEN, William POLEN.

3E:454   Date: 29 Jul 1822   RtCt: 12 Aug 1822
Jozabed WHITE to Daniel CONARD. Trust for Robert BRADEN as
security in suit by Emanuel NEWCOMER using 103a adj Wm.
SMITH, Mary FOX, P. CORDELL, Saml. GREGG.

3E:456   Date: 1 Jun 1822   RtCt: 12 Aug 1822
Israel WILLIAMS & wife Amelia of Ldn to Charles WILLIAMS of Ldn.
B/S of int. in land allotted Hannah WILLIAMS (wd/o Enos
WILLIAMS) as dower. Wit: Robert BRADEN, Samuel HOUGH Jr.
Delv. to Chas. WILLIAMS 23 Dec 1823.

3E:457   Date: 20 Apr 1822   RtCt: 12 Aug 1822
John GALLEHER & wife Sarah of Ldn to Joseph A. LLOYD of Ldn.
B/S of lot in Union adj William GALLEHER, Israel BROWN. Wit:
Wm. BRONAUGH, Francis W. LUCKETT. Delv. to atty Michael
PLAISTER pr order DBk KKK:80.

3E:458   Date: 31 Mar 1821   RtCt: 12 Aug 1822
John STOUSEBERGER and Edward MARLOW (Exors of Conrod
SHAFER dec'd) of Ldn to Hanson MARLOW of Ldn. B/S of 98a on E
side of Ferry road adj Col. CLAPHAM, Anthony AMONDS.

3E:460   Date: 21 Jun 1822   RtCt: 8 Jul 1822
John UPP of Ldn to Burr POWELL of Ldn. Trust for debt to Elizabeth
SEATON Admx of James SEATON dec'd using lot in Mdbg where

UPP resides adj Nelson GREEN. Wit: John HARRIS, Jas. WEEKS, H. SMITH.

3E:461   Date: 20 Jul 1822   RtCt: 12 Aug 1822
Isaac BROWN & wife Sarah of Ldn to Isaac NICKOLS Jr. and James HOGE of Ldn. Trust for debt to Isaac & Samuel NICKOLS using 150a (another survey gave as 178¼a) adj Robert SMITH, Dawson BROWN, Benjamin OVERFELT and 26a adj other and another adj 46a. Wit: Benjamin GRAYSON, William BRONAUGH. Delv. to Samuel NICHOLS Exors. 10 Nov 1825.

3E:464   Date: 29 Jul 1822   RtCt: 12 Aug 1822
Jozabed WHITE & wife Margaret of Ldn to Robert BRADEN of Ldn. B/S of 57a adj Wtfd (part of tract that BRADEN & WHITE prch/o Emanuel NEWCOMER Mar 1817) including 3 lots – one with brick house, one with miller's house and one adj Wtfd. Wit: Abiel JENNERS, Saml. HOUGH Jr.

3E:466   Date: 17 Jul 1822   RtCt: 12 Aug 1822
John HARDY & wife Elizabeth of Ldn to Abner GIBSON of Ldn. Trust for debt to Jacob ISH using int. in 110a farm of William GALLIHER dec'd left to Anna GALLIHER now w/o Thomas H. WEY by father Wm. and conveyed to HARDY. Wit: Cuthbert POWELL, Joseph CARR.

3E:468   Date: 25 May 1822   RtCt: 12 Aug 1822
Adam WINEGARDNER & wife Margaret of Ldn to Joshua OSBURN and Turner OSBURN of Ldn. Trust for debt to Thomas GREGG and Jehu HOLLINGSWORTH using land cnvy/b HOLLINGSWORTH. Wit: Craven OSBURN, John WHITE. Delv. to Joshua OSBURN 12 Jul 1824.

3E:470   Date: 4 Aug 1822   RtCt: 12 Aug 1822
Sheriff Burr POWELL to Benjamin GRAYSON of Ldn. B/S of 163a where insolvent debtor William FOWKE now lives under L/L (prch/o Samuel BERKLEY).

3E:472   Date: 29 Jul 1822   RtCt: 12 Aug 1822
Israel CLAYTON of Ldn to Minor REED and Mary REED of Ldn. B/S of 2a adj __ THOMAS, __ LEE's reps. Delv. to CLAYTON 8 May 1826.

3E:473   Date: 3 Aug 1822   RtCt: 12 Aug 1822
Mason MARKS & wife Hannah of Ldn to Jonah WALRAVEN of JeffVa. Trust for debt to James BEST Admr and f/o of William BEST dec'd using int. in dower land of mother Mary MARKS wd/o Abel MARKS. Wit: Craven OSBURN, John WHITE.

3E:476   Date: 17 Aug 1822   RtCt: 12 Aug 1822
David CARTER to Sydnor BAILY and Cuthbert POWELL. Trust for debt to Joseph CARR using 96a where CARTER lives former prop. of Daniel BROWN on Goose Creek adj Presley SANDERS. Wit: Caldwell CARR, John MOORE, Tho. D. L. HANSBOROUGH, Saml.

CARR. Delv. to Caldwell CARR by direction of trustee Sydnor BAILEY 10 Feb 1823.

3E:476   Date: 29 Jul 1822   RtCt: 12 Aug 1822
James HIXSON of Ldn to Stephen C. ROSZEL, Richard H. HENDERSON and Jesse TIMMS. Trust for debt to George CARTER of Oatlands using 330a except abt 8a (part of land patented to Thomas OWSLEY) adj John SINCLAIR, James SINCLAIR, James MERCER. Delv. to Wm. COCKERILL for G. CARTER pr order 18 Feb 1823.

3E:479   Date: 1 Jun 1822   RtCt: 12 Aug 1822
Lewis FRENCH of Ldn to James CRAIG of Ldn. Trust for debt to George TAVENER Jr. using 150a (dev. by father). Delv. to TAVENER 16 Jun 1823.

3E:481   Date: 30 Jul 1822   RtCt: 12 Aug 1822
Gabriel GREEN of FredVa to Meshech LACEY of Ldn. Trust for debt to Samuel CHINN using negro girl Harriet abt 14y old, brick house and lot in Mdbg adj Elizabeth BOYD (cnvy/b Samuel MURRY).

3E:482   Date: 1 Apr 1822   RtCt: 12 Aug 1822
Philip JONES & wife Ann of Ldn to David McINTOSH of Ldn. B/S of 7½a adj __ JONES, __ HIXSON. Wit: Robert BRADEN, Abiel JENNERS.

3E:484   Date: 15 Mar 1822   RtCt: 12 Aug 1822
Benjamin KIMLER of Ldn to Daniel KIMLER of Ldn. B/S of int. in lands of father John KIMLER in Ldn. Wit: Nathan[i]el POLEN, Walter ACRES, William POLEN, Daniel B. PALMER, John POLEN.

3E:485   Date: 15 Mar 1822   RtCt: 12 Aug 1822
Moses KIMLER of Burbon Co Ky to Daniel KIMLER of Ldn. B/S of int. in lands of father John KIMLER in Ldn. Wit: Nathaniel POLEN, Walter ACRES, Daniel B. PALMER, John POLEN, William POLEN.

3E:486   Date: 25 Jul 1822   RtCt: 3 Sep 1822
John DAVIS & wife Margaret of Ldn to Alexander CORDELL of Ldn. B/S of 1a (cnvy/b Adam HOUSEHOLDER) adj Sanford RAMEY. Wit: Robert BRADEN, Abiel JENNERS. Delv. to CORDELL 6 Feb 1826.

3E:487   Date: 26 Aug 1822   RtCt: 3 Sep 1822
Daniel MILLER & wife Mary of Culpeper to Aaron MILLER of Ldn. B/S of 1/6th part of land occupied by Mary HIXSON wd/o Reuben HIXSON dec'd. Delv. to Aaron MILLER 26 May 1823.

3E:488   Date: 27 Aug 1822   RtCt: 4 Sep 1822
John DREAN of Ldn to Samuel TUSTIN of Ldn. B/S of part of Lot #56 in Lsbg adj TUSTIN. Wit: Alfred A. ESKRIDGE, R. St. CLAIR, E. G. HAMILTON.

3E:490   Date: 31 Aug 1822   RtCt: 4 Sep 1822
Benjamin W. PERRY of Ldn to John A. BINNS of Ldn. BoS for slaves for life Hannah and her children Trueman, Wesley, Gerard, Mary, Emely, Harriett and a younger unnamed female child (same

ones cnvy/b PERRY in trust to Joshua TAYLOR). Wit: R. K. WATTS Jr., Martin CORDELL. Delv. to Chas. BINNS in whom the title is now vested 24 Jan 1836.

3E:490   Date: 29 Jul 1822   RtCt: 4 Sep 1822
Robert BRADEN & wife Elizabeth of Ldn to Jozabed WHITE of Ldn. B/S of 103a (prch/o Mary FOX) adj FOX, Wm. SMITH, Samuel GREGG. Wit: Abiel JENNERS, Saml. HOUGH Jr.

3E:492   Date: 29 Jul 1822   RtCt: 4 Sep 1822
Robert BRADEN & wife Elizabeth of Ldn to Jozabed WHITE of Ldn. B/S of lot in Wtfd (prch/o Wm. YATES) adj Mahlon JANNEY, Wm. HOUGH. Wit: Abiel JENNERS, Saml. HOUGH Jr.

3E:493   Date: 21 Oct 1821   RtCt: 5 Sep 1822
Ebenezer GRUBB of Ldn (as trustee for Thomas KIDWELL & wife Elizabeth in debt to David POTTS) of Ldn to Valentine JACOBS of Ldn. B/S of 16a (held in trust) adj __ KOONTZ, __ NEAR, __ CLENDENING. Wit: Craven OSBURNE, John WHITE. Delv. pr order 27 Nov 1834.

3E:496   Date: 6 Sep 1822   RtCt: 6 Sep 1822
Joseph T. NEWTON & wife Nelly of Ldn to Richard H. HENDERSON of Ldn. B/S of 7a where NEWTON lives (payment first made to Henry CRAINE as stipulated by NEWTON having prch/o him) adj Enoch HARPER. Wit: Presley CORDELL, Thomas SANDERS.

3E:497   Date: 10 Aug 1821   RtCt: 5 Sep 1822
Joseph T. NEWTON & wife Nelly of Ldn to Samuel M. EDWARDS of Ldn. B/S of 22a Lot #2 and #3 in survey adj __ MISKELL and also 2a Lot #1. Wit: Presley CORDELL, Thomas SANDERS.

3E:499   Date: 10 Feb 1822   RtCt: 25 Sep 1822
John WHITE and Craven OSBORN (as trustees of Isaac LARROWE in Oct 1818 then in Ldn) of Ldn to John A. MARMADUKE of Ldn. B/S of 42a from trust. Delv. pr order to Wm. HOUGH 22 Apr 1825.

3E:500   Date: 6 Sep 1820   RtCt: 6 Sep 1822
David SAUGHBAUGH/SAURBAUGH to Thomas J. MARLOW. Trust for debt to Michael EVERHART using farm animals, household items.

3E:502   Date: 6 Sep 1822   RtCt: 8 Sep 1822
Samuel A. TILLETT and Saml. M. EDWARDS. Agreement – TILLETT cnvy/b deed of trust to EDWARDS merchandize he bought of John GRAY of Lsbg now in possession of John F. CLARKE at Post William in Galatin Co Ky. CLARKE may have sold some items, notes and accts transferred to EDWARDS.

3E:503   Date: 6 Sep 1822   RtCt: 6 Sep 1822
Samuel A. TILLETT to Samuel M. EDWARDS. Trust for debt to Samuel CARR, Nancy TILLETT, John CARR, Thomas SWANN, Thomas SAUNDERS, B. GILPIN & son, Thomas RUSSELL, Samuel

HAMMETT and John DRISH using merchandise bought of John GRAY of Lsbg [see above]. Delv. pr order 2 Jul 1829.

3E:505   Date: 6 Sep 1822   RtCt: 6 Sep 1822
Archibald McVICKERS of Hampshire Co Va to Josiah L. DREAN of WashDC. Trust for Fleet SMITH and __ MOORE using int. in trust by Jonas POTTS & wife Nancy to Benjamin SHRIEVE and Joshua OSBURN as security for McVICKERS on Admr of Hester McVICKERS dec'd in WashDC.

3E:506   Date: 29 Jul 1822   RtCt: 6 Sep 1822
Israel CLAYTON of Ldn to Robert CHEW of Ldn. B/S of 45¼a Lot #4 and 51¾a Lot #18 in __ survey. DBk QQQ:206.

3E:508   Date: 9 Sep 1822   RtCt: 9 Sep 1822
Jesse McVEIGH and Richard H. HENDERSON. Bond on McVEIGH as Commr. of the Revenue of the 2nd District.

3E:508   Date: 9 Sep 1822   RtCt: 9 Sep 1822
Jesse TIMMS and George CARTER. Bond on TIMMS as Commr. of the Revenue of the 1st District.

3E:509   Date: 10 Sep 1822   RtCt: 10 Sep 1822
Charles BINNS clerk of ct and Rich'd H. HENDERSON. Bond on BINNS to collect taxes.

3E:509   Date: 20 Jun 1822   RtCt: 30 Aug 1822
Britton SANDERS of Ldn to Saml. M. EDWARDS of Ldn. Trust for debt to John CARR, John J. HARDING, Thos. SANDERS, Charles GULLATT, George SINCLAIR, Jno. McCABE and Richard H. HENDERSON ass'ee of Jos. BEARD Admr of Robert WRENN dec'd using farm animals, household items, slaves Rosa and Betty.

3E:511   Date: 3 Aug 1822   RtCt: 12 Aug 1822
Daniel SHOEMAKER & wife Priscilla of Ldn to Simon SHOEMAKER Sr. of Ldn. B/S of 1a adj Margaret SAUNDERS, both SHOEMAKERS. Wit: Abiel JENNERS, Samuel HOUGH Jr. Delv. to Simon Sr. 29 Mar 1836.

3E:513   Date: 20 May 1822   RtCt: 12 Aug 1822
John JANNEY 3rd of Hllb to Thomas PHILIPS and Joseph BOND of Wtfd. Trust for debt to Mordica MILLER and W. H. MILLER as firm of Mordica Miller and son of AlexDC using 66a adj Samuel CLENDENING, Benjamin LESLIE.

3E:515   Date: 10 Jun 1822   RtCt: 20 Aug 1822
Britton SAUNDERS of Ldn to Samuel M. EDWARDS of Ldn. Trust for debt to George L. LACKLAND and Sam'l HOUGH Jr. (Admr of Silas WHERRY dec'd) using farm animals and items.

3E:516   Date: 29 Jul 1822   RtCt: 26 Aug 1822
James HIXSON of Ldn to Richard H. HENDERSON, Stephen C. ROZEL and Jesse TIMMS. Trust for debt to Eliza A. BARRY using 330a on little river (part of tract patented to Thomas OWSLEY) adj John SINCLAIR. Delv. to Jesse TIMMS 13 May 1823.

3E:518 Date: 29 Jun 1822 RtCt: 12 Aug 1822
James MOUNT (trustee of Daniel BROWN for debt to William
HOGUE who sold trust to Saml. BROWN) of Ldn to Samuel
BROWN of Ldn. B/S of 9¼a (cnvy/b Stephen McGEATH) on paved
road leading to Snicker's Gap. Wit: Wm. BRONAUGH, Francis W.
LUCKETT. Delv. pr order 23 Mar 1836.

3E:519 Date: 29 Mar 1822 RtCt: 26 Aug 1822
Edward HAZEL & wife Elizabeth of Ldn to Lewis M. SMITH of Ldn.
Trust for debt to William NOLAND using 2a cnvy/b NOLAND. Wit:
Thomas SMARR, Henry McKENZEE, Abraham BROWN, Presley
CORDELL, Saml. M. EDWARDS. Delv. to NOLAND 31 Mar 1824.

3E:521 Date: 27 Jul 1822 RtCt: 26 Aug 1822
Watts MARKS of Jefferson Co Ky to Thomas MARKS of Ldn. B/S of
int. in land occupied by Mary MARKS wd/o Abel MARKS in right of
dower.

3E:523 Date: 29 Mar 1822 RtCt: 26 Aug 1822
William NOLAND & wife Catharine of Ldn to Edward HAZEL of Ldn.
B/S of 2a at Ashby's Gap Turnpike road adj Aldie. Wit: Francis
THOMPSON, James SMARR, Thomas SMARR, Presley CORDELL,
Saml. M. EDWARDS.

3E:524 Date: 29 Mar 1822 RtCt: 26 Aug 1822
James STEPHENSON & wife Sarah of Ldn to Lewis M. SMITH of
Ldn. Trust for debt to William NOLAND using 3 rood lot cnvy/b
NOLAND and farm and household items. Wit: Thos. H. KIRBY,
Henry McKENZIE, Thomas SMARR, Presley CORDELL, Saml. M.
EDWARDS. Delv. pr order ___

3E:526 Date: 17 Aug 1822 RtCt: 26 Aug 1822
William VICKERS & wife Anna of Ldn to Gurley READER of Ldn.
Trust for debt to Joseph & Samuel HATCHER of Ldn using 104¼a
adj __ DULANEY. Wit: Francis W. LUCKETT, William BRONAUGH.
Delv. pr order 8 Mar 1825.

3E:528 Date: 26 Jul 1822 RtCt: 26 Aug 1822
Lewis ELLZEY of Ldn to Craven OSBURN of Ldn. Trust for Joshua
OSBURN as security using int. as heir in lands of Thomazen
ELLZEY late of Ffx. Wit: Hector OSBURN, Norval OSBURN, Benj.
SHREVE Jr. Delv. to Joshua OSBURN 16 May 1823.

3E:529 Date: 29 Aug 1822 RtCt: 29 Aug 1822
Frederick BROOKS of PrWm to John W. TYLER of PrWm. Trust for
debt to Barnaby CANNON and John MACRAE assignees of David
ROSS using 2a.

3E:530 Date: 24 May 1822 RtCt: 29 Aug 1822
Thomas GREGG (S.H.) & wife Ann of Ldn to Jehu
HOLLINGSWORTH of Ldn. B/S of 87¾a (cnvy/b Mark GORES) adj
Lewis ELLZEY and 2a (cnvy/b Lewis ELLZEY) adj the other. Wit:

Cravan OSBURN, John WHITE. Delv. to HOLLINGSWORTH 3 May 1824.

3F:001 Date: 21 Mar 1822 RtCt: 10 Jun 1822
Reuben SCHOOLEY and Thomas PHILIPS (Exors of David LACEY dec'd) of Ldn to Jesse RICE & wife Thurza of Ldn. B/S of 150a (from suit of Nov 1821 Jesse RICE agst Reuben SCHOOLEY & Thomas PHILIPS Exors of David LACEY dec'd, Nathaniel MANNING & wife Uphamiah, Thomas GRIGGS & wife Castalina, William PAXTON & wife Didamia and Sarah LACEY). Delv. to RICE 28 Dec 1825.

3F:002 Date: 13 Jul 1822 RtCt: 2 Sep 1822
John McKNIGHT of Ldn to James RUST of Ldn. Trust for debt to John PANCOAST Sr. using 28a (from div. of land of father William McKNIGHT dec'd). Wit: John PANCOAST Jr., John GREGG, Eli TAVENER.

3F:003 Date: 10 Aug 1822 RtCt: 30 Aug 1822
Charles Fenton MERCER of Ldn to Pres. and Directors of Ashby Gap Turnpike Co. B/S of ½a (need to move first gate closer to Aldie, lists rules for charging toll to Aldie area residents.) Delv. pr order of Burr POWELL Pres of Co. on ___.

3F:004 Date: 31 Aug 1822 RtCt: 31 Aug 1822
Bennett MARKS of Ldn to John C. BAZZIL and George W. PETTIT of Ldn. B/S of 24a on Valentine's Branch nr Blue Ridge adj Thomas WHITE, Wm. BROWN.

3F:005 Date: 31 Aug 1822 RtCt: 21 Aug 1822
John C. BAZZILL & wife Mary and George W. PETITT of Ldn to Joshua OSBURN of Ldn. Trust for debt to Bennett MARKS using above 24a.

3F:006 Date: 1 Jul 1822 RtCt: 21 Aug 1822
Samuel BROWN of Ldn to Daniel JANNEY of Ldn. Trust for debt to William HOGE using 10¼a (cnvy/b James MOUNT & wife Hannah). Delv. to HOGE 22 Mar 1828.

3F:007 Date: 31 Aug 1822 RtCt: 31 Aug 1822
John C. BAZZILL & wife Mary and George W. PETITT of Ldn to Joshua OSBURN of Ldn. Trust for debt to Thomas JAMES using 36a on Valentine's branch nr Blue Ridge adj John WARNER, Alexander HARRISON, William BROWN.

3F:008 Date: 1 Aug 1822 RtCt: 3 Sep 1822
John DAVIS & wife Margaret of Ldn to Alexander CORDELL of Ldn. B/S of 1a adj Daniel STONE (cnvy/b Frederick COOPER & wife Molly). Wit: Robert BRADEN, Samuel HOUGH Jr. Delv. to A. CORDELL 6 Feb 1826.

3F:009 Date: 3 Jun 1822 RtCt: 9 Sep 1822
Joseph HARPER & wife Eliza, John SLAUGHTER & wife Sarah and Charles HARPER of Albamarle Co Va to Charles BENNETT of Ldn.

B/S of lot in Lsbg leased by Joseph JANNEY to William MOXLEY and willed to JANNEY's dau Sarah. Same rent to BENNETT.

3F:010   Date: 10 Sep 1822   RtCt: 10 Sep 1822
Frederick BROOKS of Ldn to George RICHARDS of Ldn. Trust for debt to Michael D. YOUNG of BaltMd using int. in 25a lease from Mathew RUST to BROOKS with 2 story stone building, 1 story frame house, carding machine and fulling mill.

3F:011   Date: 23 Jul 1822   RtCt: 9 Sep 1822
John UPP of Mdbg to Burr POWELL. Trust for Sarah UPP (w/o John and d/o Thomas CHINN, permitting sale of 141a in Fqr from father) with John giving up all his claims to her property. Delv. to H. SMITH pr order of B. POWELL on ___.

3F:012   Date: 24 May 1822   RtCt: 10 Sep 1822
Jehu HOLLINGSWORTH & wife Senior of Ldn to Adam WINEGARNER of Ldn. B/S of 136a (cnvy/b John HESKETT) adj Gidney CLERKs land, __ McKNIGHT, George LEWIS. Wit: Craven OSBURN, John WHITE. Delv. to WINEGARNER 3 Jan 1824.

3F:013   Date: 5 Sep 1822   RtCt: 6 Sep 1822
David SARBAUGH of Ldn to Thomas J. MARLOW of Ldn. Trust for John S. MARLOW as security on note to Babel WELLS using farm animals and items.

3F:013   Date: 11 Sep 1823   RtCt: 12 Sep 1822
Joseph EIDSON of Ldn to John SINCLAIR of Ldn. Trust for debt to Joseph HOGUE using negro woman Susan abt 13y old now hired to James IDEN until 24 Dec next. Delv. to B. W. HARRISON pr order.

3F:014   Date: 13 Sep 1822   RtCt: 12 Sep 1822
Miller HOGUE & wife Tacey of Ldn to Hugh SMITH of Ldn. Trust for debt to Joseph HOGUE using 26¼a on small branch of Goose Creek prch/o Joseph EIDSON, adj Moses WILSON, Dennis McCARTY, Handy's Mill road. Wit: Presley CORDELL, Saml. M. EDWARDS. Delv. to Jos. HOGE 22 Dec 1824.

3F:016   Date: 31 Aug 1822   RtCt: 12 Sep 1822
Joseph EIDSON & wife Elizabeth of Ldn to Miller HOGUE of Ldn. B/S of 26¼a as above. Wit: Leven LUCKETT, A. GIBSON. Delv. to HOGE 23 May 1824.

3F:017   Date: 13 Sep 1822   RtCt: 13 Sep 1822
Charles B. HAMILTON and John HAMILTON of Ldn to Jno. A. BINNS of Ldn. BoS for negro slave Helen.

3F:017   Date: 17 Sep 1822   RtCt: 17 Sep 1822
Tasker C. QUINLAN of Ldn to Thomas Randolph MOTT of Ldn. B/S of 324a between Goose Creek and Little River adj Geo. CARTER. Gives plat. Delv. to MOTT 19 Aug 1823.

3F:019   Date: 13 Sep 1822   RtCt: 12 Sep 1822
John UPP & wife Sarah of Mdbg to Humphrey B. POWELL of Ldn. Trust for debt to Noble BEVERIDGE and Hiram McVEIGH using 84a

adj Jane WEATHERLY and Lot #22 in Mdbg with stables. Wit:
Leven LUCKETT, A. GIBSON.

3F:020   Date: 9 Sep 1822   RtCt: 19 Sep 1822
David ALEXANDER & wife Elizabeth of Ldn to Daniel HAINS of Fqr.
Trust for debt to William RANDALL of Fqr using 16a (prch/o
RANDALL) on turnpike road from Aldie to Snickers Ferry adj
Elizabeth GARRETT, George W. McCARTY, (part sold to Samuel
TRAYHERN). Wit: Leven LUCKETT, A. GIBSON.

3F:022   Date: 11 Sep 1822   RtCt: 20 Sep 1822
George B. WHITING & wife Frances H. of Ldn to Portia HODGSON
of Ldn. B/S of 4¼a 'Goshen' (prch/o Israel LACEY) on old turnpike
road. Relinquishment of trust by William COOKE.

3F:023   Date: 11 Sep 1822   RtCt: 14 Oct 1822
Edmund J. LEE & wife Sally of AlexDC to Thomas KIDWELL of Ldn.
B/S of 50a adj __ CONARD and 68a adj __ CONARD, __
DEMORY. Wit: Jacob HOFFMAN, E. J. LEE Jr., Lucy LEE. Delv. to
KIDWELL 25 Jun 1823.

3F:025   Date: 21 Sep 1822   RtCt: 23 Sep 1822
Peter C. RUST of Ldn to Edwin C. BROWN of Ldn. Trust for debt to
Hannah MITCHELL of Lancaster Co Va using 197a where RUST
now resides adj Hiram SEATON, Jno. VIOLETT. Delv. to BROWN
12 Aug 1823.

3F:026   Date: 21 Sep 1822   RtCt: 24 Sep 1822
George HEAD & wife Mary of Ldn to Jacob FADELY of Ldn. B/S of
lot in Lsbg on W side of Liberty St adj William HEAD, __
CALDWELL. Wit: Presley CORDELL, Thomas SANDERS. Delv. to
FADELY 16 Apr 1834.

3F:028   Date: 21 Mar 1822   RtCt: 24 Sep 1822
John SURGHNOR & wife Elizabeth of Ldn to George HEAD of Ldn.
B/S of lot in Lsbg on Loudoun St (DBk AA:29, lot sold to George
RHINE by Patrick CAVINS). Wit: Presley CORDELL, Thomas
SANDERS.

3F:029   Date: 25 Sep 1822   RtCt: 25 Sep 1822
Daniel LOVETT of Ldn to Samuel CARR of Ldn. Trust for debt to
William HALL using 150a. Delv. to CARR 4 Oct 1827.

3F:029   Date: 25 Sep 1822   RtCt: 25 Sep 1822
William A. BINNS of Ldn to Samuel CARR of Ldn. Trust for debt to
William HALL using 200a where BINNS now resides (dev. from
father Charles BINNS).

3F:030   Date: 25 Jul 1822   RtCt: 25 Sep 1822
Henry CLAGETT & wife July of Ldn to William TAYLOR of Ldn. B/S
of 43a on Tuscarora adj W side of Mdbg road. Delv. to Joseph
MEAD pr order of B. J. TAYLOR 23 May 1836.

3F:031   Date: 21 Oct 1822   RtCt: 1 Oct 1822
Evan LLOYD of Fqr and Mary Ann LLOYD of PrWm to Daniel P.
CONARD of Ldn. B/S of 1¼a (cnvy/b William NOLAND Apr 1819 to
James LLOYD now dec'd). Delv. pr order 21 Sep 1835.

3F:032   Date: 22 Jul 1822   RtCt: 1 Oct 1822
Evan LLOYD of PrWm and Mary Ann LLOYD to Samuel M.
EDWARDS of Lsbg. PoA for sales of house and lot in Aldie and
unimproved lot in Aldie as heir of brother James LLOYD dec'd. Wit:
Presley CORDELL, John MARTIN, John H. MONROE.

3F:033   Date: 26 Jun 1822   RtCt: 1 Oct 1822
Jehu HOLLINGSWORTH of Ldn to Stacey TAYLOR of Ldn. Trust
for debt to Amos BEANS using lot cnvy/b Thomas GREGG (S.H.)
May 1822. Delv. to James L. HAMILTON pr order 27 May 1830.

3F:034   Date: 21 Sep 1822   RtCt: 1 Oct 1822
Nathaniel MANNING & wife Euphamia of Ldn to Zachariah DULANY
of Ldn. Trust for debt to Amos BEANS using lot (cnvy/b George
JANNEY & wife Susanna) adj Major BRADEN, John WRIGHT. Wit:
Abiel JENNERS, Robert BRADEN. Delv. to DULANEY 27 Mar 1826.

3F:036   Date: 1 Oct 1822   RtCt: 1 Oct 1822
William CARR of Ldn to James BROWN of Ldn. LS of lot on W side
of Liberty St adj Geo. HEAD, Samuel MURRAY dec'd, Joshua
RYLEY.

3F:037   Date: 30 Sep 1822   RtCt: 2 Oct 1822
Thomas JONES & wife Sarah of Ldn to John MARKS of Ldn. B/S of
land (allotted to Jones from Samuel Harnedor ARNETT dec'd) on
road from Drake's mill to Snickers Gap Road nr Joshua GREGG.

3F:038   Date: 30 Sep 1822   RtCt: 2 Oct 1822
Yeoman John MARKS & wife Lydia of Ldn to yeoman Stephen
McPHERSON (of William) of Ldn. B/S of 191a (allotted by father
Elisha MARKS dec'd) adj Ury GRADY, Jer. GILL, Barton EWERS,
Joshua GREGG, and 3 lots (cnvy/b Barton EWERS, Thomas
JONES and Isaiah MARKS) and 50a adj Benjamin
STRINGFELLOW, Samuel DUNKIN. Wit: Benj. GRAYSON, N. C.
WILLIAMS. Delv. to John MARKS pr order of Stephen
McPHERSON 1 Apr 1824.

3F:040   Date: 30 Sep 1822   RtCt: 3 Oct 1822
George Mason CHICHESTER of Ldn to Thomas GASSAWAY of
Ldn. B/S of 370a where CHICHESTER now resides (cnvy/b Isaac S.
WHITE) adj C. P. TUTT, __ BALL, __ MASON. Wit: Robert
BENTLEY, Alfred A. ESKRIDGE, A. R. St. CLAIR. Delv. to
GASSAWAY 1 Apr 1840.

3F:041   Date: 30 Sep 1822   RtCt: 3 Oct 1822
Thomas GASSAWAY & wife Henrietta of Ldn to George Mason
CHICHESTER of Ldn. B/S of 166a (using above land as payment)
adj __ STOUSABERGER. Wit: A. R. St. CLAIR, Alfred A.

ESKRIDGE, Robert BENTLEY, John McCORMICK, Presley
CORDELL. Delv. to CHICHESTER 14 May 1824.

3F:043 Date: 4 Oct 1822 RtCt: 4 Oct 1822
Richard H. HENDERSON of Ldn to George JANNEY of MontMd.
Release of trust for debt to George RUST Jr. on 190a.

3F:043 Date: 26 Apr 1822 RtCt: 4 Oct 1822
Jeremiah W. BRONAUGH of Georgetown D.C. to Daniel KURTZ of
Georgetown D.C. Trust for debt to Bank of Columbia using 150a adj
William BRONAUGH. Wit: John PETER, Thomas CORCORAN.
Delv. to S. M. EDWARDS pr order from Pres of Bank 23 Jun 1832.

3F:045 Date: 7 Oct 1822 RtCt: 7 Oct 1822
Fanny BOOTH Jr. of Ldn to John BOOTH Jr of Ldn. B/S of 6a adj __
BROOKS, __ MULL and all int. in land of Fanny BOOTH wd/o
James BOOTH dec'd. Wit: S. BLINCOE.

3F:046 Date: 15 Sep 1822 RtCt: 8 Oct 1822
Thomas KIDWELL & wife Elizabeth of Ldn to John J. MATHIAS of
Ldn. Trust for debt to Edmund J. LEE of AlexDC using 50a and 68a.
Wit: Ebenezer GRUBB, Craven OSBURN. Delv. to MATHIAS 14 Oct
1823.

3F:049 Date: 8 Oct 1822 RtCt: 8 Oct 1822
Richard MILTON of Ldn to Francis STRIBLING Jr. Trust for debt to
John B. TAYLOR, James HEATON and John A. MARMADUKE
using farm and household items.

3F:050 Date: 25 Sep 1822 RtCt: 8 Oct 1822
William HERBERT agent of estate of Richard DeBUTTS dec'd to
Thomas SWAYNE of Ldn. Release of mortgage (DBk CCC:253) on
190a.

3F:051 Date: 5 Oct 1822 RtCt: 8 Oct 1822
Thomas SWAYNE to William CASTLEMAN Jr. B/S of 190a on NW
fork of Goose Creek adj Amos GIBSON, __ MEAD, David SMITH,
__ WILLIAMS. Delv. to CASTLEMAN 25 Oct 1825.

3F:053 Date: 5 Oct 1822 RtCt: 8 Oct 1822
William CASTLEMAN Jr. & wife Ury of Frederick Co to Thomas
SWANN of Ldn. B/S of 190a (as security for 3/7ths of mill and land
in case of deficiency). Wit: Geo. H. NORRIS, Treadwell SMITH.

3F:054 Date: 24 Apr 1822 RtCt: 11 Oct 1822
Tinsman Josias M. CLARK of Union to yeoman Edmund LOVETT of
Ldn. B/S of ¼a in Union (lot #4 in div. of James RUST dec'd).

3F:055 Date: 1 Mar 1822 RtCt: 11 Oct 1822
Jane WEATHERBY formerly McFARLAND and William SWART &
wife Elizabeth to Oliver DUNHAM/DENHAM. B/S of ½a Lot #21 in
Mdbg (cnvy/b Leven POWELL to John McFARLAND dev. to Jane
and John McFARLING with John conveying his share to SWART).
Wit: Burr POWELL, Edwin C. BROWN, John SIDEBOTTOM, Amos

GULIC, Robert CHIN, James WICKS, Francis W. LUCKETT, Cuthbert POWELL.

3F:057   Date: 17 Sep 1822   RtCt: 12 Oct 1822
Jane McCABE of Lsbg to Samuel M. BOSS of Ldn. B/S of part of Lot #1 on S side of Loudoun St. (allotted in decree in Jane agst James HAMILTON in div. of Robert HAMILTON the elder dec'd) adj Isaac HARRIS, Mathew WEATHERLY. Delv. to BOSS 30 Aug 1823.

3F:058   Date: 26 Aug 1822   RtCt: 14 Oct 1822
Catharine PRICE/RICE (wd/o Isaac dec'd and apptd Guardian in Apr 1822 of her infant children Rebecca, Enoch Marmaduke, Nancy, John Chilton, Frankey, Isaac Jackson and James Harrison and of Clarke Co Ky to William NIBLICK of Clarke Co Ky. PoA for monies as heir of Isaac RICE dec'd from estate of James RICE dec'd late of Va.

3F:061   Date: 14 Feb 1822   RtCt: 12 Oct 1822
Daniel C. JOHNSON of Ldn and Brittanna S. LOMAX wd/o of Lawson LOMAX dec'd of Ldn. Marriage contract – transfers her personal household items in trust to Lucinda MORRIS; if he dies first she retains possesses, if she dies first her will dictates disposal. Wit: James McDANIEL, John MORRIS, Joseph W. INGLE.

3F:063   Date: 14 Oct 1822   RtCt: 14 Oct 1822
Thomas J. DORSEY, Jno. ROSE and John A. BINNS. Bond on DORSEY, ordained by Christian society of Methodists to solemnize marriages.

3F:063   Date: 11 Nov 1822   RtCt: 11 Oct [Nov?] 1822
John ROSE, Benjamin SHREVE, Robert MOFFETT, Joseph MEAD, Richard H. HENDERSON and George RUST Jr. Bond on ROSE as Sheriff to collect militia fines.

3F:064   Date: 11 Nov 1822   RtCt: 11 Nov 1822
John ROSE, Benjamin SHREVE, Robert MOFFETT, Joseph MEAD, Richard H. HENDERSON and Geo. RUST Jr. Bond on ROSE as Sheriff to collect officers fees.

3F:065   Date: 11 Nov 1822   RtCt: 11 Nov 1822
John ROSE, Benjamin SHREVE, Robert MOFFETT, Joseph MEAD, Richard H. HENDERSON and George RUST Jr. Bond on ROSE as Sheriff to collect poor rate.

3F:065   Date: 9 Nov 1822   RtCt: 11 Nov 1822
Timothy TAYLOR. Oath as Captain in 56th Reg 6th Brig and 2nd Div. of malitia of Va. Wit: Jno. WHITE.

3F:066   Date: 11 Nov 1822   RtCt: 11 Nov 1822
Daniel COCKRILL. Oath as Lt. in 56th Reg 6th Brig and 2nd Div. of malitia of Va. Wit: Jno. WHITE.

3F:066   Date: 11 Nov 1822   RtCt: 11 Nov 1822
Charles TAYLOR. Oath as Major in 5th Reg of V.M. Wit: R. BRADEN.

3F:066   Date: 27 Jul 1822   RtCt: 11 Nov 1822
John ROSE. Appointed Sheriff of Ldn.

3F:067   Date: 10 Nov 1822   RtCt: 11 Nov 1822
Frances/Fanny HARRIS of Ldn. DoE for slave London Chavas. Wit: Catharine GREENLEASE, James TIPPETT.

3F:067   Date: 8 Nov 1822   RtCt: 12 Nov 1822
Hamilton ROGERS. Oath as ensign in 56th Reg 6th Brig and 2nd Div. of malitia of Va. Wit: Abner GIBSON.

3F:067   Date: 11 Nov 1822   RtCt: 12 Nov 1822
Prisoners in Loudoun: John CAVENS & Margaret CRIDER (debtors), Henry BENEDUM, Elizabeth BECKETT (for peace breaking), Nace a free man of colour (for stealing), Nat a slave (for running at large and hiring himself), black girl the property of Elias THRASHER taken under execution by Benjamin SHREVE.

3F:068   Date: 12 Nov 1822   RtCt: 12 Nov 1822
Charles DUNKIN, Jesse TIMMS and James BEAVERS. Bond on DUNKIN as constable.

3F:068   Date: 11 Nov 1822   RtCt: 11 Nov 1822
Peter C. RUST, William GILMORE and William WILKINSON. Bond on RUST as constable.

3F:069   Date: 6 Nov 1822   RtCt: 7 Nov 1822
Richard H. HENDERSON (trustee of Daniel C. BOSS of Pittsburg Pa for benefit of James BROWN of Pittsburg Pa) of Ldn to Samuel M. BOSS. B/S of und. int. in lot & buildings on NW corner of Loudoun & King Sts. (from estate of Peter BOSS dec'd) adj Charles B. BALL. Delv. to BOSS 7 Jul 1822.

3F:069   Date: 12 Oct 1822   RtCt: 9 Nov 1822
Joseph THOMAS of Ldn to Nathan NICKOLS Jr. of Ldn. B/S of 10a nr Blue Ridge where David NICKOLS now lives (part of tract formerly of George NICKOLS dec'd) adj Phillip THOMAS. Wit: Joshua OSBURN, George W. PETTIT, Richard ASHTON. Delv. to NICKOLS Jr. ___.

3F:070   Date: 6 Nov 1820 [22?]   RtCt: 6 Nov 1822
Thomas FORTUNE of PrWm to Garner FORTUNE of PrWm. Trust for use of James JENNINGS & wife Elizabeth and dau. Hannah by former wife using negro Coly, Stephen, James, Susan and Maria and farm and household items (purchased by Thomas of JANNINGS).

3F:071   Date: 2 Nov 1822   RtCt: 6 Nov 1822
James JENNINGS of Ldn to Thomas FORTUNE of PrWm. BoS of above mentioned slaves and items and corn now due him of Mrs. Portia HODGSON of AlexDC.

3F:072 Date: 17 Jun 1820 RtCt: 14 Oct 1822
William H. WEY & wife Annah of Ldn to John HARDY of Ldn. B/S of int. in 110a farm of William GALLEHER dec'd (f/o Annah) adj Union. Wit: Wm. BRONAUGH, Francis W. LUCKETT.

3F:073 Date: 12 Oct 1822 RtCt: 14 Oct 1822
John HARDY & wife Elizabeth of Ldn to Eli C. GALLEHER of Ldn. B/S of above mentioned int. in 110a farm. Wit: Joseph CARR, Cuthbert POWELL.

3F:074 Date: 15 Oct 1822 RtCt: 15 Oct 1822
Westly JENKINS & wife Nancy of Ldn to Benjamin SHREVE of Ldn. B/S of und. int. in lands of Josiah MOFFETT Jr. (f/o Nancy) on Secolon Run adj Peter OAYTER, Thomas R. MOTT, heirs of Landon CARTER. Wit: Thomas FOUCH, James H. HAMILTON. Delv. to SHREVE 11 Mar 1824.

3F:076 Date: 15 May 1822 RtCt: 16 Oct 1822
Eli H. HANDY of Ldn to Samuel DISHMAN of Ldn. B/S of 5¾a (prch/o James CHURCH) adj William DENNY, John TOWPERMAN, Handy's Mill dam. Wit: John SINCLAIR, William CODE, James T. DISHMAN.

3F:077 Date: 17 Oct 1822 RtCt: 17 Oct 1822
Frederick HANDSHY of Ldn to Samuel DAWSON of Ldn. Trust for debt to Thomas GASSAWAY using 250a on short hill nr point of mountain (cnvy/b John HOPKINS).

3F:078 Date: 15 Oct 1822 RtCt: 17 Oct 1822
Frederick HANDSHY of Ldn to Thomas J. MARLOW of Ldn. Trust for securing bail for payment to Foundren BACKHAM, Edward WAGER, Roger HUMPHREY using farm animals, farm and household items.

3F:079 Date: 16 Oct 1822 RtCt: 18 Oct 1822
Robert BRADEN & wife Elizabeth of Ldn to Richard H. HENDERSON of Ldn. Trust for debt to Bank of Alexandria (as firm of Braden Morgan & Co of Alex) using 150a adj John NICKLIN, John CUMMINGS, Sandford RAMEY, __ McGARRICK. Wit: Abiel JENNERS, Samuel HOUGH Jr. Delv. to HENDERSON ___.

3F:081 Date: 18 Oct 1822 RtCt: 19 Oct 1822
Edward DORSEY of Ldn to Richard H. HENDERSON of Ldn. Trust for debt to David SHAWEN surviving partner of D. Shawen & Co and Thomas George and Thomas using 2 lots in Wtfd with brick house and barn and 2¼a meadow lot adj William H. HOUGH. Wit: Benjamin SHREVE Jr., H'y H. HAMILTON, A. R. St. CLAIR. Delv. to HENDERSON 23 Sep 1823.

3F:082 Date: 18 Oct 1822 RtCt: 21 Oct 1822
James W. HENSHAW of Ldn to Thomas MORRALLEE of Ldn. LS of 1a between William CARR and heirs of Edward RINKER dec'd

(cnvy/b Bernard HOUGH Admr dbn of Patrick CAVAN dec'd). Wit: Jos. GAMBLE.

3F:083   Date: 16 Oct 1822   RtCt: 23 Oct 1822
Thomas TAYLOR & wife Penellope of Ldn to Thomas GASSAWAY of Ldn. B/S of 1/7th und. share of estate of Henry TAYLOR dec'd on W side of Cotoctin Creek except lot sold by Mrs. Ann TAYLOR to Levi COLLINS now in possession of Jacob CARNES. Wit: John HAMILTON, Samuel DAWSON.

3F:084   Date: 21 Aug 1822   RtCt: 25 Oct 1822
John MANLY & wife Sarah of Ldn to John MANN of Ldn. B/S of 97a (part of tract allotted to Sarah of estate of Thomas STUMP dec'd) adj John WENNER, Joseph STUMP. Wit: Robert BRADEN, Abiel JENNERS. Delv. to MANN 25 Feb 1825.

3F:085   Date: 24 Oct 1822   RtCt: 26 Oct 1822
Gabriel MEGEATH & wife Martha of Ldn to Stephen MEGEATH of Ldn. B/S of 2a (cnvy/b William HOGUE & wife Mary, Mary MEGEATH, Wm. H. HANDY & wife Ellenor and Stephen MEGEATH) adj James MEGEATH dec'd, __ ROSZEL. Wit: William BRONAUGH, N. C. WILLIAMS. Delv. pr order 3 Mar 1825.

3F:087   Date: 17 Oct 1822   RtCt: 26 Oct 1822
Stephen MEGEATH & wife Rebecca of Ldn to Mahlon CRAVEN of Ldn. B/S of 127a adj Samuel BROWN's Mill, Joseph GARRETT. Wit: John SINCLAIR, James SINCLAIR, William HOGE, William BRONAUGH, Notley C. WILLIAMS. Delv. to CRAVEN 3 Mar 1825.

3F:088   Date: 5 Apr 1815   RtCt: 29 Oct 1822
Timothy TAYLOR & wife Achsah of Ldn to William TAYLOR of Ldn. B/S of 31a on main road from Snickers Gap to Israel JANNEY's mill adj Samuel RUSSELL, __ JOHNSON. Wit: L. ELLZEY, Thomas GREGG, Thomas PRICE.

3F:089   Date: 5 Apr 1815   RtCt: 29 Oct 1822
Timothy TAYLOR & wife Achsah of Ldn to Charles TAYLOR of Ldn. B/S of 42a on NW fork of Goose Creek adj __ McILHANEY, __ RUSSELL. Wit: L. ELLZEY, Thomas GREGG, Thomas PRICE. Delv. to Chs. TAYLOR 31 Mar 1834.

3F:091   Date: 25 Oct 1822   RtCt: 29 Oct 1822
Catharine NOLAND of Ldn to John BAYLY of Ldn. Trust for debt to Thomas TRIPLETT of Fqr using rights to 328a (cnvy/b TRIPLETT to husband William NOLAND in Oct 1819). Wit: Leven LUCKETT, Ariss BUCKNER.

3F:092   Date: 10 Jul 1822   RtCt: 31 Oct 1822
John A. WASHINGTON (s/o Edward WASHINGTON dec'd) of Ldn to Richard H. HENDERSON of Ldn. Trust for debt to Eli OFFUTT of Ffx (Edward dec'd indebted to John WRIGHT, Solomon PARKER ass'ee of WRIGHT) using old negro woman Lilly, man Adam, woman Eliza. Delv. to HENDERSON 1 Mar 1824.

3F:093   Date: 28 Sep 1822   RtCt: 1 Nov 1822
John L. GILL & wife Hannah of Ldn to George M. GRAYSON of Ldn.
Trust for James WORNELL of Ldn as security for GILL as constable
using 1½a (house & lot cnvy/b Richard CLARKE & wife Catharine).
Wit: Benjamin GRAYSON, John W. GRAYSON.

3F:095   Date: 23 Oct 1822   RtCt: 2 Nov 1822
David ALEXANDER & wife Elizabeth of Ldn to Caleb N. GALLEHER
of Ldn. B/S of 14a adj Samuel TRAYHERN, Elizabeth GARRETT.
Wit: Notley C. WILLIAMS, William BRONAUGH. Delv. to
GALLEHER 1 Aug 1836.

3F:096   Date: 6 Nov 1822   RtCt: 6 Nov 1822
David BOSS of Lsbg to John MARTIN of Lsbg. Trust for debt to
Mary BOSS of Lsbg using household items. Wit: Caleb C.
SUTHERLAND., S. M. BOSS.

3F:097   Date: 27 Jun 1822   RtCt: 13 Nov 1822
William McKIM (McKIM in jail in Henrico Co in suit of Joseph
KIMBROUGH for debt) of Richmond (a distributee of William H.
McKIM dec'd) to Sheriff Burr POWELL. B/S of 130a on Elklick Creek
(William H. McKIM a nephew of William McKIM dec'd died seized
and intestate) and all int. in estate of William H. McKIM. Wit: William
PRICE, Joseph H. MAYO, Herbert A. CLAIBURN, Robert G.
SCOTT. Delv. to Dpty Shff Horace LUCKETT 6 Sep 1823.

3F:098   Date: 8 Apr 1822   RtCt: 11 Nov 1822
George TURNER Jr. & wife Sarah of Ldn to Jonathan CARTER of
Ldn. B/S of 230a (cnvy/b several heirs of Geo. NIXON dec'd) (title
not sufficient but making other conveyances necessary to perfect it).
Acknowledgement by TURNER in Frederick Co. Ct. Wit: John
HAMILTON, Thos. GASSAWAY.

3F:099   Date: 23 Oct 1822   RtCt: 11 Nov 1822
Thomas GASSAWAY & wife Henrietta of Ldn to John HAMILTON of
Ldn. B/S of und. 1/7th share of real estate of Henry TAYLOR dec'd in
Taylor Town and 1/7th share of land on W side of Catocton Creek
(except lot sold by Mrs. Mary Ann TAYLOR). Wit: John
McCORMICK, Presly CORDELL. Delv. pr order 9 Aug 1824.

3F:100   Date: 15 Oct 1822   RtCt: 11 Nov 1822
Joseph C. WRIGHT of Ldn to blood nephew and niece Charles E.
PAXON and Rachel A. PAXON (ch/o Samuel PAXON &
Martha/Marthey sister of Joseph). Gift of negro man Samuel, boy
Washington, horse and saddle. Wit: James D. FRENCH, George W.
HENRY. Delv. to Samuel PAXON 12 Nov 1828.

3F:101   Date: 11 Nov 1822   RtCt: 11 Nov 1822
Jacob ISH of Ldn to William BEVERIDGE of Ldn. Trust for benefit of
dau Lucinda ADAMS and her children using negro boy Alfred abt
19y old, girl Nancy abt 6y old, farm animals, farm and household

items. Wit: William K. ISH, Thomas C. ROACH, Frederick BROOKS.
Delv. to BEVERIDGE 17 Sep 1827.

3F:102   Date: 11 Nov 1822   RtCt: 11 Nov 1822
Martin Norris McDANIEL & wife Nancy of Ldn to James McILHANY
and Burr W. HARRISON of Ldn. Trust for debt to Francis
STRIBLING using 173a (subject to dower of Mrs. Margaret
McILHANY on NW fork of Goose Creek adj Stephen WILSON,
Solomon DAVIS.

3F:104   Date: 15 Oct 1822   RtCt: 11 Nov 1822
David ALEXANDER & wife Elizabeth of Ldn to Samuel TRAYHERN
of Ldn. B/S of 10a (prch/o William RANDALL allotted in div. of John
JOHNSTON dec'd) adj George W. McCARTY, Capt. Dennis
McCARTY. Wit: William BRONAUGH, Francis W. LUCKETT.

3F:105   Date: 18 Apr 1820   RtCt: 11 Nov 1822
Francis STRIBLING & wife Cecelia of Ldn to Martin Norris
McDANIEL of Ldn. B/S of 173a on NW fork of Goose Creek adj
Stephen WILSON, Richard COPELAND, Solomon DAVIS. Wit:
Craven OSBURN, John WHITE. Delv. to McDANIEL 25 Aug 1823.

3F:107   Date: 1 Jul 1822   RtCt: 11 Nov 1822
Wm. BRONAUGH (under direction of Ezekiel MOUNT) to John
MOUNT. Release of trust (DBk CCC:123).

3F:107   Date: 2 Nov 1822   RtCt: 11 Nov 1822
William PAXSON Jr. of Ldn to Isaac WALKER of Ldn. Trust for debt
to Samuel PAXSON using lot in Wtfd (prch/o Joseph STEER & wife
Sarah Feb 1819) adj Richard CHILTON, Edward DORSEY, __
SMALLWOOD. Delv. pr order 8 Aug 1823.

3F:108   Date: 27 Sep 1822   RtCt: 11 Nov 1822
William BRONAUGH to Daniel BROWN. Release of trust for debt to
Stephen McGEATH and John WINER on 52a.

3F:109   Date: 1 Jul 1822   RtCt: 11 Nov 1822
William BRONAUGH (under direction of Stephen MEGEATH) to
John MOUNT. Release of trust (DBk CCC:121).

3F:109   Date: 23 Sep 1822   RtCt: 11 Dec 1822
Solomon VICKROY & wife Elizabeth of Muskingum Co Ohio to John
GEORGE and Frederick SLATES of Ldn. B/S of 2a adj __
ROARBAUGH, TANKERVILLE. Wit: Wm. H. MOORE. Delv. to
SLATES 30 Jan 1828.

3F:111   Date: 2 Nov 1822   RtCt: 11 Nov 1822
Jacob DIVINE of Ldn to Peyton HOUGH and Joseph BOND of Ldn.
Trust for debt to John DODD using lot in Wtfd and household items.

3F:113   Date: 9 Nov 1822   RtCt: 11 Nov 1822
Craven A. COPELAND (as Admr of Robert HERRON dec'd) to
David POTTS. B/S of balance of term of lease on 100a (Mar 1787
George W. FAIRFAX to Robert HERRON L/L on said HERRON,
David W. HERRON and William EVANS. Robert died 10 Nov 1820)

adj David WILLIAMS, Arthur McCHRISTLY, Nathan POTTS. Wit: Thomas DORRELL, Robert HAMILTON, David HAMILTON. Delv. to POTTS 13 Sep 1823.

3F:114 Date: 19 Jul 1821 RtCt: 12 Nov 1822
William NOLAND & wife Catharine of Ldn to William SAFFER of PrWm. B/S of 176a adj __ WILCOXEN, James LEWIS, little river turnpike road. Wit: Ariss BUCKNER, John BAILEY. Delv. to SAFFER 22 Apr 1826.

3F:115 Date: 6 Nov 1822 RtCt: 11 Nov 1822
Samuel RICHARDSON & wife Catharine of Shenandoah Co Va to John SURGHNOR of Lsbg. B/S of lot with frame house on S side of Royal St in Lsbg (prch/o Sam BUCK) adj H. GLASSGOW, Samuel M. EDWARDS, J. RILEY. Delv. to SURGHNOR 21 Feb 1832.

3F:117 Date: 13 Nov 1822 RtCt: 11 Nov 1822
Jacob THOMAS of FredMd to John THOMAS of Ldn. B/S of int. in 138a in Piedmont (as heirs of Peter VIRTZ dec'd) adj John ROLER, __ BELTZ, __ RITCHE, __ RHOBACK.

3F:118 Date: 26 Aug 1822 RtCt: 13 Nov 1822
Daniel MILLER & wife Mary of Culpeper Co Va to John JANNEY of Ldn. B/S of 75a (except ¼a for burying ground, inherited by Mary as heir of Reuben HIXON dec'd). Delv. to JANNEY 10 Sep 1829.

3F:119 Date: 27 Aug 1822 RtCt: 11 Nov 1822
John BOOTH Sr. of Ldn to George MULL of Ldn. B/S of 13a (bought of estate of Margaret RIDENBAUGH dec'd) adj David MULL, George SHULTZ, George COOPER, William WENNER. Delv. to Abel MALONY pr order 13 Jun 1836.

3F:120 Date: 14 Nov 1822 RtCt: 14 Nov 1822
Robert CHAMBERS of Star Co Ohio to John MANN of Ldn. B/S of 26a int. in 200a (devised from will of Robert BOOTH dec'd to dau Anna CHAMBERS and passed to her son William CHAMBERS and from William CHAMBERS who died intestate to children including Robert, DBk A:24). Delv. to MANN 8 Feb 1827.

3F:121 Date: 31 May 1821 RtCt: 16 Nov 1822
Yeoman Thomas CLOWES & wife Ann of Ldn to yeoman Joseph CLOWES of Ldn. B/S of 96a (from div. of their father Joseph CLOWES dec'd). Wit: Notley C. WILLIAMS, John W. GRAYSON. Delv. to Joseph CLOWES 24 Oct 1823.

3F:123 Date: 31 May 1822 RtCt: 16 Nov 1822
Yeoman Joseph CLOWES & wife Mary of Ldn to yeoman Joshua GORE of Ldn. B/S of 12a S of Lsbg road (inherited from father) adj GORE. Wit: Presley CORDELL, Thomas SANDERS. Delv. to GORE 25 Mar 1824.

3F:124 Date: 31 May 1822 RtCt: 16 Nov 1822
Thomas CLOWES & wife Ann and Joseph CLOWES & wife Mary of Ldn to Thomas HUGHES of Ldn. B/S of 24a (cnvy/b George

TAVENOR Jr.) adj Thomas CLOWES. Wit: N. C. WILLIAMS, John W. GRAYSON, Presley CORDELL, Thomas SANDERS. Delv. pr order 18 Nov 1823.

3F:126   Date: 16 Nov 1822   RtCt: 18 Nov 1822
Samuel M. BOSS of Lsbg to John H. MONROE of Lsbg. LS of lot on N side of Royal St. adj Mathew WEATHERLY, John MATHIAS, John MARTIN. Delv. to James L. HAMILTON 18 Mar 1830.

3F:127   Date: 14 Nov 1822   RtCt: 18 Nov 1822
Fleet SMITH & wife Jane of Washington to John HAMILTON of Lsbg. B/S of lot in Lsbg on S side of Market St. adj Thos. GASSAWAY. Wit: Enoch REYNOLDS, Wm. HEWITT. Delv. to HAMILTON 10 Nov 1824.

3F:129   Date: 23 Nov 1822   RtCt: 23 Nov 1822
John McCORMICK & wife Mary of Ldn to Charles BINNS of Ldn. B/S of lot in Lsbg adj BINNS on Liberty St, school house lot, Joseph HILLARD. Wit: Presley CORDELL, Saml. M. EDWARDS.

3F:130   Date: 11 Nov 1822   RtCt: 23 Nov 1822
John SHAW of Lsbg to John S. EDWARDS of Lsbg. LS of lot on Back St in Lsbg adj James HAMILTON, Henry PEERS.

3F:131   Date: 21 Nov 1822   RtCt: 23 Nov 1822
Joseph PURSELL of Ldn to Joseph MEAD of Ldn. Trust for Shff Benjamin SHREVE in execution of John FISHELL using 90a adj Cunard NEAR dec'd, Mrs. JACOBS. Wit: Benj. SHREVE Jr., John HOUGH, Absolem COCKERILL.

3F:132   Date: 5 Sep 1822   RtCt: 26 Nov 1822
Thomas SWANN and Enoch MASON to James GREENLEASE of Ldn. Release of trust for debt to William Dudley DIGGS on 333a (DBk 22:345). Delv. to GREENLEASE 2 Dec 1825.

3F:134   Date: 28 Nov 1822   RtCt: 28 Nov 1822
Benjamin MAULSBY of Ldn to George RICHARDS of Ldn. Trust for debt to James L. MARTIN using lot on N side of Markett St. in Lsbg adj MAULSBY.

3F:135   Date: 4 Dec 1822   RtCt: 4 Dec 1822
James GREENLEASE & wife Catharine of Ldn to Saml. M. EDWARDS of Ldn. Trust for debt to Christopher FRYE of Ldn using 320a 'Digges Valley' (residue of lot in DBk 22:362) less 13a sold to Enos GARRETT. Wit: John McCORMICK, Presley CORDELL.

3F:137   Date: 31 May 1822   RtCt: 6 Dec 1822
Yeoman Thomas CLOWES & wife Ann of Ldn to William S. EACHES of Ldn. B/S of 2a (from father Joseph CLOWES dec'd) on Lsbg road adj Constantine HUGHES, Joshua GORE. Wit: N. C. WILLIAMS, John W. GRAYSON. Delv. to EACHES 9 Feb 1824.

3F:138   Date: 31 Oct 1822   RtCt: 6 Dec 1822
James W. DOWNING Jr. & wife Elizabeth of FredVa to Thompson FURR of Ldn. Trust for debt to William LITTLETON of Ldn using

slaves Peter & wife Hannah and their children James, Armstead, Delila and Evelina. Wit: Benjamin GRAYSON, John W. GRAYSON. Delv. to Rich'd K. LITTLETON pr order 13 Dec 1823.

3F:139 Date: 22 Jul 1822 RtCt: 7 Nov 1822
Daniel C. BOSS (s/o Peter BOSS dec'd) & wife Margaret of Pittsburg Pa to Richard H. HENDERSON of Lsbg. Trust for use of James BROWN of Pittsburg Pa using lot and brick house NE corner of Loudoun and King Sts in Lsbg adj Robert HOUGH, Charles BALL, Joshua RILEY, Samuel M. EDWARDS (Peter BOSS died seized of leaving 1/3 to widow Mary and rest divided to heirs Peter, Saml. M., Abraham J., David and said Daniel C. and Mary HAWKE now MARTIN and William HAWKE children and heirs of Margaret HAWKE dec'd d/o Peter dec'd and Samuel BOSS son of Jacob BOSS dec'd a s/o Peter dec'd). Wit: C. BINNS, Thomas A. MOORE, Saml. M. BOSS. Delv. to S. M. BOSS 7 Jul 1823.

3F:141 Date: 20 Sep 1822 RtCt: 10 Dec 1822
Jane JOHNSON. DoE to negro Henley who is now 21y old (sold previous to 25 Jan 1806 by Col. Simon TRIPLETT to James JOHNSON). Wit: John WILSON, Moses ROBINSON, James THOMPSON.

3F:141 Date: 21 Dec 1822 RtCt: 21 Dec 1822
David CONNER & wife Nancy of Ldn to Samuel M. EDWARDS of Ldn. Trust for debt to William CARR of Ldn using lot with log house on N side of Royal St in Lsbg.

3F:142 Date: 2 Jan 1823 RtCt: 2 Jan 1823
John J. MATHIAS. Commissioned as surveyor of Ldn. Delv. to MATHIAS 21 May 1828.

3F:143 Date: 13 Jan 1823 RtCt: 13 Jan 1823
John J. MATHIAS, John H. McCABE, Samuel CLAPHAM and Samuel M. EDWARDS. Bond on MATHIAS as surveyor.

3F:144 Date: 26 Dec 1822 RtCt: 13 Jan 1823
John PAXSON. Qualified as 2nd Lt. in 2nd Reg of Cavalry of Va Malitia.

3F:144 Date: 13 Jan 1823 RtCt: 13 Jan 1823
George H. ALDER, Joseph RICHARDSON and Jno. MARKS. Bond on ALDER as constable.

3F:144 Date: 13 Jan 1823 RtCt: 13 Jan 1823
Alexander CORDELL, Geo. W. SHAWEN and Geo. SANDERS. Bond on CORDELL as constable.

3F:145 Date: 11 Apr 1822 RtCt: 11 Jan 1823
Peter RICKARD & wife Elizabeth, Simon RICKARD & wife Mary, Catharine MILLER and Michael MILLER of Ldn to George RICKARD of Ldn. B/S of 6a Lot #1 and #4, 7a Lot #7 and #18, 6a Lot #3 and #15, 7a Lot #6 and #16 (from div. of estate of Adam HOUSEHOLDER dec'd later the estate of widow Susannah dec'd).

Appearance in Culpeper Co by Simon RICKARD. Appearance in Fqr of Peter RICKARD, Catharine MILLER and Michael RICKARD. Delv. to Geo. RICKARD 9 Jun 1824.

3F:147   Date: 14 Oct 1822   RtCt: 14 Oct 1822
Samuel M. BOSS of Lsbg to John MARTIN of Lsbg. LS of lot on Loudoun St in Lsbg adj Isaac HARRIS, __ COOPER.

3F:148   Date: 8 Oct 1822   RtCt: 14 Oct 1822
Levi BARTON & wife Sarah of Fqr to Samuel TORBERT of Ldn. B/S of 5¼a on Hunger Run (prch/o Jonathan CARTER) on road to Aldie adj Amos FURGUSON, nr Mathias Hays' house. Wit: Mathias HAYS, James TORBERT, William J. CARTER. Delv. to TORBERT 13 Jan 1824.

3F:149   Date: 4 Jun 1822   RtCt: 14 Oct 1822
John UTTERBACK Jr. & wife Catharine of Fqr to Amos DUNHAM of Ldn. B/S of int. in land of John VIOLETT dec'd (grandfather of Catharine) prch/o John CARTER formerly held under LS to Elijah VIOLETT now in poss. of DUNHAM. Wit: A. GIBSON, Francis W. LUCKETT.

3F:151   Date: 14 Sep 1822   RtCt: 14 Oct 1822
Enoch TRIPLETT & wife Mary of Ldn to Samuel SINGLETON of Ldn. B/S of 35a on S side of Goose Creek (inherited from father). Wit: Francis W. LUCKETT, A. GIBSON.

3F:152   Date: 7 Oct 1822   RtCt: 14 Oct 1822
Usher SKINNER & wife Rebecca of Ldn to John HATCHER of Ldn. Trust for debt to Thomas FRED Jr. using 30¼a. Wit: William BRONAUGH, Francis W. LUCKETT.

3F:153   Date: 20 Mar 1822   RtCt: 14 Oct 1822
Joseph CARR of Ldn to Randall CASHELL of Ldn. LS of 2a in Upperville adj Sarah CANNON, John GIBSON.

3F:156   Date: 16 Oct 1822   RtCt: 16 Oct 1822
Richard PRESGRAVES of Ldn to Samuel M. EDWARDS of Ldn. Trust for William THRIFT as security on bond to Bernard HOOE using negro boy Harry, boy Sanford and girl Armenia.

3F:157   Date: 16 Mar 1822   RtCt: 7 Aug/16 Oct 1822
Andrew CAMPBELL & wife Jane of Ldn to Sampson BLINCOE of Ldn. Trust for debt to William CARR using ½ of 140a adj __ WILKINSON, __ GARRETT. Wit: Samuel D. LESLIE, A. R. St. CLAIR, Thomas JACOBS, Thomas SANDERS, Presley CORDELL, William CHILTON, E. G. HAMILTON. Delv. to CARR 1 Apr 1826.

3F:159   Date: 3 Jun 1822   RtCt: 14 Oct 1822
H. B. POWELL (as trustee for James SIMPSON & wife Elizabeth in debt to Isaac LAKE Sept 1817) of Ldn to Noble BEVERIDGE of Ldn. B/S of 150a.

3F:159   Date: 15 Oct 1822   RtCt: 15 Oct 1822
John DEMORY of Ldn to John NISEWANGER of Ldn. B/S of 14a
adj John REMER, Phillip GROVES, James NEAR. Delv. to
NISESWANGER 10 Aug 1824.

3F:160   Date: 14 Oct 1822   RtCt: 15 Oct 1822
Hiland CROWE to Robert McINTOSH. Trust for Robert McINTOSH
and John GRAVES as security on executions to Joseph TULEY
ass'ee of Geo. A. RALLS, Shff commission, MASON's Exors, __
HEATH, __ HOPWOOD, SMALLEY's Exors, Shff Horace LUCKETT
using 313a (100a of William GROVE tact and 213a prch/o Geo. N.
RALLS) and slaves George, Steven, Rachel, Sarah, Mary, Lucy &
her children Lydia, Ellen, James and Jane, farm animals, household
items. Wit: William CHILTON, Horace LUCKETT, Richard
PRESGRAVES.

3F:162   Date: 7 Dec 1822   RtCt: 7 Dec 1822
William H. HANDY of Ldn to L. P. W. BALCH and Samuel
HATCHER of Ldn. Trust for debt to Samuel NICKOLLS using 5a
(Lot #2 in div. of John HANDY dec'd). Wit: E. G. HAMILTON, H'y H.
HAMILTON, Alfred A. ESKRIDGE. Delv. to NICHOLS Exors 10 Nov
1825.

3F:163   Date: 2 Oct 1822   RtCt: 11 Nov 1822
William HERBERT of Ffx to James DULANY of Ldn. B/S of 99a (part
in JeffVa) on top of Blue ridge mountain, adj heirs of Mertho
SULLIVAN, __ SHRIVER. Wit: Jonah SANDS, Eli TAVENNER,
David REECE, Andrew HOSPITAL. Delv. to DULANY 26 Mar 1825.

3F:164   Date: 27 Sep 1822   RtCt: 9 Dec 1822
John VIOLETT Jr. of Ldn to Elijah ANDERSON. Trust for Edward
CARTER as security in notes to Noble BEVERIDGE, Peter P.
RUST, Hugh SMITH, Lewis FRENCH and Jacob SILCOTT, Jacob
NISEWANGER using land where VIOLETT now lives adj Peter C.
RUST, Enoch TRIPLETT, Martin BRENT (except 1a where William
TAYLOR built a house he intends to convey in trust for use of dau
Elizabeth TAYLOR and her children). Delv. to Geo. E. LLOYD pr
order of ANDERSON 11 Dec 1823.

3F:166   Date: 11 May 1822   RtCt: 11 Dec 1822
Jacob WALTMAN & wife Mary to Alexander CORDELL and Geo. W.
SHAWEN. Trust for debt to Adam HOUSHOLDER using 115a adj
John COMPHER, Frederick COOPER, Geo. BAKER. Wit: Ruth
HOUSEHOLDER, Mahala HOUSEHOLDER, Mary
HOUSEHOLDER, Robert BRADEN, Abiel JENNERS. Delv. to Adam
HOUSEHOLDER 8 Jan 1826.

3F:168   Date: 30 Nov 1822   RtCt: 13 Dec 1822
Peter BENEDUM of Ldn and John BENEDUM of Ldn. Agreement –
to void all deeds, notes, etc. between them. Wit: E. G. HAMILTON,
Alfred A. ESKRIDGE, A. R. St. CLAIR.

3F:169   Date: 13 Dec 1822   RtCt: 13 Dec 1822
Peter BENEDUM of Ldn to Samuel M. EDWARDS of Ldn. Trust for
benefit of Catharine BENEDUM w/o Peter using 100a adj Charles
BINNS, William A. BINNS, Thomas N. BINNS, __ SANDERS in
place of a dower and after her death for benefit of Manuel
BENEDUM, Mariah QUICK & her son Armstead T. M. QUICK. Wit:
E. G. HAMILTON, Alfred A. ESKRIDGE, A. R. St. CLAIR.

3F:170   Date: 4 May 1822   RtCt: 13 Dec 1822
Peter BENEDUM & wife Catharine of Ldn to John G. WATT of Ldn.
B/S of 20a adj S. M. EDWARDS, Charles BINNS. Wit: Samuel M.
EDWARDS, John H. McCABE. Delv. to WATT 25 Jul 1823.

3F:171   Date: 13 Dec 1822   RtCt: 13 Dec 1822
Peter BENEDUM & wife Catharine of Ldn to Jacob CARNICLE of
Ldn. B/S of 1a adj __ MEAD, on road from Lsbg to George KOONS
old place, L. CORNWELL. Wit: John H. McCABE, Samuel M.
EDWARDS. Delv. to CARNICLE 8 Feb 1832.

3F:173   Date: 13 Dec 1822   RtCt: 13 Dec 1822
Peter BENEDUM & wife Catharine of Ldn to Loveless CONWELL of
Ldn. B/S of 2a on NW side of road from Lsbg to Geo NIXSON's old
place adj Charles BINNS. Wit: J. H. McCABE, Samuel M.
EDWARDS.

3F:174   Date: 11 Dec 1822   RtCt: 13 Dec 1822
Thomas GREGG & wife Ann of Ldn to Isaac NICHOLLS Jr. and
James HOGE of Ldn. Trust for debt to Isaac & Samuel NICHOLLS
using 339a adj Dunkin McLEAN, road to Mahlon HOUGH's mill. Wit:
Lucinda WELLS, John COLLINS, Phebe NICHOLLS. Delv. to Saml.
NICHOLL Exors 10 Nov 1825.

3F:176   Date: 223 Nov 1822   RtCt: 13 Jan 1823
John VANBUSKIRK of Cumberland, Allegany Co Md to Isaac
BAKER of Winchester, FredVa. PoA for sale of merchant and saw
mill on Goose Creek formerly "Ball's Mill tract" (cnvy/b Joseph
TIDBALL). Wit: Jno. McNEILL, Charles T. BRODHAG.

3F:177   Date: 17 Oct 1822   RtCt: 13 Dec 1822
Mahlon CRAVEN & wife Hannah of Ldn to William HOGE of Ldn.
Trust for debt to Stephen McGEATH using 127a on Beaverdam
where CRAVEN now lives (prch/o said McGEATH). Wit: John
SINCLAIR, John WYNN, James SINCLAIR, William BRONAUGH,
N. C. WILLIAMS. Delv. to HOGE pr order of McGEATH 5 Sep 1825.

3F:179   Date: 3 Dec 1822   RtCt: 14 Dec 1822
Richard H. HENDERSON of Ldn to James GREENLEASE of Ldn.
Release of trust of Jun 1819 for debt to Samuel M. EDWARDS on
72a. Wit: E. G. HAMILTON, Henry PEERS, Thomas A. MOORE.

3F:179 Date: 14 Dec 1822 RtCt: 14 Dec 1822
Thomas J. NOLAND of Ldn to Richard H. HENDERSON. Trust for debt to George COLEMAN of AlexDC using ½a Lot #61 on Mercer & E St. in Aldie adj Miss LACEY. Delv. to HENDERSON 13 Oct 1824.

3F:181 Date: 1 Jul 1822 RtCt: 14 Dec 1822
William NOLAND & wife Catharine of Ldn to Thomas J. NOLAND of Ldn. B/S of Lot #61 on Mercer & E St. in Aldie. Wit: John McCORMICK, Samuel M. EDWARDS.

3F:182 Date: 12 Dec 1822 RtCt: 14 Dec 1822
Thomas MARKS of Ldn to Joshua OSBURN of Ldn. Trust for debt to Thomas JAMES of Ldn using 52¼a nr Blue Ridge (Lot #2 in div. of Abel MARKS dec'd allotted to Watts MARKS and conveyed to Thomas).

3F:183 Date: 1 Feb 1817 RtCt: 16 Dec 1822
William DARNE of Ldn to Samuel M. EDWARDS. Trust for benefit of Mary SANDERS (w/o Presley SANDERS Jr of Lsbg) using slave female Suckey with child Ann. With Thomas SANDERS, John SANDERS.

3F:184 Date: 4 Nov 1822 RtCt: 16 Dec 1822
William S. CALDWELL & wife Sarah of Todd Co Ky to Joseph CALDWELL of Trigg Co Ky. B/S of lot on S side of Market St. (prch/o Charles DRISH Nov 1817) adj Sally RYAN, Presbyterian meeting house.

3F:185 Date: 16 Dec 1822 RtCt: 17 Dec 1822
Mahlon GIBSON of Ldn to Hugh SMITH of Ldn. Trust for David CARTER and Meshack LACEY as security on debt to Burr POWELL using und. ¼th of merchant mill and 25a on Panther Skin Run from father John GIBSON.

3F:187 Date: 5 Dec 1822 RtCt: 18 Dec 1822
Isaac WRIGHT (Admr & distributee of William WRIGHT dec'd) to board of trustees of Lsbg Academy. Release of rights to "academy lot".

3F:187 Date: 21 Dec 1822 RtCt: 21 Dec 1822
William WOLFORD of Ldn to L. P. W. BALCH of Ldn. Trust for debt to Jacob WALTMAN 2nd using 95a where WOLFORD resides. Wit: E. G. HAMILTON, A. R. St. CLAIR, Alfred A. ESKRIDGE. Delv. to BALCH 8 Feb 1824.

3F:188 Date: 21 Dec 1822 RtCt: 21 Dec 1822
William CARR & wife Mary of Ldn to David CONNOR of Ldn. B/S of lot on N side of Royal St in Lsbg adj Robt. FULTON, Benjamin SHREVE.

3F:189 Date: 26 Dec 1822 RtCt: 26 Dec 1822
Presley CORDELL of Ldn to Joseph HILLEARD of Ldn. LS of 24 feet on Market St. in Lsbg.

3F:190   Date: 31 Dec 1822   RtCt: 31 Dec 1822
James MONROE to Sampson BLINCOE and Samuel CARR. Trust for debt to William CARR using farm animals, farm and household items.

3F:191   Date: 25 Dec 1822   RtCt: 3 Jan 1823
Charles CRIM of Ldn to Jacob CRIM of Ldn. Release of trust on 111a.

3F:192   Date: 3 Jan 1823   RtCt: 3 Jan 1823
Francis W. LUCKETT (trustee of James MACKLIN & wife Mary) of Ldn to James LLOYD of AlexDC. B/S of 124a on Goose Creek (failed to pay trust of Mar 1818 for debt to George JANNEY). Wit: R. H. HENDERSON. Delv. pr order DBk __.

3F:193   Date: 6 Jan 1823   RtCt: 6 Jan 1823
Israel WILLIAMS of Ldn to Garrison B. FRENCH of Ldn. Trust for debt to James D. FRENCH using 93a (allotted from estate of Enos WILLIAM dec'd) adj Samuel CLAPHAM, __ HIXSON, __ POTTERFIELD.

3F:195   Date: 9 Dec 1822   RtCt: 6 Jan 1822
Jozabed WHITE & wife Margaret of Ldn to Jonathan COST of Ldn. B/S of lot and house in Wtfd (prch/o Robert BRADEN) adj Mahlon JANNEY, William HOUGH. Wit: R. BRADEN, S. HOUGH Jr. Delv. to COST 24 Jan 1824.

3F:196   Date: 4 Jan 1823   RtCt: 10 Jan 1823
John HOUGH of Lsbg to Charles SHEPHERD of Lsbg. Trust for debt to Levin SHEPHERD using household items. Wit: E. G. HAMILTON, A. R. St. CLAIR, Chas. W. BINNS.

3F:197   Date: 9 Dec 1822   RtCt: 11 Jan 1823
John S. MARLOW to John MANN of Ldn B/S of leasehold int. in land prch/o John MANLEY. Wit: Benjamin SHREVE, A. R. St. CLAIR, E. G. HAMILTON.

3F:198   Date: 16 Dec 1822   RtCt: 14 Jan 1823
Phillip SOUDER dec'd. Division – court order of 10 Nov 1822 – dower lot (100a) to widow Susannah SOUDER, Lot #1 (24a) and (1a) nr Taylor Town and Lot #6 on the mt. (4a) to Michael SOUDER, Lot #2 (19a) and Lot #4 on the mt. (4a) to Elizabeth SOUDER, Lot #3 (25a) and Lot #7 on the mt. (4a) to Anthony SOUDERS, Lot #4 (27a) and Lot #3 on the mt. (4a) to Mary SOUDERS, Lot #5 (24a) and Lot #V (7a) to Peter SOUDER, Lot #6 (27a) and Lot #1 on the mt. (4a) to Margaret COOPER infant d/o Susannah COOPER late SOUDER, Lot #7 (20a) and Lot #8 on the mt. (4a) to Peggy SOUDER, Lot #8 (28a) and Lot #2 on the mt. (4a) to Rachel COST late SOUDER, Lot #9 (28a) and Lot #5 on the mt. (4a) to John SOUDER. Gives plat. Divisors: John HAMILTON, John STOUSEBERGER, Jno. J. MATHIAS.

3F:202   Date: 20 Nov 1822   RtCt: 14 Jan 1823
William ALT dec'd. Division – Lot #1 (29a) to William ALT, Lot #2
(21a) to Elizabeth COMPHER late ALT, Lot #3 (30a) to widow
Rachel ALT, Lot #4 (26a) to Rachel SPRING late ALT, Lot #5 (27a)
to John ALT. Gives plat. Divisors: Peter SOUDER, John SLATER,
John J. MATHIAS.

3F:204   Date: 9 Dec 1822   RtCt: 13 Jan 1823
Adam CORDELL dec'd. Division – court order dated 14 Oct 1822 –
Lot #8 (18a) to widow Elizabeth CORDELL, Lot #1 (12½a) to Jacob
CORDELL, Lot #2 (12½a) to Samuel CORDELL, Lot #3 (14¾a) to
Catharine COMPHOR late CORDELL, Lot #4 (13½a) to Elizabeth,
Samuel, Sally and Mary FILLER heirs of Frederick FILLER dec'd in
right of his purchase of John CORDELL, Lot #5 (13½a) to Elizabeth
FILLER late CORDELL, Lot #6 (11¾) to Adam CORDELL, Lot #7
(11¾a) to Margaret RICHARDS late CORDELL. Gives plat. Divisors:
Edward MARLOW, Simon AKEY, Jno. J. MATHIAS.

3F:206   Date: 7 Dec 1822   RtCt: 13 Jan 1823
Joseph PURSELL & wife Susan of Ldn to Nicholas KOONCE of
Ldn. B/S of 1a (prch/o Thomas LESLIE) adj __ JACOBS, said
PURSELL. Wit: Ebenezer GRUBB, John WHITE. Delv. pr order 18
Dec 1827.

3F:208   Date: 14 Nov 1822   RtCt: 15 Jan 1823
William VICKERS & wife Anna of Ldn to Robert PATTERSON of
Ldn. B/S of lot in Millsville (part of Lot #6 known as Sebolds Lot) adj
__ BURSON, __ PLAISTER. Wit: William BRONAUGH, Francis W.
LUCKETT.

3F:209   Date: 6 Jan 1823   RtCt: 13 Jan 1823
William TAYLOR & wife Emily of FredVa to Timothy TAYLOR of
Ldn. B/S of 1a nr foot of Blue Ridge adj __ HEATON, Marcus
HUMPHREY, Thomas HUMPHREY. Wit: Treadwell SMITH, Geo. H.
NORRIS. Delv. to Timothy TAYLOR 17 Nov 1823.

3F:210   Date: 7 Jan 1823   RtCt: 13 Jan 1823
William LEACHMAN of Ldn to children Elizabeth and Dolly Ann
LEACHMAN. Gift of negro woman Lucy abt 21y old and bed and
bedding to Elizabeth and negro girl Mahala abt 10y old and bed and
bedding to Dolly Ann and negro girl Sarah Ann abt 2y old to both.
Wit: Jno. M. MONROE, James DEEVER, John VERMILLION.

3F:211   Date: 18 Nov 1822   RtCt: 13 Jan 1823
Eli McKNIGHT of Ldn to John CHAMBLIN and William E. LOVELY
of Ldn. Trust for debt to Henson ELLIOTT using all of land now
occupied by McKNIGHT.

3F:212   Date: 6 Jan 1823   RtCt: 13 Jan 1823
William TAYLOR & wife Emily of FredVa to Timothy TAYLOR Jr. of
Ldn. B/S of 31a on road from Snickers Gap to Israel JANNEY's mill
adj Thomas NICHOLLS, __ JOHNSON.

3F:214   Date: 11 Jan 1823   RtCt: 13 Jan 1823
Samuel NICHOLLS & Co of Ldn to Jehu HOLLINGSWORTH of Ldn.
B/S of 87a on Catocton Creek adj Lewis ELLZEY, James BEST,
Joshua GORE (from release of trust for debt to NICHOLLS of
Thomas GREGG of Ldn who has since sold land to
HOLLINGSWORTH).

3F:215   Date: 18 Nov 1822   RtCt: 13 Jan 1823
Andrew BEATTY & wife Mary of Ldn to George BEATTY of Ldn. B/S
of ¼a on turnpike road from nr Aldie to Snickers Gap adj William
HARDING. Wit: Burr POWELL, A. GIBSON. Delv. pr order 15 Nov
1826.

3F:216   Date: 26 Dec 1822   RtCt: 13 Jan 1823
Thomas CHINN & wife Ann Henley of Ldn to Thomas A. DENNIS of
Ldn. B/S of 1a lot above Mdbg on Ashby's Gap road. Wit: Burr
POWELL, A. GIBSON.

3F:217   Date: 15 Nov 1822   RtCt: 13 Jan 1823
William VICKERS & wife Anne of Ldn to James PATTERSON Jr and
John PATTERSON of Ldn. B/S of 22 perches prch/o Daniel
EACHES on N side of Goose Creek nr Millsville adj James
PATTERSON Jr. Wit: William BRONAUGH, Francis W. LUCKETT.

3F:218   Date: 18 Dec 1822   RtCt: 13 Jan 1823
Andrew BEATTY of Ldn to dau Kezia BEATTY of Ldn. B/S of 3a
including house where he now lives on Snickers gap turnpike adj
George BEATTY.

3F:219   Date: 14 Jan 1823   RtCt: 14 Jan 1823
Henry T. BAYNE of Ldn to Garrison B. FRENCH of Ldn. Trust for
debt to James D. FRENCH of Ldn using int. in plantation William
HOUGH bought of John HAUBRY dec'd (as a devisee in land dev.
by William HOUGH dec'd to John SCHOOLEY & wife Elizabeth and
after their death to children of Elizabeth; BAYNE m. Phebe
SCHOOLEY dau. of John and Elizabeth) and farm and household
items.

3F:220   Date: 8 Jan 1823   RtCt: 14 Jan 1823
John CARPENTER of Ldn to Stephen McPHERSON of Ldn. Trust
for debt to George KEENE using 50a where CARPENTER lives adj
William CARPENTER Sr., Minor FURR in Manner [Manor] of Leeds
and rights to leased land and slave Robert & wife Isabella and their
children Lydia, Mariah, Cytha & Richmond and Solomon abt 20y old.
Delv. to McPHERSON 15 Oct 1824.

3F:222   Date: 11 Apr 1821   RtCt: 21 Sep 1821/14 Jan 1823
Wm. H. HANDY, Wm. H. HANDY as ass'ee of Jos. HAINES who m.
my sister Maria, James MOUNT in right of wife Hannah, Eli. H.
HANDY, John C. HANDY and Given HANDY as Admr of estate of
husband John HANDY dec'd to Burr POWELL, Wm. BRONAUGH

and Thomas A. HEREFORD. Release as security on administration of estate. Wit: E. B. POWELL, James MOUNT, Abiel JENNERS.

3F:222 Date: 13 Sep 1821 RtCt: 14 Jan 1823
Abner HUMPHREY of Ldn to John JENKINS of Ldn. B/S of 140a (under trust from Benjamin JENKINS & wife Mary for debt to William JENKINS of FredVa) where JENKINS lives adj John HANN, James DILLON.

3F:224 Date: 19 Dec 1822 RtCt: 14 Jan 1823
John STEER & wife Elenor of Ldn to John BOOTH of Ldn. B/S of Lot #1 allotted to Elenor from James BOOTH dec'd and her share of dower land. Wit: R. BRADEN, Samuel HOUGH.

3F:225 Date: 15 Nov 1821 RtCt: 18 Jan 1823
Samuel M. EDWARDS of Lsbg to James THOMAS of Lsbg. B/S of Lot #3 in Lsbg sold to THOMAS by EDWARDS in July 1820 (now cnvy/b ct order in case of Alexander SUTHERLAND's Admr agst John MATHIAS and others, being part of int. of defendents in real estate of Robert HAMILTON dec'd). Delv. to THOMAS 31 Dec 1824.

3F:226 Date: 24 Aug 1820 RtCt: 18 Jan 1823
James M. GARRETT and John T. BROOKE (Admrs of James MERCER dec'd) to Mary MASON and John T. MASON devisees of Stephen T. MASON the elder dec'd. B/S of 907a.
Acknowledgements by BROOKE in Spotsylvania Co and GARRETT in Fredericksburg.

3F:228 Date: 23 Dec 1822 RtCt: 18 Jan 1823
Samuel M. EDWARDS & wife Ann of Ldn to James THOMAS of Ldn. B/S of lot on S side of Royal St. in Lsbg (cnvy/b Benjamin H. CANBY Apr 1817). Wit: John H. McCABE, Presley CORDELL. Delv. to THOMAS 31 Dec 1824.

3F:229 Date: 19 Nov 1822 RtCt: 13 Jan 1823
Jacob VIRTS of Ldn to Peter and Adam VERTS of Ldn. BoS for farm animals, farm and household items. Wit: Daniel MOCK, Jacob FAULEY, John VIRTS.

3F:230 Date: 18 Jan 1823 RtCt: 21 Jan 1823
Thomas MARKS & wife Keziah of Ldn to Joshua OSBURN and Herod OSBURN of Ldn. Trust for debt to Isaac CAMP using 150a where MARKS now lives. Wit: John WHITE, Craven OSBURN.

3F:232 Date: 6 Jul 1822 RtCt: 13 Jan 1823
William PAXSON Sr. & wife Jane to Jacob WALTMAN (of Samuel) and Alexander CORDELL. Trust for debt to John COPELAND using 123a on Kittockton Creek and 45a nearly adjoining other lot. Wit: Jno. WHITE, Jonas POTTS, Henry SNUTES Jr.

3F:233 Date: 14 Dec 1822 RtCt: 24 Jan 1823
Thomas MARKS of Ldn to Bennett MARKS of Ldn. B/S of 52¼a Lot #2 in div. of Abel MARKS dec'd.

3F:234 Date: 28 Jan 1823 RtCt: 28 Jan 1823
David SAURBAUGH to L. P. W. BALCH. Trust for debt to Michael EVERHART using crops, household item. Delv. to EVERHEART 9 Aug 1826.

3F:235 Date: 28 Jan 1823 RtCt: 28 Jan 1823
Elizabeth BOLEN of Ldn to Thomas H. WEY of Ldn. B/S of lot adj Union (cnvy/b Samuel DUNCAN). Delv. pr order ___.

3F:236 Date: 30 Jan 1823 RtCt: 29 Jan 1823
Hezekiah PERRY to Samuel CARR. Trust for debt to William CARR using household items and int. in estate of Jno. MARSHALL dec'd. Delv. to Samuel CARR 17 Jun 1828.

3F:237 Date: 29 Jan 1823 RtCt: 29 Jan 1823
Patrick B. MILHOLLEN & wife Malinda of Ldn to Robert MOFFETT of Ldn. B/S of 5a Lot #2 allotted to John MILHOLLEN. Wit: Abiel JENNERS, Samuel M. EDWARDS.

3F:238 Date: 29 Jan 1823 RtCt: 29 Jan 1823
Esther GRANT (heir of Mary GRANT dec'd) of Ldn to Patrick MILHOLLEN of Ldn. B/S of share of land that would have descended to Mary GRANT m/o Esther from her brother John MILHOLLEN. Wit: Abiel JENNERS, Reuben SCHOOLEY, Robert MOFFETT, John W. MILHOLLEN.

3F:239 Date: 28 Jan 1823 RtCt: 29 Jan 1823
Patrick MILHOLLEN & wife Malinda of Ldn to Esther GRANT of Ldn. B/S of lot adj Elijah MYERS, Richard GRIFFITH, William HOUGH. Wit: Saml. M. EDWARDS, Abiel JENNERS. Delv. to Joshua PUSEY Guard'n of Esther GRANT a lunatic 3 Jun 1841 [or 31?].

3F:240 Date: 29 Jan 1823 RtCt: 29 Jan 1823
Patrick B. MILHOLLEN of Ldn to Abiel JENNERS of Ldn. Trust for benefit of wife Malinda selling his bonds to Robert MOFFETT, Peter COOPER, John MILLER, paying off debts and investing the rest in a home for Patrick and wife. Wit: Saml. M. EDWARDS, Charles W. BINNS, Thomas A. MOORE, Reuben SCHOOLEY. Delv. to trustee Saml HOUGH 27 Apr 1825.

3F:241 Date: 29 Jan 1823 RtCt: 29 Jan 1823
Robert MOFFETT of Ldn to Patrick B. MILHOLLEN of Ldn. B/S of 260a (cnvy/b MILHOLLEN under Sup. Ct. decree)

3F:242 Date: 29 Jan 1823 RtCt: 29 Jan 1823
Patrick B. MILHOLLEN & wife Melinda of Ldn to Robert MOFFETT of Ldn. B/S of 260a adj John BALL, George RUST, __ BREWER, __ SCHOOLEY, __ GRIFFITH, __ PEUSEY, road leading to Wtfd. Wit: Abiel JENNERS, Saml. M. EDWARDS. Delv. to MOFFETT 26 Jun 1824.

3F:244 Date: 30 Jan 1823 RtCt: 30 Jan 1823
John EVANS & wife Elizabeth of Ldn to L. P. W. BALCH of Ldn. Trust for debt to John PANCOAST using 1/8th int. in 18a of father

John EVANS dec'd. Wit: John H. McCABE, Samuel M. EDWARDS.
Delv. to PANCOAST 22 Apr 1824.

3F:245   Date: 1 Feb 1823   RtCt: 3 Feb 1823

Giles HAMMETT & wife Alice of Ldn to Everett SAUNDERS of Ldn.
B/S ½a on N side of Market St in Lsbg adj Mrs. AISQUITH, Dr.
SELDON, Edward HAMMETT (conveyed to HAMMETT & Thos. R.
MOTT Nov 1818). Wit: Presley CORDELL, Saml. M. EDWARDS.

3F:247   Date: 3 Feb 1823   RtCt: 3 Feb 1823

James WINTERS of Ldn to dau Sally WINTERS of Ldn. Gift of lot
with house nr Lsbg (prch/o Thomas HEATHERLY Apr 1810, DBk
LL:303).

3F:247   Date: 2 Aug 1820   RtCt: 13 Nov 1820/4 Feb 1823

Ferdinando FAIRFAX of Ffx to Christopher SHRIVER of Ldn. B/S of
31a on Blue Ridge Mt. adj __ SULLIVAN, __ KIDWELL. Wit: Joshua
OSBURN, Abiel JENNERS, John CAMPBELL.

3F:249   Date: 13 Jul 1822   RtCt: 5 Feb 1823

Joshua B. OVERFIELD & wife Anna of Ldn to Edward B. GRADY of
Ldn. Trust for debt to Martin C. OVERFIELD of Henderson Co Ky
using 108a Lot #1 on round hill (Judith BOLLS old place) in div. of
Martin OVERFIELD, adj Nicholas OSBURN. Wit: Benjamin
GRAYSON, Notley C. WILLIAMS.

3F:250   Date: 16 Jan 1823   RtCt: 5 Feb 1823

Isaiah B. BEANS & wife Hannah of Ldn to Edward B. GRADY of
Ldn. B/S of 58½a adj __ DUNKIN, __ HANBY, __ RUSSELL and 2a
adj __ DUNKIN, __ STRINGFELLOW, __ McPHERSON. Wit:
Benjamin GRAYSON, John W. GRAYSON. Delv. pr order filed DBk
TT:177, 26 Mar 1824.

3F:252   Date: 9 Sep 1822   RtCt: 6 Feb 1823

William RANDALL & wife Rachel of Fqr to William HARDEN of Ldn.
B/S of 6a on N side of turnpike road from Aldie to Snickers ferry adj
Andrew BEATY. Wit: David ALEXANDER, George BEATY, Leven
LUCKETT, William BRONAUGH.

3F:253   Date: 4 Feb 1823   RtCt: 7 Feb 1823

John A. BINNS to Thomas R. MOTT and Samuel M. EDWARDS.
Trust for debt to Richard H. HENDERSON using land cnvy/b
HENDERSON which belonged to reps of Isaac CURRY dec'd
except 17a reserved by HENDERSON. Delv. to EDWARDS 5 Jan
1824.

3F:254   Date: 4 Feb 1823   RtCt: 7 Feb 1823

Richard H. HENDERSON & wife Orra of Ldn to John A. BINNS of
Ldn. B/S of 64a (from reps of Isaac CURRY dec'd) except 17a, adj
James RUST, __ CHILTON, __ RHODES. Wit: John McCORMICK,
Samuel M. EDWARDS.

3F:255   Date: 7 Feb 1823   RtCt: 7 Feb 1823
William KING & wife Susan of Lsbg to Leven W. SHEPHERD of
Lsbg. B/S of lot on E side of King St in Lsbg (cnvy/b John NIXON,
DBk SS:413) adj Thomas SANDERS, Richard H. HENDERSON.
Delv. to SHEPHERD 24 Oct 1825. Wit: Thomas SANDERS, Samuel
M. EDWARDS.

3F:256   Date: 3 Feb 1823   RtCt: 7 Feb 1823
Samuel M. EDWARDS, John A. BINNS and Thomas SANDERS (as
commr. in case of Joseph CURRY agst Sally CURRY) of Ldn to
Richard H. HENDERSON of Ldn. B/S of 64a of Isaac CURRY dec'd.
Delv. to HENDERSON 25 Dec 1835.

3F:257   Date: 19 Oct 1822   RtCt: 8 Jan 1823
Richard H. HENDERSON & wife Orra Moore of Lsbg to Tasker C.
QUINLAN of Lsbg. B/S of house and lot in Wtfd (sold by Aaron
SANDERS and Chas. ELGIN as trustees of Mahlon JANNEY in debt
to Thomas R. MOTT). Wit: Wilson C. SELDON, John HAMILTON.
Delv. to Thos. R. MOTT 17 Sep 1823.

3F:257   Date: 7 Dec 1820   RtCt: 7 Dec 1822/10 Feb 1823
John H. McCABE & wife Mary of Ldn to Charles BINNS of Ldn. B/S
of lot in Lsbg at Back and North Sts. Wit: John McCORMICK,
Thomas SAUNDERS. Signatures of John ROSE, John
McCORMICK, Saml. M. EDWARDS, L. P. W. BALCH, Chas. B.
BALL, Wm. M. McCARTY, Rich'd Henry LEE, John T. WILSON
(board of trustees of Lsbg Academy) authorizing McCABE to deliver
deed to BINNS. Delv. to BINNS 22 Aug 1827.

3F:259   Date: 11 Feb 1823   RtCt: 11 Feb 1823
Giles HAMMETT, John H. MONROE, Thomas SANDERS, Thomas
MORRALLEE, Saml. HAMMETT. Bond on Giles HAMMETT as
constable.

3F:260   Date: 15 Jun 1819   RtCt: 11 Feb 1823
John RUSSELL & wife Mary of Belmont Co Ohio o Mahlon MORRIS
of Ldn. B/S of 29a (1/6th part of 176a dev. by William RUSSELL
dec'd to children John, Elizabeth, Robert, William, Ruth and Thomas
RUSSELL). Wit: Levi PICKERING, Levi MILLER.

3F:261   Date: 23 Oct 1822   RtCt: 11 Feb 1823
Peter JACOBS dec'd. Division – court order dated 9 Sep 1822 –
lease place to widow Elizabeth JACOBS, Lot #1 (6a) to Valentine
JACOBS, Lot #2 (13¾a) to George JACOBS, Lot #3 (12a) to
Christianna JACOBS, Lot #4 (11½a) to Elizabeth COCKERILL late
JACOBS, Lot #5 (10a) to Peter JACOBS, Lot #6 (8½a) to Mary
JACOBS, Lot #7 (9¼a) to Reonard JACOBS, Lot #8 (10a) to Adam
JACOBS, Lot #9 (10a) to John JACOBS, Lot #10 (10a) to Christian
JACOBS. Gives plat. Divisors: John CONARD, Peter DEMORY,
Jno. J. MATHIAS.

3F:264 Date: 12 Feb 1823 RtCt: 12 Feb 1823
Martin CORDELL, Presley CORDELL and John A. BINNS. Bond on
Martin CORDELL as constable.

3F:264 Date: 10 Jan 1823 RtCt: 10 Feb 1823
Israel SMALLWOOD to Caldwell CARR. Trust for debt to Hebron
SMALLWOOD using farm animals and household items. Delv. to
CARR 8 Aug 1824.

3F:266 Date: 13 Nov 1822 RtCt: 10 Feb 1823
John MORROW & wife Jane of Wtfd to Robert BRADEN of Wtfd.
Trust for debt to John HAMMOND of Wtfd and Charles Fenton
MERCER of Aldie as security on bond using lot in Wtfd where
MORROW now lives. Wit: Abiel JENNERS, Saml. HOUGH Jr. Delv.
to Thos. A. MOORE pr order 18 Nov 1825.

3F:267 Date: 13 Aug 1818 RtCt: 10 Feb 1823
Isaac E. STEER & wife Leah of Ldn to Stephen BALL of Ldn. B/S of
87 perch lot adj BALL's purchase of Mahlon JANNEY dec'd, Martho
SULLIVAN dec'd. Wit: Robert BRADEN, Abiel JENNERS.

3F:268 Date: 25 Dec 1822 RtCt: 10 Feb 1823
Charles Fenton MERCER of Aldie to Lewis Marshall SMITH of Aldie.
B/S of 1a in Aldie (Jonah HOOD & wife Nancy purchased lot from
MERCER and build brick house where he now lives but deed was
incomplete, and has been sold to SMITH). Wit: E. G. HAMILTON,
John THOMAS, Alfred A. ESKRIDGE, Burr POWELL, A. GIBSON.

3F:270 Date: 3 Feb 1823 RtCt: 10 Feb 1823
Thomas EVANS of Ldn to sons George EVANS of JeffVa and Abner
EVANS of Ldn. Gift of farm animals, negro man Peter, farm and
household items. Wit: Mord'a THROCKMORTON, Wm.
CARRINGTON, Mathew THROCKMORTON.

3F:271 Date: 8 Feb 1823 RtCt: 11 Feb 1823
Elias THRASHER Jr. to George SYPHERD. Trust for debt to Daniel
RICHEY using household items, farm animals, share of crops on
Daniel HOUSEHOLDER's farm. Wit: John WEANING, John
BOOTH, John GEORGE.

3F:272 Date: 11 Feb 1823 RtCt: 11 Feb 1823
Richard H. HENDERSON (for use of reps of William CLAYTON
dec'd) of Ldn to Norman URTON of Hampshire Co Va. B/S of 175a
in Manor of Leeds adj reps of William L. LEE.

3F:272 Date: 12 Feb 1823 RtCt: 12 Feb 1823
William THRIFT (as commr. in suit of Mahlon MORRIS agst Hannah
WILSON Exor of Ebenezer WILSON and Hannah WILSON, Peter
PHILLIPS & wife Sally, Thomas WILSON, John WILSON, Luke
GREEN & wife Margaret, Nicholas PHILLIPS & wife Polly, Cline
FEARST & wife Jane, Conrad FEARST & wife Elizabeth, Ebenezer
COX and Kitty COX, Samuel WILSON, Hannah WILSON and Eseph

WILSON) to Mahlon MORRIS. B/S of 1a where John GLOSSER formerly lived adj John CAMPBELL.

3F:273   Date: 11 Feb 1823   RtCt: 13 Feb 1823
John CRIDLER & wife __ of Ldn to John A. BINNS of Ldn. Trust for debt to Jesse RICE using lot on N side of Market St. in Lsbg (cnvy/b John LITTLEJOHN, DBk WW:416).

3F:274   Date: 15 Feb 1823   RtCt: 18 Feb 1823
Isaac WRIGHT of Lsbg to John A. BINNS of Lsbg. Trust to Charles BINNS of Lsbg (WRIGHT rented house and lot in Lsbg until 1 Jan next) using farm and household items. Delv. to BINNS 31 Sep 1824.

3F:275   Date: 14 Nov 1822   RtCt: 17 Feb 1823
Calvin THATCHER of Ldn to Hector OSBURN and Herod OSBURN of Ldn. Trust for debt to Joshua OSBURN using 160a formerly owned by Richard THATCHER dec'd now occupied by Mahlon PURCELL under lease, adj John LOVE dec'd, James BETTS, Issachar BROWN, Jonathan HEATON. Wit: David GRIFFITH, William TAYLOR, Joseph CARRALL. Delv. pr order 29 Mar 1826, DBk 3C:499.

3F:277   Date: 1 Apr 1822   RtCt: 21 Feb 1823
Amos JANNEY of Ldn to Phillip FRY of Ldn. Mortgage on 18a adj Adam Grubb, Phillip FRY. Wit: Daniel FRY, Aquilla FRY, Christena FRY. Delv. to FRYE 7 Apr 1826.

3F:278   Date: 21 Feb 1823   RtCt: 21 Feb 1823
Edward DORSEY of Ldn to Robert MOFFETT of Ldn. Trust for Charles B. BALL as security for debt to David SHAWEN using int. in 2 lots in Wtfd. Delv. to MOFFETT 24 Sep 1823.

3F:279   Date: 10 Feb 1823   RtCt: 21 Feb 1823
Benjamin SHREVE of Ldn to Ann TAYLOR (w/o Henry TAYLOR dec'd) and Mary TAYLOR (d/o Henry TAYLOR dec'd) of Ldn. Release of trust for debt to Abraham H. COLLINS dated Jul 1819 on land Henry died seized of. Wit: R. BRADEN, William STEER, Jesse GOVER.

3F:280   Date: 27 Feb 1823   RtCt: 27 Feb 1823
John M. McCARTY of Ldn to Richard H. HENDERSON of Ldn. Trust for debt to Charles BENNETT of AlexDC using 500a on Potomac adj Samuel G. GRIFFITH dec'd, John DULIN, Mrs. Anne of Cleve LYONS. Delv. to R. J. TAYLOR 24 Oct 1825.

3F:281   Date: 7 Feb 1823   RtCt: 23 Feb 1823
Patrick McGARVICK of Ldn to son Israel McGARVICK of Ldn. Gift of 214½a where Patrick now lives (64½a cnvy/b Ferdinando FAIRFAX in Apr 1803 DBk CC:303 and 150a by Peter R. BEVERLY in Oct 1810). Delv. copy (original missing) to Israel 18 Nov 1826.

3F:282   Date: 29 Jul 1822   RtCt: 26 Feb 1823
Robert CHEW of Ldn to William BRADFIELD of Ldn. Trust for debt to Israel CLAYTON of Ldn using 49¼a Lot #4 and 51¾a Lot #18.

3F:284 Date: 16 Jan 1823 RtCt: 27 Feb 1823
Samuel CLAPHAM of Ldn to James W. FORD of StafVa. Trust for debt to Bazell GORDON using 21a (cnvy/b Wm. NOLAND Mar 1804) and 1048a (cnvy/b NOLAND Nov 1809) and 118a (cnvy/b Robert BENTLY Aug 1821) and 200a (dev. by Josias CLAPHAM) and 50a with mill (cnvy/b Fanny LEE). Delv. to John M. CHILTON pr order of GORDON 14 Apr 1827.

3F:285 Date: 27 Feb 1823 RtCt: 27 Feb 1823
James WINTERS of Ldn to dau Hester STEWART of Ldn. Gift of lot on S side of Lsbg Turnpike road nr E line of Lsbg adj Sally WINTERS.

3F:286 Date: 27 Feb 1823 RtCt: 1 Mar 1823
John WALTON & wife Martha (d/o Samuel GOURLEY dec'd) and Samuel GOURLEY (s/o Samuel dec'd) by atty John WILKINSON executed in Bucks Co Pa to Gourley REEDER. B/S int. in 103a on Beaverdam cnvy/b David LOVETT (Joseph GOURLEY of Ldn died intestate without issue, children of brother Samuel GOURLEY dec'd are entitled to one part)

3F:288 Date: 31 Aug 1822 RtCt: 1 Mar 1823
Robert ORR of Ldn to Samuel PARMER Jr. of Ldn. Trust for debt to Walter LANGLEY and William WOODFORD of Ldn using farm animals, farm and household items. Wit: David JURY, Jonathan MOORE.

3F:289 Date: 27 Jan 1823 RtCt: 1 Mar 1823
John H. CASSADAY & wife Jane W. of Ldn to Thomas DONALDSON of Ldn. B/S of 7a (cnvy/b Joshua MOXLEY Nov 1813) adj William McKNIGHT, Abiel JENNERS, Nicholas MONEY, __ JANNEY. Wit: Abiel JENNERS, S. HOUGH Jr.

3F:290 Date: 27 Jan 1823 RtCt: 1 Mar 1823
Thomas DONALDSON & wife Elizabeth of Ldn to Zachariah DULANY and Noble S. BRADEN of Ldn. Trust for debt to Abiel JENNERS using above 7a. Delv. to BRADEN 10 Aug 1825.

3F:292 Date: 1 Aug 1822 RtCt: 3 Mar 1823
Thomas HEIR & wife Jane of Ldn to Richard H. HENDERSON. Trust for debt to Reuben SCHOOLEY using house and lot in Lsbg cnvy/b SCHOOLEY. Wit: Thomas SANDERS, Saml. M. EDWARDS.

3F:294 Date: 28 Feb 1823 RtCt: 3 Mar 1823
Noah HIXSON to Martin CORDELL. Trust for debt to Adam CORDELL using his 1/6th share in mother's dower of 2½a.

3F:295 Date: 3 Mar 1823 RtCt: 3 Mar 1823
Isaac WRIGHT (insolvent debtor) of Ldn to Shff John ROSE. B/S of 10-11a on NE side of turnpike road from Lsbg to George Town (from div. of father's estate) adj Edmund J. LEE, George FEISTER and int. in lot in Haymarket PrWm and house and lot in Lsbg prch/o Robert PERFECT.

3F:296 Date: 1 Mar 1823 RtCt: 3 Mar 1823
Thomas HEIR of Ldn to George RICHARDS. Trust for debt to
William HAYMAN Jr. of George Town using ½a lot at Loudoun and
Market Sts in Lsbg and crops, farm animals, farm and household
items.

3F:297 Date: 6 Dec 1822 RtCt: 4 Mar 1823
John FEICHTER & wife Martha of Ldn to John SURGHNOR of Ldn.
B/S of lot on N side of Loudoun St in Lsbg adj SURGHNOR, James
GARNER. Wit: Henry CRANE, Peter FEICHTER, Edward HANES,
John McCORMICK, Presly CORDELL. Delv. to SURGHNORE 27
Oct 1832.

3F:299 Date: 3 Mar 1823 RtCt: 4 Mar 1823
John SHAW & wife Rebecca of Ldn to Edward HAMMETT of Ldn.
B/S of lot on E side of Back St. in Lsbg adj SURGHNOR's leased
lot, Peter ISH's leased lot. Wit: W. C. SELDON, Thomas SANDERS.

3F:300 Date: 3 Mar 1823 RtCt: 4 Mar 1823
John McCORMICK & wife Mary of Ldn to Henry POTTERFIELD of
Ldn. B/S of lot at Market & Liberty Sts in Lsbg adj Charles BINNS,
Joseph HILLIARD's stable. Wit: Saml. M. EDWARDS, Presley
CORDELL. Delv. to Admr of Henry POTTERFELD dec'd on __.

3F:301 Date: 3 Mar 1823 RtCt: 4 Mar 1823
Edward HAMMETT & wife Sarah of Ldn to John SHAW of Ldn. B/S
of lot (cnvy/b Lindza THOMAS Mar 1819) on road from Lsbg to
Haymarket adj Benjamin SHREVE, Mrs. WOODY, James RUST.
Wit: Thomas SANDERS, Samuel M. EDWARDS. Delv. to SHAW 16
Sep 1823.

3F:303 Date: 8 Dec 1822 RtCt: 4 Mar 1823
Peter FICHTER & wife Susannah of Ldn to John SURGHNOR of
Ldn. B/S of lot on Loudoun St in Lsbg adj John FICHTER, James
GARNER. Wit: Presley CORDELL, Henry CRANE, Samuel
FITZIMONS, John McCORMICK, Presley CORDELL. Delv. to
SURGHNOR 27 Oct 1832.

3F:304 Date: 4 Mar 1823 RtCt: 5 Mar 1823
John CRIDLER & wife Elizabeth of Ldn to Samuel M. EDWARDS of
Ldn. Trust for debt to William CARR using lot on NW side of Market
St. in Lsbg with brick dwelling occupied by CRIDLER. Wit: E. G.
HAMILTON, A. R. St. CLAIR, A. A. ESKRIDGE. Delv. to EDWARDS
1 ? 1825.

3F:305 Date: 1 Mar 1823 RtCt: 6 Mar 1823
Thomas BROWN to David J. COE. Trust for debt to George R.
BRISCOE using farm animals, farm and household items. Wit:
Benjamin JOHNSON, William LICKEY.

3F:306 Date: 3 Mar 1823 RtCt: 7 Mar 1823
John HAMILTON & wife ___ to Abiel JENNERS of Ldn. Trust for
debt to Jesse GOVER using und. 1/7th of real estate of Henry

TAYLOR dec'd on Kittocton Creek with mills (cnvy/b Jesse GOVER 3 Mar).

3F:308   Date: 4 Jan 1823   RtCt: 7 Mar 1823
Benjamin KENT & wife Sarah of Ldn to Stephen T. BURSON of Ldn. B/S of 15a (cnvy/b John WEST) adj Jonas JANNEY. Delv. to BURSON 10 May 1824. Wit: Burr POWELL, A. GIBSON.

3F:309   Date: 6 Mar 1823   RtCt: 7 Mar 1823
William DEVAUGH of Ldn to Isaac KELL of Alex Va. Trust for Samuel BARTLE as security in execution with Jacob HOFFMAN mayor of AlexDC using household items.

3F:310   Date: 7 Mar 1823   RtCt: 7 Mar 1823
Britton SANDERS to Erasmus G. HAMILTON. Trust for John H. McCABE and Samuel M. EDWARDS as security in prison bounds bond using farm animals.

3F:311   Date: 7 Mar 1823   RtCt: 8 Mar 1823
Charles GULLATT & wife Rebecca of Ldn to William JACOBS & wife Catharine of Ldn. B/S of Lot #57 at Liberty & Loudoun Sts in Lsbg. Wit: Thomas SANDERS, John H. McCABE. Delv. to JACOBS 3 Jul 1830.

3F:312   Date: 1 Mar 1823   RtCt: 10 Mar 1823
John WILLIAMS and William H. HOUGH of Ldn to Jesse GOVER & wife Myriam of Ldn. Release of trust of May 1819 for debt to Isaac WALKER and Jacob MENDENHALL (now dec'd Bulah MENDENHAL Admr).

3F:314   Date: 3 Mar 1823   RtCt: 10 Mar 1823
Jesse GOVER & wife Myriam of Ldn to John HAMILTON of Ldn. B/S of 1/7th int. in Taylor Town farm from Henry TAYLOR dec'd and 1/7th of tract on W side of Catocton Creek except what was cnvy/b Mrs. Ann TAYLOR to Levi COLLINS now in possession of Jacob CARNES. Wit: Robert BRADEN, Samuel HOUGH Jr. Delv. pr order 9 Aug 1824.

3F:315   Date: 12 Feb 1823   RtCt: 10 Mar 1823
Mary A. TAYLOR of Wtfd to John HAMILTON of Ldn. B/S of und. share of real estate of father Henry TAYLOR dec'd as listed above. Delv. pr order 9 Aug 1824.

3F:316   Date: 20 Feb 1823   RtCt: 11 Mar 1823
John WALTON & wife Martha late GOURLEY and Samuel GOURLEY the younger (all in Bucks Co Pa, ch/o of yeoman Samuel GOURLEY dec'd late of Moorland township, Montgomery Co Pa) to John WILKINSON of Ldn. PoA. Joseph GOURLEY br/o Samuel died intestate and without issue leaving considerable estate to brothers children. Wit: Hiram WALTON, Jabez WILSON.

3F:318   Date: 11 Mar 1823   RtCt: 11 Mar 1823
Joseph PURSELL (insolvent debtor) of Ldn to Shff John ROSE. B/S of 90a subject to trust to Joseph MEAD for benefit of Benjamin SHREVE.

3F:319   Date: 15 Feb 1823   RtCt: 18 Feb 1823
Isaac WRIGHT & wife Susan of Lsbg to John A. BINNS. Trust for John J. MATHIAS as security in debt to Mrs. Mary MASON for hire of negro Barney & wife Charlotte using int. in lot of Robert PURFECT dec'd 11a on Lsbg paved road adj Edmund J. LEE and bricks in kiln. Delv. to Saml. M. EDWARDS pr Jno. A. BINNS 26 Aug 1823.

3F:320   Date: ___   RtCt: 10 Mar 1823
Thomas NICHOLS of Ldn to Joseph HOUGH of Ldn. Release of trust of Mar 1823 for debt to Abel JANNEY.

3F:321   Date: 8 Mar 1823   RtCt: 10 Mar 1823
Mahlon MORRIS & wife Catharine of Ldn to Elizabeth WRIGHT of Ldn. B/S of 1a where John GLOSSER formerly lived adj John CAMPBELL. Wit: Craven OSBURN, John WHITE. Delv. to Isaac TALLY who m. Eliz. WRIGHT 10 Oct 1835.

3F:322   Date: 7 Feb 1823   RtCt: 10 Mar 1823
William NOLAND & wife Catharine to Burr POWELL and James HIXSON, Cuthbert POWELL, Phillip BURWELL & Nathaniel BURWELL (pres. and directors of Ashby Gap Turnpike Company). B/S of ½a adj Mathew ADAM, __ NOLAND. Wit: Francis W. LUCKETT, A. GIBSON. Delv. to treasurer A. GIBSON 14 Nov 1832.

3F:323   Date: 18 May 1821   RtCt: 12 Nov 1821
Thomson MASON of Ldn to Richard SMITH. Trust for loan from Bank of the U.S. with note endorsed by William T. T. MASON and George GRAHAM using 462½a 'Liberia' where MASON lives. Wit: Wm. SANDERS, William S. SANDERS, Andrew HALL.

3F:325   Date: __ Jun 1822   RtCt: 10 Mar 1823
William H. DORSEY & wife Judith of Ldn to Richard H. HENDERSON of Ldn. Trust for debt to THOMAS GEORGE and THOMAS of BaltMd using house & lot in Union. Wit: Wm. BRONAUGH, John W. GRAYSON.

3F:327   Date: 15 Dec 1822   RtCt: 10 Mar 1823
Samuel JACKSON of Ldn to Geo. W. HENRY of Ldn. BoS for farm animals, farm and household items. Wit: Jozabed WHITE. Delv. to HENRY 29 Mar 1824.

3F:328   Date: 11 Feb 1823   RtCt: 10 Mar 1823
George LEE of Ldn to John MARSHALL of Ldn. B/S of 511a on upper side of Broad run (Book RR page 168) sold by commrs. of George LEE dec'd to pay debts in Mar 1814 when George LEE was an infant under 21a old. Wit: Jno. J. MATHIAS, A. R. St. CLAIR, A. A. ESKRIDGE.

3F:329   Date: 10 __ 1823   RtCt: 10 Mar 1823
Joseph HOUGH & wife Deborah of Ldn to Enos TRAHERN of Ldn. B/S of 6a on NW fork of Goose Creek. Wit: John WHITE, Craven OSBURN.

3F:330   Date: 9 Jun 1816   RtCt: 10 Mar 1823
Henry JENKINS & wife Margaret of Ldn to Elias JENKINS of Ldn. B/S of 16¼a on NE side of Alexandria road. Wit: Robert ELGIN, Charles THRIFT, Gustavus ELGIN, John McCORMICK, Thomas GREGG. Delv. to JENKINS 17 Jul 1824.

3F:331   Date: 17 Jan 1823   RtCt: 10 Mar 1823
William VICKERS & wife Anna of Ldn to Jacob ISH of Ldn. B/S of 2a lot now occupied by Joseph HIBBS adj __ WORNELL, __ VICKERS. Wit: Burr POWELL, A. GIBSON. Delv. to Robt. A. ISH his son 15 Aug 1832.

3F:332   Date: 18 Mar 1823   RtCt: 11 Mar 1823
Jehu HOLLINGSWORTH & wife Senior of Ldn to James HEATON of Ldn. B/S of 114 pole lot adj HEATON nr corner of grave yard most adj to the baptist church, Samuel PURSELL. Wit: John WHITE, Craven OSBURN.

3F:334   Date: 16 Jan 1823   RtCt: 12 May 1823
Isaiah B. BEANS & wife Hannah of Ldn to Abner G. HUMPHREY of Ldn. Trust for debt to Abner and John G. HUMPHREY (Exors of Thomas HUMPHREY dec'd) using 156a adj Joel OSBURN, __ HUMPHREY, __ TAYLOR. Wit: Benjamin GRAYSON, John W. GRAYSON. Delv. to John G. HUMPHREY 31 Jan 1828.

3F:336   Date: 16 Jan 1823   RtCt: 12 Mar 1823
Edward B. GRADY & wife Sarah of Ldn to Abner G. HUMPHREY of Ldn. Trust for debt to Abner and John G. HUMPHREY (Exors of Thomas HUMPHREY dec'd) using 58½a adj __ DUNKIN, __ HANDY, __ RUSSELL, R. CHEW. Wit: Benjamin GRAYSON, John W. GRAYSON. Delv. pr order 18 Oct 1827.

3F:337   Date: 9 Jan 1823   RtCt: 15 Jan 1823
George TAVENNER Sr. of Ldn to son James TAVENNER of Ldn. Agreement – James accepts payment for 95a where he now lives in lieu of receiving it from will of said James [George ?]. Will give up possession next 1 Sept. Wit: Jonah SANDS, Charles B. HAMILTON.

3F:338   Date: 12 Mar 1823   RtCt: 13 Mar 1823
John LIVINGSTON of Ldn to Daniel STONE of Ldn. Trust for debt to Robert BRADEN, James D. FRENCH, Isaac B. BEALE, Isaac E. STEER, Mahlon SCHOOLEY, Samuel PEIRPOINT, Jonas P. SCHOOLEY, John SCHOOLEY, Francis STRIBLING using ½a Lots #52 & #53 in Wtfd with brick house and frame shop.

3F:340   Date: 13 Nov 1822   RtCt: 14 Mar 1823
Burr G. POWELL of Ldn to Humphrey B. POWELL of Ldn. Trust for debt to Maria A. POWELL using int. in 415a derived from

grandfather subject to his mother's dower, adj Elizabeth BAKER, David FULTON, John RICHARDS, Thomas W. POWELL. Delv. to Cuthbert POWELL 31 Aug 1824.

3F:341   Date: 15 Mar 1823   RtCt: 15 Mar 1823
John THOMAS of Lsbg to John SHAFER Jr. Gift of farm animals, household items.

3F:341   Date: 31 Jul 1822   RtCt: 15 Mar 1823
Alexander KERR cashier at Bank of Metropolis in WashDC to James HIXSON. Release of trust of Jul 1821. Wit: O. B. BROWN, E. REYNOLDS.

3F:342   Date: 15 Mar 1823   RtCt: 15 Mar 1823
James HIXSON of Ldn to Stephen C. ROSZEL, Jesse TIMMS and Richard H. HENDERSON of Ldn. Trust for debt to George CARTER of Oatlands using 330a (except 8a conveyed to GIBSON and VERNON and Benjamin HIXSON) on Little River (part of tract patented to Thomas OWSLEY) adj John SINCLAIR. Delv. to CARTER 26 Mar 1824.

3F:344   Date: 13 Mar 1823   RtCt: 22 Mar 1823
John MARTIN of Ldn to John GALLEHER of Ldn. Trust for debt to George E. LLOYD of Union using a horse.

3F:345   Date: 25 Mar 1823   RtCt: 25 Mar 1823
Burr W. HARRISON & wife Sally H. of Ldn to Thomas MOSS of Ldn. B/S of 167a adj James ALLEN. Wit: Presley CORDELL, Samuel M. EDWARDS. Delv. to Edward HAMMETT pr order 9 Oct 1823.

3F:346   Date: 1 Jan 1822   RtCt: 22 Mar 1823
Peter BENEDUM of Ldn to Samuel M. EDWARDS of Ldn. B/S of 1a (part of conveyance from Thomas N. BINNS and Bernard HOUGH Admrs of Patrick CAVINS) adj __ THORNTON, __ HEREFORD.

3F:347   Date: 21 Mar 1823   RtCt: 24 Mar 1823
Samuel LAYCOCK of Ldn to John A. BINNS of Ldn. Trust for debt to John MURRAY of Lsbg using farm and household items.

3F:348   Date: 21 Mar 1823   RtCt: 27 Mar 1823
Samuel TUSTIN of Ldn to Thomas SANDERS of Ldn. Trust for debt to Samuel M. EDWARDS using lot on E side of Liberty St (bought from John DRAIN) with brick house, coach shop and blacksmith shop, adj John DRAIN, Thomas BIRKBY, heirs of William R. TAYLOR.

3F:349   Date: 21 Feb 1823   RtCt: 27 Mar 1823
John H. CASSADAY to Noble BRADEN and David CONRAD. Trust for debt to Samuel HOUGH Jr. using household items and crops.

3F:351   Date: 8 Mar 1823   RtCt: 27 Mar 1823
Aaron DAILEY of Ldn to son Samuel DAILEY. BoS for farm animals, household items. Wit: William CHILTON, John H. CANBY.

3F:351 Date: 13 Mar 1823 RtCt: 31 Mar 1823
Joseph HILLIARD of Ldn to James F. NEWTON of Ldn. B/S of 30a
(cnvy/b Presley CORDELL trustee of Silas REESE).

3F:352 Date: 15 Nov 1822 RtCt: 31 Mar 1823
Valentine JACOBS of Ldn to Thomas HALL of Ldn. B/S of 8a
(cnvy/b Thomas KIDWELL) on E side of Blue Ridge adj George
KOONCE, __ NEER.

3F:353 Date: 1 Apr 1823 RtCt: 1 Apr 1823
John S. HARL of Ldn to L. P. W. BALCH of Lsbg. Trust for debt to
John M. WILSON using farm animals and items.

3F:354 Date: 30 Jan 1823 RtCt: 2 Apr 1823
John PARMER of Ldn to Mary TAYLOR of Ldn. B/S of 1 rood lot in
Wtfd (part of 2 lots cnvy/b John B. STEVENS Jun 1816 and Apr
1817) adj Isaac WALKER, Samuel HOUGH Jr and 14½ sq pole lot
adj Saml HOUGH Jr, __ SAPPINGTON. Delv. to Jacob LEMON pr
order 5 May 1858.

3F:355 Date: 3 Mar 1823 RtCt: 2 Apr 1823
John HAMILTON & wife __ to William H. HOUGH of Ldn. Trust for
debt to Mary TAYLOR using und. 1/7th int. in real estate of Henry
TAYLOR dec'd on Kottocton Creek.

3F:357 Date: 24 Mar 1823 RtCt: 3 Apr 1823
John MORAN of Ldn to Bernard NICKINGS of Ldn. B/S of ¾a above
Mdbg on Ashby's Gap turnpike adj __ POWELL. Delv. to NICKINS
16 Jan 1827.

3F:358 Date: 21 Mar 1823 RtCt: 3 Apr 1823
John C. HANDY of Ldn to James MOUNT of Ldn. Trust for debt to
Joseph HAINS of Fqr using int. in land which brother Eli Heaton
HANDY died possessed adj Enoch FRANCIS, and horse prch/o
Joseph HAINS. Delv. to MOUNT 9 Jun 1830.

3F:359 Date: 15 Mar 1823 RtCt: 3 Apr 1823
Margaret UNDERWOOD wd/o Samuel UNDERWOOD dec'd of Ldn.
Relinquishment of dower for $600 paid by Samuel UNDERWOOD
s/o Samuel dec'd for land adj Archibald MORRISON.

3F:359 Date: 9 Nov 1822 RtCt: 4 Apr 1823
John RICHARDS of Ldn to Robert MOFFETT of Ldn. B/S of int.
(conveyed to John by Sampson RICHARDS in right of his wife
Elizabeth d/o Henry TAYLOR dec'd) in land of Henry TAYLOR
dec'd. Wit: John HAMILTON, Thomas GASSAWAY. Delv. to
MOFFETT 23 Aug 1824.

3F:361 Date: 4 Apr 1823 RtCt: 5 Apr 1823
Thomas STEPHENS of Ldn to Valentine V. PURCELL of Ldn. BoS
for farm animals, farm and household items, grain in ground at place
where he lived owned by Phillip FRYE. Wit: John BRADEN, Burr
BRADEN.

3F:362 Date: 22 Mar 1823 RtCt: 9 Apr 1823
Peter BENEDUM of Ldn to William CARR of Ldn. B/S of 63 perch lot
(part of tract leased by James HEREFORD in 1798 transferred to
BENEDUM in Jun 1815, DBk SS:428) adj John G. WATT. Wit: Saml.
M. EDWARDS, Chas. G. ESKRIDGE, Alfred A. ESKRIDGE, E. G.
HAMILTON. Delv. pr order 23 Nov 1827.

3F:362 Date: 24 Oct 1822 RtCt: 9 Apr 1823
George LEE of Ldn to Thomas VEALE and John VEALE of Ldn. B/S
of 359a between Goose Creek and broad run (leased by Thomas L.
LEE to William VEAL) and 7a adj lot. Wit: E. G. HAMILTON, A. R.
St. CLAIR, Jno. J. MATHIAS. Delv. to heirs of VEALS 11 Jan 1853.

3F:364 Date: 25 Mar 1823 RtCt: 9 Apr 1823
Joseph CAVANS & wife Ann/Nancy of Ldn to Jozabed WHITE of
Ldn. B/S of 12a (allotted to wd/o Ann CLEMENTS as dower from
land of Joseph CAVANS dec'd) and 63a Lot #1. Wit: R. BRADEN,
Samuel HOUGH Jr. Delv. to WHITE 1 Nov 1824.

3F:365 Date: 10 Apr 1823 RtCt: 11 Apr 1823
Isaac NICKOLLS and Samuel NICKOLLS of Ldn to Mathew
MITCHELL of Lsbg. B/S of 3 lots in Lsbg, 1 at W corner of Martin
KITZMILLER's lot on Loudoun St. adj James RUST; the Littlejohns
stable lot at Royal and Back Sts; the 3rd on S side of Royal St.

3F:366 Date: 9 Apr 1823 RtCt: 11 Apr 1823
Mathew MITCHELL of Ldn to Isaac NICKOLLS and Samuel
NICKOLLS of Ldn. B/S of 3 lots as above. Delv. to Saml. NICHOLS
Exors 10 Nov 1825.

3F:368 Date: 23 Dec 1822 RtCt: 14 Apr 1823
William COOKE lately of Ldn but now of Fetecianna Parish
Louisianna to George M. CHICHESTER of Ldn. B/S of und. ½ of
43a 'Spring Mill' property with merchant mill adj Fayette BALL
(prch/o Charles B. BALL by COOKE and Israel LACEY). Wit: Henry
FLOWER, J. PARKENS Sr. Delv. to CHICHESTER 27 Jun 1827.

3F:369 Date: 15 Apr 1823 RtCt: 15 Apr 1823
John WEEDON, Jacob SILCOTT, Benjamin MITCHELL Jr. and E.
M. LANE. Bond on WEEDON as constable.

3F:370 Date: 27 Mar 1823 RtCt: 15 Apr 1823
Town of Upperville. Report of addition to Upperville. Commrs.
Cuthbert POWELL, Josiah TIDBALL, Wm. C. FITZHUGH, survey by
Seth SMITH. Laid off on 20a from lands of Joseph CARR extending
to Ashby Gap Turnpike to John FLEMING's lot, to John JAMES
Shop lot.

3F:371 Date: 14 Sep 1811 RtCt: 12 May 1812/14 Apr 1823
Isaac BROWN & wife Sarah of Ldn to John WILKINSON of Ldn. B/S
of 9a on Beaver Dam (prch/o Nathaniel CRAWFORD & wife Sarah
Jan 1803). Wit: Stephen C. ROSZELL, William BRONAUGH, Benj.
GRAYSON. Delv. to Seth SMITH pr WILKINSON's order ___.

3F:372   Date: 6 Mar 1823   RtCt: 14 Apr 1823
Abner GIBSON (commr. in cause of 8 Feb 1820 of Burr POWELL
and Cuthbert POWELL Exors of Leven POWELL dec'd agst
Catharine LANE wd/o Joseph LANE) to Burr POWELL. B/S of Lot
#4 in Mdbg.

3F:373   Date: 3 Oct 1822   RtCt: 14 Apr 1823
Caleb N. GALLEHER & wife Lucinda of Ldn to William GALLEHER
Jr of Ldn. B/S of int. in 110a farm of father William GALLEHER dec'd
adj Union. Wit: A. GIBSON, William BRONAUGH.

3F:374   Date: 1 Feb 1823   RtCt: 14 Apr 1823
Thomas GRIMES of Ldn to Isaac E. STEER. Trust for debt to John
LACEY of Ldn using lot in new addition of Wtfd (this day cnvy/b
James MOORE, Asa MOORE & John WILLIAMS). Wit: Abiel. S.
HOUGH Jr.

3F:376   Date: 1 Feb 1823   RtCt: 14 Apr 1823
James MOORE, Asa MOORE and John WILLIAMS (Exors of
Mahlon JANNEY dec'd) of Ldn to Thomas GRIMES of Ldn. B/S of
Lot #24 in new addition to Wtfd. Delv. 9 Sep 1824.

3F:377   Date: 31 Mar 1823   RtCt: 14 Apr 1823
Thomas MARKS & wife Keziah of Ldn to Stacey TAYLOR of Ldn.
Trust for debt to Samuel BEANS using 2a (cnvy/b Stephen REED
May 1803) and 19a (cnvy/b Vincent KEITH May 1804). Wit: Noah
HATCHER, Marks WATKINS, Nathaniel PARNEY, Craven
OSBURN, John WHITE. Delv. to TAYLOR 12 Nov 1825.

3F:379   Date: 29 Mar 1823   RtCt: 14 Apr 1823
John S. MONDAY to George RUST Jr. BoS (for debts and rent) for
farm animals, household items.

3F:380   Date: 7 Apr 1823   RtCt: 14 Apr 1823
Sampson RICHARDS & wife Elizabeth of Ldn to Robert MOFFETT
of Ldn. B/S of und. 1/7th share of real estate of Henry TAYLOR dec'd
on W side of Catocton now in possession of Jacob CARNES. Wit:
John HAMILTON, Samuel DAWSON. Delv. to MOFFETT 23 Aug
1824.

3F:381   Date: 16 Nov 1823   RtCt: 14 Apr 1823
Henry PLAISTER Sr. of Ldn to son Henry PLAISTER Jr. of Ldn. B/S
of 63a (cnvy/b Benjamin OVERFIELD 1797) adj __ BRONAUGH, __
DUNKIN, wd/o James REED and 41a allotted to John REED,
Thomas REED and Moses BROWN & wife Mary in div. of James
REED dec'd (except those in Union) and conveyed to PLAISTER.
Delv. to H. PLAISTER Jr. 4 Oct 1824.

3F:382   Date: 12 Apr 1823   RtCt: 14 Apr 1823
Samuel RINKER of Ldn to John K. LITTLETON of Ldn. BoS for farm
animals, farm and household items. Wit: Margaret WEADEN,
Leonard R. POSTON. Delv. to LITTLETON 4 Nov 1825.

3F:383   Date: 7 Apr 1823   RtCt: 14 Apr 1823
Elijah VIOLETT of Ldn to James VIOLETT of Ldn. Gift of all his personal and real estate. Includes negro Toney, Sarah, Ralph & Eliza. Del'v. pr order 5 Jun 1830.

3F:384   Date: 16 Nov 1822   RtCt: 14 Apr 1823
Elizabeth WILKINSON wd/o Joseph WILKINSON of Ldn to Henry PLAISTER Jr of Ldn. B/S of her allotment of land nr Union from father James REED dec'd (exclusive of town lit and her int. in widows dower). Delv. to PLAISTER Jr. 4 Oct 1824.

3F:385   Date: 28 Aug 1822   RtCt: 14 Apr 1823
William NOLAND & wife Catharine of Ldn to John TAYLOR of Ldn. B/S of ½a Lot #73 on Mercer St. in Aldie. Wit: Lewis M. SMITH, Robert BAGLY, Benj. R. LACEY, Burr POWELL, Abner GIBSON.

3F:386   Date: 17 Jun 1822   RtCt: 14 Apr 1823
Isaiah ROMINE. Having lived with Lydia REED in intamacy and not being married during which time she had children Isaiah, Minor, Rebeccah, Mahala and Thurza, he acknowledges the children as his. Considers them fully legitimate. Wit: Robert WYNN.

3F:387   Date: 25 Jan 1823   RtCt: 15 Apr 1823
George JANNEY & wife Susanna of Ldn and Elisha JANNEY & wife Lydia of Ffx to Richard H. HENDERSON of Ldn. Trust for debt of both JANNEYs to John LLOYD of AlexVa using 63a 'Millsville tract' and 124a adj lot (cnvy/b John LLOYD Jan 1823). Wit: William BRONAUGH, Francis W. LUCKETT. Delv. pr order __.

3F:389   Date: 5 Nov 1822   RtCt: 17 Apr 1823
Daniel BROWN & wife Rachel of Ldn to Samuel BROWN of Ldn. B/S of 2a on N side of Goose Creek (prch/o Ezekel MOUNT) adj MOUNT, Jonathan CARTER. Wit: William BRONAUGH, Notley C. WILLIAMS.

3F:391   Date: 23 Dec 1822   RtCt: 17 Apr 1823
Daniel BROWN & wife Rachel of Ldn to Samuel BROWN of Ldn. B/S of 17¾a (prch/o Silas REESE) on Goose Creek (1a condemned on land of Dennis McCARTY for abutting a mill dam). Wit: Phebe BROWN, Susan BROWN, William BRONAUGH, Notley C. WILLIAMS.

3F:392   Date: 1 Oct 1821   RtCt: 12 May 1823
John CARTER & wife Jamimia of Belmont Co Ohio to George CARTER of Ldn. B/S of und. int. in land of father Richard CARTER dec'd on Hogback Mt. (prch/o Colon AULD or John RAMSEY). Wit: John BOYD, Eleazer EVANS.

3F:394   Date: __ 1823   RtCt: 23 Apr 1823
William DERRY & wife Barbara of Ldn to John RYMMER of Ldn. B/S of 6a on W side of short hill adj __ PRINCE, John DEMORY. Wit: Craven OSBURN, John WHITE.

3F:395   Date: 1 Apr 1823   RtCt: 24 Apr 1823
Isaac EATON & wife Malinda of Ldn to John VANSICKLER and
Abraham SKILMAN of Ldn. Trust for debt to William
LICKLEY/LICKEY of Ldn using 1a at NE corner of Loudoun and
Balm St. Wit: George LICKEY, George A. McPHERSON, Robert H.
SEARES, Presley CORDELL, Saml. M. EDWARDS. Delv. to
LICKEY 26 Aug 1825.

3F:397   Date: 20 Apr 1823   RtCt: 24 Apr 1823
William LICKEY & wife Abigal of Ldn to Isaac EATON of Ldn. B/S of
25a on Catockton Mt. adj LICKEY, William COE, Charles SMITH,
John C. LICKEY. Wit: George LICKEY, George A. McPHERSON,
Robert H. SEARES, Presley CORDELL, Saml. M. EDWARDS. Delv.
to Wm. LICKEY pr order 17 Sep 1823.

3F:399   Date: 31 Sep 1822   RtCt: 26 Apr 1823
Abigail ADAMS of Ldn to John STOUSABERGER of Ldn. B/S of
2½a adj STOUSABERGER, heirs of John COMPHER dec'd. Delv.
to Jacob STOUTSENBERGER Exor of his father 24 Mar 1848.

3F:399   Date: 11 May 1821   RtCt: 19 Apr 1823
Robert J. TAYLOR and Charles T. CHAPMAN of AlexVa to
Benjamin C. ASHTON and Richard C. NORTON (as trustees of
James L. McKENNA Mar 1818). Release of trust for debt to Charles
T. CHAPMAN to transfer to ASHTON and NORTON. Delv. to
Thomson MASON 16 Sep 1825.

3F:401   Date: 15 Jan 1823   RtCt: 30 Apr 1823
John P. DUVAL & wife Ann F. of Fqr to Thomas R. MOTT of Lsbg.
B/S of 57a (allotted to Ann F. as devisee of William CARR Sr. dec'd)
on Little River, adj Dr. John SPENCE. Wit: Burr POWELL, A.
GIBSON.

3F:402   Date: 12 Feb 1823   RtCt: 2 May 1823
John W. DAVIS & wife Elizabeth of Ldn to Andrew HESSER of Ldn.
B/S of Elizabeth's share from land of father Andrew HESSER dec'd.
Wit: Notley C. WILLIAMS, William BRONAUGH.

3F:404   Date: 2 May 1823   RtCt: 2 May 1823
Henry T. BAYNE (insolvent debtor in jail) to Shff John ROSE. B/S of
land (bought of Exors of John HAWLEY dec'd) devised by William
HOUGH dec'd to John SCHOOLEY & wife Elizabeth then to their
children, BAYNES m. Phebe SCHOOLEY d/o John & Elizabeth (for
execution from John SURGNOR).

3F:404   Date: 19 Sep 1818   RtCt: 9 Feb 1819/3 May 1823
John LEWIS of Ldn to Johnson CLEVELAND of Ldn. Trust for debt
to John H. LEWIS of Jeff Va using 240a where LEWIS now resides
adj Charles LEWIS, William B. HARRISON. Wit: Charles LEWIS,
Robert W. NEWMAN, Coleman LEWIS. Delv. to Chas. GULLATT pr
order 5 Oct 1835.

3F:405   Date: 23 Apr 1823   RtCt: 5 May 1823
Thomas CHINN & wife Ann A. of Ldn to William SWARTS of Ldn. LS of 1a above Mdbg adj Robert CHINN and adj 1¼a where Robert CHINN now resides (see next entry). Wit: Burr POWELL, A. GIBSON.

3F:407   Date: 23 Apr 1823   RtCt: 5 May 1823
Thomas CHINN & wife Nancy of Ldn to Richard, George and William CHINN (infant s/o Robert CHINN & wife Sydney of Ldn). Gift of 1¼a on Ashby's Gap turnpike road. Wit: Burr POWELL, A. GIBSON.

3F:408   Date: 3 May 1823   RtCt: 6 May 1823
Joseph BOND of Wtfd to Daniel STONE and Noble S. BRADEN of Wtfd. Trust for debt to Peyton HOUGH of Ldn using 5a tanyard lot in Wtfd (prch/o Washington and Peyton HOUGH) adj Amasa HOUGH, Robert BRADEN, William PAXSON, Margaret HIXSON. Delv. to Geo. VINSELL pr order 30 Jul 1828.

3F:410   Date: 15 Apr 1823   RtCt: 7 May 1823
George E. LLOYD of Ldn to Richard H. HENDERSON of Ldn. Trust for debt to Sabrett E. SCOTT of Georgetown DC using 21a (cnvy/b Thomas KENT) adj Isaac KENT. Delv. to HENDERSON 11 Feb 1826.

3F:411   Date: __ May 1823   RtCt: 8 May 1823
William D. DRISH & wife Harriet to Henry CLAGGETT. CoE for Harriet for B/S of 30 Dec 1820 (DBk CCC:283). Wit: John McCORMICK and John McCABE.

3F:412   Date: 8 May 1823   RtCt: 8 May 1823
Edward HAZEL (insolvent debtor in jail) of Ldn to Shff John ROSE. B/S of 2a in Aldie on Ashbys Gap Turnpike (for debts to Thomas GHEEN).

3F:412   Date: 7 May 1823   RtCt: 9 May 1823
Isaac EATON & wife Malinda of Ldn to William MISKELL of Ldn. B/S of 3½a lots in Mt. Gilead – Lot #9 at NE corner of Loudoun and College, Lot #11 on Loudoun St, Lot #20 at SE corner of Centre and Water St. Wit: John McCORMICK, Samuel M. EDWARDS.

3F:414   Date: 7 May 1823   RtCt: 9 May 1823
William MISKELL to George RICHARDS. Trust for debt to John SURGHNOR and John DRISH ass'ee of James THOMAS, David WETHERLY and Bernard GILPIN and son using ¼a lot on Market St in Lsbg (prch/o John CRIDLER) and lot in new settlement of Mt. Gilead and ½a Lot #11, #20 and #9 with unfinished log house (prch/o Isaac EATON).

3F:415   Date: 8 May 1823   RtCt: 9 May 1823
Mary HIXSON wd/o Reuben HIXSON dec'd of Ldn to Peter COMPHER of Ldn. B/S of int. in 26+a (purchased by COMPHER from Presley WILLIAMS). Delv. to COMPHER 18 Jun 1825.

3F:416   Date: 2 May 1823   RtCt: 10 May 1823
John H. CASSADAY & wife Jane of Ldn to Joshua OSBURN and
Craven OSBURN of Ldn. Trust for Charles G. EDWARDS as
security for debt to William STEER of Benjamin, Jacob COST, Abiel
JENNERS, estate of William WRIGHT dec'd using ¾a nr friends
meeting house, adj farm of Dr. J. H. McCABE, Samuel HOUGH Jr.,
grave yard, __ MOORE, __ PHILLIPS and another lot in Wtfd adj
Peter BOGGESS, Robert Braden's mill race (except int. of Henry
WALKER) and another lot in Wtfd adj __ MORROW, Samuel
HENDERSON, George W. HENRY and negro man Isaac,
household items. Wit: Robert BRADEN, Abiel JENNERS.

3F:418   Date: 10 Jul 1823   RtCt: 10 May 1823
Elizabeth POTTER of Ldn to Charles Burgess BALL of Ldn. B/S of
lot on N side of Loudoun St in Lsbg.

3F:419   Date: 26 Mar 1823   RtCt: 12 May 1823
Thomas STEVENS. Oath as Lt. Col. in 56th Reg of Va Militia.

3F:419   Date: 6 Feb 1821   RtCt: 12 May 1823
Enos GARRETT & wife Eleanor of Ldn to John A. BINNS of Ldn.
Trust for debt to Conrad BITZER using 202a (part of Wm. Dudley
Diggs valley tract) and 51¼a.

3F:420   Date: 19 Dec 1815   RtCt: 12 May 1823
Daniel DUTY of Bath Co Ky to John K. LITTLETON of Ldn. PoA to
recover negro man belonging to DUTY claimed by Richard KEENE
of Ldn. Delv. to LITTLETON 4 Nov 1825.

3F:421   Date: 25 Dec 1821   RtCt: 14 Apr 1823
Ludwell LEE to James L. McKENNA. B/S of 133a on new turnpike
road from Lsbg to Broad Run adj __ WHALEY. Recorded DBk
CCC:240.

3F:422   Date: 9 May 1823   RtCt: 12 May 1823
Samuel TRAHERN of Ldn to Caleb N. GALLEHER of Ldn. B/S of
10a adj Snickers Gap Turnpike Road, Washington McCARTY. Delv.
to GALLEHER 1 Aug 1836.

3F:423   Date: 12 May 1823   RtCt: 12 May 1823
Reuben BAYLEY of Ldn to Michael EVERHART of Ldn. Trust for
Philip EVERHART as security using farm animals, household items.

3F:424   Date: 31 May 1822   RtCt: 12 May 1823
George S. MARKS & wife Mahala of Ldn to Thomas CLOWES of
Ldn. B/S of 204a adj John DUNKIN, road to Drake's mill, Mathias
HANN, Benjamin JACKSON, Thomas DRAKE, John MARKS. Wit:
Notley C. WILLIAMS, John W. GRAYSON.

3F:425   Date: 25 Apr 1823   RtCt: 12 May 1823
Timothy TAYLOR Jr. & wife Harriet of Ldn to John TEMPLER of
Ldn. Trust for debt to Swithin NICHOLS using 31a on road from
Snickers Gap to Israel JANNEY's mill adj Thomas NICHOLLS,
Johnson LANE. Wit: Craven OSBURN, John WHITE.

3F:427   Date: 13 May 1823   RtCt: 13 May 1823
John DAVISON (insolvent debtor) of Ldn to Shff John ROSE. B/S of
½a lot & log house on N side of Washington St. in Mdbg.

3F:428   Date: 12 May 1823   RtCt: 4 May 1823
L. P. W. BALCH (as trustee for John SHAFER dated Dec 1820) of
Ldn to Samuel McPHERSON of Ldn. B/S of lot (prch/o Dr. Isaac
HOUGH by SHAFER) sold by BALCH at auction to Phillip HEATER
who sold to McPHERSON. Delv. to McPHERSON 6 Aug 1824.

3F:429   Date: 13 May 1823   RtCt: 14 May 1823
Nicholas OSBURN & wife Elizabeth S. of Ldn to Lewis P. W. BALCH
of Ldn. B/S of 128a (prch/o James WARFORD as dev. from John
WARFORD) adj Enos POTTS, Benjamin PARMER, Lewis LYDER.
Wit: Notley C. WILLIAMS, Craven OSBURN. Delv. to BALCH 3 Oct
1823.

3F:430   Date: 15 May 1820   RtCt: 15 May 1823
George M. CHICHESTER of Ldn to Charles P. TUTT of Ldn. B/S of
lot on S side of Cornwall St. in Lsbg adj DRISH's stable.

3F:431   Date: 16 May 1823   RtCt: 16 May 1823
John RALPH of Ldn to Hugh SMITH of Ldn. Trust for John MARKS
as security in debts to Thomas A. DENNIS, Mary HARN assignee of
Jesse McVEIGH, Stephen R. MOUNT, Richard H. HENDERSON
using 105a between John BAILEY and James ALLEN and house &
lot in Bloomfield occupied by RALPH. Delv. to SMITH 23 Apr 1834.

3F:432   Date: 25 Mar 1823   RtCt: 17 May 1823
William DERRY & wife Barbara of Ldn to Levi WAT(T)ERS of Ldn.
B/S of 10a on W side of Short Hill adj __ DEMORY. Wit: John
WHITE, Craven OSBURN. Delv. pr order 16 Mar 1825.

3F:433   Date: 12 Dec 1822   RtCt: 10 Feb 1823
John SINCLAIR of Ldn to Richard H. HENDERSON of Ldn. Trust for
James SANGSTER as security in judgment agst SINCLAIR by
Richard RATCLIFFE of Ffx using int. in 4y LS in mill and farm of
William H. HANDY assigned to SINCLAIR by Stephen McGEATH,
negro woman Suckey, farm animals, farm and household items. Wit:
Thos. R. MOTT, Hy H. HAMILTON, E. G. HAMILTON.

3F:434   Date: 11 Apr 1823   RtCt: 19 May 1823
Wilson Carey SELDON Sr. & wife Mary B. of Ldn to Richard Henry
LEE of Ldn. B/S of 239a (bought of Exors of Robert CARTER dec'd)
adj __ HOUGH, __ CLAGGETT, Benjamin SHREVE and 86a adj
Mary FOSTER's patent, __ SHREVE. Wit: John McCORMICK,
James H. HAMILTON.

3F:436   Date: 10 Apr 1823   RtCt: 20 May 1823
Jacob COMPHER of Ldn to Simon YEACA of Ldn. B/S of 13a share
of land from father Peter COMPHER dec'd. Wit: John HAMILTON,
Saml. STOUSABERGER, Michael THOMPSON, George ROW.
Delv. to YEACA 13 Dec 1823.

3F:437   Date: 20 May 1823   RtCt: 20 May 1823
James BRADFIELD of Ldn to Calvin THATCHER of Ldn. B/S of 60a
(prch/o James McILHANEY Sept 1798, after deducting 158a). Delv.
to THATCHER 17 Sep 1825.

3F:438   Date: 20 May 1823   RtCt: 20 May 1823
Calvin THATCHER of Ldn to James BRADFIELD of Ldn. B/S of
160a (formerly of Richard THATCHER dec'd) adj John LOVE dec'd,
James BEST, Issacher BROWN, James HEATON. Delv. to
BRADFIELD 15 Nov 1823.

3F:439   Date: 20 May 1823   RtCt: 20 May 1823
Calvin THATCHER of Ldn to L. P. W. BALCH and James P.
BRADFIELD of Ldn. Trust for using 98a (THATCHER sold 160a to
James BRADFIELD with liens on land from THATCHER to Joshua
OSBURN and Charles CHAMBLIN for use of Henson ELLIOTT and
Hector & Herod OSBURN for use of Joshua OSBURN). Delv. to
BRADFIELD 15 Nov 1823.

3F:440   Date: 20 May 1823   RtCt: 20 May 1823
Calvin THATCHER of Ldn to L. P. W. BALCH and James P.
BRADFIELD of Ldn. Trust for debt to James BRADFIELD using 98a
(cnvy/b BRADFIELD). Delv. to BRADFIELD 15 Nov 1823.

3F:441   Date: 13 Jan 1823   RtCt: 21 May 1823
Jacob WATERS of Ldn to Erasmus G. HAMILTON of Ldn. Trust for
debt to John James MATHIAS using 24a (cnvy/b MATHIAS). Wit:
Chs. G. ESKRIDGE, E. G. HAMILTON, Alfred A. ESKRIDGE. Delv.
to MATHIAS 23 Sep 1825.

3F:442   Date: 13 Jan 1823   RtCt: 21 May 1823
John J. MATHIAS of Ldn to Jacob WALTERS/WATERS of Ldn. B/S
of 24a on W side of short hill. Delv. to WATERS 27 Dec 1825.

3F:443   Date: 26 Feb 1823   RtCt: 22 May 1823
Thomas DONALDSON & wife Elizabeth to Noble S. BRADEN and
Z. DULANY. Trust for debt to Samuel HOUGH using 7a (prch/o
John H. CASSADAY) on Cotoctin adj William WRIGHT (JENNERS),
Nicholas MONEY, __ JANNEY and 2 other small lots and farm and
household items. Wit: R. BRADEN, Abiel JENNERS.

3F:445   Date: 19 Feb 1823   RtCt: 23 May 1823
Edmund B. CAVILER & wife Juliet A. of Champaighn Co Ohio to
James BOWLES of Ldn. B/S of und. int. in real estate of John
VIOLETT dec'd (allotted to John W. VIOLETT and Juliet Ann ch/o
Benjamin VIOLETT dec'd and devisee of John dec'd). Wit: Saml.
McCORD, David VANCE. Delv. to BOWLES 28 Jan 1836.

3F:446   Date: ___   RtCt: 23 May 1823
Randolph RHODES and Samuel RHODES. Agreement – not
wishing to sell land of Tholemiah derived by Ls from Bushrod
WASHINGTON 1796 as covenant forbids assignment, Samuel to

hold in name of reps of Tholemiah dec'd paying the rent and with Randolph selling crops paying Samuel 1/3.

3F:447   Date: 2 Jan 1823   RtCt: 3 Jan 1823

Daniel EACHES (trustee of George BURSON & wife Susanna Dec 1817) of Ldn to John LLOYD of AlexVa. B/S of 65a in Millville when BURSON failed to pay. Wit: Rich'd H. HENDERSON, Sydnor BAILEY, Aaron BURSON, Francis W. LUCKETT. Delv. pr order ___.

3F:448   Date: __ 1822   RtCt: 23 May 1823

Richard Henry LEE & wife Mary D. of Ldn to Henry CLAGETT of Ldn. B/S of 134¼a (prch/o Wilson C. SELDON Sr.) adj Barnard HOUGH.

3F:449   Date: 8 Oct 1822   RtCt: 24 May 1823

Levi BARTON & wife Sarah of Fqr to Mathias HAYS of Ldn. B/S of 1a where he now lives adj Amos FERGUSON, James SWARTS, road passing by his house to Aldie. Wit: William J. CARTER, Samuel TORBERT, James TORBERT. Delv. to HAYS 18 Oct 1823.

3F:450   Date: 14 Nov 1822   RtCt: 30 May 1823

Fleet SMITH & wife Jane of WashDC to Thomas GASSAWAY of Lsbg. B/S of lot in Lsbg adj __ HAMILTON, James WOOD, Gotham WRIGHT, Wright's stable, Saunders' stable. Wit: Wm. HERVETT, Enoch REYNOLDS.

3F:452   Date: 23 May 1823   RtCt: 30 May 1823

Henry CLAGETT & wife Julia of Ldn to Richard Henry LEE of Ldn. B/S of Lot #17 at Market and Back St in Lsbg. Wit: Presley CORDELL, Saml. M. EDWARDS.

3F:453   Date: 28 May 1822   RtCt: 30 May 1823

Henry CLAGETT & wife Julia of Ldn to Richard Henry LEE of Ldn. B/S of 3¼a adj __ SHREVE, __ CLAGETT. Wit: Presley CORDELL, Saml. M. EDWARDS.

3F:454   Date: 20 May 1823   RtCt: 30 May 1823

John SHAW of Lsbg to Benjamin W. PERRY of Lsbg. LS of lot on Back St in Lsbg.

3F:455   Date: 25 Oct 1822   RtCt: 30 May 1823

Mahlon NICHOLLS Jr. & wife Sarah of Ldn to Samuel LODGE of Ldn. B/S of 25a (part of prch/o William LODGE) adj Edward CUNARD Jr. dec'd, Samuel LODGE. Wit: C. C. OSBURN Jr., John NICHOLLS, Henson ELLIOTT, Craven OSBURN, John WHITE. Delv. to LODGE 10 Feb 1825.

3F:456   Date: 31 May 1823   RtCt: 2 Jun 1823

William PARMER of Harrison Co Ohio to Daniel KIMBLER of Ldn. B/S of 26a (part from father Phillip PARMER dec'd with trust to Benjamin JAMES) adj Benjamin JAMES, 6a he sold to Catharine PARMER.

3F:457   Date: 31 May 1823   RtCt: 2 Jun 1823
William PARMER of Harrison Co Ohio to Catharine PARMER of
Ldn. B/S of 6a as above.

3F:458   Date: 2 Jun 1823   RtCt: 2 Jun 1823
Newman SETTLE & wife Elizabeth of Ldn to James LEWIS and
Johnson CLEVELAND of Ldn. Trust for debt to Charles LEWIS
using 240a where SETTLE now lives (dev. by father Reuben
SETTLE dec'd). Wit: Richard H. HENDERSON, Horace LUCKETT,
Thomas A. MOORE. Delv. to LEWIS 27 Nov 1823.

3F:459   Date: 8 Mar 1823   RtCt: 2 Jun 1823
Henry RUSSELL & wife Matilda of Ldn to Ezekiel CHAMBLIN of
Ldn. B/S of 116a between Blue ridge and short hill adj E. GRUBB,
Adam GRUBB, __ LESLIE. Wit: Ebenezer GRUBB, John WHITE.
Delv. to Nelson CHAMBLIN one of the heirs 15 Aug 1832.

3F:460   Date: 29 Jan 1821   RtCt: 4 Jun 1823
Usher SKINNER & wife Rebecca of Ldn to William HANN of Ldn.
B/S of 22a (prch/o Daniel BROWN) adj Thomas KENT, __
BALDWIN, __ BURSON. Wit: Wm. BRONAUGH, Ben. GRAYSON.

3F:461   Date: 20 May 1823   RtCt: 4 Jun 1823
William H. HANDY of Ldn to Townsend McVEIGH of Ldn. B/S of 11a
on S side of Goose Creek adj Edward WILSON. Delv. to McVEIGH
11 May 1824.

3F:463   Date: 9 Jun 1823   RtCt: 9 Jun 1823
William CLENDENING, Robert RUSSELL and Edward DOWLING.
Bond on CLENDENING as constable.

3F:463   Date: 21 May 1823   RtCt: 7 Jun 1823
John MANN & wife Mary of Ldn to Hervey COGSILL of Ldn. B/S of
1a (cnvy/b Geo. MANN Sr). Wit: R. BRADEN, S. HOUGH Jr. Delv.
pr order 12 Feb 1828.

3F:464   Date: 5 May 1823   RtCt: 9 Jun 1823
Thomas JANNEY & wife Sarah E. of AlexDC to Robert J. TAYLOR
of AlexDC. Trust for debt to Bank of Potomac using und. share of
mill and 80a (LS from William HERBERT Jr. and from Jonathan
SCHOLFIELD to James and Alexander DUER) on Goose Creek
below lime kiln. Wit: Chirs.? NEALE. Delv. to TAYLOR 1 Apr 1824.

3F:467   Date: 16 Nov 1823   RtCt: 9 Jun 1823
Nancy MERSHON, Richard HUTCHISON & wife Elizabeth, William
R. COLLINS & wife Margaret, Elizabeth HUTCHISON and John
HUTCHISON of Ldn and James HUTCHISON & wife Nancy and Eli
HUTCHISON of Ffx and Enoch HUTCHISON & wife Abigail of
Gurnsey Co Ohio to Charles B. O'BANNION of Fqr. B/S of 185a in
Ldn and Ffx on little river turnpike road. Wit: Charles LEWIS, John
BAYLEY.

3F:469   Date: 9 Jun 1823   RtCt: 9 Jun 1823
William ROSE, Johnson CLEVELAND and Richard H.
HENDERSON. Bond on ROSE as constable.

3F:470   Date: 13 Jun 1823   RtCt: 13 Jun 1823
Benjamin MAULSBY (insolvent debtor) to Shff John ROSE. B/S of
house and lot in Lsbg (cnvy/b William KIRK).

3F:470   Date: 21 May 1823   RtCt: 13 Jun 1823
Jacob SUMMERS. Oath as Capt of Militia.

3F:470   Date: 21 May 1823   RtCt: 13 Jun 1823
Dean JAMES. Oath as Lt. of Militia.

3F:470   Date: 9 Jul 1807   RtCt: 13 Mar 1811/9 Jun 1823
Mary BAILEY wd/o Tarpley BAILY dec'd late of Berkley Co Va and
Lewis BAILY only child of Tarpley to George RUST of Ldn. B/S of 2
tracts of land as directed by Berkley Co Ct. Wit: Geo. POTTER, Jas.
SANDERS, John POTTER.

3F:471   Date: 23 Nov 1822   RtCt: 9 Jun 1823
Hanson DUTTON & wife Elizabeth of Ldn to Charles LEWIS of Ldn.
B/S of und. landed estate and widow's dower of Jacob JAMES
dec'd. Wit: Wm. B. HARRISON, Johnston CLEVELAND. Delv. to
Jas. CAYLOR pr order of LEWIS 25 Oct 1832.

3F:472   Date: 7 Jun 1823   RtCt: 9 Jun 1823
William LYNE of Ldn to Samuel HALLEY of Ldn. Trust for debt to
Charles LEWIS using negro slave David.

3F:473   Date: 17 Sep 1822   RtCt: 10 Jun 1823
Burr POWELL (trustee of David GIBSON Sept 1804) of Ldn to Hugh
SMITH of Ldn. B/S of 202¾a (prch/o James HIXSON) on Little River
less 1a as condemned for use of James HIXSON. Delv. to SMITH 2
Aug 1836.

3F:474   Date: 22 May 1823   RtCt: 10 Jun 1823
Frederick HANDSHEY & wife Catharine and David NEAR of Ldn to
Hiram CARNEY of Ldn. B/S of 10a on W side of short hill mt nr
Potomac and 2a Wit: Ebenezer GRUBB, John WHITE. Delv. to
CARNEY 10 Apr 1826.

3F:476   Date: 11 Jun 1823   RtCt: 11 Jun 1823
Aquilla MEAD & wife Lavinia of Ldn to Thomas ROGERS of Ldn.
Trust for debt to William HOLMES of Ldn using 7a where MEAD
resides and Blackstone JANNEY. Wit: T. P. KNOX, E. G.
HAMILTON, Alfred A. ESKRIDGE, John McCORMICK, John H.
McCABE. Delv. to ROGERS 29 Apr 1824.

3F:477   Date: 25 Feb 1823   RtCt: 11 Jun 1823
James JONES, Jeremiah JONES & wife Mary of Ohio to William
PAXSON of Ldn. Bond to confirm sale – JONESes sold PAXSON
und. right (each 1/10th) to grist mill and lot and 5a on Blue Ridge per
agreement in hands of Jonathan MATHEWS. Wit: Saml.
LAFFERTY, Joseph KINNAN.

3F:478 Date: 12 Jun 1823 RtCt: 12 Jun 1823
William ALT & wife Susannah of Ldn to David EVELAND of Ldn. B/S
of 5¼a adj __ EDWARDS. Wit: Presley CORDELL, Samuel M.
EDWARDS. Delv. to EVELAND 3 Mar 1826.

3F:480 Date: 4 Jan 1823 RtCt: 12 Jun 1823
William ALT & wife Susannah of Ldn to John ALT of Ldn. B/S of
29¼a (Lot #1 ¼ share of land from father William ALT dec'd) adj __
STONEBURNER. Wit: Saml. M. EDWARDS, L. BEARD, Charles W.
BINNS, A. R. St. CLAIR, E. G. HAMILTON, Presley CORDELL.
Delv. to Jno. ALT 17 Apr 1824.

3F:481 Date: 12 Jun 1823 RtCt: 12 Jun 1823
Elizabeth JONES and Phillippa JONES of Ldn to William D. DRISH
of Ldn. BoS on 21 Jan 1822 for negro slave for life Kate with her son
James [also states her said two children]. Phillippa now of age and
can consent.

3F:482 Date: 11 Jun 1823 RtCt: 12 Jun 1823
Phillippa E. W. JONES of Ldn to mother Elizabeth JONES. Trust for
Elizabeth JONES (for any debts on her account) using 17a
(encumbered with dower of Elizabeth from husband John JONES
dec'd, f/o Phillippa) adj William CARR, and slaves for life Richard,
Peg and her children Mary, Edward, Margaret, Abbey and Jim,
Mime and her children Violett, Barbara, Mary and Kate, Winny and
her children Leanna and Rose, Philles and her child William and
Sinah, Peter and Reuben. Wit: S. BLINCOE, John H. McCABE,
Mark WOOD.

3F:483 Date: 26 Sep 1822 RtCt: 26 Sep 1823
Jno. A. BINNS and James GARNER – Agreement – BINNS sells to
GARNER lot adj Lsbg he prch/o John MINES; GARNER now
transfers to Chs. P. TUTTS with note given to BINNS. BINNS get to
take crop and give GARNER ½ and GARNER possession of land in
one year. Wit: B. HOUGH, Alfred A. ESKRIDGE, E. G. HAMILTON.
Delv. to GARNER 23 Oct 1823.

3F:483 Date: 25 Mar 1823 RtCt: 13 Jun 1823
Benjamin C. CRUPPER & wife Penelope of Ldn to James MILLER
of Ldn. B/S of 1/3 int. in land on turnpike road below Mdbg of
Richard CRUPPER Sr. grandfather of Benjamin who is one of three
children of Richard CRUPPER Jr. dec'd who was son of Richard
CRUPPER the elder dec'd. Wit: Benjamin GRAYSON, John W.
GRAYSON.

3F:484 Date: 11 Nov 1822 RtCt: 14 Jul 1823
Henry SHOVER of Union Co Ohio to son Frederick SHOVER of
Union Co Ohio. PoA to receive from Christian SANDBOWER and
Simon SHOVER Admrs of Adam SHOVER dec'd (Henry is oldest
legatee) of Ldn. Wit: William PRICE, Jeptha PEASLEE. Delv. to
Frederick SHOVER 9 Apr 1824

3F:486   Date: 16 Jun 1823   RtCt: 16 Jun 1823
Edmund LOVETT of Ldn to Daniel JANNEY. Trust for debt to Jesse HOGE using 1/3 of crop growing in field rented to Isaac POTTS. Wit: William M. McCARTY.

3F:487   Date: __ 1822   RtCt: 16 Jun 1823
George JANNEY of MontMd to David SMITH of Ldn. B/S of 2a on NW fork of Goose Creek adj SMITH, Benjamin BRADFIELD. Delv. to SMITH 24 Nov 1824

3F:488   Date: 25 Jan 1823   RtCt: 16 Jun 1823
John LLOYD & wife Anne Harriet of AlexDC to George JANNEY of Ldn and Elisha JANNEY of Ffx. B/S of smaller tracts with mill totaling 63a in Millville and 124a adj. Wit: Chs. J. CATLETT and Chr. NEALE. Delv. to Abel JANNEY pr order 20 Apr 1825.

3F:489   Date: 3 May 1823   RtCt: 14 Jun 1823
Peyton HOUGH of Ldn to Joseph BOND of Ldn. B/S of ½ of 5a lot and tanyard in Wtfd (dev. to Peyton and his brother Washington by their grandfather William HOUGH dec'd) adj Amasa HOUGH, John BALL Jr., Robt BRADEN, William PAXSON, Mary HIXSON dec'd.

3F:490   Date: 20 Jun 1823   RtCt: 23 Jun 1823
Sythe ATWELL of Mdbg to Humphrey B. POWELL of Mdbg. Trust to secure John BOYD in possession of young negro woman slave for life Fanny sold to BOYD this day using lot in Mdbg (cnvy/b John BOYD).

3F:491   Date: 20 Jun 1823   RtCt: 23 Jun 1823
John BOYD & wife Elizabeth of Mdbg to Sythe ATWELL of Ldn. B/S of part of Lot #54 in Mdbg at Jay and Marshall St. Wit: Burr POWELL, Abner GIBSON. Delv. to E. S. SHORT pr order 14 Nov 1853

3F:493   Date: 21 Jun 1823   RtCt: 21 Jun 1823
James WINTERS (insolvent debtor) of Ldn to Shff John ROSE. B/S of lot and tenement on S side of Loudoun St in Lsbg adj Thomas HEIR (execution in suit of William D. DRISH) Wit: Samuel M. EDWARDS, Presley CORDELL.

3F:493   Date: 6 May 1823   RtCt: 19 Jun 1823
Thomas H. WEY & wife Annah of Ldn to Samuel TRAHERN of Ldn. B/S of lot adj Union (cnvy/b Elizabeth BOWLIN Jan 1823) adj BOWLIN. Wit: A. GIBSON, Leven LUCKETT.

3F:494   Date: 25 Jun 1823   RtCt: 25 Jun 1823
David BEALE of Ldn to Amos BEALE of Ldn. B/S of 105a adj 'Diggs Valley'. Delv. to Amos BEALE 24 Apr 1824.

3F:495   Date: 5 Apr 1821   RtCt: 27 Jun 1823
William NOLAND & wife Catharine of Ldn to Samuel TODD of Ldn. B/S of 1a Lot #35, #36, #37 & #38 in Aldie. Wit: Francis C. NOLAND, Francis THOMPSON, Thomas NOLAND, Lewis M. SMITH, Durr POWELL, A. GIBSON.

3F:497   Date: 16 Jun 1823   RtCt: 27 June 1823
Mathew ADAMS & wife Susan L. of Ldn to Humphrey B. POWELL
of Ldn. Trust for debt to Samuel HATCHER using und. half of 253a
(where he now resides, from father James MERCER dec'd). Wit:
Burr POWELL, A. GIBSON. Delv. to Thos. ROGERS Admr of
HATCHER 23 Jan 1827.

3F:498   Date: 27 Jun 1823   RtCt: 27 Jun 1823
Samuel HAMMETT of Ldn to Giles HAMMETT. Samuel prch/o Dpty
Shff Benjamin SHREVE personal property of brother Giles; loaning
Giles household items. Wit: Richard H. HENDERSON.

3F:498   Date: 5 Jun 1823   RtCt: 30 Jun 1823
John S. EDWARDS of Ldn to John KLINE of Ldn. Mortgage of int. in
unexpired LS of lot on Back St. in Lsbg (leased from John SHAW)
and household items. Wit: Daniel DULANY.

3F:499   Date: 4 Jun 1823   RtCt: 30 Jun 1823
John N. T. G. E. KEENE gentleman & wife Harriet of Mdbg to H. B.
POWELL of Ldn. Trust for John BOYD as security for KEENE as
constable using int. in lot in Union (cnvy/b carpenter John
JOHNSON Jun 1822). Wit: Francis W. LUCKETT, A. GIBSON.

3F:501   Date: ___   RtCt: 7 Dec 1820/12 May 1823
John T. MASON and Mary MASON devisees of Stephen Thompson
MASON dec'd. to James HIXSON and Thomas WEEKS. B/S of
907a adj __ HEREFORD, __ POWELL. (from suit in Sup Ct
Winchester). Wit: Wm. T. T. MASON, George WASHINGTON,
Richard B. MASON, Thomson MASON, George M. CHICHESTER,
John HOUGH.

3F:503   Date: 8 Nov 1822   RtCt: 12 Jul 1823
William G. McKINNY & wife Nancy of Harrison Co Va to David
GALLEHER of Ldn. B/S of int. in land of grandfather William
GALLAHER dec'd and ½ of lot in Union cnvy/b Wm. GALLAHER
dec'd to William and his brother George Wm. McKINNY.

3F:504   Date: 16 Jun 1823   RtCt: 14 Jul 1823
Joshua LLOYD & wife Mary of Belmont Co Ohio to Conrad BITZER
of Ldn. B/S of 143a where Thomas TRIBBY now lives adj BITZER,
Jonah SANDS, William NICHOLS, Mahlon WATERS (from Mary
LLOYD w/o Joshua a legatee of Eli NICHOLS dec'd late of Belmont
Co Ohio). Wit: Israel BROWN, James GILL.

3F:506   Date: 5 Apr 1823   RtCt: 14 Jul 1823
Hamilton ROGERS. Oath as Capt. in 56 Reg 6th Brigade 2nd Div. of
Va Militia.

3F:506   Date: 14 Jul 1823   RtCt: 14 Jul 1823
John ROSE, Benjamin SHREVE, Towns'd McVEIGH, Hugh SMITH,
William THRIFT and Robert MOFFETT. Bond on ROSE as Sheriff to
collect levies.

3G:001   Date: 22 Jul 1823   RtCt: 24 Jul 1823
Abner GIBSON (commr. in ct decree for heirs of Thomas WEEKS)
to James HIXSON of Ldn. B/S of land purchased by HIXSON and
WEEKS from reps of Stephens Thompson MASON dec'd cnvy/b
Widow Mary MASON and John Thompson MASON br/o Stephens.

3G:002   Date: 3 Mar 1823   RtCt: 23 Jul 1823
John SHAW and Isaac KENT & wife Hetty. Agreement – SHAW
leased to KENT wooden house and lot lately prch/o Edw'd
HAMMATT on S side of Lsbg for their lifetime if they make the rent
payment. Delv. to KENT Jr. 21 Nov 1825.

3G:003   Date: 26 May 1823   RtCt: 9 Jun 1823
John W. JACKSON to Samuel KALB. Trust for debt to John CULP
using household items. Delv. to CULP 7 Feb 1825.

3G:004   Date: 7 Jun 1823   RtCt: 9 Jun 1823
William LYNE of Ldn to Charles LEWIS of Ldn. Trust for debt to
KERR & FITZHUGH using 1a occupied by Saml. & John H.
HALLEY. Delv. to Lewis 11 Jul 1825.

3G:006   Date: 27 Nov 1816   RtCt: 11 Aug 1823
Joshua OSBURN and John WHITE of Ldn to Eli PEIRPOINT and
David SMITH (Exors of Thomas LOVE dec'd) and his heirs. Release
of trust for debt to Solomon DAVIS of MontMd.

3G:007   Date: 18 Mar 1818   RtCt: 11 Aug 1823
Lewis SHECKLES of Ldn to Benjamin JACKSON of Ldn. Trust for
debt to John MARKS using household items. Wit: John RALPH,
Thomas EWERS.

3G:008   Date: 8 Jan 1821   RtCt: 12 Jan 1822
Bazil NEWMAN of Ldn to John J. MATHIAS of Ldn. Trust for debt to
William AULT using 57a above Goose Creek.

3G:009   Date: 1 Jul 1820   RtCt: 11 Mar 1822
George TAVENDER Jr. & wife Sarah and Jonah & Nancy
TAVENDER ch/o Patty TAVENDER dec'd of Ldn to Thomas
BISCOE. B/S of 19a Lot #4 allotted to Joseph WHITE & wife on
Goose Creek (part of estate of George NIXON the elder dec'd not
devised in will) and adj Lot #6 allotted to heirs of George
TAVENDER and Patty TAVENDER and Lot #7 allotted to George
TAVENDER by prch/o John NIXON totaling 26a. Wit: R. BRADEN,
Abiel JENNERS.

3G:011   Date: 20 Jun 1823   RtCt: 20 Jun 1823
Peter ISH of Ldn to Joseph MEAD of Ldn. Trust for debt to Benjamin
SHREVE using household items. Delv. to SHREVE Jr. 21 Jun 1824.

3G:012   Date: 6 Mar 1823   RtCt: 12 Jun 1823
Walter LANGLEY & wife Susannah of Ldn to William BRADFIELD of
Ldn. B/S of 10a adj R. MARSHALL. Wit: Craven OSBURN, John
WHITE. Delv. to BRADFIELD 27 Dec 1826.

3G:014   Date: 14 Mar 1823   RtCt: 14 Jul 1823
William NOLAND of Ldn to Walter LANGLEY of Ldn. Release of trust for debt to George POTTER. Wit: Danl. P. CONARD, Lewis M. SMITH, Wm. B. CORDELL.

3G:014   Date: 18 Dec 1822   RtCt: 14 Jul 1823
Jacob LUKE & wife Sarah of FredVa to William BRADFIELD of Ldn. B/S of 75 pole lot in Pumpkin Town [Snicker's Gap] on turnpike road from Snickers Gap adj Jno. HOUGHFMAN, Amos CLAYTON, Patsey CLAYTON. Delv. to BRADFIELD 27 Dec 1826.

3G:016   Date: 8 Mar 1823   RtCt: 14 Jul 1823
Alfred H. POWELL & wife Nancy of Winchester, FredVa to Uriel GLASSCOCK of Ldn. B/S of 403a adj heirs of Leven POWELL Jr. dec'd, __ BRONAUGH. Delv. to GLASSCOCK 27 Jan 1827.

3G:018   Date: 15 Apr 1823   RtCt: 14 Jul 1823
Uriel GLASSCOCK & wife Nancy of Ldn to Burr POWELL. Trust for debt to Alfred H. POWELL using 403a as above. Wit: Wm. BRONAUGH, Francis W. LUCKETT.

3G:021   Date: 3 May 1823   RtCt: 21 Jul 1823
Samuel N. GALLEHER & wife Phebe of Ldn to Joseph A. LLOYD of Ldn. B/S of 10a (from div. of William GALLEHER dec'd). Wit: Leven LUCKETT, A. GIBSON. Delv. to Michael PLAISTER pr order DBk KKK:80.

3G:023   Date: 20 Feb 1821   RtCt: 24 Jul 1821/11 Aug 1823
Mahlon JANNEY of Ldn to Philip FRY of Ldn. Mortgage on 18a (prch/o Anthony CUNARD) adj Westwood T. MASON. Wit: Amos JANNEY, Daniel FRY.

3G:024   Date: 26 Jul 1823   RtCt: 26 Jul 1823
Stephenson HIXSON of Ldn to Richard H. HENDERSON. Trust for debt to A. H. CLARKE, Samuel M. BOSS & Patterson WRIGHT using land where HIXSON now lives. Wit: Saml. HAMMETT, Noah HIXSON, Thomas A. MOORE.

3G:025   Date: 14 Jul 1823   RtCt: 11 Aug 1823
William HENDERSON potter & wife Mary (d/o Daniel LOSCH dec'd) of PhilPa to son David HENDERSON. PoA for matters in DC, Md and Va. Wit: M. RAWN. Wil. M. KENNEDY.

3G:026   Date: 30 Jul 1823   RtCt: 30 Jul 1823
Jacob FADELY & wife Mary and William JACOBS & wife Catharine/Kitty of Ldn to Bernard GILPIN of MontMd. B/S of lot and house (cnvy/b John SHAW to dau Catharine now JACOBS Apr 1819, she now being 21y old) in Lsbg on W side of King St. adj Joseph BEARD, Thos. SANDERS, __ TAYLOR. Wit: John H. McCABE, Thomas SANDERS.

3G:028   Date: 26 Jul 1823   RtCt: 30 Jul 1823
George RUST Jr. & wife Maria C. of Ldn to William M. McCARTY of Ldn. B/S of 36a on E side of Caroline Road adj __ MURRAY. Wit: Thomas SAUNDERS, John H. McCABE.

3G:029   Date: 30 Jul 1823   RtCt: 30 Jul 1823
Bernard GILPIN & wife Latecia of MontMd to Samuel M. EDWARDS of Ldn. Trust for debt to Jacob FADLEY using land cnvy/b FADLEY. Wit: John H. McCABE, Thomas SANDERS.

3G:032   Date: 29 Jul 1823   RtCt: 20 Jul 1823
Charles P. TUTT of Ldn to William T. T. MASON and George M. CHICHESTER of Ldn. Trust for William T. T. MASON and George M. CHICHESTER as endorsers on bank notes using share of land prch/o Isaac LAROWE and 21a prch/o Stephen BALL and lot in Lsbg and slaves Dennis, Phil, Dick, Milly, Hannah, Lydia and James and slaves Jack, Martha, James, Eleanor, Maria, Willis, Margaret, Thomas, Eliza, John and Patty left in New Orleans to be sold by Archibald R. TAYLOR and horses, crops, farm and household items. Delv. to CHICHESTER 16 May 1827.

3G:035   Date: 12 May 1823   RtCt: 31 Jul 1823
Samuel McPHERSON & wife Mary of Ldn to Samuel M. EDWARDS of Ldn. Trust for debt to Lewis P. W. BALCH using saw mill and land late property of John SHAFER. Wit: Robert BRADEN, Saml. HOUGH Jr. Delv. to BALCH 21 Jan 1826.

3G:037   Date: 30 Jul 1823   RtCt: 2 Aug 1823
John PANCOAST Jr of Ldn to John H. BUTCHER. Release of trust of Jun 1818 for John PANCOAST Sr.

3G:037   Date: 13 Jun 1823   RtCt: 1 Aug 1823
Elizabeth POTTERFIELD of Ldn to Simon SHOEMAKER of Ldn. B/S of 15a (laid off as widow's dower from Jacob EMERY dec'd) where Elizabeth now lives. Delv. to SHOEMAKER 10 Apr 1822.

3G:038   Date: 30 Jul 1823   RtCt: 2 Aug 1823
John H. BUTCHER of Ldn to William WILSON of Ldn. Trust for debt to Joshua PANCOAST using 108a. Wit: A. G. WATERMAN, A. A. ESKRIDGE, Levi C. CORDELL. Delv. to PANCOAST 15 Sep 1824

3G:040   Date: 5 Jun 1823   RtCt: 4 Aug 1823
John N. T. G. E. KEENE of Ldn to Benjamin MITCHELL Jr. of Ldn. Trust for debt to Thornton WALKER household items.

3G:041   Date: 28 Jul 1823   RtCt: 4 Aug 1823
John M. HART & wife Deborah of Randolph Co Va to Hiram SEATON of Ldn. B/S of 41½a (Lot #6 devised of farm formerly owned by John VIOLETT dec'd) on Pantherskin below Clifton Mills. Delv. to SEATON 28 Jan 1825.

3G:042 Date: 8 Aug 1823 RtCt: 8 Aug 1823
Samuel CARR & wife Lucy of Lsbg to William GILMORE of Ldn. B/S of 10a (prch/o Stephen COOKE) adj GILMORE. Wit: Presley CORDELL, Thomas SANDERS.

3G:044 Date: 31 Mar 1821 RtCt: 11 Feb 1822/9 Aug 1823
Hannah WILSON wd/o Ebenezer WILSON dec'd of Ldn to Amos HARVEY of Ldn. B/S of __a adj where John CASE lives, Thomas HOUGH, Thomas LESLIE. Wit: William THOMPSON, Isaac TALLEY, Jesse EVANS. Delv. to HARVEY 28 Feb 1827.

3G:045 Date: 21 Feb 1821 RtCt: 11 Aug 1823
Charles SHEPHERD dec'd. Division of slaves by court order of 12 Feb 1821 – negro man Jim abt 30y old and girl Milley abt 11y old to Chas. SHEPHERD Admr of Jas. SHEPHERD dec'd; man Admiral abt 46y old, woman Jinney abt 53y old & not healthy and girl Patsey abt 12y old to Chas. SHEPHERD in his own right; woman Minta abt 30y old, boy Lewis abt 10y old, boy Jim abt 2y old to Leven SHEPHERD; man Dick abt 47y old, girl Maria abt 7y old, boy Charles abt 4y old to John SHEPHERD. Divisors: Saml. M. EDWARDS, John CARR, Arch'd MAINS.

3G:046 Date: 14 Aug 1823 RtCt: 14 Aug 1823
Christian SANDBOWER, Adam SANDBOWER, Michael SANDBOWER and Philip EVERHEART of Ldn to Presley CORDELL, Samuel M. EDWARDS, Abner GIBSON & James H. HAMILTON justices of Ldn. Bond on Christian and Adam as Admrs of John SANDBOWER dec'd in bond to Samuel MURREY, Stephen C. ROSZELL, Isaac HOUGH and Abiel JENNERS. Wit: L. P. W. BALCH.

3G:047 Date: 14 Aug 1823 RtCt: 14 Aug 1823
Fielding BROWN (insolvent debtor) of Ldn to Shff John ROSE. B/S of int. in ¼ section of land in Scioto Co Oh on waters of Little Scioto (prch/o Saml. HAMMET) and int. in lot & blacksmith shop in Lsbg leased from John SHAW.

3G:048 Date: 3 Apr 1823 RtCt: 14 Aug 1823
Leonard THOMAS dec'd. Division – Lot #1 (3a) to widow, Lot #2 (1a) to Elizabeth THOMAS, Lot #3 (1a) to Martha THOMAS, Lot #4 (1a) to Anne THOMAS, Lot #5 (1a) to Sarah THOMAS now FEICHTER, Lot #6 (1a) to Abby THOMAS now ANDERSON. Gives plat. Divisors: Daniel LOVETT, Thomas CARR.

3G:049 Date: 15 Aug 1823 RtCt: 15 Aug 1823
James D. FRENCH, Daniel STONE, Garrison B. FRENCH & Wm. CHILTON. Bond on James D. FRENCH as constable.

3G:049 Date: 23 Dec 1822 RtCt: 2 Jan/26 Jul 1823
Job JENKINS of Ldn to L. P. W. BALCH of Ldn. Trust for debt to Theodore JENKINS of FredMd using und. int. in estate of father Job JENKINS Sr. dec'd derived from will of William JENKINS dec'd). Wit:

Geo. MARLOW, William COLE, Hanson MARLOW, E. G.
HAMILTON, A. R. St. CLAIR, Julius HAMILTON. Delv. to BALCH 12
Sep 1823.

3G:051   Date: 20 Jan 1823   RtCt: 11 Aug 1823
Samuel QUEEN & wife Mary of Columbiana Co Ohio to John
HESSER & David HESSER of Ldn. B/S of Mary's und. int. from
father Andrew HESSER dec'd.

3G:052   Date: 2 Aug 1823   RtCt: 11 Aug 1823
Philip JONES of Ldn to Hugh SMITH of Ldn. B/S of 31a allotted from
father William JONES dec'd (except what was sold to Sampson
BLINCOE) and int. in mother's widow's dower. Delv. to SMITH 2
Aug 1836.

3G:053   Date: 4 Jun 1823   RtCt: 11 Aug 1823
Jonah NICKOLS of Ldn to Nathaniel NICKOLS of Ldn. B/S of 11a
(Lot #5 in div. of George NICKOLS dec'd) on Blue Ridge adj
Thomas NICKOLS, Tamar TRACEY. Delv. to Nath'l NICKOLS 13
Aug 1829.

3G:054   Date: 10 May 1823   RtCt: 11 Aug 1823
Samuel BEANS & wife Pleasant of Ldn to Mahlon TAYLOR of Ldn.
Trust for debt to Samuel HUGHES using land on Kittocton Creek
cnvy/b HUGHES. Wit: Stacey TAYLOR, Thomas MORRIS, Isaiah B.
BEANS, Craven OSBURN, John WHITE.

3G:057   Date: 31 Jul 1823   RtCt: 12 Aug 1823
Matthew RUST & wife Patsey of Ldn to H. B. POWELL of Ldn. Trust
for debt to Hugh SMITH using 475a two miles from Aldie on Little
River where he now lives, adj Sarah JONES, Amos FERGUSON,
Owen SULLIVAN. Wit: Sydnor B. RUST, Jas. T. RUST, Elizabeth B.
RUST, Burr POWELL, A. GIBSON. Delv. to SMITH 13 Aug 1824.

3G:058   Date: 15 Feb 1823   RtCt: 12 Aug 1823
Betsey TEBBS of PrWm to William RUST of Ldn. B/S of her life
estate in 336a and 313a in Fqr and Ldn of Wm. CARR Sr. dec'd
(son Foushee TEBBS wants to sell his und. share to RUST). Delv.
to RUST 28 Nov 1823.

3G:059   Date: 12 Aug 1823   RtCt: 12 Aug 1823
Edwin C. BROWN. DoE for slaves Venus abt 34y old & her child
Stephen Wesley abt 18m old.

3G:060   Date: 22 May 1823   RtCt: 12 Aug 1823
Frederick HANDSHY & wife Catharine of Ldn to Philip GROVE of
Ldn. B/S of 15a adj Hiram CARNEY, summit of short hill mt. Wit:
Ebenezer GRUBB, John WHITE. Delv. to GROVE 28 Aug 1824.

3G:061   Date: 8 Apr 1823   RtCt: 12 Aug 1823
James RUST & wife Sally of Ldn to Sarah R. POWELL of Ldn. B/S
of 35a (part of dower assigned Sarah out of Thomas W. POWELL's
part nr Blue Ridge beq. to Thomas and Burr POWELL by L.
POWELL doc'd) adj road from John RICHARDS to Gibson's mill.

Wit: Thos. SANDERS, Saml. M. EDWARDS. Delv. to Cuth. POWELL 25 Mar 1825.

3G:063   Date: 18 Jul 1822   RtCt: 12 Aug 1823
James RUST & wife Sally of Ldn to Charles CHAMBLING of Ldn. B/S of 40a on Goose Creek (from 96a RUST and CHAMBLING prch/o T. & J. EDMONDSON). Wit: Thos. SANDERS, Saml. M. EDWARDS.

3G:064   Date: 10 Jun 1823   RtCt: 12 Aug 1823
John CARPENTER of Ldn to Benjamin GRAYSON Jr. Trust for debt to George KEEN & John HATCHER (Admrs. of Phineas THOMAS dec'd) using 70a in Manor of Leeds adj William CARPENTER Jr., Minor FURR, Elijah COCHRAN.

3G:066   Date: 11 Mar 1823   RtCt: 12 Aug 1823
George BEATTY of Ldn to George TURNER of Ldn. Trust for debt to Osburn BEATTY of Culpeper Co Va using negro woman Ann & her 2 children Clarissa and Daniel. Wit: Asa ROGERS.

3G:067   Date: 20 Jun 1823   RtCt: 12 Aug 1823
James RUST & wife Sally of Ldn to George RUST Jr of Ldn. B/S of 36a on Carolina Road nr Lsbg adj __ MURRAY, __ SELDON, __ HOUGH. Wit: Thos. SANDERS, Saml. M. EDWARDS.

3G:069   Date: 24 Jul 1823   RtCt: 12 Aug 1823
John BRADY & wife Sarah of Ldn to Townshend McVEIGH of Ldn. Trust for debt to Elizabeth BOYD of Ldn using Lot #17 & #23 in Mdbg (prch/o BOYD, where she lately resided), adj Jno. UPP, Nelson GREEN, Jno. BRADY. Wit: Burr POWELL, Abner GIBSON. Delv. to Jesse McVEIGH 11 Apr 1832.

3G:071   Date: 12 Aug 1823   RtCt: 12 Aug 1823
Thomas H. STEPHENS of Ldn to L. P. W. BALCH of Lsbg. Trust for debt to John GEORGE using 1a with 2-story log house (prch/o David LOVETT). Wit: E. G. HAMILTON, Benj. SHREVE, B. SHREVE Jr. Delv. to BALCH 29 Jan 1825.

3G:072   Date: 8 Apr 1823   RtCt: 12 Aug 1823
John DAY & wife Catharine of Green Co Pa to John BOOTH Jr. of Ldn. B/S of 5a (Lot #4 and int. in dower of Fanny BOOTH wd/o of James BOOTH dec'd). Wit: Joab BAILY, Corbly GARARD.

3G:074   Date: 13 Feb 1823   RtCt: 12 Aug 1823
Foushee TEBBS & wife Margaret of PrWm to William RUST of Ldn. B/S of 336a in Fqr (from div. of William CARR Sr. dec'd) and 313a in Ldn from div. Delv. to RUST 28 Nov 1823.

3G:075   Date: 8 Apr 1823   RtCt: 12 Aug 1823
Sarah R. POWELL of Ldn to James RUST of Ldn. B/S of int. in 35a from Thomas W. POWELL's portion bequeathed him by grandfather Leven POWELL and sold to James RUST.

3G:076 Date: 9 Aug 1823 RtCt: 13 Aug 1823
Peter TOWPERMAN & wife Elizabeth of Ldn to William COAD of Ldn. B/S of 1a where COAD now lives adj __ BITZER, __ BALDWIN, road from Handy's Mill to Mdbg. Wit: Burr POWELL, A. GIBSON. Delv. to COAD 21 Sep 1829.

3G:078 Date: 13 Aug 1823 RtCt: 13 Aug 1823
Samuel TUSTIN of Ldn to Saml. M. EDWARDS of Ldn. Trust for Thomas BIRKBY and Caleb SUTHERLAND as security on bond to D. Shff Benj. SHREVE in suit of James BROWN ass'ee of Saml. M. BOSS using household items.

3G:079 Date: 12 Aug 1823 RtCt: 13 Aug 1823
Peter FICHTER & wife Susannah of Ldn to Philip NELSON of Ldn. B/S of lot on N side of Loudoun St in Lsbg adj John SURGENOR, Samuel HARPER, James GARNER. Wit: Presley CORDELL, Saml. M. EDWARDS. Delv. to NELSON 6 Dec 1823.

3G:081 Date: 14 Aug 1823 RtCt: 14 Aug 1823
Samuel TUSTIN of Ldn to John DRAIN of Ldn. Mortgage of lot on Liberty St in Lsbg with brick house, blacksmith shop (cnvy/b DRAIN) adj DRAIN, Thos. BIRKBY, heirs of __ TAYLOR, S. BLINCOE.

3G:082 Date: 14 Aug 1823 RtCt: 14 Aug 1823
Charles P. TUTT of Ldn to William Temple T. MASON and George M. CHICHESTER of Ldn. Trust to MASON and CHICHESTER using household items. Wit: R. H. HENDERSON, Simon SHOEMAKER, Thomas A. MOORE. Delv. to CHICHESTER 16 May 1827.

3G:083 Date: 14 Aug 1823 RtCt: 14 Aug 1823
Mandley T. RUST of Ldn to Hugh SMITH. Trust for debt to Noble BEVERIDGE using int. in estate of Mrs. Susanna CHILTON dec'd of Ldn and estate of Thos. CHILTON dec'd of Ldn. Delv. to H. H. HAMILTON pr order 1 Jul 1850.

3G:084 Date: 14 Aug 1823 RtCt: 15 Aug 1823
George FICHTER & wife Sarah to John MOOR. Trust for debt to Saml. CARR using ¾a (prch/o Simon A. BINNS) on turnpike road from Lsbg to Georgetown where FICHTER now lives adj heirs of Silas REESE dec'd. Wit: James NEWTON, Jacob FADLEY, Presley SAUNDERS.

3G:086 Date: 16 Sep 1806 RtCt: 9 Feb 1807/20 Aug 1823
John PURCELL & wife Mary of Ldn to William CRAIG of Ldn. B/S of 13¾a adj James CRAIG, George TAVENER, Jacob BROWN. Wit: William HOLMES, Levi TATE, Nathan BROWN.

3G:087 Date: 22 May 1823 RtCt: 22 Aug 1823
Robert CAMPBELL & wife Jane of Ldn to Robert BENTLEY of Ldn. B/S of 67a in 'Digg's Valley' (prch/o James CAMPBELL Aug 1820). Wit: Presley CORDELL, Saml. M. EDWARDS.

3G:089   Date: 22 Aug 1823   RtCt: 22 Aug 1823
Joseph GORE of Ldn to William VICKERS of Ldn. Release of trust of Apr 1816 for debt to John NEWLON. Wit: E. G. HAMILTON, Alfred A. ESKRIDGE, Henry PEERS.

3G:089   Date: 14 Aug 1823   RtCt: 22 Aug 1823
Ignatius NORRIS of Ldn to Wm. H. McNAB. BoS for stove and pipe. Wit: Wm. CHILTON, John MURRY.

3G:090   Date: 1 Jan 1822   RtCt: 23 Aug 1823
William HANN & wife Mary of Ldn to John J. HARDING (Pres. of Board of Overseers of the Poor of Ldn with overseers Aaron SANDERS, James MOORE, Joseph DANIEL, James COCHRAN, Seth SMITH, David LEWIS, George B. WHITING & John DULIN). B/S of 22a (cnvy/b Usher SKINNER Jan 1821) adj Thos. KENT, __ BALDWIN, __ BURSON. Wit: William BRONAUGH, John W. GRAYSON.

3G:091   Date: 23 Aug 1823   RtCt: 23 Aug 1823
Fanny EDWARDS and Saml. M. EDWARDS & wife Ann of Ldn to Saml. M. BOSS of Ldn. B/S of lot on Liberty St in Lsbg (cnvy/b Saml. MURREY) adj Joshua RILEY, Saml. MURREY. Wit: William CARR, Presley CORDELL. Delv. to BOSS 16 Jan 1824.

3G:093   Date: 3 May 1823   RtCt: 15 Aug 1823
D. Shff Benjamin SHREVE to William CLENDENING and Samuel CLENDENING of Ldn. B/S of 90a (from trust of Joseph PURCEL of Mar 1823). Delv. to Thos. R. CLENDENING pr order 29 Aug 1856.

3G:094   Date: 22 Aug 1823   RtCt: 25 Aug 1823
Thomas LEWIS and Sarah LEWIS (ch/o Nancy LEWIS dec'd) of Ldn to Hiram SEATON of Ldn. B/S of int. in und. 197a where Capt. Peter RUST lives and holds estate during life of Charles LEWIS (f/o Thomas & Sarah). Delv. to SEATON 21 Oct 1840.

3G:095   Date: 19 Feb 1823   RtCt: 25 Aug 1823
William RUST & wife Elizabeth to Lemuel HUTCHISON. B/S of 60a (prch/o Chas. S. CARTER) adj Mr. BUCKNER. Wit: John B. ARMISTEAD, Josiah TIDBALL.

3G:096   Date: 1 Apr 1823   RtCt: 25 Aug 1823
John BIRKIT & wife Mary of Ldn to Thomas HOUGH of Ldn. Trust for debt to John UNDERWOOD of Ldn using house & lot in Hllb cnvy/b UNDERWOOD now occupied by Margaret UNDERWOOD. Wit: Craven OSBURN, John CHAMBLIN, Turner OSBURN. Delv. to UNDERWOOD 4 Mar 1824.

3G:097   Date: 1 Apr 1823   RtCt: 25 Aug 1823
John UNDERWOOD of Ldn to John BIRKIT of Ldn. B/S of ¼a lot on road from Purcel's Mill (bought of John HOUGH in 1816). Wit: Craven OSBURN, John CHAMBLIN, Turner OSBURN. Delv. to BIRKETT 6 Apr 1825.

3G:098   Date: 25 Aug 1823   RtCt: 25 Aug 1823
Samuel TUSTIN (insolvent debtor) of Lsbg to Shff John ROSE. B/S
of int. in his house & lot in Lsbg (debt to Jos. HILLIARD ass'ee for
use of Burr W. HARRISON, subject to trust for Samuel M. EDWARD
& mortgage to John DRAIN).

3G:099   Date: 25 Aug 1823   RtCt: 27 Aug 1823
Wm. J. HANLEY to Caleb C. SUTHERLAND. BoS for household
items. Wit: Robert GARDNER, Wm. SEEDERS.

3G:099   Date: 25 Aug 1823   RtCt: 27 Aug 1823
Thomas JACKSON of Ldn to Anthony CONARD Sr. of Ldn. BoS for
horse and household items.

3G:100   Date: 17 Jul 1823   RtCt: 29 Aug 1823
Isaac FRY & wife Hannah of Ldn to Seth SMITH of Ldn. Trust for
debt to Mahlon SCHOFIELD using 1a nr Union where FRY now
resides (cnvy/b Isaac COWGILL). Wit: Seth SMITH, Willis F.
TRIPLETT, John JOHNSON, Benj. GRAYSON, John W.
GRAYSON. Delv. to SMITH 13 Aug 1824.

3G:102   Date: 7 Aug 1823   RtCt: 30 Aug 1823
Edward RALPH of Ldn to Samuel M. BOSS of Ldn. Trust for debt to
James HAMILTON of Ldn using household items. Wit: Geo. K. FOX,
Saml. G. HAMILTON. Delv. to BOSS 18 Jan 1824.

3G:102   Date: 14 May 1823   RtCt: 30 Aug 1823
L. P. W. BALCH of Ldn to Notley C. WILLIAMS of Ldn. Trust for debt
to Nicholas OSBURNE using 128a (prch/o OSBURNE). Wit: E. G.
HAMILTON, Alfred A. ESKRIDGE, Alfred LUCKETT.

3G:103   Date: 12 Feb 1823   RtCt: 1 Sep 1823
Andrew HESSER of Ldn to Thomas POULTON of Ldn. Trust for
debt to John W. DAVIS using land formerly held by Andrew
HESSER dec'd and cnvy/b John W. DAVIS & wife Elizabeth.

3G:105   Date: 11 Apr 1823   RtCt: 14 Apr/2 Sep 1823
Martin KITZMILLER & wife Elizabeth of Ldn to Isaac NICKOLS Jr.
and James HOGE. Trust for debt to Isaac & Samuel NICKOLS using
2a in Lsbg adj Fortney's smith shop. Wit: Stephen C. ROZELL,
Presley CORDELL. Delv. to Saml. NICHOLS Exors 10 Nov 1825.

3G:107   Date: 29 Apr 1823   RtCt: 11 Jul/2 Sep 1823
Lewis HUTCHISON & wife Keziah and Joshua HUTCHISON of Ffx
to William ROSE of Ldn. B/S of 25a. Wit: Johnston CLEVELAND,
Chas. LEWIS, Sampson HUTCHISON.

3G:108   Date: 29 Apr 1823   RtCt: 11 Jul 1823
Joshua HUTCHISON and William ROSE & wife Mary of Ldn to
Lewis HUTCHISON of Ldn. B/S of 259a adj Thos. W. LEE, Wm.
ROSE. Wit: Johnston CLEVELAND, Chas. LEWIS, Sampson
HUTCHISON.

3G:109   Date: 25 Aug 1823   RtCt: 2 Sep 1823
Hugh MOFFETT of Ldn to Saml. BUCK and Saml. M. EDWARDS of
Ldn. Trust for debt to Susan BELTZ using farm and household
items. Wit: E. G. HAMILTON, Alfred A. ESKRIDGE, Jno. J.
MATHIAS.

3G:111   Date: 29 Apr 1820   RtCt: 11 Jul/2 Sep 1823
Lewis HUTCHISON & wife Keziah, William ROSE & wife Mary of
Ldn and Joshua HUTCHISON of Ffx to Thomas William LEE of Ldn.
B/S of 80a adj William ELLZEY. Wit: Johnston CLEVELAND, Chas.
LEWIS, Sampson HUTCHISON.

3G:112   Date: 1 Sep 1823   RtCt: 2 Sep 1823
Samuel C. B McCLELLAND & wife Matilda of Ldn to Saml. M. BOSS
of Ldn. B/S of und. 1/8th int. of lot with 2 houses on King St. in Lsbg
(of Thos. JACOBS dec'd f/o Matilda) adj Jas. MILES, Chas. BINNS,
Jos. GORE. Wit: Presley CORDELL, Saml. M. EDWARDS. Delv. to
BOSS 16 Jan 1824

3G:113   Date: 26 Aug 1823   RtCt: 3 Sep 1823
John A BINNS (trustee of Isaac WRIGHT) to John H. CANBY (as
trustee of Polley CHANEY). B/S of lot in Lsbg (trust of DBk FFF:319,
late property of Robert PERFECT dec'd) adj Mr. HAWKE.

3G:114   Date: 4 Sep 1823   RtCt: 4 Sep 1823
Samuel STERRIT of Ldn to Otho R. BEATTY of Ldn. Trust for debt
to Presley CORDELL using numerous watches, farm and household
items. Delv. to CORDELL 3 Jan 1826.

3G:116   Date: 4 Sep 1823   RtCt: 4 Sep 1823
James McDONAUGH of Lsbg to Jno. A. BINNS of Lsbg. Trust for
Charles G. ESKRIDGE of Lsbg as security on bonds to Alsey
TAYLOR using farm and household items.

3G:117   Date: 4 Sep 1823   RtCt: 4 Sep 1823
Amos BEALE of Ldn to David BEALE & wife Hannah of Ldn. L/L of
house and garden they now occupy (cnvy/b David in Jun 1823).
Delv. to D. BEALLE 17 Aug 1824.

3G:118   Date: 4 Sep 1823   RtCt: 4 Sep 1823
William HAMMERLY of Ldn to Samuel CARR of Ldn. Trust for debt
to James BROWN using negro slave for life Dick abt 10y old. Wit: E.
G. HAMILTON, A. A. ESKRIDGE.

3G:119   Date: 20 Aug 1823   RtCt: 6 Sep 1823
William DAILEY of Ldn to L. P. W. BALCH of Ldn. Trust for debt to
David MARTIN of Ldn using farm and household items. Wit: E. G.
HAMILTON, Julius HAMILTON, Alfred A. ESKRIDGE.

3G:120   Date: 30 Aug 1823   RtCt: 3 Aug/5 Sep 1823
Manley T. RUST of Ldn to Hugh SMITH of Ldn. Trust for debt to Eli
OFFUTT of Ffx (RUST and OFFUTT are business partners in Lsbg
with debts in PhilPa and BaltMd) using int. in estate of Mrs. Susanna

CHILTON dec'd of Ldn and of estate of Thomas CHILTON dec'd of Ldn (RUST m. Sally d/o Thomas & Susanna).

3G:122   Date: 29 Aug 1823   RtCt: 6 Sep 1823
Jacob WIRTZ of Ldn to John BOOTH of Ldn. B/S of 4072 perch lot at foot of Short Hill adj BOOTH. Wit: Jno. J. MATHIAS, L. BEARD, Alfred A. ESKRIDGE.

3G:123   Date: 27 Aug 1823   RtCt: 6 Sep 1823
Nathan NICKOLS & wife Sarah of Ldn to Thomas JAMES of Ldn. B/S of 10a. Wit: E. G. HAMILTON, B. SHREVE Jr., Alfred A. ESKRIDGE. Delv. to JAMES 16 Feb 1825.

3G:124   Date: 26 Aug 1823   RtCt: 8 Sep 1823
John A. BINNS (trustee of Isaac WRIGHT) of Ldn to William JOHNSON of Ldn. B/S of lot in Lsbg formerly of Robert PERFECT dec'd (from trust of Feb 1823, DBk FFF:319).

3G:125   Date: 9 Sep 1823   RtCt: 8 [?] Sept 1823
Jacob RAZOR (Admr wwa of John JENKINS dec'd) and Edward MARLOW. Bound to Theodore JENKINS for bond to Wm. ELLZEY, Jno. WHITE, Abner GIBSON & C. OSBURN for administration. Delv. to JENKINS 14 Feb 1825.

3G:125   Date: 9 Sep 1823   RtCt: 8 [?] Sept 1823
Jacob RAZOR (Admr wwa of John JENKINS) and Edward MARLOW. Bound to Theodore JENKINS as security for bond to __ ROSZEL, __ WHITE, __ BAYLY & __ GIBSON. Delv. to JENKINS 14 Feb 1825.

3G:126   Date: 8 Sep 1823   RtCt: 8 Sep 1823
Jesse TIMMS and Gusta's ELGIN. Bond on TIMMS as Commissioner of Revenue for 1st district.

3G:126   Date: 8 Sep 1823   RtCt: 8 Sep 1823
Jesse McVEIGH and Lewis M. SMITH. Bond on McVEIGH as Commissioner of Revenue for 2nd district.

3G:126   Date: 7 Jul 1823   RtCt: 2 Sep 1823
Fewell A. PERRY of Ffx to Wm. M. McCARTY of Ldn. BoS for negro woman Sally & her 2 children Mary & Jack. Wit: John R. CATON, Delv. to McCARTY on ___.

3G:127   Date: 27 May 1823   RtCt: 6 Sep 1823
Mary HIXON of Ldn to Catharine HIXON of Ldn. B/S of 48a (allotted to Catharine in div. of Reuben HIXON dec'd, being full share of her father's real estate a part of tract that Mary prch/o Hugh HOLMES Esqr). Delv. to HIXON 17 Aug 1829.

3G:128   Date: 16 Jan 1823   RtCt: 9 Sep 1823
Abner HUMPHREY & John G. HUMPHREY (Exor of Thomas HUMPHREY dec'd) of Ldn to Isaiah B. BEANS of Ldn. B/S of 156a (part of property of Thomas HUMPHREY dec'd less ¼a given to build school). Delv. to BEANS 21 Mar 1828.

3G:129   **Date: 11 Apr 1823**   **RtCt: 14 Apr/2 Sep 1823**
Matthew MITCHELL & wife Elizabeth of Ldn to Isaac NICKOLS Jr &
James HOGE of Ldn. Trust for debt to Isaac & Samuel NICKOLS
using 3 lots in Lsbg – 6¼a adj Martin KITZMARTIN on Loudoun St,
Littlejohn stable lot at Royal & Back sts, and 1 rood lot on S side of
Royal St. Wit: Stephen C. ROSZEL, Presley CORDELL. Delv. to
Saml. NICHOLLS Exors 3 Dec 1825.

3G:132   **Date: 30 Aug 1823**   **RtCt: 13 Oct 1823**
Henry ASHTON of WashDC to George THOMAS of WashDC.
Mortgage on 3295a in Ldn on Broad Run (dev. by father Henry
Alexander ASHTON of King George Co). Wit: Wm. HEWITT, Tho.
CARBERY.

3G:134   **Date: 15 Sep 1823**   **RtCt: 16 Sep 1823**
Samuel HAMMATT & wife Winefred of Ldn to John SHAW of Ldn.
B/S of ¼a (cnvy/b Wm. KIRK) on N side of Market St. in Lsbg adj
late prop. of Benjamin MAULSBY. Wit: Thos. SANDERS, Saml. M.
EDWARDS. Delv. to SHAW 2 Feb 1824.

3G:136   **Date: 15 Sep 1823**   **RtCt: 16 Sep 1823**
John SHAW & wife Rebecca of Ldn to Edward HAMMETT of Ldn.
B/S of lot on Back St in Lsbg. Wit: Thomas SANDERS, Saml. M.
EDWARDS.

3G:137   **Date: 29 Jun 1823**   **RtCt: 18 Sep 1823**
Samuel CLAPHAM & wife Elizabeth of Ldn to Henry CLAGETT of
Ldn. B/S of house & lot in Lsbg (prch/o James H. HAMILTON Jul
1817, DBk VV:112) adj John McCORMICK, William DRISH, John J.
HARDING. Wit: Henry PEERS, Alfred A. ESKRIDGE, Chas. G.
ESKRIDGE, Saml. DAWSON, James M. LEWIS.

3G:139   **Date: 17 Sep 1823**   **RtCt: 17 Sep 1823**
Tasker Carter QUINLAN of Ldn to Thomas Randolph MOTT of Ldn.
B/S of house & lot in Wtfd (cnvy/b Rich'd H. HENDERSON Oct
1822, DBk FFF:257).

3G:140   **Date: 30 Jan 1823**   **RtCt: 23 Sep 1823**
George RICKARD & wife Catharine of Ldn to Zach'h DULANY of
Ldn. Trust for debt to Peter COMPHER Jr. of Ldn using lots prch/o
Gideon HOUSEHOLDER Jan 1823 – 10½a Lot #5 in div. of Adam
HOUSEHOLDER dec'd, 1a Lot #5 and 4a Lot #11 in div. of
Susanna HOUSEHOLDER dec'd. and 4¼a Lot #17 2a Lot #4
(allotted to RICKARD from Susan HOUSEHOLDER dec'd) and also
2a Lot #1, 2a Lot #7, 4¼a Lot #18 allotted to Simon RICKARD and
2a Lot #6 and 2a Lot #3 allotted to John MILLER. Wit: Robert
BRADEN, Abiel JENNERS.

3G:142   **Date: 17 Feb 1823**   **RtCt: 23 Sep 1823**
George RICKARD & wife Catharine of Ldn to Peter COMPHER of
Ldn. B/S of 12¼a (Lots #14 & #15) adj Soloman HOUSEHOLDER.
Wit: R. BRADEN, Abiel JENNERS. Delv. to COMPHER 4 Feb 1828.

3G:144   Date: 24 Sep 1823   RtCt: 24 Sep 1823
John R. ANDERSON & wife Abby of Ldn to John Gill WATTS of Ldn. B/S of Abby's 1a share (LS of Aug 1798 from James HEREFORD to Patrick CAVANS, memo of Jan 1803 said to divide land, assigned to Leonard THOMAS who has now departed intestate leaving a wife and several children, including Abby). Wit: John McCORMICK, John H. McCABE. Delv. to WATT on ___.

3G:146   Date: 9 Jan 1812   RtCt: 10 Mar 1812/27 Sep 1823
John TRIPLETT of Ldn to Patrick McINTYRE of Lsbg. Bond to occupy for 3y house & lot where McINTYRE lives and use of negro woman Nelly (Alexander McINTYRE dec'd dev. land to wife then to son Charles who died before he was 21y without issue so descended to siblings John McINTYRE, Alexander McINTYRE, Daniel McINTYRE, Catharine BENTLEY, Patrick McINTYRE, Elizabeth TRIPLETT & William McINTYRE; TRIPLETT purchased rights of Alexander & William and sold his 3 shares to McINTYRE). Wit: S. BLINCOE, Josiah HALL, Mark WOOD.

3G:147   Date: 29 Sep 1823   RtCt: 29 Sep 1823
John J. MATHIAS of Ldn to Levi WARTERS/WATERS of Ldn. B/S of 19a on W side of Short Hill adj __ DERRY, Jacob WATERS. Delv. to WATERS 29 Mar 1825.

3G:148   Date: 28 Aug 1823   RtCt: 29 Sep 1823
Bushrod WASHINGTON & wife Ann of Ffx to William REEDER, Isaac BROWN, Joseph LOVETT, George KEENE, Jacob SILCOTT, Amos HIBBS, Samuel SMITH, Samuel DUNKIN, John WILKINSON, Elijah ANDERSON, Henry PLAISTER Jr., Samuel BEAVERS, Samuel RICHARDS and other heirs of Richard RICHARDS dec'd, Isaac FRY and other heirs of Isaac COWGILL dec'd and David GALLIHER & other heirs of William GALLEHER dec'd of Ldn. B/S of numerous parcels sold but not conveyed (deed of Oct 1785 from Thomas BLACKBURN of PrWm to Spencer GRAYSON ½ for use of Nathaniel CRAWFORD & wife Sarah and other ½ for use of Bushrod WASHINGTON & wife Ann of 2328a and they sold the land in separate parcels to William REEDER, Isaac BROWN, Thomas RUSSELL, Isaac COWGILL, Samuel DUNKIN, Richard RICHARDS, Michael EBLIN, Amos HIBBS, Jacob SILCOTT, Robert McCORMICK, William GALLIHER, John WILKINSON, Samuel BOYD, Samuel SMITH, James REED, William CARTER and William MARTIN. CRAWFORD executed deeds but WASHINGTON did not).

3G:150   Date: 27 Aug 1823   RtCt: 30 Sep 1823
Peter FICHTER & wife Susan of Ldn to Samuel HARPER of Ldn. B/S of lot (prch/o John CRIDELER) on N side of Loudoun St in Lsbg adj __ EMBERSON, __ GARNER. Wit: John McCORMICK, Presley CORDELL.

3G:152   Date: 1 Oct 1823   RtCt: 1 Oct 1823
Benjamin WHITE of Ldn to Edward OWENS. Loan of farm animals, farm and household items. Wit: S. BLINCOE, Eli TAVENNER, Presley CORDELL.

3G:152   Date: 30 Sep 1823   RtCt: 4 Oct 1823
George W. HENRY of Ldn to Zachariah DULANEY and Burr POWELL of Ldn. Trust for debt to Jozabed WHITE of Ldn using 103a adj William SMITH, Presley CORDELL, Mary FOX, Samuel GREGG.

3G:154   Date: 26 Sep 1823   RtCt: 4 Oct 1823
D. Shff Benjamin SHREVE Jr. to Henry PEERS of Ldn. A/L of int. of Fielding BROWN in blacksmith ship on Back St. in Lsbg (execution in name of Henry C. SLADE, with Richard H. HENDERSON requesting assignment). Wit: Rich'd H. HENDERSON, Benj. SHREVE Jr.

3G:155   Date: 9 May 1823   RtCt: 4 Oct 1823
Samuel HUGHES & wife Elizabeth of Ldn to Samuel BEANS of Ldn. B/S of 64a (part cnvy/b Thomas LOVE, part by Thomas HUGHES) on S branch of Kittocton Creek adj Jesse SILCOTT, __ POULSON, Thomas HUGHES, Amos BEANS. Wit: Stacey TAYLOR, Thomas MORRIS, Isaiah B. BEANS, Craven OSBURN, John WHITE. Delv. to BEANS 16 Nov 1844.

3G:157   Date: 16 Jun 1823   RtCt: 6 Oct 1823
Nelson GREEN & wife Jane and Francis HARRISON of Ldn and Gabriel GREEN & wife Elizabeth of FredVa to Mesheck LACEY of Ldn. Trust for Samuel CHINN as security for Nelson (who was not to leave Ldn but did and now there are penalties) using Lot #61 in Mdbg. Wit: Burr POWELL, A. GIBSON.

3G:159   Date: 23 Aug 1823   RtCt: 10 Oct 1823
John DEMORY of Ldn to Thomas KIDWELL of Ldn. B/S of 2a on W side of Short Hill (from Oct 1819 trust from Samuel GRAVES, DBk ZZ:306). Wit: Charles HAMILTON, E. G. HAMILTON, Alfred A. ESKRIDGE.

3G:160   Date: 26 Jul 1823   RtCt: 10 Oct 1823
William M. McCARTY & wife Emily R. of Ldn to George RUST Jr of Ldn. B/S of int. dev. to Emily by her brother Stephen T. MASON dec'd which he received from devisees of his father. Wit: Thomas SANDERS, Saml. M. EDWARDS.

3G:161   Date: 20 Sep 1823   RtCt: 11 Oct 1823
Samuel MORAN & wife Arret of Warren Co Ohio to Presley CORDELL of Ldn. B/S of und. ½ of lease on 300a (Richard CONNER dec'd died seized of L/L on 300a of 2 leases executed by John CARLYLE attorney for G. W. FAIRFAX in May 1762 and 2 A/L by John SCHOOLEY (s/o Samuel SCHOOLEY dec'd in Dec 1795). Wit: Henry HANK, Nathaniel HUNT.

3G:163   Date: 4 Oct 1823   RtCt: 11 Oct 1823
William GHEEN & wife Narcissa and son James GHEEN of Ldn to
Charles TURNER of Ldn. Trust for debt to William WILKINSON
using 1/6th int. devised by William SUDDITH to Narcissa GHEEN
and at her death to her six children of which James is one. Wit: Wm.
BRONAUGH, Francis W. LUCKETT. Delv. to WILKINSON 20 Apr
1829.

3G:165   Date: 30 Oct 1823   RtCt: 6 Oct 1823
Peter ISH and John SHAW of Lsbg to George HEAD of Lsbg. LS of
lot on N side of Market St in Lsbg. Wit: W. D. DRISH. Delv. to SHAW
21 May 1825 pr order.

3G:167   Date: 13 Oct 1823   RtCt: 13 Oct 1823
Garrison B. FRENCH, Jas. D. FRENCH & Jno. HOLMES. Bond on
Garrison B. FRENCH as constable.

3G:167   Date: 12 May 1823   RtCt: 13 Oct 1823
Hercules Dunkin and Sarah DUNKIN (d/o Amos HOUGH dec'd late
of Washington Co Pa who was s/o John HOUGH dec'd late of Ldn)
of Adams Co Ohio to Joseph HOUGH of Butler Co Ohio. PoA. Wit:
J. PATTERSON, Wm. CRUMPTON.

3G:169   Date: 4 Mar 1823   RtCt: 13 Oct 1823
John HOUGH, John JACKSON & wife Ann and Ruth ROSS of
Butler Co Ohio (ch/o Amos HOUGH dec'd late of Washington Co Pa
who was s/o John HOUGH dec'd late of Ldn) to Joseph HOUGH of
Butler Co Ohio. PoA. Wit: Ezekiel McCONNELL, P. LATHAM, Saml.
QUAIL.

3G:172   Date: 20 Jan 1823   RtCt: 13 Oct 1823
Dr. William GREENLEASE dec'd late of Butler Co Ohio. Letter of
administration to Joseph HOUGH with inventory and appraisal by
Samuel MILLIKEN, Hugh WILSON and James McBRIDE
freeholders of said county.

3G:172   Date: 7 Jul 1823   RtCt: 13 Oct 1823
Alison C. LOOKER (Admr of Benjamin HOUGH dec'd late of Ross
Co Ohio who was a child of Amos HOUGH dec'd late of Washington
Co Pa who was s/o John HOUGH dec'd late of Ldn) to Joseph
HOUGH of Butler Co Ohio. PoA. Wit: John A. FULTON, Levin BELT.

3G:174   Date: 1 Feb 1823   RtCt: 13 Oct 1823
Jonathan CARTER & wife Elizabeth of Ldn to George LOVE of Fqr.
Trust for debt to Conrad BITZER using 100a on S side of
Beaverdam adj John VERNON, __ CARR, __ HAINES, __
McMULLIN. Wit: William BRONAUGH, Francis W. LUCKETT.

3G:176   Date: 5 Aug 1822   RtCt: 13 Oct 1823
Lewis GRIGSBY (trustee for Stephen McPHERSON) to Isaac
NICKOLS Jr. & James HOGE of Ldn. B/S of land involved in trust
(debt of Thomas GREGG and Isaac & Samuel NICKOLS to
McPHERSON but failed to pay). Wit: Troy WELLS, John COLLINS.

3G:176   Date: 30 Jan 1823   RtCt: 13 Oct 1823
Abraham HAWLING & wife Mary Ann (d/o Thomas ODEN & wife Martha) to Jacob SUMMERS. B/S of 1/10th of 19¼a dower (Thomas died intestate and Martha received 1/3 of estate, Martha has now also died) adj James McKIM dec'd, John HUTCHISON.
Acknowledged by HAWLING in Albemarle Co Va. Delv. 8 Sep 1828.

3G:178   Date: 13 Sep 1823   RtCt: 13 Oct 1823
Daniel COOPER & wife Elizabeth of Ldn to Samuel WILLIAMS of Ldn. B/S of 14a (formerly of Thomas LESLIE). Wit: Abiel JENNERS, Saml. HOUGH.

3G:179   Date: 4 Jun 1823   RtCt: 13 Oct 1823
John MARTIN Jr. (devisee of Edward MARTIN of Ldn) to James BOWLES of Ldn. B/S of ¼ int. in 45a (from grandfather John VIOLETT dec'd left to dau Elizabeth MARTIN m/o John Jr.) including widow's dower.

3G:180   Date: 10 Oct 1823   RtCt: 13 Oct 1823
Katharine LANE of Ldn to Epaminondas M. LANE of Ldn. B/S of land allotted by div. of estate of Flavius J. LANE dec'd.

3G:181   Date: 24 Jul 1823   RtCt: 13 Oct 1823
Epaminondas M. LANE of Ldn to John CRAINE Jr of Fqr. B/S of 102a (part of allotted land from Col. Joseph LANE dec'd).

3G:182   Date: 13 Oct 1823   RtCt: 13 Oct 1823
George COOPER & wife Mary of Ldn to John JANNEY of Ldn. B/S of 80 perches nr Lutheran Church in the German Settlement adj Aaron MILLER, Peter VIRTZ.

3G:183   Date: 11 Oct 1823   RtCt: 13 Oct 1823
Benjamin MITCHELL Jr. & wife Martha of Ldn to Epaminondas M. LANE of Ldn. B/S of Martha's int. in land where mother Mrs. Katharine LANE lives as dower from husband Col. Joseph LANE dec'd and as rep of her brother Flavius J. LANE dec'd who died intestate. Wit: William BRONAUGH, Francis W. LUCKETT.

3G:184   Date: 26 Aug 1823   RtCt: 13 Oct 1823
Benjamin FLOWERS of Ldn to Eli GALLAHER of Ldn. Trust for debt to John GALLAHER surviving partner of Hatcher & Galleher using farm animals, farm and household items. Delv. to Wm. BRONAUGH pr order of GALLEHER on ___.

3G:185   Date: 10 Sep 1823   RtCt: 13 Oct 1823
Amos HARVEY & wife Elizabeth of Ldn to Craven OSBURN & John A. MARMADUKE. Trust for debt to James McILHANY using 80a where HARVEY lives (prch/o Mahlon MORRIS heirs of Ebenezer WILSON). Wit: Ebenezer GRUBB, John WHITE.

3G:188   Date: 16 Jan 1823   RtCt: 13 Oct 1823
Abner HUMPHREY and John G. HUMPHREY (Exors wwa of Thomas HUMPHREY dec'd) of Ldn to Joseph DANIEL of Ldn. B/S of 146a adj Mason MARKS. Delv. to DANIEL 8 Jul 1825.

3G:189 Date: 16 Jan 1823 RtCt: 13 Oct 1823
Joseph DANIEL & wife Tacy of Ldn to Abner HUMPHREY of Ldn. Trust for debt to Abner HUMPHREY and John G. HUMPHREY (Exors wwa of Thomas Humphrey dec'd) using 146a as above. Wit: Burr POWELL, A. GIBSON. Delv. to John G. HUMPHREY 31 Jan 1828.

3G:191 Date: 16 Sep 1823 RtCt: 14 Oct 1823
John BROWN & wife Margaret of Ldn to Craven OSBURN and John A. MARMADUKE of Ldn. Trust for debt to James McILHANY using 73¾a (dev. to Margaret by father Thomas DAVIS dec'd) on NW side of short hill where BROWN now lives adj William GRUBB, John BAKER. Wit: Ebenezer GRUBB, John WHITE.

3G:193 Date: 16 Oct 1823 RtCt: 16 Oct 1823
Samuel TUSTIN of Lsbg to Thomas SANDERS of Lsbg. Trust for debt to Isaac TUSTIN of PhilPa using carryall and harness.

3G:194 Date: 8 Oct 1823 RtCt: 13 Oct 1823
William J. BRONAUGH of Ldn to Francis W. LUCKETT of Ldn. Trust for father William BRONAUGH as security for debts to Noble BEVERIDGE using 200a (cnvy/b father) and negro man Peter, man Joe, boy Washington abt 14y old, boy Ben abt 8y old, old woman Hannah and farm animals, farm and household items. Wit: Jno. W. T. BRONAUGH, Jere. W. BRONAUGH Jr., P. H. W. BRONAUGH. Delv. to LUCKETT 11 Oct 1827.

3G:195 Date: 30 Nov 1822 RtCt: 23 Oct 1823
John BENEDUM & wife Mary of Ldn to Peter BENEDUM of Ldn. B/S of 105a (cnvy/b Peter to John Nov 1819, DBk ZZ:244).

3G:196 Date: 23 Sep 1823 RtCt: 24 Oct 1823
William JOHNSON & wife Margaret of Lsbg to Richard H. HENDERSON of Ldn. Trust for debt to Joseph MANDEVILLE and Samuel B. LARMOUR under firm of Mandeville & Larmour of AlexVA using lot on King St in Lsbg adj James WOOD, Jotham WRIGHT. Wit: John McCORMICK, Presley CORDELL.

3G:198 Date: 23 Oct 1823 RtCt: 24 Oct 1823
Thomas SANDERS of Ldn to Peter OATYER of Ldn. B/S of lot on E side of Liberty St. (trust of Mar 1823 from Samuel TUSTIN who defaulted, DBk FFF:304). Wit: H. Peers, E. G. HAMILTON, E. HAMMAT.

3G:199 Date: 17 Oct 1822 RtCt: 25 Oct 1823
Robert A. LACEY of Ldn to Enos WILDMAN of Ldn. B/S of lot at King and Royal Sts in Lsbg (purchased by Israel LACEY now dec'd f/o Robert A. from Jacob FADELY)

3G:200 Date: 25 Oct 1823 RtCt: 25 Oct 1823
Robert A. LACEY of Ldn to Enos WILDMAN of Ldn. B/S of und. 1/7th part of und. ½ of 40a (as heir of father Israel LACEY dec'd) adj

Potomack River, Fayette BALL, 'Big Spring Mill lot'. Delv. to WILDMAN 11 Jun 1828. Wit: Presley CORDELL.

3G:201   Date: 25 Oct 1823   RtCt: 25 Oct 1823
Robert A. LACEY of Ldn to George M. CHICHESTER of Ldn. B/S of 1/6th of 1/14th int. in 40a of Armistead John LACEY dec'd adj Potomack River, Fayette BALL. Delv. to CHICHESTER 11 May 1826.

3G:202   Date: 20 Sep 1823   RtCt: 25 Oct 1823
George BRITTON & wife Rebecca of Culpeper Co Va to Robert MOFFETT of Ldn. B/S of int. in land of John MILHOLLAND dec'd (through Rebecca's mother Nancy BREWER dec'd sister of MILHOLLAND). Delv. to MOFFETT 10 Apr 1841.

3G:204   Date: 16 Apr 1823   RtCt: 31 Oct 1823
Isaac LAFFERTY of JeffVa to Catharine A. DERHAM of Ldn. BoS for negro Sybil and Philip her child. Wit: C. BINNS, Elizabeth D. BINNS.

3G:204   Date: 4 Nov 1823   RtCt: 4 Nov 1823
Aaron SANDERS of Ldn to Jonathan BUTCHER and Rich'd H. HENDERSON of Ldn. Trust for debt to Phineas JANNEY and Joseph JANNEY Jr. (Exors of John JANNEY of AlexDC) using 3 contiguous lots (155a, 87a, 42a) where SANDERS lives. Delv. to Jos. JANNEY pr order of HENDERSON 6 Oct 1824.

3G:205   Date: 27 Oct 1823   RtCt: 4 Nov 1823
James WOOD & wife Margaret of Lsbg to Richard H. HENDERSON of Lsbg. Trust for debt to Joseph MANDEVILLE and Saml. B. LARMOUR under firm of Mandeville & Larmour of AlexDC using lot with 2 story house used as office by Wm. M. McCARTY and Wm. JENNERS on S side of Market St in Lsbg adj Geo. M. CHICHESTER, Wm. WRIGHT dec'd, Wm. JOHNSON, Jotham WRIGHT. Wit: Presley CORDELL, Saml. M. EDWARDS.

3G:207   Date: 31 Oct 1823   RtCt: 6 Nov 1823
David CARTER of Ldn to Daniel VERNON and William BRONAUGH of Ldn. Trust for debt to James CARTER, Daniel P. CONRAD with Jonathan CARTER as security, Charles BINNS, Sarah LEWIS, Gourley READER Admr of Pleasant LIVINGSTON dec'd, John CHEW, estate of Presley SAUNDERS dec'd, Wm. FRANCE Admr of Mahlon CARTER dec'd, Noble BEVERIDGE, McVeigh & Co., Joseph CARR, Peyton HARDEN, John GRIGSBY, estate of James MASH dec'd, Enoch FURR, George LOVE for benefit of his sisters, Augustine LOVE, Richard COLEMAN using 125a (bought of Augustine LOVE, except 28a sold to Andrew B. McMULLEN and subject to lease to Micajah TRIPLETT for 5y) and 92½a.

3G:211   Date: ___ 1823   RtCt: 8 Nov 1823
Joseph WOOD of Ldn to Joshua PEWSEY of Ldn. Trust for debt to James NIXON, Abiel JENNERS as security on note, John H.

McCABE, Lambert MYERS using 30a (cnvy/b Exors of Mahlon JANNEY dec'd). Delv. to PEWSEY 20 Feb 1824.

3G:213   Date: 10 Nov 1823   RtCt: 10 Nov 1823
John ROSE, Benj'n SHREVE, Robert MOFFETT, George RUST Jr., Richard H. HENDERSON, William THRIFT & Joseph MEAD. Bond on ROSE as sheriff to collect levies.

3G:215   Date: 10 Nov 1823   RtCt: 10 Nov 1823
John ROSE, Benj'n SHREVE, Robert MOFFETT, George RUST Jr., Richard H. HENDERSON, William THRIFT & Joseph MEAD. Bond on ROSE as sheriff to collect officers fees.

3G:216   Date: 20 Sep 1823   RtCt: 10 Nov 1823
William CHAMBLIN dec'd. Division – Lot #1 (25a) and slaves Hiram, Sall, Alfred, Peyton & Juliet as dower to widow Catharine JACOBS, Lot #2 (24a) and slaves Ellzey, Cato & Eveline to Maria JACOBS, Lot #3 (24a) and slaves Lydia, Lee & Francis to William CHAMBLIN, Lot #4 (22a) and slaves Clarey, Richard, Stephen & Chilton to Norval CHAMBLIN. Gives plat. Divisors: Abner HUMPHREY, Wm. BRONAUGH, Daniel VERNON.

3G:218   Date: 19 Jul 1823   RtCt: 10 Nov 1823
Robert DAGG dec'd. Report of sale – court order of 12 May 1823 in suit of James DAGG agst Jno. L. DAGG directing sale of real estate and slaves. Lots #26 & #32 in Mdbg to John L. DAGG (representing Saml. DAGG) with Edmund B. GRADY (Guardian of Susan, Clarissa & James DAGG) being present. Slave Miria abt 22y old & her son Alfred abt 2y old to Edward B. GRADY. Distributions of bonds, etc. to James DAGG, Mary Jane DAGG, Sarah DAGG, Susan DAGG, Clarissa DAGG, Jno. L. DAGG, Saml. DAGG. Divisors: Jesse McVEIGH, Hugh ROGERS, James HIXSON, Burr POWELL.

3G:220   Date: 13 Nov 1823   RtCt: 13 Nov 1823
Benj'n SHREVE, Rich'd H. HENDERSON, Robert MOFFETT. Bond to Thos. FOUCH, Wm. CARR, Abiel JENNERS & S'l. M. EDWARDS on SHREVE appointed committee in charge of estate of Harriet CRAVEN a lunatic. SHREVE replaces Edward DULIN who has left Va and labours under a mental derangement.

3G:220   Date: 12 Jun 1823   RtCt: 10 Nov 1823
William VICKERS of Ldn to son-in-law William RICHARDS of Ldn. Gift of negro girl Maria 8y old (gave to RICHARDS at m. with dau. Margaret). Delv. to RICHARDS 7 Feb 1826.

3G:221   Date: 5 Nov 1823   RtCt: 10 Nov 1823
John McPHERSON to John HAMES. Bond of $5/yr for 5y for use of household items, and cow. Wit: Caldwell CARR, Jonathan GIBSON.

3G:221   Date: 8 Nov 1823   RtCt: 10 Nov 1823
John W. HEREFORD & wife Juliet to Ann Catharine HEREFORD, Mary Ann HEREFORD, Margaret A. HEREFORD, John B. HEREFORD, Francis H. HEREFORD & Matthew C. HEREFORD.

B/S of int. in land in Ldn & Fqr in div. of Francis HEREFORD dec'd late of Fqr with John W. HEREFORD & wife Juliet getting 154a adj Wm. WILLIAMSON, John CRAINE & heirs of Wm. HALE dec'd which they sold to John CRAINE and John SCANTLING with other distributees agreeing. Wit: Burr POWELL, A. GIBSON.

3G:223   Date: 6 Mar 1823   RtCt: 10 Nov 1823
Walter LANGLEY & wife Susanna of Ldn to Stephen GARRETT of Ldn. B/S of ½a Lots #82 & #83 on Mercer St in Aldie. Wit: Craven OSBURN, John WHITE. Delv. to GARRETT 20 Dec 1824.

3G:224   Date: 19 Jul 1823   RtCt: 10 Nov 1823
Jesse McVEIGH, Hugh ROGERS, James HIXSON & Burr POWELL (commrs in distribution to heirs of Robert DAGG dec'd) to John L. DAGG. B/S of Lot #26 & #32 in Mdbg. Delv. pr order 11 Apr 1825.

3G:226   Date: 6 Nov 1823   RtCt: 10 Nov 1823
Daniel C. JOHNSON of Ldn to Humphrey B. POWELL. Trust for debt to Abner GIBSON using late wife Ann's int. in estate of father Richard CRUPPER dec'd of Ldn (Ann died leaving only child John Richard).

3G:227   Date: 1 Nov 1823   RtCt: 11 Nov 1823
William LICKEY & wife Abigail of Ldn to Ezra BOLON of Ldn. B/S of 125a on E side of N fork of Beaverdam on road to N. Fork Meeting House. Wit: Saml. M. EDWARDS, Presley CORDELL. Delv. to BOLON 20 Oct 1824.

3G:228   Date: 16 Oct 1823   RtCt: 11 Nov 1823
Stephen McPHERSON & wife Cecelia of Ldn to Jonathan EWERS of Ldn. Trust to secure payment of legacies (Elisha MARKS dev. to son Isaiah MARKS and he should pay legacies, some still unpaid and has sold land, part was passed to John MARKS who conveyed to McPHERSON, so John MARKS is indebts to heirs of Isaiah MARKS – his children Elisha, Lucinda, David & John MARKS). Wit: Notley C. WILLIAMS, John W. GRAYSON. Delv. to EWERS 9 Nov 1824.

3G:231   Date: 13 Apr 1823   RtCt: 11 Nov 1823
Elizabeth WILKINSON wd/o Joseph WILKINSON dec'd of Ldn to Edmund LOVETT of Ldn. B/S of ¼a Lot #2 in div. of lands of her father James REED dec'd in Union.

3G:232   Date: 13 Nov 1823   RtCt: 14 Nov 1823
David CONARD of Ldn to Jozabed WHITE of Ldn. Release of trust for debt to Robert BRADEN dated July 1822 on 103a.

3G:233   Date: 21 May 1823   RtCt: 14 Nov 1823
Jozabed WHITE & wife Margaret of Ldn to George W. HENRY of Ldn. B/S of 103a adj William SMITH, Mary FOX, P. CORDELL, S. GREGG, Matthew BEANS. Wit: Robt. BRADEN, Saml. HOUGH Jr. Delv. to HENRY 27 Dec 1828.

3G:234   Date: 15 Nov 1823   RtCt: 15 Nov 1823
John R. ADAMS (insolvent debtor) of Ldn to Shff John ROSE. B/S of 200a prch/o Samuel ADAMS.

3G:235   Date: 30 Aug 1823   RtCt: 17 Nov 1823
Malinda BOWERS of FredVa to Thornton WALKER of Ldn. B/S of 25½a Lot #4 allotted from estate of Reuben TRIPLETT dec'd. Delv. to WALKER 25 Feb 1825.

3G:237   Date: 13 Nov 1823   RtCt: 17 Nov 1823
George RICHARD (trustee of William MISKELL) to John DRISH. B/S of lot on Market St in Lsbg and ½a Lot #11 & #20 in Mt. Gilead (from trust of May 1823).

3G:238   Date: 27 Aug 1823   RtCt: 17 Nov 1823
John JOHNSON of Ldn to Thornton WALKER of Ldn. B/S of 19¼a Lot #2 allotted from estate of Reuben TRIPLETT dec'd. Delv. to WALKER 25 Feb 1825.

3G:239   Date: 8 May 1823   RtCt: 21 Nov 1823
Samuel TRAHERN of Ldn to Caleb N. GALLEHER of Ldn. Trust for debt to Thomas H. WEY using lot in Union cnvy/b WEY. Delv. to Thos. SANDERS Exor of P. SANDERS dec'd pr rec't 8 May 1826.

3G:240   Date: 25 Dec 1822   RtCt: 22 Nov 1823
Ludwell LEE to James L. McKENNA. B/S of 133a at new turnpike road from Lsbg to Broad Run adj __ WHALEY. Delv. to Thomson MASON 7 Sep 1825.

3G:241   Date: 22 Nov 1823   RtCt: 24 Nov 1823
Samuel M. EDWARDS (trustee of John WALKER of FredMd) to Charles BINNS of Ldn. Release of trust of Sep 1820.

3G:242   Date: 11 Nov 1823   RtCt: 22 Nov 1823
John UPP & wife Sarah of Mdbg to Mesheck Lacey of Mdbg. Trust for debt to Conrad BITZER using house & lot in Mdbg where UPP resides. Wit: Burr POWELL, A. GIBSON. Delv. to BITZER 30 Apr 1827.

3G:244   Date: 31 Nov 1822   RtCt: 24 Nov 1823
Peter BENEDUM & wife Catharine of Ldn to John BENEDUM of Ldn. B/S of 100a adj Wm. A. BINNS. Wit: Jno. H. McCABE, Saml. M. EDWARDS.

3G:246   Date: 31 Nov 1822   RtCt: 24 Nov 1823
John BENEDUM of Ldn to Saml. M. EDWARDS of Ldn. Trust for debt to Peter BENEDUM using 100a as above.

3G:248   Date: 8 Nov 1823   RtCt: 25 Nov 1823
Robert ONEALE of Ldn to Silas GARRETT of Ldn. Trustee for debt to Joseph GARRETT using farm animals, household items.

3G:248   Date: 26 Nov 1823   RtCt: 26 Nov 1823
Thomas JACKSON of Ldn to Anthony CUNNARD/CONARD Jr. BoS for farm animals, household items, crops. Wit: Saml. HAMMETT, B. SHREVE Jr.

3G:250   Date: 14 May 1823   RtCt: 28 Nov 1823
Amos GIBSON & wife Hannah, Elisha JANNEY & wife Mary, their son John JANNEY and Mahlon GIBSON (heirs & reps of John GIBSON dec'd) and Hugh SMITH & wife Elizabeth (who purchased Israel GIBSON's share which was sold by trust) of Ldn to Daniel EACHES of Ldn. B/S of Lot #1 & part of Lot #2 in div. (25a) of estate of John GIBSON dec'd where he resided, adj Joseph & James GIBSON dec'd, William RICHARDS. Wit: Craven OSBURN, John W. GRAYSON. Delv. pr order filed by Edw'd L. FANT 12 Jun 1829.

3G:253   Date: 18 Nov 1823   RtCt: 1 Dec 1823
Joshua RILEY of Lsbg to Saml. CARR and Sampson BLINCOE of Lsbg. Trust for debt to William CARR using ½a Lot #59 in Lsbg except small part cnvy/b John QUICK and life estate of Mrs. ELLIOT in small log house.

3G:255   Date: 2 Dec 1823   RtCt: 2 Dec 1823
Daniel LEWIS of Lsbg to John H. MONROE of Lsbg. Trust for debt to Samuel M. BOSS using household items. Delv. to BOSS 12 Jan 1827.

3G:256   Date: 3 Dec 1823   RtCt: 3 Dec 1823
Samuel DAWSON (trustee of Jacob KIMERLIE) of Ldn to Thomas GASSAWAY of Ldn. B/S of 61a (from trust dated Oct 1820, DBk BBB:198).

3G:257   Date: 4 Dec 1823   RtCt: 5 Dec 1823
Edward DORSEY of Ldn to Benjamin SHREVE of Ldn. Trust for debt to Henry GUNNELL (Admr of Robert GUNNELL dec'd), Jesse GOVER assignee of George W. HENRY using ½a lot in new addition of Wtfd on W end of Presbyterian meeting house lot adj William NETTLE, John MORROW, Robert BRADEN.

3G:258   Date: 12 Aug 1822   RtCt: 6 Dec 1823
Fleet SMITH & wife Jane of WashDC to William D. DRISH of Ldn. B/S of 2a nr Lsbg adj Dr. C. B. BALL, Dr. SELDEN.

3G:259   Date: 14 Oct 1823   RtCt: 6 Dec 1823
Hugh SMITH (trustee of Manly T. RUST) of Ldn to Eli OFFUTT of Ffx. B/S of int. in estate of Mrs. Susanna CHILTON dec'd and Thos. CHILTON dec'd (from m. to Sally CHILTON d/o Susanna & Thomas, trust of Aug 1823). Wit: A. GIBSON, Burr POWELL. Delv. to OFFUTT 6 Aug 1830.

3G:262   Date: 8 Dec 1823   RtCt: 8 Dec 1823
L. P. W. BALCH, William THRIFT and H. B. POWELL. Bond on BALCH as treasurer of board of school commrs. of Loudoun Co.

3G:262   Date: 28 Nov 1823   RtCt: 8 Dec 1823
Henry SANDERS dec'd. Renunciation of will by widow Patience
SANDERS. Wit: Thomas SANDERS, Evritt SAUNDERS.

3G:263   Date: 8 Dec 1823   RtCt: 8 Dec 1823
Evritt SAUNDERS, Thomas SANDERS, Saml. HAMMETT. Bond on
SAUNDERS as constable.

3G:263   Date: 6 Dec 1823   RtCt: 6 Dec 1823
Elizabeth JONES of Ldn to Hugh SMITH of Ldn. B/S of 17½a adj
SMITH, William CARR (descended to Philippa E. W. JONES now
LAWRENCE d/o John JONES and said Elizabeth then conveyed to
Elizabeth in trust). Delv. to SMITH 2 Aug 1830.

3G:264   Date: 28 Nov 1823   RtCt: 8 Dec 1823
Alexander M. BRISCOE & wife Matilda P. of PrWm to George M.
CHICHESTER of Ldn. B/S of 40a with merchant mill (1/6th or 1/14th
of land and mill) on Potomac adj Fayette BALL.

3G:266   Date: 9 Apr 1823   RtCt: __ Dec 1823
Joseph GORE of Ldn to William VICKERS of Ldn. Release of trust
of Apr 1816 to John NEWLON & wife Ruth of Culpeper Co Va on
80a.

3G:267   Date: 14 Oct 1823   RtCt: 8 Dec 1823
Enos TRAHERN & wife Sarah R. of Ldn to George SAGERS of Ldn.
B/S of 6a on NW fork of Goose Creek. Wit: Notley C. WILLIAMS,
William BRONAUGH. Delv. to SAGERS 1 Feb 1825.

3G:269   Date: 8 Dec 1823   RtCt: 8 Jun 1823
John MORROW (insolvent debtor) of Wtfd to Shff John ROSE. B/S
of house & ¼a lot and 2a lot separated from the other by an alley
and deeds of trust (executions by Braden Morgan &CO ass'ees of
David CONRAD who was assignee of John HAINS?, Francis
STRIBLING, Daniel W. GRIFFITH).

3G:270   Date: 28 Nov 1823   RtCt: 8 Dec 1823
D. Shff Benjamin SHREVE Jr. to Samuel M. EDWARDS of Ldn. B/S
of lot on S side of Loudoun St in Lsbg (from insolvent James
WINTERS, Jun 1823) adj Thos. HEIR. Delv. to B. SHREVE Jr. 27
Nov 1824.

3G:271   Date: 8 Aug 1823   RtCt: 8 Dec 1823
Mesheck LACEY of Ldn to Naomi LACEY, Huldah LACEY & Ruth
LACEY of Ldn. Gift of all int. in estate of Tacey LACEY dec'd late of
Ldn.

3G:272   Date: 10 Apr 1823   RtCt: 8 Dec 1823
George JANNEY & wife Susannah and Elisha JANNEY & wife Lydia
of Ldn to Joseph BURSON of Ldn. B/S of 1a on SE side of Goose
Creek opposite Janney's Mill where Robert MOOR now resides. Wit:
William BRONAUGH, Francis W. LUCKETT. Delv. pr order 22 Sep
1828.

3G:273 Date: 27 Aug 1821 RtCt: 8 Dec 1823
Joseph WOOD & wife Lydia of Ldn to John MORROW of JeffVa.
B/S of 2a in Wtfd (formerly part of Mahlon JANNEY dec'd land) adj
John B. STEVENS, __ BRADEN, __ WHITE.

3G:274 Date: 23 Oct 1823 RtCt: 8 Dec 1823
John CRIDELER & wife Elizabeth of Ldn to Saml. M. EDWARDS of
Ldn. Trust of lot on N side of Market St in Lsbg for use of Elizabeth
SERVICK w/o Christian SERWICK during her life and then to their
children with no encumbrances from Christian Wit: John
McCORMICK, Presley CORDELL. Delv to Jno. J. MATHIAS pr order
S. M. EDWARDS 18 Jan 1828.

3G:276 Date: 4 Feb 1823 RtCt: 8 Dec 1823
Elijah HALL (trustee in deed of Jul 1821 from John W. GRAYSON
for use of R. HALL) to Richard HALL of Hampshire Co Va. B/S of
85a on Beaverdam adj GRAYSON, Abner HUMPHREY.

3G:277 Date: 7 May 1823 RtCt: 8 Dec 1823
Richard HALL & wife Winnefred of Hampshire Co Va to Matthew
CARPENTER of Ldn. B/S of 84½a (from above deed) on
Beaverdam run adj Benjamin GRAYSON, Dempsey CARTER,
Abner HUMPHREY.

3G:279 Date: 13 Sep 1823 RtCt: 8 Dec 1823
Timothy TAYLOR Jr. & wife Harriet of Ldn to Jonathan HEATON of
Ldn. B/S of int. in real estate of Abner OSBURN dec'd willed to dau
Patience now w/o HEATON (assigned to TAYLOR from 1819 suit in
Winchester agst James HEATON, Nicholas OSBURN, Joel
OSBURN, Abner OSBURN & Jonathan HEATON heirs of Abner
OSBURN dec'd). Wit: Craven OSBURN, John WHITE. Delv. to
HEATON 22 Mar 1825.

3G:281 Date: 14 Sep 1822 RtCt: 8 Dec 1823
George B. WHITING & wife Frances of Ldn to James SWARTS Sr.
and dau Matilda Simpson and sons Barnet and Alexander SWARTS
of Ldn. B/S of 496¾a 'Goshen' (less 4¾a for Mrs. Portia
HODGSON) where WHITING resides prch/o Israel LACEY dec'd.
Wit: Charles LEWIS, Ariss BUCKNER. Delv. to Jas. Sr. 22 Mar
1830.

3G:283 Date: 10 Dec 1823 RtCt: 10 Jun 1823
Charles VERMILLION to Saml. CARR. Trust for debt to George F.
THORNTON for use of John M. McCARTY using horse, farm and
household items, notes on Elizabeth BROWN, Joseph B. WEBB.

3G:285 Date: 4 Jun 1823 RtCt: 8 Dec 1823
Jehu BRADLEY & wife Mary (d/o Sally VANHORN) of Ldn to Robert
COE of Ldn. BoS for woman slave Gracey (gift of 30 Mar 1807 by
Jacob G. PEARCE to Sally VANHORN during her life then to heirs).
Wit: David J. COE, Robt. BOGUE, John W. COE. Delv. to COE 17
Nov 1828.

3G:286   Date: 29 Nov 1823   RtCt: 13 Dec 1823
Charles GULLATT & wife Rebecca of Lsbg to Dr. John T. WILSON
of Lsbg. B/S of lot on Loudoun St in Lsbg adj Samuel M.
EDWARDS. Wit: Thos. SANDERS, Saml. M. EDWARDS.

3G:287   Date: 20 Mar 1810   RtCt: 14 May 1810/13 Dec 1823
Thomas JOHNSON of FredMd and Thomas JOHNSON (s/o James)
of Ldn to William NOLAND of Ldn. B/S of 7a on Awbrey's Spring.
Wit: Jacob DELLINGER, foreign name, Daniel EMERY.

3G:288   Date: 15 Dec 1823   RtCt: 15 Dec 1823
Betsey CLIFFORD to John J. MATHIAS. Trust for debt to Samuel
CARR using house & lot she may have at death of father Alexander
COOPER on SE corner of Loudoun & Back St in Lsbg late property
of Jane HAMILTON dec'd and now occupied by COOPER. Wit:
James H. HAMILTON, John MOOR, S. M. BOSS. Delv. to CARR 3
Nov 1827.

3G:290   Date: 13 Dec 1823   RtCt: 15 Dec 1823
William MISKELL of Ldn to Samuel M. BOSS of Lsbg. Trust for debt
to Aaron DAILEY of Ldn using farm and household items (distressed
by constable Everitt SANDERS for debt to Benjamin SHREVE and
MISKELL gave bond to DAILEY).

3G:291   Date: 10 Dec 1823   RtCt: 16 Dec 1823
John C. BAZZIL & wife Mary of Ldn to Thomas JAMES of Ldn. B/S
of 24a with merchant mill on Valentine's branch adj __ WARNER,
Thomas JAMES, William BROWN. Wit: John WHITE, Craven
OSBURN. Delv. pr order 5 Nov 1825.

3G:292   Date: 10 Dec 1823   RtCt: 16 Dec 1823
John C. BAZZIL & wife Mary of Ldn to Thomas JAMES of Ldn. B/S
of 12a with saw mill & grist mill on Valentine's branch nr Blue Ridge.
Wit: Craven OSBURN, John WHITE. Delv. pr order 5 Nov 1825.

3G:294   Date: 18 Dec 1823   RtCt: 18 Dec 1823
William DRISH and Barbara STONEBURNER. Agreement made
between STONEBURNER and DRISH before their marriage that in
case of death their own family gets the decedents property.
Document was written by S. BLINCOE, signed and given to
DRISH's son-in-law Wm. KIRK to deliver to court, but KIRK moved
to Ohio without doing. Trust given to Saml. M. EDWARDS of their
possessions to see that wishes are carried out and relinquishment of
dower. Wit: Thomas SANDERS, Presley CORDELL.

3G:295   Date: 14 Dec 1823   RtCt: 20 Dec 1823
John MARTIN Jr. of Ldn to Joseph A. LLOYD of Ldn. Trust for debt
to George E. LLOYD using farm animals, crops, household items.
Wit: Wm. BRONAUGH, Wm. J. BRONAUGH.

3G:296   Date: 15 Dec 1823   RtCt: 20 Dec 1823
Deputy Francis M. BECKWITH to John Thomson BROOKS. B/S of
134a described in mortgage of DOWNEY to William McREYNOLDS

of 8 Mar 1814 (from case of James BELL agst Robert DOWNEY & wife Barbara and Thompson BROOKS Admr. of Richard BROOKS dec'd Nov 1822)

3G:297 Date: 6 Jul 1823 RtCt: 22 Dec 1823
Samuel TODD of Aldie to William BEATTY of Aldie. B/S of 10a on Barton's branch of Little River adj BEATTY, Amos FERGUSON.

3G:298 Date: 15 Oct 1823 RtCt: 26 Feb 1823
Thomas KIDWELL & wife Elizabeth of Ldn to James STUBBLEFIELD of JeffVa. B/S of 119¼a on W side of Short Hill (purchased part from John MATHIAS and part from Edmund J. LEE) adj __ CUNNARD, __ DEMORY. Wit: Ebenezer GRUBB, John WHITE.

3G:300 Date: 31 Dec 1823 RtCt: 21 Dec 1823
Anna ROSZEL. DoE for slaves Cyrus, Nancy, Suckey, Betsey and Milley (from Stephen C. ROSZEL dec'd by deed from Sarah ROSZEL and other distributees). Wit: R. H. HENDERSON, Alex'r HENDERSON.

3G:301 Date: 12 Nov 1823 RtCt: 27 Nov 1823
Stacey TAYLOR and David REESE (trustee of Thomas NICHOLS) of Ldn to John BROWN of Ldn. Release of trust for debt to Thomas NICHOLS on 114½a.

3G:302 Date: 8 Jan 1823 RtCt: 27 Dec 1823
Gideon HOUSEHOLDER & wife Julia (signed Juliana, CoE gives as Lydia) of Ldn to George RICKARD of Ldn. B/S of 10½a (Lot #5 in div. of Susannah & Adam HOUSEHOLDER) adj David AXLINE and 4a. Wit: Robert BRADEN, Samuel HOUGH Jr. Delv. to RICKARD 9 Jun 1824.

3G:304 Date: 30 Dec 1823 RtCt: 30 Dec 1823
John BENEDUM & wife Mary of Ldn to Thomas HALL of Ldn. B/S of 1a. Delv. to HALL 30 May 1842.

3G:305 Date: 12 Jan 1824 RtCt: 12 Jan 1824
John VIOLETT (insolvent debtor) to Shff John ROSE. B/S of 143a (descended to wife Mary formerly LEWIS as distributee of James LEWIS dec'd) (executions by Thomas SQUIRES, Samuel SINGLETON).

3G:305 Date: 2 Jan 1824 RtCt: 30 Jan 1824
Samuel HARPER to John MOOR. Trust for debt to Saml CARR using lot in Lsbg (prch/o Peter FICHTER)

3G:307 Date: 3 Jan 1824 RtCt: 5 Jan 1824
Aaron DAILEY of Ldn to Saml. M. EDWARDS. Trust for debt to Samuel DAILEY & John DAILEY of Ldn using land on N side of Lsbg turnpike (cnvy/b Isaac WRIGHT May 1820 DBk AAA:366, less ½a to Lsbg Turnpike Co. Delv. to Saml. DAILEY 23 Jan 1828.

3G:308   Date: 8 Dec 1823   RtCt: 5 Jan 1824
John MARKS & wife Lydia of Ldn to James ALLEN of Ldn. B/S of
105a (cnvy/b Hugh SMITH as trustee) adj John BAILY. Wit: John W.
GRAYSON, Benjamin GRAYSON. Delv. to John F. ALLEN Admr. 19
May 1859.

3G:310   Date: 8 Dec 1823   RtCt: 5 Jan 1824
Hugh SMITH (trustee of John RALPH for debt to Jesse McVEIGH)
of Ldn to John MARKS of Ldn. B/S of 105a.

3G:311   Date: 26 Jul 1822   RtCt: 6 Jan 1824
Henry CLAGETT & wife Juliet of Ldn to Presley CORDELL of Ldn.
B/S of part of Lot #23 on S side of Market St in Lsbg adj Capt. John
HAMILTON, heirs of Lee DURHAM dec'd. Wit: John McCORMICK,
Saml. M. EDWARDS.

3G:313   Date: 22 Oct 1823   RtCt: 8 Jan 1824
Presley CORDELL & wife Amelia of Ldn to William D. DRISH of Ldn.
B/S of lot on S side of Market St. in Lsbg adj Capt. John
HAMILTON, reps of Lee DURHAM dec'd. Wit: John McCORMICK,
Saml. M. EDWARDS.

3G:314   Date: 1 Aug 1823   RtCt: 8 Jan 1824
Thomas BRABHAM Jr. of Ldn to Thomas BRABHAM Sr. of FredVa.
BoS for household items. Wit: H. W. BRABHAM, Sarah BRABHAM.

3G:315   Date: 8 Jan 1824   RtCt: 8 Jan 1824
William DRISH of Ldn to son John DRISH, John HAMMERLY & wife
Jane and William KIRK & wife Nancy (daus of William DRISH) of
Ldn. Gift of lot on W side of King St in Lsbg adj James L. MARTIN,
John McCORMICK, Henry CLAGETT (for William's use during his
lifetime).

3G:316   Date: 1 Jan 1824   RtCt: 9 Jan 1824
John SHAW of Lsbg to Joseph HILLIARD of Lsbg. LS of lot on Back
St in Lsbg (formerly leased to Benj. W. PERRY who did not pay).

3G:318   Date: 7 Jan 1824   RtCt: 9 Jan 1824
Samuel DUNKIN & wife Anne of Ldn to Stephen McPHERSON of
Ldn. B/S of 59a adj Isaiah MARKS, Edward B. GRADY, Samuel
SINCLAIR. Wit: N. C. WILLIAMS, John W. GRAYSON. Delv. to
McPHERSON 27 Mar 1829.

3G:319   Date: 23 Jun 1823   RtCt: 10 Jan 1824
Stephen T. BURSON & wife Rebecca of Ldn to Richard H.
HENDERSON of Ldn. Trust for debt to Charles Bird & Co of PhilPa
using 15a (cnvy/b Benjamin KENT. Wit: H. H. HAMILTON, Tho. R.
MOTT, Saml. M. EDWARDS, Leven LUCKETT, A. GIBSON. Delv.
to HENDERSON 13 Jan 1825.

3G:321   Date: 12 Jan 1824   RtCt: 12 Jan 1824
Norval CHAMBLIN, George MARKS & Mason CHAMBLIN. Bond on
CHAMBLIN as constable.

3G:321   Date: 12 Jan 1824   RtCt: 12 Jan 1824
Jared CHAMBLIN, Mason CHAMBLIN & Charles TAYLOR. Bond on Jared CHAMBLIN as constable.

3G:322   Date: 10 Jan 1824   RtCt: 10 Jan 1824
John CRIDLER & wife Elizabeth of Ldn to Edward HAMMAT of Ldn. Trust for Samuel M. EDWARDS as security in executions by Nathan GREGG, Jno. YOUNG's Admr., Arch'd MAINS using lot on N side of Market St in Lsbg where CRIDLER resides with 2-story house and wood house occupied by Danl. HOWELL and horse and household items. Wit: John H. McCABE, Presley CORDELL. Delv. to EDWARDS 4 Jan 1825.

3G:324   Date: 29 Oct 1823   RtCt: 12 Jan 1824
Reuben TRIPLETT dec'd. Division of 231¼a where he formerly lived adj __ GLASCOCK, __ BRONAUGH, __ GALLEHER, __ DUNKIN, __ JACOBS, __ WALKER – Lot #1 (12a) & wood lot #1 (6½a) to John TRIPLETT, Lot #2 (19a¼) & wood lot #2 (6½a) to John KEENE for use of John JOHNSTON, Lot #3 (32a) to Jos. EIDSON & wife Elizabeth late TRIPLETT, Lot #4 (25½a) to Malinda BOWERS, Lot #5 (26a) to W. ROSZEL & wife C. late TRIPLETT, Lot #6 (25¾a) to Willis TRIPLETT, Lot #7 (25¾) to Roderick TRIPLETT, Lot #8 (19¼a) & wood lot #8 (6½a) to Reuben TRIPLETT, Lot #9 (19¼a) & wood lot #9 (6½) to Thornton WALKER & wife Frances late TRIPLETT; and house & lot on main st in Mdbg to Felix TRIPLETT; house & lot on back st in Mdbg to ch/o Delilah CHURCH; house & lot in Union to Margaret TRIPLETT. Gives plat and details. Divisors: Ben MITCHELL Jr., Henry PLASTER, Daniel VERNON.

3G:327   Date: 21 Aug 1822   RtCt: 11 Jan 1824
Charles P. TUTT to Elizabeth SULLIVAN (wd/o Murtho SULLIVAN dec'd). A/L with Alexander WHITAKER to take off his corn crop but Elizabeth to seed there in the fall. Wit: Peyton R. PAGE, Geo. M. CHICHESTER.

3G:328   Date: 20 Dec 1823   RtCt: 12 Jan 1824
Daniel McGAHY & wife Dorcas of Ldn to Robert BARRATT of Ldn. B/S of 2a (prch/o Jacob KEMERLE). Wit: Saml. DAWSON, Thos. GASSAWAY.

3G:330   Date: 13 Jan 1824   RtCt: 13 Jan 1824
Valentine Frederick SHOVER with PoA from Henry SHOVER & Rosannah SHOVER (devisees of Adam SHOVER late of Ldn) of Union Co Ohio to George SHOVER of Ldn. B/S of 48½a Lot #2 in div. of Adam's estate. Delv. to SHOVER 5 Sep 1826.

3G:331   Date: 25 Jul 1823   RtCt: 9 Feb 1824
Henry SHOVER and Rosannah SHOVER of Union Co Ohio to Valentine Frederick SHOVER of Union Co Ohio. PoA.

3G:332   Date: 17 Oct 1823   RtCt: 9 Feb 1824
Joseph CO(O)MBS & wife Eleanor of Wayne Co Ohio to Sarah BROWN, Mariah NICHOLS, Phebe BROWN, John Harman BROWN, Martha Ann BROWN, William Harman BROWN and Mary Ann BROWN (ch/o Nathan BROWN dec'd of Ldn). B/S of 1/6 int. in 150a nr N Fork of Goose Creek from wll of Andrew COOMBS dec'd (COMBS sold to Marthan [Martha Ann?] BROWN). Wit: Bengamin GOWLEVOT, Lewis GUNSTOFF.

3G:334   Date: 19 Jan 1824   RtCt: 19 Jan 1824
Jacob WILLIAMS of DC to Enoch FRANCIS of Ldn. B/S of ¼a on Market St in Lsbg adj Charles BINNS (prch/o Francis TRIPLETT).

3G:335   Date: 28 Oct 1823   RtCt: 19 Jan 1824
Reuben MURRY of Fqr and Sydnor BAILEY of Ldn (trustees of John MARTIN for debt to Alex SEATON, Joseph CARR) to William BENTON of Ldn. B/S of 12a lot (cnvy/b James POWELL), 12a lot (cnvy/b Pierce NOLAND) and 12a (cnvy/b John KILE).

3G:336   Date: 17 Jan 1824   RtCt: 19 Jan 1824
Gainer PIERCE to Isaac and Samuel NICHOLS Trust for debt to Joseph HOGUE using carding machines and picker.

3G:337   Date: 29 Oct 1823   RtCt: 19 Jan 1824
William BENTON of Ldn to Reuben MURRY of Fqr. Trust for debt to Alexander SEATON using three 12a lots (prch/o heirs of Elisha POWELL).

3G:338   Date: 14 Jan 1824   RtCt: 17 Jan 1824
Samuel M. EDWARDS & wife Ann of Ldn to Robert BENTLY of Ldn. B/S of 67a in Diggs Valley (cnvy/b Jas. CAMPBELL to R. H. HENDERSON trustee for benefit of EDWARDS). Wit: Richard H. HENDERSON, E. G. HAMILTON, L. BEARD, John McCORMACK, John H. McCABE.

3G:340   Date: 17 Jan 1824   RtCt: 17 Jan 1824
John MARTIN of Ldn to John H. MONROE of Ldn. Trust for debt to John M. McCARTY using leased lot (14 Oct 1822, DBk FFF:147) on S side of Loudoun St in Lsbg adj Isaac HARRIS, reps of Mrs. COOPER. Delv. to S. M. BOSS pr McCARTY 23 Dec 1837.

3G:342   Date: 17 Dec 1823   RtCt: 16 Jan 1824
Yeoman William VICKERS & wife Anna of Ldn to Enoch TRIPLETT of Ldn. B/S of 100a (using relinquishment of bond executed by James MONTEITH in favour of Enoch TRIPLETT abt 1787 granting LS of 100a adj Joanna LEWIS, now acquired by VICKERS) adj late Mason FRENCH. Wit: William BRONAUGH, Francis W. LUCKETT.

3G:343   Date: 12 Jan 1824   RtCt: 7 Feb 1822
Edward B. GRADY of Ldn to Abel JANNEY of Ldn. B/S of 8a (part of tract formerly held by Mary OVERFIELD) adj Jehu BURSON, Martin OVERFIELD. Wit: E. G. HAMILTON, Samuel HAMMAT, Alfred A. ESKRIDGE. Delv. to JANNEY 20 Jan 1826

3G:344   Date: __ Sep 1823   RtCt: 7 Feb 1824
John A. BINNS (trustee of Isaac WRIGHT, DBk FFF:319) of Ldn to
John J. MATHIAS of Ldn. B/S of 13a on turnpike road adj Edward J.
LEE.

3G:345   Date: 16 Oct 1823   RtCt: 24 Jan 1824
Willis TRIPLETT of Ldn to Samuel BEAVERS of Ldn. B/S of 25¾a
Lot #6 in div. of land of Reuben TRIPLETT dec'd. Delv. to Thomas
BEAVERS Exor. of Samuel BEAVERS 16 Mar 1839.

3G:346   Date: 24 Jan 1824   RtCt: 24 Jan 1824
Daniel DEAKINS to Robert RUSSELL. Trust for debt to Christian
JACOBS using household items.

3G:347   Date: 24 Jan 1824   RtCt: 6 Feb 1824
George E. LLOYD & wife Ruth of Ldn to Samuel DUNKIN of Ldn.
B/S of 22a (prch/o Thomas KENT) adj poor house.

3G:348   Date: 23 Jan 1824   RtCt: 24 Jan 1824
William NOLAND to Samuel DAWSON. Receipt for payment in
deficiency of 14+a in purchase of supposed 303a.

3G:348   Date: 2 Feb 1824   RtCt: 6 Feb 1823
Charles WILLIAMS of Ldn to Samuel M. EDWARDS of Ldn. Trust
for debt to Elizabeth STEER and Samuel CLAPHAM (Admrs of
Isaac STEER dec'd) using negro man Oll alias Oliver, woman
Malinda & her child Sarna Lazette (allotted to WILLIAMS as share of
Isaac dec'd slaves in right of m. to dau. Mary STEER)

3G:350   Date: 2 Feb 1824   RtCt: 6 Feb 1824
Elenor STEER of Ldn to Samuel M. EDWARDS of Ldn. Trust for
debt to Elizabeth STEER & Samuel CLAPHAM (Admrs of Isaac
STEER dec'd) using negro woman Pat & her child Armstead, boy
Lewis, girl Malinda (allotted from estate of Isaac dec'd)

3G:352   Date: 20 Dec 1823   RtCt: 7 Feb 1824
David McGAHY of Ldn to Samuel DAWSON of Ldn. Trust for debt to
Thomas GASSAWAY using lot prch/o GASSAWAY. Wit: Samuel M.
EDWARDS, William JENNERS, Alfred A. ESKRIDGE.

3G:354   Date: 20 Dec 1823   RtCt: 7 Feb 1824
Robert BARRATT & wife Mary of Ldn to Samuel DAWSON of Ldn.
Trust for debt to Thomas GASSAWAY using 2a (cnvy/b David
McGAHY). Wit: Alfred A. ESKRIDGE, Alfred LUCKETT, Robt. H.
MATHIAS, Samuel M. EDWARDS, William JENNERS.

3G:356   Date: 4 Feb 1824   RtCt: 6 Feb 1824
Elizabeth BOLEN of Ldn to Nancy LOVETT of Ldn. B/S of lot in
Union (cnvy/b Samuel DUNKIN) adj Samuel TRAYHERN. Wit:
William DUNKEN, William M. LLOYD, Aaron BURSON, G. E.
LLOYD. Delv to Seth SMITH pr order 13 Mar 1833.

3G:357   Date: 3 Feb 1824   RtCt: 6 Feb 1824
George E. LLOYD of Ldn to William DUNKIN of Ldn. Trust for
Samuel DUNKIN as security for debt to John ROBERTS, Joseph
JANNEY, Henry SLADE using farm and household items.

3G:358   Date: 29 Mar 1823   RtCt: 23 Nov 1823/6 Feb 1824
Thomas KENT of Ldn to George E. LLOYD of Ldn. B/S of 21a adj
Peter HANN, George BURSON. Wit: Jacob SILCOTT, Joseph A.
LLOYD, William DUNKIN, William H. DORSEY, William TRIPLETT.

3G:360   Date: 12 Jan 1824   RtCt: 12 Jan 1824
Stephen G. ROSZEL of Ldn. DoE for negro girl Kuzziah abt 16y old
to be free after 1 Jan 1829, girl Susan abt 14y old to be free at end
of 1 Jan 1831.

3G:360   Date: 16 Jan 1824   RtCt: 16 Jan 1824
Matthew GATES of Ldn to George RICHARDS of Ldn. Trust for debt
to John SURGHENOR using household items. Delv. to
SURGHENOR 6 Sep 1825.

3G:361   Date: 14 Jan 1824   RtCt: 14 Jan 1824
Richard H. HENDERSON (trustee of James CAMPBELL, Jun 1819
DBk YY:350 for 130a in Diggs Valley) of Ldn to Samuel M.
EDWARDS of Ldn. B/S of 67a adj R. BENTLEY, __ GARRET. Wit:
E. G. HAMILTON, L. BEARD, A. A. ESKRIDGE. Delv. to EDWARDS
25 Mar 1853.

3G:363   Date: 20 Dec 1822   RtCt: ___
David CARTER to Sydnor BAILEY and Cuthbert POWELL. Trust for
debt to John JAMES using 92½a on N side of Goose Creek
(formerly belonging to Augustin[e] LOVE) on road from Lsbg to
Coe's Mill. Wit: Coldwell CARR, Peter CARR, John HANDY.

3G:365   Date: 21 Oct 1823   RtCt: 13 Jan 1824
Mathias HAYS & wife Rhoda of Ldn to Samuel TORBERT of Ldn.
B/S of 1a where he now lives adj Amos FERGUSON, James
SWARTS, road to Aldie (TORBERT to hawl HAYS, family & goods
to Ohio). Wit: Leven LUCKETT, Abner GIBSON.

3G:366   Date: 23 Sep 1823   RtCt: 13 Jan 1824
Jonah PEUGH of Ldn to Elisha PEUGH of Ldn. Trust for rent using
corn crop, carpentry tools. Wit: William BRONAUGH. Delv. to Saml.
PEUGH by order of R. BARTON __.

3G:367   Date: 13 Jan 1824   RtCt: 12 Jan 1824
Abraham VICKERS to Wm. VICKERS. Trust for Mary VICKERS as
security on bonds to B. WHITE using work horses.

3G:368   Date: 18 Oct 1823   RtCt: 12 Jan 1824
John VANANDER & wife Elizabeth of Ldn to William WILKINSON of
Ldn. B/S of int. in 10a of Thomas VANANDER dec'd. Wit: William
BRONAUGH, Francis W. LUCKETT. Delv. pr order __.

3G:369 Date: 4 Sep 1823 RtCt: 12 Jan 1824
John MOUNT & wife Mary Ann of Ldn to Ezekiel MOUNT of Ldn.
B/S of 3¾a (prch/o Fielding LYNN) adj Jesse BURSON. Wit: William
BRONAUGH, Francis W. LUCKETT.

3G:371 Date: 24 Aug 1823 RtCt: 13 Jan 1824
David CARTER of Ldn to Andrew B. McMULLEN of Ldn. B/S of 94a
adj Johnathan CARTER, Gainer PIERCE, Thomas BISCOE. Delv.
to John SINCLAIR pr order 27 Apr 1827.

3G:372 Date: __ Jan 1824 RtCt: 20 Jan 1824
William DEVAUGHN of Ldn to Charles W. D. BINNS of Ldn. Trust
for debt to Rebecca PASQUALL using household items.

3G:374 Date: 17 Jan 1824 RtCt: 20 Jan 1824
Samuel CLAPHAM (trustee of Jonas POTTS for debt to Jemimah
HOLLINGSWORTH, Sept 1804, DBk EE:343) of Ldn to David
WEATHERLY of Ldn. B/S of 217a (now property of John R. ADAMS
and Peter BEMANDAFFER, bought at auction by Thos. R. MOTT
and conveyed to WEATHERLY) adj __ ELGIN, Samuel TILLETT.
Delv. to WEATHERLY 21 Sep 1842.

3G:375 Date: 21 Jan 1824 RtCt: 21 Jan 1824
John DRISH (of William) of Ldn to John HAMMERLY of Ldn. B/S of
und. 1/3 of lot & house on W side of King st in Lsbg adj James F.
MARTIN, Dr. Henry CLAGETT, __ FADELEY, __ McCORMICK.

3G:376 Date: 5 Jan 1824 RtCt: 23 Jan 1824
Johnathan CARTER & wife Elizabeth of Ldn to Isaac NICHOLS Jr. &
James HOGE. Trust for debt to Isaac & Samuel NICHOLS using
192¼a on Goose Creek on road from Brown's Mill to beaverdam
and main road from Little river to Snickersville adj Francis WRENN,
Jesse HARRIS. Wit: William BRONAUGH, Francis W. LUCKETT.
Delv. to Saml. NICHOLS Exors 10 Nov 1825.

3G:379 Date: 22 Jan 1824 RtCt: 23 Jan 1824
John WRIGHT & wife Margaret of Ldn to Robert CAMPBELL of Ldn.
B/S of Lots #4, #7, #9, #10, part of #12, #13, #16, #19, #21, #24,
#27, & #30 nr Leesburg under LS from James HEREFORD dec'd to
Patrick CAVEN (dev. to Margaret SANFORD now WRIGHT by
James HEREFORD). Wit: John WHITE, Robert BRADEN. Delv. to
CAMPBELL 7 Nov 1826.

3G:380 Date: 20 Sep 1823 RtCt: 23 Jan 1824
Reuben SCHOOLEY and Thomas PHILIPS (Exors of David LACEY
dec'd) of Ldn to Richard H. HENDERSON of Ldn. B/S of 8a (from
estate of David dec'd) adj __ RICE, __ BINNS. Wit: E. G.
HAMILTON, Julious HAMILTON, A. A. ESKRIDGE.

3G:381 Date: 19 Jan 1824 RtCt: 19 Jan 1824
Enoch FRANCIS of Ldn to Jacob WILLIAMS. BoS for negro woman
Lucy a slave for life w/o said Jacob abt 45y old. Wit: John MOORE,
James SINCLAIR. Delv. to WILLIAMS ___.

3G:382 Date: 11 Oct 1823 RtCt: 28 Jan 1824
John J. MATHIAS (trustee of Wadsworth SHEPHERD Dec 1821, DBk DDD:358) of Ldn to William ALT of Ldn. B/S of 14¾a (prch/o ALT) adj David EVELIN.

3G:383 Date: 7 Nov 1823 RtCt: 30 Jan 1824
Joseph TAYLOR & wife Lydia of Ldn to Thomas NICHOLS and James McDANIEL. Trust for debt to heirs of Thomas HUGHES using land prch/o heirs of Thomas HUGHS dec'd Oct 1823. Wit: Ebenezer GRUBB, John WHITE.

3G:385 Date: 29 Jan 1824 RtCt: 4 Feb 1824
Johnathan COST of Ldn to Simon AKEY. Trust for debt to Simon AKEY using household items.

3G:386 Date: 3 Feb 1824 RtCt: 3 Feb 1824
Casper JOHNSON of Ldn to Adam BARR. Loan of farm and household items. First loan of Oct 1820, later added items bought at sale by constable Joseph HAWKINS, horse bought of Samuel TRIPLETT 3 Feb 1824.

3G:386 Date: 28 Jan 1824 RtCt: 2 Feb 1824
Matthew RUST & wife Patsey/Martha of Ldn to Hugh SMITH of Ldn. Trust for debt to Noble BEVERIDGE using land where RUST resides adj Sarah JONES, Owen SULLIVAN dec'd, Lewis BIRKIBY. Wit: Sydnor B. RUST, Burr POWELL, Abner GIBSON. Delv. to SMITH 13 Aug 1827.

3G:388 Date: 2 Feb 1824 RtCt: 6 Feb 1824
Joseph CRAVEN of Ldn to Samuel M. EDWARDS of Ldn. Trust for debt to Elizabeth STEER and Samuel CLAPHAM (Admrs of Isaac STEER dec'd) using slave woman Titus & her 3 children Lee, Dinah & James Wm. (allotted to CRAVEN from estate of Isaac dec'd in right of wife Hannah late STEER who has also died)

3G:390 Date: 20 Dec 1823 RtCt: 29 Jan 1824
Thomas GASSAWAY & wife Henrietta of Ldn to David McGAHY of Ldn. B/S of 3-4a (cnvy/b Jacob KEMERLY). Wit: Towns'd McVEIGH, A. A. ESKRIDGE, William JENNERS, Thomas SANDERS, Samuel EDWARDS. Delv. to McGAHY 8 Mar 1830.

3G:392 Date: 10 Dec 1823 RtCt: 30 Jan 1824
George LOVE (trustee of Mary LOVE d/o Augustine LOVE dec'd) to David CARTER. Release of trust on 28½a purchased by Andrew B. McMULLIN from CARTER.

3G:393 Date: 29 Jan 1824 RtCt: 1 Feb 1824
John SHAW of Lsbg to Henry DODEZ of Ldn. LS of lot on N side of Market St in Lsbg adj Bengamin MAULSBY.

3G:395 Date: 18 Jun 1823 RtCt: 30 Jan 1824
Margaret THOMAS w/o John THOMAS of Ldn to Lewis P. W. BALCH of Ldn. B/S of 138a (cnvy/b John SHAFER May 1815). Delv. to BALCH 21 Jan 1826.

3G:396   Date: 27 May 1823   RtCt: 24 Jan 1824
Mary HIXSON wd/o Reuben HIXON dec'd to Aaron MILLER. B/S of dower portions, subject to life estate, of lots from div. of estate of Reuben HIXON dec'd which Aaron has prch/o other heirs. Also signed by Catharine HIXON. Delv. to MILLER 6 Jun 1826.

3G:398   Date: 29 May 1820   RtCt: 9 Feb 1824
Betsey TEBBS of Dumfries in PrWm and John B. VASHON of Lsbg. Agreement – TEBBS delivered to VASHON negro woman Anne & her 2 children and VASHON to pay annually. Richard H. HENDERSON and John A. BINNS are security for these payments using the slaves. Trusts not to encumber the slaves.

3G:399   Date: 2 Feb 1824   RtCt: 6 Feb 1824
Moses DOWDELL of Ldn to Samuel M. EDWARDS. Trust for debt to Elizabeth STEER & Samuel CLAPHAM (Admrs of Isaac STEER dec'd) using negro man Lunnon & wife Nancy, boy Elias, woman Ann & her child Lunnon [?], girl Francis (DOWDELL's allotment from estate of Isaac dec'd).

3G:401   Date: 25 Feb 1824   RtCt: 5 Mar 1824
Charles ELGIN and Aaron SANDERS (trustees of George H. SINCLAIR dated Apr 1820) of Ldn to David COONRAD of Ldn. B/S of land SINCLAIR prch/o Mahlon JANNEY. Wit: Samuel M. EDWARDS, Bengamin SHREVE, E. G. HAMILTON, Bengamin SHREVE Jr., Henry PEERS.

3G:402   Date: 5 Dec 1823   RtCt: 6 Dec 1823/6 Mar 1824
Stephen W. ROSZEL of Ldn to Samuel M. EDWARDS of Ldn. Trust for debt to Anna ROSZEL (Admr of Stephen C. ROSZEL dec'd) using 360a 'mountain farm' (where Stephen W. resides) from Stephen C. dec'd adj Glebe land where John DUNN now resides and und. int. in 100-200a lot where his mother Sarah ROSZEL resides and und. int. as rep of brother Stephen C. ROSZEL dec'd in negro man Cyrus, Dick, Daniel, Ben, Bob, James, Samuel, woman Nancy, Susanna, Betsey, Phebe, Peggy & infant child Amey, Betty, boys Jacob, Moses, Henry, Anderson & Bill and girls Mary, Mahaly, Milly, Keziah, Fanny, Delilah, Syllia & Susanna and children Sarah, Ann, Elizabeth, Washington, Margaret, Ann and Rhoda and well as any bonds and notes. Wit: Robert HUNTER, Margret MARTIN, Eli OFFUTT. Delv. to EDWARDS 19 Jun 1828.

3G:404   Date: 21 Feb 1824   RtCt: 5 Mar 1824
Mahlon JANNEY & wife Rachael of Ldn to David COONRAD of Ldn. B/S of 150a (JANNEY sold land to George H. SINCLAIR in 1820 who gave in trust to Charles ELGIN & Aaron SANDERS who sold it to COONRAD) adj Abr. B. T. MASON. Wit: Samuel M. EDWARDS, Henry PEERS, Bengamin SHREVE, E. G. HAMILTON, B. SHREVE Jr., Thomas SANDERS.

3G:405   Date: 28 Feb 1824   RtCt: 2 Mar 1824

George TAVENER Jr. & wife Sarah (late SMALLWOOD wd/o Leven SMALLWOOD) of Ldn to Samuel M. EDWARDS of Ldn. Trust for debt to John THOMAS of Ldn using und. int. in estate of Leven SMALLWOOD dec'd (Sarah apptd guardian on 9 May 1814 for Emiline, Eleanorah, Amanda & Sarah Ann Smallwood orphans of Leven SMALLWOOD dec'd with Joseph PASTOR? & John THOMAS as her security). Wit: Jacob CRIDLER, Peter ISH, James MILLS, John H. McCABE, Presley CORDELL. Delv. to THOMAS 18 Oct 1833.

3G:407   Date: 17 Nov 1823   RtCt: 3 Mar 1824

Anthony CIMMINGS of Tuskaraura Co Ohio and John DAVIS & wife Rebecca late CIMMINGS of Harrison Co Ohio to Richard H. HENDERSON of Ldn. B/S of several lots in div. of estate of father Thomas CIMMINGS dec'd. Wit: James CHRISTY, John NIXON, Samuel PEEPELS. Delv. to HENDERSON 25 Dec 1835.

3G:409   Date: 28 Feb 1824   RtCt: 3 Mar 1824

Nathaniel MANNING of Ldn to William SUMMERS of Ldn. Trust for debt to Samuel BEANS (MANNING in arrears with customers of his flour mill William GRAHAM, Peter COST, John WRIGHT, Hezekiah SHAW, John KERNER, Jacob COST) using crops including on farm of Evan EVANS.

3G:410   Date: __ Feb 1824   RtCt: 13 Feb 1824

John CRIDLER of Ldn to Edward HAMMAT of Ldn. Trust for debt to Samuel M. BOSS using household items.

3G:411   Date: 20 Feb 1824   RtCt: 28 Feb 1824

Britton SANDERS to Samuel M. EDWARDS. Trust for debt to Samuel HOUGH & George L. LOCKLAND (Admrs of Silas WHERRY dec'd), Dr. John WILSON, Samuel CARR, Thomas BURGHBY, John GRAY, Enos WILDMAN & Elizabeth WHEERY using crops.

3G:412   Date: 12 Jan 1824   RtCt: 27 Feb 1824

Abiel JENNERS of Ldn to Charles DUGLASS of Ldn. Trust for debt to John GRAY using land prch/o heirs of William WRIGHT dec'd. Wit: Samuel M. EDWARDS, E. G. HAMILTON, Alfred A. ESKRIDGE.

3G:414   Date: 13 Jan 1824   RtCt: 23 Feb 1824

George SHOVER to James McILHANY. Trust for debt to Valentine F. SHOVER using 48½a (Lot #2 in div. of estate of Adam SHOVER dec'd).

3G:415   Date: 20 Feb 1824   RtCt: 21 Feb 1824

Samuel CHINN & wife Emily of Ldn to Noble BEVERIDGE of Ldn. B/S of 50a adj Maj. Burr POWELL, Mrs. CHILTON, Mrs. MIDDLETON. Wit: Burr POWELL, A. GIBSON.

3G:417   Date: 20 Dec 1823   RtCt: 20 Jan 1824
William NOLAND & wife Catharine of Ldn to Thomas TRIPLETT of
Ldn. B/S of 328a (Lot #7 allotted to Margaret TRIPLETT). Wit:
Thomas J. NOLAND, William H. NOLAND, Burr POWELL, Francis
W. LUCKETT.

3G:418   Date: 14 Feb 1824   RtCt: 17 Feb 1824
Thomas DRAKE of Ldn to James HOGE of Ldn. Trust for debt to
Henry ELLIS of Perry Co Ohio using 25a nr house where Phenias
THOMAS formerly lived, adj Stephen McPHERSON. Wit: N. C.
WILLIAMS, George MARKS, Garret WALKER. Delv. to Wm. HOGE
Admr of Jas. HOGE dec'd 14 Mar 1829.

3G:419   Date: 12 Dec 1823   RtCt: 12 Dec 1823/20 Feb 1824
John McCORMICK & wife Mary of Ldn to Thomas R. MOTT and
Benjamin SHREVE of Ldn. Trust for Richard H. HENDERSON as
endorser on notes for debts to Powhatan Manu. Co and George
Carsen & Co using 60a (prch/o David LACEY dec'd) in Kittockten
Mt. nr Lsbg adj Archibald MEANS and unoccupied brick house and
lot in Lsbg formerly occupied by Fielding BROWN. Wit: Samuel M.
EDWARDS, James H. HAMILTON.

3G:420   Date: 16 Feb 1824   RtCt: 16 Feb 1824
John BENEDUM & wife Mary of Ldn to Anthony CUMMINGS. B/S of
100a (cnvy/b Peter BENEDUM) adj William A. BINNS. Wit: Presley
CORDELL, Samuel M. EDWARDS. Delv. to CUMMINGS 1 Dec
1827.

3G:422   Date: 14 Feb 1824   RtCt: 14 Feb 1824
John BEATY of Ldn to Mandley T. RUST of Ldn. Loan of farm
animals, household items.

3G:422   Date: 28 Jan 1824   RtCt: 14 Feb 1824
Johnathan COST & wife Martha Ann of Ldn to Peter COST of Ldn.
B/S of house and lot (prch/o Josabed WHITE) adj Mahlon JANNEY,
William HOUGH, Mary FOX. Wit: Robert BRADEN, Samuel
HOUGH.

3G:423   Date: 15 Jan 1824   RtCt: 16 Feb 1824
William KIRK & wife Nancy of Guernsey Co Ohio to William D.
DRISH of Ldn. B/S of und. 1/3 int. in house & lot (recently owned by
William DRISH) on King St in Lsbg adj Jacob FADLEY, James L.
MARTIN. Delv. pr order 30 May 1825.

3G:425   Date: 10 Feb 1824   RtCt: 13 Feb 1824
John UTTERBACK & wife Catharine of Fqr to Hiram SEATON of
Ldn. B/S of 56a (allotted to Jemima FENTON and her children in div.
of land of John VIOLETT dec'd). Wit: William BRONAUGH, Francis
W. LUCKETT. Delv. to SEATON 21 Oct 1840.

3G:426   Date: 13 Feb 1824   RtCt: 112 Feb 1824
Edward DORSEY of Ldn to Abiel JENNERS and Robert BRADEN of
Ldn. Trust for debt to James D. FRENCH with Josabed WHITE,

Robert BRADEN, John McCORMICK, David SHAWON, Abiel JENNERS, John E. PALMER, John WRIGHT, James HIGDEN, John BRADEN, George Mason CHICHESTER and Samuel HOUGH as security using int. in lot in Wtfd prch/o Exors of Mahlon JANNEY dec'd. Delv. to J. BRADEN Ecr JENNERS & Jno. WRIGHT 31 Aug 1832.

3G:427   Date: 4 Feb 1824   RtCt: 9 Feb 1824
Amos FERGUSON of Ldn to Lewis BERKELEY of Ldn. B/S of 150a. Wit: William NOLAND, Daniel P. COONRAD, John BRITT, R. H. LITTLE. Delv. pr order 30 Apr 1825.

3G:428   Date: 18 Apr 1822   RtCt: 14 Feb 1824
John CRIDLER & wife Elizabeth of Lsbg to John DRISH of Lsbg. B/S of 14a (Lot #7 allotted Susannah FICHTER w/o Peter FICHTER in div. of estate of Jacob STONEBURNER, DBk YY:304) adj Dr. SELDON. Wit: William D. DRISH, G. Martin CORDELL, William ELGIN Jr.

3G:429   Date: 10 Feb 1824   RtCt: 10 Feb 1824
John BENEDUM of Ldn to James CARR of Ldn. Trust for debt to Anthony CUMMINGS and Thomas CARR using crops. Delv. to Thos. CARR Admr. of James CARR dec'd 8 Jan 1831.

3G:430   Date: 31 Jan 1823   RtCt: 8 Feb 1824
Peter SOUDER & wife Barbary of Ldn to John AMICK of Hanover Co Pa. B/S of 24a (from div. of lands of father Philip SOUDER). Wit: Abiel JENNER, Samuel DAWSON. Delv. to AMICK 6 Apr 1838.

3G:431   Date: 28 Jan 1824   RtCt: 9 Feb 1824
Henry THOMAS of Ldn to Benjamin MITCHELL Jr. of Ldn. Trust for debt to Thornton WALKER using slave woman Nancy THOMAS (prch/o John MITCHELL of Fqr who prch/o Col. George LOVE). Delv. to WALKER 19 Dec 1825.

3G:432   Date: 15 Jun 1823   RtCt: 9 Feb 1824
Daniel COOPER & wife Elizabeth of Ldn to Mary HAINES of Ldn. B/S of 14a (cnvy/b Thomas LESLIE) on SE side of Short Hill adj __ McILHANY, Samuel WILLIAMS. Wit: Samuel HOUGH, Abiel JENNERS.

3G:433   Date: 22 Dec 1823   RtCt: 12 Jab 1824
Benjamin B. THORNTON & wife Hannah of Ldn to Robert FULTON of Ldn. B/S of part of Lot #8 in Lsbg and part of adj lot formerly prop. of John WILDMAN & wife Elener. Wit: Wesley CARR, William JONES, William FULTON.

3G:435   Date: 30 Oct 1823   RtCt: 9 Feb 1824
Elias LACEY & wife Mary P. of Ldn to Naomi LACEY, Huldah LACEY and Ruth LACEY of Ldn. B/S of int. in estate of Tacy LACEY dec'd late of Ldn. Wit: Lewis M. SMITH, Richard H. NEALL, Misheck LACEY, Burr POWELL, Abner GIBSON.

3G:436   Date: 10 Feb 1823   RtCt: 12 Mar 1824
Adam SHOVER dec'd. Division – Lot #1 (33a) and Lot #7 wood lot
(9a) to Adam SHOVER, Catharine SHETMAN w/o John SHETMAN,
George SHOVER & Catharine [also given as Charlotte] SHOVER
ch/o George SHOVER dec'd, Lot #2 (48½a) and Lot #9 (4a) and Lot
#10 wood lot (13½a) to Henry SHOVER, Lot #3 (47½a) to John
SHOVER, Jacob SHOVER, Mary Magdelen [also given as Mary
Nancy Daline] SHOVER, Elizabeth SARBAUGH w/o John
SARBAUGH, Adam SHOVER, Sopha SHOVER and George
SHOVER ch/o Simon SHOVER dec'd, Lot #4 (45a) and Lot #11
(13½a short hill) to Simon SHOVER, Sophia ROWSEY w/o Daniel
ROWSEY, Catharine WILLER w/o Henry WILLER and Barbara
SHOVER ch/o Peter SHOVER dec'd, Lot #5 (48a) and Lot #8 (4a) to
Mary MICHAEL, Lot #6 (46a) to Susan SHOVER. Gives plat.
Divisors: R. BRADEN, John S. MARLOW.

3G:439   Date: 17 Jan 1824   RtCt: 9 Feb 1824
Usher SKINNER of Ldn to William BRONAUGH of Ldn. Trust for
negroes Abea her dau Fianthe? & son Simon, Fanny and her son
Howard a boy abt 1y old, horses, sundry items.

3G:440   Date: 31 Jan 1823   RtCt: 9 Feb 1824
Anthony SOUDER & wife Lucucey/Lucrecy? of Ldn to Elizabeth
SOUDER of Ldn. B/S of 25a Lot #3 adj Elizabeth with 4a Lot #7 on
Catoctin Mt (from div. of father Philip SOWDERS). Wit: Abiel
JENNERS, Samuel DAWSON. Delv. to Peter WINE husband of
Eliz'th 21 May 1825.

3G:441   Date: 31 Jan 1824   RtCt: 9 Feb 1824
Peter SOUDER & wife Barbary of Ldn to Michael SOUDER of Ldn.
B/S of 99a 6a and 7a (bought or allotted from father Philip SOUDER
and formerly owned by Catharine COST?). Wit: Samuel DAWSON,
Abiel JENNERS. Delv. to Michael SOUDER 19 May 1827.

3G:443   Date: 21 Jan 1824   RtCt: 9 Jan 1824
Samuel LESLIE (Exor of Thomas LESLIE dec'd) of Ldn to Daniel
and Patrick BOLAND of Ldn. BoS for negro Lucinda abt 12y old.
Wit: John CRIM, Eliza B. COGSILL..

3G:444   Date: 2 Feb 1824   RtCt: 9 Feb 1824
Richard H. HENDERSON (trustee of Edward DORSEY of Wtfd, Oct
1822) of Lsbg to Conrad BITZER of Ldn. B/S of two adj lots with
brick house in Wtfd. Delv. to BITZER 29 Apr 1825.

3G:444   Date: 31 Jan 1823   RtCt: 9 Feb 1824
Michael SOUDER & wife Susanna of Ldn to mother Susanna
SOUDER of Ldn. B/S of 24a Lot #1 and 4a mt. Lot #6 in div. of lands
of father Philip SOUDERS. Wit: Abiel JENNERS, Samuel DAWSON.

3G:446   Date: 29 Nov 1823   RtCt: 9 Feb 1824
William NOLAND & wife Catharine of Ldn to Naomai LACEY,
Huldah LACEY and Ruth LACEY of Ldn. B/S of Lot #62, #63 and

part of #64 in Aldie (between lot of mother Matilda LACEY and Lot #61 of Thomas J. NOLAND). Wit: Thomas ROBINSON, James SWART, James T. RUST, Burr POWELL, Abner GIBSON.

3G:447 Date: 9 Feb 1824 RtCt: 9 Feb 1824
John A. BINNS & wife Mary Maria of Ldn to Edmund LOVETT of Ldn. B/S of ½a Lot #9 in new settlement of Mt. Gilead. Wit: John McCORMICK, Thomas SANDERS. Delv. pr order 7 Mar 1825.

3G:448 Date: 30 Aug 1823 RtCt: 9 Feb 1824
Thornton WALKER & wife Fanny of Ldn to Malinda BOWERS of FredVa. B/S of lot in Union (cnvy/b Caleb N. GALLAHER). Wit: William BRONAUGH, John W. GRAYSON.

3G:450 Date: 9 Feb 1824 RtCt: 9 Feb 1824
Joshua GORE of Ldn to heirs of John EVANS dec'd late of Ldn. Release of trust of 1814 (DBk SS:40) for debt to Isaac & Samuel NICHOLS (other trustee Thomas GREGG is now dec'd).

3G:451 Date: 5 Feb 1820 RtCt: 8 Mar 1824
John MOORE. Commission as Capt in 56th Reg 6th Brig 2nd Div of Va Militia. Delv. 29 May 1827.

3G:451 Date: 12 Mar 1824 RtCt: 12 Mar 1824
Edward HAMMAT and John H. MONROE. Bond on HAMMAT as constable.

3G:451 Date: 12 Mar 1824 RtCt: 12 Mar 1824
Samuel HAMET and Robert BENTLEY. Bond on HAMET as constable.

3G:452 Date: 8 Mar 1824 RtCt: 8 Mar 1824
George RUST. Qualification as Brigadier General of 6th Brig 2nd Div of Va Militia.

3G:452 Date: 27 Feb 1824 RtCt: 28 Feb 1824
John CRIDLER to Samuel M. EDWARDS. Trust for debt to James GARNER using horse.

3G:453 Date: 28 Feb 1824 RtCt: 3 Mar 1824
Nathaniel MANNING of Ldn to Joshua OSBURN and William SUMMERS of Ldn. Trust for debt to James NIXON, Daniel EACHES, WHITE and CLENDENING, James SHIRLEY, Isaac SHOWALTER, Carver WILLIS, Beverley WAUGH, Ebenezer GRUBB, Sarah NIXON, David POTTS, William TAYLOR, Presley CORDELL, Thomas PHILIPS, Morris OSBURN, Mary FOX, Patrick McGARICK, William BROWN, James McGARICK, Walter WOODYARD, Paxton BEANS, __ DILLOW, Isaac WALKER, Christopher GROOVER, Peter DEMORY, John WRIGHT, Joshua OSBURN, David LOVETT using 180a (cnvy/b George JANNEY and __ EACHES) adj John WRIGHT, Robert BRADEN, Joseph LEWIS and int. in estate of David LACEY dec'd and claims agst Thomas GRIGGS and Lsbg Turnpike Co stock and household items. Wit:

John WHITE, Craven OSBURN. Delv. pr order to Jno. JANNEY 25 Aug 1825.

3G:455   Date: 9 Mar 1824   RtCt: 9 Mar 1824
Joseph HAWKINS, Daniel LOVETT, John A. BINNS and William SWART. Bond on HAWKINS as constable.

3G:455   Date: 29 Jan 1824   RtCt: 9 Feb 1824
George W. SHAWEN & wife Jane of Ldn to David SHAWEN of Ldn. B/S of int. in 143a¼a (purchased by Cornelius SHAWEN now dec'd their father of Peter SANDERS in Dec 1815) and int. 38a (cnvy/b Aaron SANDERS after death of Cornelius) adj Chas. P. TUTT, Chas. F. MERCER, Aaron SANDERS, William GREGG, Samuel & Isaac NICHOLS. Wit: Robert BRADEN, Samuel HOUGH. Delv. to Saml M. EDWARD 26 Jul 1839.

3G:457   Date: 6 Jan 1824   RtCt: 9 Feb 1824
George RICHARDS (trustee of William MISKELL, May 1823) of Ldn to John A. BINNS of Ldn. B/S of ½a Lot #9 in new settlement of Mt. Gilead.

3G:458   Date: 15 Feb 1823   RtCt: 9 Feb 1824
David LOVETT of Ldn to Alexander CORDELL of Ldn. B/S of ½a Lot #16 & #17 (cnvy/b Peter R. BEVERLY). Wit: Samuel TURNER, Turner OSBURN, John BALL.

3G:459   Date: 19 Jul 1823   RtCt: 9 Feb 1824
Thomas TORBERT & wife Mary of Ldn to John TORBERT of Ldn. B/S of 1½a adj Thomas A. HEREFORD, Joseph FRED (part of 14a recovered from Jenkin PHILIPS by Samuel BUTCHER s/o Samuel dec'd). Wit: Bengamin GRAYSON, John W. GRAYSON. Delv. to Jno. TORBERT 31 Nov 1831.

3G:461   Date: 12 Jun 1823   RtCt: 9 Feb 1824
William VICKERS of Ldn to son-in-law John G. HUMPHREY of Ldn. Gift of negro girl Harriet 7y old (given to HUMPHREY when he m. dau. Mary).

3G:461   Date: 1 Apr 1824   RtCt: 1 Apr 1824
Martin CORDELL & wife Martha of Ldn to Alexander CORDELL of Ldn. B/S of lot in Lsbg (prch/o John DRISH) on road from Lsbg to Nolland's Ferry on Potomac, adj John MANSFIELD, __ DRISH. Wit: Wm. ELLZY, Wm. F. HARRISON.

3G:463   Date: 10 Mar 1824   RtCt: 11 Mar 1824
Peter BENEDUM & wife Catherine of Ldn to Elisabeth BENEDUM w/o Henry BENEDUM, Sarah Ann BENEDUM, Manuel BENEDUM, William Henry BENEDUM and Mary Catherine BENEDUM ch/o Elizabeth and Henry of Ldn. B/S of 49a adj __ VIRTZ, __ CUMMINGS. Wit: John W. GRAYSON, Saml. M. EDWARDS. Delv. to Elizabeth 3 Aug 1839.

3G:464   Date: 31 Jan 1824   RtCt: 9 Feb 1824
William NOLAND & wife Catherine of Ldn to James SWART of Ldn. B/S of 140a. Delv. to SWART 23 Apr 1833.

3G:465   Date: 9 Feb 1824   RtCt: 9 Mar 1824
Nathaniel MANNING & wife Euphemia of Ldn to James COPELAND of Ldn. B/S of 2a (part of tract prch/o George JANNEY) adj John WRIGHT. Wit: Robert BRADEN, John WHITE. Delv. to H. ADAMS pr order 14 Apr 1832.

3G:467   Date: 10 Mar 1824   RtCt: 10 Mar 1824
Peter BENEDUM & wife Catherine of Ldn to Henry BENEDUM of Ldn. B/S of 105a (less 3a conveyed to Jacob CONWELL) adj Charles BINNS, Wm. A. BINNS. Wit: John W. GRAYSON, Saml. M. EDWARDS.

3G:468   Date: 10 Mar 1824   RtCt: 10 Mar 1824
Charles BINNS & wife Hannah of Ldn to Charles W. D. BINNS of Ldn. Gift of lot on Loudoun St in Lsbg adj Charles GULATT.

3G:468   Date: 10 Mar 1824   RtCt: 10 Mar 1824
Henry BENEDUM & wife Elisabeth of Ldn to Robert R. HOUGH of Ldn. Trust of 102a (cnvy/b Peter BENEDUM) for benefit of Catharine BENEDUM w/o Peter then for Maria QUICK and Manuel BENEDUM of Ldn or Maria's son Armistead T. QUICK. Delv. to R. R. HOUGH 27 Mar 1827.

3G:469   Date: 3 Apr 1824   RtCt: 5 Apr 1824
Benjamin WAR of Ldn to George W. FRENCH. Trust for debt to James D. FRENCH using household items.

3G:470   Date: 17 Jan 1824   RtCt: 9 Feb 1824
Mathew RUST of Ldn to Sydnor B. RUST of Ldn. LS of 435a on Little River where Mathew lives (25a under lien to Frederick BROOKS and 205a under incumbrance of trust for benefit of James RUST) and negroes Nanncy?, Charles, Peter, Jerry, George, Fenton and Napoleon and farm and household items. Wit: Danl. MARMADUKE, Stephen J. BURSON, John DOWDELL. Delv. to Sydnor B. RUST 15 Sep 1827.

3G:471   Date: 9 Feb 1824   RtCt: 9 Feb 1824
Edward DORSEY & wife __ of Wtfd to Joseph MEADE of Ldn. Trust to D. Shff Benjamin SHREVE Sr. for executions by Richard SLADE ass'ee of Jesse GROVES, Jesse GROVES ass'ee of George W. HENRY?, Wm. PAXSON and Jacob R. THOMAS, Henry GUNNEL Admr wwa of Robert GUNNELL dec'd, James D. FRENCH using lot prch/o Charles ELLGIN Apr 1818, and ½a adj Presbyterian meeting house and 1½a adj Wm. KETTLE, John MORROW, Robert BRADEN and int. in grist and saw mills.

3G:473   Date: 13 Mar 1824   RtCt: 13 Mar 1824
Peter BENEDUM to Robert R. HOUGH Trust for debt to Henry BENEDUM using farm and household items.

3G:474   Date: 20 Mar 1824   RtCt: 22 Mar 1824
George K. FOX & wife Jane of Ldn to Samuel M. EDWARDS of Ldn.
Trust for debt to Samuel M. BOSS using ¼a (cnvy/b by Saml. G.
HAMILTON) on S side of Cornwall St in Lsbg adj John BENTON,
Wm. DOWLING. Delv. to BOSS 9 Mar 1833.

3G:475   Date: 13 Mar 1824   RtCt: 13 Mar 1824
John WALKER & wife Abigail of Ldn to Jonathan EWERS of Ldn.
B/S of 13¾a (prch/o Edward CATING Sept 1817) adj Jessee
HUMPHREY.

3G:476   Date: 15 Oct 1823   RtCt: 8 Mar 1824
Samuel COCKREL & wife Elisabeth of Ldn to Valentine JACOBS of
Ldn. B/S of 11¾a between short hill and Blue Ridge adj Peter
JACOBS, Elisabeth JACOBS. Wit: David CUNNARD, Thomas
KIDWELL, Peter JACOBS. Delv. to JACOBS 6 Jun 1831.

3G:477   Date: 18 Feb 1824   RtCt: 12 Apr 1824
Samuel RICHARDS of Ldn to Hannah TRIPLETT of Ldn. Trust of
household items for use by Micaijah TRIPLETT.

3G:478   Date: 13 Dec 1823   RtCt: 12 Apr 1824
Gainer PIERCE of Ldn to William J. BRONAUGH of Ldn. Trust for
debt to Henry ELLIS, Garret WALKER using farm items, carding
machine. William BRONAUGH, Joseph Wm. BRONAUGH, Geo. W.
BRONAUGH.

3G:478   Date: 6 Sep 1823   RtCt: 12 Apr 1824
James W. DOWNING to John K. LITTLETON. BoS for slaves Peter
& wife Hannah and their children, Evline, Armstead and Susan. Wit:
Sydnor BALEY, Lenoard [Leonard] R. POSTON, James KEAN.
Delv. to LITTLETON 4 Nov 1825.

3G:479   Date: 9 Feb 1824   RtCt: 12 Apr 1824
Nathaniel MANNING & wife Euphemia of Ldn to Andrew
THOMPSON of Ldn. B/S of 30a (part of land prch/o George
JANNEY) adj William SUMMERS, John WRIGHT. Wit: Robert
BRADEN, John WHITE.

3G:480   Date: 24 Mar 1824   RtCt: 12 Apr 1824
Henry STEVENS & wife Eleanor of Ldn to James L. McKENNY of
Ffx. B/S of 33a with grist and saw mill on Broad Run known as
Clifton Mills in exchange for 227a in PrWm). Wit: Johnston
CLEVELAND, Abiel JENNERS. Delv. to Thomson F. MASON 6 Sep
1825.

3G:482   Date: 28 Nov 1823   RtCt: 12 Apr 1824
David CARTER of Ldn to James McCRAY of Ldn. B/S of 1¾a
(cnvy/b Alfred CLEMM in 1820) on road from Schoffields Mill to
Lsbg.

3G:482   Date: 15 Nov 1817   RtCt: 13 Apr 1824
Benjamin TRACY & wife Nancy, Evritt TRACY & wife Thamer of Ldn
to James NICHOLS of Ldn. B/S of 152a (from George NICHOLS

dec'd f/o the wives, subject to right of dower). Wit: Joshua OSBORN, John WHITE.

3G:483 Date: 2 Feb 1824 RtCt: ___
Abner HUMPHREY of Ldn to Joshua OSBURN of Ldn. Trust for benefit of Margaret HUMPHREY w/o Marcus HUMPHREY of Ldn using negro man Jim. Wit: John G. HUMPHREY, Abner G. HUMPHREY, Thomas J. HUMPHREY.

3G:484 Date: 25 ___ 1824 RtCt: 14 Apr 1824
Roderick TRIPLETT & wife Mary of Ldn to Samuel BEAVERS of Ldn. B/S of 25¾a (Lot #7 in div. of lands of Reuben TRIPLETT dec'd) adj David GALLAHER. Wit: W. BRONAUGH, Francis W. LUCKETT. Delv. to Thomas BEAVERS Exor. of Saml. 16 Mar 1839.

3G:486 Date: 6 Mar 1824 RtCt: 14 Apr 1824
Charles TRUSSEL to John FLEMING. Relinquishes rights to estate of Archibald FLEMING Sr. dec'd. Wit: William FLEMING, Jesse FLEMING. Delv. to FLEMING 8 Aug 1826.

3G:486 Date: 18 Jul 1822 RtCt: 10 May 1824
George MULL & wife Catherine of Warner Co Ohio to William WOODFORD of Ldn. B/S of 157a adj Michael COOPER, George SHOEMAKER, Siman SHOEMAKER. Wit: John MARTIN, John M. HOUSTON, Benjamin SAGER.

3G:487 Date: 6 Jan 1824 RtCt: 14 Apr 1824
George SMITH & wife Eve of Ldn to Absalom VANVACTOR of Ldn. B/S of 1a between short hill and Blue Ridge adj Mathias PRINCE. Wit: Ebenezer GRUBB, John WHITE. Delv. to VANVACTOR 7 Oct 1826.

3G:488 Date: 15 Apr 1824 RtCt: 15 Apr 1824
David CARTER of Ldn to Shff John ROSE. Conveys int. in deed of trust from CARTER to Daniel VERNON and William BRONAUGH dated Oct 1823, DBk GGG:207.

3G:489 Date: 19 Apr 1824 RtCt: 20 Apr 1824
William RICHARDS & wife Lydia of Ldn to John RICHARDS and George M. GRAYSON of Ldn. Trust for debt to John W. CLARK, Abel GOURLY, Jesse RICHARDS, Isaac RICHARD & Thomas RICHARDS using 121¼a (cnvy/b Benjamin GRAYSON) on Beaverdam adj John NICHOLLS. Wit: Benjamin GRAYSON, John W. GRAYSON. Delv. to Seth SMITH pr order 9 Oct 1848.

3G:490 Date: 16 Apr 1824 RtCt: 21 Apr 1824
Benjamin DANIEL & wife Sydney of Ldn to Stacy TAYLOR and Joshua PANCOAST of Ldn. Trust for debt to Joshua GREGG using 106½a adj John LOVE. Wit: Craven OSBURNE, John WHITE. Delv. to PANCOAST 14 May 1827.

3G:492 Date: 23 Apr 1824 RtCt: 23 Apr 1824
Yardley TAYLOR & wife Hannah and Betsey BROWN (daus. of Richard BROWN dec'd as is Sarah w/o Benjamin BROWN) of Ldn to

Benjamin BROWN of Ldn. B/S of und. 2/3s of lands of Richard BROWN dec'd who prch/o William ROBERTS, adj __ VANDEVER. Wit: John McCORMACK, Saml. M. EDWARDS. Delv. to Benj. BROWN 20 Nov 1829.

3G:493 Date: 26 Apr 1824 RtCt: 26 Apr 1824
Gainer PIERCE of Ldn to James HOGE of Ldn. Trust for debt to Isaac & Samuel NICHOLS using 1a adj lot with house where George LAMBERT resides, James SWART and 5¼a. Wit: Aron BURSON. Delv. to Saml. NICHOLS Exors 10 Nov 1825.

3G:494 Date: 10 Jan 1824 RtCt: 26 Apr 1824
Samuel TORBET of Fqr to Gainer PIERCE of Ldn. B/S of 1a (cnvy/b Mathias HAYS) where George LAMBERT lives adj Amos FERGUSON, James SWART, road to Aldie and 5¼a adj lot. Delv. to PIERCE 15 Nov 1825.

3G:495 Date: 2 Feb 1824 RtCt: 29 Apr 1824
Richard H. HENDERSON (trustee of Edward DORSEY, Oct 1822) of Lsbg to William CLINE of Lsbg. B/S of lot in Wtfd adj William H. HOUGH.

3G:497 Date: 30 Apr 1824 RtCt: 30 Apr 1824
Honor TILLET of Ldn to dau. Peggy TILLET of Ldn. Gift of negro boy slave for life Jesse s/o Fanny abt 5y old and to grandsons Giles Erasmus TILLET & Samuel TILLET sons of her son Samuel A. TILLET featherbed and some furniture. Wit: Saml. CARR, Jno. MOOR, James F. NEWTON.

3G:496 Date: 30 Apr 1824 RtCt: 30 Apr 1824
Eli BOWLING/BOLON of Ldn to Thomas JONES of Ldn. Trust for debt to Rich. JONES using negro slave Dotio?, farm animals, furniture.

3G:497 Date: 30 Apr 1823 RtCt: 30 Apr 1824
Joel OSBURN of Ldn to George RUST Jr of Ldn. Release of trust for debt to Morris OSBURN in Apr 1823, DBk EEE:99.

3G:498 Date: 30 Apr 1824 RtCt: 30 Apr 1824
Henry CLAGETT of Ldn to George RUST Jr of Ldn. Release of trust of Jun 1820 for debt to William T. T. MASON and Thomson MASON (Exors of A. T. MASON) using 503a.

3G:499 Date: __ Apr 1823 RtCt: 1 May 1824
John CARR of Ldn to George RUST Jr of Ldn. Release of trust of May 1819, DBk ZZ:284, for debt to Joseph CALDWELL using 323a.

3G:499 Date: 5 May 1824 RtCt: 8 May 1824
Samuel DUNKIN & wife Anna of Ldn to Price JACOBS of Ldn. B/S of 89a nr Union adj Henery PLASTER, Capt. Benjamin MITCHEL, Elisabeth HAWLEY. Wit: Wm. BRONAUGH, John W. GRAYSON. Delv. to JACOBS 10 Nov 1830.

3G:501   Date: 10 Jan 1824   RtCt: 11 May 1824
Casper ECKHART dec'd. Division – Lot #1 (188a) to widow Ann ECKHART, Lot #2 (128a) with mill to ___. Suit of John HEIS & wife Catherine late COOPER, Adam COOPER & Geo. Cooper agst widow Ann ECKHART. Discovered that 100a of land cnvy/b Elisha GREGG in Feb 1798 to ECKHART – Ann entitled to half. Gives plat. Divisors Aaron SANDERS, Charles ELGIN, Wm. GIBSON.

3G:503   Date: 9 Jun 1823   RtCt: 7 May 1824
John T. STRIDER of Ldn to Tolliver P. GRANTHEM. Trust on household items, interests in estate of Henery NY[SW]ANGER Sr. dec'd and Thomas NISWANGER dec'd and Catherine NISWANGER and stone house on NE side of said estate. Wit: William GREEN, E. G. HAMILTON, Henry PEERS, Alfred A. ESKRIDGE. Delv. to pr GRANTHAM's order 14 Nov 1825.

3G:504   Date: 2 Jan 1824   RtCt: 5 May 1824
Thomas SANDERS of Ldn to Henry SANDERS at present of U.S. Army. B/S of lot (cnvy/b Wm. AUSTIN, DBk UU:265) in Lsbg with building occupied by Enos WILDMAN as tavern adj Saml. CARR, __ BOSS, __ McCABE. Delv. to Henry SAUNDERS 5 Oct 1846.

3G:505   Date: 1 May 1824   RtCt: 3 May 1824
Middleton ROBY to James B. WILSON. Trust for debt to John BURSON using household items.

3G:505   Date: 24 Apr 1824   RtCt: 10 May 1824
John McCORMACK by PoA from Nancy JOHNSON of Ldn. Col for slave Mary abt 10y old of yellow complexion, born and raised in St. Marys Co Md.

3G:506   Date: 10 May 1824   RtCt: 10 May 1824
John BOYD, John BRADY & Amos FERGUSON. Bond on BOYD as constable.

3G:506   Date: 15 Jan 1821   RtCt: 12 Feb 1821/10 May 1824
Robert ARMSTEAD of Ldn to John G. HISLOP of Petersburg, Dinwiddie Co Va and Richard H. HENDERSON of Ldn. Trust for benefit of Frances ARMISTEAD (will of Mrs. Isabella HISLOP dated 27 Sep 1820 beq. to Frances ARMSTEAD w/o Robert all her estate during her lifetime). Wit: Edmund TYLER, Elias LACEY, Colin M. BRISCOE.

3G:507   Date: 8 Jan 1824   RtCt: 10 May 1824
Catherine DYER now resident of Va. Col for negro man Abraham abt 28y old, girl Marian abt 15y old (both born and raised in MontMd), woman Peg alias Margaret abt 47 or 48y old (born and raised in Charles Co Md).

3G:507   Date: 6 May 1824   RtCt: ___
George COOPER of Ldn. DoE for slave woman Virgin abt 38y old, her dau. Patty 7y old and her 2 other children Sal abt 4y old and Polly abt 2y old.

3G:507   Date: 6 May 1824   RtCt: ___
Ann ECKHART of Ldn. DoE for slave woman Milly abt 18y old, Jane
9y old, Lewis 3y old and Mary turning 1y old.

3G:508   Date: 12 Nov 1823   RtCt: 8 May 1824
Timothy TAYLOR & Stacy TAYLOR trustee and Robert RUSSEL
Exor of Samuel RUSSEL dec'd of Ldn to Thomas NICHOLLS of
Ldn. Release of trust of Oct 1817. Wit: Geo. H. ALDERS, Joel
CRAVEN, Wm. WILSON.

3G:509   Date: 18 Apr 1820   RtCt: 12 Apr 1824
Thomas H. KIRBY of Ldn to Thomas J. NOLAND of Ldn. Trust for
debt to William NOLAND of Ldn using Lot #39, #40, #41 & #42 in
Aldie (cnvy/b William NOLAND).

3H:001   Date: 26 Mar 1824   RtCt: 26 Mar 1824
Henry CLAGETT & wife Juliet/Julia of Ldn to Henry SAUNDERS
(now of the U.S. Army) of Ldn. B/S of part of Lot #14 in Lsbg (cnvy/b
Wm. WOODDY Mar 1806, DBk GG:276) with 2 story framed house
on N side of Loudoun St. between Bernard HOUGH and James L.
MARTIN. Wit: John McCORMICK, Thomas SAUNDERS.

3H:003   Date: 31 Jan 1824   RtCt: 9 Mar 1824
Joshua GREGG and Lewis LYDER of Ldn to Nicholas OSBURNE of
Ldn. Release of trust of Mar 1818 on 125a for debt to James
WARFORD. Wit: N. C. WILLIAMS, Joshua PANCOAST, Stephen
McPHERSON.

3H:004   Date: 6 Mar 1814   RtCt: 26 Mar 1824
Thomas CHINN Sr. & wife Ann H. of Ldn to Richard H.
HENDERSON of Ldn. Trust for debt to Amos JOHNSON of Fqr
using 95a where CHINN now resides adj Ashbys Gap turnpike road,
Reuben MURRAY, Samuel CHINN, H. B. POWELL. Wit: Edwin C.
BROWN, Enos W. NEWTON, A. G. TEBBET.

3H:006   Date: 27 Mar 1824   RtCt: 27 Mar 1824
John CRIDELER/CRIDLER of Ldn to Edward HAMMAT of Ldn.
Trust for debt to David OGDEN of Ldn using household items.

3H:007   Date: 22 Dec 1818   RtCt: 27 Mar 1824
John SIMPSON & wife Nancy of Ldn to brother French SIMPSON of
Ldn. B/S of 20½a (cnvy/b brother James SIMPSON) adj French,
Samuel SIMPSON, ___ LOVETT. Wit: John JONES, Edmund
LOVETT, John LUM, John McCORMICK, Saml. M. EDWARDS.

3H:009   Date: 22 Dec 1818   RtCt: 27 Mar 1824
French SIMPSON & wife Elizabeth of Ldn to brother John SIMPSON
of Ldn. B/S of 3a (allotted from will of mother Mary SIMPSON
dec'd). Wit: Edmund LOVETT, John LUM, John McCORMICK,
Saml. M. EDWARDS.

3H:010   Date: 16 Oct 1823   RtCt: 12 Apr 1824
Gov. James PLEASANTS Jr. to James L. McKENNA. Patent -
survey made 8 May 1821, warrant #6959 issued 13 Nov 1820,

grants 20a including 8 islands in Broad run. Delv. to Thomson MASON 6 Sep 1825.

3H:011   Date: 11 Sep 1805   RtCt: 12 Feb 1824
Thomas Ludwell LEE and Landon CARTER (Exor of George CARTER dec'd of StafVa) of RichVa to John DRISH of Ldn. B/S of 8a on N side of Loudoun St in Lsbg. Wit: John LYONS, John B. RATHIE, Jno. MATHIAS. Delv. to DRISH 27 Feb 1827.

3H:013   Date: 12 Oct 1822   RtCt: 27 Mar 1824
William MORAN Sr. DoE for negro man John abt 40y old. Wit: R. H. HENDERSON, Hy. H. HAMILTON.

3H:014   Date: 21 Dec 1816   RtCt: 11 Aug 1817/29 Mar 1824
Ch. J. LOVE to John HUTCHISON. B/S of 6a adj John KEMBLER, heirs of Maj. F. TURNER. Wit: Lewis AMBLER, Thomas HUTCHISON, John BRAGG. Delv. pr order 1 Apr 1828.

3H:014   Date: 27 Dec 1823   RtCt: 12 Apr 1824
Elezeir B. COGSIL. Oath as Lt. in 56th Reg 6th Brig. 2nd Div. of Militia of Va.

3H:015   Date: 9 Feb 1824   RtCt: 29 Mar 1824
Townshend McVEIGH (trustee of James T. RUST) of Ldn to Asa ROGERS of Ldn. B/S of ½a Lots #80 & 81 with house in Aldie (prch/o William NOLAND by RUST). Delv. to ROGERS 12 Jan 1832.

3H:016   Date: 7 Jan 1824   RtCt: 29 Mar 1824
Richard JONES to Hugh SMITH. B/S of 35½a (Lot #6 in div. of father William JONES dec'd). Wit: Rich'd COCKRAN, John C. SULLIVAN, Gourley REEDER. Delv. to SMITH 2 Aug 1836.

3H:017   Date: 20 Feb 1824   RtCt: 29 Mar 1824
Nathaniel MANNING & wife Euphama of Ldn to Lambert MYERS of Ldn. B/S of 10a (part of purchase from George JANNEY) adj Andrew THOMPSON, Nathaniel GREGG. Wit: Craven OSBURN, John WHITE. Delv. to MYRES 1 Sept 1824.

3H:019   Date: 14 Feb 1824   RtCt: 29 Mar 1824
Nathaniel MANNING & wife Euphama of Ldn to Nathan GREGG of Ldn. B/S of 3a (part of purchase from George JANNEY) adj And'w THOMPSON. Wit: Craven OSBURN, John WHITE. Delv. to GREGG 31 Oct 1825.

3H:021   Date: 26 Mar 1824   RtCt: 29 Mar 1824
John SIMPSON & wife Nancy of Ldn to Edmund LOVETT of Ldn. B/S of 171a (residue of 5 tracts containing 125a, 9a, 16a, 37a, 3a less 20a to French SIMPSON). Wit: John McCORMICK, Saml. M. EDWARDS.

3H:023   Date: 26 Mar 1824   RtCt: 29 Mar 1824
John SIMPSON & wife Nancy of Ldn to Jesse TIMMS of Ldn. Trust for debt to George CARTER of Oatlands using 194a. Wit: John McCORMICK, Saml. M. EDWARDS. Delv. to W. L. COCKERELL agent for George CARTER.

3H:026   Date: 26 Mar 1824   RtCt: 29 Mar 1824
John JONES and William LICKEY of Ldn to Edmund LOVETT of Ldn. Release of trust of 8 May 1817 (DBk VV:261) using 57½a for debt to James SIMPSON. Wit: G'o. CARTER.

3H:028   Date: 26 Mar 1824   RtCt: 29 Mar 1824
Edmund LOVETT & wife Elizabeth of Ldn to John SIMPSON of Ldn. B/S of 194a (residue of 2 tracts, 156a & 57a less 19a sold by LOVETT & his late wife Christian to George CARTER of Oatlands). Wit: Saml. M. EDWARDS, John McCORMICK, Saml. M. EDWARDS.

3H:030   Date: 5 Feb 1824   RtCt: 10 Mar 1824
John VIOLETT & wife Mary of Ldn to William SILCOTT Jr. of Ldn. Trust of 140-150a (given to Mary in div. of estate of her father James LEWIS dec'd) for benefit of Mary (sale taking place under deed of trust from VIOLETT to Elijah ANDERSON for benefit of Edward CARTER). Wit: Burr POWELL, Abner GIBSON. Delv. to Jacob SILCOTT pr order 29 Mar 1825.

3H:032   Date: 2 Feb 1824   RtCt: 29 Mar 1824
Elizabeth STEER of Ldn to Saml. M. EDWARDS of Ldn. Trust for debt to Saml. CLAPHAM (Admr of Isaac STEER dec'd) using negro man slave Dick, Godfrey & Frank, girl Delpha (allotted to Elizabeth as dower). Wit: E. G. HAMILTON, Charles WILLIAM, Alfred A. ESKRIDGE.

3H:034   Date: 26 Mar 1824   RtCt: 29 Mar 1824
Townshend McVEIGH of Ldn to Edmund LOVETT of Ldn. Release of trust of 12 Jan 1824 on 156a for debt to Stephen McPHERSON.

3H:035   Date: 26 Mar 1824   RtCt: 29 Mar 1824
Edmund LOVETT & wife Elizabeth of Ldn to Townshend McVEIGH of Ldn. Trust for debt to John SIMPSON of Ldn & Stephen McPHERSON using ¾a in Union (1/3 cnvy/b George MARKS Nov 1821, DBk DDD:257, 1/3 by Josiah M. CLARKE Sept 182,2 DBk FFF:54 & 1/3 by Elizabeth WILKINSON Apr 1823, DBk GGG:231) and 171a (cnvy/b John SIMPSON). Wit: John McCORMICK, Saml. M. EDWARDS. Delv. to Hugh SMITH 11 Aug 1846.

3H:039   Date: 20 Mar 1824   RtCt: 30 Mar 1824
Hugh WILEY & wife Jane of Ldn to H. B. POWELL of Ldn. Trust for debt to Isaac RADCLIFFE (Admr of James GUN dec'd) using 6a (cnvy/b Thomas ATWELL Jan 1810 to Hugh Sr. and then to Hugh Jr. May 1811). Wit: Burr POWELL, Abner GIBSON. Delv. to POWELL pr order ___.

3H:041   Date: 24 Nov 1823   RtCt: 29 Mar 1824
William CHILTON of Ldn to Lloyd NOLAND of Ldn. Trust for debt to Burr & Cuthbert POWELL using household items and infant [slave] children Richard son of Jenny and Lewis son of Maria. Wit: Hy. H. HAMILTON, William H. McNABB.

3H:043   Date: 9 Sep 1823   RtCt: 1 Apr 1824
Mary GALLEHER of Ldn to Eli C. GALLEHER of Ldn. Trust of 10a (allotted to Mary from div. of father Wm. GALLEHER dec'd) & dower int. of mother Mary GALLEHER in ½a in Union, and household items.

3H:044   Date: 10 Mar 1824   RtCt: 12 Mar 1824
Benjamin HAGERMAN & wife Violinda to Humphrey B. POWELL. Trust for debts to John WITHERS, Abner GIBSON, Noble BEVERIDGE, John C. SULLIVAN & Amos SKINNER using 20¾a (part in Ldn, part in Fqr, prch/o Charles F. MERCER Sep 1817, DBk VV:187) and 51a (DBk RR:294). Wit: John McCORMICK, Saml. M. EDWARDS. Delv. to A. GIBSON pr order 4 Jun 1825.

3H:048   Date: 31 Mar 1824   RtCt: 2 Apr 1824
Nancy L. PIERPOINT of Ldn to John BRADEN of Ldn. Trust for debt to Sarah LOVE of Ldn using household items.

3H:049   Date: 2 Apr 1824   RtCt: 2 Apr 1824
Job JENKINS of Ldn to William JENKINS of Ldn. B/S of int. in real estate of father Job JENKINS (inherited as heir of Job JENKINS dec'd and was dev. to Job JENKINS Sr. by will of William JENKINS dec'd).

3H:050   Date: 2 Mar 1824   RtCt: 2 Apr 1824
George W. SHAWEN & wife Jane of Ldn to David ENGLISH of WashDC. Trust for debt to James EAKEN of WashDC using 2 lots which formed parcel of estate of father Cornelius SHAWEN dec'd (partition with George & brother David) – 141a adj Sandford RAMEY, Thomas DAVIS, Margaret SANDERS and nearly adj 12¼a adj Henry DAY, Joseph SMITH, Reuben HIXSON, and 37a. Wit: Robert BRADEN, Abiel JENNERS. Delv. to Jas. HAMILTON 27 Feb 1830.

3H:054   Date: 2 Mar 1823   RtCt: 5 Apr 1824
Benjamin BRADFIELD & wife Rachel of Ldn to John BRADFIELD and Jonathan N. BRADFIELD of Ldn. B/S of 104a adj Stephen WILSON, __ McILHANY, Bernard TAYLOR, James COCHRAN.

3H:055   Date: 18 Feb 1824   RtCt: 5 Apr 1824
John N. T. G. E. KEENE & wife Harriot/Harriett of Ldn to Samuel HAMMONTREE of Ldn. B/S of lot in Union (cnvy/b John JOHNSON in Jun 1820) adj Thornton WALKER, Nathan HARRIS, Lewis HUNT, __ BALDWIN. Wit: Wm. BRONAUGH, Wm. H. DORSEY.

3H:057   Date: 28 Jan 1824   RtCt: 5 Apr 1824
H. B. POWELL to John N. T. G. E. KEENE. Release of trust of Jun 1823 for debt to John BOYD.

3H:058   Date: 26 Jan 1824   RtCt: 5 Apr 1824
John N. T. G. E. KEENE & wife Harriet of Ldn to Mahlon BALDWIN of Ldn. B/S of lot in Union (cnvy/b John JOHNSON in Jun 1820). Wit: Wm. BRONAUGH, Francis W. LUCKETT.

3H:059   Date: 30 Mar 1824   RtCt: 5 Apr 1824
Richard WEADON & wife Fanny/Frances of Fqr to William
WEADON of Fqr. B/S of ¾a in Union.

3H:061   Date: 9 Apr 1824   RtCt: 9 Apr 1824
John WADE of Ldn to Robert WADE Jr. of Ldn. Trust for debt to
Robert WADE Sr. using farm animals, household items.

3H:062   Date: 7 Apr 1824   RtCt: 8 Apr 1824
Eve TOWNER of Ldn to John SURGHNOR of Ldn. B/S of Lot #62 in
Lsbg (cnvy/b Benjamin T. TOWNER May 1819, DBk YY:238) (for
annuity to begin at death of her mother; while mother is alive Eve in
possession of premises). Wit: H. H. HAMILTON, E. G. HAMILTON,
Alfred A. ESKRIDGE. Delv. to SURGHNOR 27 Oct 1832.

3H:063   Date: 20 Mar 1824   RtCt: 8 Apr 1824
John CRIDLER (insolvent) to Samuel M. BOSS. Deed of transfer of
estate – house & lot on Market and Air Sts conveyed in trust to
Saml. M. EDWARDS, numerous debts, household items, note from
Saml. MULLEN. Wit: E. G. HAMILTON, Saml. M. EDWARDS, A. A.
ESKRIDGE. Delv to BOSS 8 Aug 1827.

3H:065   Date: 26 Feb 1824   RtCt: 8 Mar 1824
Joseph GAMBLE & John BELL (commr. from chancery in
Winchester) to Robert SHERRARD of Hampshire Co Va. B/S of
151a on E side of Kittoctan Mt adj __ MOFFETT, __ GARRETT
(cnvy/b Archibald McVICKER to Jonas POTTS, then to Benjamin
SHREVE and Joshua OSBURN in trust). Delv. to SHERRARD 2 Mar
1827.

3H:067   Date: 6 Mar 1824   RtCt: 8 Mar 1824
James BRADFIELD of Ldn to James P. BRADFIELD of Ldn. B/S of
160a (formerly belonging to Richard THATCHER now dec'd) adj late
John LOVE, James BEST, Isachar BROWN, James HEATON. Wit:
Daniel JAMES. Delv. to J. P. BRADFIELD 20 Apr 1824.

3H:068   Date: 21 Feb 1824   RtCt: 8 Mar 1824
Stephen GREGG & wife Harriet of Ldn to James JOHNSON of Ldn.
B/S of 1½a in Bloomfield (cnvy/b Abner HUMPHREY) adj John G.
HUMPHREY, John RALPH. Wit: Benj'n GRAYSON, John W.
GRAYSON.

3H:070   Date: 1 Sep 1823   RtCt: 8 Mar 1824
William LITTLETON to John K. LITTLETON. Assignment of rights to
named slaves ___ except James and Delilah (reference to be had to
DBk FFF:138). Wit: Saml. BEAVERS, Eliza BEAVERS. Delv. to Jno.
K. LITTLETON 4 Dec 1825.

3H:070   Date: 28 Feb 1824   RtCt: 8 Mar 1824
James HIXSON & wife Mary of Ldn to Benjamin HIXSON of Ldn.
B/S of 9¼a on both sides of Little River (prch/o James SIXLAIR
[SINCLAIR], adj turnpike road, Mrs. JONES, school house,

exclusive of bed of river 9¼a and including river 9¾a. Wit: Burr POWELL, A. GIBSON. Delv. to B. HIXON 8 Jul 1825.

3H:072   Date: 28 Feb 1824   RtCt: 8 Mar 1824
James HIXSON & wife Mary of Ldn to William ROGERS of Ldn. B/S of 212¼a (part prch/o MASON's heirs) on Little River adj John COCHRAN, __ POWELL. Wit: Burr POWELL, A. GIBSON. Delv. to ROGERS 30 Jan 1827.

3H:074   Date: 28 Feb 1824   RtCt: 8 Mar 1824
James HIXSON & wife Mary of Ldn to Sandford ROGERS of Ldn. B/S of 189a (part of prch/o MASON's heirs) adj Benjamin HIXSON, __ RUST, __ SULLIVAN, __ HEREFORD. Wit: Burr POWELL, A. GIBSON. Delv. to C. B. ROGERS pr order filed 5P 407, Feb 23/66?

3H:076   Date: 28 Feb 1824   RtCt: 8 Mar 1824
James HIXSON & wife Mary of Ldn to Benjamin HIXSON of Ldn. B/S of 180¼a (part of prch/o MASON's heirs) on Little River adj Sandford ROGERS, __ RUST, __ HEREFORD, __ SULLIVAN. Wit: Burr POWELL, A. GIBSON. Delv. to B. HIXON 8 Jul 1825.

3H:078   Date: 1 Jan 1824   RtCt: 8 Mar 1824
Anthony CONNARD & wife Mary of Ldn to David CONRAD of Ldn. B/S of 212a where Anthony resides (prch/o George MOULS and Abraham MASON) adj Philip HEATER, Thompson MASON, Dr. MARLOW, Col. Chas. ELGIN. Wit: Robert BRADEN, Abiel JENNERS. Delv. pr order filed DBk HHH:78, Nov 24th 1829.

3H:080   Date: 12 Feb 1824   RtCt: 8 Mar 1824
Thomas PHILIPS and Isaac WALKER of Ldn to George JANNEY & wife Susanna of Ldn. Release of trust of Apr 1816 for debt to William BIRDSALL.

3H:081   Date: 27 Jan 1824   RtCt: 8 Mar 1824
Henry RUSSELL & wife Matilda of Ldn to Daniel STONE and George HARRIS of Ldn. Trust for debt to Peter & Adam WERTZ of Ldn using 16¼a adj John BINNS and 16¼a (prch/o Asa MOORE) adj Ebenezer GRUBB and 27a on Cactotin Creek. Wit: Robert BRADEN, Abiel JENNERS.

3H:084   Date: 1 Apr 1823   RtCt: 8 Mar 1824
David SHAWEN of Ldn to George W. HENRY of Ldn. B/S of ½a in new addition to Wtfd (prch/o William STEER) adj William H. HOUGH, __ HAMMONTREE.

3H:085   Date: 16 Feb 1824   RtCt: 8 Mar 1824
Robert M. POWELL of Ldn to William BENTON of Ldn. B/S of int. in land which Ann LILLY of Ky holds a life estate as dower from late husband Elisha POWELL dec'd (1/7th share to son Robert M.) and 1/6th share of father's land allotted to brother Elisha POWELL dec'd and Robert's share from brother's right to dower land.

3H:087 Date: 27 Jan 1824 RtCt: 8 Mar 1824
Peter WERTZ/VIRTZ and Adam WERTZ (Exors of Conrad WERTZ dec'd) of Ldn to Henry RUSSELL of Ldn. B/S of 126¾a adj John BINNS and 16¼a (prch/o Asa MOORE) adj Ebenezer GRUBB, and 27a (prch/o William PAXON). Wit: Daniel STONE, William RUSSELL, George HARRIS Jr. Delv. to RUSSELL 20 May 1826.

3H:088 Date: 8 Mar 1824 RtCt: 8 Mar 1824
John SURGHNOR of Lsbg to John S. PEARCE of Ldn. LS of lot as Market & Back Sts in Lsbg. Delv. to PEARCE 10 Aug 1825.

3H:090 Date: 5 Jan 1824 RtCt: 8 Mar 1824
John LEWIS & wife Mary of Bracken Co Ky to William BENTON of Ldn. B/S of 250a (4/5th of land dev. by father William MARTIN dec'd to his children John, Edward, Andrew, Robert and Mary now Mary LEWIS) adj Guy KILE, __ LANE, __ ANDERSON, Robert & Edward MARTIN, __ LUCKETT.

3H:092 Date: 6 Mar 1824 RtCt: 8 Mar 1824
James P. BRADFIELD & wife Elizabeth of Ldn to Daniel JAMES & Calvin THATCHER of Ldn. Trust for debt to James BRADFIELD using 160a. Delv. to James BRADFIELD 10 Mar 1825.

3H:094 Date: 5 Mar 1824 RtCt: 8 Mar 1824
Gainer PIERCE of Ldn to William J. BRONAUGH of Ldn. Trust for debt to Jonathan CARTER using farm animals, household items.

3H:095 Date: 9 Mar 1804 [24?] RtCt: 9 Mar 1824
John CRIDLER & wife Elizabeth of Ldn to John M. McCARTY of Ldn. Trust for debt to William M. McCARTY (Admr of Joseph BEARD dec'd) of Ldn using lot (prch/o Saml. MULLEN) on S side of Market & E side of Air in Lsbg with wooden building now occupied by Daniel HOWELL.

3H:096 Date: 21 Nov 1823 RtCt: 9 Mar 1824
Burr G. POWELL of Ldn to Cuthbert POWELL of Ldn. B/S of 415a (½ of land left by will of Col. Leven POWELL div. between Burr G. POWELL and his brother Thomas W. POWELL) nr Blue Ridge adj Mrs. Elizabeth BAKER, David FULTON, John RICHARDS, Thomas W. POWELL, Jeffries branch. Delv. to C. POWELL 15 Mar 1824.

3H:098 Date: 10 Dec 1823 RtCt: 12 Apr 1824
Sandford HUTCHISON of Ffx to Joshua HUTCHISON of Ffx. Trust for debt to Thomas William LEE of Ldn using 124a (cnvy/b Jeremiah HUTCHISON & wife Mary Ann, Dec 1823). Wit: Chs. LEWIS, J. CLEVELAND, Elijah HUTCHISON.

3H:099 Date: 1 Apr 1824 RtCt: 12 Apr 1824
Townshend D. PEYTON & wife Sarah M. of Ldn to son Richard F. PEYTON. B/S of 250a (cnvy/b Francis HEREFORD & Ann C. HEREFORD, Dec 1817). Wit: Leven LUCKETT, A. GIBSON.

3H:101   Date: 12 Nov 1823   RtCt: 12 Apr 1824
Samuel HUGHES & wife Elizabeth, Elisha HUGHES & wife Fanny, Mathew HUGHES and Lydia HUGHES by Thomas HUGHES their attorney, Sarah HUGHES wd/o Thomas HUGHES dec'd, Hannah BROOKBANK, Thomas BROOKBANK & wife Elizabeth, Thomas HUGHES & wife Ruth, Maria HUGHES and John HUGHES (heirs at law of said Thomas HUGHES dec'd) to Amos BEANS. B/S of 17½a on waters of Kittocton Creek adj Samuel BEANS, Amos BEANS. Wit: Ebenezer GRUBB, John WHITE. Delv. to Amos BEANS 28 Oct 1829.

3H:103   Date: 12 Nov 1823   RtCt: 12 Apr 1824
Samuel HUGHES & wife Elizabeth, Elisha HUGHES & wife Fanny, Mathew HUGHES and Lydia HUGHES by Thomas HUGHES their attorney, Sarah HUGHES wd/o Thomas HUGHES dec'd, Hannah BROOKBANK, Thomas BROOKBANK & wife Elizabeth, Thomas HUGHES & wife Ruth, Maria HUGHES and John HUGHES (heirs at law of said Thomas HUGHES dec'd) to Abraham HOWSER of Ldn. B/S of 50a 'mill lot' on Kittocton Creek, adj Joseph TAYLOR, Amos BEANS, Samuel BEANS. Wit: Ebenezer GRUBB, John WHITE. Delv. to John GOODING 9 Jul 1840 per order.

3H:106   Date: 18 Oct 1812   RtCt: 12 Apr 1824
Samuel HUGHES & wife Elizabeth, Elisha HUGHES & wife Fanny, Mathew HUGHES and Lydia HUGHES by Thomas HUGHES their attorney, Sarah HUGHES wd/o Thomas HUGHES dec'd, Hannah BROOKBANK, Thomas BROOKBANK & wife Elizabeth, Thomas HUGHES & wife Ruth, Maria HUGHES and John HUGHES (heirs at law of said Thomas HUGHES dec'd) to Joseph TAYLOR of Ldn. B/S of 94a (part of tract cnvy/b William BEANS) nr S fork of Kittocton Creek, adj Samuel BEANS, James LOVE, __ POULSON. Wit: Ebenezer GRUBB, John WHITE. Delv. to TAYLOR 3 Nov 1828.

3H:108   Date: 10 Dec 1823   RtCt: 12 Apr 1824
Jeremiah HUTCHISON & wife Mary Ann to Sandford HUTCHISON of Ffx. B/S of 77a and 46a adj Lsbg and Centreville Rd. Wit: Charles LEWIS, Johnston CLEVELAND.

3H:110   Date: 30 Mar 1824   RtCt: 12 Apr 1824
Aaron MILLER & wife Mary of Ldn to Benjamin GRUBB of Ldn. B/S of 69a adj __ MINK, __ HICKMAN, John JANNEY, __ RICHARDS; and 25a on E side of Short Hill Mt adj __ JANNEY, __ VINTON. Wit: Robert BRADEN, Abiel JENNERS. Delv. 14 Mar 1825, recorded in DBk KKK:[017].

3H:112   Date: 7 Jun 1824   RtCt: 14 Jun 1824
Ramey G. SANDERS. Oath at Major in 57th Reg 6th Brig 2nd Div. of Militia.

3H:112   Date: 7 Jun 1824   RtCt: 8 Jun 1824
John CARNEY of Lsbg to Saml M. EDWARDS and William KING of Lsbg. Trust to EDWARDS and KING as endorsers on note to Valley

Bank at Lsbg using household items. Wit: Charles W. D. BINNS, F. J. KIMMY?. Delv. to EDWARDS 29 Sep 1827.

3H:113 Date: 13 May 1824 RtCt: 7 Jun 1824
Edwin C. BROWN. Name used in trust of 21 Sep 1822 between Peter R. RUST of Ldn and Edwin C. BROWN of Ldn. BROWN states name was only used in trust for Hannah MITCHELL of Lancaster Co Va and requests his name be removed.

3H:114 Date: 29 Apr 1824 RtCt: 5 Jun 1824
James BEANS of Ldn to David F. BEALL of Ldn. B/S of 6a (to correct error in deed of Apr 14, 1795 from William PAXON to BEANS; PAXON conveyed to Edward CUNNARD Apr 1796, then BEALL purchased). Wit: Stacy TAYLOR, Chas. TURNER, Alfred WRIGHT. Delv. pr order 18 May 1829.

3H:115 Date: 1 Jun 1824 RtCt: 4 Jun 1824
Francis W. LUCKETT of Ldn (trustee of David CARTER, Oct 1818) to Conrad BITZER of Ldn (assignee of George LOVE as trustee for the benefit of wife Mary LOVE and Martha, Sarah, and Jane H. LOVE d/o Augustine LOVE). B/S of 98a (125a less 27a released to Andrew McMULLEN). Wit: Joseph HOCKINGS, Micajah TRIPLETT, Jonathan CARTER. Delv. to BITZER 2 Mar 1829.

3H:117 Date: 1 Apr 1824 RtCt: 3 Jun 1824
William NETTLE of Wtfd to David CONRAD of Wtfd. B/S of lot in Wtfd (cnvy/b Edward DORSEY, Apr 1816) adj John WILLIAMS stable lot. Delv. pr order filed DBk HHH:78, 25 Nov 1829.

3H:118 Date: 3 Jun 1824 RtCt: 3 Jun 1824
Lewis ELLSEY to Joshua OSBURNE. Trust for debt to Thomas MARKS using farm where ELLSEY formerly lived now occupied by Mahlon MORRIS, negro girl Sarah & her children Betty & her children [?]. Delv. to OSBURNE 22 Oct 1825.

3H:118 Date: 21 Apr 1824 RtCt: 2 Jun 1824
Abel JAMES & wife Sarah of Ldn to Andrew HEATT/HEATH of Ldn. B/S of their 1/13th int. in Loudoun estate of William SMALLEY dec'd late of Ldn and their 1/5th int. in estate of Andrew HEATT [HEATH] Sr. dec'd in Ldn, Ffx and PrWm. Wit: Charles LEWIS, Aris BUCKNER.

3H:120 Date: 31 May 1824 RtCt: 3 May 1824
James H. HAMILTON & wife Margaret of Ldn to Benjamin SHREIVE Jr. of Ldn. Trust for debt to Rich'd H. HENDERSON of Ldn using 230a (prch/o reps of George NIXON dec'd). Wit: John McCORMACK, Saml. M. EDWARDS.

3H:121 Date: 28 May 1824 RtCt: 31 May 1824
William CHILTON & wife Sarah N. to John BURTON. B/S of 10a (prch/o Rev. John MINES) adj John McCORMACK, Daniel LACEY. Wit: John H. McCABE, Saml. M. EDWARDS. Delv. to BURTON 2 Sep 1825.

3H:122   Date: 24 May 1824   RtCt: 31 May 1824
Benjamin GRAYSON & wife Nancy of Ldn to George M. GRAYSON
of Ldn. Trust for debt to William FRANCIS of Licking Co Ohio using
220a adj John P. DULANY, Henry CARTER, Eaches mill, John
RICHARDS, George NOBLE. Wit: Francis W. LUCKETT, Wm. H.
DORSEY.

3H:125   Date: 31 May 1824   RtCt: 31 May 1824
Rich'd H. HENDERSON & wife Orra Moore of Ldn to Ann ECKHART
of Ldn. B/S of 1a lot in Lsbg on N side of Market St., adj Isaac a man
of colour, Charles BINNS, lot Mrs. ECKHART prch/o the wd/o
William WRIGHT. Wit: Wilson C. SELDON, Saml. M. EDWARDS.
Delv. to A. SANDERS formerly ECKHART 22 Feb 1829.

3H:126   Date: 28 Jan 1824   RtCt: 22 May 1824
George E. LLOYD & wife Ruth and William DUNKIN of Ldn to
Joseph TORREYSON of Ldn. B/S of Lot #1 in Union (from div. of
land of James REED dec'd) adj Isaac BROWN, lot assigned to
Joseph & Elizabeth WILKINSON in div. Wit: Aron BURSON, Samuel
DUNKIN, Elsey R. OVERFIELD, Isaac BROWN Jr.

3H:127   Date: 28 May 1824   RtCt: 28 May 1824
James McBRIDE (insolvent debtor, executions by William
HERBERT Admr. of Ferdinando FAIRFAX) to Shff John ROSE. B/S
of land mentioned in schedule [none listed].

3H:127   Date: 22 May 1824   RtCt: 22 May 1824
John WORSLEY to Abiel JENNERS. Release of trust of Mar 1817
for debt to William COCKING.

3H:129   Date: 6 May 1824   RtCt: 10 May 1824
James MILLER of Ldn to John WEADON of Ldn. Trust for debt to
James JOHNSTON using horse, household items, int. in estate of
Richard CRUPPER dec'd. Delv. to JOHNSON 12 Nov 1827.

3H:130   Date: 17 May 1824   RtCt: 31 May 1824
George RUST & wife Maria C. of Ldn to Robert RAY of NY City.
Trust for debt to Nathaniel PRIME of NY City using 503a on
Potomac River and 322a nr Wtfd (cnvy/b Joseph CALDWELL) and
42a nr Lsbg and 44a on road from Lsbg to Noland's Ferry. Wit: R. R.
WARD, John EASTMOND, Abiel JENNERS, Saml. HOUGH. Delv.
to Jno. HAMILTON pr order 28 Aug 1825.

3H:134   Date: 31 Dec 1823   RtCt: 20 May 1824
John HUFFMAN & wife Phebe of Ldn to William BRADFIELD of
Ldn. B/S of 80 sq poles in Snickers Gap. Wit: Benjamin GRAYSON,
John A. GRAYSON. Delv. to BRADFIELD 27 Dec 1826.

3H:136   Date: 13 Mar 1824   RtCt: 20 May 1824
Robert CHEW of Ldn to Ruel MARSHALL of Ldn. B/S of 80 poles nr
Snickers Gap.

3H:137   Date: 17 Feb 1824   RtCt: 10 May 1824
William H. HOUGH & wife Mary Ann of Ldn to Lambert MYERS of Ldn. B/S of lot in Wtfd (cnvy/b John WILLIAMS & wife and James MOORE) adj David CONRAD, Lewis KLEIN. Wit: Abiel JENNERS, Saml. HOUGH. Delv. to MYRES 1 Sep 1826.

3H:139   Date: 14 Nov 1818   RtCt: 10 May 1824
Moses BROWN & wife Mary to George E. LLOYD and William DUNKIN. B/S of Lot #1 in Union (in div. of James REED dec'd) adj Isaac BROWN, lot assigned Joseph and Elisabeth WILKINSON. Wit: Wm. BRONAUGH, Francis W. LUCKETT.

3H:140   Date: 18 Mar 1824   RtCt: 10 May 1824
Alexander M. BRISCOE & wife Matilda P. of PrWm to Naomai LACEY, Huldah LACEY and Ruth LACEY of Ldn. B/S of int. in estate of Tracy LACEY dec'd and int. which John LACEY dec'd had in estate of Tracy LACEY.

3H:141   Date: 5 Dec 1822   RtCt: 11 May 1824
H. B. POWELL to Matthew ADAMS & wife Susan L. Release of trust of May 1818 for debt to Samuel HATCHER and Joseph HATCHER.

3H:143   Date: 1 May 1824   RtCt: 10 May 1824
Abraham FULTON of Ldn to Asa ROGERS of Ldn. Trust for debt to Horrace LUCKETT of Ldn using brick house and adj lots in Aldie on S side of Little River turnpike road where Abraham now lives.

3H:144   Date: 11 May 1824   RtCt: 11 May 1824
Isaac EATON & wife Malinda of Ldn to Robert R. HOUGH of Ldn. B/S of ½a Lot #12 in Mt. Gilead on Loudoun St. Wit: John McCORMACK, John H. McCABE.

3H:146   Date: 28 Apr 1824   RtCt: 14 May 1824
Christopher NEALE & wife Harriot of AlexDC to Craven Peyton THOMPSON and Israel Peyton THOMPSON of AlexDC. B/S of 242a (cnvy/b Ferdinando FAIRFAX, Nov 1819) on E side of Blue Ridge adj Hugh THOMPSON, John CAMPBELL. Gives plat. Wit: James CARSON, J. SAVITT, Joseph B. LADD.

3H:150   Date: 21 Apr 1824   RtCt: 15 May 1824
Thomas BIRKBY & wife Sarah of Lsbg to Ignatius ELGIN of Ldn. B/S of ½a Lot #4 in West addition to Lsbg on S side of Cornwall St. Delv. to ELGIN 7 Jan 1826.

3H:151   Date: 13 Feb 1824   RtCt: 19 May 1824
Mandly T. RUST & wife Sally (late Sally CHILTON d/o Thomas and Susana CHILTON dec'd) and Richard H. HENDERSON (trustee for Sally) to Saml. M. EDWARDS of Ldn. Trust for debt to Eli OFFUTT of Ldn using int. in claims to estates of Thomas & Susana CHILTON dec'd. Wit: Saml. DAWSON, James M. LEWIS. Delv. to OFFUTT 20 Dec 1827.

3H:155   Date: 13 Feb 1824   RtCt: 19 May 1824
Eli OFFUTT & wife Margaret of Ffx to Rich'd H. HENDERSON
(trustee of Sally RUST) of Ldn. B/S of int. in estates of Thomas &
Susana CHILTON dec'd as in above deed. Wit: Saml. DAWSON,
James M. LEWIS. Delv. to OFFUTT pr order 14 Jan 1829.

3H:157   Date: 17 Jun 1823   RtCt: 27 Jun 1823/8 Jun 1824
John THOMAS Jr. of Ldn to L. P. W. BALCH and Samuel
HATCHER of Ldn. Trust for debt to John PANCOAST Sr. of Ldn
using 150a (prch/o John THOMAS Sr. July 1821). Delv. to BALCH 8
Feb 1826.

3H:159   Date: 10 Jun 1824   RtCt: 10 Jun 1824
George RICHARD of Ldn to George COOPER of Ldn. B/S of 4a (Lot
#11 in timber lotts in div. of Susan HOUSEHOLDER estate allotted
to Gideon HOUSEHOLDER and sold to G. RICHARD). Delv. to
COOPER 2 Oct 1837.

3H:160   Date: 15 Jun 1824   RtCt: 16 Jun 1824
John A. BINNS of Lsbg to Charles W. D. BINNS of Lsbg. Trust for
debt to Charles BINNS of Lsbg using negro boy Lewis, woman Sally
& her 3 daus. Betsy, Mary & Charlott, farm animals, household
items. Taken out by Jas. A. BINNS in the presence of Chas.
BINNS.

3H:162   Date: 10 Feb 1824   RtCt: 14 Jun 1824
Peter COOPER & wife Nancy of Ldn to Saml. M. EDWARDS of Ldn.
Trust for William THRIFT of Ldn as security in suit of Robert
MOFFETT using und. 1/9th share of 94a in German Settlement (from
will of father Michael COOPER dec'd) adj Wm. WOLFE, Polly
HIXON, Peter SANDERS. Wit: Thomas A. MOORE, H. SMITH, A. A.
ESKRIDGE.

3H:164   Date: 10 Jan 1824   RtCt: 11 May 1824
Ann ECKART of Ldn to Catharine HIERS (w/o John HIERS late
Catherine COOPER), George COOPER and Adam COOPER of
PhilPa. B/S of (by suit of Dec 1823) 128a including mill from 216a
and 100a (from will of Caspar ECKHART dec'd late of Ldn,
purchased jointly Feb 1798 from Elisha GREGG).

3H:166   Date: 6 Mar 1824   RtCt: 8 May 1824
Charles CRIM Jr. of Ldn to William CLENDENING of Ldn. Trust for
debt to George ABB [ABEL] Sr. of Ldn using grain, farm animals and
items, household items. Wit: George ABEL Jr., Adam ABEL, Marcus
BLINCOE.

3H:168   Date: 1 Jul 1823   RtCt: 11 Aug 1824
Coleman LEWIS to Charles GULATT. Trust for debt to David LEWIS
using horse.

3H:170   Date: 12 Mar 1824   RtCt: 10 May 1824
Calvin THATCHER of Ldn to L. P. W. BALCH and James P.
BRADFIELD of Ldn. Trust for debt to James BRADFIELD of Ldn

using 98a (cnvy/b BRADFIELD May 1823). Delv. to BALCH 3 Jun 1825.

3H:171   Date: 10 May 1824   RtCt: 10 May 1824

Samuel M. EDWARDS of Ldn to Thomas PHILLIPS and Thomas PHILIPS & Joseph BOND (as Exors of Asa MOORE) of Ldn. B/S of 1 moriety of 6a & 2a in Wtfd to PHILIPS and 1 moriety to Exors of Asa MOORE (in suit of PHILIPS and BOND agst Daniel JANNEY). PHILIPS and Asa MOORE dec'd were copartners in firm of Moore & Philips. Delv. to PHILIPS 16 Sep 1828.

3H:173   Date: 14 Jun 1824   RtCt: 14 Jun 1824

Daniel COCKREL. Oath as Captain in 56th Reg 6th Brig 2nd Div of Loudoun Militia.

3H:173   Date: 18 Jun 1824   RtCt: 18 Jun 1824

Saml. HAMMET. Certificate dated 29 May 1824 appointing him coronet of a Troop of Cavalry in the 2nd Reg and 2nd Div of Va Militia.

3H:173   Date: 16 Jun 1824   RtCt: 18 Jun 1824

Asa ROGERS. Oath as Captain in 56th Reg 6th Brig 2nd Div of Va Militia.

3H:174   Date: 15 Jun 1824   RtCt: 15 Jun 1824

Burr WEEKS. Oath as Lt. in 56th Reg of Loudoun Militia.

3H:174   Date: 10 Jun 1824   RtCt: 14 Jun 1824

Saml. M. EDWARDS. Oath as Lt. Col. in 56th Reg 6th Brig 2nd div of Va Militia.

3H:174   Date: 10 Jun 1824   RtCt: 14 Jun 1824

William JENNERS. Oath as Capt. in 57th Reg 6th Brig 2nd Div of Va Militia.

3H:175   Date: 10 May 1798   RtCt: 24 Jun 1824

John Tasker CARTER of WstmVA and George Fairfax LEE of WstmVa. Exchange of Mt. Pleasant land in WestmVa for 3408a on Goose Creek (from father Robert CARTER Esq). Wit: Jno. Jas. MAUND, George GAINER, Henry LEE.

3H:177   Date: 19 Aug 1815   RtCt: 15 Jun 1824

Josiah MOFFETT Jr. dec'd. Division - 110a Lot #1 to reps of Josiah MOFFETT Jr. dec'd (widow Fanny MOFFETT, Thomas J., Nancy, Hannah, Martha, Elizabeth, Josiah, Sally & Milly MOFFETT); 110a Lot #2 to Robert MOFFETT. Divisors: Abner WILLIAMS, Ignatius ELGIN, Samuel DONOHOE, Enoch FRANCIS. Gives plat.

3H:179   Date: ___   RtCt: 15 Jun 1824

Daniel BOLAND. Report on alien born in Simpledary Parish of Minagh, County of Tipperary, age 28 years, of Ireland, allegiance to King of Great Britain & Ireland, migrated from County of Tipperary, intends to live nr Lsbg.

3H:180   Date: 2 Apr 1824   RtCt: 14 Jun 1824
Mathew BEANS dec'd. Widow's dower – 100 poles [Plat says 13a].
Gives plat. Divisors: R. BRADEN, Lambert MYERS, James LEVI.

3H:181   Date: 16 Jun 1824   RtCt: 12 Jun 1824
John THOMAS Jr. & wife Elizabeth of Ldn to William LODGE of Ldn.
B/S of 150a adj Joseph JANNEY, William LODGE. Wit: Benjamin
GRAYSON, John W. GRAYSON. Delv. to A. ROGER 10 Jan 1826.

3H:183   Date: 11 Jun 1824   RtCt: 12 Jun 1824
Leah THOMAS (w/o John THOMAS Sr.) of Ldn to William LODGE of
Ldn. B/S of her claim to above 150a (cnvy/b John Sr. to John Jr., Jul
1821). Delv. to LODGE 16 Oct 1825.

3H:185   Date: 11 Jun 1824   RtCt: 12 Jun 1824
William LODGE Sr. & wife Christina of Ldn to John THOMAS Jr. of
Ldn. B/S of 159a in Columbiana Co Ohio, Section No. 34 of
Township No. 12 in Range No. 2 (prch/o Isaac JAMES & wife Sarah
Jun 1807, DBk A:223). Delv. Wit: Benjamin GRAYSON, John W.
GRAYSON. Delv. to John Jr. 18 May 1825.

3H:187   Date: 11 May 1824   RtCt: 12 Jun 1824
Thomas KIDWELL & wife Elisabeth of Ldn to Jacob SHRIVER of
Ldn. B/S of 40a Lots #24 & #25 on W side of Short Hill, adj John
CUNNARD. Wit: Saml. M. EDWARDS, B. SHRIVER Jr., A. A.
ESKRIDGE, Jno. J. MATHIAS, Ebenezer GRUBB, John WHITE.
Delv. to SHRIVER 9 Mar 1829.

3H:189   Date: 28 May 1824   RtCt: 4 Jun 1824
John J. STULL of Georgetown DC and John ROSE of Ldn to
Thomson MASON of Ldn. Release of trust of Nov 1821 for debt to
Farmer Mechanics Bank.

3H:192   Date: 10 Jan 1824   RtCt: 11 May 1824
John HIES [HIERS?] & wife Catherine (late Catherine COOPER),
Adam COOPER & wife Susana and George COOPER of PhilPa to
Ann ECKHART of Ldn. B/S of 188a (beq. by Casper ECKHART
dec'd to sister [listed as dau in will] Catherine and her children).
Delv. to Ann SANDERS formerly EKHART 22 Feb 1829.

3H:195   Date: 3 Dec 1822   RtCt: 10 Mar 1824
Joseph PURCELL of Ldn to Stacy TAYLOR and Samuel PURCELL
Jr. of Ldn. Trust for debt to Valentine V. PURSELL using 107a below
Blue Ridge (prch/o Thomas LESLIE). Wit: David LOVETT, Thomas
WHITE, John HOUGH.

3H:198   Date: 22 Apr 1824   RtCt: 20 [?] Apr 1824
Benjamin BRADFIELD of Ldn to L. P. W. BALCH and John GREGG
of Ldn. Trust for debt to John PANCOAST Jr. of Ldn using 154a.
Delv. to PANCOAST 26 May 1825.

3H:199   Date: __ 1824   RtCt: 8 Mar 1824
George TAVENER Sr., Robert BRADEN and Stacy TAYLOR of Ldn
to Joseph TAVENER of Ldn. Release of trust of Sept 1807 for debt
to George TAVENER Sr.

3H:201   Date: 5 Jun 1824   RtCt: 12 Jun 1824
Richard H. LEE of Ldn to Saml. M. EDWARDS of Ldn. Trust for debt
to John J. HARDING & Robt. BENTLY of Ldn using lot in Lsbg
(cnvy/b Dr. Henery CLAGETT & wife Julia). Delv. to EDWARDS 13
May 1825.

3H:203   Date: 5 Jan 1824   RtCt: 14 Jun 1824
Pierce NOLAND & wife Mary of Hampshire Co Va to John KILE Jr of
Ldn. B/S of int. in land which Mary's father Elisha POWELL died
seized and was allotted as dower to widow Anne POWELL and her
share of land from death of brother Elisha POWELL dec'd. Delv. to
B. MITCHELL Jr. pr order 9 May 1824.

3H:204   Date: 10 Jun 1824   RtCt: 14 Jun 1824
Samuel MURRAY & wife Mary Ann of Ldn to Samuel SINGLETON
of Ldn. Trust for debt to Samuel SINGLETON using 26a (prch/o
Simon BINNS) and 1a (prch/o Wm. A. BINNS), crops, $300 to come
from estate of father William MURRY dec'd, 2 negro men & 1
woman (Phil, Adam & Jerry), farm and household items. Wit: John
McCORMACK, Thomas SANDERS.

3H:206   Date: 12 Jul 1824   RtCt: 12 Jul 1824
John ROSE, Benjamin SHRIEVE, Robert MOFFETT and William
THRIFT are bound to justices John McCORMACK, Jno. H.
McCABE, Saml. M. EDWARDS & Thomas SANDERS. Bond on
ROSE as Sheriff to collect levies.

3H:207   Date: 22 Jun 1824   RtCt: 12 Jul 1824
Timothy TAYLOR Jr. Oath as Major in 56th Reg 6th Brig 2nd Div of Va
Militia.

3H:207   Date: 22 Jun 1824   RtCt: 12 Jul 1824
Charles TAYLOR. Oath as Colonel of 56th Reg 6th Brig 2nd Div of Va
Militia.

3H:208   Date: 12 Jul 1824   RtCt: 12 Jul 1824
Erasmus G. HAMILTON and Richard H. HENDERSON. Bond on
Hamilton as Notary Public.

3H:208   Date: 11 Mar 1824   RtCt: 14 Jun 1824
Thomas MARKS & wife Keziah of Ldn to Stacy TAYLOR and
Valentine V. PURCELL of Ldn. Trust for debt to Noah HATCHER
using 150a. Wit: Craven OSBURN, John WHITE.

3H:211   Date: 29 Nov 1823   RtCt: 14 Jun 1824
George W. McKINNY of Harrison Co to William GALLEHER of Ldn.
B/S of int. allotted him from grandfather William GALLEHER dec'd
as part which widow Mary GALLAHER holds a life estate and his ½
or ½a lot in Union.

3H:212   Date: 28 Apr 1824   RtCt: 14 Jun 1824
William W. LAWRENCE of Ldn to Elizabeth JONES of Ldn. BoS of secretary and plants. Wit: John C. LYON. Delv. to Jno. H. McCABE for Mrs. JONES 7 Jul 1828.

3H:213   Date: 17 May 1824   RtCt: 14 Jun 1824
William RICHARDS & [wife] Lydia RICHARDS of Ldn to Joseph CARR of Ldn. B/S of 226a (less 14½a sold to Amos GIBSON) adj turnpike road, Clifton Mill, Joseph LEWIS, heirs of John GIBSON dec'd. Wit: John W. GRAYSON, Cuthbert POWELL. Delv. to CARR 14 May 1826.

3H:215   Date: 1 Apr 1824   RtCt: 14 Jun 1824
David CONRAD & wife Sarah E. of Ldn to William NETTLE of Ldn. B/S of 150a (cnvy/b Mahlon JANNEY with Charles ELGIN and Aron SANDERS as trustees of Geo. H. SINCLAIR, Feb 1824). Wit: Robert BRADEN, Abiel JENNERS. Delv. to NETTLE 4 Nov 1833.

3H:217   Date: 23 Mar 1824   RtCt: 14 Jun 1824
Gainer PIERCE & wife Sarah of Ldn to William J. BRONAUGH of Ldn. Trust for debt to James HOGE using 1a where George LAMBERT lives and adjoining 5¼a. Wit: William BRONAUGH. Delv. to Jas. HOGE 12 Dec 1825.

3H:219   Date: 29 Dec 1823   RtCt: 14 Jun 1824
William W. LAWRENCE to Elizabeth JONES. BoS for farm and household items. Wit: Deskin D. MONROE. Delv. to Jno. H. McCABE for Mrs. JONES 7 Feb 1828.

3H:220   Date: 1 Jun 1824   RtCt: 14 Jun 1824
Burr POWELL and Cuthbert POWELL to Abel JANNEY. Release of trust dated Sept 1811 for debt to Robert M. POWELL.

3H:221   Date: 7 Jun 1824   RtCt: 14 Jun 1824
William ELLZEY of Ldn to Conrad ROLLER, John ROLLER & Daniel ROLLER of Ldn. B/S of 121a adj Michael STREAM, George & Jacob VERTS. Wit: Frederick SLEETS [SLATES?], William COLE, Solomon HOUSEHOLDER. Delv. to Conrad ROLLER 30 Jan 1828.

3H:222   Date: __ June 1824   RtCt: 15 Jun 1824
Mary McINTYRE of Ldn to Samuel M. BOSS of Ldn. Trust for John T. WILSON and Presly CORDELL of Ldn as security in letter of Admr. for estate of Patrick McINTYRE dec'd using negro man Davy, woman Aga or Agnis & her child Edmund, household items.

3H:224   Date: 5 May 1824   RtCt: 16 Jun 1824
Samuel DUNKIN & wife Anna of Ldn to Henery HUTCHISON of Ldn. B/S of 101a nr Union adj Wm. BRONAUGH, Benjamin MITCHELL. Wit: William BRONAUGH, John W. GRAYSON. Delv. to HUTCHISON 12 Jul 1830.

3H:226   Date: 31 May 1824   RtCt: 17 Jun 1824
Benjamin WAR of Ldn to George W. FRENCH. Trust for debt to James D. FRENCH using cow and calf.

3H:227   Date: 10 Jun 1824   RtCt: 18 Jun 1824
Enoch FRANCIS & wife Anna of Ldn to President, Directors and Co
of the Leesburg Turnpike Road. B/S of bridge on old Alexandria
road and ¼a (former property of William WILSON condemned for
abutting the bridge on W side of Goose Creek) and ¼a on E side of
Goose Creek including toll house and lands on farm of FRANCIS
where road was constructed and rights to stone. Wit: Burr POWELL,
A. GIBSON.

3H:228   Date: 17 Jun 1824   RtCt: 19 Jun 1824
Craven OSBURN and Stacy TAYLOR to David LOVETT. Release of
trust of Sep 1817 for debt to Jonathan TRIBBY and George
TRIBBY.

3H:230   Date: 15 Jun 1824   RtCt: 19 Jun 1824
Mortimer McILHANY & wife Mary A. of Ldn to David LOVETT of Ldn.
B/S of Mortimer's int. in land of sister Elisabeth dec'd (76a Lot #2
and 16a Lot #3 in div.). Wit: Craven OSBURN, John WHITE.

3H:232   Date: 22 Jun 1824   RtCt: 22 Jun 1824
Isaac EATON & wife Malinda of Ldn to George RICHARDS of Ldn.
Trust for debt to Otho R. BEATTY of Ldn using 20a (part of 2 tracts
prch/o John and William LICKEY) adj Mt. Gilead, Charles SMITH,
William COE, and farm animals, household items. Wit: John
McCORMACK, Saml. M. EDWARDS. Delv. pr order 17 Dec 1833.

3H:236   Date: 12 May 1823   RtCt: 22 Jun 1824
Joseph WOOD & wife Lydia of Ldn to Joshua PUSEY of Ldn. Trust
for debt to James NIXON of Ldn with Abiel JENNERS as security
using 80a (with exception of race from Factory Mill to Braden's Mill
race in Wtfd). Wit: Robert BRADEN, Abiel JENNERS.

3H:239   Date: 2 Jun 1824   RtCt: 24 Jun 1824
William PAXON & wife Jane of Ldn to Elizabeth TALLEY (w/o Isaac
TALLEY) of Ldn. B/S of 5a adj Simon MATHEWS. Wit: Robert
BRADEN, Abiel JENNERS. Delv. to Anthony WRIGHT s/o Elizabeth
TALLEY 15 Oct 1835.

3H:241   Date: __ 1824   RtCt: 25 Jun 1824
George RICHARD of Ldn to Daniel HOUSEHOLDER of Ldn. B/S of
4a (part of land of Susanah HOUSEHOLDER dec'd) adj Ruth
JANNEY, Adam GRUBB, Peter COMPHER. Delv. to
HOUSEHOLDER 2 Apr 1830.

3H:242   Date: 24 Jun 1824   RtCt: 28 Jun 1824
Eli McKNIGHT & wife Ally of Ldn to Stacy TAYLOR and Joshua
GREGG of Ldn. Trust for debt to Joshua PANCOAST using 51a
(allotted from div. of father's estate) adj David LOVETT, Lewis
LYDER and 35a (prch/o James LARUE and 35a (prch/o William
BROWN) and 10a (prch/o Thomas JAMES) and 2a (prch/o Deborah
McKNIGHT). Wit: Craven OSBURN, John WHITE. Delv. to
PANCOAST 28 Aug 1827.

3H:245 Date: 14 Jun 1824 RtCt: 1 Jul 1824
Gainer PIERCE of Ldn to John W. BAKER of Georgetown DC. Trust for debt to Thomas A. NICHOLSON and Gideon DAVIS (with PIERCE as security for Jesse S. DRAKE) using 87½a on N side of Goose Creek adj old turnpike road to Snickers Gap. Wit: Danl. BUSSARD, Walter NEWTON.

3H:248 Date: 22 Nov 1823 RtCt: 25 May/1 Jul 1824
Susannah SETTLE and Newman SETTLE & wife Elisabeth of Ldn to Amos SKINNER of Ldn. B/S of 243a adj James SWART, Daniel SETTLE, Richard McGRAW. Wit: William THRIFT, Chas. GULATT, Wm. ROSE, Horace LUCKETT, Charles LEWIS, John BAYLY. Delv. to A. SKINNER 13 May 1825.

3H:250 Date: 26 Jun 1824 RtCt: 3 Jul 1824
Jozabed WHITE & wife Margaret to Richard H. HENDERSON. Trust for debt to John McPHERSON & John BRIN (under firm of McPherson & Brin) and Jonathan JANNEY & John JANNEY using 47a nr Hllb (share in land of father Josiah WHITE dec'd) adj William WHITE, Washington WHITE, his sisters Elisabeth and Rachael WHITE, J. McILHANY, John WHARTON. Wit: John WHITE, Robert BRADEN. Delv. to HENDERSON 21 July 1828.

3H:253 Date: 3 Jul 1824 RtCt: 3 Jul 1824
Robert CAMPBELL of Ldn to Henery COST of FredMd. Trust for debt to COST using 25a (cnvy/b John WRIGHT). Wit: S. BLINCOE, Thos. MORRALLE, James STONE.

3H:254 Date: 19 Jun 1824 RtCt: 5 Jul 1824
Isaac STEER of Ldn to Thomas PHILIPS of Ldn. B/S of 1a and 25 poles (lots cnvy/b Thos. PHILLIPS and Jos. BOND Exors of Asa MOORE dec'd). Delv. to PHILIPS 9 Jul 1832.

3H:256 Date: 19 Jun 1824 RtCt: 5 Jul 1824
Thomas PHILLIPS and Joseph BOND (Exors of Asa MOORE dec'd) of Ldn to Ann MOORE of Ldn. B/S of 100 pole lot in Wtfd lately occupied by Asa MOORE dec'd, adj Thomas PHILIPS, Amasa HOUGH, Edward STABLER.

3H:258 Date: 18 Jun 1824 RtCt: 10 Jul 1824
William CHILTON & wife Sarah of Ldn to Burr POWELL & Cuthbert POWELL (CHILTON's securities in trust of May 1821) of Ldn. B/S of 606a (cnvy/b FAIRFAX in Aug 1804) nr Carter's Mill on Goose Creek. Wit: Francis W. LUCKETT, A. GIBSON. Delv. to C. POWELL 15 May 1827.

3H:262 Date: 15 Jun 1824 RtCt: 5 Jul 1824
Thomas PHILIPS and Joseph BOND (Exors of Asa MOORE dec'd) of Ldn to Isaac STEER of Ldn. B/S of 25 pole lot in Wtfd adj Moore and Philips tanyard, Amasa HOUGH.

3H:264   Date: 28 May 1824   RtCt: 7 Jul 1824
John HAMMAT of Fqr and Samuel HAMMAT of Ldn (Exors of George HAMMAT dec'd late of Ldn) to John BURTON of Ldn. B/S of 46a nr Lsbg (prch/o Benjamin EDWARDS dec'd) on NE side of road from Lsbg to Williams Shop. Delv. to BURTON 2 Sep 1825.

3H:266   Date: 15 Jun 1824   RtCt: 5 Jul 1824
Thomas PHILIPS and Joseph BOND (Exors of Asa MOORE dec'd) of Ldn to Isaac STEER of Ldn. B/S of 40a adj Robert BRADEN, Thomas PHILIPS, William PAXON.

3H:269   Date: 19 Jun 1824   RtCt: 5 Jul 1824
Isaac STEER of Ldn to Thomas PHILIPS of Ldn. B/S of 40a (as above). Delv. to PHILIPS 9 Jul 1832.

3H:271   Date: 14 May 1824   RtCt: 16 Jun 1824
John HIES(S) & Catherine HIES(S), Adam COOPER of PhilPa and George COOPER of Ldn. DoE for negro slaves Virgin & her 3 children, Patty, Sarah & Mary (allotted in div. of Caspar ECKART slaves).

3H:272   Date: 7 Jun 1824   RtCt: 7 Jun 1824
Wm. HAWKE Jr. Released Saml. M. BOSS as security for John MARTIN, Guardian of HAWKE. Delv. to BOSS 3 Feb 1826.

3H:272   Date: 4 Jun 1824   RtCt: 12 Jul 1824
Thomson MASON & wife Ann of Ldn to Jno. J. STULL of DC and John ROSE of Ldn. Trust for debt to Farmers Mechanics Bank using 562½a 'Liberia' where MASON now lives. Wit: Samuel CLAPHAM, James H. HAMILTON. Delv. Clem't COX? pr. C. SMITH's order 16 Feb 1826.

3H:276   Date: 12 Jul 1824   RtCt: 12 Jul 1824
Samuel M. EDWARDS of Ldn to Thomas PHILIPS and Thomas PHILIPS & Joseph BOND (Exors of Asa MOORE dec'd). B/S of 2a (purchased by PHILIPS and MOORE as copartners, 1 moriety to PHILIPS and 1 moriety to PHILIPS and BOND as Exors). Delv. to BOND and PHILIPS 17 Sep 1828.

3H:278   Date: 6 Apr 1824   RtCt: 14 Jun 1824
Samuel CLAPHAM & wife Elisabeth of Ldn to Saml. NIXON and Andrew S. ANDERSON of Ldn. Trust for debt to William GREGG of Ldn using 300a where Samuel now resides (devised from father Josiah CLAPHAM dec'd) adj Mr. JOHNSON, Moses DOWDLE, Joseph CRAVEN. Delv. to John SCHOOLEY Exor of Wm. GREGG dec'd 16 Nov 1827.

3H:281   Date: 28 Jul 1824   RtCt: 28 Jul 1824
Gainer PIERCE (insolvent) to Sheriff John ROSE. B/S of 113½a (prch/o Jonathan CARTER and subject to trust), int. in 6¼a with house nr Aldie (bought from Saml. TALBOT and subject to trust),

(executions by James COSTER, Stephen McPHERSON, Mahlon PURCELL, Wm. SILVER, Robt. BENTLY). Wit: John McCORMACK.

3H:282 Date: 28 Jul 1824 RtCt: 9 Aug 1824
John SURGENOR. Commission as Ensign of a Co of Light Infantry in 2nd Batt of 57th Reg 6th Brig 2nd Div of Va Militia.

3H:282 Date: 7 Jul 1823 RtCt: 20 Jul 1824
Fewell A. PERRY of Ffx to Wm. M. McCARTY of Ldn. BoS for negro woman Sally & her children Mary and Jack. Wit: John R. CATON.

3H:283 Date: 6 Mar 1824 RtCt: 27 Jul 1824
Sarah DONOHOE of Ldn. DoE for negro slave woman Amy abt 25y old (freed after 1 Jan 1830), girl Elisabeth 5y old (freed after 1 Jan 1844), girl Sarah Anna 3y old (freed after 1 Jan 1846) and any increase when they reach 25y old, black boy Benjamin abt 16y old (freed 1 Jan 1834 or 54?), black boy George Washington 1y old (freed 1 Jan 1850). Wit: Robt. R. HOUGH, Sarah C. HOUGH.

3H:284 Date: 19 Jul 1824 RtCt: 20 Jul 1824
James HIXON & wife Mary of Ldn to Richard H. HENDERSON, Jesse TIMMS and Joseph DANIEL of Ldn. Trust for debt to George CARTER of Oatlands using 330a (less 8a) on Little River (part of tract patented to Thomas OWSLEY) adj John SINCLAIR. Wit: Burr POWELL, A. GIBSON. Delv. to W. L. COCKERELL agent for Geo. CARTER ___.

3H:286 Date: 19 Jul 1824 RtCt: 19 Jul 1824
Charles DRISH & wife Susanah of Ldn to John THOMAS of Ldn. B/S of lot in Lsbg at NW intersection of Cornwall & Church St. Wit: Ebenezer GRUBB, Saml. M. EDWARDS. Delv. to THOMAS 12 Apr 1832.

3H:289 Date: 17 Jul 1824 RtCt: 17 Jul 1824
Elias [otherwise called Ellis] JENKINS of Ldn to Richard H. HENDERSON of Ldn. Trust for debts to Joseph JANNEY of AlexDC, John GUNNEL of Ffx and John CANBY of Ldn using 7a (cnvy/b Jos. T. NEWTON, Mar 1821). Wit: Saml. M. EDWARDS, B. SHREVE Jr.

3H:291 Date: 16 Jul 1824 RtCt: 15 Jul 1824
Notley C. WILLIAMS & wife Elisabeth S. of Ldn to Lewis P. W. BALCH of Lsbg. Release of trust of May 1823 for debt to Nicholas OSBURN.

3H:292 Date: 23 Jun 1824 RtCt: 9 Aug 1824
Roger CHEW. Appointed 2nd Lt. of a Troop of Cavalry in 2nd Reg 2nd Div. of Va Militia.

3H:293 Date: 9 Aug 1824 RtCt: 9 Aug 1824
Mosses GUILICK and William GILMORE bound to Charles LEWIS, Thomas FRENCH, Robert BRADEN and William CARR as Justices of Peace of Ldn. Bond on GUILICK to execute will of John MUDD dec'd with other exor Thomas GREGG executed bond to Johnson

CLEVELAND, Aris BUCKNER, S. C. ROZZELL and Abiel JENNER, Justices of Ldn.

3H:294   Date: 12 Jul 1824   RtCt: 13 Aug 1824
Samuel M. EDWARDS. Bond on EDWARDS as Notary Publick.

3H:294   Date: 18 Sep 1803   RtCt: 8 Dec 1823/12 Aug 1824
Thomas Ludwell LEE of Ldn and Landon CARTER of RichVa (Exors of George CARTER dec'd) to James CROSS of Ldn. B/S of 153¾a adj M. HARRISON, R. JENKINS. Wit: John McCORMICK, John LITTLEJOHN, Samuel HOUGH, Jno. MATHIAS.

3H:297   Date: 22 Jul 1824   RtCt: 9 Aug 1824
John MOORE. Qualified as Captain of a Company of Light Infantry in 2nd Batt 57th Reg 6th Brig 2nd Div of Va Militia.

3H:297   Date: 8 Aug 1824   RtCt: 9 Aug 1824
Charles DOUGLAS. Qualified as Captain in 57th Reg 6th Brig 2nd Div. of Va Militia. Delv. to DOUGLAS 19 May 1825.

3H:298   Date: 29 Jun 1824   RtCt: 9 Aug 1824
Thomas R. SAUNDERS. Qualified as Captain in 57th Reg 6th Brig 2nd Div of Va Militia.

3H:299   Date: 27 Jul 1824   RtCt: 27 Jul 1824
Stacy HAINS of Ldn to John M. McCARTY of Ldn. Trust for debt to Edmund CAMMACK of Georgetown DC and Thomas W. LANGTON of MontMd using 14a on turnpike road abt 1m below Lsbg and farm and household items. Wit: Jas. McILHANY, Lewis BEARD, Enos WILDMAN.

3H:300   Date: 29 Jul 1824   RtCt: 2 Aug 1824
George GUILICK & wife Sarah of Ldn to Richard H. HENDERSON, Humphrey POWELL and Jesse TIMMS of Ldn. Trust for debt to George CARTER of Oatlands using 101¾a on road from ford of Little River to Snickers Gap. Wit: Burr POWELL, A. GIBSON. Delv. to W. L. COCKERILL agent for Geo. CARTER ___.

3H:303   Date: 31 Jul 1824   RtCt: 31 Aug 1824
Thomas JAMES & wife Mary of Ldn to John C. BAZILL of Ldn. B/S of 24a on both sides of Valentines branch nr Blue Ridge adj James' saw mill, Thomas WHITE, heirs of William BROWN. Wit: John WHITE, Craven OSBURN.

3H:305   Date: 20 May 1824   RtCt: 5 Aug 1824
John POULSON & wife Hannah of Ldn to David GOODIN of Ldn. B/S of 10a nr S branch of Kittocton Creek (Lot #6 in div. of estate of Jasper POULSON dec'd). Wit: John McCORMICK, Presley CORDELL.

3H:307   Date: 10 Jun 1824   RtCt: 12 Jul 1824
Burr POWELL (with Samuel DISHMAN & wife Elisabeth and John JOHNSTON & wife Hester/Esther wd/o William T. DISHMAN) of Ldn to Enos W. NEWTON of Ldn. B/S of ½a Lots #47 & #48 in Mdbg (William T. DISHMAN prch/o POWELL and began building houses

but died before done and in debt, leaving a widow without a child who with his father Samuel DISHMAN let property be forfeited over to POWELL). Wit: Francis W. LUCKETT, Abner GIBSON, William BRONAUGH, Wm. H. DORSEY.

3H:311   Date: 5 Aug 1824   RtCt: 6 Aug 1824
John WRIGHT & wife Peggy of Ldn to Sarah ELLZEY of Ldn. B/S of 52a (residue of tract dev. to Peggy late Peggy SANFORD by late James HEREFORD dec'd) abt ½ mile W of Lsbg nr Federal hill, __ HEREFORD, __THORNTON, __ CAMPBELL. Wit: Abiel JENNERS, Robert BRADEN.

3H:314   Date: 6 Aug 1824   RtCt: 6 Aug 1824
John MOUNT of Ldn to Jonathan CARTER of Ldn. Trust to Jacob SILCOT of Ldn as security in suit of John W. COE agt Wm. SMITH & Jas. MOUNT using crops.

3H:315   Date: 11 Jun 1824   RtCt: 12 Jul 1824
Walter LANGLY & wife Susanah of Ldn to Timothy CARRINGTON of Ldn. B/S of 5a on Blue Ridge Mt. adj __ BRADFIELD, R. CHEW. Wit: Ben. GRAYSON, John W. GRAYSON.

3H:317   Date: 17 Apr 1824   RtCt: 10 May 1824
Mary VIOLETT (w/o John VIOLETT) and William SILCOTT & wife Sally of Ldn to Hiram SEATON of Ldn. B/S of 20a adj heirs of Charles LEWIS, __ SEATON. Wm. BRONAUGH, Francis W. LUCKETT. Delv. to SEATON 28 Oct 1839.

3H:319   Date: 11 Jun 1824   RtCt: ___
Amos CLAYTON & wife Elisabeth of Ldn to Timothy CARRINGTON of Ldn. B/S of ¼a in pumpkin town on turnpike road through Snickers Gap adj Mrs. HODGERSON, Notley C. WILLIAMS. Wit: Benj. GRAYSON, John W. GRAYSON. Delv. to CARRINGTON 4 Jun 1827.

3H:321   Date: 11 Jun 1824   RtCt: 12 Jul 1824
Martha CLAYTON of Ldn to Timothy CARRINGTON of Ldn. B/S of 66 sq poles in pumpkin town on turnpike road through Snickers Gap, adj Mr. WILLIAMS. Wit: William EVENS, Heaton PEARCE, William GALLOWAY. Delv. to CARRINGTON 4 Jun 1827.

3H:323   Date: 28 Jul 1824   RtCt: 28 Jul 1824
Joseph DANIEL of Ldn to Richard H. HENDERSON, Humphrey POWELL and Jesse TIMMS of Ldn. Trust for debt to George CARTER of Oatlands using 150a (cnvy/b James SINCLAIR Sep 1814).

3H:325   Date: 26 Jul 1824   RtCt: 26 Jul 1824
Mosses GUILICK of Ldn to Richard H. HENDERSON, Humphrey POWELL and Jesse TIMMS of Ldn. Trust for debt to George CARTER of Oatlands using 300a where GUILICK now lives (from will of father John GUILICK rec. 12 Sep 1808). Wit: W. L. COCKERILL. Delv. to W. L. COCKERILL agent for CARTER ___.

3H:326   Date: 13 Aug 1824   RtCt: 13 Aug 1824
George JANNEY of Ldn to L. P. W. BALCH of Ldn. Trust for debt to
William SMITH of Ldn using 584a in Monongalia Co Va (prch/o
Abraham BAKER), farm animals, crops, household items. Delv. to
BALCH 8 Feb 1826.

3H:328   Date: 8 Jan 1808   RtCt: 13 Oct 1823/4 Jun 1824
John McILHANY Jr. & wife Harriet of Ldn to Elizabeth McILHANY of
Ldn. B/S of land (from estate of James McILHANY dec'd) on NW
fork of Goose Creek where David F. BEALE now lives. Wit: John
McILHANY, Stacy TAYLOR, Lewis ELLSEY.

3H:329   Date: 28 Jul 1824   RtCt: 28 Jul 1824
Thomas F. TEBBS of Fqr to Charles G. ESKRIDGE of Ldn. Trust for
debt to John GRAY of Ldn using 200a (allotted to TEBBS in div. of
William CARR dec'd of PrWm) adj William RUST, William TEBBS,
Jno. P. DUVALL, Carolina road, Little River.

3H:331   Date: 10 Jun 1824   RtCt: 10 Aug 1824
Enos W. NEWTON & wife Sarah of Mdbg to Humphrey B. POWELL.
Trust for debt to Burr POWELL of Ldn for use of heirs of William T.
DISHMAN using Lot #47 & #48 in Mdbg. Wit: Francis W. LUCKETT,
Abner GIBSON. Delv. to pr order of B. POWELL 2 May 1829.

3H:333   Date: 19 Jun 1824   RtCt: 12 Aug 1824
John McCORMACK and Archibald MAINS (Exors of George
ROWAN dec'd) of Ldn to Jesse RICE of Ldn. B/S of lot in Lsbg on S
side of Loudoun St.

3H:334   Date: 7 Aug 1824   RtCt: 9 Aug 1824
Garrett WALKER & wife Ruth of Ldn to Isaac and Samuel NICHOLS
of Ldn. Trust for debt to James HOGE and Isaac NICHOLS Jr. of
Ldn using l17a on Beaverdam adj James BROWN, Widow
VANHORNE's dower lot, Samuel BROWN; and other lot (cnvy/b L.
P. W. BALCH Jan 1819, DBk XX:295). Wit: William BRONAUGH,
William H. DORSEY. Delv. to Saml. NICHOL's Exors 10 Nov 1825.

3H:337   Date: 7 Aug 1824   RtCt: 9 Aug 1824
Sophia WALKER, Garrot WALKER & wife Ruth, Joseph WALKER &
wife Mary, William WALKER & wife Nancy, John WALKER & wife
Abigail, James WELSH & wife Mary, Benjamin WALKER & wife
Elisabeth, Thomas GORE & wife Sarah of Ldn to Isaac and Samuel
NICHOLS of Ldn. Trust for debt to James HOGUE and Isaac
NICHOLS Jr. of Ldn using 169a on Beaverdam. Wit: William
BRONAUGH, William H. DORSEY. Delv. to Saml. NICHOL's Exors
14 Nov 1825.

3H:342   Date: 2 Jul 1824   RtCt: 9 Aug 1824
Edmund SMITH & wife Elisabeth of Ldn to Lewis M. SMITH of Ldn.
B/S of lot on N side of Mercer St in Aldie adj SMITH (prch/o George
PELTER). Wit: Burr POWELL, A. GIBSON.

3H:343   Date: 11 Jun 1824   RtCt: ___
George PELTER & wife Catherine of Frederick Co to Edmund SMITH of Ldn. B/S of ½a Lots #20, #21 & #22 in Aldie on N side of Mercer St.

3H:345   Date: 112 Jun 1824   RtCt: 9 Aug 1824
William PAXON Jr. & wife Diademia of Ldn to Andrew S. ANDERSON of Wtfd. B/S of lot in Wtfd (cnvy/b Joseph STEER) adj Richard CHILTON, Edward DORSEY, __ SMALLWOOD. Wit: R. BRADEN, Abiel JENNERS. Delv. pr order 4 Feb 1834.

3H:347   Date: 1 Aug 1824   RtCt: 9 Aug 1824
William SILCOTT & wife Sarah of Ldn to Hiram SEATON of Ldn. B/S of 20a adj Charles LEWIS. Wit: Cuthbert POWELL, Joseph CARR.

3H:349   Date: __ 1824   RtCt: 9 Aug 1824
William S. EACHES & wife Ann of Ldn to Joseph LUKE of Ldn. B/S of 2a (part of land inherited by Thomas CLOWES) adj Lsbg road, Joshua GORE, Constantine HUGHES, Thomas HUGHES. Wit: John McCORMICK, James H. HAMILTON. Delv. to LUKE 19 Aug 1826.

3H:350   Date: 19 Jun 1824   RtCt: 9 Aug 1824
William McMULLIN & wife Elisabeth of Ldn to Fielding LYNN of Ldn. B/S of 8a on Beaverdam adj John MOUNT, Jesse BURSON, Ezekiel MOUNT. Wit: John SINCLAIR, Wm. SMITH, James LYNN, Burr POWELL, Abner GIBSON. Delv. to John SINCLAIR pr order 11 Jul 1836.

3H:352   Date: 10 May 1824   RtCt: 9 Aug 1824
Shff John ROSE to William SILCOTT of Ldn. B/S of 143a (cnvy/b insolvent Jno. VIOLETT Jan 1824, descended to his wife Mary formerly Mary LEWIS as distributee of James LEWIS dec'd) adj Enoch TRIPLETT, Saml. SINGLETON.

3H:354   Date: 28 Jul 1824   RtCt: 9 Aug 1824
Tunis SLACK of Ldn to Sydnor BAILY of Ldn. Trust for debt to Abraham L. SLACK using farm animals, household items.

3H:355   Date: 17 Nov 1823   RtCt: 9 Aug 1824
Stephen McPHERSON Jr & wife Cecilia of Ldn to Abner G. HUMPHREY of Ldn. B/S of 44a (cnvy/b William CARTER) adj Dempsey CARTER, Jacob DRAKE, Abner HUMPHREY, William CARTER. Wit: Saml. M. EDWARDS.

3H:357   Date: 13 Jun 1824   RtCt: 9 Aug 1824
John P. DUVALL of Fqr to Nelson GREEN of Ldn. Release of trust for debt to Gabriel GREEN & Fanny HARRISON of Ldn using

3H:358   Date: 22 May 1824   RtCt: 9 Aug 1824
William PAXON Sr. & wife Jane of Ldn to Samuel PAXON of Ldn. B/S of 35a (part of land prch/o John HOUGH) on road leading to Wtfd, adj Isaac STEER. Wit: Robert BRADEN, Abiel JENNERS. Delv. to Saml. PAXON 28 Dec 1827.

3H:360   Date: 20 Nov 1823   RtCt: 8 Dec 1823/9 Aug 1824
Elijah GLASCOCK & wife Joice to Cuthbert POWELL of Ldn. Trust for debt to Joseph CARR using 230a adj Danl. THOMPSON, Wm. FITZHUGH. Wit: Burr WEEKS, John GLASCOCK, Caldwell CARR. Delv. to C. CARR 12 Apr 1827.

3H:362   Date: 31 Jul 1824   RtCt: 9 Aug 1824
John C. BAZZILL & wife Mary of Ldn to Joshua OSBURN of Ldn. Trust for debt to Thomas JAMES of Ldn using 24a on both sides of Valentine branch nr blue ridge adj heirs of William BROWN. Wit: Craven OSBURN, John WHITE. Delv. to Thomas JAMES 25 Aug 1828.

3H:364   Date: 19 Jun 1824   RtCt: 19 Jun/9 Aug 1824
David LOVETT of Ldn to Isaac, Samuel & Swithen NICHOLS of Ldn. Trust for debt to Isaac NICHOLS Jr. & James HOGE of Ldn using 183½a on NW fork of Goose Creek nr Thatchers mill; and 76a (cnvy/b Mortimore McILHANY); and 16a adj __ BRADFIELD; and 92a (cnvy/b Charles J. KILGORE of MontMd). Delv. to Saml. NICHOL's Exor. 10 Nov 1825.

3H:367   Date: __ 1824   RtCt: 9 Aug 1824
Timothy TAYLOR & wife Achsa of Ldn to Joel OSBURN Jr. of Ldn. Trust for debt to Morris OSBURN using 200a on NW fork of Goose Creek where TAYLOR lives. Wit: Craven OSBURN, John WHITE. Delv. to Morris OSBURN 8 Jun 1825.

3H:369   Date: 4 Jun 1824   RtCt: 9 Aug 1824
Amos HARVEY & wife Elisabeth to John A. MARMADUKE and Samuel CLENDENING. Trust for debt to William CLENDENING using 3a (cnvy/b Wm. PAXON) adj John CAMPBELL, James MEHANY [McILHANEY]. Wit: Craven OSBURN, John WHITE.

3H:372   Date: 9 Aug 1824   RtCt: 9 Aug 1824
Amos JANNEY to James McILHANY. Trust for debt to Philip HEATON and Joseph JANNEY of AlexDC using 130a.

3H:374   Date: 10 Aug 1824   RtCt: 10 Aug 1824
Isaac WRIGHT (Guardian of James Wm. STEWART) of Ldn to William LOYD of Ldn. Stewart bound to LOYD as taylor apprentice for 5 years from 10 Aug 1824. Wit: Thomas GLEESAR?

3H:375   Date: 4 Feb 1824   RtCt: 10 Aug 1824
Joseph MEADE & wife Elisabeth and Richard H. HENDERSON of Ldn to William SMITH (assignee of MEADE) of Ldn. B/S 104½a (prch/o George JANNEY May 1820) adj Bernard TAYLOR, A. GIBSON, Israel JANNEY. Wit: John McCORMICK, Presly CORDELL. Delv. to SMITH 10 Mar 1826.

3H:377   Date: 11 Aug 1824   RtCt: 11 Aug 1824
Emanuel WALTMAN to John GEORGE. Trust for debt to Jacob SMITH and Susanah SMITH using 11a (Lot #4 in survey for

Ferdinando FAIRFAX) adj __ BOOTH. Delv. to Jno. GEORGE 1 Feb 1833.

3H:378 Date: 29 Jun 1824 RtCt: 13 Aug 1824

Isaac BROWN & wife Sarah of Ldn to Jonas JANNEY Jr. B/S of ½a in Union adj Isaac BROWN, Samuel DUNKIN, __ GALLAHER, Asa TRAHORN. Wit: William BRONAUGH, Wm. H. DORSEY. Delv. to JANNEY 29 Oct 1830.

3H:380 Date: 1 Jun 1824 RtCt: 14 Aug 1824

Gustavus ELGIN of Ldn to daughter Nancy DULIN & her children. Loan of negro woman Nancy & her child, negro Jim (former prop. of son-in-law Edward DULIN purchased at sale by Dpty. Benj. SHRIEVE and constable Evritt SANDERS) and farm animals and household items. Wit: C. GULATT, Jno. A. BINNS.

3H:381 Date: 13 Aug 1824 RtCt: 14 Aug 1824

William RUST & wife Elisabeth of Fqr to Noble BEVERIDGE of Ldn. B/S of 91½a (allotted to Thomas CHINN in div. of father Thomas CHINN dec'd and conveyed to RUST May 1824) nr Mdbg adj Burr POWELL; and ½a (cnvy/b Thomas A. DENNIS Aug 1824). Wit: Leven LUCKETT, Abner GIBSON. Delv. to BEVERIDGE Jun 1833.

3H:383 Date: 16 Aug 1824 RtCt: 17 Aug 1824

Samuel NOLAND of Ldn to Lloyd NOLAND of Fqr. Trust for debt to Noble BEVERIDGE, Hiram McVEIGH, John J. HARDING, Burr POWELL, Lloyd NOLAND, Elisabeth NOLAND, Edwin C. BROWN, Thomas BROWN, Townsend D. PEYTON using 75a island in Potomac nr Noland Ferry, 50a (from div. of father Thomas NOLAND dec'd) adj Samuel CLAPHAM, Elisabeth NOLAND, Burr POWELL, negro boy Charles abt 18y old (conveyed as a security to Elisabeth NOLAND). Delv. to Lloyd NOLAND 26 Nov 1826.

3H:385 Date: 14 May 1824 RtCt: 17 Aug 1824

Thomas CHINN & wife Ann H. of Ldn to William RUST of Fqr. B/S of 71a nr Mdbg adj Burr POWELL (allotted to CHINN in div. of father Thomas CHINN dec'd except that conveyed to Barney MECKINS & Robert CHINN). Wit: Burr POWELL, A. GIBSON.

3H:387 Date: 13 Aug 1824 RtCt: 17 Aug 1824

William A. DENNIS & wife Lettice of Ldn to William RUST of Fqr. B/S of ½a on Ashby Gap turnpike road (part of tract allotted Thomas CHINN in div. of father Thomas CHINN dec'd and conveyed to DENNIS). Wit: Abner GIBSON, Leven LUCKETT.

3H:388 Date: 13 Aug 1824 RtCt: 17 Aug 1824

William RUST & wife Elisabeth of Fqr to William A. DENNIS of Ldn. B/S of 313a (prch/o Dr. Foushe TEBBS) adj heirs of John TYLER dec'd. Wit: Leven LUCKETT, Abner GIBSON. Delv. 12 Dec 1825.

3H:390 Date: 16 Aug 1824 RtCt: 17 Aug 1824

Ebenezer GRUBB of Ldn to Andrew HILLMAN of Ldn. Mortgage on 113a adj Peter GIDEON, __ EVANS. Wit: Samuel NEER.

3H:392 Date: 6 Apr 1824 RtCt: 17 Aug 1824
Charles P. TUTT & wife Ann Mason and George M. CHICHESTER
of Ldn to William CLINE of Ldn. B/S of 1 rood lot on S side of
Cornwall St in Lsbg adj John DRISH. Wit: Saml. CLAPHAM, Saml.
DAWSON.

3H:393 Date: 14 May 1824 RtCt: 19 Aug 1824
William A. DENNIS & wife Catherine/Kitty of Ldn to Elias L. CHINN,
Ann M. CHINN, Catherine M. CHINN, Martha CHINN & Francis
CHINN (ch/o Thomas & Ann M. CHINN) of Ldn. B/S of 91¼a adj
Samuel DISHMAN, Silas BEATTY. Wit: Burr POWELL, Abner
GIBSON.

3H:395 Date: 17 Aug 1824 RtCt: 21 Aug 1824
Caldwell CARR (trustee of Elisabeth GIBSON for her as guardian of
her infant children with securities Abner GIBSON, Isaac NICHOLS,
William NICHOLS, Stephen WILSON) of Upperville, Ldn to Samuel
PEACH of AlexDC. B/S of 14½a (PEACH a child of GIBSON). Wit:
John H. ASHBY, William MILTON, Wm. WRIGHT.

3H:396 Date: 14 Jan 1824 RtCt: 21 Aug 1824
Elisabeth GIBSON of Ldn to Samuel PEACH of AlexDC. B/S of
14½a adj William RICHARDS (cnvy/b Mosses GIBSON), adj James
GIBSON, heirs of Jno. GIBSON dec'd. Conveyed to PEACH on
acct. of a legacy left Rebeca GIBSON w/o PEACH by her father.
Delv. to PEACH 2 Sep 1826.

3H:398 Date: 26 Aug 1824 RtCt: 27 Aug 1824
Rich'd H. HENDERSON and Thos. R. MOTT of Ldn to Samuel
CLAPHAM & wife Elisabeth of Ldn. Release of trust of Jun 1824 for
debt to Chandler PRICE using 'Eagles Nest' former residence of
Samuel's father.

3H:398 Date: 30 Aug 1824 RtCt: 30 Aug 1824
Charles DRISH & wife Susanah of Ldn to William D. DRISH of Ldn.
B/S of lot in Lsbg on W side of King St. (cnvy/b Sampson BLINCOE
and Richard H. HENDERSON as commrs., May 1815). Wit: John H.
McCABE, Presley CORDELL.

3H:400 Date: 13 Aug 1824 RtCt: 30 Aug 1824
William VICKERS of Ldn to Daniel EACHES of Ldn. Trust for debt to
Joseph CARR using 100a (except 18a sold to Enoch TRIPLETT) adj
Mason FRENCH and 31a (prch/o Whitman LEITH) adj Elisha
POWELL. Delv. to Caldwell CARR agt for J. CARR 14 Nov 1828.

3H:402 Date: 30 Aug 1824 RtCt: 30 Aug 1824
Charles DRISH & wife Susanah of Ldn to William KING (Admr of
Henry GLASCOW dec'd) of Ldn. B/S of lot on E side of King St in
Lsbg with house now occupied by Thomas WILLIAMS adj John
SURGINOR's boot and shoe factory, Robt. BENTLEY. Wit: John H.
McCABE, Presley CORDELL.

3H:403   Date: 30 Aug 1824   RtCt: 30 Aug 1824
William D. DRISH & wife Harrriet of Ldn to James L. MARTIN of Ldn. Trust for debt to Charles DRISH using lot on W side of King St [see DBk 3H:398].

3H:404   Date: 8 Jan 1824   RtCt: 31 Aug 1824
Ann COLEMAN of Ldn to niece Frances Ann NEWMAN of Ldn. Gift of negro girl Charlott 3-4y old slave for life. Wit: Jas. R. COLEMAN, Johnston COLEMAN.

3H:405   Date: 17 Jun 1824   RtCt: 1 Sep 1824
Stephen W. ROZIL & wife Catherine of Ldn to Samuel BEVERS of Ldn. B/S of 26a (Lot #5 from allotment in div. of Reuben TRIPLETT dec'd). Wit: William BRONAUGH, William H. DORSEY. Delv. to Thomas BEAVERS Exor. of Samuel BEAVERS 16 Mar 1839.

3H:407   Date: 18 Jun 1824   RtCt: 1 Sep 1824
Samuel BEVERS & wife Sarah of Ldn to Benjamin MITCHELL Jr. of Ldn. Trust for debt to Stephen W. ROSZIL using above land. Wit: William BRONAUGH, William H. DORSEY.

3H:408   Date: 1 Sep 1824   RtCt: 1 Sep 1824
Edward HAMMATT of Ldn to John S. PEARCE of Ldn. B/S of lot in Lsbg adj lot leased by John SHAW to John SURGHNOR then to PEARCE on Back St. Delv. to Pearce 20 Oct 1825.

3H:409   Date: 8 Sep 1823   RtCt: 2 Sep 1824
James B. SPENCE late of Ldn to wife Nancy SPENCE. PoA to sell lot devised to her by her father James BOOTH dec'd.

3H:410   Date: 10 May 1788   RtCt: 3 Sep 1824
Samuel HOUGH & wife Ann to William TAYLOR. B/S of lot on King St in Lsbg adj TAYLOR's stone house, Samuel MURRY's stone greenery. Wit: Pat. CRAVEN, John LITTLEJOHN, James HAMILTON.

3H:411   Date: 25 Apr 1822   RtCt: 13 Aug 1822/4 Sep 1824
William HERBERT of Ffx to John NEER Jr. of Ldn. B/S of 12a on Potomac River adj Catherine NICEWANGER, John CUNNARD. Wit: Philip GROOVE, William DERRY, John CONARD, Jonathan CONARD, George SMITH. Delv. pr order 6 Jun 1827.

3H:412   Date: 21 May 1824   RtCt: 6 Sep 1824
Charles BINNS (surviving trustee with John MATHIAS now dec'd, Dec 1808, DBk KK:145, of William WOODY now dec'd) to Elisabeth WOODY (wd/o William WOODY). B/S of late residence on N side of Loudoun St in Lsbg. Delv. to C. BINNS ___.

3H:413   Date: 21 Aug 1824   RtCt: 28 Aug 1824
John LIND of FredMd to Margaret BOGEN (w/o John BOGEN) now of Ldn. Loan of farm animals, household items. Wit: George VINSEL, John VINSEL.

3H:414   Date: 10 Sep 1824   RtCt: 10 Sep 1824
Benedict WENNER and Adam SLATZ/SLATES & wife Sevilla (late WENNER) of Ldn to John WENNER of Ldn. B/S of int. in estate of late William WENNER dec'd –farm where he lived and wood land on E side of Short Hill totaling 227a. Wit: John McCORMICK, Saml. M. EDWARDS.

3H:415   Date: 15 Jun 1824   RtCt: 15 Jun/10 Sep 1824
Richard H. HENDERSON & S. BLINCOE to Henery PEERS & Eleanor PEERS. Release of trust of Nov 1817 for debt to Francis TRIPLETT Sr.

3H:416   Date: 11 Sep 1824   RtCt: 11 Sep 1824
Thomas N. HARDING of Ldn to William EAGLE of Ldn. Trust for debt to Thomas McGILL of MontMd using farm animals, household items.

3H:416   Date: 11 Aug 1824   RtCt: 13 Sep 1824
Jonathan BURSON of Preble Co Ohio to Seth SMITH of Ldn. PoA including for note from Isaac & James BROWN and Lewis P. W. BALCH.

3H:418   Date: 13 Sep 1824   RtCt: 13 Sep 1824
Jesse TIMMS and Geo. CARTER. Bond on TIMMS as Commissioner of Revenue in 1st District.

3H:418   Date: 7 Sep 1822 [24?]   RtCt: 13 Sep 1824
Jesse McVEIGH and Joshua OSBURN. Bond on McVEIGH as Commissioner of Revenue in 2nd District.

3H:419   Date: 2 Feb 1824   RtCt: 13 Sep 1824
Frederick HANDSHY & wife Catherine of Ldn to James STUBBLEFIELD of JeffVa. B/S of 170a on Potomac River to top of Short Hill Mt, adj Hiram KERNEY [McKENNEY?], __ FRAZIER. Wit: D. LONG, John MOLER. Delv. pr order 7 Jul 1831.

3H:421   Date: 9 Sep 1824   RtCt: 13 Sep 1824
John NEAR & wife Eve of Ldn to James STUBLEFIELD of JeffVa. B/S of 4a in Ldn and JeffVa on Potomac, adj Mdbg road. Wit: Durett LONG, John S. GALLAHER.

3H:423   Date: 10 Aug 1824   RtCt: 13 Sep 1824
John McCORMICK and William CHILTON (trustees of Mosses GIBSON for benefit of James H. HAMILTON) of Lsbg and David ENGLISH (trustee of James H. HAMILTON of Ldn for use of James EAKINS of DC) to Joseph CARR. B/S of all land in previous trusts. Wit: J. MOORE Jr., Saml. CLAPHAM, Jno. WHITE. Delv. to Caldwell CARR 13 Feb 1826.

3H:425   Date: 22 May 1824   RtCt: 6 Sep 1824
Elizabeth WOODY to Joseph CARTER. Trust for debt to John SIMPSON & Isaiah POTTS using lot & house on N side of Loudoun St in Lsbg between Mrs. DONAHOE & Chas. GULATT. Delv. to C. BINNS 3 Mar 1826.

3l:001 Date: 2 Jun 1824 RtCt: 11 Oct 1824
Thomson F. MASON and Daniel MINOR of AlexDC to Edmund J. LEE & wife Sally of AlexDC. Release of trust for Daniel MINOR as endorser on note. Delv. to E. J. LEE 6 Sep 1825.

3l:003 Date: 31 Aug 1824 RtCt: 13 Sep 1824
Caldwell WRIGHT of Ldn to Abiel JENNERS of Ldn. B/S of ¼ und. share in 2 tracts of father William WRIGHT dec'd – 103a (cnvy/b Moses CALDWELL Feb 1796) and 31a (cnvy/b Anthony CONARD and Philip MOUL Jun 1811)

3l:004 Date: 7 Aug 1824 RtCt: 13 Sep 1824
John PAXON & wife Ann of Ldn to David SHAWEN of Ldn. B/S of 105a (prch/o William PAXON, Apr 1822) adj __ JONES, John JANNEY, Jno. A. BINNS dec'd. Wit: R. BRADEN, Presly CORDELL.

3l:005 Date: 10 May 1824 RtCt: 13 Sep 1824
Robert BRADEN of Ldn to Noble S BRADEN of Ldn. B/S of lot with stone building in Wtfd (prch/o William PAXON). Delv. to N. S. BRADEN 26 Sep 1850.

3l:006 Date: 10 May 1824 RtCt: 13 Sep 1824
Robert BRADEN of Ldn to Burr BRADEN of Ldn. B/S of 3/8a in Hllb (cnvy/b John B. STEVENS, Jun 1809).

3l:007 Date: __ 1824 RtCt: 17 Sep 1824
Jesse TIMMS (trustee of Edward KELLY) of Ldn to George CARTER of Oatlands. B/S of 522a (Oct 1817 Edward KELLY conveyed to Jesse TIMMS and Sampson BLINCOE in trust for debt to CARTER). Delv. to W. L. COCKERILL agent for Geo. CARTER. .

3l:008 Date: 15 Sep 1824 RtCt: 17 Sep 1824
George SA(U)NDERS & wife Elisabeth to Joshua PUSEY and Sampson BLINCOE. Trust for debt to James NIXON (assigned note from George JANNEY) using 72a adj Margaret SAUNDERS, John SAUNDERS; and land prch/o John SAUNDERS. Wit: Henery PEERS, Tasker C. QUINLIN, Cyrus SAUNDERS, Abiel JENNERS, Samuel HOUGH. Delv. to PUSEY 27 May 1826.

3l:011 Date: 18 Sep 1824 RtCt: 27 Sep 1824
David SHAWEN of Ldn to Isaac WALKER of Ldn. B/S of 105a (prch/o John PAXON) adj John JANNEY, John A. BINNS dec'd. Delv. to Isaac WALKER on ___.

3l:012 Date: 2 Jan 1824 RtCt: 27 Sep 1824
Samuel WALTMAN & wife Catherine of Lsbg to Jacob WALTMAN of Ldn. B/S of 1/8th share of 109a of Samuel WALTMAN dec'd (subject to dower of late Widow now w/o Levi PRINCE) on Catockton Creek adj William PAXON, John HAMILTON.

3l:014 Date: 31 Aug 1824 RtCt: 28 Sep 1824
Henery CARTER & wife Sarah and Richard CARTER & wife Deborah of Ldn to Isaac and Samuel NICHOLS. Trust for debt to

Isaac NICHOLS Jr. using 54a and 72a and 100a. Wit: Benjamin GRAYSON, John W. GRAYSON. Delv. to Saml. NICHOLS Exor. 10 Nov 1825.

3I:017   Date: 13 Mar 1824   RtCt: 29 Sep 1824
James SAUNDERS & wife Prescilla of Berkly Co Va, Presly SAUNDERS & wife Mary, Evritt SAUNDERS & wife Susan, Ramey G. SAUNDERS, Cyrus SAUNDERS, John SAUNDERS, Gunnel SAUNDERS & Edith SAUNDERS of Ldn and Henery SAUNDERS (now of the U.S. Army) of Ldn to Thomas SAUNDERS of Ldn (all ch/o Henery SAUNDERS dec'd). B/S of all rights to estate of father subject to dower. Wit: James H. HAMILTON, Saml. M. EDWARDS.

3I:019   Date: 1 Oct 1824   RtCt: 1 Oct 1824
Judson EMBERSON of Ldn to Saml. M. EDWARDS of Ldn. Trust for James GILMORE of Ldn as security with Henery H. HAMITT for Mathew MITCHELL using household items, horse, crops.

3I:021   Date: 30 Sep 1824   RtCt: 30 Sep 1824
Alfred G. CARTER, William G. CARTER and Robert CARTER (ch/o Robert CARTER dec'd formerly of Sudley) to George HANCOCK (creditor of Robert dec'd). B/S of 650a Delv. pr order __.

3I:022   Date: 1 Oct 1824   RtCt: 3 Oct 1824
Charles WILLIAMS & wife Mary of Ldn to Sydnah WILLIAMS and Eleanor STEER of Ldn. B/S of land prch/o Mosses DOWDALL & wife Sarah (her int. in estate of father Isaac STEER dec'd). Wit: John H. McCABE, Saml. M. EDWARDS. Delv. pr order 2 Jan 1826.

3I:023   Date: 1 Oct 1824   RtCt: 2 Oct 1824
Mosses DOWDALL & wife Sarah of Ldn to Charles WILLIAMS of Ldn. B/S of Sarah's 135a int. in real estate of father Isaac STEER dec'd (in consideration for WILLIAMS' int. in lands of father Enos WILLIAMS dec'd). Wit: John H. McCABE, Saml. M. EDWARDS. Delv. to WILLIAMS 26 Aug 1825.

3I:025   Date: 1 Oct 1824   RtCt: 2 Oct 1824
Charles WILLIAMS & wife Mary of Ldn to William GILMORE and Rich'd H. HENDERSON (trustees of Sarah DOWDALL). B/S of 56a and 2 wood lots from father's estate. Wit: John H. McCABE, Saml. M. EDWARDS. Delv. to HENDERSON 24 Nov 1826.

3I:026   Date: 2 Oct 1824   RtCt: 2 Oct 1824
John BEATTY of Ldn to Susan Elisabeth RUST of Ldn. BoS for farm animals. Wit: S. BLINCOE, P. SAUNDERS, W. D. DRISH.

3I:027   Date: 4 Oct 1824   RtCt: 4 Oct 1824
Thomas HUMPHREY of Ldn to Jonathan EWERS of Ldn. B/S of 13¾a (Lot #6 in div. of Jesse HUMPHREY dec'd). Wit: S. BLINCOE, Joseph HUMPHREY, David J. EATON.

3I:028   Date: 28 Sep 1824   RtCt: 17 Oct 1824
John SA(U)NDERS late of Ldn now of Westmoreland Co Pa to George SANDERS of Ldn. B/S of 101a (purchased by George &

John of George JANNEY, Jun 1818) adj Margaret SANDERS, Archibald MORRISON, Elijah PEACOCK, Francis McKENNY. Wit: S. H. MONTGOMERY, James SLOAN, John NEWELLS?. Delv. to George SAUNDERS 13 Apr 1830.

3I:029   Date: 25 Sep 1824   RtCt: 11 Oct 1824
Amos GUILICK. Oath as Ensign in 57th Reg 6th Brig 2nd Div. of Va Militia.

3I:030   Date: 2 Oct 1824   RtCt: 11 Oct 1824
John J. MATHIAS. Appointment as Lt. of a Company of Light Infantry in 2nd Batt of 57th Reg 6th Brig 2nd Div of Va Militia.

3I:030   Date: 11 Oct 1824   RtCt: 11 Oct 1824
William FITZIMONS, Archibald MAINES and S. EDMONDS. Bond on FIZTIMONS as constable.

3I:030   Date: 11 Oct 1824   RtCt: 11 Oct 1824
Thomas Jefferson BENNETT, James BROWN, Charles H. HAMILTON and George W. SHAWEN. Bond on BENNETT as constable.

3I:031   Date: __ 1824   RtCt: 13 Sep 1824
William NICHOLS of Ldn to Joseph TAVENER of Ldn. B/S of 2 rood lot adj William NICHOLS, Joseph TAVENER (part of land cnvy/b Jesse THATCHER). Delv. to TAVENER 2 Jun 1834.

3I:032   Court order Date: 13 Aug 1822   RtCt: 11 Oct 1824
Isaac STEER dec'd. Division – 91a Lots #5, #6 & #7 and 6a Lot #8 of Big Spring Farm to widow Elisabeth STEER; 105a Lot #1 to James CRAVEN & his children Joseph, Isaac and Eleanor (of Hannah CRAVEN dec'd); 135a Lot #2 to Mosses DOWDALL & wife Sarah; 111a Lot #3 to Chas. WILLIAMS & wife Sarah; 131a Lot #4 to Eleanor STEER. Divisors: Aron SANDERS, Thomas SANDERS, Saml. M. EDWARDS. Gives plat.

3I:036   Date: 7 Oct 1824   RtCt: 11 Oct 1824
Michael BOGER dec'd. Division – 134½a widow's dower; 27¾a Lot #1 and 10a Lot #1 on Short Hill to Michael BOGER; 33a Lot #2 and 11a Lot #2 on Short Hill to Jacob BOGER; 33a Lot #3 and 13a Lot #3 on Short Hill to Samuel BOGER; 41a Lot #4 to Philip BOGER; 40¼a Lot #5 to John BOGER; 21a Lot #6 and Lot #6 [on Short Hill?] to Mary BOGER; 29a Lot #7 and 11¼a Wood Lot #7 to Elisabeth BOGER; 37a Lot #8 to Mary AMICK late Mary BOGER; 92a Lot #9 to children of __ ARNOLD late __ BOGER. Divisors: John HAMILTON, Peter STUCK, Jno. J. MATHIAS. Gives plat.

3I:039   Date: 12 Aug 1824   RtCt: 11 Oct 1824
William WENNER dec'd. Division – 34a and 3a lot on Short Hill to widow's dower; 15a Lot #1 and 1a Lot #1 on Short Hill to Daniel WENNER; 17¼a Lot #2 to Joseph WENNER; 16½a Lot #3 to Charlott WENNER; 19a Lot #4 to John WENNER; 15¾a Lot #5 and 2½a Lot #5 [on Short Hill?] to Geo. WENNER; 11a Lot #6 and 1a

Lot #6 at foot of Short Hill to Jonathan WENNER; 16a Lot #7 and 1½a Lot #7 on Short Hill to Benedick WENNER; 16a Lot #8 and 1½a Lot #8 on Short Hill to Sybyia WENNER now Sybyia SLATS; 15a Lot #9 to Solomon WENNER; 14a Lot #10 to Wm. WENNER; 15½a Lot #11 to Catherine WENNER; 10a Lot #12 and 1½a Lot #12 on Short Hill to Mary WENNER. Divisors: John HAMILTON, John BOOTH, Adam SANBOWER, Jno. J. MATHIAS. Gives plat.

3I:043 Date: 19 Feb 1824 RtCt: 23 Oct 1824
William EMBERSON & wife Mary Ann of AlexDC and Judson EMBERSON & wife Elisabeth of Ldn to William CARR. B/S of lot in Lsbg on N side of Loudoun St. adj Saml. MURRY, James GAINER. Wit: Thos. SANDERS, Saml. M. EDWARDS.

3I:045 Date: 12 Feb 1824 RtCt: 11 Oct 1824
Usher SKINNER & wife Rebeca of Ldn to Thomas FRED Jr of Ldn. B/S of 30¼a (cnvy/b Daniel BROWN) where FRED now resides, adj Poor of Ldn, John HANN, John BALDWIN, Thomas TRAHORN. Wit: Benj. GRAYSON, John W. GRAYSON. Delv. to FRED 18 Oct 1832.

3I:046 Date: 11 Oct 1824 RtCt: 11 Oct 1824
George LEE and Maria(h) C. LEE of Ldn to Sarah SNYDER (wd/o Peter SNYDER dec'd) and Jane Elisabeth SNYDER, Catherine Smith SNYDER, William Henery SNYDER and Elisabeth Ann SNYDER (ch/o Peter dec'd) of Ldn. B/S of 152a (Peter dec'd bought of LEE without making a deed) adj __ LAFABER, __ DAWSON. Wit: Charles DAWSON, Philip HOUSER, Peter OATAYAR. Delv. to Wm. Henry SNYDER 26 Jun 1843.

3I:047 Date: 25 Aug 1824 RtCt: ___
William A. ROGERS & wife Susanah (d/o Pierce BAYLY the elder) to William P. BAYLY. B/S of int. of brother Pierce BAYLY the younger - Pierce BAYLY the Elder of Ldn dev. to son Pierce BAYLY land prch/o James MURRY, Joseph BENNET and William MURRY Sep 1791; Pierce the younger died intestate. Wit: John CATHER and William LAKE Jr. in Harrison Co Va.

3I:049 Date: 11 Feb 1824 RtCt: 11 Oct 1824
Walter LANGLEY & wife Susan M. of Ldn to George PELTER of FredVa. B/S of ½a Lot #20, #21 & #22 on N side of Mercer St in Aldie. Wit: Robert ARMISTEAD, William NOLAND.

3I:050 Date: 7 Aug 1824 RtCt: 12 Oct 1824
Benjamin MOFFETT & wife Malinda of Fqr to Robert MOFFETT of Ldn. B/S of remaining part of Lot #16 in Mdbg not sold to Nelson GREEN (prch/o Amos JOHNSON and Burr POWELL) adj Whitacre Lot #16. Wit: Burr POWELL, Abner GIBSON.

3I:051 Date: 26 Apr 1824 RtCt: 14 Oct 1824
Thomson MASON of Ldn to Charles G. ESKRIDGE of Ldn. Trust for debt to John H. CANBY of Ldn using 562½a. Wit: A. A. ESKRIDGE, E. G. HAMILTON, Henery PEERS.

3I:053   Date: 5 Oct 1824   RtCt: 18 Oct 1824
Edmund LOVETT & wife Elisabeth of Ldn to Hugh SMITH of Ldn.
B/S of 171a (cnvy/b John SIMPSON Mar 1824). Wit: John
McCORMICK, Saml. M. EDWARDS. Delv. to SMITH 2 Aug 1836.

3I:055   Date: 18 Oct 1824   RtCt: 18 Oct 1824
Ann THOMAS of Ldn to John S. PEARCE of Ldn. B/S of 1a Lot #3
from div. of Leonard THOMAS dec'd f/o Ann (part of 999y lease
from P. CAVINS). Wit: Thomas HIR [HEIR?], Thomas McCARTY,
Henery ORAM. Delv. to PIERCE 10 Aug 1825.

3I:056   Date: ___   RtCt: 18 Oct 1824
L. P. W. BALCH and Samuel HATCHER of Ldn to John THOMAS Jr
of Ldn. Release of trust of Jun 1823 for debt to John PANCOAST Sr
on 150a. Delv. to William LODGE 16 Oct 1825.

3I:057   Date: 21 Feb 1824   RtCt: 18 Oct 1824
James JOHNSTON of Ldn to Thomas A. HEREFORD of Ldn. Trust
for debt to Isaac and Samuel NICHOLS using 1½a in Bloomfield adj
John RALPH. Delv. to Isaac NICKOLS Exor of S. NICKOLS ___.

3I:058   Date: 19 Oct 1824   RtCt: 19 Oct 1824
Mary DAVIS of Ldn to James McILHANY of Ldn. B/S of 32a or 33a
(assigned from div. of James McILHANY dec'd; part of 'White Oak
Bottom') adj McILHANY, Mrs. GREGG.

3I:059   Date: 14 Oct 1824   RtCt: 21 Oct 1824
Richard H. HENDERSON (trustees of Thomas J. NOLAND, Dec
1822) of Ldn to George COLEMAN of AlexDC. B/S of ½a Lot #61 in
Aldie adj Miss LACEYs.

3I:060   Date: 23 Oct 1824   RtCt: 23 Oct 1824
William CARR & wife Mary of Ldn to Peter OACHER of Ldn. B/S of
¼a on W extremity of Loudoun St on E side of Air St. in Lsbg. Wit:
Thomas SANDERS, Saml. M. EDWARDS.

3I:061   Date: 23 Oct 1824   RtCt: 23 Oct 1824
Joseph S. HICKMAN attorney for Joseph HICKMAN Sr. & wife Jane
of Franklin Co Ohio to John H. BUTCHER of Ldn. B/S of 135a und.
1/6th of claim as heirs of Elisabeth BURKINS (w/o John BURKINS,
d/o Samuel BUTCHER dec'd) now in possession of John BURKINS;
adj James PHILIPS, Benj. OVERFIELD, Jenkins PHILIPS; and adj
254a und. claim (as heir of John BUTCHER dec'd, conveyed to his
father Samuel dec'd Jun 1768) now in possession of James
CURRILL.

3I:063   Date: 24 Aug 1824   RtCt: 25 Oct 1825
Ann WRIGHT and Isaac WRIGHT of Ldn to Ann ECK(H)ART of Ldn.
B/S of 1a on N side of Market St extended from Lsbg where old poor
house stood (part of land allotted to Ann in div. of William WRIGHT
dec'd). Delv. to Ann SANDERS formerly EKHART 22 Feb 1829.

3l:064 Date: 21 Oct 1824 RtCt: 27 Oct 1824
Thomas Jefferson BENNETT of Ldn to Andrew S. ANDERSON of Ldn. Trust for debt to Joseph WOOD of Ldn using int. in land adj John WESTLY and Obed PIERPONT formerly owned by James HAMILTON Sr and beq. to his dau. Mary HAMILTON; and interest in land purchased by Charles BENNETT (now dec'd) from __ LACEY adj other lot; and int. in land in Wood Co Va on Little Knowa beq. by Charles BENNETT Sr. dec'd.

3l:065 Date: 3 Sep 1824 RtCt: 28 Oct 1824
Richard H. LEE of Ldn to Henery CLAGETT of Lsbg. B/S of 183a adj Gillmore's Mill pond, __ HOUGH.

3l:067 Date: 30 Oct 1824 RtCt: 30 Oct 1824
James THOMAS of Ldn to John BURTON of Ldn. B/S of 5a abt 1 mile W of Lsbg on N side of road across mt. to VANDEVENTERs, adj BURTON, __ HAMMETT. Delv. to BURTON 2 Sep 1825.

3l:068 Date: 30 Oct 1824 RtCt: 30 Oct 1824
Israel WILKINSON & wife Macha of Ldn to John BURTON of Ldn. B/S of 1a abt 1 mile W of Lsbg on N side of side of road across mt. to VANDEVENTERs, adj __ CHILTON. Wit: John McCORMACK, Saml. M. EDWARDS. Delv. to BURTON 2 Sep 1825.

3l:069 Date: 30 Oct 1824 RtCt: 30 Oct 1824
James THOMAS of Ldn to John J. MATHIAS of Ldn. Trust for debt to Israel WILKINSON using int. in land prch/o WILKINSON and part from John BURTON. Delv. to MATHIAS 28 Jun 1827.

3l:070 Date: 1 May 1824 RtCt: 1 Nov 1824
Thomas DRAKE (trustees of Moses WILSON in debt to William WINN, Nov 1821) of Ldn to John HATCHER of Ldn. B/S of 50a adj Dennis McCARTY, John RUSSEL.

3l:071 Date: 1 Sep 1824 RtCt: 1 Nov 1824
Cuthbert POWELL & wife Catherine of Ldn to Burr POWELL of Ldn. Trust for debt to Charles BENNETT of AlexDC using 800a adj David FULTON. Wit: William ELLZEY, John WHITE. Delv. pr order to J. T. GRIFFITH 10 Apr 1826.

3l:073 Date: 22 Apr 1824 RtCt: 1 Nov 1824
Craven WALKER & wife Alice of Ldn to Thornton WALKER of Ldn. B/S of ½a in Union (cnvy/b Thornton WALKER Apr 1821) and ¼a in Union (cnvy/b Michael PLASTER Dec 1820). Wit: Francis W. LUCKETT, John W. GRAYSON. Delv. to WALKER 19 Mar 1829.

3l:075 Date: 21 Dec 1820 RtCt: 1 Nov 1824
John SHAVER & wife Mary of Ldn to William WERTZ Jr of Ldn. B/S of 88¾a (cnvy/b Michael SHAVER, Mar 1812) adj Potomac River, Wm. WINNER, Christian BEAGLE. Wit: Robert BRADEN, Abiel JENNERS, Ebenezer GRUBB, John WHITE. Delv. to Wm. VIRTS 23 Jul 1825.

3I:077   Date: 12 Aug 1824   RtCt: 1 Nov 1824
Jesse RICE & wife Kirsa of Ldn to Archibald MAINS of Ldn. B/S of
lot & house In Lsbg on S side of Loudoun St (cnvy/b MAINS and
John McCORMACK Exors of George ROWAN dec'd, Jun 1824).
Wit: John WHITE, Presly CORDELL.

3I:078   Date: 10 Jun 1824   RtCt: 2 Nov 1824
George RICHARD of Ldn to Gidian HOUSHOLDER of Ldn. B/S of 8
lots divided among reps of Adam HOUSEHOLDER dec'd – 2a Lots
#1, #3, #4, #5, #6, #7, and Lots #9 and 10½a House Lot #5, totaling
30a. Delv. to G. HOUSEHOLDER 7 Feb 1828.

3I:079   Date: 1 Sep 1824   RtCt: 7 Sep 1824
Presly CORDELL & wife Amelia of Ldn to Amos BEALE of Ldn.
Trust for debt to David BEALE of Ldn using 306a adj __
SCHOOLEY lease, __ RAMEY, R. BRADEN.

3I:081   Date: 2 Nov 1824   RtCt: 3 Nov 1824
Charles BINNS of Ldn to Burr POWELL, Cuthbert POWELL and
Alfred H. POWELL (trustees of S. H. CHILTON). BoS of farm
animals prch/o William CHILTON Esq.

3I:081   Date: 26 Oct 1824   RtCt: 4 Oct 1824
George JANNEY of Ldn to Samuel GILPIN of Ldn. Trust for debt to
Bernard GILPIN of MontMd as bail in chancery using household
items.

3I:082   Date: 5 Nov 1824   RtCt: 5 Nov 1824
Tasker C. QUINLIN of Ldn to Thomas R. MOTT of Ldn. Trust for
debt to William HAMILTON of Charles Co Md using 798a
(descended from father Hugh QUINLIN dec'd). Delv. to Jas.
McILHANY and E. G. HAMILTON the trustees appointed by court 25
Dec 1828.

3I:084   Date: 5 Nov 1824   RtCt: 5 Nov 1824
Tasker C. QUINLIN of Ldn to Thomas R. MOTT of Ldn. Trust for
debt to Richard H. HENDERSON and James McILHANY of Ldn
(with above trust) using 181a Limestone Lot, 272¾a Mrs.
TRIPLETT's Lot and 214½a DANIEL's Lot. Delv. to Jas. McILHANY
on ___.

3I:085   Date: 19 Mar 1824   RtCt: 11 Oct 1824
Thomas MARKS & wife Keziah of Ldn to Stacy TAYLOR and
Valentine V. PURCELL of Ldn. Trust for debt to Edmund F.
CARTER using 150a adj __ RAMSAY. Wit: Craven OSBURNE,
John WHITE.

3I:087   Date: 11 Oct 1824   RtCt: 11 Oct 1824
Peyton R. PAGE of Ldn to Presly SANDERS of Ldn. Trust for
Samuel M. EDWARDS of Ldn as security on note to Saml. HALL of
Ldn using farm animals. Delv. to EDWARDS 27 Oct 1827.

3I:088   Date: 10 Dec 1823   RtCt: 11 Oct 1824
Thomson MASON & wife Ann of Ldn to Rich'd H. HENDERSON of
Ldn. Trust for debt to Samuel DAWSON, Samuel M. EDWARDS and
William T. T. MASON of Ldn using 562½a 'Siberia' [Liberia] where
MASON lives.

3I:090   Date: ___   RtCt: ___
James McILHANY dec'd. Division of dower – #1 - farm called Martin
SIDDLERs Ruth GREGG ? Stony point and 57a of Short Hill to
Nathaniel DAVIDSON & wife Nancy; #2 - 48a farm where dec'd
resided and lot where mulatto man Jacob MORE? resides to
Mortimore McILHANY the youngest child; #3 - farms occupied by
NICHOLS, MOLIN, CASEY & CRADICK adj other land to Elisabeth
McILHANY; #4 – walnut level now occupied by Edward SANDERS,
lots occupied by Lewis ELLZEY & Warner TURNERs lot, KIDWELLs
lot and 77¾a on Short Hill to Louisa McILHANY; #5 – farms
occupied by Zachariah OWENS, Henery WINEGARNER & his son
Herbert WINEGARNER, Benj. WHITACRE and Joseph WHITACRE
and 18a out of Danl. HANLY Lot on the E side, 31a of WILSONs
Lot adj OWENS to Cecelia McILHANY; #6 – JOHNSON Lott,
CRAVENS Lott and SMITHs Lott which were divided from Jos.
WHITACREs Lott, Henery WINEGARNERs & OWENS to John
McILHANY; # 7 – JAMES Lott, HEARTs Lott & CARLISLEs Lot at
upper end of Goose Creek Tract divided from the 6th share to Lewis
ELLZEY & wife Rosana; #8 – Lotts occupied by RICHARDSON and
ALDER divided form the 7th and 9th share to James McILHANY; # 9
– Loots occupied by OGDEN and one adj occupied by PEACOCK
and son to Mary McILHANY; dower of widow Margaret McILHANY –
Stony Point where Ruth GREGG resides and part of lott occupied by
HAWKINS including mansion house, wood lot on side of Short Hill,
additional lots also listed. [long accts]. Memo of lands: 200a Siddlers
Lot, 115a Martins?, 141 Morriss, 114 Ruth Gregg, 153a Hawkins,
25a Mountain Lot, 138a Jacob Lott, 361a home place, 209a James
Lot, 135a Hanly, 180a Johnson, 310a Winegarner & son, 170a Benj.
WHITACRE, 160a Jas. WHITACRE, 134a Esekiel SMITH, 48a
Mountain Lot, 102a Lovet Lot, 115a Turner, 113a Mccarty, 344a Hill
Land unencumbered, 140a Stony point, 182a Walnut Level, 400a
Ellzy & Warner, 506a Nicholas Molen Casey & Cradler, 210a Ogdon
Lot, 122a Alder Lot, 173a Peacock and son, 191a Richardson, 204a
Griffith, 221a Dorrel & Pearce, 276a Reed & Earnest, 123a White
Oak Bottom, 178a Kidwell's Lot, 184a Heart & Carlisle, 267a Wilson,
130a Yellis Craven, 157a Olbins, 500a Ridge land bt of Wilson.
Divisors: Edward M. DANIEL, W. ELLZEY, James HAMILTON. No
plat given.

3I:097   Date: 8 Nov 1824   RtCt: 19 Nov 1824
Prisons in custody of Sheriff John ROSE and jailor Samuel
HAMMETT: Debtors Henery H. HAMILTON, James MONROE,

Robert CHEW, runaway negro Henery, Harriet charged with murder. Wit: Geo. RICHARDS.

3I:098   Date: 10 Nov 1824   RtCt: 10 Nov 1824
Peter C. RUST, Wm. GILMORE and Wm. THRIFT. Bond on RUST as constable.

3I:098   Date: 10 Nov 1824   RtCt: 10 Nov 1824
Court order of 8 Mar 1824 to Jacob SLATER Jr. and Michael SLATER in case of Anthony SLATER vs John SLATERs Admrs. ordered sale of negro Rachael & her 4 children from estate of John SLATER dec'd. Rachael and 2 youngest children sold to William SLATER, Dewarner sold to George SLATER, young Hannah sold to Jacob SLATER Sr.

3I:099   Date: 8 Nov 1824   RtCt: 8 Nov 1824
French SIMPSON. Qualified as Lt. in 57th Reg 6th Brig 2nd Div of Va Militia.

3I:099   Date: 26 Jul 1824   RtCt: 8 Nov 1824
William BRADFIELD. Qualified as Captain of a Troop of Cavalry in 2nd Reg 2nd Div of Va Militia.

3I:099   Date: 2 Jul 1824   RtCt: 8 Nov 1824
Commission of Ludwell LEE as Sheriff of Ldn.

3I:100   Date: 2 Jul 1824   RtCt: ___
Geo. LEE, Hamilton ROGERS, Horrace LUCKETT, Wm. THRIFT, Ludwell LEE, Aris BUCKNER, John M. McCARTY, Leven LUCKETT. Bond on Ludwell LEE as Sheriff to collect levies.

3I:101   Date: 2 Jul 1824   RtCt: ___
Geo. LEE, Hamilton ROGERS, Horrace LUCKETT, Wm. THRIFT, Ludwell LEE, Aris BUCKNER, John M. McCARTY, Leven LUCKETT. Bond on Ludwell LEE as Sheriff to collect taxes.

3I:101   Date: 2 Jul 1824   RtCt: ___
Geo. LEE, Hamilton ROGERS, Horrace LUCKETT, Wm. THRIFT, Ludwell LEE, Aris BUCKNER, John M. McCARTY, Leven LUCKETT. Bond on Ludwell LEE as Sheriff to collect officers pay.

3I:102   Date: 8 Nov 1824   RtCt: 8 Nov 1824
L. P. W. BALCH, Townsend McVEIGH and Hugh SMITH. Bond on BALCH as treasurer of the Board of School Commrs.

3I:103   Date: 10 Sep 1824   RtCt: ___
Thomas LEISLE [LESLIE?] dec'd. Division of land not directly willed – 220a in lot of Wm. MATHIAS on Blue Ridge, part of John EVANS' lot, 194½a 'Springfield' lot formerly William OSBURNEs' left to her mother Ann LESLIE, 106a lot on side of Blue Ridge, log house and lot in Hllb, lot between the Hills subject to life estate of mother adj lands of David POTTS and John BAKER to dau. Caroline Frances LEISLE now w/o Jacob SHUTT; 240a and 67a, stone house in Hllb, wood lot to Amanda O. LEISLE. Richard H. HENDERSON was

appointed Guardian ad litem to Amanda O. LEISLE in chancery. Divisors: John WHITE, David LOVETT, Joshua OSBURN.

3I:105 Date: 9 Nov 1824 RtCt: 9 Nov 1824
Peyton POWELL, Wm. WILKINSON, Charles TURNER. Bond on POWELL as constable.

3I:105 Date: 9 Nov 1824 RtCt: 9 Nov 1824
Jason DAVIS and Joseph DANIEL bound to Thomas PHILIPS and Joseph BOND (Exors of Asa MOORE dec'd). Bond on DAVIS as Guardian of Polly DAVIS.

3I:106 Date: 13 Nov 1824 RtCt: 13 Nov 1824
Charles DUNCAN, Benj. DUNCAN and Benjamin BRIDGES. Bond on Charles DUNCAN as constable.

3I:107 Date: 25 Aug 1824 RtCt: 8 Nov 1824
Joseph HICKMAN & wife Jane of Franklin Co Ohio to son Joseph S. HICKMAN of Franklin Co Ohio. PoA. Wit: J. R. PARISH, W. T. MERTIN, Wm. STIERWOLT.

3I:109 Date: 2 Dec 1824 RtCt: 9 Dec 1824
John F. SAPPINGTON & wife Mary of Ldn to Benjamin SHRIEVE Jr. of Ldn. Trust for debt to Jacob WALTMAN Jr. of Ldn and as security for debts to Jno. KALB, John SCHOOLEY, George W. FRENCH Admr of James D. FRENCH using ¼a in Wtfd (DBk RR:14), ½a (DBk VV:13), 2-story house on Main St Wtfd (DBk TT:258), and 2 lots in new addition to Wtfd (DBk VV:14). Delv. to SHRIEVE 27 Jan 1826.

3I:110 Date: 17 Jul 1824 RtCt: 6 Nov 1824
Norman URTON of Hampshire Co Va to George M. GRAYSON of Ldn. Trust for debt to Enoch FURR of Ldn using 190a a foot of S side of Blue Ridge adj Robert RUSSEL, Amos CLAYTON, Potia HODGSON. Delv. to FURR 5 Aug 1826.

3I:112 Date: 5 Nov 1824 RtCt: 5 Nov 1824
John WEST of Ldn to L. P. W. BALCH and John GREGG of Ldn. Trust for debt to John PANCOST Jr. of Ldn using 183a where WEST resides.

3I:114 Date: 5 Jun 1824 RtCt: 8 Nov 1824
Mahlon MORRIS & wife Catherine, Amos HENRY & wife Elisabeth, Robert RUSSEL, William CLENDENING & wife Ruth, William RUSSEL & wife Nancy and Thomas RUSSEL & wife Mary of Ldn to Michael ARNOLD of Ldn. B/S of 88a adj Thomas RUSSEL, __ COPELAND, __ McILHANY, nr great road from Hllb to AlexVa. Wit: John WHITE, Craven OSBURN. Delv. to ARNOLD 1 Jan 1829.

3I:116 Date: 9 Aug 1824 RtCt: 8 Nov 1824
Edward B. GRADY of Ldn to Peter C. RUST of Ldn. Trust for debt to Abner JURY of Ldn using farm and household items prch/o JURY.

3I:117 Date: 10 Jun 1824 RtCt: 8 Nov 1824
Henery SETTLE & wife Margaret of Ldn bound to Adrian SWART. Bond for SWART's 1/8th part of real estate of Henery's father. Wit: John SIMPSON, Linna A. SETTLE, John SWARTS.

3I:118 Date: 11 Nov 1824 RtCt: 8 Nov 1824
Charles SMITH of Ldn to Saml. M. EDWARDS of Ldn. Trust for debt to John SIMPSON of Ldn using negro slave men Joe and Bidwell.

3I:120 Date: 22 Apr 1823 RtCt: 8 Nov 1824
George CARTER & wife Helen, Wm. CARTER & wife Margaret, Charles CARTER and Samuel CARTER of Ldn to William CARR of Ldn. B/S of 155a adj __ GREENUP. Wit: James H. HAMILTON, Presly CORDELL, David COPWELL, Stephen C. ROSZEL. Delv. to William CARR 1 Aug 1827.

3I:122 Date: 19 Feb 1823 RtCt: 8 Nov 1824
William RUST & wife Elisabeth to Foushee TEBBS. B/S of 540a in PrWm and Ldn formerly belonging to Chas. L. CARTER known as 'Tecumseh.' Wit: John B. ARMISTEAD, Josiah TIDBALL.

3I:124 Date: 8 Apr 1824 RtCt: 10 Nov 1824
John STOUTSEBERGER & wife Margaret to Jacob COMPHER of Ldn. B/S of 1¾a adj Henery TAYLOR, Peter STONEBURNER. Wit: John HAMILTON, Samuel DAWSON. Delv. to COMPHER 14 Oct 1833.

3I:125 Date: 9 Nov 1824 RtCt: 11 Nov 1824
Edmund LOVETT & wife Elisabeth to Saml. M. EDWARDS. Trust to Daniel LOVETT, William LICKEY, John JONES, John SIMPSON, Isaiah POTTS and French SIMPSON as securities in executions using 2a lot with log house and blacksmith shop in Mt. Gilead (prch/o Isaac EATON) and ¾a with 2 houses and a shop in Union (prch/o Stephen McPHERSON and J. M. CLARKE). Wit: William CARR, James H. HAMILTON.

3I:127 Date: 13 Mar 1824 RtCt: 12 Nov 1824
Elisha JANNEY Jr of Ldn to John SMITH of Ldn. Trust for debt to William SMITH of Ldn using and household items. Wit: Jonas SMITH, Travis GLASSCOCK.

3I:129 Date: 4 Mar 1824 RtCt: 12 Nov 1824
William PAXON & wife Jane of Ldn to Valentine PURCELL of Ldn. B/S of 45a (½ of 85a) on side of mountain (prch/o J. DANIELS' Exors). Wit: R. BRADEN, Abiel JENNERS. Delv. to PURSELL 21 Jun 1826.

3I:131 Date: 13 Nov 1824 RtCt: 13 Nov 1824
Michael COOPER of Ldn to Thomas WHITE of Ldn. Trust for debt to Simon SHOEMAKER of Ldn using farm animals, household items.

3l:131   Date: 7 Feb 1823   RtCt: 19 Nov 1824
Pattrick McGAVICK of Ldn to son Israel McGAVICK of Ldn. Gift two lots totaling 214½a where Pattrick now lives (DBk CC:303 and DBk MM:404).

3l:133   Date: __ Dec 1824   RtCt: 13 Dec 1824
John A. BINNS & wife Mary M. of Ldn to Charles Wm. D. BINNS of Ldn. Trust to Samuel M. EDWARDS as security in debt to Conrad BITZER assignee of Richard JEFFERIES using lot on S side of Loudoun St in Lsbg cnvy/b John A. by father C. BINNS. Delv. to EDWARDS 8 Apr 1837.

3l:135   Date: 22 Nov 1824   RtCt: 22 Nov 1824
Thomas RUSSELL (insolvent) to Sheriff Ludwell LEE. B/S of lot in Lsbg prch/o John CRIDLER (do to executions at suit of ALDRIDGE & HIGDON assignee of Samuel CARR, John BRIN assignee of Saml. M. BOSS, John MINES assignee of Wm. D. DRISH assignee of Wm. McALLISTER).

3l:135   Date: 4 Aug 1824   RtCt: 20 Nov 1824
Philip THOMAS of Ldn to Jefferson C. THOMAS of Ldn. B/S of 30a at foot of Blue Ridge.

3l:137   Date: 4 Sep 1824   RtCt: 20 Nov 1824
Isaiah PAYNE & wife Judah of Ldn to Jefferson C. THOMAS of Ldn. B/S of 2½a adj Thomas JAMES. Wit: Craven OSBURNE, John WHITE. Delv. pr order 5 Sep 1825.

3l:138   Date: 25 Mar 1824   RtCt: 20 Nov 1824
James L. McKENNA & wife Anne Cecilia of Ffx to Jonah THOMPSON of AlexDC. Trust for debt to Bank of Alexandria using 33a with grist mill and saw mill on Broad Run in Ldn.

3l:141   Date: 25 Nov 1824   RtCt: 25 Nov 1824
Benjamin H. CANBY by attorney John H. CANBY of Ldn to Jacob FADELY. B/S of ½a in Lsbg on King St, adj Chas. B. BALL dec'd.

3l:142   Date: 26 Nov 1824   RtCt: 26 Nov 1824
John H. CANBY and Francis DAWSON (in trust from Isaac WRIGHT, DBk GGG:113, for benefit of Polly CHANY late DAWSON of Ldn to William JOHNS(T)ON of Ldn. B/S of lot in Lsbg (Polly died intestate and Francis DAWSON is her only child and heir).

3l:144   Date: 30 Oct 1824   RtCt: 29 Nov 1824
William HUNT & wife Rebecca of Fqr to Lawson OSBURNE of Ldn. B/S of 18¼a nr E side of Mdbg Road, adj Joshua OVERFIELD. Wit: Burr POWELL, A. GIBSON. Delv. to OSBURN 15 Apr 1828.

3l:146   Date: 26 Nov 1824   RtCt: 2 Dec 1824
Nicholas OSBURNE & wife Elisabeth S. of Ldn to Lewis P. W. BALCH of Ldn. B/S of 128a adj Enoss POTTS, Benjamin PALMER. Wit: Craven OSBURNE, John WHITE. Delv. to BALCH 29 Sep 1825.

3I:148   Date: 8 May 1824   RtCt: 3 Dec 1824
Timothy TAYLOR & wife Harriet B. of Ldn to James HEATON, Joel OSBURN and Abner OSBURN of Ldn. B/S of share from estate of Abner OSBURN dec'd in agreement from suit in Winchester Dist. of Jun 1822. Wit: Craven OSBURN, John WHITE.

3I:150   Date: 17 Jul 1823   RtCt: 6 Dec 1824
Charles Fenton MERCER of Aldie to William BEATTY of Aldie. B/S of lot on S side of Loudoun St in Lsbg (DBk GGG:270) adj Thomas HIER.

3I:152   Date: 1 Dec 1824   RtCt: 1 Dec 1824
James SANDFORD of Ldn to Sheriff Ludwell LEE. Transfer of interest in 160a originally leased in 1792 by Jacob REMEY to Thomas HARPER for the lives of Jacob REMEY and his sons John & James (lease bought by Sandford of Thos. HERBERT Admr of James HERBERT dec'd).

3I:152   Date: 24 May 1824   RtCt: 7 Dec 1824
William NOLAND & wife Catherine of Ldn to Daniel P. CONRAD of Ldn. B/S of ½a Lot #72 on Mercer St in Aldie. Wit: Jonah HOOD, John HOCKING, Thos. ROBINSON, Leven LUCKETT, A. GIBSON.

3I:154   Date: 8 Dec 1824   RtCt: 8 Dec 1824
Peter SAUNDERS of Ldn to James McILHANY of Ldn. Trust to George SAUNDERS of Ldn as security on note to Elijah PEACOCK using int. in crops on Thomson MASON's farm. Wit: R. H. HENDERSON, Saml. HAMMATT, Jno. THOMAS.

3I:155   Date: 18 Oct 1824   RtCt: 12 Nov/10 Dec 1824
Caspar JOHNSON & wife Martha of Ldn to Horrace LUCKETT of Ldn. Trust for debt to Jacob ISH of Ldn using 161a on Goose Creek (prch/o John WILSON, Jan 1816). Wit: Saml. M. EDWARDS, Alfred A. ESKRIDGE, William KING, John MCCORMICK.

3I:157   Date: 13 Jun 1824   RtCt: 10 Dec 1824
Mosses MILLER & wife Christena of Montgomery Co Ohio to Adam MILLER and Jesse MILLER of Ldn. B/S of int. in 250a estate of Peter MILLER Sr. late of Ldn dev. to wife Catherine in her life. Wit: John TOLKERTH, Aron BAKER.

3I:159   Date: 17 Feb 1824   RtCt: 13 Dec 1824
Seth BARDWELL & wife Nancy of Clark Co Ohio and Nancy BARDWELL late Nancy JONES ch/o William JONES dec'd late of JeffVa to William PAXTON of Ldn. B/S of mill and 5a under Blue ridge now in PAXTON's possession (formerly prop. of William JONES dec'd). Wit: Samuel LAFFERTY, Joseph KINNON.

3I:161   Date: 24 Nov 1824   RtCt: 13 Dec 1824
Daniel JAMES. Oath as ensign in 56th Reg 6th Brig 2nd Div of Va Militia.

3I:162   Date: 23 Jun 1824   RtCt: 13 Dec 1824
Ira McCAFFREY & wife Sarah (heirs of John VIOLETT dec'd of Belmont Co OH) to James BOLES of Ldn. B/S of und. ¼ of 45a of Sarah's grandfather John VIOLETT dec'd. Delv. to Jas. BOWLES 19 Aug 1831.

3I:164   Date: 7 Jan 1825   RtCt: 7 Jan 1825
Thomson MASON of Ldn to Wm. T. T. MASON and David LOVETT of Ldn. Trust to Joshua OSBURN and Lydia, Jonathan & Albert HEATON (Admrs of estate of Dr. James HEATON) as security in bond to Wm. A. G. DADE using slaves Jere Sr. & sons Jere & John, John, Normy, Sarah, Charlotte, Eliza, Wilford, Letty, Henerietta, Philip, Molly, Lydia & Maddison.

3I:165   Date: 22 Dec 1824   RtCt: 22 Dec 1824
George COX of Ldn (insolvent) to Shff Ludwell LEE. B/S of und. 1/10th part in 130-140a of estate of Hugh FULTON dec'd late of Ldn (in custody due to executions for debts to John SCHOOLEY, George WHITMORE, John WALTERS) nr Valley Meeting House, adj Caspar ECKART, Elisha GREGG, Aaron SAUNDERS.

3I:166   Date: 1 Jan 1825   RtCt: 1 Jan 1825
William F. LUCKETT of Ldn to Edwin C. BROWN of Ldn. Trust for debt to Noble BEVERIDGE using 170a (cnvy/b Leven LUCKETT Sr.) where LUCKETT lives adj Francis W. LUCKETT. Delv. pr order 5 Feb 1829.

3I:168   Date: 11 Dec 1824   RtCt: 13 Dec 1824
Elias JAMES & wife Ruth and Jonathan JAMES & wife Polly of Ldn to Daniel JAMES of Ldn. B/S of 87½a nr W fork of Goose Creek (part of land of Elisabeth McILHANY dec'd allotted to her mother Margaret McILHANY conveyed to JAMES' May 1819). Wit: Craven OSBURNE, John WHITE. Delv. to Danl. JAMES 23 Sep 1825.

3I:170   Date: 18 Oct 1824   RtCt: 7 Jan 1825
William CLINE of Lsbg to Lewis KLINE of Wtfd. LS for 999y of 2½a in Wtfd adj Edward DORSEY. Wit: Presly SAUNDERS, Aaron SAUNDERS, Thos. R. SAUNDERS. Delv. to KLINE 14 Nov 1825.

3I:172   Date: 27 Dec 1824   RtCt: 28 Dec 1824
Peter SANDERS to Thomson MASON of Ldn. Assigns right to crop of rye growing on MASON's farm. (from assignment of George SANDERS to Thomson MASON of trust from Peter to James McILHANY) Wit: S. BLINCOE, Saml. HAMMATT, Jacob HOUSER, Wm. CHILTON.

3I:173   Date: 27 Dec 1824   RtCt: 27 Dec 1824
George SAUNDERS to Thomson MASON of Ldn. Transfers right to trust given by Peter SANDERS to James McILHANY. Wit: S. BLINCOE, Wm. CHILTON, Eli JANNEY.

3l:174   Date: 30 Oct 1824   RtCt: 23 Dec 1824
Israel WILKINSON & wife Macha of Ldn to James THOMAS of Ldn.
B/S of 7a abt 1 mile W of Lsbg on N side of road from Lsbg across
the mountain. Wit: John McCORMICK, Samuel M. EDWARDS.

3l:176   Date: 3 Jan 1825   RtCt: 7 Jan 1825
Peter BEMASDAFER & wife Susan of Ldn to Philip RAH(A)N Sr. of
Adam Co Pa. B/S of 1000a with merchant, grist and saw mill (cnvy/b
Saml. ADAMS Jun 1813, DBk ZZ:274). Wit: John McCORMICK,
John H. McCABE.

3l:178   Date: 18 Sep 1824   RtCt: 23 Dec 1824
William AMBLER & wife Susan of Ldn to Lewis AMBLER of Ldn. B/S
of 89½a in Ldn and Ffx, adj Stephen DANIEL, John HUTCHISON.
Wit: Wm. B. HARRISON, Johnston CLEVELAND.

3l:180   Date: 10 Jul 1824   RtCt: 23 Dec 1824
Isaac EATON & wife Malinda of Ldn to Uree HANDY (late EATON)
of Ldn. B/S of ½a lot in Mt. Gilead on Loudoun St. Wit: William
LICKEY, Thomas POLLINGS, Rowena HOLMES, Thomas
SANDERS, William CARR, James H. HAMILTON.

3l:182   Date: 1 Oct 1824   RtCt: 18 Dec 1824
William CHILTON & wife Sarah to Richard H. HENDERSON. B/S of
2 adj lots (62a and 46a) nr Lsbg prch/o George RUST Jr, on road
from Coblers Gap to Ellis Williams shop, adj Jesse RICE. Wit: John
McCORMICK, Saml. M. EDWARDS. Delv. to HENDERSON 25 Dec
1835.

3l:184   Date: 20 Dec 1824   RtCt: 20 Dec 18224
Peter SAUNDERS to Margaret SANDERS. BoS for farm animals
and geer (included in trust to Robert MOFFETT for benefit of Geo.
SAUNDERS as bail in suit of Jacob HOUSER) and household items
in Ohio.

3l:185   Date: 16 Dec 1824   RtCt: 16 Dec 1824
Peter SANDERS of Ldn to Robert MOFFETT of Ldn. Trust for
George SANDERS of Ldn as bail in suit of Jacob HOUSER using
horses.

3l:186   Date: 7 Aug 1824   RtCt: 13 Sep/1 Oct 1824
John PAXON & wife Ann of Ldn to Samuel HOUGH and Burr
BRADEN of Ldn. Trust for debt to David SHAWEN using 19a nr
Catoctin Creek adj __ BALL, __ TRITAPAUGH; and 41a adj land
formerly Nathan BALL's, formerly Henery HORNE, __ BAGLEY, __
BINNS, __ SHAWEN; and 12a on E side of Beaverdam Creek adj C.
SHAWEN; and 19¼a adj Conrad VIRTS, Reuben HIXON; and 5a on
Catoctin Creek; and 9a adj Catoctin; and 33½a adj __ COOPER.
Wit: Robert BRADEN, Presly CORDELL.

3l:192   Date: 2 Dec 1824   RtCt: 3 Jan 1825
John ALT & wife Polly of Ldn to John J. MATHIAS and George
RICHARD of Ldn. Trust for debt to John COMPHER using lots from

div. of estate of Wm. ALT dec'd (29a Lot #1 allotted William ALT; Lot #2 to Elisabeth COMPHOR late Elisabeth ALT (both prch/o John ALT); Lot #5 to John ALT). Delv. to COMPHER __. Wit: E. GRUBB, Saml. HOUGH.

3I:194   Date: 18 Dec 1820   RtCt: 3 Jan 1825
John SHAFFER/SHAVER & wife Mary of Ldn to William VIRTS Jr. of Ldn. Trust for debt to Conrad BITZER ass'ee of Presley WILLIAMS, James NIXON, Philip SWANK, Catherine SWANK Jr., George SHOEMAKER, Simon SHOEMAKER and David AXLINE using 121a (prch/o George SWANK, Mar 1806), 152½a (prch/o Henery WOOLF, Nov 1804), 61½a (prch/o Earl of Tankerville and Henery A. BENNETT, Jun 1791), 55½a (prch/o Ferdinando FAIRFAX, Feb 1803). Wit: Robert BRADEN, Abiel JENNERS, Ebenezer GRUBB, Saml. HOUGH. Recorded before in DBk BBB:393.

3I:202   Date: 11 Mar 1824   RtCt: 12 Nov 1824
Thomas MARKS of Ldn to Thomas GREGG of Ldn. Trust for debt to Valentine V. PURCELL using negro woman Charity abt 24-25y old and boys Grandison 12y old and Calvin 10y old.

3I:204   Date: 24 Nov 1824   RtCt: 31 Dec 1824
Henery LOYD, Thomas WEST, William LANCASTER, Lot SLACK and Polly WEST (ch/o Uree WEST of Bedford Co Va, grandchildren of Thomas HUMPHREY dec'd late of Ldn who beq. to them in will of 1 May 1822) to Humphrey WEST of Montgomery Co Va. PoA to rec. beq. from Admr. Abner & John HUMPHREYS. Wit: David SAUNDERS, Armistead OTEY.

3I:205   Date: 29 Dec 1824   RtCt: 29 Dec 1824
Israel CLAYTON to Ruel MARSHAL. Confirmation of sale of 101a adj Punkin Town to Robert CHEW who sold ½a to Ruel MARSHAL. Wit: R. H. HENDERSON, Wm. CHILTON, Saml. HAMMATT.

3I:206   Date: 29 Jul 1822   RtCt: 6 Sep/29 Dec 1824
Israel CLAYTON of Ldn to Robert CHEW of Ldn. B/S of 49¼a Lot #4 on turnpike road adj. C. URTON and 51¾a Lot #18 in late survey. Recorded before DBk EEE:506.

3I:208   Date: 29 Jul 1822   RtCt: 26 Feb 1823/29 Dec 1824
Robert CHEW of Ldn to William BRADFIELD of Ldn. Trust for debt to Israel CLAYTON using above land. Delv. to BRADFIELD 27 Dec 1826.

3I:210   Date: 19 Nov 1824   RtCt: 28 Dec 1824
Peter SA(U)NDERS of Ldn to Samuel HOUGH of Ldn. B/S of 183a (cnvy/b Saml. HOUGH) adj Wm. H. HOUGH, Robert BRADEN, heirs of Michael COOPER, Margaret SAUNDERS, Joseph POSTON.

3I:212   Date: 25 Dec 1824   RtCt: 28 Dec 1824
Wm. H. HOUGH and David SHAWEN (trustees of Peter SANDERS, Mar 1819, in favor of Lydia, Mary, Sarah & Samuel HOUGH) to Peter SAUNDERS. Release of trust on 180a.

3I:215   Date: 1 May 1824   RtCt: 13 Dec 1824
Isaac WALKER and Noble S. BRADEN (trustees of Nero LAWSON, Feb 1821, for debt to Edward DORSEY) of Ldn to John WILLIAMS (ass'ee of Edward DORSEY) of Ldn. B/S of lot in Wtfd adj Nathan MINOR.

3I:217   Date: 27 Mar 1824   RtCt: 15 Dec 1824
Edward B. GRADY & wife Sarah to Abijah SANDS. B/S of 14a (cnvy/b Isaiah MARKS) adj __ McPHERSON; and 58½a (cnvy/b Isaiah B. BEANS); and 2a (cnvy/b Isaiah B. BEANS). Wit: Francis W. LUCKETT, John W. GRAYSON.

3I:220   Date: 27 Mar 1824   RtCt: 13 Dec 1824
Abijah SANDS & wife Elisabeth to Edward B. GRADY. B/S of 90a (Lot #2 and part of Lot #3 in div. of James GRADY dec'd) adj GRADY, Notley C. WILLIAMS. Wit: Francis W. LUCKETT, John W. GRAYSON.

3I:222   Date: 13 Dec 1824   RtCt: 13 Dec 1824
Shff Ludwell LEE to Samuel UNDERWOOD of Ldn. B/S of 62a below Goose Creek on NE side of road from Lsbg to Georgetown DC, adj Mrs. VEALE.

3I:223   Date: 13 Dec 1824   RtCt: 13 Dec 1824
Peyton R. PAGE to L. P. W. BALCH. Trust for debt to David CARR of Ldn using farm animals.

3I:225   Date: 28 Dec 1824   RtCt: 1 Jan 1824 [25]
William P. FOX & wife Catherine E. of Ldn to Zackariah DULANY of Ldn. Trust for debt to Jozabed WHITE using 90a (cnvy/b WHITE, Dec 1824). Wit: Saml. HOUGH, Presly CORDELL.

3I:227   Date: __ Dec 1824   RtCt: 1 Jan 1825
Jozabed WHITE & wife Margaret of Ldn to William P. FOX of Ldn. B/S of 12a Lot #6, 63a Lot #1 on road from Wtfd to Mrs. LACEY's farm (except rights Mary GARRETT will have at death of Ann CLEMENTS, both cnvy/b Joseph CAVIN, Mar 1823), and 10a adj Lot #1 (prch/o Zackariah DULANY). Wit: Saml. HOUGH, Presly CORDELL. Delv. to FOX 26 Oct 1826.

3I:230   Date: 28 Dec 1824   RtCt: 1 Jan 1825
Zackariah DULANY & wife Mary E. of Ldn to Jozabed WHITE of Ldn. B/S of 10a. Wit: Samuel HOUGH, Presly CORDELL.

3I:232   Date: 13 Dec 1824   RtCt: 13 Dec 1824
Daniel LOVETT and William LICKEY of Ldn and Stephen McPHERSON of Ldn. Agreement – McPHERSON has trust on land which Townsend McVEIGH is trustee given by Edmund LOVETT, judgments have been ordered against Edmund LOVETT with Daniel and Wm. as security; McPHERSON agrees not to enforce the trust for another 5 years with Daniel & Wm. paying an annual int.

3I:233   Date: 27 Nov 1824   RtCt: 13 Dec 1824
William CARTER & wife Margaret of Ldn to George CARTER of Ldn.
B/S of 1/9th und. part of 17a (Wm. CATER, George CARTER &
others inherited from Richard CARTER dec'd), adj __ GRAYSON.
Wit: John McCORMICK, Wm. CARR.

3I:235   Date: 1 Nov 1824   RtCt: 13 Dec 1824
Samuel TURNER & wife Amanda of Ldn to John A. MARMADUKE
and Samuel CLENDENING of Ldn. Trust for debt to Henery
RUSSELL of Ldn using 87a (cnvy/b heirs of Wm. RUSSEL dec'd,
Oct 1824). Wit: Craven OSBURNE, John WHITE. Delv. to H.
RUSSELL 20 May 1826.

3I:239   Date: 7 Jul 1824   RtCt: 13 Dec 1824
Isaac EATON & wife Malinda of Ldn to William P. EATON of Ldn.
B/S of ½a Lot #28 in Mt. Gilead on Loudoun St. Wit: William
LICKEY, Thomas ROLLINGS, Rowena HOLMES, Thomas
SANDERS, William CARR, James H. HAMILTON.

3I:241   Date: 9 Mar 1823   RtCt: 13 Dec 1824
Ezekiel CHAMBLING & wife Elisabeth of Ldn to John A.
MARMADUKE and Saml. CLENDENING of Ldn. Trust for debt to
Henery RUSSELL using 116a (cnvy/b RUSSELL Mar 1823). Delv. to
H. RUSSELL 20 May 1826.

3I:244   Date: 13 Jan 1825   RtCt: 13 Jan 1825
Mary COE, Samuel TILLETT, Samuel CARR & John W. COE bound
to Robert COE as security in bond to justices Stephen C. ROSSELL,
Robert BRADEN, John BAILY & Abner GIBSON for Mary COE as
Guardian of Mary E. COE, Emily J. COE and Elisabeth Ann COE
orphans of Edward M. COE dec'd.

3I:246   Date: 13 Jan 1825   RtCt: 13 Jan 1825
Mary COE, Samuel TILLETT, Samuel CARR & John W. COE bound
to justices John McCORMICK, William B. HARRISON, John W.
GRAYSON and Saml. M. EDWARDS for Mary COE as Admr of
estate of Edward M. COE dec'd with bond payable to Stephen C.
ROSSELL, Robert BRADEN, John BAILY & Abner GIBSON.

3I:247   Date: 12 Jan 1825   RtCt: 13 Jan 1825
George H. ALDER, John H. BUTCHER and Joshua B. OVERFIELD.
Bond on ALDER as constable.

3I:248   Date: 26 Jul 1824   RtCt: 14 Feb 1825
John WOLFORD of Ldn to Wm. H. HOUGH and Thos. PHILIPS of
Ldn. Trust for debt to Wm. STEER (Admr of John HOUGH dec'd)
using 25a (cnvy/b Commr. Saml. M. EDWARDS, subject to dower of
Elisabeth HOUGH wd/o John HOUGH dec'd). Wit: R. H.
HENDERSON, Thos. R. MOTT, E. G. HAMILTON. Delv. to STEER
14 Dec 1826.

3I:251   Date: 9 Oct 1788   RtCt: 14 Apr 1789/1 Nov 1824
James CURRELL of Ldn to William GUNNELL (trustee of Frances CURRELL w/o James). Trust for benefit of Frances during her life using slaves Sutton, Adam, Juno, Dinah, Mary, Anthony, Harry, Judy, Alice and Charlotte, farm animals, farm and household items. Wit: John COCKERILLE, Edward DULIN, Francis DULIN. Recorded before in DBk R:175.

3I:253   Date: 31 Dec 1824   RtCt: 31 Dec 1824
John MOUNT (insolvent) of Ldn to Sheriff Ludwell LEE. B/S of 102a (for executions by James SWART ass'ee of And'w B. McMULLEN agst MOUNT and Jacob WINCUP his appearance bail).

3I:254   Date: 10 Sep 1824   RtCt: 10 Jan 1825
John WALKER & wife Abigail of Ldn to Benjamin WALKER of Ldn. B/S of 20a (from div. of estate of Benjamin WALKER dec'd). Wit: Francis W. LUCKETT, William H. DORSEY. Delv. pr order 3 Jul 1830.

3I:256   Date: 14 Aug 1824   RtCt: 10 Jan 1825
William RANDALL & wife Rachael of Fqr to Andrew B. McMULLEN of Ldn. B/S of 8¾a (allotted in div. of John JOHNSTON dec'd) on N side of Goose Creek. Wit: Burr POWELL, A. GIBSON.

3I:258   Date: 13 Dec 1824   RtCt: 10 Jan 1825
Philip S. KING & wife Martha T. of Culpeper Co Va to Oliver DENHAM of Ldn. B/S of Lot #11 in Mdbg (cnvy/b Leven POWELL Mar 1806 to Aaron GRANT under rent charge and since GRANT's death allotted as dower to widow Martha T. now KING). Wit: Burr POWELL, Abner GIBSON.

3I:260   Date: 16 Aug 1824   RtCt: 10 Jan 1825
John IDEN & wife Hannah, James IDEN & wife Margaret, David DANIEL & wife Elisabeth and Samuel RUSSELL of Ldn to Samuel DUNKIN of Ldn. B/S of __ a - John & Hannah IDEN's and James & Margaret IDEN's share in lands of the wives' father Thomas RUSSELL dec'd; and David & Eliz. DANIEL's land conveyed to David by his father John DANIEL & wife; and Samuel RUSSELL's share conveyed to him by his brothers Benjamin and Neil RUSSELL. Wit: William BRONAUGH, Francis W. LUCKETT.

3I:263   Date: 10 Sep 1824   RtCt: 10 Jan 1825
John WALKER & wife Abigail of Ldn to Garrett WALKER of Ldn. B/S of int. in 40a at the death of mother Sarah VANHORN (dower from John VANHORN dec'd) & brother. Wit: Francis W. LUCKETT, William H. DORSEY. Delv. to Garrett WALKER 22 Jul 1847.

3I:265   Date: 15 Feb 1825   RtCt: 15 Feb 1825
Augustine M. SANDFORD, Robert SANDFORD and Robert MOFFETT. Bond on Augustine M. as constable.

3I:266   Date: 4 Aug 1824   RtCt: 15 Feb 1825
John HOUGH dec'd. Allotment of 5a dower to widow Elisabeth HOUGH from land allotted to John HOUGH dec'd out of estate of Wm. HOUGH dec'd. Small drawing. Divisors: John HAMILTON Jr., Beniah WHITE, James WHITE.

3I:267   Date: 13 Jul 1824   RtCt: 15 Feb 1825
Commr Samuel M. EDWARDS (chancery suit of Wm. STEER agst Jno. WOODFORD, July 1824) of Ldn to John WOOLFORD of Ldn. B/S of 25a (subject to dower of Elisabeth HOUGH, wd/o John HOUGH dec'd) adj WOOLFORD, John JACKSON, __ DAWSON's heirs.

3I:269   Date: 14 Jul 1825   RtCt: 14 Feb 1825
Benjamin SHRIEVE Jr. Qualified as Captain of a company of artillery in the 2nd Reg 2nd Div of Va Militia.

3I:269   Date: 13 Jan 1824   RtCt: 14 Feb 1825
Thomas RUSSELL & wife Elisabeth of Belmont Co Ohio to William VICKERS of Ldn. B/S of rights to und. 122a from father Thomas RUSSELL dec'd late of Ldn. Wit: J. JOHNSON, Mosses COULTER.

3I:272   Date: 20 Dec 1824   RtCt: 10 Jan 1825
John HAMILTON & wife Winefred of Ldn to Robert RAY of NY City. Trust for debt to Nathaniel PRIME of NY City using land on both sides of Cotecton Creek abt 3 miles from Potomac (cnvy/b Peter STONEBURNER, Oct 1818). Wit: R. R. WARD, Jesse HOYT.

3I:277   Date: 27 Jan 1825   RtCt: 26 Jan 1826
Jonathan JAMES of Ldn to Shff Ludwell LEE. B/S of 1/3 of 87½a (purchased jointly by Elias, Jonathan and Daniel JAMES of Margaret McILHANY) where father Jonathan JAMES the Elder now lives (for execution from Henery BROOKBANK, Henery B. DEGEN with Elias JAMES as appearance bail). Wit: Asa ROGERS, Daniel JAMES.

3I:278   Date: 29 Jan 1825   RtCt: 29 Jan 1825
James B. SPENCE & wife Nancy to James BOOTH of Ldn. B/S of 5a Lot #2 in div. of James BOOTH dec'd and rights to dower of Frances BOOTH the wd/o James BOOTH dec'd. Wit: Ebenezer GRUBB, Saml. M. GRUBB. Delv. to BOOTH 28 Sep 1840.

3I:281   Date: 2 Feb 1825   RtCt: 2 Feb 1825
Saml. CARR of Lsbg to Samuel HARPER of Lsbg. Release of trust for debt to James BROWN.

3I:282   Date: 1 Feb 1825   RtCt: 10 Feb 1825
Joseph WOOD & wife Lydia and Robert BRADEN of Ldn to William H. HOUGH of Ldn. B/S of 1a in new addition to Wtfd (prch/o Exors of Mahlon JANNEY dec'd). Wit: Presly CORDELL, Saml. HOUGH. Delv. to HOUGH 13 Apr 1829.

3I:284   Date: 1 Jan 1824   RtCt: 11 Feb 1825
John Gill WATT & wife Dewana of Ldn to Samuel M. EDWARDS & wife Ann of Ldn. B/S of (paid with real estate) und. 1/3 of 2a with

buildings on N side of Markett St in Lsbg now occupied by EDWARDS adj John THOMAS, John DRISH, court house (conveyed to Dewana then Dewana BINNS, Winifred HAMILTON & Jane WILDMAN & Ann B. HAMILTON, Dewana & Winifred with 1/3 each, and Jane & Ann with 1/6th each by Charles BENNETT, DBk TT:302, 319). Wit: John H. McCABE, Thomas SANDERS. Delv. to EDWARDS 12 Jun 1833.

3I:287   Date: 1 Jan 1824   RtCt: 11 Feb 1825
Samuel M. EDWARDS & wife Ann of Ldn to John Gill WATT of Ldn. B/S of (using above land for payment) 2a adj Jno. M. KLINE on N side of Market St. and 6a on W side of Air St. Lsbg (except ground rents from lease made by James HEREFORD to Pat CRAVEN for 999y and lease for life by James HEORFORD (sic) to Wm. BLINSTONE alias McCABE for lives of said Wm., his wife Elisabeth now Elisabeth SPATES and their son John). Wit: John H. McCABE, Thomas SANDERS.

3I:290   Date: 7 Aug 1824   RtCt: 10 Jan 1825
Thomas PHILIPS and Joseph BOND (Exors of Asa MOORE dec'd) of Ldn to Ann MOORE of Ldn. B/S of 2a Lot #2 nr Wtfd adj Thomas LACEY dec'd, James D. FRENCH, and HOUGH and McCABE, meeting house lot. Delv. to Noble S. BRADEN pr order of Exor ___.

3I:292   Date: 11 Sep 1824   RtCt: 14 Jan 1825
Robert ROBERTS & wife Nancy of Ldn to Thomas R. MOTT and Samuel M. EDWARDS of Ldn. Trust for debt to Richard H. HENDERSON using 1+a house and lot now occupied by ROBERTS (prch/o John LICKEY and 24+a lease lot of Benjamin TOMKINS (prch/o James RUST). Wit: John McCORMICK, Thomas SANDERS.

3I:294   Date: 27 Jan 1825   RtCt: 26 Jan 1825
Peter BENEDUM (insolvent) to Shff Ludwell LEE. B/S of int. (probably none) in dower of his wife in lands of former husband Jno. YAINTS dec'd in state of Md and in land he conveyed March last to Henery BENEDUM with wife and children in Ldn.

3I:294   Date: 22 Jan 1825   RtCt: 22 Jan 1825
Shff Ludwell LEE to Samuel CARR. B/S of lot in Lsbg (purchased by insolvent Thomas RUSSELL of John CRIDLER, then conveyed Nov 1824 to Shff.)

3I:296   Date: 20 Jan 1825   RtCt: 20 Jan 1825
Elias JAMES (insolvent) to Shff Ludwell LEE. B/S of 1/3 of 87½a (suits agst JAMES by Henery BROOKBANK, Henery B. DEAGEN, Wm. TAYLOR Guardian of T. M. McILHANY). Wit: S. BLINCOE, Saml. HAMMETT, Timothy TAYLOR.

3I:298   Date: 24 Nov 1824   RtCt: 18 Jan 1825
Mary DAVIS of Ldn to George M. FRYE of Ldn. B/S of 88a Lot #9 in div. of Elisabeth McILHANY dec'd.

3I:300 Date: 13 Jan 1825 RtCt: 20 Jan 1825
William F. CLARK of Ldn to Benjamin GRAYSON of Ldn. Trust for debt to James JOHNSON using household items.

3I:302 Date: 11 Jan 1825 RtCt: 13 Jan 1825
Samuel C. BOSS of Ldn to Charles THORNTON of Ldn. Trust for John BEATTY of Ldn as security to Wm. D. DRISH using negro slave boys Lewis and Jim. Wit: R. H. HENDERSON, William JENNERS, Alfred A. ESKRIDGE.

3I:304 Date: 15 Jan 1825 RtCt: 15 Jan 1825
John D. PERRY of Ldn to Saml. M. EDWARDS of Ldn. Trust for debt to Joseph HILLEARD of Ldn using farm and household items, woman slave Susan.

3I:306 Date: 15 Jan 1825 RtCt: 15 Jan 1825
Isaiah POTTS & wife Elisabeth of Ldn to Jesse HOGUE of Ldn. Trust for William HOGUE of Ldn as security on notes to Elisabeth WHITE, Ann WHITE since dec'd, Joseph TAVENDER rep of Ann WHITE dec'd using 136a (DBk SS:159). Wit: John McCORMICK, Saml. M. EDWARDS. Delv. to Wm. HOGUE 15 Dec 1826.

3I:310 Date: 29 Jan 1825 RtCt: 14 Feb 1825
Alexander M. BRISCOE & wife Matilda P. of PrWm to George M. CHICHESTER of Ldn. B/S of Matilda's right in estate of father Israel LACEY dec'd of Ldn (except int. in land on Ohio river, int. in house and lot in Lsbg, their 1/7th and 1/6th of 1/7th part of big Spring Mill they have already sold), and int. in estate of Armistead John LACEY dec'd. Wit: Jesse EWELL, J. HUTCHISON in PrWm.

3I:312 Date: 11 Jan 1825 RtCt: 14 Mar 1825
Commr. Francis W. LUCKETT to Joshua B. DUNKIN and Samuel DUNKIN. B/S of 125a whereof Thomas RUSSELL Sr. died. Samuel RICHARDS is appointed Guardian ad Litem for Peyton RUSSELL infant defendant in case to be heard 11 Jan 1825. Und. shares of the deft. to be sold. Gives terms required for sale. Francis W. LUCKETT appointed Commr. for sale.

3I:314 Date: 23 Jun 1824 RtCt: 14 Mar 1825
Irey McCAFFREY & wife Sarah of Belmont Co Ohio (heirs at law of John VIOLETT dec'd) to Amos DENHAM of Ldn. B/S of lease lot formerly held by Elijah VIOLETT but now by DENHAM.

3I:316 Date: 14 Mar 1825 RtCt: 14 Mar 1825
Charles L. CLOWES, James BROWN and John BROWN. Bond on CLOWES as constable.

3I:317 Date: 14 Mar 1825 RtCt: 14 Mar 1825
Daniel WINE, John HAMILTON and Wm. STEER bound to justices Ariss BUCKNER, Abner GIBSON, Thomas H. GASSOWAY and Charles LEWIS. WINE, an Exor of will of Jacob WINE dec'd executed bond payable to Thomas FOUCH, Wm. A. HARRISON,

Wm. CARR and Samuel M. EDWARDS. HAMILTON and STEER as security. Wit: William JENNERS.

3I:318 Date: 15 Mar 1825 RtCt: 15 Mar 1825
Martin CORDELL, William CARR and Presly CORDELL. Bond on Martin CORDELL as constable.

3I:319 Date: 11 Mar 1825 RtCt: 11 Mar 1825
John CRIDLER (insolvent) to Shff Ludwell LEE. B/S of remaining int. in lot on Market and Air Sts in Lsbg.

3I:320 Date: 20 Feb 1825 RtCt: 10 Mar 1825
Leonard THOMAS & wife Elisabeth (late HICKMAN, d/o Peter HICKMAN dec'd) to Presly SAUNDERS. Trust for debt to Benjamin MILES, John HICKMAN & Henery HICKMAN using und. 1/12th int. in 577a of Peter HICKMAN dec'd. Wit: Saml. DAWSON, Saml. M. EDWARDS. Delv. to SAUNDERS 5 May 1837.

3I:323 Date: 9 Mar 1825 RtCt: 9 Mar 1825
James H. HAMILTON & wife Margaret of Ldn to John DRISH of Ldn. B/S of 14a (cnvy/b Henery SANDERS July 1820, DBk BBB:215). Wit: John H. McCABE, Saml. M. EDWARDS. Delv. to DRISH 30 May 1826.

3I:325 Date: 8 Mar 1825 RtCt: 8 Mar 1825
John UNDERWOOD of Ldn to Samuel UNDERWOOD of Ldn. Trust for debt to Margaret UNDERWOOD of Ldn using negro man Peter abt 38y old, farm animals and items, crops.

3I:327 Date: 12 Mar 1825 RtCt: 12 Mar 1825
Edmund LOVETT (insolvent) to Shff Ludwell LEE. B/S of lot in Mt. Gilead (cnvy/b Jno. A. BINNS) and int. in house and lot in Mt. Gilead he gave for a public school house (executions by Rachael BIRDSALL Admr of Whitson BIRDSALL dec'd).

3I:328 Date: 3 Mar 1825 RtCt: 8 Mar 1825
William VICKERS of Ldn to John W. GRAYSON of Ldn. Trust for debt to Samuel HATCHER and Gourley REEDER (Admr of Joseph HATCHER dec'd) using 107a where VICKERS now resides as his Home place; 31a of wood land adj Edward CARTER (prch/o Wheatman LEATH; int. in 80a adj Lewis FRENCH, Enoch TRIPLETT, Edward HALL (prch/o Enos MONTEITH). Delv. to Thos. ROGERS Admr of HATCHER 27 Sep 1831.

3I:330 Date: 7 Mar 1825 RtCt: 7 Mar 1825
William P. FOX of Ldn to Elisabeth SULLIVAN of Ldn. Trust for debt using farm animals and items. Wit: Isaac LAROWE, Ellisabeth B. SULLIVAN, Rebeca E. SULLIVAN.

3I:332 Date: 15 Jan 1825 RtCt: 7 Mar 1825
Jehu HOLLINGSWORTH & wife Senior of Ldn to Jonathan HEATON of Ldn. B/S of 35½a adj __ TAYLOR, __ FAIRFAX, James BEST. Wit: John WHITE, Craven OSBURNE. Delv. to HEATON 10 Feb 1829.

3I:334 Date: 4 Jan 1825 RtCt: 7 Mar 1825
Ellisabeth SULLIVAN to William Parkerson FOX. Memo – if SULLIVAN demands goods from trust above then give and pay rent for balance. Wit: Ellisabeth B. SULLIVAN, Rebeca E. SULLIVAN.

3I:335 Date: 5 Mar 1825 RtCt: 5 Mar 1825
Henson ELLIOTT of Ldn to Calvin THATCHER of Ldn. Trust for debt to Catharine E. BROWN, Joshua OSBURNE as security in debt to Anna JAMES, Herod OSBURNE as security for debt to Turner OSBURNE, debt to Nathan NICHOLS Jr., William BROWN, Eli PAIRPOINT, Walter A. SMITH of Fqr, Abel JANNEY, Charles J. KILGOUR of MontMd, George MARKS, Nathan NICHOLS Sr. as security to John WHITE Admr of Jonah WHITE dec'd, John A. MARMADUKE using horses, crops, int. (if any) in lease he prch/o Isaac YOUNG for 108a nr Scotland Mills, farm and household items.

3I:339 Date: 25 Feb 1825 RtCt: 3 Mar 1825
Phebe R. DONOHOE of Mdbg to Edwin C. BROWN of Mdbg. Trust for debt to Waterman and Campbell using household items, animals.

3I:340 Date: 19 Feb 1825 RtCt: 2 Mar 1825
Aaron MILLER & wife Mary of Ldn to Simon SHOEMAKER Sr. of Ldn. B/S of 7a on E side of Short Hill (cnvy/b Catherine MILLER, Adam MILLER & wife Elisabeth and Jesse MILLER & wife Rebeca), adj __ CRIM, __ GRUBB, __ MORRISON. Wit: Craven OSBURNE, John WHITE. Delv. to SHOEMAKER 8 Jun 1835.

3I:343 Date: 22 Feb 1825 RtCt: 3 Mar 1825
Nancy JAMES and Smith JAMES. Marriage contract – Nancy possesses negro girl Charlott, household items, farm animals, 61a of land from her father William JAMES dec'd and to enjoy them during her marriage. She is entitled to her dist. share of estate of dec'd brother William JAMES as yet und. and a child's part of estate held by her mother Abigail JAMES as dower. Items put in trust with Dean JAMES and John JAMES for Nancy's use during the marriage. If she leaves no will, it goes to any children, and if none, to her brothers and sisters.

3I:346 Date: 1 Feb 1825 RtCt: 19 Feb 1825
Robert RUSSELL & wife Mary of Ldn to Isaac NICHOLS Jr. and James HOGE of Ldn. Trust for debt to Isaac and Samuel NICKOLS of Ldn using 194a to the E of Blue Ridge. Wit: Benjamin GRAYSON, John W. GRAYSON. Delv. to Saml. NICHOLS' Exors 10 Nov 1825.

3I:350 Date: 26 Nov 1824 RtCt: 14 Feb 1825
Gabriel GREEN & wife Elizabeth of FredVa to John HOCKINGS and Thomas SOBEY of Ldn. B/S of ½a Lot #86 & #86 on Mercer St in Aldie (cnvy/b William NOLAND). Wit: Burr POWELL, A. GIBSON. Delv. pr order 25 Mar 1830.

3I:353 Date: 26 Jan 1825 RtCt: 2 Mar 1825
Catherine MILLER, Adam MILLER & wife Ellisabeth and Jesse
MILLER and wife Rebeca of Ldn to Aaron MILLER of Ldn. B/S of
22a (cnvy/b JANNEY to Peter MILLER dec'd) adj __ STATLER, __
HARDACRE, __ GRUBB, __ FRYE. Wit: Craven OSBURNE, John
WHITE.

3I:355 Date: 12 Nov 1824 RtCt: 1 Mar 1825
William ALT & wife Susanah of Ldn to Samuel M. EDWARDS of
Ldn. Trust for debt to John COMPHER of Ldn using 118a (DBk
XX:260) and 150a (DBk TT:356). Wit: Chas. G. ESKRIDGE, Alfred
A. ESKRIDGE, Wm. B. HARRISON, Burr W. HARRISON, Thos. R.
MOTT, John McCORMICK, Thomas SANDERS.

3I:359 Date: 28 Jan 1825 RtCt: 25 Feb 1825
Norval CHAMBLIN & wife Sarah W. T. of Ldn to Price JACOBS of
Ldn. B/S of 30a (land allotted from div. of father William CHAMBLIN
dec'd, land allotted to mother Catherine JACOBS as dower and int.
in lot which free woman of colour Lucy TRIPLETT holds a life
estate).

3I:361 Date: 26 Feb 1825 RtCt: 26 Feb 1825
Hannah MOFFETT of Ldn to Robert MOFFETT of Ldn. B/S of 1/7th
part of land her father Josiah MOFFETT died seized of, on secolon
run adj Peter OAYTER, Thos. R. MOTT, heirs of Landon CARTER.

3I:363 Date: 16 Feb 1825 RtCt: 16 Feb 1825
Rebeca CRAIG of Ldn to Joseph HART of Ldn. B/S of 1¼a on road
from Daniel JANNEY's Mill by the front of John Purcell's house and
front of Hart's house to Canby's Mill.

3I:364 Date: 17 Jan 1825 RtCt: 25 Feb 1825
Abraham VERNON of Westfallen Township Chester Co Pa to Jonah
TAVENER of Ldn. PoA for transactions with estate of Daniel
VERNON dec'd late of Ldn. Wit: L. P. W. BALCH, Alfred A.
ESKRIDGE, William H. HOOE.

3I:365 Date: 18 Dec 1820 RtCt: 24 Feb 1825
John SHAFFER & wife Mary of Ldn to Lewis P. W. BALCH of Lsbg.
Trust for debt to John THOMAS of Lsbg, Peter COMPHOR,
Frederick SLATZ, John GEORGE, Emanuel WALTMAN Sr., Philip
HEATON of Ldn using 11a with grist mill (prch/o Dr. Isaac HOUGH,
Mar 1819) and 70a with grist mill formerly occupied by John BALL
(prch/o Presly WILLIAMS) adj Peter COMPHER, William HOUGH
dec'd, Isaac BALL's lot, school house lot, Sandford RAMEY dec'd,
Reuben HIXON dec'd; and 138a (prch/o Jacob VIRTS, etc May
1815) adj John ROLLER, __ ROHORBACK. Wit: Samuel HOUGH,
Saml. M. EDWARDS.

3I:372 Date: 10 Feb 1824 RtCt: 20 Feb 1825
Singleton CHAMBERS & wife Mariah, Mescheck KIRBY & wife Mary
and Edmund CHAMBERS (ch/o John CHAMBERS who was s/o

William CHAMBERS) of JeffVa to John GEORGE of Ldn. B/S of land dev. in will of Robert BOOTH dated 20 Sep 1759 – 60a to son John BOOTH, then to heirs of Thomas STUMP and William CHAMBERS. Delv. to GEORGE 7 Mar 1828.

3I:374 Date: 5 Jul 1823 RtCt: 19 Feb 1825
Presly SAUNDERS to Henery SAUNDERS and Gunnell SAUNDERS. Trust for debt to Everett SAUNDERS with Henery SAUNDERS Sr. dec'd as security using household items.

3I:377 Date: 16 Feb 1825 RtCt: 17 Feb 1825
Thomas CLEWS & wife Nancy of Ldn to George MARKS. of Ldn B/S of 204a (cnvy/b MARKS May 1822, DBk FFF:424). Wit: John W. GRAYSON, Wm. H. DORSEY.

3I:379 Date: __ Mar 1825 RtCt: 11 Mar 1825
William E. LOVELY of Ldn to John CHAMBLING of Ldn. Trust for debt to Jefferson C. THOMAS and Thomas JAMES (Exors of Philip THOMAS dec'd), Anne JAMES, Joseph THOMAS, John C. BAZZILL, John CHEW, Hanson ELLIOTT and Philip THOMAS as securities, George KEENE and John HATCHER as Exors of Phineas THOMAS dec'd, Mahlon PURSELL with Andrew SORMAN as security using farm animals, crops. Wit: S. BLINCOE, Thomas JONES, Richard C. McCARTY.

3I:382 Date: 12 Nov 1824 RtCt: 14 Feb 1825
Leven LUCKETT of Ldn to heirs of Henery SETTLE dec'd. Release of mortgage of Nov 1812, DBk PP:353. Wit: Horrace LUCKETT, Asa ROGERS, Burr WEEKS.

3I:383 Date: 29 Jan 1825 RtCt: 14 Feb 1825
Joshua HUTCHISON of Ffx to William AMBLAR of Ldn. B/S of 204a (using 55a in Ffx for purchase) adj John LEWIS, Mrs. BERKLY, __ BATY. Delv. to AMBLER 2 Dec 1828.

3I:385 Date: 29 Jan 1825 RtCt: 11 Feb 1825
William AMBLAR & wife Susan of Ldn to Joshua HUTCHISON of Ffx. B/S of 136a in Ldn and Ffx (using 100a in Ldn and $300 for 81a by PoA by William ROE of Ross Co Ohio to AMBLAR) adj Stephen DANIEL, Lewis AMBLAR, John HUTCHISON, Sandford HUTCHISON, late B. HUTCHISON. Wit: Charles LEWIS, Johnston CLEVELAND. Delv. pr order 8 Mar 1830.

3I:387 Date: 2 Dec 1824 RtCt: 13 Dec 1824/14 Feb 1825
Wayne McKENNIE, Mary McKENNIE and Henery ADAMS & wife Priscilla (late McKENNIE) to James McILHANY. Trust for debt by late Francis McKENNIE to Elijah PEACOCK using 97a adj James NIXON, John HAMILTON Jr. and 25a wood land on NW side of Short Hill. Wit: B. WHITE, Johnson IRWIN, John HAMILTON Jr.

3I:390 Date: 23 Jul 1824 RtCt: 14 Feb 1825
Lott BARR and Nimrod BARR (grandchildren of George NIXON the elder dec'd and ch/o Hannah BARR dec'd formerly NIXON) of Ldn to

Martha HOMBS of Ldn. B/S of 16a (und. int. in land of George
NIXON the elder dec'd) on Beaverdam adj James DUER, William
CARR, __ COE, Thomas BROWN. Wit: Micajah TRIPLETT, Saml.
TRIPLETT, Thomas LEONARD, George BARR, James DEWAR.

3I:391   Date: 14 Feb 1825   RtCt: 14 Feb 1825
Luke HILTON of Ldn to Eli JANNEY of Ldn. Trust for Charles B.
HAMILTON of Ldn as security on bond to John BRADEN (Exor of
Ab[i]el JENNERS dec'd) using horse bought last Nov of BRADEN as
Exor.

3I:393   Date: 5 May 1817   RtCt: 14 Feb 1825
Abraham SKILLMAN & wife Violinda of Ldn to Abel JANNEY of Ldn.
B/S of 155a (prch/o Francis TITUS) on Beaverdam adj __ GIBSON,
__ CARR. Wit: Jas. SIMPSON, James BEAVERS. Delv. to JANNEY
27 Jan 1826.

3I:395   Date: 29 Jan 1825   RtCt: 14 Feb 1825
William AMBLAR & wife Susan of Ldn to John HUTCHISON of Ldn.
B/S of 97a adj Lewis AMBLAR, Sandford HUTCHISON, Joshua
HUTCHISON. Wit: Charles LEWIS, Johnston CLEVELAND. Delv. pr
order DBk HHH:14, 1 Apr __.

3I:397   Date: 24 Apr 1824   RtCt: 14 Feb 1825
Thomas NICHOLS and Isaac NICHOLS (Exors of Isaac NICHOLS
dec'd) of Ldn to Mahlon WALTERS of Ldn. B/S of 19a (from tract
cnvy/b gift from Thomas NICHOLS of Newcastle Co Pa Jan 1776 to
son Isaac NICHOLS of Ldn, DBk L:78). Wit: James McDOWOLL,
Giles BROWN, Timothy TAYLOR Jr. Delv. to WA[L]TERS 9 Oct
1826.

3I:399   Date: 16 Feb 1825   RtCt: 14 Mar 1825
S. A. JACKSON & wife Sarah of Ldn to Mason OSBURNE of Ldn.
Trust for debt to Morris OSBURNE using 22a with new stone house
(part of farm of George NICHOLS dec'd). Wit: John WHITE, Craven
OSBURNE. Delv. to M. OSBURNE 24 May 1827.

3I:403   Date: 5 Mar 1825   RtCt: 5 May 1825
Samuel A. JACKSON of Ldn to Calvin THATCHER of Ldn. Trust for
debt to Samuel CLENDENING, Hiram & Townsend McVEIGH, John
JANNEY, John PURCELL, Josiah WALRAVEN, Nathan NICHOLS
Jr., Thomas TRIPLETT using int. in 25a (part assigned his wife
Sarah formerly Sarah NICHOLS and part prch/o Thomas NICHOLS)
and household items.

3I:406   Date: 4 Mar 1825   RtCt: 6 Apr 1825
William CANBY of Ldn to Samuel GILPIN of Ldn. Trust for debt to
Charles CANBY of BaltMD using crops, farm and household items.
Delv. to GILPIN 12 Nov 1825.

3I:407   Date: __   RtCt: 11 Apr 1825
Jacob MILLER. Oath as Lt in __ Batt 56th Reg of Va Militia.
Wm. RUSSELL. Oath as Ensign in same.

3I:408   Date: 8 Apr 1825   RtCt: 8 Apr 1825
Thomas H. STEPHENS (insolvent) to Shff Ludwell LEE. B/S of
house and lot in German Settlement (after satisfying trust) and
house and 2 lots in Berlin Md (suit of John STOUSBERGER and
Edward MARLOW Exors of Conrad SHAFFER dec'd).

3I:409   Date: 7 Apr 1825   RtCt: 7 Apr 1825
Stephen WILSON & wife Hannah P. of MontMD to William WILSON
of Ldn. B/S of 100a (69a of which was transferred by Aaron
HOLLOWAY Dec 1821, DBk EEE:143) on NW fork of Goose Creek
adj Benjamin DANIELS, Abdon DILLON, Richard COPELAND,
Thomas GREGG. Wit: Wilson C. SELDEN, John McCORMICK.
Delv. to William WILSON 10 Jul 1837.

3I:412   Date: 8 Feb 1825   RtCt: 15 Feb 1825
David WEATHERLY & wife Elisabeth A. of Ffx to George W.
HUNTER. Trust for debt (purchased land, DBk GGG:374, with funds
from Peter) to Peter WEATHERLY (not yet a citizen of U.S. by
naturalization) using 217a. Wit: John McCORMICK, Saml. M.
EDWARDS. Delv. pr order 18 Apr 1836.

3I:414   Date: 10 Jul 1824   RtCt: 6 Apr 1825
Isaac EATON & wife Malinda of Ldn to Samuel GILPIN of Ldn. B/S
of ½a Lot #34 in Mt. Gilead nr Loudoun and Back St. Wit: William
LICKEY, Thomas ROLLINGS, Rowena HOLMES, Thomas
SANDERS, William CARR, James H. HAMILTON.

3I:417   Date: 26 Feb 1825   RtCt: 6 Apr 1825
Burr POWELL & wife Catherine of Ldn to Cuthbert POWELL of Ldn.
B/S of und. share in 610a (cnvy/b William CHILTON to Burr and
Cuthbert POWELL as tenants in common Jun 1824) adj James
MONROE, George CARTER, Tasker C. QUINLIN, Thomas R.
MOTT. Wit: Francis W. LUCKETT. Delv. to C. POWELL 12 May
1827.

3I:419   Date: 5 Apr 1825   RtCt: 5 Apr 1825
Joseph DANIEL of Ldn to Richard H. HENDERSON, Humphrey
POWELL and Jessee TIMMS of Ldn. Trust for debt to George
CARTER of Oatlands using 150a (cnvy/b James SINCLAIR Sept
1804). Wit: Saml. BUCK, E. G. HAMILTON.

3I:422   Date: 9 Apr 1821   RtCt: 4 Apr 1825
William VICKERS yeoman of Ldn to William RICHARDS Jr. (h/o
Margaret who is d/o VICKERS) of Ldn. LS of 109a (cnvy/b Jonathan
CARTER) during her lifetime. Wit: Seth SMITH, Thomas KING,
Richard CARTER.

3I:422   Date: 25 Nov 1824   RtCt: 29 Mar 1825
Aaron BURSON of Ldn to Thomas TRAHERN of Ldn. Release of
trust of May 1815 for debt to James TRAHERN.

3I:423 Date: 15 Mar 1816 RtCt: 29 Mar 1825
Thomas PARKER, Robert J. TAYLOR and Richard H.
HENDERSON (Commrs. of Sup. Ct in case of Thomas SWAN and
Edmund J. LEE Admrs of Wm. B. PAGE dec'd against Ferdinando
FAIRFAX, Jul 1814) to Ebenezer GRUBB. B/S of 113a Beezers Lot
adj Peter GIDEON, __ EVANS and 3a Spring Lot adj Beezers Lot,
__ CLENDENING.

3I:426 Date: 15 Mar 1816 RtCt: 3 Mar 1825
Thomas PARKER, Robert J. TAYLOR and Richard H.
HENDERSON (Commrs. of Sup. Ct in case of Thomas SWAN and
Edmund J. LEE Admrs of Wm. B. PAGE dec'd against Ferdinando
FAIRFAX, Jul 1814) to Joshua OSBURNE of Ldn. B/S of 155a
'Warners Lot' adj __ OREM, Wm. HOWELL, Jos. OSBURNE. Delv.
to OSBURNE 10 Jun 1826. Gives plat.

3I:428 Date: 12 Mar 1825 RtCt: 28 Mar 1825
Joseph BURSON & wife Mary of Ldn to son John BURSON of Ldn.
B/S of 134a (agrees to maintain his parents with profits from farm)
adj Poor House farm, Cyrus BURSON, John WHITACRE. Wit:
William BRONAUGH, Wm. H. DORSEY.

3K:001 Date: 12 Feb 1825 RtCt: 19 Feb 1825
Usher SKINNER of Ldn to William BRONAUGH of Ldn. Trust for
debt to Sally BRONAUGH of Ldn using farm animals and items.

3K:002 Date: 10 Feb 1825 RtCt: 11 Mar 1825
John LEWIS and Mary LEWIS of Ldn to Peter RUST Jr of Ldn. B/S
of 1/6th int. each in 197a (less 19½a recovered of BROWN) of
mother Nancy late wife of Charles LEWIS from her father James
LEWIS.

3K:003 Date: 28 Feb 1825 RtCt: 14 Mar 1825
Charles LEWIS of Ldn to Johnston CLEVELAND of Ldn. B/S of
320a 'Plainfield tract' (cnvy/b Nathan HUTCHISON) adj Nancy
JONES, heirs of George BERKLEY. Wit: Robt. M. NEWMAN,
Johnston J. COLEMAN, Jonathan LEWIS.

3K:004 Date: 14 Feb 1825 RtCt: 14 Mar 1825
Charles LEWIS (Commr. of suit of 18 Dec 1824) to Jacob
SUMMERS. B/S of 185a (belonging to heirs of Henry SETTLE) adj
William LYNE. Delv. to SUMMERS 23 Sep 1828.

3K:005 Date: 1 Mar 1825 RtCt: 14 Mar 1825
Shff Ludwell LEE to Daniel JAMES of Ldn. B/S of int. in 87½a where
Jonathan JAMES the elder now resides (cnvy/b Margaret
McILHANY to Elias, Jonathan and Daniel JAMES , then to Shff by
them Jan 1825) Delv. to JAMES 25 Aug 1826.

3K:006 Date: 9 Feb 1825 RtCt: 14 Mar 1825
Thomas NICHOLS of Ldn to S. A. JACKSON of Ldn. B/S of 11a adj
__ KILGORE, Tho. JAMES.

3K:007   Date: 22 Feb 1825   RtCt: 14 Mar 1825

William VICKERS & wife Anna of Ldn to Francis W. LUCKETT of Ldn. Trust for debt to William RICHARDS Jr. of Ldn using 80a (cnvy/b John NEWLON, Apr 1816) and 16a (cnvy/b Robert M. POWELL, May 1821); and upper part of 1a Lot #3 in Millville, and ½a upper end of Lot #6, and ¼a Lots #1 and #3 on N side of Main St, and lower end of Lot #4, and 1a lower end of Lot #5. Delv. to LUCKETT 20 Jan 1826.

3K:009   Date: 8 Mar 1825   RtCt: 14 Mar 1825

Ariss BUCKNER & wife Lucy of Ldn to James L. McKENNA of Ffx. Trust for debt to Bank of Alexandria using 1400a where BUCKNER resides. Wit: Charles LEWIS, John BAYLY. Delv. pr order 14 Feb 1832.

3K:012   Date: 14 Mar 1825   RtCt: 14 Mar 1825

Sarah HUMPHREY wd/o Jacob HUMPHREY dec'd of Ldn to son Thomas L. HUMPHREY. B/S of land unintentionally conveyed to Sarah, May 1822, DBk EEE:279. Delv. to HUMPHREY 22 Dec 1825.

3K:013   Date: 24 Jan 1825   RtCt: 14 Mar 1825

Charles WILLIAMS & wife Mary of Ldn to Syddnah WILLIAMS of Ldn. B/S of int. in 2/6th of land allotted to Hannah WILLIAMS relict of Enos WILLIAMS dec'd as dower. Wit: Saml. CLAPHAM, Saml. DAWSON. Delv. to Sydnor WILLIAMS 10 Apr 1828.

3K:014   Date: 14 Feb 1825   RtCt: 14 Mar 1825

Jacob SUMMERS & wife Elizabeth to James LEWIS and Samuel HALLEY. Trust for debt to Charles LEWIS (Commr for Henry SETTLE dec'd) using 185a adj Wm. LEWIS, Joshua LEE. Wit: Ariss BUCKNER, John BAYLY.

3K:017   Date: 30 Mar 1824   RtCt: 14 Mar 1825

Aaron MILLER & wife Mary of Ldn to Benjamin GRUBB of Ldn. B/S of 69a adj GRUBB, __ MINK, __ HICKMAN, __ RICHARDS, John JANNEY, George COOPER; and 25a on E side of Short Hill mt. (prch/o John HANKS' heirs) adj Isaac HOUGH. Filed with the relinq. of dower among the deeds of Oct 1825.

3K:019   Date: 18 Feb 1825   RtCt: 14 Mar 1825

George SHOVER of Ldn to Noble BRADEN of Ldn. Trust for debt to Robert BRADEN using 13½a. Wit: W. F. BRADEN, D. SHAWEN, D. CONRAD, Geo. W. HENRY.

3K:021   Date: 7 Aug 1824   RtCt: 14 Mar 1825

Garrett WALKER & wife Ruth of Ldn to James HOGE and Thomas GORE of Ldn. Trust for Gabriel MEGEATH as security on bond to Sophia WALKER using int. in land of father Benjamin WALKER dec'd (prch/o heirs of Lovell JACKSON, except 1½a sold to William WALKER). Wit: Wm. BRONAUGH, Wm. H. DORSEY.

3K:023 Date: 16 Feb 1822 RtCt: 14 Mar 1825
Eli McKNIGHT & wife Alley of Ldn to Robert CARLISLE of Ldn. B/S
of 2a on NW fork of Goose Creek, adj __ LIDER, Thomas JAMES.

3K:025 Date: 14 Mar 1825 RtCt: 14 Mar 1825
Charles BINNS & wife Martha of Ldn to Robert MOFFETT of Ldn.
B/S of Martha's und. int. of land of father Josiah MOFFETT dec'd,
on Secolon run adj Peter OATYER, Thos. R. MOTT, heirs of Landon
CARTER. Wit: Abner GIBSON, James M. LEWIS.

3K:027 Date: 2 Mar 1825 RtCt: 14 Mar 1825
Thomas L. HUMPHREY & wife Sarah of Ldn to mother Sarah
HUMPHREY. B/S of 43a (additional land as dower and to
compensate for advances to Thomas L.; deed exec. May 1822
suppose to be 43a but was not) adj John WILLIAMS, John
WILKINSON, John HATCHER, John BROWN. Wit: Wm.
BRONAUGH, Wm. H. DORSEY. Delv. to Wm. HUMPHREY 3 Dec
1825.

3K:029 Date: 15 Mar 1825 RtCt: 15 Mar 1829
L. P. W. BALCH (trustee of John SHAFER, Dec 1820) of Ldn to
John CONNARD of Ldn. B/S of 119a (138a cnvy/b Jacob VIRTZ
May 1815 to SHAFER, one share was not conveyed). Delv. to John
CONARD 16 Jan 1829.

3K:030 Date: 15 Mar 1825 RtCt: 15 Mar 1825
French GARRISON to John ANKERS. Trust for debt to Wm.
ELLZEY for grain, Anna ROZELL with Jacob FADELY and George
SHRYOCK as securities at sale of Stephen C. ROZELL dec'd, note
to James MILLER with Jacob SILCOTT as security using farm and
household items.

3K:033 Date: 16 Mar 1825 RtCt: 10 [?] Mar 1825
Ann THOMAS d/o Leonard THOMAS dec'd of Ldn to James
MATEER of Ldn. B/S of int. in dower leased land where her mother
now lives. Delv. pr order filed 6 Feb 1833.

3K:034 Date: 15 Mar 1825 RtCt: 18 Mar 1825
Yeoman David GALLEHER & wife Elizabeth of Ldn to Thornton
WALKER of Ldn. B/S of 2a adj Seth SMITH, H. PLAISTER; and 3a
wood lot #5 in div. of William GALLEHER dec'd, both nr Union. Wit:
William BRONAUGH, Francis W. LUCKETT.

3K:036 Date: 21 Mar 1825 RtCt: 21 Mar 1825
Enos GARRETT of Ldn to John TRIBBY, Thomas TRIBBY and
Eleanor McFARLAND (ch/o Thomas TRIBBY Sr dec'd) and Thomas
TRIBBY, Eleanor THOMPSON, William TRIBBY, Jesse TRIBBY,
Mason TRIBBY, Sarah TRIBBY, Nancy TRIBBY, Ruth TRIBBY,
Mary TRIBBY & Martha TRIBBY (ch/o James TRIBBY s/o Thomas
TRIBBY Sr dec'd) and David REECE (Exor of Thomas TRIBBY Sr
dec'd). Release of trust of July 1807 for debt to Enos GARRETT on
158a.

3K:038   Date: 28 Feb 1825   RtCt: 21 Mar 1825
William VICKERS of Ldn to Gourley REEDER of Ldn. LS of 100a
where Vickers now lives (prch/o William LYONS) with an addition of
7a. Delv. to REEDER 5 Oct 1826.

3K:039   Date: 15 Mar 1825   RtCt: 21 Mar 1825
Nicholas OSBURN of Ldn to Enos WILDMAN of Ldn. Trust for debt
to Notley C. WILLIAMS using slaves Bill, Uriah, Poll, Violett, Mariah,
John, William, Sam, Harriet, Charlot, Squire & Poll's infant child; and
int. in any slaves which might descend from und. slaves in
possession of James CURRELL which he might be entitled to from
trust given by James CURRELL to William GUNNELL the 3rd for
benefit of his wife, Frances CURRELL, her children & grandchildren;
and farm animals and items, household items.

3K:041   Date: 19 Mar 1825   RtCt: 21 Mar 1825
Thomas L. HUMPHREY & wife Sarah of Ldn to William C. PALMER
and Mason P. CHAMBLIN merchants trading under Palmer &
Chamblin of Ldn. B/S of 52a adj John WILLIAMS, John
WILKINSON, John HATCHER. Wit: Benjn. GRAYSON, Wm. H.
DORSEY.

3K:043   Date: 15 Mar 1825   RtCt: 22 Mar 1825
Thornton WALKER & wife Fanny of Ldn to Samuel BEVERS of Ldn.
B/S of 25½a (from original tract of Reuben TRIPLETT dec'd, cnvy/b
Melinda BEAVERS, Aug 1823). Wit: Wm. BRONAUGH, Francis W.
LUCKETT.

3K:044   Date: 11 Mar 1825   RtCt: 22 Mar 1825
William STONE to Mahlon MORRIS and Josh'a REID. Trust for debt
to Isaac CAMP using crops, animals, farm and household items.

3K:047   Date: 22 Mar 1825   RtCt: 22 Mar 1825
Sandford FLING (Admr of George FLING dec'd) of Ldn to Dr.
George LEE of Ldn. BoS for negro woman Violett 41-42y old & her
son 8-9m old.

3K:048   Date: 7 Apr 1819   RtCt: 23 Mar 1825
John SHAW Jr. of Ldn to father John SHAW and mother Rebecca
SHAW. PoA to sell or occupy themselves a house & lot in Lsbg (gift
from father Apr 1819). Wit: Catharine SHAW. Statement of 29 Nov
1824 states John Jr. now of legal age.

3K:049   Date: 10 Mar 1825   RtCt: 23 Mar 1825
John CRANE & wife Elizabeth of Fqr to Elijah ANDERSON of Ldn.
B/S of 5a adj ANDERSON, John KILE, Vickers REEDER. Delv. to
Anderson 2 Apr 1832.

3K:051   Date: 7 Mar 1825   RtCt: 16 Mar 1825
Britton SANDERS and Ann ECKHART (wd/o Casper ECKHART
dec'd). Marriage will soon occur and Ann has considerable assets –
house & lot on King St in Lsbg adj Wm. CLINE & David OGDEN; 2a
W of Lsbg (bought from Richard H. HENDERSON & Ann WRIGHT);

190a (from will of father Elisha GREGG dec'd); negro man Jim, boy Frank, boy Henry (from late husband), woman Hannah & her child Bill or William bought by her from Aaron SAUNDERS slaves for life, woman Rose, woman Betty & her child Maria slaves for life bought by her from Britton SANDERS; farm animals, farm and household items. She to maintain holdings and if she does not designate in a will then Sanders to enjoy them after her death, except 190a (to go to legal heirs). Items held in trust to Charles GULATT & Saml. M. EDWARDS. Wit: Edward HAMMETT, James GILMORE, George HAMMETT. Delv. to EDWARDS 7 Jan 1827.

3K:055   Date: 24 Mar 1825   RtCt: 24 Mar 1825
James ATWELL to Jesse ATWELL. Trust for Jesse as security in sundry cases using farm animals, farm and household items. Wit: W. A. BINNS, James MATEER, Wm. KING.

3K:056   Date: 23 Mar 1825   RtCt: 24 Mar 1825
Blacksmith Joseph TORRISON of Union to Josias M. CLARK. Trust for Dr. David E. BROWN as security in debt to Robert H. MILLER of AlexDC using lot in Union with store and blacksmith shop (cnvy/b Dunkin & Lloyd).

3K:057   Date: 26 Mar 1825   RtCt: 25 Mar 1825
John SHAW Jr. of Ldn to John SHAW of Ldn. B/S of brick house & lot at Loudoun & King Sts in Lsbg (gift from John).

3K:058   Date: ___ 1825   RtCt: 9 Jun 1825
William CHILTON of Lsbg to Lloyd NOLAND. Trust for debt to Burr POWELL and Cuthbert POWELL using ½a lot & house in Lsbg where he lives and slaves Jesse, Matilda, Maria & her infant Alfred, Jane [,?] Harriet, Wilson & Lewis and household items. Delv. to Burr W. HARRISON pr order of Burr POWELL 24 Jan 1826.

3K:062   Date: 12 Mar 1825   RtCt: 28 Mar 1825
Joseph BURSON & wife Mary of Ldn to son Cyrus BURSON of Ldn. B/S of 134a (subject to payment of ½ legacies from will dated Aug 1819 to be paid to wife Mary and his other children) adj Wm. FARR, Samuel PEUGH, John & Cyrus BURSON. Wit: William BRONAUGH, Wm. H. DORSEY. Delv. to Cyrus BURSON 27 Sep 1826.

3K:063   Date: 15 Mar 1825   RtCt: 22 Mar 1825
Thornton WALKER & wife Fanny of Ldn to David GALLEHER of Ldn. B/S of 4 lots totaling 51¼a (part of original tract of Reuben TRIPLETT dec'd cnvy/b John JOHNSON, Aug 1823). Wit: Wm. BRONAUGH, Francis W. LUCKETT. Delv. to GALLEHER 29 Oct 1828.

3K:065   Date: 11 Feb 1825   RtCt: 8 Apr 1825
Christopher NEALE & wife Harriet of AlexDC to John W. MASSIE of AlexDC. B/S of Lots #1-5 in Hllb containing 156a (for purpose of paying debt by NEALE & Philip TRIPLETT late joint merchants in

firm of Triplett & Neale at Richmond. Delv. to R. H. HENDERSON pr order 23 Feb 1827.

3K:068   Date: 1 Jan 1825   RtCt: 9 Apr 1825
Richard H. HENDERSON (trustee of Henly BOGGESS, Dec 1819) of Lsbg to Charles McKNIGHT of AlexDC. B/S of 220a adj George NOBLE, George RUST, Herod THOMAS. Delv. pr order 1 Jul 1829.

3K:069   Date: 29 Nov 1823   RtCt: 11 Apr 1825
David GALLEHER & wife Elizabeth of Ldn to William GALLEHER of Ldn. B/S of ½ of lot in Union (cnvy/b William G. McKENNEY – his share from grandfather William GALLEHER dec'd). Wit: William BRONAUGH, Francis W. LUCKETT.

3K:071   Date: 5 Apr 1825   RtCt: 11 Apr 1825
Yeoman Samuel BEAVERS & wife Sarah of Ldn to Henry PLAISTER Jr of Ldn. B/S of int. in lands of James REED dec'd late of Ldn as dower to widow Rebecca REED (DBk YY:201, DBk BBB:437). Wit: William BRONAUGH, Francis W. LUCKETT.

3K:073   Date: 7 Apr 1825   RtCt: 11 Apr 1825
Hugh ROGERS of Ldn to William L. POWELL of Ldn. B/S of part of Lots #17 & 23 in Mdbg (cnvy/b Nelson GREGG for securing a debt to Elizabeth BOYD). Wit: Asa ROGERS, James H. McVEIGH, Burr WEEKS.

3K:074   Date: 5 Apr 1825   RtCt: 11 Apr 1825
William VICKERS of Ldn to Seth SMITH of Ldn. Trust for debt to Jacob SILCOTT of Ldn using 93a adj William REEDER, Elijah ANDERSON, James WORNELL (prch/o Jonathan CARTER) and his 1/12th int. in estate of Thomas RUSSELL dec'd (cnvy/b Thomas RUSSELL Jr.)

3K:075   Date: 25 Feb 1825   RtCt: 11 Apr 1825
John BOGER & wife Margaret of Ldn to Peter COMPHER, Peter FRY, Samuel PRILL and John MANN of Ldn. Trust for debt to Peter COMPHER using 25 perches (cnvy/b Amos JANNEY) adj Lutheran Church lot, George COOPER. Wit: Saml. DAWSON, Saml. M. EDWARDS.

3K:077   Date: 2 Mar 1825   RtCt: 11 Apr 1825
William McMULLIN & wife Elizabeth of Ldn to Fielding LYNN of Ldn. B/S of 10a on Beaverdam (where William lives, part of land allotted in div. of father Alexander McMULLIN dec'd). Wit: Burr POWELL, Wm. BRONAUGH. Delv. to John SINCLAIR pr order 11 Jul 1836.

3K:079   Date: 21 Jan 1825   RtCt: 11 Apr 1825
Robert J. TAYLOR (trustee as security for Martin BRENT debt to Charles BENNETT) of AlexDC to Hiram SEATON of Ldn. B/S of 15a adj __ DULANEY.

3K:080   Date: 30 Sep 1824   RtCt: 11 Apr 1825
Mary GALLEHER of Ldn to Joseph A. LLOYD. B/S of ½a lot in Union adj William GALLEHER, Samuel DUNKIN, James REID. Delv. to Michael PLAISTER pr order ___.

3K:081   Date: 18 Apr 1821   RtCt: 11 Apr 1825
Stephen WILSON & wife Hannah P. of Ldn to David JAMES of Ldn. B/S of 50a (at NE end of tract WILSON prch/o estate of William WEST dec'd) adj Timothy TAYLOR, Rufus UPDIKE. Wit: Stacey TAYLOR, David SMITH, Chas. TAYLOR, James COCHRAN Jr. Delv. to David JAMES 24 May 1827.

3K:083   Date: 15 Dec 1824   RtCt: 11 Apr 1825
Sydnor BAILEY and Cuthbert POWELL (trustees of David CARTER, Aug 1822) of Ldn to Joseph CARR of Ldn. B/S of 96a (prch/o David BROWN) on Goose Creek adj Presley SAUNDERS dec'd. Delv. to CARR 13 Feb 1826.

3K:084   Date: 2 Apr 1825   RtCt: 11 Apr 1825
Benjamin DANIEL (br/o William DANIEL) & wife Sidney of Ldn to Richard ADAMS of Ldn. B/S of 106½a (see DBk KK:7; occupied for the present year by Jonah PURCELL). Wit: John McCORMICK, Saml. M. EDWARDS.

3K:087   Date: 26 Feb 1825   RtCt: 11 Apr 1825
Samuel HOGUE & wife Mary of Ldn to Thomas ROGERS of Ldn. Trust for debt to Conrad BITZER with William HOLMES and Elijah HOLMES as security using und. share of land of Joseph HOLMES dec'd subject to dower. Wit: William CARR, James H. HAMILTON.

3K:089   Date: __ Mar 1825   RtCt: 25 Mar/11 Apr 1825
Joshua and Craven OSBURN (Exors of Landon OSBURN dec'd) of Ldn to Jane POTTS of Ldn. B/S of 160a (from tract of Landon dec'd now in possession of Turner OSBURN, purchased by Landon of Exors of William OSBURN) adj Craven OSBURN, Nathan POTTS dec'd. Wit: Jos. B. FOX, Edward MORELAND, Amanda O. FOX. Mailed to grantee pr order 5 Mar 1855.

3K:091   Date: 30 Aug 1824   RtCt: 30 Mar 1825
Thomas TRAHERN of Ldn to Samuel HATCHER of Ldn. Trust for debt to John PANCOAST Jr. using 53¼a (cnvy/b Philip FRY). Wit: Jos. BENNETT, Lewis COHAGAN, William SHAVOURS. Delv. to PANCOAST 1 Jun 1826.

3K:092   Date: 12 Apr 1825   RtCt: 12 Apr 1825
John ODEN & wife Margaret to William ODEN. B/S of int. in __a held by father Thomas ODEN in his life now occupied by Jacob SUMMERS which was assigned to his mother Martha ODEN as dower (in his right as heir, as purchaser of Richard W. ODEN's part, and his int. in Vincent ODEN's part who died intestate without wife or child).

3K:093   Date: 2 Apr 1825   RtCt: 12 Apr 1825
Mahlon JANNEY & wife Rachel of Ldn to Jeremiah T. MILLER of Ldn. Trust for debt to David REESE using 107a (prch/o David REECE Exor of Thomas TRIBBY dec'd, subject to dower of Mary TRIBBY) adj William BROWN, Joseph LEWIS, __ HUGHES. Wit: John WHITE, Presley CORDELL.

3K:095   Date: 13 Apr 1825   RtCt: 13 Apr 1825
Abraham SKILLMAN to [Thomas BROWN]. Release of trust – see DBk VV:141.

3K:095   Date: 13 Apr 1825   RtCt: 13 Apr 1825
Thomas BROWN of Ldn to Saml. B. T. CALDWELL of Ldn. Trust for debt to Chancery BROOKS of BaltMd using __a (cnvy/b Abraham SKILLMAN 181? and in another deed from George NIXON 18??). Delv to CALDWELL 14 Apr 1828.

3K:097   Date: 16 Apr 1825   RtCt: 16 Apr 1825
Daniel LOVETT of Ldn to George CARTER of Ldn. B/S of 3a adj CARTER, Wm. CARR on S side of road from Oatlands Mills to Mr. John NIXON's Mill. Delv. to CARTER 5 Jun 1827.

3K:099   Date: 16 Apr 1825   RtCt: 10 Apr 1825
Daniel LOVETT of Ldn to Richard H. HENDERSON, Thomas R. MOTT, Sampson BLINCOE of Ldn. Trust for debt to George CARTER of Oatlands using 150a devised by father Daniel LOVETT dec'd. Delv. to Jesse TIMMS pr order verbally of Geo. CARTER 5 Jun 1827.

3K:101   Date: 15 Apr 1825   RtCt: 16 Apr 1825
David MILBOURN of Ldn to James SINCLAIR of Ldn. Trust for debt to Aquilla MEAD using farm and household items. Wit: S. B. T. CALDWELL, Jno. MARTIN, R. G. SAUNDERS. Delv. to SINCLAIR 21 Mar 1826.

3K:103   Date: 19 Apr 1825   RtCt: 19 Apr 1825
Samuel CROOKS of Ldn to Connard LONG of Ldn. Trust for debt to Charles CROOKS using int. in 22¼a entitled to by marriage with Margaret d/o Lewis LYDER and 1/9th of dower of Mary LYDER in 90a life estate.

3K:105   Date: 18 Apr 1825   RtCt: 19 Apr 1825
Samuel CROOKS of Ldn to Connard LONG of Ldn. Trust for debt to Charles CROOKS using farm animals and items, crops, household items.

3K:107   Date: 17 Apr 1823   RtCt: 22 Apr 1825
James McKEMIE and Eli McKEMIE (sons of Nancy McKEMIE) to George SMITH. Release of 5a (to perfect title from 1822 of Francis McKEMIE late of Ldn to SMITH as widow Nancy McKEMIE is now suppose to be deceased and was entitled to 1/5th of land) Wit: L. ELLZEY, Joseph C. WRIGHT, Thos. WILKINSON, Isaac THOMAS. Delv. to SMITH 13 Nov 1829.

3K:108   Date: 2 Apr 1825   RtCt: 23 Apr 1825
William VICKERS of Ldn to John W. GRAYSON of Ldn. Trust for John G. HUMPHREY & William RICHARDS as security for Shff Hugh SMITH for benefit of J. THOMSON of AlexDC, debts to Exors of Abner HUMPHREY, Leah MONTEATH of StaffVa, Daniel EACHES, Patsy LEITH of Ohio (now Patsy REEDER), Edmund JONES, Abraham BROWN, James JOHNSON, Jacob REEDER, David SIMPSON, Noble BEVERIDGE, William BROWN & Jacob ISH using negro boy Landon, farm animals, farm and household items. Delv. pr order 9 May 1826.

3K:111   Date: 4 Mar 1825   RtCt: 23 Apr 1825
John DUNKIN & wife Ruth of Ldn to David E. BROWN of Ldn. Trust as security for debt to Isaac BROWN and Samuel DUNKIN using 90¼a (part of Philip FRY's tract) adj George MARKS, Benjn. JACKSON, Thos. TRAYHERN.

3K:113   Date: 22 Mar 1825   RtCt: 25 Apr 1825
James MONROE & wife Eliza to Alexander KERR Cashier of Bank. Trust for debt to Bank of Metropolis using 250a where MONROE resides at Little River nr Aldie. Wit: William WATERS, Jno. N. MOULDER.

3K:116   Date: 19 Apr 1825   RtCt: 26 Apr 1825
Benjamin DANIEL of Ldn to William DANIEL of Ldn. BoS for note of Richard ADAMS, note of Charles BINNS and John A. BINNS, farm animals, farm and household items. Wit: Fras. STRIBLING, H. ELLIOTT.

3K:117   Date: 23 Apr 1825   RtCt: 26 Apr 1825
John A. MARMADUKE & wife Catharine of Ldn to George M. CHICHESTER of Ldn. B/S of 42a on Potomac adj Dr. SELDON. Wit: Craven OSBURN, John WHITE. Delv. to CHICHESTER 10 Apr 1832.

3K:119   Date: 26 Apr 1825   RtCt: 26 Apr 1825
John SHAVER and David AXLINE. Agreement – 15 Jun 1791 SHAVER purchased 61½a from Henry A. BENNETT. On 16 Feb 1803, DBk CC:227, Shaver purchased 55½a in Piedmont from Ferdinando FAIRFAX. On 12 Nov 1804, DBk UU:18, SHAVER purchased land from Henry WOLF in Cattocton Manor formerly leased for lives. On 5 Mar 1806 SHAVER purchased 121a, DBk HH:321, of Philip SWANK, etc. AXLINE is now bound as security for SHAVER to Conrad BITZER with SHAVER owing many others and has trust using all land to William VERTZ. Agrees for AXLINE to rent out land until they are sold. Wit: S. BLINCOE, John THOMAS, John CARNEY.

3K:122   Date: 26 Mar 1825   RtCt: 29 Apr 1825
Robert BRADEN and Daniel STONE (trustees of Edward DORSEY & wife Mary, Dec 1820) of Ldn to James NIXON of Ldn. B/S of 19a

on Cotocton Creek adj William JANNEY. Wit: Presley CORDELL, Samuel HOUGH.

3K:124 Date: 21 Apr 1825 RtCt: 30 Apr 1825
Fayette BALL of Ldn to Richard H. HENDERSON, Lewis P. W. BALCH and Burr W. HARRISON of Lsbg. Trust for debt to George CARTER of Oatlands using 300a 'Big Spring Tract' on W side of road from Lsbg to Noland's ferry adj Thos. SWANN, C. P. TUTT, Thos. GASSAWAY, 'Rasberry Plane Estate'. Delv. to CARTER pr Jesse TIMMS 5 Jun 1827.

3K:128 Date: 5 May 1825 RtCt: 19 May 1825
Samuel CLAPHAM & wife Elizabeth of Ldn to James B. MURRAY of NY City. Trust for debt to Chatham Fire Insurance Co. of NY City using 68a where Thomas AWBRY lately lived adj Thomas AWBRY, John SEMPLE, Thomas GEORGE and plantation where Frederick WYSELL then lived; and 300a adj Mrs. JOHNSON, __ KIMELY, __ STEER; and 150a adj Elizabeth MORRIS, Mary RICHARDSON. Recorded from copy original being sent on to the Insurance Co. Wit: J. Warren BRAKETT, Joseph CRAVEN, George W. DOTY, W. D. MATTBY, James M. LEWIS, Samuel DAWSON.

3K:135 Date: 28 Apr 1825 RtCt: 4 May 1825
Archibald MAINS of Ldn to Richard H. HENDERSON of Ldn. B/S of fraction of an acre – the eastern extremity of fence on side of road from Lsbg across mountain by Jesse RICE. Delv. to HENDERSON on Christmas day, a day on which every fellow has a right to have holiday, 1835.

3K:136 Date: 19 Feb 1825 RtCt: 5 May 1825
George FITCHTER & wife Sally of Ldn to Samuel CARR of Ldn. B/S of 4a on NE side of turnpike road from Lsbg to Goose Creek Bridge adj Edmund J. LEE. Wit: S. M. BOSS, Gunnell SAUNDERS, John McCORMICK, Saml. M. EDWARDS.

3K:138 Date: 2 May 1825 RtCt: 2 May 1825
John COOPER & wife Magdalena of Ldn to Jacob SHOEMAKER of Ldn. B/S of 44a (allotted Magdalena late HICKMAN in div. of father Peter HICKMAN Sr dec'd). Delv. to SHOEMAKER 26 Feb 1827.

3K:141 Date: 9 May 1825 RtCt: 9 May 1825
John WINE, Jacob WALTMAN and Henry RUSSELL bound to justices of peace Johnson CLEVELAND, Abner GIBSON, Thomas SANDERS & Thomas GASSAWAY. Bond on WINE as Exor of Jacob WINE dec'd with bonds payable to Thomas FOUCH, Wm. B. HARRISON, Wm. CARR and Saml. M. EDWARDS.

3K:142 Date: 10 May 1825 RtCt: 10 May 1825
Charles CRIM dec'd. Division – court order dated 12 Apr 1825; 100¾a Lot #1 to widow's dower; 33a Lot #2 to Jacob CRIM; 30a Lot #3 to Adam CRIM; 30a Lot #4 to Daniel CRIM, 21a Lot #5 to Martin HARGAR; 30a Lot #7 to Mary SAWYER, 8a Lot #6 to John CRIM;

29a Lot #8 to Michael KIDWILER; 25a Lot #9 to Abraham CRIM; 33a Lot #10 to John WITTEMAN; 33a Lot #11 to Mordecai HARDACRE; 33¾a Lot #12 to Chas. CRIM; 51a Lot #13 to Jno. CASE; 5a Lot #14 to John CRIM; 15a Lot #15 to Martin HARGAR; 6a Lot #16 to Jacob CRIM. Gives plats. Divisors: Thomas WHITE, John GEORGE, Aaron MILLER.

3K:146   Date: 9 May 1825   RtCt: 9 May 1825
John WEADON, Benjamin MITCHELL, Jacob SILCOTT & William WEADON. Bond on John WEADON as constable.

3K:147   Date: 12 Apr 1825   RtCt: 18 May 1825
David JAMES & wife Charlotte of Ldn to Charles TAYLOR and Timothy TAYLOR of Ldn. Trust for debt to David HANDLEY using 50a (cnvy/b Stephen WILSON, Apr 1821) adj Jas. BRADFIELD, Rufus UPDIKE. Wit: Craven OSBURN, John WHITE. Delv. to HANDLEY 18 Feb 1830.

3K:150   Date: 16 Apr 1825   RtCt: 9 May 1825
William GULICK & wife Mary of Ldn to Francis W. LUCKETT of Ldn. Trust for debt to Levin LUCKETT of Ldn using 29a (cnvy/b Leven LUCKETT) on mt. adj C. F. MERCER, Moses GULICK, Leven LUCKETT. Wit: Burr POWELL, Abner GIBSON. Delv. pr order 17 Jan 1828.

3K:153   Date: 1 Nov 1824   RtCt: 9 May 1825
Charles SHEPHERD of Lsbg to Samuel M. EDWARDS of Ldn. Trust for debt to Thomas R. MOTT of Lsbg using lot (cnvy/b Thomas R. SAUNDERS) in Lsbg adj Rev. Jno. G. WATT on S side of Cornwell St.

3K:154   Date: 13 Jun 1825   RtCt: 13 Jun 1825
Wm. ROSE, Charles LEWIS and Ariss BUCKNER. Bond on ROSE as constable in 1st District.

3K:155   Date: 13 Jun 1825   RtCt: 13 Jun 1825
William CLENDENNING, George W. SHAWEN & Robert RUSSELL. Bond on CLENDENNING as constable.

3K:156   Date: 8 Jun 1825   RtCt: 12 Jun 1825
Andrew MONROE of Ldn to John Alexander BINNS of Ldn. B/S of int. in estate of father John MONROE dec'd and mother Sarah MONROE lately dec'd, farm and household items.

3K:157   Date: 30 May 1825   RtCt: 1 Jun 1825
David GALLEHER & wife Ellisabeth of Ldn to Isaac NICHOLS Jr. and James HOGE. Trust for debt to Isaac Sr. and Samuel NICHOLS of Ldn using 103a. Wit: John W. GRAYSON, William H. DORSEY. Delv. to Exors of Isaac NICHOLS dec'd 28 Jul 1826.

3K:160   Date: 30 May 1825   RtCt: 1 Jun 1826 [25]
Mahlon CRAVEN & wife Hannah of Ldn to Isaac NICHOLS Jr. & James HOGE of Ldn. Trust for debt to Isaac & Samuel NICHOLS using 127a on Snickers Gap Turnpike road. Wit: John W.

GRAYSON, Wm. H. DORSEY. Delv. to Exors of Isaac NICHOLS dec'd 28 Jul 1826.

3K:164 Date: 10 Mar 1825 RtCt: __ Jun 1825
Robert BRADEN & wife Ellizabeth of Ldn and John MORGAN & Joseph EACHES lately copartners in firm of Braden Morgan & Co. to Colin AULD & Wm. H. MILLER of AlexDC. Trust for debt to Bank of Alexandria using all of notes (long list) to Co and 58a lot with water grist mill and saw mill in Wtfd and miller's house. Wit: Saml. HOUGH, Presly CORDELL.

3K:174 Date: 3 May 1825 RtCt: 1 Jun 1825
William BRONAUGH & wife Jane of Ldn to Isaac NICHOLS Jr. and James HOGE of Ldn. Trust for debt to Samuel and Isaac NICHOLS using 250a (inherited from father William BRONAUGH dec'd). Wit: John W. GRAYSON, Wm. H. DORSEY. Delv. to Exors of Isaac NICHOLS dec'd 28 Jul 1826.

3K:176 Date: 9 May 1825 RtCt: 9 May 1825
George JANNEY of Ldn to Notley C. WILLIAMS of Ldn. B/S of 278a (cnvy/b Daniel EACHES and by JANNEY to WILLIAMS, 9 Dec 1816) adj James GRADY. Delv. to WILLIAMS 25 Feb 1830.

3K:178 Date: __ 1825 RtCt: 9 May 1825.
Abraham SKILLMAN of Ldn to Jesse MALLIN of Ldn. B/S of 1½a on road by N. Fork Meeting House adj Jesse ATWELL, Mrs. BROWN. Delv. to Jesse MALLON 12 Apr 1831.

3K:180 Date: 22 Feb 1823 RtCt: 9 May 1825
John COMPHER & wife Ellizabeth of Ldn to John ALT of Ldn. B/S of 21a (¼ part allotted to Ellizabeth late ALT from father William ALT dec'd). Wit: Ebenezer GRUBB, Saml. HOUGH. Delv. to John ALT 17 Aug 1826.

3K:182 Date: 7 May 1825 RtCt: 9 May 1825
Joshua OSBURNE and Craven OSBURNE (Exors of Landon OSBURN dec'd) of Ldn to Jane POTTS of Ldn. B/S of 2a adj POTTS and 7a adj POTTS.

3K:184 Date: 9 May 1825 RtCt: 9 May 1825
Charles STOVIN of Ldn. DoE for slave Edward RILEY.

3K:184 Date: 18 Feb 1825 RtCt: 9 May 1825
John SPICER of Ldn. DoE for Robert VALLENTINE, black complexion, abt 42y old. Wit: S. A. JACKSON, Nathan NICHOLS Jr., Robert CARLISLE.

3K:185 Date: 1 Nov 1824 RtCt: 9 May 1825
Charles SHEPHERD & wife Ellizabeth of Lsbg to Thomas R. MOTT of Ldn. B/S of house & lot in Lsbg on N side of Loudoun St adj Saml. M. BOSS. Wit: S. HOUGH, E. G. HAMILTON, Wm. T. T. MASON, Thomas SANDERS, Saml. M. EDWARDS.

3K:186   Date: 4 May 1825   RtCt: 9 May 1825
George JANNEY of Ldn to Abel JANNEY of Ldn. B/S of 53a 'Millville tract' (3 small tract united) with valuable mills & improvements with rents due cording and other machines; and adj 124a.

3K:188   Date: 13 Apr 1825   RtCt: 9 May 1825
Townshend D. PEYTON & wife Sarah M. of Ldn to Horrace LUCKETT of Ldn. B/S of 10a on W side of mt. when Snickers Gap Turnpike road crosses the same. Wit: Burr POWELL, Abner GIBSON. Delv. to LUCKETT __.

3K:190   Date: 9 May 1825   RtCt: 13 May 1826 [25]
Philip RHAN(N) Sr. & wife Catherine of Adams Co Pa to William CLINE of Ldn. B/S of 100a (cnvy/b Peter BEMASDAFFER, Jan 1825) including merchant and saw mills on both side of Goose Creek adj __ BLINCOE. Wit: R. McKINNY, Jacob KELLER. Delv. to CLINE 19 Sep 1826.

3K:193   Date: 28 Aug 1824   RtCt: 9 May 1825
Catherine NOLAND (w/o William NOLAND) of Ldn to James SWART Jr of Ldn. B/S of 139a adj Adam GUILICK, __ BERKLY. Delv. to SWART 23 Apr 1833.

3K:195   Date: 12 Mar 1825   RtCt: 12 May 1825
Saml. M. EDWARDS to Moses DOWDELL. Release of trust of Feb 1824 for debt to (Admr of Isaac STEER) of slaves London & wife Nance, Ann & her child London, boy Elias and girl Fanny/Frances. DOWDLE has sold slave to Chas. WILLIAMS.

3K:195   Date: 2 Apr 1825   RtCt: 17 May 1825
David REECE (Exor of Thomas TRIBBY Sr dec'd) of Ldn to Mahlon JANNEY of Ldn. B/S of 107a (subject to 21a dower of widow Mary TRIBBY) adj Joseph LEWIS, William BROWN, __ HUGHES. Delv. 28 Aug 1827.

3K:198   Date: 2 Mar 1825   RtCt: 18 May 1825
George M. FRYE & wife Mary of FredVa to James L. MARTIN of Ldn. B/S of 423a at foot of Short Hill adj Joshua WHITE (part of land assigned to Mary formerly Mary McILHANEY from land of father James McILHANEY dec'd).

3K:200   Date: 1 Jan 1824   RtCt: 18 May 1825
John Gill WATT & wife Dewanner of Ldn to James L. MARTIN of Ldn. Trust for debt to Christopher FRYE now of Mont Md using 22a (cnvy/b Peter BENEDUM by assign. Jun 1822, DBk EEE:321) and 20a (DBk FFF:170) and 2a and 5a (cnvy/b Saml. M. EDWARDS). Wit: John H. McCABE, Thomas SANDERS.

3K:206   Date: 3 Mar 1825   RtCt: 18 May 1825
James L. MARTIN & wife Sally A. P. of Ldn to George Michael FRYE & wife Mary of FredVa. B/S of 423a. Wit: John H. McCABE, Saml. M. EDWARDS. Delv. to FRYE 28 Mar 1833.

3K:208 Date: 10 May 1825 RtCt: 21 May 1825
John SANDERS & wife Leana late of Ldn to George SANDERS.
Relinquishment of dower for B/S of __ 1824 of 101a adj Archibald
MORRISON, Margaret SANDERS. Wit: A. JOHNSTON, Robt.
MONTGOMERY, John Y. BAULEY. Delv. to Geo. SAUNDERS 17
May 1827.

3K:209 Date: 22 Feb 1825 RtCt: 21 May 1825
John HATCHER & wife Sarah of Ldn to James B. WILSON of Ldn.
B/S of 42a on Goose Creek where Moses WILSON now lives, adj
Hugh ROGERS, Edward WILSON. Wit: William BRONAUGH, Wm.
F. DORSEY. Delv. to WILSON 13 Jan 1827.

3K:212 Date: 14 May 1825 RtCt: 21 May 1825
Edward HAMMATT & wife Ellizabeth of Ldn to Richard H.
HENDERSON of Ldn. B/S of 3a W (formerly of George HAMMATT
f/o Edward) of Lsbg on road from Lsbg to Ellis Williams' Shop, adj
Charles BINNS. Wit: John McCORMICK, Saml. M. EDWARDS.
Delv. to HENDERSON 25 Dec 1835.

3K:213 Date: 14 May 1825 RtCt: 21 May 1825
Robert BRADEN of Ldn to John WRIGHT and Burr BRADEN of Ldn.
Trust for debt to John BRADEN, estate of Joseph BRADEN dec'd,
James NIXON, Noble S. BRADEN using 128a adj John BRADEN,
Mary FOX (prch/o agents of Earl of Tankerville) and 140a (3 lots) adj
John BRADEN, George WARNER; and 30a (2 wood lots) on
Cotocton Mt.; and rights to 96a under lease of Saml. EVANS dec'd
and rights to 26a where Mathias SMITLEY holds a L/L; and house &
lot in Hllb; and house and lot in Snickers Gap; and 159a adj E.
GRUBB, Saml. HOUGH which Joseph WILKINSON formerly held a
lease.

3K:216 Date: 25 Apr 1825 RtCt: 21 May 1825
Robert BRADEN of Ldn to John BRADEN & Noble S. BRADEN of
Ldn. Trust for debt to William BROWN, heirs of Isaac RICE of Ky,
estate of Thomas LACEY dec'd, Mary FOX, Jane DODD, David
SHAWEN, John STABLER, Thompson F. MASON, James RUST,
Joseph SPOONS, William TEMPLE, C. J. P. THOMPSON, Mordecai
MILLER & son, Wm. D. DIGGS (nr. $6000 total) using 138a in
German Settlement adj John GEORGE; 90a (2 timber lots) on Short
Hill adj Edmund JENNINGS; 9a (2 lots) with brick house and mill adj
John BRADEN; 4a with stone house occupied by the miller; rights to
land where widow MILLER now lives and 20a adj lot; 3 houses and
lots in Wtfd.

3K:220 Date: 2 May 1825 RtCt: 24 May 1825
Joseph CANBY of RichVA and William CANBY & wife Sarah of Ldn
to Levi G. EWERS of Ldn. B/S of 61a (in trust from Saml GREGG &
wife Hannah, Jun 1822, DBk EEE:356, for benefit of Sarah w/o
William CANBY). Wit: John H. McCABE, Saml. M. EDWARDS. Delv.
to EWERS 9 Sep 1839.

3K:224 Date: 25 May 1825 RtCt: 25 May 1825
Daniel BROWN (insolvent) to Shff Ludwell LEE. B/S of 17¾a (prch/o Silas REESE) and 2½a (prch/o Ezekiel MOUNT) on Goose Creek and cnvy/b Daniel to his son Saml. BROWN (for execution by Jno. CHEW). Wit: Samuel BROWN. Delv. to Burr WEEKS 15 Jun 1826.

3K:225 Date: 19 May 1825 RtCt: 1 Jun 1825
Christopher FRYE & wife Margaret of Ldn to John Gill WATT of Ldn. B/S of lot on S side of Cornwall St in Lsbg (cnvy/b George SHEID May 1822, DBk EEE:237) with house, kitchen & stable. Wit: Thos. SANDERS, Saml. M. EDWARDS.

3K:227 Date: 29 Apr 1825 RtCt: 1 Jun 1825
Isaac BROWN Jr. & wife Ann (formerly Ann NIXON) now of FredVa to Samuel BROWN of Winchester. B/S of 9½a formerly belonging to George NIXON dec'd grandfather of Ann as heir of father Jonah NIXON dec'd, adj Jonathan CARTER on Goose Creek. Delv. to Saml. BROWN 17 Oct 1827.

3K:230 Date: 7 Jan 1819 RtCt: 3 Jun 1825
Levi WILLIAMS & wife Sarah of Ldn to David Fendall BEALL of Ldn. B/S of 63a (prch/o Enos POTTS) adj Isaac & Samuel NICHOLS, James BEANS, David SMITH. Wit: David SMITH, Lewis GRIGSBY, Nathaniel GRIGSBY, John W. GRAYSON, William H. DORSEY.

3K:232 Date: 3 Jun 1825 RtCt: 3 Jun 1825
Michael HICKMAN & wife Catherine of Ldn to Jacob SHUMAKER of Ldn. B/S of 40 perches (formerly belonging to Peter HICKMAN dec'd). Wit: Saml. M. EDWARDS, Jno. ROSE. Delv. to SHOEMAKER 26 Feb 1827.

3K:234 Date: 3 Jun 1825 RtCt: 4 Jun 1825
Samuel NOLAND to Lloyd NOLAND. B/S 50a (of all the land included in 3 islands obtained in div. of father Thomas NOLAND estate near Nolands ferry in Potomac within Md). Aug 1824 Saml. conveyed this to LLOYD as security to Noble BEVERIDGE. Islands were then sold to William EAGLE who has since died.

3K:236 Date: 1 Jun 1825 RtCt: 4 Jun 1825
Mordecai HARDACRE & wife Barbara of Ldn to Thomas WHITE of Ldn. B/S of 3a adj Peter MILLER dec'd, __ MILLER, __ GRUBB, __ FRYE. Wit: Ebenezer GRUBB, John WHITE. Delv. to WHITE 20 May 1836.

3K:238 Date: 4 Jun 1825 RtCt: 6 Jun 1825
Benjamin BRADFIELD & wife Rachael of Ldn to Thomas EMERSON of Ldn. B/S of 10a adj Joseph GORE, Joseph MEAD. Wit: William CARR, James H. HAMILTON. Delv. to EMBERSON 24 Mar 1837.

3K:240   Date: 4 Jun 1825   RtCt: 6 Jun 1825
Benjamin BRADFIELD & wife Rachael of Ldn to Daniel COCKERILL
of Ldn. B/S of ¾a adj Bernard TAYLOR. Delv. to COCKERILLE 11
Apr 1830.

3K:242   Date: 13 Apr 1825   RtCt: 8 Jun 1825
Leven LUCKETT & wife Leticia of Ldn to Horace LUCKETT of Ldn.
B/S of 32a adj G. W. McCARTY, __ BEATTY, Snickers Gap old
turnpike road, Wm. & Mosses GUILICK. Wit: Francis W. LUCKETT,
William BRONAUGH. Delv. to H. LUCKETT __.

3K:244   Date: 23 Aug 1824   RtCt: 14 Jun 1825
Reed POULTON. Qualified as 1st Lt. of Troop of Cavalry in 2nd Reg
2nd Div of Va Militia.

3K:244   Date: 31 Dec 1824   RtCt: 14 Jun 1825
Amos HARVEY. Qualified as Capt. in 56th Reg 6th Brig 2nd Div of Va
Militia.

3K:245   Date: 14 Aug 1824   RtCt: 14 Jun 1825
John JOHNSTON of Shelby Co Ky to son William JOHNSTON of
Shelby Co Ky. PoA for business with Mosses GUILICK &c Exor with
myself of estate of John GUILICK late of Ldn and in settling widow's
dower; and to convey int. in land in Wood Co Va originally conveyed
to GUILICK for 500a and devised by John GUILICK dec'd to my wife
Sarah now dec'd; and to secure his portion from Admrs of estate of
Hugh JOHNSTON dec'd late of Ldn.

3K:246   Date: 4 Jun 1825   RtCt: 9 Jul 1825
John McCORMICK & wife Mary of Ldn to James B. MURRAY of NY
City. Trust for debt to Chatham Fire Insurance Co. of NY City using
lot on NE corner of Market & King Sts in Lsbg. Wit: John L. NIXON,
Wm. KING, Gilbert S. MERRITT, Edward MERRITT, William
ELLZEY, Saml. M. EDWARDS.

3K:251   Date: 4 Jun 1825   RtCt: 25 Jun 1825
John DRISH & wife Ellenor of Ldn to James B. MURRAY of NY City.
Trust for debt to Chatham Fire Insurance Co. of NY City using lot
with house on E side of King St in Lsbg (cnvy/b Pattrick McINTYRE,
Dec 1813). Wit: John J. MASON, John McCORMICK, Gilbert S.
MOUNT, John H. McCABE, Saml. M. EDWARDS. Delv. to John
DRISH pr order.

3K:255   Date: 4 Jun 1825   RtCt: 16 Jun 1825
William KING & wife Susan of Ldn to James B. MURRAY of NY City.
Trust for debt to Chatham Fire Insurance Co. of NY City using lot on
W side of King St in Lsbg (cnvy/b John MUNROE, Sept 1820). Wit:
Edward MER[R]ITT, Gilbert MOUNT, William ELLZEY, Samuel M.
EDWARDS. Forwarded to MURRAY ___.

3K:259   Date: 14 Jun 1825   RtCt: 9 Jul 1825
Farmer Westwood T. MASON & wife Ann of Ldn to James B. Murray
of NY City. Trust for debt to Chatham Fire Insurance Co. of NY City

using 301¼a abt 6 miles N of Lsbg and 1 mile from the Potomac, adj Westwood T. MASON, Wm. T. T. MASON, Alfred BELT, Thompson MASON. Gives plat. Wit: G. WASHINGTON, John L. MASON, John ROSE, John McCORMICK. Forwarded to MURRAY __.

3K:263   Date: 13 Aug 1823   RtCt: 9 Jul 1825
Colin AULD of AlexDC to William LYLE Jr of AlexDC. B/S of dividend of 366a prch/o John MUNRO by Robert LYLE Sr. which was assigned to AULT then awarded in DC court to William Jr.

3K:265   Date: 2 Aug 1824   RtCt: 9 Jul 1825
William LYLE Jr. (s/o Robert LYLE dec'd) of AlexDC to Colin AULD of AlexDC. Mortgage for above 366a. Delv. to AULD 11 Jan 1827.

3K:267   Date: 30 Apr 1825   RtCt: 9 Jul 1825
Henery HICKMAN & wife Mary of Ldn to John HICKMAN of Ldn. B/S of 45¼a Lot #4 and 6¼a allotted to Henery in div. of estate of Peter HICKMAN dec'd. Wit: Presley CORDELL, Saml. HOUGH. Delv. to Jno. HICKMAN 12 Feb 1827.

3K:269   Date: 30 Apr 1825   RtCt: 9 Jul 1825
Adam MINK & wife Sarah of Ldn to John HICKMAN of Ldn. B/S of 49a Lot #3 allotted to Sarah in div. of estate of Peter HICKMAN dec'd. Wit: Presley CORDELL, Saml. HOUGH. Delv. to HICKMAN 12 Feb 1827.

3K:270   Date: 21 May 1825   RtCt: 9 Jul 1825
Peter COST & wife Mary of Ldn to Jonathan COST of Ldn. B/S of house and lot in Wtfd (prch/o Jonathan COST). Wit: John WHITE, Craven OSBURNE.

3K:272   Date: 18 May 1824   RtCt: 4 Jul 1825
Townshend D. PEYTON & wife Sarah of Ldn to Hugh SMITH of Ldn. B/S of 13a (prch/o B. POWELL trustee of David GIBSON) adj Peyton HIXON, Ashbys Gap turnpike road. Wit: Leven LUCKETT, Francis W. LUCKETT. Delv. to SMITH 2 Aug 1836.

3K:273   Date: 16 Jun 1825   RtCt: 4 Jul 1825
Casper JOHNSON & wife Martha of Ldn to Horrace LUCKETT of Ldn. Trust for debt to Jacob ISH of Ldn using 161a. Wit: Charles LEWIS, John BAYLEY.

3K:275   Date: 12 Apr 1825   RtCt: 12 Jun 1825
George TAVENER Jr. of Ldn to Eli TAVENER of Ldn. B/S of 18a on road to Wtfd adj Stacey JANNEY, Joseph TAVENER. Wit: Jonah SANDS, C. B. HAMILTON, Rawleigh T. CHINN, Hiram TAVENER.

3K:276   Date: 15 Jun 1825   RtCt: 25 Jun 1825
William D. DRISH & wife Harriet of Ldn to Richard H. HENDERSON of Ldn. B/S of house and lot (cnvy/b John DRISH) in Lsbg on Cornwall and King Sts. Wit: Thomas FOUCH, Saml. M. EDWARDS.

3K:277   Date: 20 Jun 1825   RtCt: 20 Jun 1825
William B. HARRISON & wife Penelope of Ldn to Burr W. HARRISON of Ldn. Trust for debt to Asa ROGERS using 300a

'Soldiers Repose' where HARRISON lives on Broad Run and adj 317a on S side of Broad Run called "Mahoney's Tract now occupied by Thos. GHEEN. Wit: John H. McCABE, Saml. M. EDWARDS. Delv. to ROGERS 28 Apr 1828.

3K:279   Date: 20 Jun 1825   RtCt: 20 Jun 1825
William B. HARRISON & wife Penelope of Ldn to Burr W. HARRISON of Ldn. Trust for debt to Benj. SHRIEVE Jr. and Robert MOFFETT using 300a 'Soldiers Repose' where HARRISON lives on Broad Run and adj 317a on S side of Broad Run called "Mahoney's Tract now occupied by Thos. GHEEN. Wit: John H. McCABE, Saml. M. EDWARDS. Delv. to SHRIEVE 10 Mar 1829.

3K:282   Date: 26 May 1825   RtCt: 24 Jun 1825
Samuel BERKLY of JeffVa to John K. LITTLETON of Ldn. Trust for debt to Enoch FURR of Ldn using negro slave James abt 25y old, household items; and int. in estate of father Samuel BERKLY dec'd late of Ky and estate of brother Benjamin BERKLY dec'd. Delv. to LITTLETON 8 Aug 1839.

3K:283   Date: 10 Jun 1825   RtCt: 18 Jun 1825
Deborah JENNERS (wd/o Abiel JENNERS dec'd) of Ldn to Samuel B. HARRIS of Ldn. B/S of right of dower to land sold to HARRIS by John BRADEN (Exor of Abiel).

3K:285   Date: 10 Jun 1825   RtCt: 18 Jun 1825
John BRADEN (Exor of Abiel JENNERS dec'd) of Ldn to Samuel B. HARRIS of Ldn. B/S of 103a (cnvy/b William WRIGHT) adj George GREGG, __ NICHOLS, Andrew BROWN; and 31a on Kittockton mt adj Presly SAUNDERS, John ROSE; and 250a (cnvy/b George TAVENDER Jr, Sep 1819) adj Wm. McGEATH, Joseph JANNEY dec'd. Delv. to HARRIS __.

3K:287   Date: 25 Mar 1825   RtCt: 18 Jun 1825
George RICHARD of Ldn to Peter COMPHER of Ldn. B/S of 5a (part of tract where RICHARD now resides).

3K:288   Date: 10 Jun 1825   RtCt: 18 Jun 1825
Samuel B. HARRIS & wife Ann to David SHAWEN and Noble S. BRADEN. Trust for debt to John BRADEN (Exor of Abiel JENNERS dec'd) using land bought of BRADEN as Exor. Wit: Presley CORDELL, Samuel HOUGH. Delv. to Jno. BRADEN 21 Jan 1833.

3K:290   Date: 1 May 1825   RtCt: 15 Jun 1825
James CUMMINGS of Tuscaroura Co Ohio to Richard H. HENDERSON of Ldn. B/S of int. (1/9th) of land of father Thomas CUMMINGS dec'd. Delv. to HENDERSON 25 Dec 1835.

3K:291   Date: 15 Jun 1825   RtCt: 15 Jun 1825
Jacob WALTMAN and John WENNER (Exors of Manuel WALTMAN dec'd) of Ldn to Adam SANBOWER of Ldn. B/S of 57a at mouth of Catockton Creek at Potomac. Delv. to SANBOWER 6 Jan 1829.

3K:292 Date: 16 May 1825 RtCt: 15 Jun 1825
Leonard THOMAS & wife Elizabeth of Ldn to George BEAMER of
Ldn. B/S of 43a adj Henery HICKMAN, Peter HICKMAN, __
MARLOW, __ CHICHESTER; and 4a Lot #4 (allotted to Elizabeth as
c/o Peter HICKMAN Sr. dec'd) on W side of Kottockton mt. adj
Jacob SLATER, Jno. SLATER, Peter FRYE. Delv. to BEAMER 24
Nov 1827. Wit: Saml HOUGH, Presley CORDELL.

3K:294 Date: 8 Aug 1818 RtCt: 15 Jun 1825
Stephen McPHERSON to Turner & Herod OSBURNE.
Relinquishment of claim – purchased 173a but survey measured
only 167a, OSBURNEs credited McPHERSON for the deficiency.
Wit: N. C. WILLIAMS, Charles RUSSELL.

3K:294 Date: 4 Jun 1825 RtCt: 15 Jun 1825
H. B. POWELL (trustee of Nelson GREEN, Jul 1822 for debt to
Abner GIBSON) of Ldn to Ann GREEN (Admr of George GREEN
dec'd of FredVa) by agent A. W. BOWIE. B/S of lot with brick house
formerly occupied by Nelson GREEN now Dr. TRIPLETT on
Madison St in Mdbg (cnvy/b Amos JOHNSON to GREEN). Mailed to
Chas. T. GREEN, Warrenton, Va 3 Jan 1868.

3K:295 Date: 8 Aug 1818 RtCt: 12 Jun 1825
William WINN to Turner and Herrod OSBURNE. Relinquishment of
claim - deed for land where WINN lives was made for 116a but
survey says 112a; OSBURNEs credited WINN. Wit: N. C.
WILLIAMS, Charles RUSSELL.

3K:296 Date: 14 Jun 1825 RtCt: 14 Jun 1825
John M. EDWARDS of Ldn to Charles G. EDWARDS of Ldn. B/S of
450a (as heir of Benjamin EDWARDS dec'd except dower of widow
[incorrectly stated as wife of John M. EDWARDS]).

3K:298 Date: 13 Jun 1825 RtCt: 13 Jun 1825
John STATLER of Ldn. DoE for slave Calvin RAMSEY.

3K:298 Date: 9 May 1825 RtCt: 13 Jun 1825
Shff Ludwell LEE to Rebecca BIRDSALL, __ BIRDSALL and __
BIRDSALL. B/S of lots and house for purpose of a public school in
Mt Gilead (former property of Edmund LOVETT now in jail under
execution from Rachel BIRDSALL and others Admrs. of Whitson
BIRDSALL).

3K:299 Date: 13 Apr 1825 RtCt: 12 Jun 1825
Leven LUCKETT & wife Lettitia of Ldn to William GULICK of Ldn.
B/S of 29a adj Moses GULICK on side of mountain. Wit: Burr
POWELL, Abner GIBSON.

3K:302 Date: 13 Jun 1825 RtCt: 13 Jun 1825
John JONES to Thomas SA(U)NDERS. Trust for debt to John
SAUNDERS using 153a adj George CARTER, John SIMPSON,
Casper JOHNSTON, Hugh SMITH. Delv. to Thomas SAUNDERS 4
Jan 1827.

3K:304 Date: 29 Apr 1825 RtCt: 13 Jun 1825
William BEATTY & wife Rebecca of Ldn to Lewis BERKLEY of Ldn.
B/S of 1a adj William NOLAND, Mathew RUST; and 10a. Wit: Burr
POWELL, A. GIBSON. Delv. to BERKLY 11 Sep 1834.

3K:306 Date: 25 May 1825 RtCt: 13 Jun 1825
Daniel BROWN and Ann WATKINS (wd/o William WATKINS dec'd).
Marriage contract – Mahlon CRAVEN as trustee for what Ann's 1/3
of 14a in Hampshire and personal property she wants to use for
support of herself, BROWN, and her 4 children Louisa WATKINS,
Bernard WATKINS, Sarah Ann WATKINS and Elender WATKINS.
At her death her property goes to any new children, and if none, to
the current children. Wit: Stephen McPHERSON Jr., John WYNN,
Thomas C. GREGG. Delv. pr order 11 Aug 1834.

3K:308 Date: 4 Jun 1825 RtCt: 13 Jun 1825
Thomas GREGG to Richard H. HENDERSON. Trust for debt to
James McILHANY using 339a where GREGG resides adj James
McILHANY, Lewis ELLZEY.

3K:310 Date: 14 Apr 1825 RtCt: 12 Jun 1825
Eli TAVENER & wife Nancy of Ldn to Jonah SANDS of Ldn. Trust
for debt to George TAVENER Sr. using 18a on road to Wtfd adj
Stacey JANNEY, Joseph TAVENER.

3K:312 Date: 13 Jun 1825 RtCt: 13 Jun 1825
Margaret SAUNDERS of Ldn to Isaac NICKOLS Jr and James
HOGE of Ldn. Trust for debt to Isaac & Samuel NICKOLS of Ldn
using 4 lots – 50¾a, 4a, 13a and ¾a. Delv. to HOGE __.

3K:316 Date: 27 Apr 1825 RtCt: 13 Jun 1825
James MOUNT & wife Hannah of Ldn to Given HANDY of Ldn. B/S
of int. in 140a Lot #1 (formerly owned by Eli Heaton HANDY allotted
to him after death of his father John HANDY) on Goose Creek. Wit:
William BRONAUGH, Wm. H. DORSEY.

3K:318 Date: 4 Jun 1825 RtCt: 13 Jun 1825
Bernard TAYLOR & wife Sarah of Ldn to Samuel IDEN & wife Sarah
of Ldn. B/S of ¾a adj Abdon DILLON, Walker KERRICK. Wit:
William CARR, James H. HAMILTON.

3K:320 Date: 8 Nov 1824 RtCt: 13 Jun 1825
Samuel IDEN & wife Sarah of Ldn to Henry GRIGGS of Ldn. B/S of
3a adj Samuel IDEN, Abdon DILLON, heirs of Henry SMITH. Wit:
Bernard TAYLOR, James DICKERSON, Hezekiah GLASCOCK,
William CARR, James H. HAMILTON. Delv. to Exor Danl.
COCKERILL 11 Apr 1831.

3K:322 Date: 13 Dec 1823 RtCt: 12 Jun 1825
John CONRAD (signed CONARD) to Ebenezer GRUBB and
Edward DOWLIN. Release of trust of Oct 1817 on 184a for debt to
Valentine MILLER. Wit: John POTTS, Jesse NEER, Saml. NEER,
Presley WIGGINTON, Daniel CRIM.

3K:324 Date: 28 May 1825 RtCt: 12 Jun 1825
Isaac EATON & wife Malinda of Ldn to George TAVENER (of Richard) of Ldn. B/S of 2¼a in Mt. Gilead (EATON sold to Edmund LOVETT but made no deed, at whose request and that of William LICKEY who bought at sale under trust by LOVETT to Saml. M. EDWARDS for benefit of Daniel LOVETT) on road from Martha HOLMES to Coe's Mill. Wit: William CARR, James H. HAMILTON. Delv. to TAVENER 21 May 1845.

3K:327 Date: 24 Nov 1824 RtCt: 12 Jun 1825
Amos NEER & wife Sarah of Clarke Co Ohio to Ebenezer GRUBB of Ldn. B/S of 1/3 int. in farm of Jonathan CONARD dec'd no in occupation of Edward PAINTER (h/o Julianna PAINTER former w/o Jonathan dec'd) between Blue Ridge & Short Hill adj Ebenezer GRUBB, heirs of Peter JACOBS dec'd. Wit: Saml. LAFFERTY, Joseph KENNAN.

3K:330 Date: 19 May 1825 RtCt: 9 Jun 1825
Edmund J. LEE & wife Sally of AlexDC to John HOOFF of AlexDC. Trust for debt to Farmers Bank of AlexDC with John LLOYD and Colin AULD as endorsers using 575a 'Ellerslie' abt 2 miles from Lsbg with the turnpike road passing thru (cnvy/b William WILSON); and slaves on said farm Bob, George, Ralph, Daniel, Tom, little Phil, Jack, Molly, Margaret, Amy, Eliza, Rin? or Rose? & Thomas. Delv. to AULD pr order 11 Jan 1827.

3K:335 Date: 21 May 1822 RtCt: 11 Jul 1825
Colin AULD to John SHAW & wife Rebecca of Ldn. Release of trust for debt to James DUNLAP (DBk EEE:218).

3K:335 Date: 30 Dec 1824 RtCt: 11 Jul 1825
David GIBSON of Ldn to Richard H. HENDERSON of Ldn. Trust for debt to Nancy GIBSON of Ldn using his 1/5th int. in 40-50a estate of Rebecca VERNON dec'd wd/o Daniel VERNON dec'd with water grist mill. (David received funds from Elizabeth FOSTER for land belonging to Nancy in PrWm as security for Nancy with deed of trust to Burr POWELL for benefit of Nancy, 220a where David then lived, still in his possession, property of his father Thomas GIBSON dec'd, which David has created a prior lien for monies due to his brother & sisters whom he purchased their interests).

3K:338 Date: 3 Jun 1825 RtCt: 11 Jul 1825
John SHAW & wife Rebecca of Ldn to Erasmus G. HAMILTON of Ldn. B/S of lot in Lsbg on E side of Back St. Wit: Thomas SANDERS, Saml. M. EDWARDS.

3K:340 Date: 13 Jul 1825 RtCt: 13 Jul 1825
Robert R. HOUGH (trustee Peter BENEDOM & wife) of Ldn to Benj. SHREVE Jr. of Ldn. Trust for debt to Benjamin SHREVE Jr. renting for 4y to him the plantation where BENEDUM now resides, with crops. SHREVE released personal prop. of BENEDOM purchased at sale for benefit of wife of sd. Peter and later him.

3K:341   Date: 16 Feb 1825   RtCt: 28 Jul 1825
Eli McKNIGHT & wife Ally of Ldn to Joseph HOUGH of Ldn. B/S of
1½a (from farm of McKNIGHT). Wit: Craven OSBURN, John
WHITE. Delv. to HOUGH 10 Aug 1829.

3K:343   Date: 2 Jun 1825   RtCt: 16 Jul 1825
Samuel SAWYER & wife Mary of Harrison Co Ohio to Edward
HUGHES of Ldn. Trust for benefit of Daniel BOLAND (until he
becomes a citizen of U.S.) using 30a adj __ COOPER; with John
CRIM to carry away crops. Wit: Isaac ALLEN, Thomas B. CARTER,
Wm. GLANDEN. Delv. to BOLAND 6 Feb 1829.

3K:347   Date: 1 Jun 1825   RtCt: 15 Jul 1825
George HEAD and John SHAW of Lsbg to Simon SMALE of Lsbg.
LS of 999y of lot on N side of Market St in Lsbg. Wit: Alfred A.
ESKRIDGE, John J. MATHIAS, Roberdeau ANNIN.

3K:349   Date: 30 Jul 1825   RtCt: 3 Aug 1825
David E. BROWN and Alice GIBSON, Samuel PEACH & wife
Rebecca Ann late GIBSON (who with Mahlon GIBSON were next
heirs to Emily Jackson BROWN dec'd) to Mahlon GIBSON. B/S of
all their int. in estate of Emily J. BROWN in real estate of her father
John GIBSON dec'd (David & wife Emily J. agreed to convey Emily's
int. to Mahlon, and she requested it on her death bed). Wit: Benj.
GRAYSON, Wm. H. DORSEY.

3K:351   Date: 23 Mar 1825   RtCt: 11 Apr/ 3 Aug 1825
Samuel MURRAY of Ldn to Jno. A. BINNS of Lsbg. Trust for Wm. A.
BINNS of Ldn as security on note to Jno. WORSELEY Exor of Chas.
BENNETT dec'd and to Thomas SAUNDERS Exor of Henry
SAUNDERS dec'd using crops growing at Oatlands. Wit: Chas.
BINNS 3rd, Simon A. BINNS Jr.

3K:352   Date: 14 May 1825   RtCt: 8 Aug 1825
Joseph CARR of Ldn to John FLEMING of Ldn. B/S of ¼a in
Upperville. Mailed to B. R. GLASCOCK, atty 11/15/24.

3K:355   Date: 8 Jun 1825   RtCt: 8 Aug 1825
Thomas H. LUCKETT of Fqr to Henry F. LUCKETT of Ldn. Trust for
debt to Daniel HARTMAN of Winchester, Levi L. STEPHENSON
with William F. LUCKETT as security using negroes James, Sally
and Etty, farm animals, household items.

3K:357   Date: 10 Aug 1825   RtCt: 11 Aug 1825
Thomson MASON to David LOVETT. Trust for Joshua OSBURNE
and William T. T. MASON as security on bond to Wm. A. G. DADE
using negro slaves Jere Sr. & his sons Jere & John, John, Nanny,
Sarah, Charlotte, Eliza, Wilford, Letty, Henrietta, Philip, Molly, Essex
and Lucy. Wit: R. H. HENDERSON, E. G. HAMILTON, Tho. R.
MOTT.

3K:359 Date: 20 Jun 1825 RtCt: 15 Aug 1825
Jane L. MORROW of JeffVa to William MORROW of JeffVa. B/S of 2a 'out' lot adj John R. STEVENS, __ BRADEN, __ WHITE (cnvy/b __ WOOD to John MORROW now dead).

3K:360 Date: 30 Oct 1824 RtCt: 22 Aug 1825
Jacob TOWNER of Lsbg to John SURGHNOR of Lsbg. B/S of Lot #62 in Lsbg (cnvy/b Jacob TOWNER Sr to Jacob Jr. Sep 1792, DBk W:136). Wit: Geo. RICHARDS, Edward HAMMAT, John MARTIN. Delv. to SURGHNOR 27 Oct 1832.

3K:361 Date: 23 Aug 1825 RtCt: 23 Aug 1825
Rich'd H. HENDERSON (trustee of Stephen T. BURSON in debt to Chas. Bird & Co of PhilPa) of Ldn to John PANCOAST Jr of Ldn. B/S of 15a adj Jonas JANNEY, John WEST erroneously called in said deed of trust Abel JANNEY & Samuel WEST.

3K:363 Date: 24 Aug 1825 RtCt: 25 Aug 1825
William VERTZ/WERTZ Jr. (trustee of John SHAFER, Dec 1820) of Ldn to Joshua PUSEY of Ldn. B/S of 61½a and 55 ½a (prch/o FAIRFAX, Feb 1803) adj Michael BOGER, __ RICHEY, __ BOGER, Peter HICKMAN. Wit: L. P. W. BALCH, Robert MOFFETT, David AXLINE. Delv. to PUSEY 15 Feb 1828.

3K:366 Date: 24 Aug 1825 RtCt: 25 Aug 1825
William VERTZ/WERTZ Jr. of (trustee of John SHAFER, Dec 1820) of Ldn to Conrad BITZER of Ldn. B/S of 152½a adj __ WOOLF, __ STONEBURNER, John FAWLEY, Peter STUCK.

3K:368 Date: 24 Aug 1825 RtCt: 25 Aug 1825
William VERTZ/WERTZ Jr. (trustee of John SHAFER, Dec 1820) of Ldn to Conard BITZER of Ldn. B/S of 121a adj __ HOFF.

3K:369 Date: 17 Aug 1825 RtCt: 25 Aug 1825
John W. MILHOLLEN (s/o Esther) of Ldn to Robert MOFFETT of Ldn. B/S of int. in lands of which uncle John MILHOLLIN dec'd the brother of mother Esther MILHOLLIN dec'd possessed, and und. int. in 8a purchased by mother Esther dec'd of Patrick B. MILHOLLIN (no deed recorded) on Cotocton Mt adj George RUST Jr. Wit: Noble S. BRADEN, D. SHAWEN, Jesse GOVER, Wm. F. BRADEN. Delv. to MOFFET 10 Apr 1841.

3K:371 Date: 25 Aug 1825 RtCt: 25 Aug 1825
Benjamin DANIEL of Ldn to Joseph DANIEL of Ldn. B/S of int. in lease right of tract where Thomas LOVE now lives, made by Thomas LOVE Sr. to Benjamin DANIEL & wife Jane May 1806, DBk GG:426.

3K:372 Date: 2 Apr 1825 RtCt: 25 Aug 1825
Levi WATERS & wife Sarah of Ldn to William CLENDENING. Trust for debt to Michael DERRY using 1a adj George SMITH, Jacob FILLAR (cnvy/b DERRY, Apr 1825). Wit: Craven OSBURN, John WHITE. Delv. DERRY's order filed 2 Apr 1828.

3K:376   Date: 26 Aug 1825   RtCt: 26 Aug 1825
George SHOVER of Ldn to L. P. W. BALCH of Ldn. Trust for debt to
Frederick ROLLER with Jacob SMITH as security using 48½a (int.
of Henry SHOVER in estate of Adam SHOVER dec'd) and 13½a
wood lot #10 in div. of real estate of Adam SHOVER dec'd.

3K:378   Date: 16 Aug 1825   RtCt: 26 Aug 1825
Miller HOGUE & wife Tacey of Ldn to H. B. POWELL of Ldn. Trust
for debt to Joseph HOGUE using 26¼a (cnvy/b Moses WILSON,
Oct 1819). Wit: Leven LUCKETT, A. GIBSON.

3K:380   Date: 2 Aug 1824   RtCt: 31 Aug 1825
George HEAD of Ldn to George RICHARDS of Ldn. Trust for debt to
Lydia HEAD using farm and household items.

3K:382   Date: 30 Oct 1824   RtCt: 2 Sep 1825
John BURTON & wife Sophiah of Ldn to James THOMAS of Ldn.
B/S of 5a abt 1 mile W of Lsbg on road across mt. to
VANDEVANDERs. Wit: John McCORMICK, Presley CORDELL.

3K:384   Date: 22 Aug 1825   RtCt: 2 Sep 1825
James NIXON of Ldn to William D. DRISH and Rowena ELGIN
(Admrs of Charles ELGIN dec'd). B/S of 14a (Thos. M. BINNS now
dec'd sold to Chas. ELGIN now dec'd, set apart to Eliz. S. BINNS
out of estate of uncle John A. BINNS who was br/o Thomas N.; then
sold to Edward DORSEY, then to NIXON by trust from Robert
BRADEN & Daniel STONE). Wit: Joshua PUSEY, Samuel NIXON,
James W. NIXON.

3K:386   Date: 2 Sep 1825   RtCt: 5 Sep 1825
John BURTON & wife Sophia of Ldn to Thomas F. TEBBS of Ldn.
B/S of __a W of Lsbg where BURTON now lives (46a+ were cnvy/b
John and Samuel HAMMET to BURTON May 1824; 10a by William
CHILTON May 1824; 5a by James THOMAS Oct 1824; 1a by Israel
WILKINSON Oct 1824; 7a by William CHILTON with legal title to
reps of David LACEY dec'd but equitable title to BURTON). Wit:
Rich'd H. HENDERSON, Alexr. HENDERSON, E. G. HAMILTON,
John McCORMICK, Presley CORDELL.

3K:388   Date: 12 Mar 1825   RtCt: 5 Sep 1825
Daniel JAMES of Ldn to William HOGUE of Ldn. Trust for debt to
Daniel JANNEY of Ldn using 87½a (sold to Elias, Jonathan Jr. and
Daniel JAMES by Margaret McILHANY, May 1819).

3K:390   Date: 19 May 1825   RtCt: 5 Sep 1825
John T. BROOKE at present of AlexDC to William THRIFT of Ldn.
B/S of 140a where THRIFT lives (cnvy/b MARSHALL of Ct. in case
BELL assignee of REYNOLDS against Richard BROOKE). Wit:
Rich'd H. HENDERSON, E. G. HAMILTON, Chas. G. ESKRIDGE,
Alfred A. ESKRIDGE.

3K:391 Date: 31 Aug 1825 RtCt: 5 Sep 1825
John S. MARLOW & wife Ann E. of Ldn to Henry FRAZIER of FredMd. B/S of 70a adj Jacob WALTMAN, Thos. J. MARLOW, ___ WENNER, ___ SANBOWER. Wit: John HAMILTON, Geo. W. SHAWEN. Delv. pr order 15 Aug 1830.

3K:393 Date: 6 Aug 1825 RtCt: 8 Aug 1825
Eleanor LEITH of Ldn to son Theodorick LEITH. Gift of all her int. in property of mother dec'd and estate of her father Edward VIOLETT who died many years before. Wit: Charles LEWIS, Margaret LEITH, Wm. G. LEITH.

3K:394 Date: 5 Aug 1825 RtCt: 10 Sep 1825
John BRADEN (Exor of Abiel JENNERS dec'd) and Deborah JENNERS of Ldn to Joseph COX of Ldn. B/S of 6a (formerly in poss. of Benjamin KINS, purchase by JENNERS of George TAVENER Jr).

3K:396 Date: 12 Sep 1825 RtCt: 12 Sep 1825
Emanuel WALTMAN, Jacob SMITH & Jacob WALTMAN Jr. Bond on Emanuel WALTMAN as constable.

3K:396 Date: 12 Sep 1825 RtCt: 12 Sep 1825
Jesse TIMMS and George CARTER. Bond on TIMMS as Commissioner of Revenue in 1st district.

3K:397 Date: 12 Sep 1825 RtCt: 12 Sep 1825
Jesse McVEIGH and H. SMITH. Bond on McVEIGH as Commissioner of Revenue in 2nd district.

3K:398 Date: 25 Aug 1825 RtCt: 12 Sep 1825
George W. SHAWEN. Qualified as Lt. in 57th Reg 6th Brig 2nd Div Va Militia. Delv. to SHAWEN 2 Apr 1829.

3K:399 Date: 14 Jul 1825 RtCt: 12 Sep 1825
Robert BRADEN of Ldn to Burr BRADEN of Ldn. B/S of 178¼a (bought of Peter R. BEVERLY with 2 small lots bought of Wm. VERTZ & Wm. SMITH) adj John WRIGHT, William VERTZ, Edward McDANIEL, William SMITH, John NICKLIN.

3K:401 Date: 2 Feb 1825 RtCt: 12 Sep 1825
Eli JANNEY and Mahlon WALTERS (Exors of Blackstone JANNEY dec'd) of Ldn to Jesse HURST of Ldn. B/S of 20½a (cnvy/b Stephen WILSON, DBk II:348) nr Goose Creek meeting house, adj Mary WILSON. Delv. to HURST 21 Nov 1827.

3K:403 Date: 21 May 1825 RtCt: 12 Sep 1825
Amos CLAYTON & wife Elizabeth of Ldn to Robert CHEW, William BRADFIELD, Timothy CARRINGTON, William WOODFORD & Townsend CLAYTON (trustee of Robert M. H. CHEW. B/S of ½a (for purpose of building a house for a public school and place of divine worship) on SE side of Blue Ridge and S side of Snickersville, adj N. C. WILLIAMS, ___ CARRINGTON, ___ BRADFIELD. Wit: Timothy

CARRINGTON, Town. CLAYTON, Craven OSBURN, Wm. H. DORSEY. Delv. pr order of Wm. BRADFIELD 29 Jun 1845.

3K:405   Date: 29 Aug 1825   RtCt: 12 Sep 1825
Benjamin B. THORNTON & wife Hannah to Robert FULTON. Relinq. of dower for deed of 22 Dec 1823. Note: deed from B. B. THORNTON husband of above named Hannah recorded DBk GGG:433. Delv. Robert FULLER 12 Nov 1827.

3K:405   Date: 12 Sep 1825   RtCt: 12 Sep 1825
Joseph POSTON of Ldn to William CHILTON of Ldn. Trust for Elijah PEACOCK as security on bonds to Henry J. FRY using 103a where POSTON now lives adj __ HOUGH, __ HAMILTON.

3K:406   Date: 27 Aug 1825   RtCt: 12 Sep 1825
Benjamin WALKER & wife Elizabeth of Ldn to James SWART Jr of Ldn. Trust for debt to James SWARTS using 2 lots totaling 45a (allotted to Benj. & brother John from estate of Benjamin WALKER Sr. dec'd). Wit: William BRONAUGH, Wm. H. DORSEY. Delv. pr order 31 Aug 1827.

3K:409   Date: __ 1825   RtCt: 12 Sep 1825
Hugh SMITH to Miller HOGUE & wife Tacey. Release of trust of Sep 1822 for debt to Joseph HOGUE using 26¼a. Wit: Joseph HOGUE.

3K:410   Date: 14 Jul 1825   RtCt: 12 Sep 1825
Burr BRADEN of Ldn to John BRADEN of Ldn. Trust for debt to George TAVENER Sr. using land bought of Robert BRADEN, adj John WRIGHT, Wm. VERTZ.

3K:413   Date: 16 May 1825   RtCt: 12 Sep 1825
Jacob SILCOTT of Ldn to George M. GRAYSON of Ldn. Trust for debt to Joshua GORE of Ldn using 144a (occupied by SILCOTT as a farm) adj Amos HIBBS, John P. DULANEY, heirs of Samuel SMITH dec'd. Delv. to Joshua OSBORNE one of Exors 10 Sep 1833.

3K:415   Date: 2 Apr 1825   RtCt: 12 Sep 1825
Michael DERRY & wife Ann Barbara of Ldn to Levi WALTERS/WATERS of Ldn. B/S of 1a between Short Hill & Blue Ridge, on road to Harper's Ferry adj George SMITH. Wit: Ebenezer GRUBB, John WHITE. Delv. to Levi WATERS 2 Apr 1828.

3K:417   Date: 13 Sep 1825   RtCt: 13 Sep 1825
Garrison P. FRENCH, Andrew CAMPBELL and John HOLMES. Bond on FRENCH as constable.

3K:418   Date: 4 Jun 1825   RtCt: 17 Sep 1825
Benjamin BRADFIELD & wife Rachel of Ldn to James COCHRAN Jr of Ldn. B/S of 1a. Wit: William CARR, James H. HAMILTON.

3L:001   Date: 11 Oct 1825   RtCt: 11 Oct 1825
Samuel UNDERWOOD, Richard H. LEE, Samuel CARR. Bond on UNDERWOOD as constable.

3L:001   Date: 6 Sep 1825   RtCt: 7 Oct 1825
John McKINLEY & wife Elizabeth and Mary ARMISTEAD of Madison Co, Alabama to Eliza D. PEYTON of King George Co Va. B/S of 1 moiety of 83a in Ashton's patent. Delv. to William ELLZEY pr order 17 Oct 1828.

3L:004   Date: 5 Sep 1825   RtCt: 4 Oct 1825
David YOUNG of Ldn to Joshua PANCOAST of Ldn. B/S of 102a (as in trust from John MOUNT & wife Mary Ann to YOUNG).

3L:006   Date: 28 Sep 1825   RtCt: 5 Oct 1825
John DUNKIN & wife Ruth of Ldn to Samuel BECK of FredVa. B/S of 90a where DUNKIN resides adj George MARKS, Thomas TRAHORN. Wit: Benjamin GRAYSON, John W. GRAYSON. Delv. pr order 12 Mar 1831.

3L:008   Date: 16 Sep 1825   RtCt: 1 Oct 1825
Casper JOHNSON & wife Martha of Ldn to Thomas SANDERS (Exor of Presley SANDERS Sr, dec'd). B/S of 10a with stone house (Adam BARR & wife Precious of Ldn gave in trust to Richard H. HENDERSON for benefit of John ROBERTS and Amos JOHNSON, DBk CCC:285 and failed to pay) adj SANDERS dec'd. Wit: John SIMPSON, John BAYLY.

3L:011   Date: 3 Oct 1825   RtCt: 10 Oct 1825
Stephen R. MOUNT. Oath as Lt in 56th Reg, 6th Brig, 2nd Div of Va Militia.

3L:012   Date: 10 Oct 1825   RtCt: 11 Oct 1825
John CARPENTER. Relinquishment as Exor of will of father William CARPENTER dec'd over to George KEEN.

3L:012   Date: 17 Sep 1825   RtCt: 23 Oct 1825
Isaac WALKER & wife Susan of Ldn to Robert BRADEN of Ldn. B/S of Lot # 35 & #50 (prch/o Exor of Mahlon JANNEY dec'd) in new addition to Wtfd adj Lewis KLINE. Wit: Presley CORDELL, Saml. HOUGH. Delv. to N. S. BRADEN Exor 18 Dec 1838.

3L:015   Date: 17 Sep 1825   RtCt: 23 Sep 1825
Mahlon JANNEY of Ldn to Noble S. BRADEN and Wm. NETTLE of Ldn. Trust for debt to Robert BRADEN using 21a with saw mill adj Wtfd. Delv. to Noble S. BRADEN 20 Mar 1828.

3L:018   Date: 24 Sep 1825   RtCt: 24 Sep 1825
William C. LUCKETT of Ldn to Charles STOVIN of Ldn. B/S of land from father Samuel LUCKETT dec'd in right of dec'd wife Sally by her father Josias CLAPHAM dec'd – Samuel with 2nd wife Rebecca, Benjamin JACKSON & wife Ellisabeth and Josias CLAPHAM sold in Mar 1819 to William LYNE but wasn't legal to do so because William was under age).

3L:020   Date: 19 Sep 1825   RtCt: 19 Sep 1825
Joseph T. NEWTON & wife Nelly of Ldn to son James F. NEWTON
of Ldn. B/S of 176a on Goose Creek adj Ellis JENKINS. Wit: John
McCORMICK, Jno. J. MATHIAS.

3L:023   Date: 15 Nov 1825   RtCt: 15 Nov 1825
Lewis P. W. BALCH, Humphrey B. POWELL and John M.
McCARTY to Pres. & Directors of the Library Fund. Bond on BALCH
as treasurer.

3L:024   Date: 29 Aug 1812   RtCt: 16 Nov 1825
John MUSTIN & wife Blanch of FredVa to James MONROE of
Albermarle Co Va. B/S of land on Little River (dev. to Blanch by
father Joseph JONES dec'd of Ldn and share of his brother James
TYLER dec'd; JONES was indebted in mortgage to British House of
Commons represented by Daniel GRINNAN of FredVa).

3L:028   Date: 6 Sep 1825   RtCt: ___
John WALTMAN dec'd. Division- Lot #1 (24a) to daughter Ellisabeth
MILLER; Lot #2 (38a) to Samuel WALTMAN; widow Peggy
WALTMAN dower (48a); Lot #3 (30a) & Lot #5 (7a wood lot) to
David WALTMAN; Lot #4 (40a) to Maria WALTMAN. Gives plat.
Divisors: Robert BRADEN, Jacob EVERHART, Fred'k SLATES.

3L:032   Date: 19 Sep 1825   RtCt: 19 Sep 1825
James SURGENOR to William CHILTON. Trust for debt to John
SURGENOR & John E. DANGERFIELD using household items.
Delv. to CHILTON 26 Jun 1829.

3L:034   Date: 22 Jun 1825   RtCt: ___
John SLATER dec'd. Division – Lot #1 (27a) & mountain Lot #1
(7½a) to Susanah SOUDER; Lot #2 (27a) & mountain Lot #2 (6½a)
to William SLATER; Lot #3 (8a) to Michael SLATER; Lot #6 (9½) to
Jacob SLATER; Lot #7 (26a) to George SLATER; Lot #8 (23a) &
mountain Lot #3 (4½a) to Anthony SLATER; Lot #4 (27½a) &
mountain Lot #4 (7½a) to Mary HICKMAN late SLATER; Lot #5
(26a) & mountain Lot #5 (10½a) to heirs & reps of Ellisabeth SMITH
dec'd late SLATER. Gives plat. Divisors: John COMPHER, John
HAMILTON, Jno. J. MATHIAS.

3L:039   Date: 22 Sep 1825   RtCt: 5 Oct 1825
John N. T. G. E. KEENE of Ldn to Thornton WALKER of Ldn. Trust
for to Stephen Wesley ROSZILL for bond on KEENE as constable
using household items.

3L:041   Date: 9 Sep 1825   RtCt: 10 Oct 1825
Lewis FRENCH & wife Sarah and Ann FRENCH wd/o Mason
FRENCH dec'd of Ldn to Samuel MURRAY of Fqr. B/S of 157a on
Goose Creek (willed to Lewis by father Mason dec'd) adj William
VICKERS. Wit: Wm. BRONAUGH, Francis W. LUCKETT.

3L:043   Date: 17 Aug 1825   RtCt: 10 Oct 1825

Richard Henry LEE of Ldn to Richard H. HENDERSON of Ldn. Trust for debt to Daniel SHEFFY of Augusta Co Va using 33½a on W side of road from Lsbg to Aldie and Mdbg adj Robert J. TAYLOR, Henry CLAGGETT, William MEADE, and house & lot in Lsbg at Market & Back Sts. opposite Sampson BLINCOE.

3L:045   Date: 8 Oct 1825   RtCt: 10 Oct 1825

John J. MATHIAS of Ldn to William CARR of Ldn. B/S of 200a on E side of Blue Ridge adj Henry ORAM, Joshua OSBURNE, __ CLIP, David POTTS. Delv. to D. CARR late purchaser 4 Jun 1845.

3L:047   Date: 12 Oct 1825   RtCt: 12 Oct 1825

Aaron MILLER & wife Mary of Ldn. CoE for deed of 30 Mar 1824. Delv. to B. GRUBB 27 Jun 1826

3L:048   Date: 11 Oct 1825   RtCt: 12 Oct 1825

Enoch FRANCIS of Ldn to Richard Henry LEE of Ldn. Release of mortgage in DBk UU:265.

3L:049   Date: 25 Jul 1825   RtCt: 12 Oct 1825

William SMARR of Ldn to John SMARR of Ldn. B/S of land cnvy/b BEAVERS Apr 1823 (from trust of William BENTON to BEAVERS for debt to John BEVERIDGE).

3L:051   Date: 3 Oct 1825   RtCt: 16 Oct 1825

Philip COOPER & wife Ellisabeth of Ldn to Jacob WILTER of Washington Co Md. B/S of 104a (cnvy/b Absalom KALB, Mar 1819) adj heirs of Daniel SHOEMAKER dec'd, Jeremiah PURDIM, Charles CRIMM, George COOPER, heirs of Jacob EMORY dec'd. Wit: John HAMILTON, Geo. W. SHAWEN. Delv. pr order 24 Aug 1829.

3L:053   Date: 1 May 1825   RtCt: 18 Oct 1825

James L. MARTIN of Lsbg to Joseph HUNT of Lsbg. B/S of lot on upper end of Loudoun St opposite Mrs. FORTNEY's smith shop. Delv. pr order 9 Feb 1828.

3L:055   Date: 19 Oct 1825   RtCt: 20 Oct 1825

David GREENWALL of Lsbg to John A. BINNS of Lsbg. Trust for debt to James MATEER using 1a on King St in Lsbg. Delv. to BINNS 14 Dec 1826.

3L:056   Date: 20 Oct 1825   RtCt: 22 Oct 1825

William FARR & wife Rachael of Ldn to Sarah Ann HUMPHREY (d/o Rachael). Gift of Rachel's int. in land of her father Jesse HUMPHREY dec'd (dower land to widow Mary). Wit: Benjamin GRAYSON, John W. GRAYSON.

3L:058   Date: 20 Oct 1825   RtCt: 22 Oct 1825

William FARR & wife Rachael of Ldn to El(l)ijah FARR of Ldn. B/S of 14¾a & 4¾a Lots #2 & #3 in div. of Jesse HUMPHREY dec'd allotted to Rachael HUMPHREY. Wit: Benjamin GRAYSON, John W. GRAYSON. Delv. pr order to Cyrus BURSON 9 Mar 1828.

3L:060   Date: 14 May 1825   RtCt: 24 Oct 1825
John GIBSON & wife Rachael of Ldn to Thomas W. SMITH of Ldn.
B/S of 4a on Pantherskin (part of land of Joseph GIBSON dec'd f/o
John where John and Thomas as partners erected a mill). Wit:
Francis W. LUCKETT, John W. GRAYSON. Delv. to SMITH 15 Apr
1828.

3L:063   Date: 30 Jul 1825   RtCt: 24 Oct 1825
Mahlon GIBSON of Ldn to Thomas W. SMITH of Ldn. B/S of land of
John GIBSON dec'd allotted to David E. BROWN and conveyed to
Mahlon). Delv. to SMITH 15 Apr 1828.

3L:064   Date: 2 Apr 1825   RtCt: 25 Oct 1825.
John NEER Jr. & wife Eve of Ldn to John CONRAD of Ldn. B/S of
20 poles of land on Potomac at pt. of mt. on road to Harding's Ferry.
Wit: Ebenezer GRUBB, John WHITE. Delv. to Jno. CONARD
[CONRAD] 16 Jan 1829.

3L:066   Date: 25 Oct 1825   RtCt: 26 Oct 1825
Leven W. SHEPHERD & wife Catherine of Ldn to Editha
SAUNDERS of Ldn. B/S of part of lot on E side of King St in Lsbg
(conveyed in Feb 1823 by Wm. KING & wife Susan) adj Thomas
SAUNDERS, Richard H. HENDERSON. Wit: Saml. M. EDWARDS,
John J. MATHIAS, A. A. ESKRIDGE, William J. JONES, Roberdeau
ANNIN.

3L:068   Date: 19 Sep 1825   RtCt: 27 Oct 1825
Jeremiah McVEIGH & wife Sarah of Ldn to Isaiah ROMINE of Ldn.
B/S of Sarah's int. dower land of Rebeca ROMINE w/o of father
John ROMINE dec'd, adj Jonathan EWERS, Edward B. GRADY on
Snickers Gap Turnpike Road. Wit: Benjamin GRAYSON, John W.
GRAYSON. Delv. to Minor ROMINE 25 Sep 1837 pr order.

3L:070   Date: 23 Apr 1825   RtCt: 10 Oct 1825
John L. DAGG of Ldn to Richard COCHRANE of Mdbg. B/S of Lot
#26 in Mdbg. Wit: Francis W. LUCKETT, Edward B. GRADY, Peter
C. RUST. Delv. pr order 27 Feb 1829.

3L:071   Date: 27 Nov 1823   RtCt: 27 Oct 1825
Meshack LACEY (trustee of Nelson GREEN for benefit Samuel
CHINN in Jun 1823) of Ldn to George GREEN of FredVa. B/S of Lot
#61 in Mdbg. Delv. to M. BOWIE 24 Feb 1826.

3L:073   Date: 9 Mar 1825   RtCt: 29 Oct 1825
Thomas BROWN and Thomas H. KIRBY of Ldn to Juliann, Elvira
and Margaret McKENZIE d/o Henry McKENZIE of Ldn. Gift of
household items. Wit: John SKILLMAN, George R. BRISCOE,
Dennis McCARTY.

3L:074   Date: 1 Nov 1825   RtCt: 1 Nov 1825
Peter COST & wife Mary of Ldn to John NIXON of Ldn. B/S of __a
on Secolon adj Mahlon GARNER, Jonathan NIXON. Wit: John H.
McCABE, John J. MATHIAS.

3L:077   Date: 1 Nov 1825   RtCt: 1 Nov 1825
John NIXON & wife Nancy of Ldn to Peter COST of Ldn. B/S of 5a (Lot #7 in div. of estate of George NIXON the elder dec'd cnvy/b George the younger to John in Mar 1818). Wit: John H. McCABE, Jno. J. MATHIAS. Delv. to COST 23 Mar 1827.

3L:079   Date: 1 Nov 1825   RtCt: 1 Nov 1825
James H. HAMILTON & wife Margaret of Ldn to Peter COST of Ldn. B/S of 164a (prch/o heirs of George NIXON dec'd). Wit: John H. McCABE, John J. MATHIAS. Delv. to COST 23 Mar 1827.

3L:081   Date: 28 Oct 1825   RtCt: 1 Nov 1825
David ENGLISH of Georgetown D.C. to James H. HAMILTON of Ldn. Release of trust on 178a of Nov 1821 for debt to James EAKIN.

3L:083   Date: 2 Feb 1825   RtCt: 2 Nov 1825
Eli JANNEY and Mahlon WALTERS (Exors of Blackstone JANNEY dec'd) of Ldn to William BROWN of Ldn. B/S of 148a (per ct decree in Winchester in Dec 1824) adj Joseph GORE, Joseph CLEWES, Eli JANNEY, George FAIRHURST, Aquila MEADE. Delv. to BROWN 1 Jun 1826.

3L:086   Date: 27 Sep 1825   RtCt: 7 Nov 1825
Walter LANHAM of Ldn and Acquilla LANHAM of PrG to Vincent MOSS of Ldn. B/S of 250a where Walter now resides adj MOSS, Sydnor BAILEY, Elizabeth T. HARRISON, Daniel THOMAS. Wit: Josiah JONES, Thos. GETTINGS. Delv. to MOSS 16 Apr 1828.

3L:088   Date: 7 Sep 1825   RtCt: 7 Nov 1825
Samuel CLAPHAM of Ldn to Walter S. RINGOLD and Clement COX of Georgetown D.C. Trust for debt to Clement SMITH using __a on Potomac. Wit: Clement COX, Joseph CRAVEN, Job McPHERSON, John FRYE. Delv. to COX 16 Feb 1826.

3L:094   Date: 11 Mar 1825   RtCt: 9 Nov 1825
Thomas J. BENNETT & wife Susan W. of Ldn to John WAR of Ldn. B/S of 4a (formerly owned by James HAMILTON Sr and willed to Mary HAMILTON) adj John WESTLEY, Obed PAIRPOINT, John BRADEN. Wit: Wm. H. DORSEY, Wm. BRONAUGH. Delv. to WAR 11 Apr 1826.

3L:096   Date: 15 Sep 1824   RtCt: 17 Sep 1825
Margaret SAUNDERS of Ldn to Joshua PUSEY and Sampson BLINCOE of Ldn. Trust for debt to James NIXON (including bond by Margaret, John SAUNDERS and George SAUNDERS and note by Margaret, John SAUNDERS, James ROACH and Thomas WHITE) using 144a (conveyed 1804, DBk LL:394) adj Archibald MORRISON, Charles CRIM, Daniel SHOEMAKER, George SHOEMAKER. Wit: Henry PEERS, Tasker C. QUINLIN, Cyrus SAUNDERS. Delv. to PUSEY 14 Aug 1826.

3L:100   Date: 5 Jul 1825   RtCt: 5 Jul/16 Nov 1825
Samuel C. SINCLAIR of Ldn to Charles DOUGLAS and Sampson
BLINCOE of Ldn. Trust for debt to John GRAY using int. in land of
father Samuel SINCLAIR dec'd except dower of his mother Edith
SINCLAIR. Wit: Roberdeau ANNIN, William J. JONES, Chas. G.
ESKRIDGE.

3L:103   Date: __ Jan 1825   RtCt: 10 Nov 1825
Daniel GREENWALL to Lewis BEARD. Trust for debt to James
GARRISON using 1a lot on N end of King St in Lsbg. Wit: Saml. C.
SINCLAIR, G. D. SMITH, George GLEXON?

3L:106   Date: 11 Nov 1825   RtCt: 12 Nov 1825
Lewis A. BEATTY to James McILHANEY. Trust for Thomas B.
BEATTY as security on bonds to J. JONES Exor. of Sarah JONES
dec'd, of Joseph CLEWES, of Wm. M. McCARTY using farm
animals.

3L:109   Date: 13 Dec 1825   RtCt: 13 Dec 1825
Saml. M. EDWARDS, Everet SAUNDERS and Jas. RUST. Bond on
EDWARDS to perform trust for Susana ANSELL [Saml. M.
EDWARDS] apptd. committee to take charge of estate of Susanah
ANSELL an idiot.

3L:109   Date: 13 Dec 1825   RtCt: 13 Dec 1825
Everett SAUNDERS, Thos. SAUNDERS and Saml. HAMMETT.
Bond on Everett SAUNDERS as constable.

3L:110   Date: 24 Dec 1825   RtCt: 5 Dec 1825
Deborah JENNERS. DoE for negro man Samuel MIDDLETON. Wit:
D. SHAWEN, Joseph WOOD, Noble S. BRADEN, William
FITZIMONS.

3L:111   Date: 31 May 1822   RtCt: 14 Nov 1825
Yeoman Thomas CLOWES & wife Ann of Ldn to yeoman Joshua
GORE of Ldn. B/S of 31a (inherited from father Joseph CLOWES
dec'd) adj Wm. HOLMES, Constantine HUGHES, brother Joseph
CLOWES, Dr. William EACHES. Wit: N. C. WILLIAMS, John W.
GRAYSON. Delv. to GORE 25 Aug 1827.

3L:113   Date: 22 Mar 1825   RtCt: 14 Nov 1825
Joseph WALKER of Ldn to Thomas GORE of Ldn. B/S of 10a (from
div. of father Benjamin WALKER dec'd). Delv. pr order 28 Jan 1831.

3L:115   Date: 30 Jul 1825   RtCt: 14 Nov 1825
Isaac WALKER & wife Susana of Ldn to William NETTLE of Ldn.
B/S of part of lot in new addition of Wtfd (prch/o David JANNEY) adj
Saml. HOUGH, Robert BRADEN. Wit: Presley CORDELL, Saml.
HOUGH. Delv. to NETTLE 5 Mar 1839.

3L:117   Date: 14 Nov 1825   RtCt: 14 Nov 1825
Charles HAMILTON of Ldn. DoE for negro man George EDMONDS.

3L:118   Date: 1 Feb 1825   RtCt: 26 Sep 1825
Amos FERGUSON & wife Catherine of Ldn to Jonathan BEARD of
Ldn. Trust for debt to James BEAVERS using 50a & 150a cnvy/b
BEAVERS. Wit: Henry MILTON, Gainer PIERCE, Thomas MOSS.

3L:121   Date: 29 Sep 1825   RtCt: 14 Nov 1825
Samuel MURRAY & wife Mary Ann of Ldn to George RICHARDS of
Ldn. Trust for debt to Simon A. BINNS and William BINNS Jr. using
20a (prch/o Simon A. BINNS where MURRAY now resides), 1a
(bought of Wm. A. BINNS with house) and wife's int. in estate of
John A. BINNS dec'd and monies owed by Charles BINNS and int.
in estate of father William MURREY dec'd, crops, farm and
household items. Wit: David WOODY, Samuel ELGIN. Delv. to
George RICHARDS 12 Sep 1827.

3L:125   Date: 2 Apr 1825   RtCt: 14 Nov 1825
Levi WATERS & wife Sarah of Ldn to George SMITH of Ldn. B/S of
10a on W side of Short Hill adj John DEMORY. Wit: Ebenezer
GRUBB, John WHITE. Delv. to SMITH 10 Aug 1827.

3L:127   Date: 14 Nov 1825   RtCt: 14 Nov 1825
George W. HENRY of Ldn to William JENNERS of Ldn. Trust for
Charles & John HAMILTON as security for debt to John & Daniel
WINE using 103a (prch/o Jozabed WHITE) adj William SMITH, Mary
FOX, Samuel GREGG, Mathew BEANS. Delv. to Wm. M. JENNERS
by Jas. L. HAMILTON 18 Feb 1828.

3L:130   Date: 8 Dec 1824   RtCt: 30 Jul/15 Nov 1825
Benjamin REDMOND to son Andrew James and dau Mary Ann. Gift
of negro woman Harriet abt 22y old. Wit: Benjamin JAMES, Sally
JAMES, Balis S. FOLEY, David JAMES.

3L:131   Date: 25 Sep 1823   RtCt: 15 Nov 1825
Samuel DODD & wife Catherine of Ldn to Thomas GREGG of Ldn.
B/S of 6a (cnvy/b Henry HOWELL, Feb 1813) adj GREGG. Wit:
Stacy TAYLOR, Stephen GREGG, Craven OSBURNE, John
WHITE.

3L:133   Date: 16 Nov 1825   RtCt: 16 Nov 1825
James McCRAY of Ldn to Asa ROGERS of Ldn. Trust for debt to
Richard H. HENDERSON (in execution of Wm. H. HANDY) using
1¾a (prch/o David CARTER) on Goose Creek adj Andrew
McMULLEN, Jos. CARR. Delv. to ROGERS 11 Sep 1826.

3L:135   Date: 10 May 1819   RtCt: 16 Nov 1825
James MONROE of Washington D.C. to Tasker C. QUINLAN of
Ldn. B/S of 4½a on Little River. Wit: William BENTON, William
LEWIS, Adrian L. SWART.

3L:137   Date: 15 Nov 1825   RtCt: 16 Nov 1825
Humphrey B. POWELL of Ldn to Cuthbert and Burr G. POWELL of
Ldn. Release of trust of 215a for debt to Maria A. POWELL. Delv. to
C. POWELL 19 May 1827.

3L:138   Date: 4 Nov 1825   RtCt: 16 Nov 1825
Charles Fenton MERCER of Lsbg to Henry KEMP of FredMd.
Mortgage on und. moiety of 385a (conveyed to MERCER and Chas.
P. TUTT) on Kittocton Mt nr road from Noland's Ferry to Lsbg adj
Aaron SAUNDERS, John ROSE, late Col. Charles ELGIN. Delv. pr
order 20 ___.

3L:140   Date: 4 Nov 1825   RtCt: 16 Nov 1825
Humphrey B. POWELL (trustee of Burr POWELL) of Ldn to Charles
F. MERCER of Ldn. B/S of 385a.

3L:142   Date: 22 Mar 1825   RtCt: 18 Nov 1825.
Joseph WALKER of Ldn to Garrett WALKER of Ldn. B/S of int. in
40a dower of Sarah VANHORNE wd/o John VANHORN dec'd. Delv.
to Garrett WALKER 22 Jul 1847.

3L:143   Date: 1 Nov 1825   RtCt: 18 Nov 1825
Elisabeth T. HARRISON and Ann FITZHUGH of Ldn to Elisabeth
BAKER of Ldn. B/S of 100a (from div. in ct. decree of PrWm).

3L:145   Date: 17 Sep 1825   RtCt: 18 Nov 1825
Robert BRADEN & wife Elisabeth of Ldn to Lewis KLEIN. B/S of 1
rood lot in Wtfd (cnvy/b James MOORE trustee for benefit of Jesse
RICE) adj Richard CHILTON. Wit: Presly CORDELL, Saml.
HOUGH. Delv. to KLEIN 14 Aug 1826.

3L:148   Date: 28 Mar 1825   RtCt: 19 Nov 1825
William MEADE formerly of Ldn now of Campbell Co Va (trustee of
Peter COOPER & wife Nancy, Jun 1819) to John LITTLETON of
Ldn. B/S of 110½a.

3L:150   Date: 28 Mar 1825   RtCt: 19 Nov 1825
Peter COOPER & wife Nancy of Ldn to Samuel M. EDWARDS of
Ldn. Trust for debt to Robert MOFFETT using und. 2/9ths of land nr
Rehobeth (of father Michael COOPER dec'd where his widow now
resides, 1/9th prch/o brother Daniel COOPER). Wit: John
LITTLETON, Alfred A. ESKRIDGE, C. W. D. BINNS, John
McCORMICK, John H. McCABE. Delv. to Saml. HOUGH pr order 21
Feb 1827.

3L:153   Date: 30 Apr 1825   RtCt: 21 Nov 1825
Lewis AMBLER & wife Sally of Ldn to John HUTCHISON of Ldn.
B/S of 89½a in Ldn & Ffx adj John HUTCHISON, Jefferson
HUTCHISON, Stephen DANIELS. Wit: Charles LEWIS, Johnson
CLEVELAND. Delv. pr order filed DBk HHH:14 on 1 Apr 1828.

3L:154   Date: 25 Nov 1825   RtCt: 25 Nov 1825
Hiland CROWE (insolvent debtor) of Ldn to Shff Ludwell LEE. B/S of
213a on Little River turnpike road and 88-100a adj the first. Wit:
John M. McCARTY, Saml. HAMMET. Delv. to H. LUCKET 13 Jun
1826.

3L:156   Date: 6 Apr 1825   RtCt: 25 Nov 1825
John MINES & wife Eliza of Ldn to William D. DRISH of Ldn. B/S of
lot on Cornwall St in Lsbg (prch/o Michael SHRYOCK, Oct 1813).
Wit: R. G. WATERMAN, John GREY, John HANNELY. CoE of Eliza
in MontMd.

3L:158   Date: 10 Jan 1825   RtCt: 25 Nov 1825
Christopher NEALE & wife Harriett to Ralph Henry POTTS of New
York City. B/S of 4 lots containing 124a within a few miles of Hllb.
CoE in Ffx.

3L:161   Date: 1 Nov 1816   RtCt: 26 Nov 1825
John M. McCARTY & wife Ann Lucinda of Ldn to William M.
McCARTY of Ldn. B/S of 104a below Broad Run and nr Potomac
adj Ann M. and Edgar McCARTY. Wit: John McCORMICK, John H.
McCABE.

3L:163   Date: 1 Jun 1825   RtCt: 26 Nov 1825
Thomas HUGHES & wife Martha of Ldn to Mary HUGHES of Ldn.
B/S of 87a & 13a & 100a (allotted to Mary from div. from father
Constantine HUGHES who d. 11 Dec 1823). Wit: David SMITH,
William HOGE, Moses HICKS.

3L:167   Date: 30 Aug 1825   RtCt: 28 Nov 1825
Benniah WHITE & wife Frances R. of Ldn to Jacob CRIM of Ldn.
B/S of 28½a (formerly of Abel JANNEY Sr dec'd) adj CRIM, heirs of
Peter MILLER dec'd, Archibald MORRISON. Wit: Ebenezer GRUBB,
Mortimer McILHANY. Delv. to Mrs. CRIM 27 Jun 1826.

3L:170   Date: 10 Nov 1825   RtCt: 28 Nov 1825
Erasmus WEST of FredMd to James STUBBLEFIELD of JeffVa. B/S
of land on Potomac (prch/o Frederick HENSHA by West and Henry
FRAZIER). Delv. pr order DBk OOO:157 on 7 Jul 1831.

3L:173   Date: 25 Nov 1825   RtCt: 28 Nov 1825
James WEEKS of Mdbg to Elizabeth and Mary HAWLING of Ldn.
LS of 2 adj lots #31 & #42 in Mdbg.

3L:175   Date: 9 May 1825   RtCt: 2 Dec 1825
William LYNE of Ldn to Charles LEWIS of Ldn. Trust for debt to
Saml. and Jno. H. HALLY using 'Brambleton' tract where LYNE
lives. Delv. to John H. HALLEY 15 Jun 1827.

3L:177   Date: 2 Dec 1825   RtCt: 2 Dec 1825
Henry BODINE to Edward HAMMETT. Trust for Isaac
VANDEVANTER as security in suit of Thomson FOUCH using farm
animals, saw.

3L:179   Date: 29 Nov 1825   RtCt: 29 Nov 1825
Christopher C. McINTYRE to Charles W. D. BINNS. Trust for debt to
Nicholas OSBURNE using int. in estate of father Patrick McINTYRE
dec'd.

3L:181   Date: 3 Dec 1825   RtCt: 3 Dec 1825
Christopher C. McINTYRE to Richard J. FLEMING. Trust for debt to Sarah FOLEY (Admx of Presley FOLEY dec'd) using int. in estate of father Patrick McINTYRE dec'd.

3L:183   Date: 2 Dec 1825   RtCt: 2 Dec 1825
Christopher C. McINTYRE (insolvent debtor) to Shff Ludwell LEE. B/S of int. in estate of father Patrick McINTYRE dec'd (suit of Saml. M. BOSS, of SMITH & CARTER).

3L:184   Date: 10 Sep 1825   RtCt: 3 Dec 1825
Samuel MURRAY & wife Ellisabeth of Fqr to John WORNELL. Trust for debt to Lewis FRENCH using 157a prch/o Lewis & wife Sarah and Ann FRENCH wd/o Mason FRENCH dec'd. Wit: Francis W. LUCKETT, A. GIBSON. Delv. to L. FRENCH 10 Feb 1826.

3L:187   Date: 30 Nov 1825   RtCt: 3 Dec 1825
Lewis FRENCH of Ldn to John WORNELL of Ldn. Trust for debt to James WORNELL using farm animals. Delv. to Jno. WORNELL ___.

3L:189   Date: 1 Dec 1825   RtCt: 8 Dec 1825
Thomas MORALLEE (trustee of Simon SMALE & wife Elizabeth, Dec 1819) of Ldn to John SURGHENOR of Ldn. B/S of ½a on S side of Market St in Lsbg (prch/o John CRIDLER & wife Elizabeth). Wit: Saml. M. EDWARDS, James RUST. Delv. to SURGHNOR 27 Oct 1832.

3L:191   Date: 20 Dec 1825   RtCt: 12 Dec 1825
Robert BENTLEY & wife Catherine to Burr W. HARRISON. Trust for Robert J. TAYLOR, Joseph HILLIARD and John THOMAS as securities using 67a (cnvy/b Robert CAMPBELL, Aug 1823, DBk GGG:87). Wit: John McCORMICK, Saml. M. EDWARDS.

3L:195   Date: 10 Dec 1825   RtCt: 12 Dec 1825
Thomas BUCK & wife Reuhemah of FredVa to Andrew HEATH of Ldn. B/S of 250a adj William HAWLEY Jr., Elizabeth PAGET, Timothy PAGET, George HANCOCK. Wit: Charles LEWIS, John BAYLY.

3L:197   Date: 9 Dec 1825   RtCt: 12 Dec 1825
Andrew HEATH (Exor of Andrew HEATH Sr. dec'd) of Ldn to Thomas BUCK of FredVa. B/S of 250a on Elk Licking run adj George HANCOCK. Wit: Jacob SUMMERS, Lydia HEATH, Emily BROWN.

3L:199   Date: 10 Dec 1825   RtCt: 12 Dec 1825
Andrew HEATH (Exor of Andrew HEATH Sr. dec'd) of Ldn to Lydia HEATH of Ldn. B/S of 250a adj Timothy PAGET, Andrew HEATH. Delv. to John HUTCHISON pr order 28 Dec 1837.

3L:201   Date: 7 Dec 1825   RtCt: 12 Dec 1825
Thomas MARKS & wife Keziah of Ldn to Joshua OSBURNE and Volentine V. PURCELL of Ldn. Trust for debt to Lydia HEATON and

Jonathan & Albert HEATON (Admrs of James HEATON dec'd) using 19a. Wit: Thomas NICHOLS, Craven OSBURNE.

3L:205   Date: 10 Dec 1820 [25?]   RtCt: 12 Dec 1825
Turner OSBURNE of Ldn to Joshua OSBURNE of Ldn. B/S of 118a (cnvy/b Exors of Landon OSBURNE dec'd) adj Jane POTTS, __ SHUTT. Delv. to Joshua OSBURN 21 Jun 1827.

3L:207   Date: 5 Dec 1825   RtCt: 12 Dec 1825
Joshua OSBURNE and Craven OSBURNE (Exors of Landon OSBURNE dec'd) of Ldn to Turner OSBURNE of Ldn. B/S of 118a.

3L:209   Date: 5 Dec 1825   RtCt: 12 Dec 1825
James COPELAND & wife Sarah of Ldn to Urey HUMPHREY and Mary Ann HUMPHREY (heirs of Charles HUMPHREY dec'd). B/S of 14a (Charles prch/o COPELAND on 13 Jan 1819) on NW side of Short Hill adj William & James THOMPSON. Wit: John WHITE, Craven OSBURNE.

3L:211   Date: 2 Apr 1824   RtCt: 12 Dec 1825
Christian JACOBS of Ldn to Daniel CRIM of Ldn. B/S of 10a (allotted to JACOBS by commrs. of Peter JACOBS dec'd) between Short hill and Blue ridge. Delv. to CRIM 23 Dec 1828.

3L:213   Date: 31 Dec 1816   RtCt: 9 Dec 1825
Richard H. HENDERSON & wife Orra Moore of Lsbg to Samuel M. EDWARDS & wife Ann of Lsbg. B/S of 149a to EDWARDS and 153a to HENDERSON (purchased jointly of William D. DIGGS, May 1813). Wit: James RUST, Tasker C. QUINLAN.

3L:216   Date: 9 Jul 1825   RtCt: 12 Dec 1825
Martin C. OVERFIELD & wife Mary of Henderson Co Ky to Joshua B. OVERFIELD of Ldn. B/S of 148a (Lot #1 in div. of Martin & Elizabeth OVERFIELD dec'd of land on round hill). Delv. to Joshua 27 Jun 1828.

3L:219   Date: 25 Nov 1825   RtCt: 12 Dec 1825
Thomas JONES of Ldn to Hugh SMITH of Ldn. B/S of 71-72a (dev. by wills of parents William JONES dec'd and Sarah JONES dec'd) adj Isaac HUGHES, Sampson BLINCOE, brother William JONES. Delv. to SMITH 2 Aug 1836.

3L:220   Date: 31 Oct 1825   RtCt: 13 Dec 1825
Benjamin SHREVE Jr. of Ldn to James H. HAMILTON of Ldn. Release of trust for debt to Richard H. HENDERSON on 100a.

3L:221   Date: 5 Dec 1825   RtCt: 15 Dec 1825
William DELANEY & wife Rachael formerly WRIGHT of JeffVa to Jonas HEATH. Trust for benefit of Rachael using 1/8th part of land 1 mile N of Wtfd adj __ PAXON, __ McGAVOCK (Rachael's int. in estate of Patterson WRIGHT dec'd). Wit: Jno. S. GALLAHER, D. LONG.

3L:223   Date: 15 Dec 1825   RtCt: 16 Dec 1825
Augustus STONESTREET of Ldn to Elizabeth STONESTREET of Ldn. BoS of negro boy Bill abt 21y old, boy Harry abt 19y old, farm animals, farm and household items. Wit: R. G. SAUNDERS.

3L:224   Date: 1 Aug 1825   RtCt: 17 Dec 1825
John POULSON of Ldn atty for John TRIBBY & wife Lydia of Wayne Co OH to Agness POULSON of Ldn. B/S of 12a Lot #2 allotted to TRIBBY as heir of Jasper POULSON dec'd. PoA to John POULSON from William POULSON & wife Elizabeth, John TRIBBY & wife Lydia, Samuel SPENCER & wife Margaret and Elizabeth BOVAIRD of Wayne Co OH. Delv. to Agness 24 Feb 1829.

3L:227   Date: 19 Dec 1825   RtCt: 19 Dec 1825
Felix TRIPLETT of Ldn to Stephen W. ROZELL of Ldn. Trust for debt to Thornton WALKER using lot in Mdbg allotted from estate of Reuben TRIPLETT dec'd.

3L:228   Date: 20 Dec 1825   RtCt: 20 Dec 1825
Abraham M. FULTON (insolvent debtor) of Ldn to Shff Ludwell LEE. B/S of brick house and lot in Aldie subj. to trust in favor of Horace LUCKETT. Delv. to H. LUCKETT 13 Jun 1826.

3L:229   Date: 1 Nov 1819   RtCt: 23 Dec 1825
William M. McCARTY & wife Emily of Ldn to John M. McCARTY of Ldn. B/S of 59a on Potomac. Wit: John H. McCABE, Jno. J. MATHIAS.

3L:231   Date: 1 Oct 1823   RtCt: 23 Dec 1825
William M. McCARTY & wife Emily of Ldn to John M. McCARTY of Ldn. B/S of 225a on Potomac. Wit: Jno. H. McCABE, Jno. J. MATHIAS.

3L:233   Date: 3 Dec 1825   RtCt: 23 Dec 1825
Isaac KENT and John SHAW of Ldn to Elijah KENT of Ldn. LS for 999y of house and lot on S side of Lsbg on W side of Carolina road adj Mrs. WOODLEY, Benj. SHREVE, James RUST. Delv. to Jno. SHAW 8 Feb 1827.

3L:236   Date: 1 Nov 1824   RtCt: 28 Dec 1825
Thomas R. MOTT & wife Mary C. of Ldn to Thomas R. SAUNDERS of Ldn. B/S of house and lot on N side of Main St in Wtfd to E of town formerly occupied by __ TALBERT (cnvy/b Tasker C. QUINLAN). Wit: S. HOUGH, Wm. T. T. MASON, E. G. HAMILTON, Saml. M. EDWARDS, Tasker C. QUINLAN. Delv. pr order 6 Apr 1831.

3L:237   Date: 29 Aug 1825   RtCt: 29 Dec 1825
Richard H. HENDERSON & wife Orra Moore of Ldn to George RHODES of Ldn. B/S of 13a nr Lsbg (prch/o John A. BINNS). Wit: Thos. R. MOTT, Saml. M. EDWARDS. Delv. to RHODES 9 Sep 1836.

3L:239   Date: __ 1826   RtCt: 4 Jan 1826
Isaac NICHOLS Jr and James HOGE (trustees of Nathan BROWN dec'd) of Ldn to Isaac NICHOLS Sr. of Ldn. B/S of 135a adj heirs of John YOUNG dec'd formerly occupied by Thomas GREGG dec'd.

3L:241   Date: 26 Dec 1825   RtCt: 29 Dec 1825
Ludwell LEE of Ldn to Wilson C. SELDON Sr of Ldn. B/S of right of way to Eden Island on Potomac established by Thomas L. LEE from turnpike road at Muses' Shop to ford across little river to island.

3L:242   Date: 2 Apr 1817   RtCt: 12 Sep 1825
Enoch FURR Sr. & wife Sarah of Ldn to Joshua FRED of Ldn. B/S of 61a. Wit: Benj. GRAYSON, John W. GRAYSON.

3L:244   Date: 24 Nov 1808   RtCt: 9 Jan 1809/17 Sep 1825
Harriet P. HARRISON and James SURGHENOR. Marriage contract – Harriet's int. in estate of father Valentine HARRISON dec'd (und. land in Ky, slaves Milly, Cinthia, Osborne, Lewis, Pat, Reegan?, James and Nelson in possession of widow) after her death goes to her heirs but James can use while he is alive, puts in trust to Selden HARRISON. Wit: Burr POWELL, Leven D. POWELL, George NEALE, Addison HARRISON. Delv. to SURGNOR 27 Oct 1832.

3L:246   Date: 5 Jul 1825   RtCt: 8 Nov 1825
William R. SWIFT & wife Mary D. of AlexDC to Jonah F. DAVIS of AlexDC. Trust for debt to Humphrey PEAKE (Admr of Jonathan SWIFT dec'd late of AlexDC) using 1/5th int. in 214a of father Jonathan dec'd subject to dower, on Goose Creek adj Ludwell LEE, int. in 1357a in Ffx, int. in 356 in Ffx nr Lsbg road abt 5 miles from Alex. and mansion house in Alex. Delv. to H. PEAKE 13 Aug 1827.

3L:250   Date: 30 Nov 1825   RtCt: 30 Nov 1825
James HIXON of Ldn to Richard H. HENDERSON, L. P. W. BALCH and Jesse TIMMS of Ldn. Trust for debt to George CARTER of Oatlands using193a adj Sandford ROGERS, Burr POWELL, T. D. PEYTON. Delv. to TIMMS 5 Jun 1827.

3L:253   Date: 30 Nov 1825   RtCt: 30 Nov 1825
Benjamin HIXSON of Ldn to Richard H. HENDERSON, L. P. W. BALCH and Jesse TIMMS of Ldn. Trust for debt to George CARTER of Oatlands using 3a (cnvy/b James HIXON, Jan 1821) and 4a (prch/o Daniel VERNON) and 180¼a (cnvy/b James HIXON). Delv. to TIMMS 5 Jun 1827.

3L:257   Date: 10 Jan 1826   RtCt: 10 Jan 1826
L. P. W. BALCH, William THRIFT and Asa ROGERS. Bond on BALCH as treasurer of library fund.

3L:258   Date: 28 Oct 1822   RtCt: 11 Jan 1826
John VERMILLION to Wm. CARR. Inventory of property sold to CARR on 28 Oct 1822 to satisfy rent – horses.

3L:258   Date: 15 Dec 1825   RtCt: ___
James L. MARTIN (commr. in decree of case of Edward HAMMAT agst DONOHOE) to Edward HAMMAT. B/S of lot (estate of Nancy DONOHOE dec'd) on N side of Loudoun St in Lsbg with stone dwelling.

3L:259   Date: 6 Dec 1825   RtCt: 9 Jan 1826
John J. MATHIAS. Appointment as Capt. of Co. of Light Infantry in 2nd Battalion of 57th Reg 6th Brig and 2nd Div of Militia. Delv. to MATHIAS 21 May 1828.

3L:260   Date: 27 Dec 1825   RtCt: 9 Jan 1826
Ben. MITCHELL, Stephen McPHERSON Jr., Garrett WALKER. Court order of 9 Nov 1824, report on Snickers Gap Turnpike Road between Be[a]verdam Bridge and Shennandoah.

3L:261   Date: 25 Mar 1825   RtCt: 11 Jan 1826
Lewis LYDER dec'd. Division – 90a (part of lower farm where Samuel CROOK has resided) to widow's dower of Mary LYDER; upper farm lot #1 & wood lot #1 to Cornelia LYDER; upper farm lot #2 & wood lot #2 to Landon LYDER; upper farm lot #3 to Lettitia LYDER; upper farm lot #4 & wood lot #3 to Lydia LYDER; upper farm lot #5 & wood lot #4 to Lemuel LYDER; upper farm lot #6 & wood lot #5 to Jacob LYDER; upper farm lot #7 to Nancy CORRELL & husband Abraham; upper farm lot #8 to Margaret COOK & husband Samuel; lower farm residue lot #9 (31a) to Mahala LYDER. Gives detailed plat. Divisors: N. C. WILLIAMS, James JOHNSON, Jacob SILCOTT.

3L:265   Date: 1 Jan 1826   RtCt: 9 Jan 1826
Humphrey SHEPHERD & wife Catherine to P. McCORMICK Jr. Trust for debt to William CASTLEMAN Jr. using 190a on Goose Creek. Delv. to CASTLEMEN 2 Dec 1829.

3L:269   Date: 29 Dec 1825   RtCt: 9 Jan 1826
William CASTLEMAN Jr. & wife Urey of FredVa to Humphrey SHEPHERD of FredVa. B/S of 190a (cnvy/b Thomas SWAYNE Oct 1822) on NW fork of Goose Creek. Delv. to SHEPHERD 11 Aug 1834.

3L:271   Date: 24 Nov 1825   RtCt: 9 Jan 1826
Burr POWELL of Ldn to William HANNA(H) of Ldn. B/S of 1a below Mdbg and Wankepin branch adj Hugh ROGERS. Delv. pr order 23 Sep 1829.

3L:273   Date: 26 Nov 1825   RtCt: 9 Jan 1826
Burr POWELL & wife Catherine of Ldn to Abner GIBSON of Mdbg. B/S of 5a below Mdbg at Washington and Independence St. adj William HANNA. Wit: Francis W. LUCKETT, Cuthbert POWELL. Delv. to GIBSON 15 Mar 1836.

3L:276 Date: 5 Jan 1826 RtCt: 9 Jan 1826
Peter TOWPERMAN and Catesby JONES. Agreement concerning use of household items paid with farm animals, crops. Wit: Burr POWELL, Andrew TOWPERMAN. Delv. to TOWPERMAN 27 Jan 1827.

3L:277 Date: 20 Dec 1825 RtCt: 9 Jan 1826
Joseph EIDSON & wife Ellisabeth of Ldn to John GALLEHER of Ldn. B/S of 32a (Ellisabeth's share from father Reuben TRIPLETT dec'd). Wit: Burr POWELL, Abner GIBSON. Delv. to David GALLEHER 29 Oct 1828.

3L:279 Date: 9 Jan 1826 RtCt: 9 Jan 1826
Presley CORDELL of Ldn. DoE for Amy GRAYSON (slave for life).

3L:280 Date: 5 Jan 1824 RtCt: 9 Jan 1826
Pierce NOLAND & wife Mary of Hampshire Co Va to John KILE Jr of Ldn. B/S of Mary's 1/7th int. of land from father Elisha POWELL dec'd allotted widow Ann POWELL and her share from death of brother Elisha POWELL dec'd. Wit: Geo. SHARP, John STUMP.

3L:282 Date: 21 Dec 1825 RtCt: 9 Jan 1826
William GHEEN & wife Narcissa and Leroy GHEEN of Ldn to Peyton POWELL of Ldn. Trust for debt to William WILKINSON using int. in 160a dev. as life estate to Narcissa from will of William SUDDETH and Leroy's 1/6th int. Wit: Burr POWELL, A. GIBSON. Delv. to WILKINSON 20 Apr 1829.

3L:284 Date: 12 Aug 1823 RtCt: 9 Jan 1826
Joseph LEWIS (free man of colour). DoE for his wife Polly aged 34y whom he prch/o Henerietta WILLIAMS of Ffx. Wit: Asa MOORE, Daniel STONE, Thomas PHILLIPS.

3L:285 Date: 15 Dec 1825 RtCt: 9 Jan 1826
Thomas SWAYNE of Ldn to William CASTLEMAN Jr. of FredVa. Release of mortgage of Oct 1822.

3L:286 Date: 15 Aug 1825 RtCt: 9 Jan 1825
William NOLAND & wife Catherine of Ldn to Notley C. WILLIAMS of Ldn. B/S of 2½a on Ashby's Gap Turnpike opposite Mercer's Mill nr Aldie. Wit: Leven LUCKETT, A. GIBSON. Delv. to WILLIAMS 25 Feb 1830.

3L:289 Date: 21 Sep 1825 RtCt: 9 Jan 1826
Francis W. LUCKETT & wife Sarah S. of Ldn to Edward B. GRADY of Ldn. Trust of debt to John L. DAGG of PhilPa using 177a (given to Francis by father Leven LUCKETT) where LUCKETT resides adj William F. LUCKETT. Wit: William BRONAUGH, Burr POWELL. Delv. to DAGG 11 Aug 1827.

3L:291 Date: ___ 1826 RtCt: 9 Jan 1826
Micaga TRIPLETT & wife Nancy of Ldn to Samuel TRIPLETT of Ldn. Trust for delivering of flour to neighboring mills using farm animals and crops.

3L:293   Date: 5 Dec 1825   RtCt: 9 Jan 1826
Edward HALL & wife Louisa F. late Louisa DeBUTTS of Ldn to
William HERBERT (as agent for estate of Richard DeBUTTS) of
Ffx. Correction for release of mortgage (DBk CCC:253) to Thomas
SWAYNE late of Ldn on 190a.

3L:295   Date: 9 Jan 1826   RtCt: 9 Jan 1826
Hiland CROWE (insolvent debtor) of Ldn to Shff Ludwell LEE. B/S of
80-100a (debts to Joseph TULEY & others). Delv. to H. LUCKETT
13 Jun 1826.

3L:297   Date: 28 Dec 1825   RtCt: 9 Jan 1826
Hugh ROGERS & wife Mary of Ldn to Mosses WILSON of Ldn. B/S
of 1a (from trust of Moses WILSON to Jonathan CARTER and John
SINCLAIR purchased by ROGERS and Mosses' wife Tamar agrees
to relinq. dower on land sold by ROGERS to Joseph HOGUE if this
land is sold back to Mosses). Wit: Burr POWELL, Abner GIBSON.

3L:299   Date: 11 Jan 1826   RtCt: 11 Jan 1826
Simon A. BINNS of Ldn to Asa ROGERS of Ldn. Trust for debt to A.
C. CAZENOVE &c, Robert H. TAYLOR, John W. MASSIE &c, John
A. BINNS of Charles and John A. BINNS of Simon using 220a adj
Benj. SHREVE, Wm. HAWLING.

3L:301   Date: 8 Jun 1825   RtCt: 12 Dec 1825/13 Jan 1826
CATESBY Ap. Henery BALL to Zedakiah KIDWELL. B/S of land
(from Daniel and Henry SETTLES as willed to Euxlius? JONES by
grandfather John TURBERVILLE). Wit: William BALL, George
BEARD, Spencer M. BALL. Delv. 1 Mar 1833.

3L:302   Date: 14 Jan 1826   RtCt: 14 Jan 1826
Isaac EATON & wife Malinda to Richard H. HENDERSON. Trust for
debt to Edward Stabler and Son using 18a on Loudoun St. in Mt.
Gilead adj Robert COE. Wit: John J. MATHIAS, Thomas SANDERS.

3L:304   Date: 17 Jan 1826   RtCt: 16 Jan 1826
James WILLIAMS of Mercer Co Ky at present in Ldn to Ellis
WILLIAMS of Ldn. B/S of und. 1/5th part of 1/5th int. in real estate of
Mary WILLIAMS dec'd and real estate of Daniel WILLIAMS dec'd
(inherited as 2 of the 7 children of John WILLIAMS dec'd of Ldn)
now occupied by Martha WILLIAMS wd/o John. James is one of 5
children of John WILLIAMS dec'd late of Mercer Co Ky a brother of
Mary & Daniel dec'd. Delv. to Ellis WILLIAMS 13 Jul 1836.

3L:306   Date: 16 Jan 1826   RtCt: 16 Jan 1826
Martin C. OVERFIELD of Henderson Co Ky by attorney John R.
GRIGSBY to Charles TAYLOR of Ldn. B/S of int. in 26a wooded lot
of brother Hudson OVERFIELD assigned to widow. Delv. to
TAYLOR 12 Nov 1828.

3L:307   Date: 1 Dec 1825   RtCt: 16 Jan 1826
Jesse DAILEY & wife Mary of Ldn to Mary WOOD and son John
WOOD of Ldn. B/S of part of Lot #58 in Lsbg adj Simon SMALE.

Wit: John MARTIN, John SURGHNOR, John FEICHTER, Thomas SANDERS, Saml. M. EDWARDS.

3L:309   Date: 15 Apr 1824   RtCt: 17 Jan 1826
Shff John ROSE to Richard H. HENDERSON. B/S of tenement in Wtfd cnvy/b insolvent debtor John MONROE (from John HAMMOND to MONROE).

3L:310   Date: 10 Jan 1826   RtCt: 20 Jan 1826
Amos DONAHOE to John L. MARTIN. Trust for debt to Betsey MURRAY using household items.

3L:311   Date: 20 Jan 1826   RtCt: 20 Jan 1826
Patrick BOLAND to Daniel BOLAND (dissolving partnership). B/S of lot prch/o __ SAWYER & wife Mary.

3L:313   Date: 5 Aug 1825   RtCt: 24 Jan 1826
Durett LONG of JeffVA to John CUNNARD of Ldn. Trust for debt to Edward CUNNARD using 2a on Kittockton Creek in gap of Short Hill. Wit: Nathan EDMONDS, Christian MILLER. Delv. to John CONRAD 1 May 1828.

3L:314   Date: 12 Oct 1823   RtCt: 12 Dec 1803/29 Jan 1826
Zadock LANHAM of Md to Nathaniel MOSS of Ldn. B/S of 116a (from will of Aaron LANHAM dec'd) adj MOSS. Wit: Daniel THOMAS, Stephen MOSS. Delv. to Vincent MOSS 16 Apr 1828.

3L:316   Date: 14 Sep 1824   RtCt: 5 Sep 1824
Matthew MITCHELL & wife Ellizabeth to Samuel M. EDWARDS and Burr W. HARRISON. Trust for debt to John LITTLEJOHN using lots in Lsbg. Wit: Chas. G. ESKRIDGE, Alfred A. ESKRIDGE, Wm. CHILTON. Delv. to LITTLEJOHN 5 Jul 1830.

3L:323   Date: 20 Jan 1826   RtCt: 21 Jan 1826
Samuel HAMMETT agent for R. J. TAYLOR of AlexDC to Philip C. JONES of Shenandoah Co Va. BoS for slave woman Sarah aged 32y last March, her daughter Harriet aged 7y this Jan, her son Edmond aged 5y last Nov, and Thomas aged 1y the 7th of Jan 1826. Wit: A. A. ESKRIDGE.

3L:323   Date: 3 Feb 1826   RtCt: 4 Feb 1826
William HAWKE Jr. of Ldn to Samuel M. BOSS of Ldn. B/S of int. in lot with 2-story house on NE corner of Loudoun & King St. in Lsbg (from HAWKE's grandfather Peter BOSS dec'd of Lsbg – left widow Mary BOSS, Peter, Saml. M., Danl. C., Abraham J. BOSS, Saml. BOSS s/o Jacob BOSS dec'd and David BOSS, and Wm. HAWKE & sister Mary heirs of Margaret HAWKE dec'd d/o Peter dec'd) adj Robt. R. HOUGH, estate of Chas. B. BALL, James THOMAS, John SURGHINOR, Saml. M. EDWARDS. Delv. to Saml. M. BOSS 14 Apr 1826.

3L:325   Date: 28 Jan 1826   RtCt: 6 Feb 1826
Mary FOX of Ldn to Susan BURNS of Ldn. B/S of ¼a Lot #61 in Wtfd.

3L:327   Date: 6 Feb 1826   RtCt: 8 Feb 1826
Alexander CORDELL & wife Diana of Ldn to John COOPER of Ldn.
B/S of 1a on Broad run. Wit: John HAMILTON, George W.
SHAWEN. Delv. pr order filed DBk QQQ:293 on 12 Nov 1829.

3L:328   Date: 3 Oct 1825   RtCt: 10 Feb 1826
Elizabeth W. THOMAS of Ldn to Jefferson C. THOMAS of Ldn. B/S
of int. in 69a (lately belonging to Philip THOMAS dec'd) at foot & on
Blue Ridge, adj heirs of James NICHOLLS dec'd, Thomas JAMES
and 16a and 4a. Delv. to grantee 12 Jul 1861.

3L:330   Date: 1 Sep or Dec 1825   RtCt: 1 Dec 1826
Wilson Cary SELDON of Execter, Ldn to Thomas R. MOTT,
Erasmus G. HAMILTON and Charles G. ESKRIDGE of Ldn. Trust
for debt to George CARTER of Oatlands using 400a on road from
Lsbg to Execter and dwelling house. Delv. to J. TIMMS 5 Jun 1827.

3L:333   Date: 12 Nov 1825   RtCt: 15 Nov 1825
Lewis ELLZEY of FredMd to Craven OSBURNE of Ldn. Trust for
Joshua OSBURN as security on bond to __ HOBLETZELL and
James RUST for deed of trust using int. in estate of Thomazin
ELLZEY late of Ffx. Wit: Thos. DONALDSON, Thos. WILKINSON,
Thos. TAYLOR, Jno. MOUNT Jr., Samuel C. DORMAN. Delv. to J.
OSBURNE 18 Jun 1826.

3L:337   Date: 23 Dec 1825   RtCt: 16 Jan 1826
Mary WOOD wd/o Mark WOOD dec'd and son John W. WOOD of
Ldn to Jesse DAILEY of Ldn. B/S of lot in Lsbg Mark WOOD bought
of Dr. Henery CLAGETT on Back St. Wit: Jno. A. BINNS, Wm. H.
JACOBS, Jno. SHAW Jr. Delv. to DAILEY 30 Jul 1839.

3L:338   Date: 24 Sep 1825   RtCt: 25 Jan 1826
Robert COE & wife Elizabeth of Ldn to Ezra BOLIN of Ldn. B/S of 2a
(part of tract where COE lives). Wit: John SIMPSON, James H.
HAMILTON. Delv. to BOLIN 30 Nov 1826.

3L:340   Date: 28 Nov 1825   RtCt: 16 Jan 1826
Martin C. OVERFIELD of Henderson Co Ky to John R. GRIGSBY of
Henderson Co Ky. PoA.

3L:341   Date: 16 Nov 1825   RtCt: 12 Dec 1826/13 Feb 1826
George TURNER of Ldn to Asa ROGERS of Ldn. Trust for debt to
John GRIGSBY using negroes Linney, William and Hendley.

3L:342   Date: 7 Jan 1826   RtCt: 3 Feb 1826
John TODHUNTER of Jessamine Co Ky to Robert L. NELSON of
Jessamine Co Ky. PoA to receive money from Mrs. ELGIN and
William DRISH (Admrs. of Charles ELGIN dec'd) from note of Oct
1818 by ELGIN and Edward DULIN to Samuel FRANK in trust for
Mary TODHUNTER w/o John and of Mrs. Peggy EDMONS (Exor of
Sandford EDMOND dec'd of Ldn for note.

3L:344   Date: 9 Aug 1825   RtCt: 28 Nov 1825/13 Feb 1826
John GRUBB of Ldn to John HAMILTON of Ldn. Trust for Elijah
PEACOCK and John BROWN of Ldn as securities for GRUBB and
George FRITS on bonds to John MYERS of JeffVa using nr 7a
(purchased partly of Jeremiah PURDUM and part of Aaron MILLER)
adj Archibald MORRISON, and household items. See DBk PPP:131
pr ack.

3L:346   Date: 9 Feb 1826   RtCt: 9 Feb 1826
James TOWNSEND of Oatlands to George CARTER of Oatlands.
Trust of negro girl Amey lately prch/o Robert FULTON. Wit: Jesse
TIMMS. Delv. to J. TIMMS 5 Jun 1827.

3L:348   Date: ___   RtCt: 13 Mar 1826
James HEATON to son Jonathan HEATON. List of goods and
chattles given to son at marriage – farm and household items, part
in compensation for £300 Pa money left him by grandfather SMITH.
Delv. to Jas. HEATON 29 Mar 1826.

3L:348   Date: 13 Feb 1826   RtCt: 16 Feb 1826
William NORRIS (free man of colour). DoE for his dau Elizabeth
NORRIS a negro slave who was 15y old 20 Jun last. Wit: Wm. J.
Jones.

3L:349   Date: 13 Feb 1826   RtCt: 13 Feb 1826
Augustine M. SANDFORD, Robert SANDFORD and Robert
MOFFETT. Bond on Augustine as constable.

3L:349   Date: 21 Jan 1826   RtCt: 14 Feb 1826
David CHAMBLIN and David LOVETT. Bond on CHAMBLIN as
constable.

3L:350   Date: 9 May 1825   RtCt: 13 Feb 1826
Shff John ROSE by D. Shff Townsend McVEIGH to Burr WEEKS of
Ldn. B/S of 113½a (from Gainer PIERCE). Delv. to WEEKS 15 Jun
1826.

3L:352   Date: 1 Feb 1826   RtCt: 15 Feb 1826
Charles KIRK of Ldn to Enos T. BEST of Ldn. Trust for debt to Mary
LIDER using farm animals, farm and household items. Wit: Everitt
SAUNDERS. Delv. to BEST 11 Mar 1830.

3L:353   Date: 8 Feb 1826   RtCt: 16 Feb 1826
Barbara NORTON to Jonathan LOVETT. BoS for farm animals &
items, all household furniture.

3L:354   Date: 13 Jan 1826   RtCt: 13 Feb 1826
Benjamin GRAYSON (Admr of Benjamin GRAYSON Jr. dec'd) of
Ldn to George MARKS of Ldn. B/S of lot In Bloomfield (cnvy/b
Stephen McPHERSON) formerly owned and occupied by Richard
MATHEWS, adj Benjamin BARTON. Delv. to MARKS 26 Nov 1830.

3L:355   Date: 6 Jan 1826   RtCt: 20 Feb 1826
John M. McCARTY & wife Ann Lucinda of Ldn to James B.
MURRAY of New York City. Trust for debt to Chatham Fire

Insurance Co. using 560a on S side of Potomac (formerly of Daniel McCARTY the elder). Wit: Joseph C. HART, Gilbert S. MOUNT, Thomas SANDERS, John H. McCABE.

3L:361   Date: 5 May 1825   RtCt: 8 Aug 1825/13 Feb 1826
James HAMILTON of Ldn to Charles B. HAMILTON and John HAMILTON Jr. of Ldn. B/S of ¼ int. in real estate of father James HAMILTON dec'd which includes lot where John now lives adj land cultivated by Elijah PEACOCK and wood lot on Short Hill. Wit: Elijah PEACOCK, Henry ADAMS, Daniel HINES. Delv. to Chas. B. HAMILTON 8 Aug 1835.

3L:362   Date: 23 Jan 1826   RtCt: 13 Feb 1826
Ebenezer GRUBB Sr. & wife Mary of Ldn to Curtis GRUBB of Ldn. B/S of 199a (for $1250 in part of a deed of gift to son Curtis E. GRUBB – his full share of estate of E. Sr.) adj __ ARNOLD, __ HOUSEHOLDER, Peter SAUNDERS, Wm. HOUGH, Beverdam Creek. Wit: Craven OSBURNE, John WHITE. Delv. to E. GRUBB 22 Jun 1826.

3L:364   Date: 23 Jan 1826   RtCt: 13 Feb 1826
Ebenezer GRUBB Sr. & wife Mary of Ldn to Ebenezer GRUBB Jr of Ldn. B/S of 199a (for $1250 in part of a deed of gift to son Ebenezer Jr. – his full share of estate of E. Sr.) adj Wm. HOUGH. Wit: Craven OSBURNE, John WHITE. Delv. to E. GRUBB 22 Jun 1826.

3L:367   Date: 20 Jan 1826   RtCt: 4 Mar 1826
Gainer PIERCE of Ldn to James HOGE of Ldn. BoS of all household and kitchen furniture.

3L:368   Date: 17 Jan 1826   RtCt: 13 Feb 1826
George M. FRYE & wife Mary of FredVa to John WHITE of Ldn. B/S of 80a (conveyed to Mary late Mary DAVIS wd/o Solomon DAVIS dec'd before her marriage with George, descended to Mary by demise of her sister Ellizabeth McILHANEY) adj Robert WHITE, Norris McDANIEL, Milton McILHANEY, Francis STRIBLING. Delv. to WHITE 27 Jun 1827.

3L:370   Date: 22 Jul 1825   RtCt: 13 Feb 1826
Gourley REEDER (trustee of William VICKERS for debt to Joseph and Samuel HATCHER, Aug 1822) of Ldn to John G HUMPHREY of Ldn. B/S of 104¼a adj Russell's meadow.

3L:371   Date: 12 Apr 1817   RtCt: 13 Feb 1826
Zorababel WELLS and Elizabeth WELLS of Ldn to Samuel CLENDENING of Ldn. PoA to sell int. property of estate of Samuel CLENDENING dec'd

3L:372   Date: 7 Oct 1825   RtCt: 13 Feb 1826
William HOUGH & wife Jane, Wm. CLENDENING & wife Ruth, Sarah NIXON and Mary CLENDENING of Ldn to Samuel CLENDENING of Ldn. B/S of 5/6th int. in land in Hllb now in possession of Samuel (Saml. CLENDENING Sr. died possessed)

including Wm. CLENDENING's share having purchased Elizabeth WELLS' share. Wit: Craven OSBURNE, John WHITE.

3L:374 Date: 14 Feb 1825 RtCt: 13 Feb 1826
Jesse LEWELLEN of Fqr to Humphrey B. POWELL. Trust for debt to Burr POWELL with Hugh ROGERS as security using farm animals, household items. Delv. to POWELL 17 Oct 1826.

3L:376 Date: 1 Jun 1825 RtCt: 13 Feb 1826
William LYNE of Ldn to Philip L. PALMER of Ldn. B/S of 1a E of LYNE's farm 'Brambleton'. Wit: Saml. HALLEY, Jere H. HALLEY. Delv. to PALMER 7 Aug 1831.

3L:377 Date: 10 Feb 1826 RtCt: 13 Feb 1826
Phebe R. DONOHOE of Mdbg to Edwin C. BROWN of Mdbg. Trust for debt to WATERMAN and CAMPBELL using int. in estate of father John V. DONOHOE und. and in possession of mother Sarah DONOHOE. Delv. to Saml. CAMPBELL 18 Dec 1833.

3L:379 Date: 11 Feb 1826 RtCt: 20 Feb 1826
John M. McCARTY & wife Ann Lucinda of Ldn to James HIGGINS and James MONROE Jr. of New York City. Trust for Dr. William GRAYSON as security for bond to Chatham Fire Insurance Co. using 500a (descended from father Daniel McCARTY of Cedar Grove) on Potomac subject to trust of Charles BENNETT.

3L:381 Date: 21 Feb 1826 RtCt: 22 Feb 1826
Charles BINNS of Ldn to dau Hannah Sim TEBBS. Gift of negro woman Anne & her 3 children Issum, Washington and Brenda. Wit: A. A. BINNS, E. D. BINNS. Delv. to C. BINNS 5 Nov 1835.

3L:381 Date: 16 Feb 1826 RtCt: 18 Feb 1826
Simon A. BINNS & wife ___ to Chas. G. ESKRIDGE. Trust for debt to Samuel M. BOSS using 220a where BINNS now resides adj Benjamin SHREVE, Charles BINNS, estate of Wm. HAWLING dec'd. Wit: Alfred A. ESKRIDGE, William J. JONES, Henry CLIFORD.

3L:384 Date: 12 Jan 1826 RtCt: 27 Feb 1826
William COE & wife Catherine of Ldn to Richard H. HENDERSON. Trust for debt to Samuel CARR, John GRAY, Townsend McVEIGH, A. C. Cagenove &Co assignee of S. M. BOSS using 35a of land which descended to Catherine from her brother Mennan COE dec'd and conveyed to Wm. COE by Edward M. COE. Wit: John SIMPSON, Thomas ROGERS. Delv. to HENDERSON 19 Jan 1828.

3L:386 Date: ___ 1825 RtCt: 13 Feb 1826
Benjamin SHREVES of Ldn and Eli OFFUT of Ffx to William CLINE of Ldn. Release of trust of Jun 1813 on 100a for debt to Peter BEMARSDERFER. Delv. to CLINE 19 Sep 1826.

3L:387 Date: ___ 1825 RtCt: 27 Feb 1826
Eli OFFUTT of Ffx to William CLINE of Ldn. B/S of deed of trust from Peter BEMARSDAFFER dated Jun 1813 (DBk VV:266) on 100a on

Goose Creek including Adams Mill for Philip RHOAN (alias RHAN) as security on bonds to John BROOKBANK and John AVEY. Wit: Chas. G. ESKRIDGE, Alfred A. ESKRIDGE, Roberdeau ANNIN. Delv. to CLINE 19 Sep 1826.

3L:388 Date: 26 May 1824 RtCt: 26 May 1824/28 Feb 1826
Walter KERRICK & wife Deborah of Ldn to Samuel HATCHER, Thos. HUGHES and Wm. PIGGOTT of Ldn. B/S of 3a adj Benjamin BRADFIELD, Stephen WILSON, James McILHANEY's heirs. Wit: Alfred A. ESKRIDGE, L. P. W. BALCH, John THOMAS, John McCORMICK, John H. McCABE. Delv. to PIGGOTT 22 Jun 1827.

3L:390 Date: 26 May 1824 RtCt: 26 May 1824/28 Feb 1826
Walter KERRICK & wife Deborah of Ldn to Samuel HATCHER, Thomas HUGHES and Wm. PIGGOTT of Ldn. B/S of 7a adj Samuel IDEN (prch/o Bernard TAYLOR). Wit: Alfred A. ESKRIDGE, L. P. W. BALCH, John THOMAS. Delv. to PIGGOTT 22 Jun 1827.

3L:392 Date: 27 Feb 1826 RtCt: 28 Feb 1826
Lewis P. W. BALCH (as trustee on trust of Dec 1818) to Elizabeth C. COE. B/S of 42¾a with mill on Mdbg road. Wit: William J. JONES, C. W. D. BINNS, Roberdeau ANNIN.

3L:394 Date: 27 Feb 1826 RtCt: 28 Feb 1826
Ellizabeth C. COE of PrWm to L. P. W. BALCH of Ldn. Trust for debt to Conrad BITZER using 42¾a on fork of Goose Creek. Wit: C. W. D. BINNS, Roberdeau ANNIN, William JONES. Delv. to BITZER 13 Dec 1830.

3L:397 Date: ___ 1825 RtCt: 13 Feb 1826
Benjamin SHRIEVE of Ldn and Eli OFFUTT of Ffx to William CLINE of Ldn. Release of trust of Peter BEMARSDERFER for debt to Philip RHOAN alias RHAN, John BROOKBAKER alias BRUBACKER (now dec'd) using 100a. Wit: Chas. G. ESKRIDGE, Alfred A. ESKRIDGE, Roberdeau ANNIN. Delv. to CLINE 19 Sep 1826.

3L:398 Date: 24 Feb 1826 RtCt: 9 Mar 1826
John BOOTH of Jefferson Co Indiana (by his agent John BOOTH) to Philip KIST of Ldn. B/S of 2a (part of John MULL's inheritance from father David MULL but admitted BOOTH had a superior title) adj Catherine MULL. Delv. pr order 31 Aug 1832.

3L:400 Date: 10 Mar 1826 RtCt: 11 Mar 1826
Casper JOHNSON of Ldn to Benjamin JOHNS(T)ON of Ldn. BoS of negro man Henly abt 30y old, farm animals, farm and household items, crops. Wit: Edw'd. KELLY, John SWART, Robert P. SWART.

3L:401 Date: 13 Mar 1826 RtCt: 13 Mar 1826
Joseph HAWKINS, John SIMPSON, Jesse McVEIGH and John A. BINNS. Bond on HAWKINS as constable.

3L:402 Date: 15 Dec 1824 RtCt: 13 Mar 1826
Thomas LACEY and Patience LACEY (ch/o William LACEY dec'd and devisees of Thomas LACEY dec'd late of Ldn) of Belmont Co

Ohio at present in Wheeling, Ohio Co, Va to Edmund J. LEE Jr. of Wheeling Va. PoA for devises from Uncle Thomas LACEY dec'd.

3L:403   Date: 23 Dec 1825   RtCt: ___
Ludwell LEE. Commission to continue as Sheriff.

3L:402   Date: 13 Mar 1826   RtCt: 13 Mar 1826
Ludwell LEE, Aris BUCKNER, George LEE, Hugh ROGERS, Horrace LUCKETT and William THRIFT. Bond on LEE as Sheriff.

3L:404   Date: 13 Mar 1826   RtCt: 13 Mar 1826
Ludwell LEE, Aris BUCKNER, George LEE, Hugh ROGERS, Horrace LUCKETT and William THRIFT. Bond on LEE as Sheriff to collect poor rate.

3L:405   Date: 13 Mar 1826   RtCt: 13 Mar 1826
Ludwell LEE, Aris BUCKNER, George LEE, Hugh ROGERS, Horrace LUCKETT and William THRIFT. Bond on LEE as Sheriff to collect officers fees.

3M:001   Date: 28 Mar 1826   RtCt: 31 Mar 1826
Samuel CLAPHAM & wife Elizabeth of Ldn to Thomson F. MASON of DC and Richard H. HENDERSON of Ldn. Trust of all of estate and 1450a 'Eagles Rest', 300a formerly belonging to Walter BROOKES, 160a and mill on Goose Creek, 300a 'Fair Island' on the Potomac in MontMd, 100a in MontMd, 680a in Washington Co Md, 800a 'Chestnut Hill' mansion house and farm where he now lives, small 70a island in Potomac adj FredMd, slave men Bill, Shaver, Godfrey, James, Ben, Sibbey, Henry, Lewis, Bill, King and slave women Jane, Easter, Anny, Maria, Fanny, Edie, slave boys Philip, Elias, Madison, Bedford, Nathan, Frederick, Alfred, Charles, children Hiram, Daniel, Robert, Wilson, Flora, Henry, Mary, Tom, John and Elias. (Samuel's health declining and can not manage sale of estate and payment of debts). After deaths to be equally divided between nieces Betsey C. MASON w/o of Thomson F. MASON, Matilda R. PRICE, Virginia PRICE and Benjamin PRICE. Wit: Saml. C. ROSS, Mosses DOWDELL, Jno. J. MATHIAS. Delv. to HENDERSON 20 Apr 1826.

3M:008   Date: 7 Oct 1825   RtCt: 13 Feb 1826
Zorababel WELLS & wife El(l)izabeth of __ Ohio by attorney Samuel CLENDENING of Ldn to William CLENDENING of Ldn. B/S of ¾a in Hllb now in possession of Samuel CLENDENING (being 1/5th share of Ellizabeth's inheritance from father Saml. CLENDENING dec'd) adj __ MARMADUKE.

3M:009   Date: 10 Mar 1826   RtCt: 10 Mar 1826
Garret/Gerrard WINECUP of Ldn to William CAMPBELL of Ldn. Trust for debt to William using farm items. Wit: Joseph HAN, Thomas MORALLE, Henry CLAGGETT.

3M:010   Date: 31 Mar 1825   RtCt: 8 Aug 1825/13 Mar 1826
Martha HOLMES of Ldn to Henry O. CLAGETT of Ldn. B/S of 16a
on Beverdam adj James DEWAR (formerly Presly SAUNDERS),
William CARR, __ COE, Thomas BROWN (allotted to Martha from
George NIXON the elder dec'd). Wit: Francis DULIN, Nimrod BARR,
Saml. TRIPLETT. Delv. to CLAGGETT 23 Jan 1830.

3M:012   Date: 1 Oct 1826   RtCt: 13 Mar 1826
John EVANS and William EVANS of Ffx to William HUMMER of
Ldn. B/S of 14a nr line between Ldn and Ffx adj Mrs. LINDSEY. Wit:
Joseph SMITH, Racheal LATTIMORE, Thos. WILLIAMS, James
LATTIMORE, Thos. H. KERBY, Edmund CHICK, Wm. B. HAWOOD.
Delv. to Washington HUMMER 10 Dec 1827.

3M:013   Date: 21 Feb 1825   RtCt: 13 Mar 1826
William J. BRONAUGH (trustee of Gainer PIERCE) of Ldn to James
HOGE of Ldn. B/S of 87½a and 25a (default of trust).

3M:014   Date: 6 Feb 1826   RtCt: 13 Mar 1826
George TAVENER Jr. of Ldn to John CARR of Ldn. Trust for debt to
Joseph CALDWELL of Ky using lot in Wtfd (acquired by TAVENER
thru marriage with Sarah SMALLWOOD wd/o Leven SMALLWOOD
dec'd) (used in trust to Saml. M. EDWARDS for benefit of John
THOMAS). Delv. to CARR 19 Apr 1833.

3M:017   Date: 16 Mar 1826   RtCt: 13 Mar 1826
William H. BUTLER of Ldn to Henry MOFFETT of Ldn. Trust for debt
to Peter OAYTER of Ldn using farm animals, household items. Wit:
Saml. GILPIN, C. W. BUCKMASTER, Israel COMBS Jr.

3M:018   Date: 11 Mar 1826   RtCt: 13 Mar 1826
John BAKER of Ldn to David, Samuel, John Jr, Daniel, Margaret
and Nancy BAKER of Ldn. B/S to David (grain and crops), to
Samuel (cattle and farm items), to John Jr. (horse, farm items), to
Daniel (farm animals), to Margaret (farm animals, household items),
to Nancy (household items). Wit: Jesse EVANS, Amos HENRY,
Edward DOWLING, Ezekiel SHAMBLIN.

3M:020   Date: 23 Oct 1825   RtCt: 13 Mar 1826
Matthew CARPENTER & wife Harriot of Ldn to George W.
GRAYSON of Ldn. Trust for debt to Richard HALL of Hampshire Co
Va using 84½a on Beaverdam adj Benjamin GRAYSON, Abner
HUMPHREY. Wit: Benjamin GRAYSON, John W. GRAYSON. Delv.
pr order 22 Feb 1830.

3M:023   Date: 13 Dec 1825   RtCt: 13 Mar 1826
Commr Stacy TAYLOR to William SUMMERS. B/S of 1/10th part of
land of Thomas HUGHES dec'd which belonged to ch/o his son
Hugh HUGHES dec'd, subject to dower (13 Sep 1825 ct order in
case of Mary an infant agst John and Sarah HUGHES infants). Delv.
pr order 1 Jun 1827.

3M:024 Date: 6 Mar 1826 RtCt: 13 Mar 1826
George W. SEEVERS (Marshal of Sup. Co in Winchester Dist) to
Thomas DRAKE of Ldn. B/S of ¼a in Bloomfield adj Benjamin
GRAYSON and 1a in Bloomfield adj John RALPH, John G.
HUMPHREYS (from case of 5 Dec 1823 DRAKE agst Rosanna
SHARP).

3M:025 Date: 27 Dec 1825 RtCt: 14 Mar 1826
Ludwell LEE of Ldn to Eliza A. LEE of Ldn. B/S of 742a adj __
WHALEY, __ MUSE (trading for land in JeffVa). Delv. to Wilson C.
SELDEN Jr. pr order of E. A. LEE 5 Jul 1828.

3M:027 Date: 5 Dec 1825 RtCt: 14 Mar 1826
Benj'n. MITCHELL, Jno. CRAINE Jr., Peter JETT for self and as
Guardian of daughter Catherine (heirs & distributees of Col. Joseph
LANE with Admr. widow Katherine LANE). Release of estate of Col.
Leven POWELL dec'd (Burr POWELL acting Exor) of liabilities for
him as security on bonds to Katherine. Wit: Geo. C. POWELL, Jas.
CRAINE, Burr W. HARRISON.

3M:028 Date: 20 Dec 1823 RtCt: 11 Apr 1825/5 Apr 1826
William NOLAND & wife Catherine of Ldn to Richard VANPELT of
Ldn. B/S of ½a Lots #3 & #4 on Mercer St in Aldie. Wit: Mary B.
FONTAINE, Thomas J. NOLAND, William H. NOLAND. Delv. to
VANPELT 18 Apr 1826.

3M:029 Date: 21 Feb 1818 RtCt: 14 Mar 1826
Colin AULD of AlexDC to William NOLAND of Ldn. B/S of fee simple
estate nr Gum Spring held by John LEWIS Sr. under L/L of Charles
J. LOVE with LS lately purchased by NOLAND. Wit: John RAMSAY,
Peter HEWETT, Thomas NOLAND.

3M:031 Date: ___ 1826 RtCt: 15 Mar 1826
Solomon WENNER of Ldn to John WENNER of Ldn. B/S of 15a Lot
#9 in div. of land of William WENNER dec'd.

3M:033 Date: 27 Jun 1825 RtCt: 15 Mar 1826
Gustavus A. MORAN to James McCLAIN. Trust for debt to William
THRIFT (Admr of William MOREN dec'd) using slaves Philip and
Henry, horses, beds. Wit: George ELMORE, Nelson B. WILSON,
James WILSON. Delv. to THRIFT 22 Aug 1834.

3M:035 Date: 14 Mar 1826 RtCt: 15 Mar 1826
John G. HUMPHREY & wife Mary of Ldn to James JOHNSON of
Ldn. B/S of 2a on road to Bloomfield adj JOHNSON, Benjamin
GRAYSON, __ HUMPHREY. Wit: Benjamin GRAYSON, John W.
GRAYSON.

3M:037 Date: 28 Jan 1826 RtCt: 16 Mar 1826
Reuben TRIPLETT of Ldn to Price JACOBS of Ldn. B/S of land
allotted in div. of Reuben TRIPLETT dec'd. Delv. to JACOBS 8 Mar
1830.

3M:039   Date: 15 Nov 1825   RtCt: 17 Mar 1826
Joseph POSTON to James McILHANY. Trust for debt to Michael
FRYE using 103½a (cnvy/b John HOUGH Jr. to Leonard POSTEN
dec'd in Oct 1788).

3M:041   Date: 3 Oct 1825   RtCt: 23 Mar 1826
Jefferson C. THOMAS & wife Mary of Ldn to Elizabeth W. THOMAS
of Ldn. B/S of 143a adj Thomas JAMES, Widow E. CUNNARD. Wit:
John WHITE, Craven OSBURN. Delv. to T. R. CLENDENING pr
order 16 Nov 1859.

3M:043   Date: 2 Mar 1826   RtCt: 27 Mar 1826
William D. DRISH & wife Harriet of Ldn to John HAMMERLY of Ldn.
B/S of lot where DRISH resides (cnvy/b Mandley T. RUST and Eli
OFFUTT, Jun 1817) on King St in Lsbg adj Lewis P. W. BALCH,
McCABE's reps.

3M:045   Date: 2 Mar 1826   RtCt: 27 Mar 1826
John HAMMERLY & wife Jane of Ldn to William D. DRISH of Ldn.
B/S of ¼a lot (cnvy/b DRISH and part by John DRISH of William) on
W side of King St in Lsbg adj __ McCOWAT, __ FADELEY, Dr.
CLAGGETT. Wit: John McCORMICK, Saml. M. EDWARDS. Delv. to
DRISH 4 May 1826.

3M:047   Date: 2 Mar 1826   RtCt: 27 Mar 1826
William DRISH & wife Barbara of Ldn to John HAMMERLY of Ldn.
B/S of parts of Lots #19 & #20 on W side of King St in Lsbg (cnvy/b
John LITTLEJOHN, Jul 1793, DBk V:43). Wit: John McCORMICK,
Saml. M. EDWARDS.

3M:049   Date: 2 Mar 1826   RtCt: 27 Mar 1826
John HAMMERLY & wife Jane of Ldn to William DRISH of Ldn. B/S
(for natural life of DRISH & wife) of part of lot cnvy/b John DRISH &
wife in Dec 1809 (DBk LL:480), adj John DRISH, __ CORDELL.

3M:051   Date: 1 Mar 1826   RtCt: 29 Mar 1826
Amos GIBSON & wife Hannah of Ldn to Isaac NICHOLS Jr of Ldn.
B/S of 307½a adj Israel JANNEY. Wit: Charles B. HAMILTON,
Thomas ROGERS.

3M:053   Date: 27 Mar 1826   RtCt: 30 Mar 1826
Patty CARUTHERS wd/o Thomas CARUTHERS dec'd, John, Sally,
Nancy, William, Emily, Joseph and Anne CARUTHERS (infant ch/o
Thomas CARRUTHERS dec'd) and William HOLMS their Guardian
appt. 13 Feb 1826 of Ldn to James CARRUTHERS & wife Nancy of
Ldn. B/S of 76a Lot #3 in div. of James [Thomas?] CARUTHERS.
Wit: William CARR, James H. HAMILTON.

3M:056   Date: 27 Mar 1826   RtCt: 30 Mar 1826
James CARRUTHERS & wife Nancy of Ldn to Patty CARRUTHERS
wd/o Thos. CARRUTHERS dec'd, John, Sally, Nancy, William,
Emily, Joseph and Anne CARRUTHERS (infant ch/o Thomas

CARRUTHERS dec'd) and William HOLMS their Guardian of Ldn. B/S of 83a Lot #2 in div. Wit: William CARR, James H. HAMILTON.

3M:058 Date: 2 Jun 1824 RtCt: 30 Mar 1826
William PAXSON & wife Jane of Ldn to Amos HARVEY of Ldn. B/S of 3a with use of mill race (cnvy/b heirs of William JONES dec'd) adj John CAMPBELL, __ HOUGH. Wit: Robert BRADEN, Abiel JENNERS.

3M:060 Date: 28 Mar 1826 RtCt: 31 Mar 1826
Samuel C. ROSS of Ldn to Samuel DAWSON of Ldn. Trust for debt to Mrs. Elizabeth CLAPHAM for rent of farm where he lives using negro boy Lewis abt 14y old, boy James abt 10y old (both subject to mortgage to John BEATTY), animals, household items. Delv. to DAWSON 12 Jun 1826.

3M:063 Date: 3 Dec 1825 RtCt: 12 Dec 1825/5 Apr 1826
John McKNIGHT to Joseph TAYLOR and Vollentine V. PURSEL. Trust for debt to Lydia HEATON (Admr of Dr. James HEATON dec'd) using 12a adj Samuel PALMER Sr., Thomas JAMES and 1½a where McKNIGHT lives (prch/o sister Mary McKNIGHT) adj Thomas JAMES, Deborah McKNIGHT. Wit: Towns'd HEATON. Delv. to C. C. McINTYRE 18 Mar 1840.

3M:066 Date: 24 Mar 1826 RtCt: 6 Apr 1826
John ALT & wife Polly of Ldn to Joshua PEUSEY of Ldn. B/S of 77a (Lot #5 in div. of father William ALT dec'd). Wit: Saml. HOUGH, Geo. W. SHAWEN. Delv. to __ 20 Feb 1834.

3M:068 Date: 31 Jan 1825 RtCt: 8 Apr 1826
Edward HAMMATT of Ldn to Thomas MORALLEE of Ldn. B/S of lot on N side of Market St in Lsbg (from trust of Jan 1824, DBk GGG:322, of John CRIDLER & wife Ellizabeth).

3M:070 Date: 25 Mar 1826 RtCt: 8 Apr 1826
Thomas MORALLEE of Ldn to brother Michael MORALLEE of Ldn. B/S of ½ of lot on N side of Market St in Lsbg where Arthur GARNER now resides, (see above land).

3M:071 Date: 5 Mar 1826 RtCt: 8 Apr 1826
Thomas MORALLEE and Michael MORALLEE. Agreement – joint purchasers of above lot, both to get ½ of rent.

3M:072 Date: 14 Dec 1825 RtCt: 8 Apr 1826
Thomas MORALLE (trustee of Simon SMALE) of Ldn to James McDONOUGH of Ldn. B/S of W half of ½a on Market St in Lsbg (trust from John CRIDLER & wife Ellizabeth for debt to SMALE, Dec 1819, DBk BBB:147).

3M:074 Date: 5 Apr 1825 RtCt: 8 Apr 1826
James McDONOUGH & wife Kezia of Ldn to George RICHARDS of Ldn. Trust for debt to Simon SMALE using above lot. Wit: John McCORMICK, James H. HAMILTON.

3M:077 Date: 1 Apr 1826 RtCt: 10 Apr 1826
James CURRELL of Ldn to Notley C. WILLIAMS and John J.
CURRELL. BoS for negro male Kendall, farm animals, farm and
household items, crops. Wit: Thomas G. HUMPHREY, William F.
ADAMS.

3M:078 Date: 8 Apr 1826 RtCt: 10 Apr 1826
Yeoman Henry PLA(I)STER of Ldn to boot & shoemaker Thomas
JONES of Union. B/S of ¼a in Union now occupied by JONES (Lot
#6 in div. of James REED dec'd) adj Isaac BROWN, James REED,
lot owned by Thornton WALKER & occupied by John PAYNE,
Edmund LOVETT. Wit: Henery HUTCHISON, James SUTHARD,
Samuel TORRYSON.

3M:080 Date: 3 Apr 1826 RtCt: 10 Apr 1826
Susannah SMITH of Ldn to son Jacob SMITH of Ldn. B/S of 98¾a
where she now resides on Dutchman Run and 2a on Dutchman run
adj __ RHORBACK and 25a on E side of Short Hill adj Henery
PLETCHER, Peter RIDENBAUGH. Delv. to SMITH 20 Jul 1826.

3M:082 Date: 12 May 1824 RtCt: 10 Apr 1826
Thomas KIDWELL & wife Elizabeth of Ldn to Absalom
VANVACTER of Ldn. B/S of 2a on W side of Short Hill (cnvy/b John
DEMORY 23 Aug 1823). Wit: Ebenezer GRUBB, John WHITE. Delv.
to VANVACTER 7 Oct 1826.

3M:084 Date: 6 May 1825 RtCt: 10 Apr 1826
H. B. POWELL to John N. T. G. E. KEENE. Release of trust of Jun
1823 for John BOYD using houses & lots in Union.

3M:085 Date: 12 Jun 1822 RtCt: 11 Apr 1826
William H. HANDY of Fqr (late of Ldn) to John WYNN & wife
Susannah of Ldn. Release of trust for debt to Joseph HAINS.

3M:087 Date: 4 Mar 1826 RtCt: 11 Apr 1826
Gideon HOUSEHOLDER & wife Julia Ann of Ldn to Jacob ARNOLD
of Ldn. B/S of 4a adj David AXLINE. Wit: Noble S. BRADEN, Geo.
W. SHAWEN. Delv. to ARNOLD 2 Oct 1827.

3M:090 Date: ___ 1826 RtCt: 11 Apr 1826
Evelyn B. DOUGLAS and George LEE of Ldn to Jeremiah
CULLISON of Ldn. B/S of 216¼a (leased by Thomas Ludwell LEE
to Thomas WATSON in 1773 and transferred to Jeremiah
CULLISON and by will of Jeremiah CULLISON dec'd to said
Jeremiah) between Goose Creek and Broad run. Wit: Tasker C.
QUINLAN, H. PEARS, Jno. J. MATHIAS. Delv. to CULLISON 8 Jun
1826.

3M:092 Date: 11 Apr 1826 RtCt: 11 Apr 1826
Jeremiah CULLISON of Ldn to George LEE of Ldn. B/S of 18a on
Little Beverdam (part of land leased by Thomas Ludwell LEE to
Thomas WATSON in 1773, as above).

3M:093   Date: 5 Aug 1825   RtCt: 11 Apr 1826
Edward CUNNARD of Ldn to Durett LONG of JeffVa. B/S of 2a on Kittocton Creek in gap of Short Hill (cnvy/b Mahlon HOUGH, Feb 1805). Gives very small plat. Wit: Nathan EDMONDS, Christian MILLER, John CONARD.

3M:095   Date: 25 Sep 1824   RtCt: 10 Apr 1826
Mathias SMITLEY of Ldn to Noble S. BRADEN of Ldn. Trust for debt to Robert BRADEN using 30a (has L/L held of fee simple owned by R. BRADEN) adj Adam MILLER, David AXLINE. Wit: David SHAWEN, William STEER, L. W. P. HIXON, D. CONARD.

3M:098   Date: 2 May 1826   RtCt: 2 May 1826
Samuel A. TILLETT to Tasker C. QUINLAN. Release of trust. Delv. to QUINLAN 16 May 1826.

3M:098   Date: 17 Jan 1826   RtCt: 11 Apr 1826
John S. MARLOW & wife Ann of Ldn to John VINSEL of Ldn. B/S of 271a adj Capt. EVERHART. Wit: Ebenezer GRUBB, Geo. W. SHAWEN. Delv. to VINSELL 14 Jun 1827.

3M:100   Date: 11 Apr 1826   RtCt: 11 Apr 1826
William Alexander POWELL, C. POWELL and Wm. A. POWELL (Exor of Cuthbert J. POWELL Jr. dec'd), John Levin POWELL and Alfred H. POWELL (ch/o of Leven POWELL Jr.) to Burr POWELL. B/S of 9 10/16[th]a (cnvy/b Leven POWELL to Leven POWELL Jr., Oct 1806) on Federal St. Delv. to Wm. O. CHILTON pr order 24 Sep 1827.

3M:102   Date: 10 Nov 1825   RtCt: 12 Apr 1826
Joseph Hains & wife Maria to Given HANDY wd/o John HANDY dec'd. B/S of int. in estate of Eli Heaton HANDY dec'd (Lot #1 in div. of estate of John HANDY dec'd) on N side of Goose Creek. Wit: William BRONAUGH, Francis W. LUCKETT.

3M:104   Date: 10 Sep 1825   RtCt: 12 Apr 1826
William H. HANDY to Given HANDY wd/o John HANDY dec'd). B/S of int. in estate of Eli Heaton HANDY dec'd (br/o William H.) on N side of Goose Creek (Lot #1 in div. of estate of John HANDY dec'd).

3M:106   Date: 16 Mar 1826   RtCt: 12 Apr 1826
Evylen Byrd DOUGLAS, George LEE and Maria Carter LEE of Ldn to Charles BINNS. Release of negro Thomas alias Thomas JACKSON sold to BINNS by Pattrick H. DOUGLAS now dec'd. Wit: Tasker C. QUINLAN, Thomas A. MOORE. Delv. to BINNS 9 Jun 1830.

3M:107   Date: 17 Apr 1826   RtCt: 18 Apr 1826
Simon SMALE of Ldn to dau Mary SMALE of Ldn. B/S of lot on Market St. (leased from John SHAW dec'd late of Ldn, May 1822, DBk EEE:228). Delv. to P. LOTT husband of Mary SMALE 6 Apr 1835.

3M:109   Date: 19 Apr 1826   RtCt: 19 Apr 1826
Leonard THOMAS & wife Ellisabeth of Ldn to Jacob EVERHART of Ldn. Trust for debt to Benjamin GRUBB, George KAUBRICH and Joseph MILLER using 2a adj William WRIGHT, road from Wtfd to Nolands Ferry. Wit: Ebenezer GRUBB, Noble S. BRADEN. Delv. to EVERHART 8 Feb 1828.

3M:112   Date: 31 Mar 1826   RtCt: 20 Apr 1826
James H. HAMILTON to Alexander LAWRENCE. Trust for debt to John McCORMICK, Daniel LOVETT and George S. HOUGH using household items, und. int. in supposed legacy in Cochecton, Ohio.

3M:115   Date: 4 Mar 1826   RtCt: 12 Apr 1826
John Gill WATT & wife Dewanner of Lsbg to John ROSE. Trust for debt to Anne A. LAFFERTY using lot on S side of Cornwall St in Lsbg (cnvy/b George SHEID, DBk EEE:237). Wit: Thomas SANDERS, John H. McCABE. Delv. to Saml. KENNERLY Admr. 9 Oct 1835.

3M:117   Date: 22 Apr 1826   RtCt: 22 Apr 1826
Charles G. EDWARDS & wife Deborah of Ldn to William PAXSON Sr. of Ldn. B/S of 4a Lot #2 in Wtfd adj Joseph TALBOTT. Wit: Samuel HOUGH, Noble S. BRADEN. Delv. pr order 12 Jun 1830.

3M:119   Date: 23 Apr 1822   RtCt: 24 Apr 1826
Warner W. THROCKMORTON of FredVa to Mordecai THROCKMORTON & wife Sarah McCarty of Ldn. Release of trust on 400a for debt to Warner WASHINGTON. Wit: W. H. FOOTE, George TAYLOR.

3M:122   Date: 21 Apr 1826   RtCt: 25 Apr 1826
Peter BOGGESS of Ldn to Daniel STONE of Ldn. Trust for debt to John SCHOOLEY using lot where he now lives in Wtfd contiguous to the Wtfd Bridge (cnvy/b Sandford EDMONDS). Delv. to SCHOOLEY 1 Jul 1834.

3M:124   Date: 11 Jun 1822   RtCt: 14 Jan 1826
Francis STRIBLING Jr. of Ldn and James HILL of Ldn. Agreement – rent of property for 1 year in exchange for 2/5ths of crops. Wit: Thos. STEPHENS.

3M:126   Date: 22 Apr 1826   RtCt: 29 Apr 1826
Tasco/Tasker C. QUINLAN of Ldn to Samuel TILLETT of Ldn. B/S of 287a (inherited from father) on Goose Creek adj Col. MERCER. Delv. pr order 20 Jan 1838.

3M:128   Date: 8 May 1826   RtCt: 1 May 1826
William CHILTON. BoS to Burr POWELL, Cuthbert POWELL and Alfred H. POWELL (trustees of Sarah H. CHILTON) for household items cnvy/b trust to Lloyd NOLAND for benefit of Burr & Cuthbert POWELL property tax was taken by valuation of Col. Wm. ELLZEY, Dr. SELDEN and Dr. CLAGGET, slaves conveyed in trust to NOLAND (Jess, Matilda, Maria & children Louis & Fenton, Jane)

and to Adam R. ALEXANDER (slaves Alfred, Harriett and Wilson). Were previously lost before recording.

3M:129   Date: 3 May 1826   RtCt: 3 May 1826
Richard H. HENDERSON to Mary LUTZ. A/L for term of 999y - house & lot on King St in Lsbg late prop. of estate of Joseph BEARD dec'd (from execution in Sup Ct of Tiffany WYMAN &co agt Joseph BEARD's Admr) purchased at sale by D. Shff Wm. THRIFT.

3M:130   Date: 13 Apr 1826   RtCt: May 1826
John Gill WATT & wife Dewanner of Ldn to Christopher FRYE now of Baltimore Co Md. B/S of 20a in fee simple (cnvy/b Peter BENEDUM, May 1822, DBk FFF:170) and 22a under L/L and 4a adj Martin KITZMILLER, Robert ROBERTS (DBk EEE:321) and 1a under LS adj the last mt. lot of 7a (DBk GGG:144) and 6a (DBk JJJ:287) together abt 58a. Delv. to FRYE 25 Jan 1831.

3M:133   Date: 10 Apr 1826   RtCt: 4 May 1826
Jas. L. MARTIN of Ldn to John Gill WATT of Ldn. Release of trust of Jan 1824 for debt to Christopher FRYE.

3M:135   Date: 12 Nov 1803   RtCt: 9 Jan 1804/10 Apr 1826
Ferdinando FAIRFAX of JeffVa to Susanna SMITH of Ldn. B/S of 25a in Piedmont adj Henery PLETCHER, Peter RIDENBAUGH. Wit: John D. ORR, William H. HARDING, Abiel JENNERS, J. SAUNDERS, John H. CANBY, Alexander YOUNG.

3M:136   Date: 7 Jan 1826   RtCt: 10 Apr 1826
Members of the Leesburg Friendship Fire Co: Everit SAUNDERS, Samuel M. BOSS, Thomas SAUNDERS, Edward HAMMATT, William H. JACOBS, Thomas BIRKBY, John MURRAY, Joshua RILEY, George HEAD, John H. McCABE, Richard H. LEE, John H. MONROE, James L. MARTIN, Lewis BEARD, Samuel CARR, Thomas RUSSELL, Isaac HAINES, John J. HARDING, Simon SMALE, Enos WILDMAN, James THOMAS, Jacob FADELY, George RICHARDS, Sampson BLINCOE, Robert A. LACEY, Samuel HAMMATT, William SEEDERS, James GILMORE, Samuel GILPIN, William JENNERS, Gunnell SAUNDERS, Edwin A. STOVER, Thomas WILLIAMS, Thomas F. TEBBS, Caleb C. SUTHERLAND, James SINCLAIR, Giles HAMMATT, Robert McINTYRE, James SURGHNOR, Benjamin DAWES, John MARTIN, Henson SIMPSON, William L. POWELL, Henery PEERS, John JANNEY, Jacob TOWNER, Nicholas KLINE, John MORRIS, William W. HAMMONTREE, John TOWNER, Benjamin SHRIEVE Jr., John J. MATHIAS, Wilson DRISH, Tasker C. QUINLAN, Robert MATHIAS, Roberdeau ANNIN.

3M:137   Date: 8 May 1826   RtCt: 8 May 1826
John BOYD, John BRADY and Amos FERGUSON. Bond on BOYD as constable.

3M:138   Date: 13 Mar 1826   RtCt: 8 May 1826
David SMITH and Daniel JANNEY (trustees) and Bernard TAYLOR
of Ldn to Abraham SKILLMAN of Ldn. Release of trust of Aug 1817
for debt to Bernard TAYLOR using 269a (DBk VV:134).

3M:140   Date: 8 May 1826   RtCt: 8 May 1826
Lewis GRIGGSBY to Levi Gregg EWERS. Release of trust of Jan
1816 by Samuel GREGG (sold to EWERS) for debt to John and
Thomas GREGG (Exors of John GREGG dec'd) on 113a (DBk
TT:416).

3M:142   Date: 1 Apr 1826   RtCt: 8 May 1826
Bernard TAYLOR & wife Sarah of Ldn to Abraham SKILLMAN of
Ldn. B/S of 3a and __ BROWN, __ TOMLINSON. Wit: Charles B.
HAMILTON, Thomas ROGERS.

3M:143   Date: 4 Jun 1825   RtCt: 8 May 1826
Daniel COCKERILL & wife Esther of Ldn to Benjamin BRADFIELD
of Ldn. B/S of 1a adj BRADFIELD.

3M:145   Date: 28 Apr 1826   RtCt: 8 May 1826
Thomas PHILIPS (Exor of James MOORE dec'd) of Ldn to Isaac
WALKER of Ldn. B/S of 185a (prch/o George JANNEY, Nov 1817)
adj Sandford RAMEY, Pattrick McGAVICK. Delv. to WALKER 31
May 1831.

3M:147   Date: 1 Apr 1825   RtCt: 8 May 1826
Abraham SKILLMAN of Ldn to Daniel JANNEY and Henery S.
TAYLOR of Ldn. Trust for debt to George GRIMES using 150a
(cnvy/b Bernard TAYLOR, Aug 1817) nr N. Fork Meeting house on
Long Branch. Delv. to Jas. L. HAMILTON 10 Mar 1828.

3M:149   Date: 8 May 1825   RtCt: 9 May 1826
Peyton COOK of Warner Co Ky to Robert A. LACEY of Ldn. B/S of
int. (1/6th as heir of John LACEY dec'd) in 400a in Mann Co Ky on
Ohio River and Sixteen Mile Creek.(cnvy/b Charles Fenton
MERCER in July 1816 to Maria Elizabeth COOKE w/o William
COOKE, Matilda Payne BRISCOE w/o Alexander M. BRISCOE,
Mary A. LACEY, Robt. A. LACEY, Westwood LACEY, John LACEY
and Catherine LACEY heirs of Israel LACEY).

3M:151   Date: 17 Aug 1825   RtCt: 9 May 1826
John BAKER & wife Sarah of Ldn to Ebenezer GRUBB, Peter
DEMORY and John CUNNARD of Ldn. B/S of 128a Osburne Lott on
W side of Short Hill (prch/o Jacob COST) and 114a Morris' Lott and
40a Wood Lott and 70a on W side of Short Hill and 11a nr Dawson's
Spring and ¼a adj Thomas DAVIS, Wm. GRUBB.

3M:153   Date: 7 Dec 1826   RtCt: 9 May 1826
William NOLAND & wife Catherine. CoE for sale in Dec 1823.

3M:154   Date: 12 May 1826   RtCt: 12 May 1826
Saml. M. EDWARDS (trustee of William H. HANDY & wife Elleanor) of Ldn to Richard H. HENDERSON of Ldn. B/S of 147¼a (from trust of Dec 1820, DBk DDD:120).

3M:156   Date: 28 May 1825   RtCt: 16 May 1826
Henery CLAGGETT & wife Julia of Ldn to Richard H. LEE of Ldn. B/S of 33a on W side of main road from Lsbg to Aldie adj __ MEADE, __ TAYLOR. Delv. to R. J. TAYLOR pr order 28 Apr 1832.

3M:157   Date: 10 Jan 1826   RtCt: 17 May 1826
Samuel M. EDWARDS & wife Ann of Ldn to Colin AULD of AlexDC. B/S of Lot #6 with stone house between Loudoun and Royal Sts in Lsbg (cnvy/b AULD, Apr 1818, DBk WW:146). Wit: John H. McCABE, Thomas SANDERS. Delv. to AULD 4 Sep 1829.

3M:159   Date: 19 May 1826   RtCt: 19 May 1826
Robert A. LACEY of Ldn to George Mason CHICHESTER of Ldn. B/S of all int. in Big Spring Mill as heir at law of his brother Armistead John LACEY dec'd (was sold in Oct 1823 to CHICHESTER but was miscalculated). Delv. to CHICHESTER 8 Dec 1827.

3M:161   Date: 17 May 1826   RtCt: 20 May 1826
William DERRY & wife Barbara of Ldn to John DEMORY of Ldn. B/S of 1a between Blue Ridge and Short Hill adj DEMORY. Wit: Ebenezer GRUBB, John J. MATHIAS.

3M:163   Date: 22 May 1826   RtCt: 22 May 1826
Robert A. LACEY of Ldn to Enos WILDMAN of Ldn. B/S of int. (either by purchase or inheritance) in brick house and lot on King & Royal Sts in Lsbg (share as heir of brother Armistead John LACEY dec'd).

3M:164   Date: 12 Dec 1825   RtCt: 25 May 1826
Samuel PURSELL Jr. of Ldn to Stacy TAYLOR and Thomas GREGG of Ldn. Trust for debt to Valentine N. PURCELL using Lot #1 in div. of real estate of Thomas PURCEL dec'd allotted to widow as dower in Hllb. Wit :John E. PARMER, John POTTER, John BIRKITT. Delv. to V. PURCELL 28 Jun 1827.

3M:167   Date: 2 Apr 1825   RtCt: 23 May 1826
Casper EVERHART & wife Mary of Ldn to Nelson EVERHART of Ldn. B/S of 1a between Short Hill and Blue Ridge Mt. adj John WOLF, Philip DERRY. Wit: John WHITE, Craven OSBURNE. Delv. to Nelson EVERHART 17 Apr 1838.

3M:168   Date: 22 Oct 1825   RtCt: 27 May 1826
Anthony SLATER & wife Susannah of Muskingum Co Ohio to George SLATER of Ldn. B/S of 23a (Lot #8 in div. of real estate of John SLATER dec'd). Wit: John HAMILTON, George W. SHAWEN. Delv. pr order 29 Jul 1831.

3M:171   Date: 4 Mar 1826   RtCt: 27 Mar 1826
George RICKARD & wife Syvilla of Ldn to Mary HICKMAN of Ldn.
B/S of 4a (prch/o John BOWSET heir of Susannah
HOUSEHOLDER dec'd). Wit: Geo. W. SHAWEN, Noble S.
BRADEN. Delv. pr order __.

3M:172   Date: 8 Oct 1825   RtCt: 29 May 1826
William CARR & wife Mary of Ldn to John J. MATHIAS of Ldn. B/S
of 2a in E addition of Lsbg on S side of Market St (2 lots prch/o Ann
TAYLOR dec'd and Exors of George CARTER dec'd, lot prch/o Wm.
TALORE [TAYLOR], DBk II:59). Wit: Thomas SANDERS, John H.
McCABE. Delv. to MATHIAS 5 Apr 1833.

3M:175   Date: 18 Feb 1823   RtCt: 1 Jun 1826
John C. Handy of Ldn to John BALL of Ldn. B/S of 2 lots in Wtfd
(cnvy/b Joseph P. THOMAS) – one with tavern and stone house adj
Robert BRADEN and the other with stable adj Lewis KLEIN, Robert
WHITE.

3M:176   Date: 7 Nov 1825   RtCt: 1 Jun 1826
John SHEPHERD of Ldn to John A. BINNS of Ldn. Trust for debt to
William D. DRISH using lot on Cornwall St in Lsbg cnvy/b DRISH.
Taken out by Jno. A. BINNS and not examined.

3M:178   Date: 29 Apr 1826   RtCt: 5 Jun 1826
Isaac WALKER & wife Susan of Ldn to Joseph BOND and Jesse
GOVER of Ldn. Trust for debt to Thomas PHILLIPS (Exor of James
MOORE dec'd) using 185a adj Sandford RAMEY, Pattrick
McGAVACK. Delv. to WALKER 31 Mar 1829.

3M:181   Date: 25 Feb 1826   RtCt: 5 Jun 1826
Jasper EVERHART & wife Mary of Ldn to Adam EVANS of Ldn. B/S
of 2a adj John CONRAD. Wit: John WHITE, Craven OSBURNE.
Delv. to EVANS 29 Aug 1826.

3M:183   Date: 11 Nov 1825   RtCt: 5 Jun 1826
Jesse BURSON of Ldn to John BROWN of Ldn. Trust for debt to
David E. BROWN, James BROWN, Cyrus BURSON, Isaac BROWN
using farm animals, crops, all of household.

3M:184   Date: 30 May 1826   RtCt: 5 Jun 1826
Bernard S. DUFFY of FredVa to Hannah BROWN of Muskingum Co
Ohio. B/S of int. in 112a nr Scotland Mills (from William BROWN
dec'd late of Ldn to Hannah during her life then part to Charles
McKNIGHT of Ldn which he sold to DUFFY).

3M:185   Date: 14 Jun 1826   RtCt: 14 Jun 1826
John MILTABARGAR. Report on alien – born Wittenburg Co,
Germany, age 37y, allegiance to King of Prussia, emigrated from
Wittenberg Co, intends to reside in Loudoun Co.

3M:186   Date: 29 May 1826   RtCt: 7 Jun 1826
Thomas PHILIPS (Exor of James MOORE dec'd) of Ldn to Israel
MYERS and William MYERS of Ldn. B/S of 5a adj Joseph WOOD,

John WORSLEY, Isaac E. STEER. Delv. to Israel MYRES 15 Oct 1827.

3M:187   Date: 8 Jun 1826   RtCt: 8 Jun 1826
William VICKERS to Wm. RICHARD. Trust for debt to Jacob SILCOTT using 100a adj Edw'd HALL, Jno. G. HUMPHREY and 31a adj Edward CARTY, Goose Creek and 1a on S side of Millville adj Thornton WALKER, Geo. JANNEY and strip of land from 6-8a adj VICKERS, Hiram SEATON and strip of land adj SEATON, WORNELL & ANDERSON and 3 shares of stock in Snickers Gap Turnpike Road. Wit: B. WEEKS, Enos WILDMAN, Roberdeau ANNIN, William J. JONES. Delv. to the order of SILCOTT.

3M:190   Date: 8 Jun 1826   RtCt: 8 Jun 1826
John S. PEARCE & wife Jane of Ldn to Henery MILLHOLLEN of Ldn. B/S of part of tract leased from P. CAVIN for 999 years to Leonard THOMAS dec'd (cnvy/b Ann THOMAS d/o Leonard, Oct 1824, DBk JJJ:55, Lot #3 in div.). Wit: Jno. A. BINNS, Wilson C. SELDEN, Jno. McCORMICK.

3M:191   Date: 14 Oct 1825   RtCt: 8 Jun 1826
Amos GIBSON & wife Hannah, Elisha JANNEY & wife Mary late GIBSON, John FLETCHER for himself and his heirs by former wife Tacy P. formerly GIBSON representing int. of Israel GIBSON in estate of his father which he surrendered for the benefit of his creditors who together with Mahlon GIBSON were next heirs at law to Emily Jackson BROWN dec'd to Mahlon GIBSON. B/S of all int. in estate of Emily Jackson BROWN and her share in real estate of father John GIBSON dec'd. Wit: Craven OSBURNE, John WHITE.

3M:193   Date: 9 Feb 1826   RtCt: 8 Jun 1826
Elizabeth GIBSON wd/o John GIBSON dec'd late of Ldn to Thos. W. SMITH. Trust for debt to Mahlon GIBSON for advances toward settling up her Guardianship as Guardian of Mahlon and other ch/o John GIBSON dec'd using her dower of personal items.

3M:195   Date: 8 Jun 1826   RtCt: 8 Jun 1826
William VICKERS (insolvent debtor) of Ldn to Shff Ludwell LEE. B/S of 100a where VICKERS resides (bought of Enos MONTEITH subject to trust to Gourley REEDER for benefit of Samuel & Joseph HATCHER) and adj 2a and 80a on W side of 1st lot and 31a on Goose Creek subject to trust and 15½a adj William BENTON and several lots in Millville subject to trusts and 80a adj John HUMPHREY, Samuel DUNKIN and several other lots.

3M:197   Date: 6 Jun 1826   RtCt: 10 Jun 1826
Portia HODGSON of AlexDC to Robert J. TAYLOR of AlexDC. Trust for debt to Bank of Alexandria using 1262a on Bull Run purchased by William LEE Esqr of Greenspring dec'd from John PAGE Oct 1787 and devised to dau Portia and 2187a nr Snickers Gap (assigned Portia from estate of her brother William Ludwell LEE dec'd) and slaves Reuben, Higland, and Jim, Criss, Sally and

children Tom, Charles and Mary Alsey and her children Charlotte, Mosses and Jane Kitty and her children John and an infant. Delv. pr order 11 Mar 1828.

3M:201   Date: 12 Jun 1826   RtCt: 12 Jun 1826
James L. HAMILTON. Oath as Lt. in Co of Artillary Va. Militia of Loudoun Co.

3M:201   Date: 23 May 1826   RtCt: 12 Jun 1826
Mason POULTON. Oath as Lt. in Co of Artillary Va. Militia of Loudoun Co.

3M:201   Date: 9 Mar 1826   RtCt: 9 May/12 Jun 1826
Sarah ROZELL, Stephen G. ROZELL, Sarah DONOHOE, Phebe ROZELL, Stephen W. ROZELL, Nancy ROZELL (heirs and reps. of Stephen C. ROZELL). DoE if they remove within five months from date and not to return to Va – black man Samuel above 45y old and wife Betty also above 45y old. Wit: Thornton WALKER, Wm. WHITE, Michael LYNN, Benjamin WALKER.

3M:202   Date: 12 Jun 1826   RtCt: 12 Jun 1826
Lewis GRIGSBY, Arthur ORRISON and William POLEN. Bond on GRIGBSY as constable.

3M:203   Date: 7 Jun 1826   RtCt: 13 Jun 1826
William SHRIEVE. Certificate of qualification as Ensign in 57th Reg 6th Brig 2nd Div Va Militia. Delv. to SHRIEVE 8 Dec 1826.

3M:203   Date: 22 Dec 1823   RtCt: 18 Dec 1824/13 Jun 1826
Anna ROZELL to Sarah ROZELL, Stephen G. ROZELL, Sarah DONOHOE, Phebe ROZELL, Stephen W. ROZELL and Nancy ROZELL (heirs and reps. of Stephen C. ROZELL dec'd h/o Anna). Assigns her int. in slaves Jacob, Daniel, Benjamin, Kezziah, Robert, James, Amy, Fanny, Susannah, Delilah, Rhoda, Elizabeth, Sarah Ann, Washington, Margaret Ann, Lydia Phebe.

3M:204   Date: 14 Jun 1826   RtCt: 14 Jun 1826
George RICHARDS and John ROSE to President of Literary Fund. Bond on RICHARDS as treasurer.

3M:204   Date: 14 Jun 1826   RtCt: 14 Jun 1826
George RICHARDSON, J. B. OVERFIELD and William BRADFIELD. Bond on RICHARDSON as constable.

3M:206   Date: 15 Apr 1826   RtCt: 13 Jun 1826
Hugh FULTON dec'd. Division – widow's dower (44½a) to Susannah FULTON; Lot #1 (8½a) & Lot #11 (8a) to Nathaniel WRIGHT & wife Mary; Lot #2 (5½a) & Lot #12 (6a) to David FULTON; Lot #3 (15a) to Rachael MADDISON late FULTON; Lot #4 (11a) to Ellizabeth JACOBS late FULTON; Lot #5 (13½a) to Margaret FULTON; Lot #6 (13¾a) to James FULTON; Lot #7 (13¼a) to Rebecca COX late FULTON; Lot #8 (16¾a) allotted to William FULTON; Lot #9 (14½a) to Catherine CANE; Lot #10 (14½a) to Martha THOMAS late

FULTON. Divisors: Aaron SANDERS, William BROWN, Philip HEATER.

3M:211   Date: 7 Jul 1826   RtCt: 10 Jul 1826
James McDANIEL. Certificate of qualification as Ensign of 56th Reg 6th Brig 2nd Div Va Militia.

3M:211   Date: 19 May 1826   RtCt: 12 Jun 1826
William DERY of Ldn to Peter TEMERY/DEMORY of Ldn. Trust for debt to John NISEWANGER of Ldn using 87a where DERY lives adj John DEMORY, John CUNNARD, Philip GROVES, John NISWANGER, Absalom VANVACTER, Mathias PRINCE. Delv. to P. DEMORY 13 Aug 1827.

3M:213   Date: ___ 1826   RtCt: 12 Jun 1826
Jesse HOGE of Ldn to Joseph GORE of Ldn. Release of trust for debt to Isaac NICHOLS Jr., William PIGGOTT and William HOGE (Exors of Samuel NICHOLS dec'd) and Isaac NICHOLS Sr.

3M:215   Date: 1 Jun 1826   RtCt: 12 Jun 1826
James JOHNSON of Ldn to John SMARR of Ldn. B/S of 33a (Lot #4 in div. of real estate of father John JOHNSON dec'd) on 'big branch' of Goose Creek on Turnpike road adj Dennis McCARTY.

3M:216   Date: 12 Jun 1826   RtCt: 12 Jun 1826
Craven OSBURNE of Ldn. DoE for negro slave Isaiah BUCKNER abt 26y old after 1 Oct next. Wit: Saml. M. EDWARDS, Bernard TAYLOR, William NICHOLS.

3M:217   Date: 9 Apr 1825   RtCt: 12 Jun 1826
Commr Alexander S. TIDBALL (suit of Isaac BAKER and Joseph TIDBALL agst John Van BUSKIRK of 2 Dec 1823 in Winchester) to Isaac BAKER and Joseph TIDBALL of FredVa. B/S of mortgaged property called 'Ball's Mill'.

3M:218   Date: 12 Jun 1826   RtCt: 12 Jun 1826
Joshua OSBURNE of Ldn. DoE negro woman Delila abt 24y old and her 3 children Elija abt 7y old, Mary Ann abt 5y old and Maria Jane abt 2y old. Wit: Saml. M. EDWARDS, Bernard TAYLOR, William NICHOLS.

3M:219   Date: 1 Jun 1826   RtCt: 12 Jun 1826
John EVERHART & wife Sarah of Ldn to John WENNER and John GEORGE of Ldn. Trust for debt to Henry RUSE with Frederick SLATES as security using 9a.

3M:221   Date: 10 Jun 1826   RtCt: 12 Jun 1826
Joseph B. FOX & wife Amanda of Ldn to John JONES of Ldn. B/S of 2 rood lot in Hllb. Wit: Craven OSBURNE, John WHITE. Delv. to JONES 14 Jan 1828.

3M:222   Date: 15 Oct 1825   RtCt: 12 Jun 1826
Edmund SMITH & wife Elizabeth of FredVa to William ELGIN of Ldn. B/S of 1½a (cnvy/b George PELTER) with house in Aldie adj Lewis M. SMITH, Lewis BERKLEY. Wit: John BELL, Geo. REED.

3M:224 Date: 18 Mar 1826 RtCt: 12 Jun 1826
Sidnor/Sydnah WILLIAMS of Ldn to brother John WILLIAMS of Ldn.
B/S of 97a (from div. of father Enos WILLIAMS dec'd) on W side of
Catockton Creek adj Adam HOUSEHOLDER, __ BAKER,
__RAMEY. Delv. to John WILLIAMS 24 Jun 1831.

3M:226 Date: 12 Jun 1826 RtCt: 12 Jun 1826
Joseph TAVENER and Jonah TAVENER (Exors of George
TAVENER dec'd) of Ldn to Richard TAVENER of Ldn. B/S of 156a
adj George TAVENER Jr.

3M:228 Date: 30 Jan 1826 RtCt: 12 Jun 1826
William J. BRONAUGH (trustee of Gainer PIERCE) to James
HOGE. B/S of 10¼a and 1a (in trust for debt to HOGE).

3M:229 Date: 1 May 1826 RtCt: 12 Jun 1826
John W. TYLER to Nathaniel TYLER. Trust for benefit of Margaret
TEBBS w/o Foushee TEBBS using negro woman Anne & her 2
children. Wit: R. J. FLEMING.

3M:230 Date: 2 Jun 1826 RtCt: 12 Jun 1826
John BALL of Ldn to Stephen SANDS of Ldn. B/S of 2 lots in Wtfd
(cnvy/b John E. HANDY), one with tavern and shoe shop adj Robert
BRADEN, Thomas SANDERS, the other with stable adj Lewis
KLINE. Wit: Noble S. BRADEN, J. WILSON, Samuel C. DORMAN,
A. S. ANDERSON.

3M:231 Date: 3 Jun 1826 RtCt: 12 Jun 1826
Stephen SANDS of Ldn to Noble S. BRADEN. Trust for debt to John
BALL using above two lots. Wit: A. S. ANDERSON, Samuel C.
DORMAN.

3M:234 Date: 12 Jun 1826 RtCt: 12 Jun 1826
Richard TAVENER & wife Nancy of Ldn to Joseph TAVENER of
Ldn. B/S of 78a.

3M:235 Date: 6 May 1826 RtCt: 12 Jun 1826
Henery RUSE & wife Sarah of Ldn to John EVERHART of Ldn. B/S
of 9a (allotted to Sarah EVERHART now RUSE from land of father
Jacob EVERHART dec'd) on Big Dutchman, and all int. in 15a
widow's dower, and ¼ int. in 33a nr Potomac and 3a adj __ BOOTH,
__ SLATES (dev. by Jacob EVERHART to Sarah, Jacob, John and
Joseph EVERHART). Wit: Mortimore McILHANEY, Geo. W.
SHAWEN.

3M:237 Date: 1 Jun 1826 RtCt: 13 Jun 1826
William D. DRISH & wife Harriet of Ldn to James McILHANY of Ldn.
B/S of lot and house on Cornwall St in Lsbg (prch/o Rev. John
MINES Apr 1822). Wit: Thomas FOUCH, John J. MATHIAS.

3M:239 Date: 3 Jun 1826 RtCt: 13 Jun 1826
Norval CHAMBLIN & wife Sarah W. T. of Ldn to Price JACOBS of
Ldn. Trust for debt to Israel Thompson GRIFFITH using adj. lots
totaling 27a (See DBk GG:300 and DBk VV:125).

3M:241   Date: 3 Jun 1826   RtCt: 13 Jun 1826
Yeoman Henry PLAISTER of Ldn to Norval CHAMBLIN of Ldn. B/S of 3a (cnvy/b Anthony SWICK, May 1826) now occupied by SWICK adj Jonah TAVENER, James BROWN.

3M:243   Date: 24 May 1826   RtCt: 13 Jun 1826
Yeoman Anthony SWICK & wife Martha of Ldn to Henry PLAISTER of Ldn. B/S of 3a (cnvy/b James TREHORN in separate parcels, DBk GG:300 and DBk VV:125) adj Lovel JACKSON. Wit: Edward HALL, Wm. BRONAUGH.

3M:244   Date: 30 May 1826   RtCt: 13 Jun 1826
Charles G. EDWARDS of Ldn to Craven A. COPELAND of Ldn. Trust for debt to James COPELAND using house and lot in Wtfd (prch/o John H. McCABE).

3M:246   Date: 3 Oct 1825   RtCt: 14 Jun 1826
Samuel BUTCHER & wife Hannah to Samuel TORBET. CoE in Wood Co for deed of 2 Jan 1819 on 14a. Delv. to TORBERT 31 Nov 1831.

3M:247   Date: 23 Nov 1825   RtCt: 14 Jun 1826
John KEITH & wife Sarah of Fqr to Samuel TORBET of Fqr (nephew of Sarah). B/S of 170a. Wit: Benjamin GRAYSON, John W. GRAYSON.

3M:249   Date: 22 Apr 1826   RtCt: 15 Jun 1826
Benjamin MITCHELL & wife Martha of Ldn to Josiah GREGG of Ldn. Trust for debt to Gregg SIMPSON using four 20a lots (fell to different individuals in div. of land of Joseph LANE dec'd). Wit: Edward HALL, John W. GRAYSON. Delv. to Wm. BENTON pr order 11 Jan 1828.

3M:251   Date: 15 Jun 1826   RtCt: 15 Jun 1826
Shff Ludwell LEE by deputy Burr WEEKS to Timothy CARRINGTON and Roger CHEW of Ldn. B/S of 20¼a (2 lots from insolvent debtor Daniel BROWN May 1825, conveyed to BROWN by Ezekiel MOUNT and Silas REESE). Delv. to CHEW 12 Feb 1828.

3M:252   Date: 26 May 1826   RtCt: 16 Jun 1826
George BUTLER & wife Elizabeth of Ldn to Joseph WOOD of Ldn. Trust for debt to John BUTLER using ¼a adj Wtfd. Wit: Noble S. BRADEN, Saml. HOUGH. Delv. John BUTLER 13 Sep 1830.

3M:254   Date: 17 Jun 1826   RtCt: 20 Jun 1826
Caleb C. SUTHERLAND of Ldn to Richard H. HENDERSON of Ldn. Trust for debt to Benjamin SHRIEVE Jr. using int. in estate of father Alexander SUTHERLAND dec'd' and his brothers John and Thomas SUTHERLAND (Meadow lot rented to Thomas R. MOTT, large lot on road to Tuscarora, ground rent on lot of Mary LUTZ held by Lemuel CARR, fee simple on lot fronting Loudoun & King Sts with smith shop occupied chiefly by Dr. Thos. F. TEBBS). Delv. pr order 11 Jan 1831.

3M:256   Date: 8 Sep 1823   RtCt: 23 Jun 1826
Samuel CLAPHAM & wife Elizabeth of Ldn to John J. HARDING of
Ldn. B/S of part of Lot #18 on Market St. in Lsbg. Wit: Saml.
DAWSON, James M. LEWIS. Delv. to HARDING 5 Sep 1832.

3M:258   Date: 11 Mar 1826   RtCt: 30 Jun 1826
Thomas H. STEPHENS & wife Elizabeth of Ldn to George MILLER
of Ldn. B/S of ¼a Lot #9, #10, #11 & #12 in German Settlement on
E end of Lovett's farm. Wit: Ebenezer GRUBB, Craven OSBURNE.

3M:259   Date: 1 Jul 1826   RtCt: 1 Jul 1826
Charles BINNS Sr. of Ldn to Charles G ESKRIDGE of Ldn. B/S of
lot on Liberty St at North St in Lsbg. Delv. to BINNS 2 Nov 1826.

3M:261   Date: 14 Jul 1826   RtCt: 3 Aug 1826
Francis STRIBLING of FredVa to Province McCORMICK of FredVa.
Trust for debt to George W. KIGER using lot with life estate to
STRIBLING in right of marriage with his late wife Cecelia McILHANY
(see deed of trust from STRIBLING to Alexander S. TIDBALL). Delv.
to Jas. McILHANY for P. McCORMICK 21 Sep 1826.

3M:263   Date: 25 Jul 1826   RtCt: 31 Jul 1826
Albert BAYLEY & wife Sarah to John BAYLY. CoE for deed of 16
Nov 1819. Wit: Chas. LEWIS, Ariss BUCKNER. Delv. to Jno.
BAYLEY 9 Oct 1826.

3M:263   Date: 25 Jul 1826   RtCt: 31 Jul 1826
Albert BAYLY & wife Sarah. CoE for deed of 26 Jan 1821. Wit:
Charles LEWIS, Aris BUCKNER. Delv. to Jno. BAYLEY 9 Oct 1826.

3M:264   Date: 1 Aug 1826   RtCt: 4 Aug 1826
Samuel DAWSON. Acknowledgement of deed of 28 Mar 1826. Wit:
John H. McCABE, Jno. J. MATHIAS.

3M:264   Date: 5 May 1826   RtCt: 31 Jul 1826
John CARTER & wife Eliza of Fqr to Robert J. TAYLOR of AlexDC.
Trust for debt to John HONE of NY using 1033a 'Sudley' in Ffx and
Ldn nr Bull Run, Landon CARTER, Andrew HEATH's plantation.

3M:267   Date: 22 Mar 1826   RtCt: 31 Jul 1826
Price JACOBS & wife Katherine, William JACOBS & wife Maria and
William CHAMBLIN of Ldn to Joseph HUMPHREY of Ldn. B/S of
96¼a (from land of William CHAMBLIN dec'd). Wit: William
BRONAUGH, Francis W. LUCKETT. Delv. pr order 24 Mar 1827.

3M:269   Date: 12 Jul 1826   RtCt: 28 Jul 1826
Thomas PHILIPS of Ldn to Joseph WOOD of Ldn. Release of trust
for debt to Exor of James MOORE dec'd (DBk UU:82).

3M:270   Date: 26 Jul 1826   RtCt: 26 Jul 1826
John WYNN of Ldn to Shff Ludwell LEE. B/S of 109a (prch/o Joseph
HAINES) where WYNN lives.

3M:271   Date: 26 Jul 1826   RtCt: 26 Jul 1826
Jesse BURSON of Ldn to Shff Ludwell LEE. B/S of 149a (prch/o Jacob STONEBURNER).

3M:271   Date: 12 Jul 1826   RtCt: 26 Jul 1826
Joseph WOOD & wife Lyddia of Ldn to John BRADEN and Isaac E. STEER of Ldn. Trust for debt to John WORSELEY using 150a adj Asa MOORE dec'd, Elijah MYERS dec'd, James MOORE dec'd, Jonathan MYERS, William FOX dec'd. Wit: Presley CORDELL and Charles B. HAMILTON. Delv. to WORSLEY 3 Oct 1827.

3M:274   Date: 24 Jul 1826   RtCt: 24 Jul 1826
Ferdinand B. CREB(B)S of Ldn to Roberdeau ANNIN of Ldn. Trust for debt to William L. CLARKE of FredVa using Lot #18 & #24 in Mdbg and household items.

3M:275   Date: 15 Mar 1826   RtCt: 24 Jul 1826
John HARRIS & wife Elizabeth of Ldn to Berry CREBS of Ldn. B/S of Lot #18 & #24 in Mdbg (paid to John UNDERWOOD for claim on lots in Mdbg under a contract with HARRIS). Wit: Burr POWELL, A. GIBSON.

3M:276   Date: 24 Jul 1826   RtCt: 24 Jul 1826
Michael COOPER & wife Hannah of Ldn to Deborah JENNERS (wd/o Abiel) of Ldn. B/S of 1/9th int. in land of father Michael COOPER dec'd subject to life estate of mother (fulment of bond by Abiel JENNERS dec'd to COOPER of 3 Mar 1821) adj William WOOLFORD, Margaret SAUNDERS. Wit: Noble S. BRADEN, George W. SHAWEN.

3M:278   Date: 25 Apr 1826   RtCt: 20 Jul 1826
Isaac S. HONE and John HONE & wife Joanna of NY City to John CARTER late of Ldn now of Ffx. Release of trust for debt to John HONE on 1033a.

3M:280   Date: 15 Jun 1826   RtCt: 20 Jul 1826
Thomas LACEY of Bellmont Co Ohio to Joseph HOUGH of Ldn. B/S of 4a (dev. by Thomas LACEY dec'd) on N side of Bull Run adj Wm. HOUGH, Saml. HOUGH, John McCABE. Delv. to HOUGH 18 Jul 1828.

3M:281   Date: 15 Jun 1826   RtCt: 20 Jul 1826
Joseph HOUGH of Ldn to Edmund J. LEE Jr. of Ldn. Trust for debt to Thomas LACEY of Bellmont Co Ohio using above 4a.

3M:283   Date: 15 Jul 1826   RtCt: 17 Jul 1826
James L. MARTIN of Ldn to Abiel JENNERS of Ldn. Release of trust of Jan 1822 for debt to John MILLER (DBk DDD:351).

3M:284   Date: 19 Sep 1820   RtCt: 17 Jul 1826
Burr POWELL to Jacob MANN. B/S of ½a lot in Mdbg (sold to Nelson GREEN 19 Sep 1820 but GREEN couldn't pay).

3M:286   Date: 12 Jul 1826   RtCt: 12 Jul 1826
Samuel BUCK to Burr W. HARRISON. Trust for William GILMORE
(as security in LS of Big Spring Mill for 3y), Samuel BAYLEY and
Charles THORNTON (security on same LS for 2y) using negro man
Bernard, woman Hannah with infant daughter abt 3-4m, and notes.

3M:289   Date: 1 Jul 1826   RtCt: 14 Jul 1826
Lemuel HUTCHISON & wife Catherine of Fqr to Mary S.
GWATKINS and Margaret GWATKINS of PrWm. B/S of 60a
(Cassius CARTER willed to Charles S. CARTER who sold to William
RUST and RUST to HUTCHISON). Wit: Josiah TIDBALL, Jno. B.
ARMISTEAD. Delv. pr order __.

3M:290   Date: 4 Mar 1826   RtCt: 13 Jul 1826
Samuel KALB & wife Susannah of Ldn to Gideon HOUSHOLDER of
Ldn. B/S of 84a allotment from div. of Adam HOUSEHOLDER Sr.
dec'd and wife Susannah dec'd. Wit: Noble S. BRADEN, Geo. W.
SHAWEN. Delv. to HOUSEHOLDER 7 Feb 1828.

3M:292   Date: 13 Jul 1826   RtCt: 13 Jul 1826
Phineas WILLIAMS of Ldn to Sidnor WILLIAMS of Ldn. B/S of 1/6th
int. in 131a from father Enos WILLIAMS dec'd estate including
dower. Delv. to Sydnor WILLIAMS, 10 Apr 1828.

3M:293   Date: 7 Jun 1826   RtCt: 11 Jul 1826
Charles BINNS (Exor of Daniel LOSH dec'd, Exor William MAINS
now dec'd) of Ldn to James McILHANY of Ldn. B/S of Lot #35 in
Lsbg.

3M:294   Date: 19 Apr 1826   RtCt: 10 Jul 1826
Benjamin GRUBB of Ldn to Leonard THOMAS of Ldn. B/S of 2a
(cnvy/b Joseph CAVINS, Dec 1820) adj William WRIGHT.

3M:296   Date: 13 Jun 1826   RtCt: 6 Jul 1826
Joseph GREGG & wife Mary of Ldn to Silas GARRETT of Ldn. B/S
of 1a (inherited from father) adj Josiah GREGG. Wit: Thomas
NICHOLS, Thomas ROGERS. Delv. to GARRETT 11 Oct 1830.

3M:297   Date: 22 Jul 1826   RtCt: 31 Jul 1826
George and Sarah FEICHTER of Ldn to John SURGHENOR of Ldn.
Trust for debt to John FEICHTER of Ldn using ¾a with log dwelling
house nr Goose Creek Bridge (prch/o Simon A. BINNS).

3M:298   Date: 1 Aug 1826   RtCt: 1 Aug 1826
Garrison B. FRENCH of Ldn to Israel WILLIAMS of Ldn. Release of
trust of Jan 1823 for debt to James D. FRENCH on 93a.

3M:300   Date: 20 Jun 1826   RtCt: 1 Aug 1826
Dr. George LEE of Ldn to Thomas FOUCH of Ldn. B/S of 184a in
CamP adj Peter OAYTERS, George SMITH, John PILES. Delv. to
FOUCH 23 Nov 1827.

3M:301   Date: 2 Jun 1826   RtCt: 31 Jul 1826
Norval CHAMBLIN of Ldn to Price JACOBS of Ldn. BoS for male
slave Stephen. Sarah W. F. CHAMBLIN to acknowledge when she

arrives at lawful age deed from land of father Wm. CHAMBLIN dec'd.

3M:302   Date: __ Aug 1826   RtCt: 5 Aug 1826

Richard H. HENDERSON of Ldn to William JOHNSON of Ldn. Release of trust of Sep 1823 on debt to Joseph MANDEVILLE and Samuel B. LARMOUR. Wit: James McCLAIN, Roberdeau ANNIN, James STUBBLEFIELD Jr.

3M:303   Date: 5 Aug 1826   RtCt: 5 Aug 1826

William JOHNSON & wife Margaret of Ldn to Enos WILDMAN of Ldn. Trust for debt to John WORSELY using lot with 1-story building and 2-story brick dwelling house on King St in Lsbg adj James WOOD, Jotham WRIGHT. Wit: John McCORMICK, John J. MATHIAS. Delv. to WORSLEY 3 Oct 1827.

3M:306   Date: 30 Oct 1826   RtCt: 7 Aug 1826

Isaac EATON & wife Malinda of Ldn to William CARTER of Ldn. B/S of Lot #41 and ½ of Lot #44 in Mount Gilead. Wit: Robt. H. SEARS, Elkoman W. OMANSETTER, John SIMPSON, Thomas ROGERS. Delv. pr order 15 May 1834.

3M:307   Date: 10 Jul 1826   RtCt: 8 Aug 1826

Westwood A. LACEY of Ldn to Neoimi LACEY, Huldah LACEY and Ruth LACEY of Ldn. B/S of int. in real estate of Tacey LACEY dec'd and from brother Armistead John LACEY dec'd.

3M:309   Date: 26 Jul 1826   RtCt: 8 Aug 1826

Susannah CHANNEL (wd/o Dr. James CHANNEL) to Edwin C. BROWN (who m. Elizabeth only dau and heir of James dec'd). B/S of 148¾a farm nr Mdbg (cnvy/b John BAYLY Dec 1805) and house and Lot #15 in town. Delv. to BROWN 17 July 1827.

3M:310   Date: 26 Jul 1826   RtCt: 8 Aug 1826

Edwin C. BROWN & wife Elizabeth of Ldn to Humphrey B. POWELL of Ldn. Trust for Susannah CHANNEL for rest of her life using above land. Wit: Burr POWELL, A. GIBSON.

3M:312   Date: 26 Jul 1826   RtCt: 8 Aug 1826

Leven LUCKETT Jr. of Ldn to Edwin C. BROWN of Ldn. B/S of above land (cnvy/b BROWN to LUCKETT this day). Delv. to BROWN 17 Jul 1827.

3M:313   Date: 26 Jul 1826   RtCt: 8 Aug 1826

Edwin C. BROWN & wife Elizabeth of Ldn to Leven LUCKETT Jr of Ldn. B/S of above land. Wit: Burr POWELL, Abner GIBSON.

3M:314   Date: 20 Jul 1826   RtCt: 8 Aug 1826

Enos W. NEWTON & wife Sarah of Mdbg to H. B. POWELL. Trust for debt to Edwin C. BROWN using farm animals, numerous household items. Wit: Burr POWELL, Abner GIBSON. Delv. to BROWN 17 Jul 1827.

3M:317 Date: 18 Feb 1825 RtCt: 8 Aug 1826
William CHAMBERS of Stark Co Ohio as agent for Robert
CHAMBERS of same to Michael EVERHART of Ldn. B/S of 3/4a
(und. int. in 60a to heirs of STUMP & CHAMBERS). Wit: John
MOORE, Frederick SLATES, Thomas HARDY.

3M:318 Date: ___ 1826 RtCt: 9 Aug 1826
John BOOTH of Jefferson Co Indiana to John LONG of Ldn. B/S of
Lot #1 at foot of short hill in div. of David MULL dec'd.

3M:319 Date: __ Jun 1826 RtCt: 8 Aug 1826
John WENNER and Jacob WALTMAN (Exors of Emanuel
WALTMAN dec'd) of Ldn to Joseph WALTMAN of Ldn. B/S of 252a
(cnvy/b Emanuel WALTMAN dec'd) adj Jacob WALTMAN.

3M:320 Date: 9 Aug 1826 RtCt: 9 Aug 1826
Joseph WENNER of Ldn to John WENNER of Ldn. B/S of 17¼a
(Lot #2 in div. of William WENNER dec'd).and int. in widow's dower.

3M:321 Date: 3 Jun 1826 RtCt: 14 Aug 1826
Reed POULTON. Qualification as Captain of a troop of cavalry in 2nd
Reg 2nd Div of Militia. Oath on 18 Jul 1826. Delv. to POULTON 26
Oct 1826.

3M:322 Date: 26 Jul 1826 RtCt: 14 Aug 1826
Stephen R. MOUNT. Oath as Capt. in 56th Reg 6th Brig 2nd Div of Va
Militia.

3M:322 Date: 7 Aug 1826 RtCt: 14 Aug 1826
Joshua GORE Jr. Oath as Lt. in 56th Reg 6th Brig 2nd Div of Militia.

3M:322 Date: 11 Jul 1826 RtCt: 14 Aug 1826
Roger CHEW. Oath as 1st Lt. of troop of cavalry in 2nd Reg 2nd Div of
Va Militia.

3M:323 Date: 24 Jun 1826 RtCt: 14 Aug 1826
Amos GUILICK. Oath as Lt. in 57th Reg 6 Brig 2nd Div of Va Militia.

3M:323 Date: 18 Sep 1825 RtCt: 19 Sep 1825/10 Feb 1826
Saml. M. EDWARDS of Ldn to Charles BENNETT of AlexDC. BoS
of mulatto man Harry (sometimes called Henery FISHER) for 8
years than to be freed.

3M:324 Date: 9 Aug 1826 RtCt: 16 Aug 1826
Henery NICEWANGER Sr. dec'd. Division – Lot #1 (32¼a) and Lot
#2 called the Still House (6a) to widow; Lot #3 (14a) to John F.
STRIDER; Lot #4 (11a) and small lot on ridge marked #3 (2a) to
Christian NISWANGER; Lot #5 (11a) & small lot on ridge marked #5
(3a) to John NISEWANGER; Lot #6 (9½a) with small lot on ridge
marked #6 (3a) to John NICEWANGER Sr.; Lot #7 (14a) to Jacob
HOMES; Lot #8 (15½a) to Martin HARDMAN; Lot #9 (2a) to John
NICEWANGER Sr in right of wife. Gives plat. Divisors: Peter
DEMORY, Joshua OSBURN, John CONARD.

3M:328 Date: 27 Sep 1826 RtCt: 27 Sep 1826
Fauquier County – Loudoun County: Survey Report of Boundary -
Gives (difficult to read on microfilm, original held at Lsbg
courthouse) detailed plat over several pages. Some referenced
individuals include: Peter GLASSCOCK, Randolph RHODES, Isaiah
HICKS, Gourley's house, Wm. FITZHUGH, Wm. HICKMAN, Dr.
SMITH, William WILKINSON, Carter's Smith Shop, Amos DUNHAM,
Mrs. WEATHERBY, Maj. POWELL, HEREFORD heirs, Wm.
ROGERS, Hugh ROGERS, Mrs. BATTSON, Capt. John
BALTHROPE. By Cuthbert POWELL, John P. DUVALL.

3M:335 Date: 10 Aug 1826 RtCt: 10 Aug 1826
David LOVETT of Ldn to James McILHANY of Ldn. B/S of 16a
(bought of Mortimore McILHANY, part of farm now occupied by
David HANDLEY) adj Timothy TAYLOR Sr.

3M:336 Date: 10 Aug 1826 RtCt: 11 Aug 1826
James H. RUSSELL of Ldn to Aaron RUSSELL of Ldn. B/S of und.
1/9th from land of William RUSSELL dec'd except dower (dev. to
children of his last wife) on road from Hllb to Wtfd.

3M:337 Date: 6 Feb 1824 RtCt: 11 Aug 1826
Henry RUSSELL & wife Matilda of Ldn to Aaron RUSSELL and
Mahlon RUSSELL of Ldn. B/S of und. 1/9th from land of William
RUSSELL dec'd except dower (dev. to children of his last wife) on
road from Hllb to Wtfd. Wit: Robert BRADEN, Abiel JENNERS.

3M:338 Date: 5 Jun 1819 RtCt: 13 Mar/14 Aug 1826
Margaret GREEN of JeffVa to Amos HENRY of Ldn. B/S of int. in __
a (devised by father Ebenezer WILSON dec'd to his widow Hannah
WILSON for life then to children).

3M:339 Date: 12 Aug 1826 RtCt: 14 Aug 1826
Robert BRADEN & wife Elizabeth of Ldn to George WARNER of
Ldn. B/S of 14¼a (prch/o WARNER) adj Simeon HAINES dec'd.
Wit: Saml. HOUGH, Noble S. BRADEN.

3M:342 Date: 9 May 1826 RtCt: 23 Aug 1826
John H. SWEENEY of Ldn to Reazon WILLCOXEN of Ffx. BoS of
negro boy Jefferson, farm animals, farm and household items. Delv.
to WILLCOXEN on ___.

3M:343 Date: 18 Apr 1826 RtCt: 14 Aug 1826
Benjamin GRAYSON (Admr of Benjamin GRAYSON Jr. dec'd) of
Ldn to Benjamin BARTEN of Ldn. B/S of 1¼a with house on SE side
of road at W end of Bloomfield, adj Col. George MARKS. Delv. to
GRAYSON 4 Jan 1827.

3M:344 Date: 8 Aug 1826 RtCt: 14 Aug 1826
Mary PRINCE (single woman) of Ldn to Levi PRINCE of Ldn. Trust
for benefit of her children Nathan PRINCE now in 10th year of age
and John Levi PRINCE now in 5th year of age (in case of Mary's
death, until they both reach 21y old), using household items.

3M:345   Date: 15 Aug 1826   RtCt: 15 Aug 1826
Craven OSBURNE (trustee of Lewis ELLZEY) of Ldn to Joshua
OSBURN of Ldn. B/S of ELLZEY's int. in estate of Thomazin
ELLZEY dec'd (from trust of Jul 1822 for benefit of Joshua
OSBURNE). Delv. to OSBURN 6 Jul 1833.

3M:346   Date: 9 May 1826   RtCt: 14 Aug 1826
Caleb N. GALLEHER (trustee of Samuel TRAYHERN) of Ldn to
Lydia HUTCHISON of Ldn. B/S of lot adj Union (from trust for debt
to Thos. H. WEY). Wit: Samuel TORRYSON, Seth SMITH, Thomas
SANDERS.

3M:348   Date: 25 Feb 1826   RtCt: 16 Aug 1826
William ELLZEY of Ldn to Samuel POOL of Ldn. LS of __a adj __
CLEVELAND, __ ALEXANDER. Wit: Wm. MERSHON, Daniel
SETTLE, Dean JAMES.

3M:350   Date: 28 Jul 1826   RtCt: 17 Aug 1826
Charles HARDY of FredVa to Samuel M. EDWARDS of Ldn. Trust
for debt to Thomas PHILIPS Exor of James MOORE dec'd using
50a with fulling mill (formerly belonging to William JANNEY). Delv. to
EDWARDS 5 Aug 1829.

3M:351   Date: 27 Jul 1826   RtCt: 17 Aug 1826
John WILLIAMS (as surviving trustee of William JANNEY to him &
Jacob MENDENHALL for benefit of James FARQUHAR) of Ldn to
Charles HARDY of FredVa. B/S of above 50a. Delv. to HARDY 17
May 1827.

3M:353   Date: 14 Aug 1826   RtCt: 22 Aug 1826
Eli C. GALLAHER (trustee for Benj. FLOWERS for benefit of John
GALLAHER, Aug 1823) to John GALLAHER. Sale of household
items held in trust.

3M:354   Date: __ May 1825   RtCt: 5 May 1825/24 Aug 1826
Phineas JANNEY and Daniel JANNEY (Exors of Israel JANNEY
dec'd) of Ldn to William SMITH of Ldn. B/S of 97a adj Daniel
JANNEY, Amos GIBSON, Bernard TAYLOR, William EACHES. Wit:
Roberdeau ANNIN, Alfred A. ESKRIDGE, William J. JONES. Delv.
to SMITH 28 Aug 1827.

3M:356   Date: 29 Mar 1825   RtCt: 29 Mar 1825/24 Aug 1826
Phineas JANNEY and Daniel JANNEY (Exors of Israel JANNEY
dec'd) of Ldn to William EACHES of Ldn. B/S of 61a adj Solomon
GORE. Wit: Roberdeau ANNIN, Alfred A. ESKRIDGE, William J.
JONES. Delv. to EACHES 15 Sep 1835.

3M:357   Date: 16 May 1826   RtCt: 20 May 1826
John WYNN of Ldn to Mahlon CRAVEN of Ldn. Trust for debt to
William HOGE using farm animals, farm and household items. Delv.
to HOGE 13 Dec 1830.

3M:358   Date: 19 Aug 1826   RtCt: 26 Aug 1826
Barbara NORTON wd/o Nathaniel NORTON dec'd of Ldn to James
B. DUNKIN of Ldn. Trust for debt to Samuel DUNKIN with Hamilton
NORTON and Jonathan LOVETT as security using her int. in real
estate of her late husband.

3M:360   Date: 26 Aug 1826   RtCt: 28 Aug 1826
Mahlon EDWARDS of Ldn to Jacob EDWARDS of Ldn. BoS of
household items in tenement occupied by Mahlon on E side of Short
Hill. Delv. to Jacob EDWARDS 15 Jan 1827.

3M:361   Date: 29 Aug 1826   RtCt: 29 Aug 1826
Adam EVANS of Ldn to Roberdeau ANNIN of Ldn. Trust for debt to
Jacob WATERS using lot cnvy/b Jaspar EVERHART, farm animals,
personal items.

3M:362   Date: 25 Aug 1826   RtCt: 29 Aug 1826
Thomson F. MASON and Richard H. HENDERSON to Samuel M.
EDWARDS. Trust for debt to Bank of U.S. using slaves (Maria, Sam,
Bayley, Peter, Lewis, Joe, Abe, Billy Gibson, Billy Gibson Jr., old
woman Hannah, Mahala, Jane, Abb, old Pat children David, Kitty,
Betty, Min, Kit, Charles, Henry, Peter, Allen, women Jane, Matilda,
Nelly, Harriet, boys Worsely, Jerry, Edward, unnamed infant)
animals, etc. conveyed to MASON and HENDERSON in trust from
Samuel CLAPHAM. Wit: C. RATCLIFFE, Jno. MOSS, Robt.
RATCLIFF.

3M:365   Date: 12 Aug 1826   RtCt: 30 Aug 1826
William CHILTON (with Samuel CLAPHAM as security) to John J.
HARDING of Lsbg. Mortgage using books of every description
(gives long list)

3M:367   Date: 17 Aug 1826   RtCt: 30 Aug 1826
Margaret SAUNDERS of Ldn to Joshua PEUSEY and William
CLENDENING of Ldn. Trust for debt to Sarah NIXON of Ldn using
144a adj Archibald MORRISON, Charles CRIM, Jacob
SHOEMAKER, George SHOEMAKER. Wit: Thomas WHITE. Delv.
to Abraham SMITH pr order ___.

3M:370   Date: 25 Aug 1826   RtCt: 1 Sept 1826
Francis STRIBLING of FredVa to James McILHANY. Trust for debt
to ROBERTS & TAGGERT using int. in life estate arising from his
marriage with Cecelia McILHANY distrib. of James McILHANY
dec'd. Delv. to Jas. McILHANY 30 Aug 1826.

3M:372   Date: 1 Sep 1826   RtCt: 1 Sep 1826
Elias POOL of Ldn to Roberdeau ANNIN of Ldn. Trust for debt to
James L. MARTIN of Ldn using int. in crops on farm of Mrs. Honor
TILLETT.

3M:373   Date: 15 Feb 1826   RtCt: 2 Sep 1826
David E. BROWN & wife Eliza Alice late GIBSON of Ldn to Samuel
PEACH of AlexDC. B/S of 16¼a & 15a lots allotted to Eliza Alice as

ch/o John GIBSON dec'd late of Ldn and int. in dower of widow Elizabeth. Wit: William BRONAUGH, Edw'd HALL. Delv. to PEACH 11 Feb 1828.

3M:375 Date: __ Sep 1826 RtCt: 8 Sep 1826
William CHILTON of Lsbg to Lloyd NOLAND. Trust for loan from Burr POWELL, Cuthbert POWELL & Alfred H. POWELL trustees of Sarah H. CHILTON using house and lot in Lsbg where he resides. Delv. to Dr. POWELL pr order of B. POWELL 11 Oct 1827.

3M:377 Date: 22 Aug 1826 RtCt: 11 Sep 1826
John WORNELL. Oath as cornet in Co of Light Dragoons attached to 56th Reg Va Militia.

3M:377 Date: 11 Sep 1826 RtCt: 11 Sep 1826
Jesse TIMMS and George CARTER. Bond on TIMMS as Commissioner of Revenue in 1st District.

3M:378 Date: 11 Sep 1826 RtCt: 11 Sep 1826
Jesse McVEIGH and Townsend McVEIGH. Bond on Jesse as Commissioner of Revenue in 2nd District.

3M:378 Date: 18 Apr 1819 RtCt: 15 Aug 1826
William NOLAND & wife Catherine of Ldn to Jane LOVE of Ldn. B/S of ½a Lot #5 on Mercer St in Aldie. Wit: Burr POWELL, Ariss BUCKNER.

3M:380 Date: 7 Sep 1826 RtCt: 11 Sep 1826
William BATTSON (Exor of John BATTSON dec'd of Fqr) to Townsend McVEIGH of Mdbg. B/S of 157½a adj James BATTSON, Little River. Delv. to McVEIGH 13 Mar 1827.

3M:382 Date: 12 Aug 1820 [26?] RtCt: 11 Sep 1826
Francis W. LUCKETT (trustees of William VICKERS Feb 1825) of Ldn to William RICHARDS Jr. of Ldn. B/S of 80a and 15a adj William BENTON and lots in Millville (1a upper end of #3, ½a upper end of #6, ¼a #1 & #3, lower end of #4, 1a #5). Delv. to RICHARDS on ___.

3M:383 Date: 20 May 1826 RtCt: 1 Aug 1826
Mary McINTYRE of Ldn to Joseph FRED of Ldn. LS of 20a on farm where Mary resides adj Andrew CAMPBELL, Wm. WILKINSON, George YOUNG. Wit: Geo. ROACH, Thomas ROGERS, David YOUNG. Delv. to FRED 28 Feb 1828.

3M:384 Date: 11 Sep 1826 RtCt: 11 Sep 1826
L. P. W. BALCH of FredMd (trustee of John SHAFFER) to John THOMAS of Lsbg. B/S of 70a adj Peter COMPHER, German Settlement.

3M:385 Date: 31 Aug 1826 RtCt: 11 Sep 1826
John THOMAS Jr. & wife Elizabeth of Ldn to William RHODES Jr. of Columbianna Co Ohio. B/S of 159a in section #34 of township #12 in Columbiannia Co (prch/o William LODGE). Wit: Benjamin GRAYSON, John W. GRAYSON. Delv. to RHODES 3 Mar 1827.

3M:386   Date: 1 Nov 1825   RtCt: 2 Sep 1826
John P. DUVALL & wife Ann F. to James MONROE. B/S of 215a on Little River (as devisee of Wm. CARR Sr. of PrWm). Wit: Burr POWELL, A. GIBSON.

3M:389   Date: 4 Mar 1826   RtCt: 16 Sep 1826
George RICHARD & wife Syvilla of Ldn to George SHOEMAKER of Ldn. B/S of 8a (prch/o John MARTIN) adj __ HICKMAN. Wit: Geo. W. SHAWEN, Noble S. BRADEN. Delv. to SHOEMAKER 10 Sep 1835.

3M:390   Date: 1 Jun 1826   RtCt: 15 Sep 1826
Jesse BURSON to John BURSON. BoS to cover debt using crop of corn. Wit: Cyrus BURSON, Thomas M. HUMPHREY.

3M:391   Date: 20 Sep 1826   RtCt: 20 Sep 1826
Edward HAMMATT & wife Betsy of Lsbg to James L. MARTIN of Lsbg. B/S of part of Lot #58 on N side of Loudoun St in Lsbg (cnvy/b MARTIN as commr in suit of HAMMATT agst DONOHOE). Wit: Saml. M. EDWARDS, Thomas SANDERS.

3M:392   Date: 9 Mar 1826   RtCt: 20 Sep 1826
James L. MARTIN of Ldn to Edward HAMMATT of Ldn. B/S of above house & lot in Lsbg (real estate of Ann DONOHOE dec'd, from court decree of Nov 1825 in HAMMATT agst DONOHOE, cnvy/b Joshua BAKER and Sarah CAVEN, Dec 1801, DBk BB:204).

3M:393   Date: 20 Sep 1826   RtCt: 20 Sep 1826
James L. MARTIN & wife Sarah of Ldn to John SAUNDERS of Ldn. B/S of part of Lot #58 in Lsbg (see above). Wit: Thomas SANDERS, Saml. M. EDWARDS.

3M:394   Date: 23 Sep 1826   RtCt: 23 Sep 1826
James STEADMAN & wife Alcy of Ldn to Elizabeth SMITH of Ldn. B/S of her half of lot in Lsbg purchased jointly of Jno. H. McCABE, Apr 1821, DBk CCC:341. Wit: John J. MATHIAS, Samuel M. EDWARDS.

3M:396   Date: 4 Sep 1826   RtCt: 25 Sep 1826
Felix TRIPLETT of Ldn to David SIMPSON of Ldn. B/S of lot in Mdbg from div. of estate of Rewben TRIPLETT dec'd. Delv. to SIMPSON 1 Jul 1828.

3M:397   Date: 17 Aug 1826   RtCt: 30 Sep 1826
William ALT & wife Susanna of Ldn to Michael SPRING of Ldn. B/S of und. 1/4th of 30a from div. of father William ALT dec'd allotted to widow Rachael ALT. Wit: Samuel M. EDWARDS, Thomas SANDERS. Delv. to SPRING 10 Sep 1834.

3M:399   Date: 17 Aug 1826   RtCt: 30 Sep 1826
William ALT & wife Susanna of Ldn to John ALT of Ldn. B/S of 118a (cnvy/b Robert CAMPBELL, Dec 1818, DBk XX:240) and 77a (cnvy/b John DULIN, Mar 1816, DBk TT:356) less 20a (cnvy/b ALT to Basell NEWMAN, DBk ZZ:238) and less 47a (to NEWMAN, DBk

CCC:14) and less 5¼a (to David EVELAND, DBk FFF:478) and less 4a (to Saml. COX not yet conveyed). Wit: Saml. M. EDWARDS, Thomas SANDERS.

3M:401   Date: 2 Oct 1826   RtCt: 2 Oct 1826
Simon SMALE & wife Elizabeth of Lsbg to John SHAW of Lsbg. B/S of part of Lot #58 'Donohoe's Lot' in Lsbg adj SMALE's brick house on Back St. Delv. to SHAW 8 Feb 1827.

3M:403   Date: 2 Oct 1826   RtCt: 2 Oct 1826
John SHAW & wife Cynthia to George RICHARDS. Trust for debt to Simon SMALE using lot on Back St. Wit: Jno. ROSE, Jno. J. MATHIAS. Delv. pr order 1 Jul 1830.

3M:405   Date: 31 Aug 1826   RtCt: 12 Sep 1826
Daniel GREENWALL of Lsbg to Charles G. ESKRIDGE of Lsbg. Trust for debt to John GRAY of Lsbg using ½a (cnvy/b Robert R. HOUGH, DBk TT:287) and ½a (cnvy/b John NEWTON).

3M:407   Date: 14 Aug 1826   RtCt: 5 Oct 1826
Richard H. HENDERSON & wife Orra Moore of Ldn to Gourley REEDER, John G. HUMPHREY and William RICHARDS Jr. of Ldn. B/S of 100a and 80a (cnvy/b insolvent debtor William VICKERS to Shff). Delv. to HUMPHREY 11 Mar 1831.

3M:408   Date: 5 Oct 1826   RtCt: 6 Oct 1826
Peter COOPER of Ldn to John WINE of Ldn. Trust for debt to Mrs. Sally NIXON of Ldn, Joshua PEUSEY (Exor of James NIXON dec'd) as security of Jonathan COOPER, George WENNER using farm animals, household items.

3M:410   Date: 7 Oct 1826   RtCt: 7 Oct 1826
S. B. T. CALDWELL of Ldn. Cancellation of BoS from B. W. SOWERS for printing office.

3M:410   Date: 7 Aug 1826   RtCt: 9 Oct 1826
Ryland JACOBS. Qualified as Ensign in 56th Reg 6th Brig 2nd Div of Va Militia.

3M:410   Date: 13 Sep 1820   RtCt: ___
William CLAYTON dec'd. Division – Lot #1 (100½a) & Lot #14 (1a) to Amos CLAYTON; Lot #2 (50¾a) & Lot #12 (66 perches) & wood Lot #16 (50¾a) to Patty CLAYTON; Lot #3 (44a) & Lot #11 (66 perches) & Lot #17 on the ridge (51a) & Lot #7 (15a) to ___ LUKE w/o ___ LUKE; Lot #4 (49a) & Lot ___ (1¼a) & Lot #9 (2a) & Lot #18 on the ridge (51¾a) to Israel CLAYTON; Lot #5 (101a) & Lot ___ (½a) & Lot ___ (½a) to Wm. CLAYTON; Lot #6 (19) & ½ of Lot #10 to Phebe HUFFMAN w/o John HUFFMAN; Lot #8 (5a) & Lot #15 on the ridge (6a) to Mary w/o John HALLAWAY. Gives plat. Divisors: Abner HUMPHREY, Edw'd B. GRADY, Thos. A. HEREFORD. Final decree 9 Oct 1826.

INDEX

David, 107, 171, 192,
206, 237, 238
Manuel, 9

BACKHAM
Foundren, 41
BAGLEY
___, 170
BAGLY
Robert, 70
BAILEY
John, 45, 74
Mary, 78
Sydnor, 76, 110, 112,
190, 214
BAILY
Joab, 87
John, 108, 173
Lewis, 78
Sydnor, 29, 150
Tarpley, 78
BAKER
___, 247
Abraham, 149
Aron, 168
Daniel, 233
David, 233
Elisabeth, 217
Elisha, 25
Elizabeth, 66, 133
George, 49
Isaac, 50, 246
John, 98, 164, 233,
241
John W., 144
Joshua, 258
Margaret, 233
Nancy, 233
Samuel, 233
Sarah, 241
William, 8
BALCH
L. P. W., 13, 21, 24,
26, 49, 51, 56, 58,
67, 74, 75, 85, 87,
90, 91, 103, 138,
140, 149, 160,
164, 165, 172,
180, 186, 206,
207, 222, 231, 257
Lewis P. W., 3, 74,
84, 114, 146, 155,
167, 180, 193,
211, 231, 235

BALDWIN
___, 77, 88, 89, 130
John, 17, 159
Mahlon, 25, 130
BALEY
Sydnor, 123
BALL
___, 37, 170
C. B., 103
Charles, 47
Charles B., 40, 58,
60, 68, 73, 167,
226
Fayette, 68, 99, 104,
193
Henry, 225
Isaac, 12, 180
John, 56, 80, 121,
180, 243, 247
Nathan, 170
Spencer M., 225
Stephen, 59, 84
William, 225
BALTHROPE
John, 254
BALY
George, 2
BARDWELL
Nancy, 168
Seth, 168
BARR
Adam, 114, 210
George, 182
Hannah, 181
Lott, 181
Nimrod, 181, 233
Precious, 210
BARRATT
Mary, 111
Robert, 109, 111
BARRY
Eliza A., 32
BARTEN
Benjamin, 254
BARTLE
Samuel, 63
BARTON
Benjamin, 228
Levi, 48, 76
R., 112
Sarah, 48, 76
BATTSON
James, 257
John, 257

Mrs., 254
William, 257
BATY
___, 181
BAULEY
John Y., 197
BAYLEY
Albert, 249
John, 77, 200, 249
Reuben, 73
Samuel, 251
Sarah, 249
BAYLY
___, 92
Albert, 249
George, 12
John, 12, 42, 144,
185, 210, 219,
249, 252
Perce, 13
Pierce, 159
Robert, 7
Sarah, 249
Susanah, 159
William P., 12, 159
BAYNE
Henry T., 54, 71
Phebe, 54
BAYNES
Phebe, 71
BAZILL
John C., 147
BAZZIL
John C., 7, 34, 106
Mary, 106
BAZZILL
John C., 34, 151, 181
Mary, 34, 151
BEAGLE
Christian, 161
BEALE
Amos, 80, 91, 162
David, 80, 91, 162
David F., 149
Hannah, 91
Isaac B., 65
BEALL
David F., 135, 198
BEAMER
George, 202
BEANS
Amos, 37, 95, 134
Hannah, 57, 65

Isaiah B., 57, 65, 86, 92, 95, 172
James, 135, 198
Mathew, 140, 216
Matthew, 16, 101
Paxton, 120
Pleasant, 86
Samuel, 69, 86, 95, 116, 134
William, 134
BEARD
George, 225
Jonathan, 216
Joseph, 32, 83, 133, 240
L., 79, 92, 110, 112
Lewis, 147, 215, 240
BEATTY
___, 199
Andrew, 54
David, 16
George, 54, 87
John, 157, 177, 236
Kezia, 54
Lewis A., 215
Mary, 54
Osburn, 87
Otho R., 91, 143
Rebecca, 203
Silas, 153
Thomas B., 215
William, 107, 168, 203
BEATY
Andrew, 57
George, 57
John, 22, 117
BEAVERS
___, 212
Eliza, 131
James, 17, 40, 182, 216
Melinda, 187
Samuel, 94, 111, 124, 131, 154, 189
Sarah, 189
Thomas, 111, 124, 154
BECK
Samuel, 210
BECKETT
Elizabeth, 40
BECKWITH
F M , 14

Francis M., 4, 5, 14, 15, 25, 106
BELL
___, 207
James, 107
James M., 6
John, 131, 247
BELT
Alfred, 200
Levin, 96
BELTZ
___, 45
Susan, 91
BEMANDAFFER
Peter, 113
BEMARSDAFFER
Peter, 231
BEMARSDERFER
Peter, 231
BEMASDAFER
Peter, 170
Susan, 170
BEMASDAFFER
Peter, 196
BEND
William B., 23
BENEDOM
Peter, 204
BENEDUM
Catharine, 50, 102, 122
Catherine, 121, 122
Elisabeth, 121, 122
Henery, 176
Henry, 40, 121, 122
John, 14, 49, 98, 102, 107, 117, 118
Manuel, 50, 121, 122
Mary, 98, 107, 117
Mary C., 121
P., 27
Peter, 15, 20, 23, 49, 50, 66, 68, 98, 102, 117, 121, 122, 176, 196, 240
Sarah A., 121
William H., 121
BENNET
Joseph, 159
BENNETT
Charles, 34, 60, 161, 176, 189, 205, 230, 253
Henery A., 171

Henry A., 12, 192
Henry J., 10
Joseph, 190
Susan W., 214
Thomas J., 158, 161, 214
BENTLEY
Catharine, 94
Catherine, 219
R., 112
Robert, 37, 38, 88, 120, 153, 219
BENTLY
Robert, 61, 110, 141, 146
BENTON
John, 123
William, 110, 132, 133, 212, 216, 244, 248, 257
BERKELEY
Elizabeth, 23
John W., 23
Lewis, 20, 118
BERKLEY
George, 184
Lewis, 203, 247
Samuel, 29
BERKLY
___, 196
Benjamin, 201
Mrs., 181
Samuel, 201
BEST
Enos T., 228
James, 29, 54, 75, 131, 178
William, 29
BETTS
James, 60
BEVERIDGE
John, 212
Noble, 2, 7, 10, 12, 13, 19, 20, 27, 35, 48, 49, 88, 98, 99, 114, 116, 130, 152, 169, 192, 198
William, 13, 43
BEVERLY
Carter, 10
Lovely, 8
Peter R., 8, 60, 121, 208
BEVERS

Samuel, 154, 187
Sarah, 154
BINNS
___, 12, 113, 170
A. A., 230
C., 47, 99, 155, 167
C. W. D., 217, 231
Charles, 9, 31, 32,
   36, 46, 50, 58, 60,
   62, 91, 99, 102,
   110, 122, 136,
   138, 154, 162,
   186, 192, 197,
   205, 216, 225,
   230, 238, 249, 251
Charles W., 52, 56,
   79
Charles W. D., 113,
   122, 135, 138,
   167, 218
Dewanna, 176
E. D., 230
Elizabeth D., 99
Elizabeth S., 207
Hannah, 122, 230
J. A., 6
James A., 138
John, 132, 133
John A., 2, 6, 8, 15,
   16, 17, 18, 22, 30,
   35, 39, 57, 58, 59,
   60, 64, 66, 73, 79,
   91, 92, 111, 115,
   120, 121, 138,
   152, 156, 167,
   178, 192, 194,
   205, 207, 212,
   216, 221, 225,
   227, 232, 243, 244
Martha, 186
Mary M., 15, 120,
   167
Simon, 141
Simon A., 88, 205,
   216, 225, 230, 251
Thomas M., 207
Thomas N., 50, 66,
   207
W. A., 188
William, 216
William A., 36, 50,
   102, 117, 122,
   141, 205, 216
BIRD

Charles, 108
BIRDSALL
Rachael, 178
Rachel, 202
Rebecca, 202
Whitson, 178, 202
William, 132
BIRKBY
Sarah, 137
Thomas, 66, 88, 137,
   240
BIRKIBY
Lewis, 114
BIRKIT
John, 89
Mary, 89
BIRKITT
John, 242
BISCOE
James B., 25
Thomas, 82, 113
BITZER
___, 88
Conard, 206
Conrad, 73, 81, 96,
   102, 119, 135,
   167, 171, 190,
   192, 206, 231
BLACKBURN
Thomas, 94
BLAND
___, 20
BLINCOE
___, 196
Marcus, 138
S., 24, 38, 79, 88, 94,
   95, 106, 144, 155,
   157, 169, 176,
   181, 192
Sampson, 48, 52, 86,
   103, 153, 156,
   191, 212, 214,
   215, 220, 240
BLINSTONE
Elisabeth, 176
John, 176
William, 176
BODINE
Henry, 218
BOGEN
John, 154
Margaret, 154
BOGER
___, 158, 206

Elisabeth, 158
Jacob, 158
John, 158, 189
Margaret, 189
Mary, 158
Michael, 158, 206
Philip, 158
Samuel, 158
BOGGESS
Henly, 189
Peter, 73, 239
BOGUE
Robert, 105
BOLAND
Daniel, 119, 139,
   205, 226
Patrick, 119, 226
BOLEN
Elizabeth, 56, 111
BOLES
James, 169
BOLIN
Ezra, 227
BOLLS
Judith, 57
BOLON
Eli, 125
Ezra, 101
BOND
Joseph, 32, 44, 72,
   80, 139, 144, 145,
   165, 176, 243
BOOTH
___, 152, 247
Aaron, 1, 8, 11, 28
Anna, 45
Fancy, 11
Fanny, 11, 38, 87
Frances, 175
James, 11, 38, 55,
   87, 154, 175
John, 1, 11, 38, 45,
   55, 59, 87, 92,
   159, 181, 231, 253
Nancy, 154
Robert, 45, 181
Sarah, 28
BOOTHE
James, 28
John, 27
BOSHER
James, 25
BOSS
___, 126

Robert M. H., 208
Roger, 10, 146, 248, 253
CHICHESTER
___, 202
George M., 37, 68, 74, 81, 84, 88, 99, 104, 109, 118, 153, 177, 192, 242
CHICK
Edmund, 233
CHILTON
___, 57, 161
John M., 61
Mrs., 116
Richard, 6, 44, 150, 217
S. H., 162
Sally, 92, 103, 137
Sarah, 144, 170
Sarah H., 20, 240, 257
Sarah N., 135
Susana, 137, 138
Susanna, 88, 92, 103
Thomas, 88, 92, 103, 137, 138
William, 6, 13, 20, 24, 48, 49, 66, 85, 89, 129, 135, 144, 155, 162, 169, 170, 171, 183, 188, 207, 209, 211, 226, 240, 256, 257
William O., 238
CHIN
Robert, 39
CHINN
Ann A., 72
Ann H., 54, 127, 152
Ann M., 153
Catherine M., 153
Elias L., 153
Emily, 116
Emmily, 24
Francis, 153
George, 72
Martha, 153
Nancy, 72
Rawleigh T., 200
Richard, 72
Robert, 72, 152

Samuel, 24, 28, 30, 95, 116, 127, 213
Sydney, 72
Thomas, 20, 35, 54, 72, 127, 152, 153
William, 72
CHRISTY
James, 116
CHURCH
Delilah, 109
James, 41
CIMMINGS
Anthony, 116
Rebecca, 116
Thomas, 116
CLAGETT
___, 76
Henery, 141, 161, 227
Henry, 36, 76, 93, 108, 113, 125, 127
Henry O., 233
Julia, 76, 127, 141
Juliet, 108, 127
July, 36
CLAGGET
Dr., 240
CLAGGETT
___, 74
Dr., 235
Henery, 242
Henry, 72, 212, 233
Julia, 242
CLAIBURN
Herbert A., 43
CLAPHAM
Col., 28
Elisabeth, 145, 153
Elizabeth, 93, 193, 232, 236, 249
Josiah, 145
Josias, 61, 210
Sally, 210
Samuel, 26, 47, 52, 61, 93, 111, 113, 114, 115, 129, 145, 152, 153, 155, 185, 193, 214, 232, 249, 256
CLARK
John W., 124
Josias M., 38, 188
William F., 177
CLARKE

A. H., 83
Catharine, 43
J. M., 166
John F., 31
Josiah M., 129
Josias M., 4
Richard, 43
William, 6
William L., 250
CLAYTON
Amos, 83, 148, 165, 208, 259
Elisabeth, 148
Elizabeth, 208
Israel, 17, 29, 32, 60, 171, 259
Martha, 148
Patsey, 83
Patty, 259
Sarah, 17
Townsend, 208, 209
William, 17, 59, 259
CLEMENTS
Ann, 68, 172
CLEMM
Alfred, 123
CLENDENING
___, 31, 184
Mary, 230
Ruth, 165, 230
Samuel, 32, 89, 151, 173, 182, 229, 230, 233
T. R., 235
Thomas R., 89
William, 77, 89, 138, 151, 165, 206, 230, 233, 256
CLENDENNING
William, 194
CLERK
Gidney, 35
CLEVELAND
___, 255
J., 133
Johnson, 71, 77, 78, 147, 193, 217
Johnston, 20, 78, 90, 91, 123, 134, 170, 181, 182, 184
CLEWES
Joseph, 214, 215
CLEWS
Nancy, 101

Margaret, 14, 40
CRIDLER
  Elizabeth, 8, 62, 109,
    118, 133, 219,
    236, 237
  Jacob, 116
  John, 8, 60, 62, 72,
    109, 116, 118,
    120, 127, 131,
    133, 167, 176,
    178, 219, 236, 237
CRIM
  ___, 179
  Abraham, 194
  Adam, 193
  Charles, 8, 52, 138,
    193, 194, 214, 256
  Daniel, 193, 203, 220
  Jacob, 52, 193, 194,
    218
  John, 119, 193, 194,
    205
CRIMM
  Charles, 212
CROOK
  Samuel, 223
CROOKS
  Charles, 191
  Margaret, 191
  Samuel, 191
CROSS
  James, 147
CROWE
  Hiland, 49, 217, 225
CRUMPTON
  William, 96
CRUPPER
  Ann, 101
  Benjamin C., 79
  John R., 101
  Penelope, 79
  Richard, 79, 101, 136
CULLISON
  Jeremiah, 237, 238
CULP
  John, 82
CUMMINGS
  ___, 121
  Anthony, 117, 118
  James, 201
  John, 41
  Thomas, 201
CUNARD
  Anthony, 83

Edward, 76
CUNNARD
  ___, 107
  Anthony, 12
  David, 123
  E., 235
  Edward, 135, 226,
    238
  John, 140, 154, 226,
    241, 246
CURRELL
  Frances, 174, 187
  James, 174, 187, 237
  John J., 237
CURRILL
  James, 160
CURRY
  Isaac, 9, 21, 57, 58
  Joseph, 58
  Sally, 58
  Sarah, 9
CURTIS
  John, 8

DADE
  William A. G., 169,
    205
DAGG
  Clarissa, 100
  James, 100
  John L., 100, 101,
    213, 224
  Mary Jane, 100
  Robert, 100, 101
  Samuel, 100
  Sarah, 100
  Susan, 100
DAILEY
  Aaron, 66, 106, 107
  Jesse, 226, 227
  John, 107
  Mary, 226
  Samuel, 66, 107
  William, 91
DANGERFIELD
  John E., 211
DANIEL
  ___, 162
  Benjamin, 124, 190,
    192, 206
  David, 174
  Edward M., 163
  Elisabeth, 174
  Jane M., 206

John, 174
Joseph, 7, 89, 97, 98,
  146, 148, 165,
  183, 206
Sidney, 190
Stephen, 8, 170, 181
Sydney, 124
Tacy, 98
William, 190, 192
DANIELS
  Benjamin, 9, 183
  J., 166
  Stephen, 217
DARNE
  Thomas, 1
  William, 51
DAVIDSON
  Nancy, 163
  Nathaniel, 163
DAVIS
  Elizabeth, 71, 90
  Gideon, 144
  Jason, 165
  John, 30, 34, 116
  John W., 71, 90
  Jonah F., 222
  Margaret, 30, 34, 98
  Mary, 160, 176, 229
  Polly, 165
  Rebecca, 116
  Solomon, 44, 82, 229
  Thomas, 98, 130,
    241
DAVISON
  John, 74
DAWES
  Benjamin, 240
  Edward, 27
DAWSON
  ___, 175
  Charles, 21, 159
  Francis, 167
  Polly, 167
  Samuel, 26, 41, 42,
    69, 93, 103, 109,
    111, 118, 119,
    137, 138, 153,
    163, 166, 178,
    185, 189, 193,
    236, 249
  William, 19
DAY
  Catharine, 87
  Catherine, 11

Henry, 130
John, 11, 87
DEAGEN
Henery B., 176
DEAKINS
Daniel, 111
DeBUTTS
Louisa, 225
Richard, 38, 225
DEEVER
James, 53
DEGEN
Henery B., 175
DELANEY
Rachael, 220
William, 220
DELLINGER
Jacob, 106
DEMORY
___, 36, 74, 107
John, 49, 70, 95, 216,
237, 242, 246
Peter, 58, 120, 241,
246, 254
DENHAM
Amos, 177
Oliver, 14, 38, 174
DENNIS
Absalom, 2
Catherine, 153
Kitty, 2
Lettice, 2
Samuel, 2
Thomas A., 2, 54, 74,
152
W. A., 2
William A., 2, 152,
153
DENNY
William, 41
DERHAM
Catharine A., 99
DERRY
___, 94
Ann Barbara, 209
Barbara, 70, 74, 242
Michael, 206, 209
Philip, 242
William, 70, 74, 154,
242
DERY
William, 246
DESKIN
___, 20

DEVAUGH
William, 63
DEVAUGHN
William, 113
DEWAR
James, 182, 233
DICKERSON
James, 203
DIGGS
William D., 46, 197,
220
DILLON
Abdon, 183, 203
James, 55
DILLOW
___, 120
DISHMAN
Elisabeth, 147
James T., 41
Samuel, 41, 147,
148, 153
William T., 147, 149
DIVINE
Jacob, 44
DODD
Catherine, 216
Jane, 197
John, 44
S., 9
Samuel, 216
DODEZ
Henry, 114
DONAHOE
Amos, 226
Mrs., 155
DONALDSON
Elizabeth, 61, 75
Thomas, 61, 75, 227
DONOHOE
Ann, 258
John V., 230
Nancy, 223
Phebe R., 179, 230
Samuel, 139
Sarah, 146, 230, 245
DORMAN
Samuel C., 227, 247
DORRELL
Thomas, 45
DORSEY
Edward, 41, 44, 60,
103, 117, 119,
122, 125, 135,

150, 169, 172,
192, 207
Judith, 7, 64
Mary, 192
Thomas J., 39
W. H., 2
William, 186
William F., 197
William H., 7, 64,
112, 130, 136,
148, 149, 152,
154, 174, 181,
184, 185, 187,
188, 194, 195,
198, 203, 205,
209, 214
DOTY
George W., 193
DOUGLAS
___, 19
Charles, 147, 215
Evelyn B., 237
Evylen B., 238
Pattrick H., 238
William, 14, 15
DOUGLASS
William, 14
DOVE
George, 19
DOWDALL
Mosses, 157, 158
Sarah, 157, 158
DOWDELL
John, 122
Moses, 115, 196
Mosses, 232
DOWDLE
Moses, 145
DOWLIN
Edward, 203
DOWLING
Edward, 77, 233
William, 123
DOWNEY
Barbara, 107
Robert, 107
DOWNING
Elizabeth, 46
James W., 46, 123
DRAIN
John, 66, 88, 90
DRAKE
Jacob, 150
Jesse S., 144

William, 44, 233
EVELAND
David, 79, 259
EVELIN
David, 114
EVENS
William, 148
EVERHART
Capt., 238
Casper, 242
Jacob, 211, 239, 247
Jaspar, 256
Jasper, 243
John, 246, 247
Joseph, 247
Mary, 242, 243
Michael, 27, 31, 56,
  73, 253
Nelson, 242
Philip, 73
Sarah, 246, 247
EVERHEART
Philip, 85
EWELL
Jesse, 177
EWERS
Barton, 11, 12, 37
Jonathan, 9, 101,
  123, 157, 213
Levi G., 197, 241
Thomas, 82

FADELEY
___, 113, 235
FADELY
Jacob, 36, 83, 98,
  167, 186, 240
Mary, 83
FADLEY
Jacob, 84, 88, 117
FAIRFAX
___, 144, 178, 206
Ferdinando, 3, 11,
  57, 60, 136, 137,
  152, 171, 184,
  192, 240
G. W., 95
George W., 44
Thomas, 12
FAIRHURST
George, 214
FANT
Edward L., 103
FARQUHAR

James, 23, 255
FARR
Elijah, 212
Rachael, 212
William, 188, 212
FARROW
Joseph, 15
FAULEY
Jacob, 55
FAWLEY
John, 206
FEARST
Cline, 59
Conrad, 59
Elizabeth, 59
Jane, 59
FEICHTER
George, 251
John, 62, 226, 251
Martha, 62
Peter, 62
Sarah, 85, 251
FEISTER
George, 61
FENTON
Jemima, 117
FERGUSON
___, 20
Amos, 76, 86, 107,
  112, 118, 125,
  126, 216, 241
Catherine, 216
FICHTER
George, 88
John, 62
Peter, 62, 88, 94,
  107, 118
Sarah, 88
Susan, 94
Susannah, 62, 88,
  118
FIETCHER
George, 11
FILLAR
Jacob, 206
FILLER
Elizabeth, 53
Frederick, 53
Mary, 53
Sally, 53
Samuel, 53
FISHELL
John, 46
FISHER

Henery, 253
FITCHTER
George, 193
Sally, 193
FITZHUGH
Ann, 217
Ann C., 4
Harrison, 4, 5
William, 151, 254
William C., 68
FITZIMONS
Samuel, 62
William, 158, 215
FLEMING
Archibald, 124
Jesse, 124
John, 68, 124, 205
R. J., 247
Richard J., 219
William, 124
FLETCHER
John, 244
Tacy P., 244
FLING
George, 187
Sandford, 187
FLOWER
Henry, 68
FLOWERS
Benjamin, 97, 255
FOLEY
Balis S., 216
Presley, 219
Sarah, 219
FONTAINE
Mary B., 234
FOOTE
W. H., 239
FORD
James W., 61
Stephen, 11
FORTNEY
Ms., 212
FORTUNE
Garner, 40
Thomas, 40
FOSTER
Elizabeth, 204
Jeremiah, 6
Mary, 23, 74
FOUCH
Jonathan, 24

Thomas, 41, 100,
177, 193, 200,
247, 251
Thomson, 218
FOWKE
William, 29
FOX
Amanda, 246
Amanda O., 190
Catherine E., 172
George K., 90, 123
Grace, 5
Jane, 123
Joseph B., 190, 246
Mary, 15, 16, 28, 31,
95, 101, 117, 120,
197, 216, 227
William, 250
William P., 172, 178,
179
FRANCE
William, 99
FRANCES
Enoch, 18
FRANCIS
Anna, 143
Enoch, 16, 67, 110,
113, 139, 143, 212
John, 16
Lewis, 16
Thomas, 4
William, 136
FRANK
Samuel, 227
FRAZIER
___, 155
Henry, 208, 218
FRED
Joseph, 121, 257
Joshua, 222
Thomas, 48, 159
FRENCH
Ann, 211, 219
Garrison, 209
Garrison B., 52, 54,
85, 96, 251
George W., 122, 142,
165
James D., 43, 52, 54,
65, 85, 96, 117,
122, 142, 165,
176, 251
Lewis, 30, 49, 178,
211, 219

Mason, 110, 153,
211, 219
Sarah, 211, 219
Thomas, 146
FRITS
George, 228
FRY
Aquilla, 60
Christena, 60
Christopher, 24
Daniel, 60, 83
Hannah, 90
Henry J., 209
Isaac, 19, 90, 94
Peter, 189
Philip, 8, 83, 190, 192
Phillip, 60
FRYE
___, 180, 198
Christopher, 15, 46,
196, 198, 240
George M., 176, 196,
229
John, 214
Margaret, 198
Mary, 196, 229
Michael, 235
P., 8
Peter, 202
Phillip, 67
FULKISON
William, 27
FULLER
Robert, 209
FULTON
Abraham, 137
Abraham M., 221
David, 66, 133, 161,
245
Ellizabeth, 245
Hugh, 169, 245
James, 245
John A., 96
Margaret, 245
Martha, 246
Rachael, 245
Rebecca, 246
Robert, 51, 118, 209,
228
Susannah, 245
William, 118, 246
FURGUSON
Amos, 48
FURR

Enoch, 99, 165, 201,
222
Minor, 54, 87
Sarah, 222
Thompson, 46

GAINER
George, 139
James, 159
GALLAHER
___, 25, 152
Caleb N., 120
David, 124
Eli, 97
Eli C., 255
John, 97, 255
John S., 155, 220
Mary, 141
William, 81
GALLEHER
___, 5, 109
Annah, 41
Caleb N., 43, 69, 73,
102, 255
David, 81, 186, 188,
189, 194, 224
Eli C., 41, 130
Elizabeth, 186, 189
Ellisabeth, 194
John, 28, 66, 224
Lucinda, 69
Mary, 130, 190
Phebe, 83
Samuel N., 83
Sarah, 28
William, 28, 41, 69,
83, 94, 130, 141,
186, 189, 190
GALLIHER
Anna, 29
David, 94
William, 29, 94
GALLOWAY
William, 148
GAMBLE
Joseph, 42, 131
GARARD
Corbly, 87
GARDNER
Robert, 90
GARNER
___, 94
Arthur, 236

James, 62, 79, 88, 120
Mahlon, 213
GARRET
___, 112
GARRETT
___, 48, 131
Eleanor, 73
Elizabeth, 36, 43
Enos, 46, 73, 186
James M., 55
Joseph, 42, 102
Mary, 172
Silas, 17, 102, 251
Stephen, 17, 101
GARRISON
French, 186
James, 215
GASSAWAY
Henrietta, 37, 43, 114
Thomas, 37, 41, 42, 43, 46, 67, 76, 103, 109, 111, 114, 193
GASSOWAY
Thomas H., 177
GATES
Matthew, 112
GEORGE
John, 1, 11, 27, 44, 59, 87, 151, 180, 181, 194, 197, 246
Thomas, 193
GETTINGS
Thomas, 214
GHEEN
James, 96
Leroy, 224
Marcissa, 96
Narcissa, 96, 224
Thomas, 13, 72, 201
William, 96, 224
GIBSON
___, 66, 86, 92, 182
A., 3, 12, 13, 14, 17, 18, 20, 21, 24, 35, 36, 48, 54, 59, 63, 64, 65, 69, 71, 72, 80, 81, 83, 86, 88, 95, 98, 101, 102, 103, 108, 116, 130, 132, 133, 143, 144, 146, 147, 149, 151,

152, 167, 168, 174, 179, 203, 207, 219, 224, 250, 252, 258
Abner, 2, 13, 20, 23, 25, 29, 40, 69, 70, 80, 82, 85, 87, 92, 101, 112, 114, 118, 120, 129, 130, 148, 149, 150, 152, 153, 159, 173, 174, 177, 186, 193, 194, 196, 202, 223, 224, 225, 252, 253
Alice, 205
Amos, 38, 103, 142, 235, 244, 255
Ann, 101
Billy, 256
David, 78, 200, 204
Elisabeth, 153
Eliza A., 256
Elizabeth, 244, 257
Hannah, 103, 235, 244
Israel, 103, 244
James, 103, 153
John, 19, 48, 51, 103, 142, 153, 205, 213, 244, 257
Jonathan, 100
Joseph, 103, 213
Mahlon, 51, 103, 205, 213, 244
Mary, 244
Mosses, 153, 155
Nancy, 204
Rachael, 213
Rebeca, 153
Rebecca A., 205
Tacy P., 244
Thomas, 204
William, 126
GIDEON
Peter, 152, 184
GILL
Hannah, 43
James, 81
Jeremiah, 37
John L., 3, 43
GILMORE
Edward, 188

James, 157, 240
William, 6, 40, 85, 146, 157, 164, 251
GILPIN
B., 31
Bernard, 72, 83, 84, 162
Latecia, 84
Samuel, 162, 182, 183, 233, 240
GLANDEN
William, 205
GLASCOCK
___, 109
B. R., 205
Elijah, 151
Hezekiah, 203
John, 151
Joice, 151
GLASCOW
Henry, 153
GLASSCOCK
Aquilla, 7
Nancy, 83
Peter, 254
Travis, 166
Uriel, 83
GLASSGOW
H., 45
Henry, 11
GLEESAR
Thomas, 151
GLEXON
George, 215
GLOSSER
John, 60, 64
GOCHNORER
Isaac, 3
GOODIN
David, 147
GOODING
Daniel, 3
John, 134
GORDON
Bazell, 61
GORE
Joseph, 89, 91, 104, 198, 214, 246
Joshua, 45, 46, 54, 120, 150, 209, 215, 253
Sarah, 11, 149
Solomon, 255

Thomas, 11, 149,
185, 215
Truman, 26
GORES
Mark, 33
GOURLEY
___, 254
Joseph, 61, 63
Martha, 63
Samuel, 61, 63
GOURLY
Abel, 124
GOVER
Jesse, 60, 62, 63,
103, 206, 243
Myriam, 63
GOWER
John, 1
GOWLEVOT
Bengamin, 110
GRADY
Edmund B., 100
Edward B., 25, 57,
65, 100, 108, 110,
165, 172, 213,
224, 259
James, 172, 195
Sarah, 65, 172
Ury, 37
GRAHAM
George, 64
John, 22
William, 116
GRANT
Aaron, 174
Esther, 56
Martha T., 174
Mary, 56
GRANTHEM
Tolliver P., 126
GRAVES
John, 49
Samuel, 95
GRAY
John, 31, 32, 116,
149, 215, 230, 259
GRAYSON
___, 173
Alexander C., 3
Amy, 224
Bengamin, 121
Benjamin, 3, 9, 18,
19, 21, 25, 29, 37,
43, 47, 57, 65, 68,

77, 79, 87, 90,
105, 108, 124,
131, 136, 140,
148, 157, 159,
177, 179, 187,
205, 210, 212,
213, 222, 228,
234, 235, 248,
254, 257
G. M., 3
George M., 3, 43,
124, 136, 165, 209
George W., 233
John W., 3
John A., 136
John W., 9, 19, 25,
43, 45, 46, 47, 57,
64, 65, 73, 79, 89,
90, 101, 103, 105,
108, 120, 121,
122, 124, 125,
131, 140, 142,
148, 157, 159,
161, 172, 173,
178, 179, 181,
192, 194, 195,
198, 210, 212,
213, 215, 222,
234, 235, 248, 257
Nancy, 9, 136
Richard O., 9
Spencer, 94
William, 230
GREEN
Ann, 202
Charles T., 202
Elizabeth, 95, 179
Gabrial, 28
Gabriel, 24, 30, 95,
150, 179
George, 202, 213
Jane, 14, 24, 25, 95
Luke, 59
Margaret, 59, 254
Nelson, 3, 11, 14, 19,
24, 25, 29, 87, 95,
150, 159, 202,
213, 251
Rolly, 16
William, 126
GREENLEASE
Catharine, 40, 46
James, 46, 50
William, 96

GREENLEESE
James, 27
GREENUP
___, 166
GREENWALL
Daniel, 26, 215, 259
David, 212
GREGG
___, 9
Ann, 33, 50, 188
Elisha, 126, 138, 169,
188
George, 201
Hannah, 5, 22, 197
Harriet, 131
John, 23, 34, 140,
165, 241
Joseph, 12, 251
Joshua, 37, 124, 127,
143
Josiah, 22, 248, 251
Mary, 251
Mrs., 160
Nathan, 109, 128
Nathaniel, 128
Nelson, 189
Rebeccah, 19
Ruth, 163
S., 101
Samuel, 5, 6, 16, 21,
22, 23, 28, 31, 95,
197, 216, 241
Stephen, 131, 216
Susanna, 21
Thomas, 1, 18, 29,
33, 37, 42, 50, 54,
65, 96, 120, 146,
171, 183, 203,
216, 222, 241, 242
Thomas C., 203
William, 19, 121, 145
GREY
John, 218
GRIFFITH
___, 56
Daniel W., 104
David, 60
Isaac, 26
Israel T., 248
J. T., 161
Richard, 56
Samuel G., 60
GRIGGS
Castalina, 34

Henry, 203
Thomas, 34, 120
GRIGGSBY
Lewis, 23, 241
GRIGSBY
John, 99, 227
John R., 225, 227
Lewis, 96, 198, 245
Nathaniel, 198
GRIMES
George, 241
Thomas, 69
GRINNAN
Daniel, 211
GROOVE
Philip, 154
GROOVER
Christopher, 120
GROVE
Philip, 86
William, 49
GROVES
Jesse, 122
Philip, 246
Phillip, 49
GRUBB
___, 11, 179, 180,
198
Adam, 60, 77, 143
B., 212
Benjamin, 26, 134,
185, 239, 251
Curtis, 229
E., 171, 197
Ebenezer, 12, 26, 31,
38, 53, 77, 78, 86,
98, 107, 114, 120,
124, 132, 133,
134, 140, 146,
152, 161, 171,
175, 184, 195,
198, 203, 204,
209, 213, 216,
218, 229, 237,
238, 239, 241,
242, 249
John, 228
Mary, 229
Samuel M., 175
William, 98, 241
GUILICK
Adam, 196
Amos, 158, 253
George, 147

John, 148, 199
Mosses, 146, 148,
199
Sarah, 147, 199
William, 199
GULATT
C., 152
Charles, 122, 138,
144, 155, 188
GULIC
Amos, 39
GULICK
Amos, 25
Mary, 194
Moses, 194, 202
William, 194, 202
GULLATT
Charles, 32, 63, 71,
106
Rebecca, 63, 106
GUN
James, 129
GUNNEL
Henry, 122
John, 146
GUNNELL
Henry, 103
Robert, 103, 122
William, 174, 187
GUNSTOFF
Lewis, 110
GWATKINS
Margaret, 251
Mary S., 251

HAGERMAN
Benjamin, 16, 130
Violinda, 130
HAINES
___, 96
Isaac, 240
Joseph, 54, 250
Maria, 54
Mary, 118
Simeon, 254
Stacey, 28
HAINS
Daniel, 36
John, 104
Joseph, 22, 67, 237,
238
Maria, 238
Stacy, 147
HALE

William, 101
HALL
Andrew, 64
Bazil, 24
Edward, 178, 225,
244, 248, 257
Elijah, 105
Josiah, 94
Louisa F., 225
Richard, 105, 233
Samuel, 162
Thomas, 67, 107
William, 36
Winnefred, 105
HALLAWAY
John, 259
Mary, 259
HALLEY
Jere H., 230
John H., 82, 218
Samuel, 78, 82, 185,
230
HALLY
John H., 218
Samuel, 218
HAMES
John, 100
HAMET
Samuel, 120
HAMILTON
___, 76, 209
Ann B., 176
C. B., 200
Charles, 95, 215, 216
Charles B., 35, 65,
182, 229, 235,
241, 250
Charles H., 158
David, 45
E. G., 1, 9, 30, 48,
49, 50, 51, 52, 59,
62, 68, 74, 75, 78,
79, 86, 87, 89, 90,
91, 92, 95, 98,
110, 112, 113,
115, 116, 126,
129, 131, 159,
162, 173, 183,
195, 205, 207, 221
Erasmus G., 63, 75,
141, 204, 227
H. H., 88, 108, 131
Henery H., 163

Henry H., 41, 49, 74,
128, 129
James, 15, 39, 46,
90, 130, 154, 161,
163, 214, 229
James H., 4, 41, 74,
85, 93, 106, 117,
135, 145, 150,
155, 157, 166,
170, 173, 178,
183, 190, 198,
203, 204, 209,
214, 220, 227,
236, 237, 239
James L., 37, 46,
216, 241, 245
Jane, 106
John, 13, 35, 42, 43,
46, 52, 58, 62, 63,
67, 69, 74, 108,
136, 156, 158,
159, 166, 175,
177, 181, 208,
211, 212, 216,
227, 228, 229, 243
Julious, 113
Julius, 86, 91
Margaret, 135, 178,
214
Mary, 161, 214
Robert, 39, 45, 55
Samuel G., 15, 90,
123
William, 162
Winefred, 175
Winifred, 176
HAMITT
Henery H., 157
HAMMAT
Alice B., 14
E., 98
Edward, 14, 109,
116, 120, 127,
206, 223
George, 26, 145
Giles, 14
John, 145
Samuel, 110, 145
Sarah, 14
HAMMATT
Betsy, 258
Edward, 4, 82, 154,
197, 236, 240, 258
Ellizabeth, 197

George, 197
Giles, 240
Samuel, 93, 168,
169, 171, 240
Winefred, 93
HAMMERLY
Jane, 108, 235
John, 108, 113, 235
William, 91
HAMMET
John, 207
Samuel, 85, 139,
207, 217
HAMMETT
___, 161
Alice, 57
Edward, 57, 62, 66,
93, 188, 218
George, 188
Giles, 57, 58, 81
Samuel, 15, 26, 32,
58, 81, 83, 103,
104, 163, 176,
215, 226
Sarah, 62
HAMMOND
John, 59, 226
HAMMONTREE
___, 132
Samuel, 130
William W., 240
HAN
Joseph, 233
HANBY
___, 57
HANCOCK
George, 157, 219
HANDLEY
David, 194, 254
HANDSHEY
Catharine, 78
Frederick, 78
HANDSHY
Catharine, 86
Catherine, 155
Frederick, 41, 86,
155
HANDY
___, 65
Eli H., 16, 41, 54, 67,
203, 238
Elleanor, 242
Ellenor, 42
Given, 54, 203, 238

John, 16, 49, 54, 112,
203, 238
John C., 10, 54, 67,
243
John E., 247
Maria, 54
Uree, 170
W. H., 3
William H., 42, 49,
54, 74, 77, 216,
237, 238, 242
HANES
Edward, 62
HANK
Henry, 95
HANKS
Ann, 8
Catharine, 8
Cephus, 3, 8
Jeremiah, 8
John, 8, 185
Stiles, 8
Zedock, 8
HANLEY
William J., 90
HANLY
Daniel, 163
HANN
John, 55, 159
Mary, 7, 89
Mathias, 7, 73
Matthias, 25
Peter, 7, 112
William, 7, 77, 89
HANNA
William, 223
HANNAH
William, 223
HANNELY
John, 218
HANSBOROUGH
Thomas D. L., 29
HARDACRE
___, 180
Barbara, 198
Mordecai, 194, 198
HARDEN
Elizabeth, 17
Henry, 17
Peyton, 99
William, 17, 57
HARDING
Elizabeth P. B., 18

HEIR
Jane, 61
Thomas, 24, 27, 61,
62, 80, 104, 160
HEIS
Catherine, 126
John, 126
HEISKELL
John, 9
HENDERSON
Alexander, 107, 207
David, 83
Mary, 83
Orra M., 57, 58, 136,
220, 221, 259
R. H., 52, 88, 107,
128, 168, 171,
173, 177, 189, 205
Richard H., 4, 10, 13,
20, 21, 23, 26, 30,
31, 32, 38, 39, 40,
41, 42, 47, 50, 51,
57, 58, 59, 60, 61,
64, 66, 70, 72, 74,
76, 77, 78, 81, 83,
93, 95, 98, 99,
100, 108, 110,
112, 113, 115,
116, 117, 119,
125, 126, 127,
135, 136, 162,
137, 138, 141,
144, 146, 147,
148, 151, 153,
155, 157, 160,
163, 164, 170,
176, 183, 184,
187, 189, 191,
193, 197, 200,
203, 204, 206,
207, 210, 212,
213, 216, 220,
221, 222, 226,
230, 232, 240,
242, 248, 252,
256, 259
Samuel, 73
Samuel C., 19
Samuel E., 8
William, 83
HENRY
Amos, 165, 233, 254
Elisabeth, 165
Elizabeth, 10

George W., 1, 10, 43,
64, 73, 95, 101,
103, 122, 132,
185, 216
HENSHA
Frederick, 218
HENSHAW
James W., 41
HERBERT
James, 168
Thomas, 168
William, 38, 49, 77,
136, 154, 225
HEREFORD
___, 66, 81, 132,
148, 254
Ann C., 100, 133
Francis, 101, 133
Francis H., 100
James, 20, 23, 68,
94, 113, 148, 176
John B., 100
John W., 100, 101
Juliet, 100, 101
Margaret A., 100
Mary A., 100
Matthew C., 100
Thomas A., 55, 121,
160, 259
HERRON
David W., 44
Robert, 44
HERVETT
William, 76
HESKETT
___, 20
John, 35
HESSER
Andrew, 71, 86, 90
David, 86
Elizabeth, 71
John, 86
HEWETT
Peter, 234
HEWITT
William, 46, 93
HIBBS
Amos, 94, 209
Joseph, 65, 94
HICKMAN
___, 10, 134, 185,
258
Catherine, 198
Elisabeth, 178

Elizabeth, 202
Henery, 178, 200,
202
Henry, 27
Jane, 160, 165
John, 27, 178, 200
Joseph, 160, 165
Joseph S., 160, 165
Magdalena, 193
Mary, 200, 211, 243
Michael, 198
Peter, 1, 28, 178,
193, 198, 200,
202, 206
William, 254
HICKS
Isaiah, 254
Moses, 218
HIER
Thomas, 168
HIERS
Catharine, 138
Catherine, 140
John, 138, 140
HIES
Catherine, 140, 145
John, 140, 145
HIGDEN
James, 118
HIGDON
___, 167
HIGGINS
James, 230
HILL
James, 7, 239
HILLAIRD
Joseph, 62
HILLARD
Joseph, 46
HILLEARD
Joseph, 51, 177
HILLEARY
John H., 2
Perry, 2
William, 1
HILLIARD
Joseph, 13, 67, 90,
108, 219
HILLMAN
Andrew, 152
HILTON
Luke, 182
HINES
Daniel, 229

HIRST
 Elizabeth, 8
 Jesse, 8
 Richard, 8
HISLOP
 Isabella, 126
 John G., 126
HIXON
 Catharine, 92, 115
 James, 146, 222
 L. W. P., 238
 Mary, 92, 146
 Peyton, 200
 Polly, 138
 Reuben, 45, 92, 115,
  170, 180
HIXSON
 ___, 30, 52
 Benjamin, 66, 131,
  132, 222
 James, 30, 32, 64,
  66, 78, 81, 82,
  100, 101, 131, 132
 Margaret, 6, 72
 Mary, 30, 72, 80,
  115, 131, 132
 Noah, 61, 83
 Reuben, 30, 72, 130
 Stephenson, 83
 William, 6
HOBLETZELL
 ___, 227
HOCKING
 John, 168
HOCKINGS
 ___, 20
 John, 179
 Joseph, 135
HODGERSON
 Mrs., 148
HODGSON
 Portia, 36, 40, 105,
  244
 Potia, 165
HOFFMAN
 Jacob, 36, 63
HOGE
 James, 18, 29, 50,
  90, 93, 96, 113,
  117, 125, 142,
  149, 151, 179,
  185, 194, 195,
  203, 222, 229,
  233, 247

Jesse, 80, 246
Joseph, 35
William, 22, 34, 42,
 50, 117, 218, 246,
 255
HOGLAND
 ___, 28
HOGUE
 James, 4, 9, 149
 Jesse, 177
 Joseph, 35, 110, 207,
  209, 225
 Mary, 42, 190
 Miller, 35, 207, 209
 Samuel, 190
 Tacey, 35, 207, 209
 William, 18, 33, 42,
  177, 207
HOLLINGSWORTH
 Jehu, 29, 33, 35, 37,
  54, 65, 178
 Jemimah, 113
 Senior, 35, 65, 178
HOLLOWAY
 Aaron, 9, 183
 Rachel, 9
HOLMES
 ___, 22
 Elijah, 190
 Hugh, 92
 John, 22, 96, 209
 Joseph, 190
 Martha, 204, 233
 Rowena, 170, 173,
  183
 William, 78, 88, 190,
  215
HOLMS
 William, 236
HOMBS
 Martha, 182
HOMER
 Richard B., 7
HOMES
 Jacob, 253
HONE
 Isaac S., 250
 Joanna, 250
 John, 249, 250
HOOD
 Jonah, 59, 168
 Nancy, 59
HOOE
 Bernard, 48

William H., 180
HOOFF
 John, 204
HOPKINS
 John, 41
HOPWOOD
 ___, 49
HORNE
 Henery, 170
HORSEMAN
 James, 2
HOSPITAL
 Andrew, 49
HOUGH
 ___, 74, 87, 161,
  176, 209, 236
 Abiel S., 69
 Amasa, 72, 80, 144
 Amos, 96
 Ann, 154
 B., 10, 23, 79
 Barnard, 76
 Barnett, 4
 Benjamin, 27, 96
 Bernard, 42, 66, 127
 Deborah, 65
 Elisabeth, 173, 175
 George S., 239
 Isaac, 74, 85, 180,
  185
 Jane, 19, 230
 John, 46, 52, 81, 89,
  96, 140, 150, 173,
  175, 235
 Joseph, 1, 64, 65, 96,
  205, 250
 Lydia, 19, 171
 Mahlon, 50, 238
 Mary, 27, 171
 Mary Ann, 137
 Peyton, 44, 72, 80
 R. R., 122
 Robert, 47
 Robert R., 122, 137,
  146, 204, 226, 259
 S., 3, 19, 52, 61, 77,
  195, 221
 Samuel, 2, 3, 5, 6, 7,
  8, 10, 15, 19, 27,
  28, 29, 31, 32, 34,
  41, 55, 56, 59, 63,
  66, 67, 68, 73, 75,
  84, 97, 101, 107,
  116, 117, 118,

121, 136, 137,
147, 154, 156,
170, 171, 172,
175, 180, 193,
195, 197, 200,
201, 202, 210,
215, 217, 236,
239, 248, 250, 254
Sarah, 96, 171
Sarah C., 146
Thomas, 85, 89
Washington, 72, 80
William, 18, 31, 52,
54, 56, 71, 80,
117, 175, 180,
229, 230, 250
William H., 41, 63,
67, 125, 132, 137,
171, 173, 175
HOUGHFMAN
John, 83
HOUSEHOLDER
___, 229
Adam, 26, 30, 47, 93,
107, 162, 247, 251
Daniel, 59, 143
Gideon, 93, 107, 138,
237
Julia, 107
Julia A., 237
Lydia, 107
Mahala, 49
Mary, 49
Ruth, 49
Sarah, 26
Soloman, 93
Solomon, 142
Susan, 93, 138
Susanah, 143
Susanna, 93
Susannah, 26, 47,
107, 243, 251
HOUSER
Abigail, 8
Jacob, 8, 169, 170
Philip, 159
HOUSHOLDER
Adam, 11, 49
Gideon, 251
Gidian, 162
HOUSTON
John M., 124
HOWELL
___, 18

Daniel, 109, 133
Henry, 216
William, 184
HOWSER
Abigail, 27
Abraham, 134
Jacob, 27
HOYT
Jesse, 175
HUFFMAN
John, 136, 259
Mrs., 17
Phebe, 136, 259
HUGHES
___, 191, 196
Constantine, 46, 150,
215, 218
Edward, 205
Elias, 6
Elisha, 134
Elizabeth, 95, 134
Fanny, 134
Hugh, 234
Isaac, 220
John, 134, 234
Lydia, 134
Maria, 134
Martha, 218
Mary, 218, 234
Mathew, 134
Ruth, 134
Samuel, 86, 95, 134
Sarah, 134, 234
Thomas, 6, 45, 95,
114, 134, 150,
218, 231, 234
HUMMER
William, 233
HUMPHREY
___, 65, 235
Abner, 9, 55, 65, 92,
97, 98, 100, 105,
124, 131, 150,
192, 234, 259
Abner G., 65, 124,
150
Charles, 220
Jacob, 17, 185
Jesse, 157, 212
Jessee, 123
John, 244
John G., 65, 92, 97,
98, 121, 124, 131,

192, 229, 235,
244, 259
Joseph, 9, 157, 249
Marcus, 22, 53, 124
Margaret, 22, 124
Mary, 121, 212, 235
Mary A., 220
Rachael, 212
Roger, 41
Sarah, 18, 185, 186,
187
Sarah A., 212
Thomas, 6, 53, 65,
92, 97, 157, 171
Thomas G., 237
Thomas J., 124
Thomas L., 17, 18,
185, 186, 187
Thomas M., 258
Urey, 220
William, 186
HUMPHREYS
Abner, 171
David, 17, 18
John, 17, 18, 171
John G., 234
HUNT
Joseph, 212
Lewis, 4, 20, 130
Mary, 4
Nathaniel, 95
Rebecca, 167
William, 167
HUNTER
George W., 183
Robert, 115
HURST
Jesse, 208
HUTCHISON
Abigail, 1, 77
B., 181
Catherine, 251
Daniel, 25
Eli, 77
Elijah, 133
Elizabeth, 77
Enoch, 1, 77
Henery, 142, 237
J., 177
James, 77
Jefferson, 217
Jeremiah, 133, 134

John, 1, 77, 97, 128,
170, 181, 182,
217, 219
Joseph, 15
Joshua, 90, 91, 133,
181, 182
Keren, 1
Keziah, 90, 91
Lemuel, 89, 251
Lewis, 90, 91
Lydia, 255
Mary Ann, 133, 134
Nancy, 77
Nathan, 184
Richard, 77
Sampson, 90, 91
Sandford, 133, 181,
182
Sanford, 134
Thomas, 1, 128

IDEN
Hannah, 3, 174
James, 35, 174
John, 3, 174
Margaret, 174
Rebecca, 13
Samuel, 13, 203, 231
Sarah, 203
INGLE
Joseph W., 39
IRWIN
Johnson, 181
ISH
Jacob, 29, 43, 65,
168, 192, 200
Peter, 62, 82, 96, 116
Robert A., 65
William K., 44

JACKSON
Benjamin, 9, 22, 25,
73, 82, 192, 210
Ellisabeth, 210
John, 8, 96, 175
John W., 82
Lovel, 248
Lovell, 185
S. A., 11, 25, 182,
184, 195
Samuel, 64
Samuel A., 182
Sarah, 182

Thomas, 90, 103,
238
JACOBS
___, 11, 53, 109
Adam, 58
Catharine, 63, 83,
100
Catherine, 180
Christian, 58, 111,
220
Christianna, 58
Elisabeth, 123
Elizabeth, 58
Ellizabeth, 245
George, 58
John, 58
Katherine, 249
Maria, 100, 249
Mary, 58
Matilda, 91
Mrs., 46
Peter, 58, 123, 204,
220
Price, 24, 125, 180,
235, 248, 249, 252
Reonard, 58
Ryland, 259
Thomas, 48, 91
Valentine, 31, 58, 67,
123
William, 9, 63, 83,
249
William H., 227, 240
JAMES
___, 163
Abel, 135
Abigail, 179
Ann, 13
Anna, 179
Anne, 181
Benjamin, 76, 216
Charlotte, 194
Daniel, 8, 131, 133,
168, 169, 175,
184, 207
David, 7, 190, 194,
216
Dean, 1, 78, 179, 255
Elias, 169, 175, 176,
184, 207
Isaac, 140
Jacob, 13, 78
John, 19, 68, 112,
179

Jonathan, 25, 169,
175, 184, 207
Mary, 147
Nancy, 179
Polly, 169
Ruth, 169
Sally, 216
Sarah, 135, 140
Smith, 13, 179
Thomas, 34, 51, 92,
106, 143, 147,
151, 167, 181,
184, 186, 227,
235, 236
William, 1, 179
JANNEY
___, 7, 61, 75, 180
Abel, 1, 7, 64, 80,
110, 142, 179,
182, 196, 206, 218
Amos, 9, 12, 26, 60,
83, 151, 189
Blackstone, 78, 208,
214
Daniel, 22, 34, 80,
139, 180, 207,
241, 255
David, 23, 215
Eli, 169, 182, 208,
214
Elisha, 70, 80, 103,
104, 166, 244
Elizabeth, 12
Elozabeth, 26
George, 8, 37, 38,
52, 70, 80, 104,
120, 122, 123,
128, 132, 149,
151, 156, 158,
162, 195, 196,
241, 244
Israel, 42, 53, 73,
151, 235, 255
James M., 1
John, 5, 7, 12, 24, 26,
32, 45, 97, 99,
103, 121, 134,
144, 156, 182,
185, 240
Jonas, 63, 152, 206
Jonathan, 144
Joseph, 3, 6, 35, 99,
112, 140, 146,
151, 201

Catherine, 241
Daniel, 135
David, 6, 34, 113, 117, 120, 207
Elias, 118, 126
Huldah, 104, 118, 119, 137, 252
Israel, 24, 36, 68, 98, 177, 241
John, 69, 137, 241
Mary A., 241
Mary P., 118
Matilda, 120
Matilda P., 177
Meshack, 51, 213
Meshech, 30
Mesheck, 95, 104
Misheck, 118
Miss, 20, 51, 160
Mrs., 172
Naomai, 119, 137
Naomi, 104, 118
Neoimi, 252
Patience, 232
Robert A., 98, 99, 240, 241, 242
Ruth, 104, 118, 119, 137, 252
Sarah, 34
Tacey, 104, 252
Tacy, 118
Thomas, 176, 197, 232, 250
Tracy, 137
Westwood, 241
Westwood A., 252
William, 232

LACKLAND
George L., 32

LADD
Joseph B., 137

LAFABER
___, 159
William, 19

LAFFERTY
Anne A., 239
Isaac, 99
Samuel, 78, 168, 204

LAKE
Isaac, 48
William, 159

LAMBAG
Anthony, 11
Jane, 11

Joseph, 11

LAMBERT
George, 125, 142

LANCASTER
William, 171

LANE
___, 133
Catharine, 69
E. M., 68
Epaminondas M., 97
Flavius J., 97
Hardage, 2
Johnson, 73
Joseph, 69, 97, 234, 248
Katharine, 97
Katherine, 234
William H., 2, 4

LANGLEY
Susan M., 159
Susanna, 101
Susannah, 82
Walter, 17, 25, 61, 82, 83, 101, 159

LANGLY
Susanah, 148
Walter, 148

LANGTON
Thomas W., 147

LANHAM
Aaron, 226
Acquilla, 214
Walter, 214
Zadock, 226

LARMOUR
Samuel B., 98, 99, 252

LAROWE
Isaac, 84, 178

LARROWE
Isaac, 31

LARUE
James, 143

LATHAM
P., 96

LATTIMORE
James, 233
Racheal, 233

LAWRENCE
Alexander, 239
Philippa E. W., 104
William W., 142

LAWSON
Nero, 172

LAYCOCK
Samuel, 66

LEACHMAN
Dolly A., 53
Elizabeth, 53
William, 53

LEAMING
George, 8

LEATH
Wheatman, 178

LEE
___, 29
Alexander, 21
E. J., 36
Edmond J., 1
Edmund J., 36, 38, 61, 64, 107, 156, 184, 193, 204, 232, 250
Edward J., 111
Eliza A., 234
Fanny, 61
George, 19, 64, 68, 159, 164, 187, 232, 237, 238, 251
George F., 20, 139
Henry, 139
Joshua, 185
Lucy, 36
Ludwell, 21, 73, 102, 164, 167, 168, 169, 172, 174, 175, 176, 178, 183, 184, 198, 202, 217, 219, 221, 222, 225, 232, 234, 244, 248, 250
Maria C., 159, 238
Mary D., 76
Portia, 244
Richard H., 4, 58, 74, 76, 141, 161, 209, 212, 240, 242
Sally, 36, 156, 204
T. W., 20
Thomas L., 68, 128, 147, 222, 237, 238
Thomas W., 90, 91, 133
William, 244
William L., 59, 245

LEISLE
Amanda O., 164

Daniel, 36, 85, 121,
  166, 172, 191,
  204, 239
David, 1, 4, 24, 61,
  87, 120, 121, 140,
  143, 151, 165,
  169, 205, 228, 254
Edmund, 38, 80, 101,
  120, 127, 128,
  129, 160, 166,
  172, 178, 202,
  204, 237
Elisabeth, 160, 166
Elizabeth, 129
Jonathan, 228, 256
Joseph, 94
Nancy, 111
LOWELL
  H. B., 2
LOYD
  Henery, 171
  William, 151
LUCKET
  H., 217
LUCKETT
  ___, 133
  Alfred, 90, 111
  Francis W., 4, 5, 6, 7,
  12, 13, 14, 18, 19,
  20, 22, 23, 24, 25,
  28, 33, 39, 41, 44,
  48, 52, 53, 54, 64,
  70, 76, 81, 83, 96,
  97, 98, 104, 110,
  112, 113, 117,
  124, 130, 135,
  136, 137, 144,
  148, 149, 161,
  169, 172, 174,
  177, 183, 185,
  186, 187, 188,
  189, 194, 199,
  200, 211, 213,
  219, 223, 224,
  238, 249, 257
  Henry F., 205
  Horace, 43, 49, 77,
  144, 199, 221
  Horrace, 137, 164,
  168, 181, 196,
  200, 232
  Leticia, 199
  Lettitia, 202

Leven, 13, 21, 23, 24,
  25, 35, 36, 42, 57,
  80, 83, 108, 112,
  133, 152, 164,
  168, 169, 181,
  194, 199, 200,
  202, 207, 224, 252
Levin, 194
Rebecca, 210
Sally, 210
Samuel, 210
Sarah S., 18, 224
Thomas H., 205
William C., 210
William F., 169, 205,
  224
LUKE
  ___, 259
  Jacob, 17, 83
  Joseph, 150
  Sarah, 17, 83
LUM
  John, 127
LUTTRAIL
  Alexander, 23
LUTZ
  Mary, 240, 249
LYDER
  Cornelia, 223
  Jacob, 223
  Landon, 223
  Lemuel, 223
  Lettitia, 223
  Lewis, 74, 127, 143,
  191, 223
  Lydia, 223
  Mahala, 223
  Margaret, 191
  Mary, 191, 223
LYLE
  Robert, 200
  William, 200
LYNE
  William, 78, 82, 184,
  210, 218, 230
LYNN
  Fielding, 113, 150,
  189
  James, 150
  Michael, 245
LYON
  John C., 142
LYONS
  Anne, 60

Cleve, 60
John, 128
William, 187

MACKLIN
  James, 52
  Mary, 52
MACRAE
  John, 33
MADDISON
  Rachael, 245
MAGRUDER
  Ninion, 20
MAINES
  Archibald, 158
MAINS
  Archibald, 85, 109,
  149, 162, 193
  William, 251
MALLIN
  Jesse, 195
MALONY
  Abel, 45
MANDEVILLE
  Joseph, 98, 99, 252
Mandeville and
  Lannom, 23
Mandeville and
  Larmour, 98
MANLEY
  John, 26, 52
  Sarah, 26, 27
MANLY
  John, 26, 42
  Sarah, 42
MANN
  George, 77
  Jacob, 251
  John, 8, 42, 45, 52,
  77, 189
  John A., 24
  Mary, 77
MANNING
  Euphama, 128
  Euphamia, 37
  Euphemia, 122, 123
  Nathaniel, 34, 37,
  116, 120, 122,
  123, 128
  Uphamiah, 34
MANSFIELD
  John, 121
MARKS

Abel, 22, 25, 29, 33,
  51, 55
Bennet, 22
Bennett, 7, 34, 55
David, 101
Elisha, 37, 101
George, 7, 24, 108,
  117, 129, 179,
  181, 192, 210,
  228, 254
George S., 25, 73
Hannah, 29
Isaiah, 37, 101, 108,
  172
John, 9, 25, 37, 47,
  73, 74, 82, 101,
  108
Keziah, 55, 69, 141,
  162, 219
Lucinda, 101
Lydia, 22, 37, 108
Mahala, 73
Mary, 22, 29, 33
Mason, 22, 25, 29, 97
Matt, 22
Samuel, 22
Thomas, 22, 33, 51,
  55, 69, 135, 141,
  162, 171, 219
Watts, 33, 51
MARLOW
___, 202
Ann, 238
Ann E., 208
Dr., 132
Edward, 1, 12, 28,
  53, 92, 183
George, 1, 86
Hanson, 28, 86
Henson, 9
John G., 11
John S., 1, 10, 26,
  52, 119, 208, 238
JohnS., 35
Mary, 10
Thomas J., 1, 10, 31,
  35, 41, 208
MARMADUKE
___, 233
Catharine, 192
Daniel, 122
John A., 31, 38, 97,
  98, 151, 173, 179,
  192

MARSHAL
Ruel, 171
MARSHALL
___, 207
John, 56, 64
R., 82
Ruel, 136
MARTIN
Andrew, 13, 133
David, 91
Edward, 97, 133
Elizabeth, 97
James F., 113
James L., 46, 108,
  117, 127, 154,
  196, 212, 223,
  240, 250, 256, 258
John, 37, 43, 46, 48,
  66, 97, 106, 110,
  124, 133, 145,
  191, 206, 226,
  240, 258
John L., 226
Margret, 115
Mary, 47, 133
Robert, 133
Sally A. P., 196
Sarah, 258
William, 94, 133
MASH
James, 99
MASON
___, 37, 49, 132
A. T., 7, 125
Abraham, 132
Abraham B. T., 115
Ann, 145, 163, 199
Betsey C., 232
Enoch, 46
John J., 199
John L., 200
John T., 55, 81, 82
Mary, 55, 64, 81, 82
Richard B., 81
Stephen T., 55, 81,
  95
Stephens T., 82
Thompson, 132, 200
Thompson F., 197
Thomson, 64, 71, 81,
  102, 125, 128,
  140, 145, 159,
  163, 168, 169, 205

Thomson F., 123,
  156, 232, 256
Westwood T., 83,
  199, 200
William T. T., 64, 81,
  84, 88, 125, 163,
  169, 195, 200,
  205, 221
MASSIE
John W., 188, 225
MASTERSON
Charles, 22
MATEER
James, 186, 188, 212
MATHEWS
___, 7
Jonathan, 78
Richard, 228
Simon, 143
MATHIAS
John, 46, 55, 107,
  128, 147, 154
John J., 38, 47, 52,
  53, 58, 64, 68, 75,
  82, 91, 92, 94,
  105, 106, 111,
  114, 140, 158,
  159, 161, 170,
  205, 211, 212,
  213, 214, 221,
  223, 225, 232,
  238, 241, 242,
  243, 247, 249,
  252, 258, 259
Mark, 9
Robert, 241
Robert H., 111
William, 164
MATTBY
W. D., 193
MAULSBY
Bengamin, 114
Benjamin, 46, 78, 93
MAUND
John J., 139
MAYO
Joseph H., 43
McALLISTER
William, 167
McBRIDE
James, 96, 136
McCABE
___, 126, 176, 235
Elisabeth, 176

J. H., 50, 73
Jane, 39
John, 13, 32, 72, 176,
    250
John H., 16, 47, 50,
    55, 57, 58, 63, 78,
    79, 83, 84, 94,
    100, 102, 109,
    110, 116, 135,
    137, 141, 142,
    153, 157, 170,
    176, 178, 196,
    197, 199, 201,
    213, 214, 217,
    218, 221, 229,
    231, 239, 240,
    242, 243, 248,
    249, 258
Mary, 58
William, 176
McCAFFERY
John, 12
McCAFFREY
Ira, 169
Irey, 177
Sarah, 169, 177
McCARTY
Ann L., 218, 229, 230
Ann M., 218
Daniel, 229, 230
Dennis, 35, 44, 70,
    161, 213, 246
Edgar, 218
Emily, 221
Emily R., 95
G. W., 199
George W., 13, 36,
    44
John M., 60, 105,
    110, 133, 147,
    164, 211, 217,
    218, 221, 229, 230
Richard C., 181
Thomas, 160
Washington, 73
William M., 26, 27,
    58, 80, 84, 92, 95,
    99, 133, 146, 215,
    218, 221
McCHRISTLY
Arthur, 45
McClain
James, 234, 252
McCLELLAND

Matilda, 91
    Samuel C. B., 91
McCONNELL
Ezekiel, 96
McCORD
Samuel, 75
McCORMACK
John, 110, 125, 126,
    135, 137, 141,
    143, 146, 149,
    161, 162
McCORMICK
___, 113
John, 4, 6, 11, 14, 17,
    21, 22, 23, 27, 38,
    43, 46, 51, 57, 58,
    62, 65, 72, 74, 78,
    93, 94, 98, 105,
    108, 117, 118,
    120, 127, 128,
    129, 130, 147,
    150, 151, 155,
    160, 168, 170,
    173, 176, 177,
    180, 183, 190,
    193, 197, 199,
    200, 207, 211,
    217, 218, 219,
    231, 235, 237,
    239, 244, 252
Mary, 46, 62, 117,
    199
P., 223
Province, 249
Robert, 94
McCOWAT
___, 235
McCRAY
James, 123, 216
McCRUM
Robert, 9
McDANIEL
Edward, 208
James, 8, 22, 28, 39,
    114, 246
John, 20
Martin N., 44
Nancy, 44
Norris, 229
McDONAUGH
James, 91
McDONOUGH
James, 237
Kezia, 237

McDOWOLL
James, 182
McFARLAND
Eleanor, 186
John, 38
McFARLING
John, 38
McGAHY
Daniel, 109
David, 111, 114
Dorcas, 109
McGARICK
James, 120
Patrick, 120
McGARRICK
___, 41
McGARVICK
Israel, 60
Patrick, 60
McGAVACK
Pattrick, 243
McGAVICK
Israel, 167
Pattrick, 167, 241
McGAVOCK
___, 220
McGEATH
Stephen, 3, 33, 44,
    50, 74
William, 201
McGILL
Charles B., 2
Thomas, 155
McGRAW
Richard, 144
McILHANEY
___, 42
Ellizabeth, 229
James, 18, 75, 151,
    196, 215, 231
Mary, 196
Milton, 229
Mortimer, 24, 27
Mortimore, 247
T. Milton, 24
McILHANY
___, 118, 130, 165
Cecelia, 163, 249,
    256
Elisabeth, 143, 163,
    169, 176
Elizabeth, 149
Harriet, 149
J., 144

MECKINS
  Barney, 152
MEGEATH
  Gabriel, 4, 42, 185
  James, 42
  Martha, 4, 42
  Mary, 42
  Rebecca, 42
  Stephen, 42, 44
MENDENHAL
  Bulah, 63
MENDENHALL
  Jacob, 63, 255
MERCER
  C. F., 194
  Charles F., 5, 34, 59,
    121, 130, 168,
    217, 241
  Col., 239
  James, 30, 55, 81
  Joseph, 4
MERRITT
  Edward, 199
  Gilbert S., 199
MERSHON
  Ann, 20
  Joseph B., 20
  Nancy, 77
  Thomas B., 20
  William, 255
MERTIN
  W. T., 165
MICHAEL
  Mary, 119
MIDDLETON
  Maryann, 24
  Mrs., 116
  Samuel, 215
  Studly, 24
MILBOURN
  David, 191
MILES
  Benjamin, 28, 178
  James, 91
MILHOLLAND
  John, 23, 99
  Nancy, 23, 99
  Patrick B., 23
MILHOLLEN
  Esther, 206
  John, 56
  John W., 56, 206
  Malinda, 56
  Mary, 56

Melinda, 56
Patrick, 56
Patrick B., 56
MILHOLLIN
  ___, 7
  John, 206
  Patrick B., 206
MILLER
  Aaron, 5, 8, 27, 30,
    97, 115, 134, 179,
    180, 185, 194,
    212, 228
  Adam, 8, 168, 179,
    180, 238
  Catharine, 47, 48
  Catherine, 168, 179,
    180
  Christena, 168
  Christian, 226, 238
  Daniel, 30, 45
  Elisabeth, 179
  Elizabeth, 8
  Ellisabeth, 180, 211
  George, 249
  Jacob, 182
  James, 79, 136, 186
  Jeremiah T., 191
  Jesse, 168, 179, 180
  John, 9, 56, 93, 250
  Joseph, 239
  Levi, 58
  Mary, 30, 45, 134,
    179, 185, 212
  Michael, 47
  Mordecai, 197
  Mordica, 32
  Mosses, 168
  Peter, 168, 180, 198,
    218
  Rachel, 5
  Rebeca, 179, 180
  Robert H., 188
  Valentine, 203
  W. H., 32
  William H., 195
MILLHOLLEN
  Henery, 244
MILLIKEN
  Samuel, 96
MILLS
  Ezra, 21
  James, 116
MILTABARGAR
  John, 243

MILTON
  Henry, 216
  Richard, 38
  William, 153
MINES
  Eliza, 218
  John, 6, 79, 135, 167,
    218, 247
MINK
  ___, 134, 185
  Adam, 200
  Sarah, 200
MINOR
  Daniel, 11, 156
  Elizabeth, 11
  Eskridge, 11
  John, 11
  Margaret, 11
  Nancy, 11
  Nathan, 172
  Rebekah, 11
  Spencer, 11
  Thomas, 11
MISKELL
  ___, 31
  William, 72, 102, 106,
    121
MITCHEL
  Benjamin, 125
MITCHELL
  B., 141
  Ben, 109
  Benjamin, 24, 68, 84,
    97, 118, 142, 154,
    194, 223, 234, 248
  Elizabeth, 93
  Ellizabeth, 226
  Hannah, 36, 135
  John, 118
  Martha, 24, 97, 248
  Mathew, 68, 157
  Matthew, 27, 93, 226
MOCK
  Daniel, 55
MOFFETT
  ___, 131
  Benjamin, 3, 159
  Elizabeth, 139
  Fanny, 139
  Hannah, 139, 180
  Henry, 233
  Hugh, 91
  Josiah, 41, 139, 180,
    186

Malinda, 159
Martha, 139, 186
Milly, 139
Nancy, 139
Robert, 23, 39, 56,
  60, 67, 69, 81, 99,
  100, 138, 139,
  141, 159, 170,
  174, 180, 186,
  201, 206, 217, 228
Sally, 139
Thomas J., 139
MOLER
John, 155
MOLIN
___, 163
MONDAY
John S., 69
MONEY
Nicholas, 61, 75
MONROE
Andrew, 194
Deskin D., 142
Eliza, 192
James, 52, 163, 183,
  192, 211, 216,
  230, 258
John, 194, 226
John H., 37, 46, 58,
  103, 110, 120, 240
John M., 5, 6, 53
Sarah, 194
MONTEATH
Leah, 192
MONTEITH
Enos, 178, 244
James, 110
MONTGOMERY
Robert, 197
S. H., 158
MOOR
John, 27, 88, 106,
  107, 125
Robert, 104
MOORE
___, 32, 73
Ann, 176
Asa, 10, 69, 132,
  133, 139, 144,
  145, 165, 176,
  224, 250
J., 155
James, 6, 7, 17, 23,
  69, 89, 137, 217,

241, 243, 244,
  249, 250, 255
John, 1, 8, 29, 113,
  120, 147, 253
Jonathan, 61
Peter, 6
Thomas A., 1, 4, 9,
  10, 21, 23, 26, 47,
  50, 56, 59, 77, 83,
  88, 138, 239
William H., 44
MORALLE
Thomas, 233, 237
MORALLEE
Michael, 236
Thomas, 219, 236
MORAN
Arret, 95
Gustavus A., 234
John, 67
Samuel, 95
William, 128
MORE
Jacob, 163
MORELAND
Edward, 190
MOREN
William, 234
MORGAN
John, 195
MORRALLE
Thomas, 144
MORRALLEE
Thomas, 41, 58
MORRIS
Catharine, 64
Catherine, 165
Elizabeth, 193
John, 39, 240
Lucinda, 39
Mahlon, 58, 59, 60,
  64, 97, 135, 165,
  187
Thomas, 86, 95
MORRISON
___, 179
Archibald, 67, 158,
  197, 214, 218,
  228, 256
MORROW
___, 73
Jane, 59
Jane L., 206

John, 2, 59, 103, 104,
  105, 122, 206
William, 206
MOSS
John, 256
Nathaniel, 226
Stephen, 226
Thomas, 66, 216
Vincent, 214, 226
MOTT
Mary C., 221
Thomas R., 20, 35,
  41, 57, 58, 71, 74,
  93, 108, 113, 117,
  153, 162, 173,
  176, 180, 183,
  186, 191, 194,
  195, 205, 221,
  227, 248
MOUL
Philip, 156
MOULDER
John N., 192
MOULS
George, 132
MOUNT
Ezekel, 70
Ezekiel, 19, 44, 113,
  150, 198, 248
Gilbert, 199
Gilbert S., 199, 229
Hannah, 34, 54, 203
James, 19, 33, 34,
  54, 55, 67, 148,
  203
John, 14, 44, 113,
  148, 150, 174,
  210, 227
Mary A., 14, 113, 210
Sarah, 19
Stephen, 210
Stephen R., 17, 18,
  19, 24, 74, 253
MOXLEY
Joshua, 61
William, 35
MUDD
John, 146
MULL
___, 38
Catherine, 124, 231
David, 45, 231, 253
George, 45, 124
John, 231

Nancey, 16
Nancy, 7, 43, 107, 115, 122, 152, 205
Nancy Thomas, 118
Napoleon, 122
Nat, 40
Nathan, 27, 232
Nelly, 94, 256
Nelson, 222
Noaroh, 13
Normy, 169
Oliver, 111
Oll, 111
Osborne, 222
Pat, 111, 222, 256
Patsey, 85
Patty, 27, 84, 126, 145
Peg, 79, 126
Peggy, 115
Peter, 27, 47, 59, 79, 98, 122, 123, 178, 256
Peyton, 100
Phebe, 115
Phil, 84, 141, 204
Philip, 99, 169, 205, 232, 234
Philles, 79
Poll, 187
Polly, 126, 224
Presley, 27
Rachael, 164
Rachel, 49
Ralph, 70, 204
Reegan, 222
Reuben, 79, 245
Rhoda, 115, 245
Richard, 79, 100, 129
Richmond, 54
Rin, 204
Robbert, 17
Robert, 54, 232, 245
Robert Vallentine, 195
Rosa, 32
Rose, 79, 188, 204
Roy, 17
Sal, 126
Sall, 100
Sally, 92, 138, 146, 205, 245
Sam, 7, 16, 187, 256
Samuel, 43, 115, 245

Samuel Middleton, 215
Sanford, 48
Sarah, 49, 70, 115, 135, 145, 169, 205, 226
Sarah Ann, 53, 245
Sarah Anna, 146
Sarna Lazette, 111
Shaver, 232
Sibbey, 232
Simon, 119
Sinah, 79
Solomon, 54
Squire, 187
Stephen, 11, 40, 100, 252
Stephen Wesley, 86
Steven, 49
Suckey, 51, 74, 107
Susan, 26, 35, 40, 112, 123, 177
Susanna, 115
Susannah, 245
Sutton, 174
Sybil, 99
Sylla, 20
Syllia, 115
Thomas, 84, 204, 226
Thomas Jackson, 238
Thomas Turner, 24
Timothy, 27
Titus, 114
Tom, 204, 232, 245
Toney, 70
Trueman, 30
Uriah, 187
Venus, 86
Violett, 79, 187
Virgin, 126, 145
Washington, 43, 98, 115, 230, 245
Wesley, 30
Wilford, 169, 205
William, 79, 187, 188, 227
Willis, 84
Wilson, 188, 232, 240
Winny, 79
Worsely, 256
NELSON
Philip, 88

Robert L., 227
Thomas, 18
NETTLE
William, 103, 135, 142, 210, 215
NEWCOMER
Emanuel, 28, 29
NEWELLS
John, 158
NEWLON
John, 89, 104, 185
Ruth, 104
NEWMAN
Basell, 258
Bazil, 82
Frances A., 154
Robert M., 184
Robert W., 71
NEWTON
Enos W., 127, 147, 149, 252
James, 88
James F., 67, 125, 211
John, 259
Joseph T., 146
Joseph T., 31, 211
Nelly, 31, 211
Richard H., 10
Sarah, 149, 252
Walter, 144
NIBLICK
William, 39
NICEWANGER
Catherine, 154
Henery, 253
John, 253, 254
NICHOLLS
Isaac, 50
James, 227
John, 76, 124
Mahlon, 76
Phebe, 50
Samuel, 50, 54, 93
Sarah, 76
Thomas, 53, 73, 127
NICHOLS
___, 22, 163, 201
Eli, 81
George, 123, 182
Isaac, 2, 4, 9, 11, 18, 110, 113, 120, 121, 125, 149, 151, 153, 156,

Arthur, 245
Matthew, 21
OSBORN
 Craven, 31
 Joshua, 124
OSBORNE
 Joshua, 209
OSBURN
 Abner, 105, 168
 C., 92
 C. C., 76
 Cravan, 34
 Craven, 4, 18, 24, 29,
  33, 35, 38, 44, 55,
  64, 65, 69, 70, 73,
  74, 76, 82, 86, 89,
  95, 97, 98, 101,
  103, 105, 106,
  121, 128, 141,
  143, 147, 151,
  165, 168, 190,
  192, 194, 205,
  206, 209, 235
 Elizabeth S., 74
 Hector, 33, 60, 75
 Herod, 55, 60, 75
 Joel, 7, 65, 105, 125,
  151, 168
 Joshua, 18, 29, 32,
  33, 34, 40, 51, 55,
  57, 60, 73, 75, 82,
  120, 124, 131,
  151, 155, 165,
  169, 190, 220,
  227, 254, 255
 Landon, 190, 195
 Morris, 7, 120, 125,
  151
 Nicholas, 57, 74, 105,
  146, 187
 Norval, 33
 Patience, 105
 Turner, 29, 89, 121,
  190
 William, 190
OSBURNE
 Craven, 31, 124, 162,
  167, 169, 173,
  178, 179, 180,
  182, 195, 200,
  216, 220, 227,
  229, 230, 242,
  243, 244, 246,
  249, 255

Elisabeth, 167
Herod, 179, 202
Herrod, 202
J., 227
Joseph, 184
Joshua, 135, 179,
 184, 195, 205,
 212, 219, 220,
 246, 255
Landon, 220
Lawson, 167
Mason, 182
Morris, 182
Nicholas, 90, 127,
 167, 218
Turner, 179, 202, 220
William, 164
OTEY
 Armistead, 171
OVERFELT
 Benjamin, 29
OVERFIELD
 Anna, 57
 Benjamin, 69, 160
 Elizabeth, 220
 Elsey R., 136
 Hudson, 225
 J. B., 245
 Joshua, 167
 Joshua B., 3, 57,
  173, 220
 Martin, 57, 110, 220
 Martin C., 57, 220,
  225, 227
 Mary, 110, 220
OWENS
 ___, 163
 Edward, 95
 Zachariah, 163
OWSLEY
 Thomas, 30, 32, 66,
  146

PAGE
 B., 11
 John, 244
 Peyton R., 109, 162,
  172
 William B., 184
PAGET
 Elizabeth, 219
 Timothy, 219
PAINTER
 Edward, 204

Julianna, 204
PAIRPOINT
 Eli, 179
 Obed, 214
PALMER
 Abel, 24
 Benjamin, 167
 Daniel B., 28, 30
 John E., 7, 118
 Philip L., 230
 Samuel, 236
 William C., 24, 187
PANCOAST
 John, 17, 34, 56, 84,
  138, 140, 160,
  190, 206
 Joshua, 14, 84, 124,
  127, 143, 210
PANCOST
 John, 165
 Joshua, 9
PARISH
 J. R., 165
PARKENS
 J., 68
PARKER
 Solomon, 42
 Thomas, 184
PARMER
 Benjamin, 74
 Catharine, 76, 77
 John, 67
 John E., 242
 Phillip, 76
 Samuel, 61
 William, 76, 77
PARNEY
 Nathaniel, 69
PASQUALL
 Rebecca, 113
PASTOR
 Joseph, 116
PATTERSON
 J., 96
 James, 18, 54
 John, 18, 54
 Robert, 53
PATTON
 Francis L., 15, 16
PAXON
 ___, 220
 Ann, 156, 170
 Charles E., 43
 Diademia, 150

George, 78, 83
John, 78, 242
POTTERFELD
Henry, 62
POTTERFIELD
___, 52
Elizabeth, 84
Henry, 62
POTTS
David, 31, 44, 120, 164, 212
Elisabeth, 177
Enos, 74, 198
Enoss, 167
Isaac, 80
Isaiah, 155, 166, 177
Jane, 190, 195, 220
John, 203
Jonas, 32, 55, 113, 131
Nancy, 32
Nathan, 45, 190
Ralph H., 218
POULSON
___, 95, 134
Agness, 221
Elizabeth, 221
Hannah, 147
Jasper, 147, 221
John, 147, 221
William, 221
POULTON
Mason, 245
Reed, 199, 253
Thomas, 90
POWELL
___, 67, 81
Alfred H., 83, 162, 238, 240, 257
Ann, 224
Anne, 141
B., 200
Burr, 3, 5, 12, 13, 14, 15, 17, 18, 19, 20, 21, 27, 28, 29, 34, 35, 38, 43, 51, 54, 59, 63, 64, 65, 69, 70, 71, 72, 78, 80, 81, 83, 86, 87, 88, 95, 98, 100, 101, 102, 103, 114, 116, 117, 118, 120, 129, 132, 142, 143, 144,

146, 147, 149, 150, 152, 153, 159, 161, 162, 167, 174, 179, 189, 194, 196, 202, 203, 204
Burr G., 65, 133, 216
C., 238
Catharine, 12
Catherine, 3, 12, 161
Cuthbert, 3, 4, 20, 29, 39, 41, 64, 66, 68, 69, 87, 112, 133, 142, 144, 150, 151, 161, 162, 183, 188, 190, 216, 223, 240, 254, 257
Cuthbert J., 238
E. B., 55
Elisha, 110, 132, 141, 153, 224
George C., 234
H. B., 3, 7, 13, 25, 48, 81, 86, 103, 127, 129, 130, 137, 202, 207
Humphrey, 147, 148, 183
Humphrey B., 10, 12, 13, 18, 19, 20, 35, 65, 80, 81, 101, 130, 149, 211
James, 110
John L., 238
L., 18, 86
Leven, 3, 12, 17, 38, 69, 83, 87, 133, 174, 234, 238
Leven D., 222
Major, 254
Maria A., 65, 216
Mary, 141, 224
Nancy, 83
Peyton, 165, 224
Robert M., 132, 142, 185
Sarah R., 86, 87
Thomas, 86
Thomas W., 66, 86, 87, 133
William A., 238
William L., 189, 240
POWELL

Burr, 129, 149, 183, 188, 217, 222, 223, 224, 225, 230, 234, 238, 240, 250, 251, 252, 253, 257, 258
Catherine, 183, 223
Cuthbert, 129
H. B., 237, 252
Humphrey B., 216, 217, 230, 252
PRESGRAVES
Richard, 48, 49
PRICE
Benjamin, 232
Chandler, 153
Matilda R., 232
Thomas, 8, 42
Virginia, 232
William, 43, 79
PRILL
Samuel, 189
PRIME
Nathaniel, 136, 175
PRINCE
___, 70
John L., 255
Levi, 156, 254
Mary, 254
Mathias, 124, 246
Nathan, 254
PURCEL
Joseph, 89
Thomas, 242
PURCELL
John, 88, 180, 182
Jonah, 190
Joseph, 140
Mahlon, 60, 146
Mary, 88
Samuel, 140
Valentine, 166
Valentine N., 242
Valentine V., 67, 141, 162, 171
Volentine V., 219
PURDIM
Jeremaih, 212
PURDUM
Jeremiah, 228
PURFECT
Robert, 64
PURSEL
Edwin, 1

___, 42, 92
Anna, 107, 115
C., 109
Sarah, 107, 115
Stephen C., 30, 66,
  93, 107, 115, 166
Stephen G., 112
Stephen W., 115
W., 109
ROSZELL
Stephen C., 68, 85
ROSZIL
Stephen W., 154
ROSZILL
Stephen W., 211
ROW
George, 74
ROWAN
George, 149, 162
ROWSEY
Daniel, 119
Sophia, 119
ROZEL
Stephen C., 32
ROZELL
Anna, 186, 245
Nancy, 245
Phebe, 245
Sarah, 245
Stephen C., 90, 186,
  245
Stephen G., 245
Stephen W., 221, 245
ROZIL
Catherine, 154
Stephen W., 154
ROZZELL
S. C., 147
RUSE
Henry, 246, 247
Sarah, 247
RUSSEL
John, 161
Mary, 165
Nancy, 165
Robert, 127, 165
Samuel, 127
Thomas, 165
William, 165, 173
RUSSELL
___, 42, 57, 65
Aaron, 254
Benjamin, 4, 174
Charles, 202

Elisabeth, 175
Elizabeth, 58
H., 173
Henery, 173
Henry, 77, 132, 133,
  193, 254
James H., 254
John, 2, 58
Mahlon, 254
Mary, 24, 58, 179
Matilda, 77, 132, 254
Neal, 4
Neil, 174
Peyton, 177
Robert, 58, 77, 111,
  179, 194
Ruth, 58
Samuel, 4, 42, 174
Thomas, 4, 24, 31,
  58, 94, 167, 174,
  175, 176, 177,
  189, 240
William, 24, 58, 133,
  182, 254
RUST
___, 20, 132
Elisabeth, 152, 166
Elizabeth, 89
Elizabeth B., 86
George, 20, 23, 38,
  39, 56, 69, 78, 84,
  87, 95, 100, 120,
  125, 136, 170,
  189, 206
J., 18
James, 6, 7, 27, 34,
  38, 57, 62, 68, 86,
  87, 122, 176, 197,
  215, 219, 220,
  221, 227
James T., 2, 13, 86,
  120, 128
Mandley T., 88, 117,
  235
Mandly T., 2, 137
Manley T., 91
Manly T., 103
Maria C., 84, 136
Martha, 114
Mathew, 35, 122, 203
Matthew, 5, 19, 26,
  86, 114
Patsey, 86, 114
Peter, 89, 184

Peter C., 36, 40, 49,
  164, 165, 213
Peter P., 49
Peter R., 135
Sally, 86, 87, 137,
  138
Susan E., 157
Sydnor B., 86, 114,
  122
William, 18, 86, 87,
  89, 149, 152, 166,
  251
RYAN
Sally, 51
RYLEY
Joshua, 37
RYMMER
John, 70
RYMMS
John, 15

SAFFER
William, 45
SAGER
Benjamin, 124
George, 10
Mary E., 10
SAGERS
George, 104
SANBOWER
___, 208
Adam, 27, 159, 201
SANDBOWER
Adam, 85
Christian, 79, 85
John, 85
Michael, 85
SANDERS
___, 50
Aaron, 7, 16, 58, 89,
  99, 115, 121, 126,
  158, 246
Ann, 136, 140, 160
Aron, 142
Britton, 32, 63, 116,
  187
Edward, 163
Elisabeth, 156
Elizabeth, 11
Everitt, 106
Evritt, 152
George, 7, 11, 28,
  47, 156, 157, 169,
  170, 197

Henery, 178
Henry, 104, 126
James, 78
John, 7, 51, 157, 197
Leana, 197
Margaret, 130, 158,
　170, 197
Mary, 51
P., 102
Patience, 104
Peter, 7, 121, 138,
　169, 170, 171
Presley, 29, 51, 210
Presly, 162
Ramey G., 134
Susannah, 16
Thomas, 8, 14, 15,
　16, 24, 31, 32, 36,
　45, 46, 48, 51, 58,
　61, 62, 63, 66, 83,
　84, 85, 87, 93, 95,
　98, 102, 104, 106,
　114, 115, 120,
　126, 141, 158,
　159, 160, 170,
　173, 176, 180,
　183, 193, 195,
　196, 198, 202,
　204, 210, 225,
　226, 229, 239,
　242, 243, 247,
　255, 258, 259
Thomas R., 15
William, 64
William S., 64
SANDFORD
Augustine M., 174,
　228
James, 168
Robert, 174, 228
SANDS
Abigale, 6
Abijah, 172
Elisabeth, 172
Jonah, 49, 65, 81,
　200, 203
Stephen, 247
Thomas, 1
SANFORD
Margaret, 113
Peggy, 148
SANGSTER
James, 74
SAPPINGTON

___, 67
John F., 19, 165
Mary, 165
SARBAUGH
David, 35
Elizabeth, 119
John, 119
SAUNDERS
Aaron, 169, 188, 217
Britton, 32
Cyrus, 156, 157, 214
David, 171
Edith, 157
Editha, 213
Everet, 215
Everett, 57, 181, 215
Everit, 240
Everitt, 228
Evritt, 104, 157
Francis, 11
George, 168, 169,
　170, 214
Gunnel, 157
Gunnell, 181, 193,
　240
Henery, 157, 181
Henry, 127, 205
J., 240
James, 157
John, 12, 27, 156,
　157, 202, 214, 258
Margaret, 32, 156,
　171, 203, 214,
　250, 256
Mary, 157
P., 157
Peter, 8, 168, 170,
　171, 229
Prescilla, 157
Presley, 88, 99, 190
Presly, 157, 169,
　178, 181, 201, 233
R. G., 191, 221
Ramey G., 157
Susan, 157
Thomas, 31, 58, 84,
　127, 157, 202,
　205, 213, 215, 240
Thomas R., 147, 169,
　194, 221
SAURBAUGH
David, 13, 31, 56
SAVITT
J., 137

SAWYER
Mary, 193, 205, 226
Samuel, 205
SCANTLING
John, 101
SCHOFIELD
Mahlon, 90
SCHOLFIELD
Jonathan, 77
SCHOOLEY
___, 56
___, 162
Elizabeth, 54, 71
John, 54, 65, 71, 95,
　145, 165, 169, 239
Jonas P., 65
Mahlon, 65
Phebe, 54, 71
Reuben, 24, 27, 34,
　56, 61, 113
Samuel, 95
SCOTT
Robert G., 43
Sabrett E., 72
SEARES
Robert H., 71
SEARS
Robert H., 252
SEATON
___, 148, 244
Alex, 110
Alexander, 110
Elizabeth, 28
Hiram, 36, 84, 89,
　117, 148, 150,
　189, 244
James, 28
SEEDERS
William, 90, 240
SEEVERS
George W., 234
SELDEN
Dr., 103, 240
Wilson C., 10, 183,
　234, 244
SELDON
___, 87
Dr., 13, 57, 118, 192
Mary B., 4, 23, 74
W. C., 62
Wilson C., 4, 23, 58,
　74, 76, 136, 222,
　227
SEMPLE

John, 193
SERVICK
Elizabeth, 105
SERWICK
Christian, 105
SETTLE
Daniel, 144, 255
Elisabeth, 144
Elizabeth, 77
Henery, 166, 181
Henry, 184, 185
Linna A., 166
Margaret, 166
Newman, 77, 144
Reuben, 77
Susannah, 144
SETTLES
Daniel, 225
Henry, 225
SHADACRE
___, 11
SHAFER
Conrod, 28
John, 66, 74, 84, 114,
186, 206
SHAFFER
Conrad, 183
John, 9, 171, 180,
257
Mary, 180
SHAMBLIN
Ezekiel, 233
SHAREMON
James, 22
SHARP
George, 224
Rosanna, 234
SHAVER
Conrad, 12
George, 2
John, 161, 171, 192
Mary, 161, 171
Michael, 161
SHAVOURS
William, 190
SHAW
Catharine, 83, 187
Cynthia, 259
Hezekiah, 116
John, 14, 15, 16, 46,
62, 76, 81, 82, 83,
85, 93, 96, 108,
114, 154, 187,

188, 204, 205,
221, 227, 239, 259
Rebecca, 14, 62, 93,
187, 204
SHAWEN
___, 170
C., 170
Cornelious, 16
Cornelius, 121, 130
D., 185, 206, 215
David, 10, 16, 41, 60,
121, 130, 132,
156, 170, 171,
197, 201, 238
George, 5, 130
George W., 16, 47,
49, 121, 130, 158,
194, 208, 212,
227, 236, 237,
238, 243, 247,
250, 251, 258
Jane, 121, 130
SHAWON
David, 118
SHEARMAN
Joseph, 13
SHECKLES
Lewis, 82
SHEFFY
Daniel, 212
SHEID
George, 15, 198, 239
Rebeccah, 15
William, 16
SHELL
Henry G., 2
SHEPHERD
Catherine, 213, 223
Charles, 14, 52, 85,
194, 195
Ellizabeth, 195
Humphrey, 223
James, 85
John, 85, 243
Leven, 85
Leven W., 58, 213
Levin, 52
Wadsworth, 114
SHERRARD
Robert, 131
SHETMAN
Catharine, 119
John, 119
SHIRLEY

James, 120
SHIVELY
Jacob, 8
SHOEMAKER
Daniel, 32, 212, 214
George, 124, 171,
214, 256, 258
Jacob, 10, 193, 256
Priscilla, 32
Siman, 124
Simon, 32, 84, 88,
166, 171, 179
SHOMAKER
George, 8
SHORT
E. S., 80
SHOVER
Adam, 1, 79, 109,
116, 119, 207
Barbara, 119
Catharine, 119
Charlotte, 119
Frederick, 79
George, 109, 116,
119, 185, 207
Henry, 79, 109, 119,
207
Jacob, 119
John, 1, 119
Mary M., 119
Mary N. D., 119
Peter, 119
Rosannah, 109
Simon, 79, 119
Sopha, 119
Susan, 119
Valentine F., 109,
116
SHOWALTER
Isaac, 120
SHREIVE
Benjamin, 135
SHREVE
___, 76
B., 92, 103, 146
Bengamin, 115
Benjamin, 4, 8, 10,
23, 27, 33, 39, 40,
41, 46, 51, 52, 60,
62, 64, 74, 81, 82,
87, 88, 89, 95,
100, 103, 104,
106, 117, 122,

131, 204, 220,
221, 225, 230
SHREVES
Benjamin, 231
SHRIEVE
Benjamin, 32, 141,
152, 165, 175,
201, 231, 240, 248
William, 245
SHRIVER
___, 49
B., 140
Christopher, 57
Jacob, 140
SHRYOCK
George, 186
Michael, 218
SHULTZ
George, 45
SHUMAKER
Jacob, 198
SHUMATE
Murphey, 7
SHUTT
___, 220
Caroline F., 164
Jacob, 164
SIDDLER
Martin, 163
SIDEBOTTOM
John, 38
SILCOT
Jacob, 148
SILCOTT
Jacob, 49, 68, 94,
112, 129, 186,
189, 194, 209,
223, 244
Jesse, 95
Sally, 148
Sarah, 150
William, 129, 148,
150
SILVER
William, 146
SIMPSON
David, 192, 258
Elizabeth, 13, 48, 127
Emily, 13
Frederick, 16
French, 9, 16, 127,
128, 164, 166
Gregg, 248
Hanson, 16

Henson, 13, 16, 240
Isaac, 13
James, 7, 16, 48,
127, 129, 182
John, 9, 13, 16, 127,
128, 129, 155,
160, 166, 202,
210, 227, 230,
232, 252
Mary, 13, 127
Nancy, 127, 128
Samuel, 16, 127
William, 13
SINCLAIR
___, 20
Benjamin, 16
Edith, 215
George, 32
George H., 115, 142
James, 16, 30, 42,
50, 113, 131, 148,
183, 191, 240
John, 2, 19, 21, 30,
32, 35, 41, 42, 50,
66, 74, 113, 146,
150, 189, 225
Prescilla, 16
Samuel, 108, 215
Samuel C., 215
Susan, 21
SINGER
Charles, 9
SINGLETON
Samuel, 48, 107,
141, 150
SKILLMAN
Abraham, 5, 6, 182,
191, 195, 241
John, 213
Violinda, 182
SKILMAN
Abraham, 71
SKINNER
Amos, 130, 144
Nathan, 13
Peter, 13
Rebeca, 159
Rebecca, 48, 77
Usher, 48, 77, 89,
119, 159, 184
SLACK
Abraham L., 150
Lot, 171
Tunis, 150

SLADE
Henry, 112
Henry C., 95
Richard, 122
SLATER
Anthony, 164, 211,
242
Ellisabeth, 211
George, 164, 211,
242
Jacob, 164, 202, 211
John, 53, 164, 202,
211, 243
Mary, 211
Michael, 164, 211
Susannah, 242
William, 164, 211
SLATES
___, 247
Adam, 155
Frederick, 44, 142,
211, 246, 253
Sevilla, 155
SLATS
Sybyia, 159
SLATZ
Frederick, 180
SLAUGHTER
John, 34
Sarah, 34
SLEETS
Frederick, 142
SLOAN
James, 158
SMALE
Elizabeth, 219, 259
Mary, 239
Simon, 15, 205, 219,
226, 237, 239,
240, 259
SMALLEY
___, 49
William, 135
SMALLWOOD
___, 44, 150
Amanda, 116
Eleanorah, 116
Emiline, 116
Hebron, 59
Israel, 59
Leven, 116, 233
Sarah, 116, 233
Sarah A., 116
SMALWOOD

___, 6
SMARR
James, 33
John, 22, 212, 246
Thomas, 16, 33
William, 22, 212
SMITH
___, 163, 228
Abraham, 256
Ann, 9
Benjamin, 2
C., 145
Charles, 9, 71, 143, 166
Clement, 214
David, 8, 38, 80, 82, 190, 198, 218, 241
Dr., 254
Edmund, 149, 150, 247
Elisabeth, 149
Elizabeth, 103, 247, 258
Ellisabeth, 211
Emely, 9
Esekiel, 163
Eve, 124
Fleet, 13, 32, 46, 76, 103
G. D., 215
George, 12, 124, 154, 191, 206, 209, 216, 251
H., 17, 29, 35, 138, 208
Henry, 203
Hugh, 3, 35, 49, 51, 74, 78, 81, 86, 88, 91, 103, 104, 108, 114, 128, 129, 160, 164, 192, 200, 202, 209, 220
Jacob, 13, 151, 207, 208, 237
Jane, 46, 76, 103
John, 166
Jonas, 166
Joseph, 130, 233
Lewis M., 16, 25, 33, 59, 70, 80, 83, 92, 118, 149, 247
Peter, 19
Richard, 64
Robert, 29

Samuel, 1, 94, 209
Seth, 7, 22, 68, 89, 90, 111, 124, 155, 183, 186, 189, 255
Susanah, 151
Susanna, 240
Susannah, 237
Thomas W., 213, 244
Treadwell, 38, 53
Walter A., 179
William, 15, 16, 28, 31, 95, 101, 148, 149, 150, 151, 166, 208, 216, 255
Smith & Carter, 219
SMITLEY
Mathia, 238
Mathias, 197
SNUTES
Henry, 55
SNUTS
Henry, 27
SNYDER
Catherine S., 159
Elisabeth A., 159
Jane E., 159
Peter, 159
Sarah, 159
William H., 159
SOBEY
Thomas, 179
SORBAUGH
David, 13
SORMAN
Andrew, 181
SOUDER
Anthony, 119
Barbary, 118, 119
Elizabeth, 52, 119
John, 52
Lucrecy, 119
Michael, 52, 119
Peggy, 52
Peter, 52, 53, 118, 119
Philip, 118, 119
Phillip, 52
Rachel, 52
Susanah, 211
Susanna, 119
Susannah, 52
SOUDERS
Anthony, 52
Mary, 52

Philip, 119
SOWDERS
Philip, 119
SOWERS
B. W., 259
SPATES
Elisabeth, 176
SPEAKS
James, 3
SPENCE
James B., 154, 175
John, 71
Nancy, 154, 175
SPENCER
James, 11
Margaret, 221
Mary, 11
Samuel, 221
SPICER
John, 195
SPOONS
Joseph, 197
SPRING
Michael, 258
Rachel, 53
SQUIRES
Thomas, 107
ST. Clair
A. R., 37, 41, 48, 49, 50, 51, 52, 62, 64, 68, 79, 86
R., 30
STABLER
Edward, 144, 225
John, 197
STATLER
___, 180
John, 202
STEADMAN
Alcy, 258
James, 258
STEER
___, 193
Benjamin, 73
Eleanor, 157, 158
Elenor, 11, 55, 111
Elisabeth, 158
Elizabeth, 111, 114, 115, 129
Hannah, 114
Isaac, 111, 114, 115, 129, 144, 145, 150, 157, 158, 196

Isaac E., 59, 65, 69, 244, 250
John, 11, 19, 55
Joseph, 44, 150
Mary, 111
Sarah, 44, 157
William, 60, 73, 132, 173, 175, 177, 238
STEPHENS
Elizabeth, 249
Thomas, 67, 239
Thomas H., 87, 183, 249
STEPHENSON
James, 33
Levi L., 205
Sarah, 33
STERRET
S., 28
STERRIT
Samuel, 91
STEVENS
Ann H., 8
Eleanor, 8, 123
Henry, 8, 16, 123
John B., 10, 67, 105, 156
John R., 206
Thomas, 8, 73
STEVENSON
Job, 16
STEWART
Adam, 14
Hester, 61
James W., 151
STIERWOLT
William, 165
STONE
Daniel, 34, 65, 72, 85, 132, 133, 192, 207, 224, 239
James, 28, 144
Peter, 8
William, 187
STONEBURNER
___, 79, 206
Barbara, 106
Jacob, 118, 250
Peter, 166, 175
STONESTREET
Augustus, 221
Elizabeth, 221
STOUSABERGER
___, 37

Jacob, 27
John, 71
Samuel, 74
STOUSBERGER
John, 183
STOUSEBERGER
John, 28, 52
STOUTSEBERGER
John, 166
Margaret, 166
STOUTSENBERGER
Jacob, 71
John, 12
STOVER
Edwin A., 240
STOVIN
Charles, 195, 210
STREAM
Michael, 142
STRIBLING
Cecelia, 44, 249, 256
Francis, 6, 25, 38, 44, 65, 104, 192, 229, 239, 249, 256
STRIDER
John F., 253
John T., 126
STRINGFELLOW
___, 57
Benjamin, 37
STUBBLEFIELD
James, 107, 155, 218, 252
STUBLEFIELD
James, 155
STUCK
Peter, 158, 206
STULL
John J., 140, 145
STUMP
___, 253
John, 224
Joseph, 8, 27, 42
Sarah, 26
Thomas, 8, 26, 27, 42, 181
SUDDETH
William, 224
SUDDITH
William, 96
SULLIVAN
___, 57, 132
Elisabeth, 178
Elizabeth, 100

Ellisabeth, 179
Ellisabeth B., 178, 179
John C., 128, 130
Martho, 59
Mertho, 49
Murtho, 109
Owen, 5, 86, 114
Rebeca E., 178, 179
SUMMERS
Elizabeth, 185
Jacob, 78, 97, 184, 185, 190, 219
William, 116, 120, 123, 234
SURGENOR
James, 211
John, 88, 146, 211
SURGHENOR
James, 222
John, 112, 219, 251
SURGHINOR
John, 226
SURGHNOR
Elizabeth, 36
James, 240
John, 16, 36, 45, 62, 72, 131, 133, 154, 206, 226
SURGINOR
John, 153
SURGNOR
John, 71
SUTHARD
James, 237
SUTHERD
James, 4
SUTHERLAND
Alexander, 55, 248
Caleb, 88
Caleb C., 43, 90, 240, 248
John, 248
Thomas, 248
SWAN
Thomas, 184
SWANK
Catherine, 171
George, 171
Philip, 27, 171, 192
SWANN
Thomas, 4, 31, 38, 46, 193
SWART

Adrian, 166
Adrian L., 216
Elizabeth, 38
James, 5, 120, 122,
  125, 144, 174,
  196, 209
John, 5, 232
Joseph, 5
Manley, 5
Robert P., 232
William, 38, 121
SWARTS
Alexander, 105
Barnet, 105
James, 76, 105, 112
John, 166
Matilda S., 105
William, 72
SWAYNE
Thomas, 38, 223,
  224, 225
SWEENEY
John H., 254
SWICK
Anthony, 248
Martha, 248
SWIFT
Jonathan, 222
Mary D., 222
William R., 222
SYPHERD
George, 59

TALBERT
___, 221
TALBOT
Samuel, 145
TALBOTT
Henry, 28
Joseph, 239
TALLEY
Elizabeth, 143
Isaac, 85, 143
TALLY
Elizabeth, 64
Isaac, 64
TALORE
William, 243
Tankerville, 10, 12, 44
TATE
Levi, 88
TAVENDER
George, 82, 201
Jonah, 82

Joseph, 177
Nancy, 82
Patty, 82
Sarah, 82
TAVENER
Eli, 34, 200, 203
George, 21, 30, 88,
  116, 141, 200,
  203, 204, 208,
  209, 233, 247
Hiram, 200
Jonah, 17, 180, 247,
  248
Joseph, 141, 158,
  200, 203, 247
Nancy, 203, 247
Richard, 27, 204, 247
Sarah, 116
TAVENNER
Eli, 49, 95
George, 65
James, 65
Jonah, 11, 18
TAVENOR
George, 46
TAYLOR
___, 65, 83, 88, 178,
  242
Achsa, 151
Achsah, 42
Alsey, 91
Ann, 42, 60, 63, 243
Archibald R., 84
B. J., 36
Bernard, 130, 151,
  199, 203, 231,
  241, 246, 255
Charles, 25, 39, 42,
  109, 141, 190,
  194, 225
Elizabeth, 49, 67
Emily, 53
George, 239
Hannah, 124
Harriet, 73, 105
Harriet B., 168
Henery, 166
Henery S., 241
Henry, 42, 43, 60, 63,
  67, 69
John, 2, 70
John B., 38
Joseph, 114, 134,
  236

Joshua, 31
Lydia, 114
Mahlon, 86
Mary, 60, 67
Mary A., 43, 63
Penellope, 42
R. J., 60, 226, 242
Robert H., 225
Robert J., 4, 71, 77,
  184, 189, 212,
  219, 244, 249
Sarah, 203, 241
Stacey, 37, 69, 86,
  95, 107, 190
Stacy, 124, 127, 135,
  140, 141, 143,
  149, 162, 216,
  234, 242
Thomas, 42, 227
Timothy, 6, 7, 39, 42,
  53, 73, 105, 127,
  141, 151, 168,
  176, 182, 190,
  194, 254
William, 6, 36, 42, 49,
  53, 60, 120, 154,
  176, 243
William R., 66
Yardley, 124
Yardly, 18
TEBBET
A. G., 127
TEBBS
Betsey, 86, 115
Foushe, 152
Foushee, 86, 87,
  166, 247
Hannah S., 230
Margaret, 87, 247
Thomas F., 149, 207,
  240, 249
William, 149
TEMERY
Peter, 246
TEMPLE
William, 197
TEMPLER
John, 73
THATCHER
Calvin, 1, 60, 75,
  133, 138, 179, 182
Jesse, 158
Richard, 1, 60, 75,
  131

THOMAS
___, 29
Abby, 85
Ann, 160, 186, 244
Anne, 85
Daniel, 214, 226
Elisabeth, 178
Elizabeth, 85, 140,
   202, 257
Elizabeth W., 227,
   235
Ellisabeth, 239
George, 93
Henry, 118
Herod, 189
Isaac, 1, 191
Isaac P., 10
Jacob, 45
Jacob R., 122
James, 55, 72, 161,
   170, 207, 226, 240
Jefferson C., 167,
   181, 227, 235
John, 45, 59, 66, 114,
   116, 138, 140,
   146, 160, 168,
   176, 180, 192,
   219, 231, 233, 257
Joseph, 40, 181
Joseph P., 243
Leah, 140
Leonard, 27, 85, 94,
   160, 178, 186,
   202, 239, 244, 251
Lindza, 62
Margaret, 114
Martha, 85, 246
Mary, 235
Nancy, 118
Phenias, 117
Philip, 167, 181, 227
Phillip, 40
Phineas, 87, 181
Sarah, 85
Thomas George and
   Thomas, 8, 41, 64
THOMPSON
___, 7
Andrew, 123, 128
C. J. P., 197
Craven P., 137
Daniel, 151
Eleanor, 186
Francis, 33, 80

Hugh, 137
Israel P., 137
James, 47, 220
John, 27
Jonah, 167
Margaret, 27
Michael, 74
William, 85, 220
THOMSON
J., 192
THORNTON
___, 66, 148
Benjamin B., 118,
   209
Charles, 16, 177, 251
Felix H., 9
George F., 105
Hannah, 118, 209
Thomas, 17
THRASHER
Elias, 1, 10, 40, 59
Sally, 10
Sarah, 10
THRIFT
Charles, 65
William, 13, 17, 48,
   59, 81, 100, 103,
   138, 141, 144,
   164, 207, 222,
   232, 234, 240
THROCKMORTON
Mathew, 59
Mordecai, 21, 59, 239
Sarah M., 21, 239
Warner W., 21, 239
TIDBALL
Alexander S., 246,
   249
Joseph, 50, 246
Josiah, 68, 89, 166,
   251
TILLET
Giles E., 125
Honor, 125
Peggy, 125
Samuel, 125
Samuel A., 125
TILLETT
Honor, 256
Nancy, 31
Samuel, 113, 173,
   239
Samuel A., 31, 238
TIMMS

J., 227
Jesse, 26, 30, 32, 40,
   66, 92, 128, 146,
   147, 148, 155,
   156, 191, 193,
   208, 222, 228, 257
Jessee, 183
TIPPETT
James, 40
TITUS
Francis, 182
Tunis, 17
TODD
Samuel, 80, 107
TODHUNTER
John, 227
Mary, 228
TOLKERTH
John, 168
TOMKINS
Benjamin, 176
TOMLINSON
___, 241
TORBERT
James, 5, 48, 76
John, 121
Mary, 121
Samuel, 48, 76, 112
Thomas, 121
TORBET
Samuel, 125, 248
TORREYSON
Joseph, 136
TORRISON
Joseph, 188
TORRYSON
Samuel, 237, 255
TOWNER
Benjamin T., 131
Eve, 131
Jacob, 206, 240
John, 240
TOWNSEND
James, 228
TOWPERMAN
Andrew, 224
Elizabeth, 88
John, 41
Peter, 88, 224
TRACEY
Tamar, 86
TRACY
Benjamin, 123
Evritt, 123

Nancy, 123
Thamer, 123
TRAHERN
Enos, 65, 104
James, 183
Samuel, 73, 80, 102
Sarah R., 104
Thomas, 183, 190
TRAHORN
Asa, 152
Thomas, 159, 210
TRAYHERN
Samuel, 36, 43, 44,
111, 255
Thomas, 192
TREHORN
James, 248
TRIBBY
George, 143
James, 186
Jesse, 186
John, 186, 221
Jonathan, 143
Lydia, 221
Martha, 186
Mary, 186, 191, 196
Mason, 186
Nancy, 186
Ruth, 186
Sarah, 186
Thomas, 81, 186,
191, 196
William, 186
TRIPLETT
___, 162
C., 109
Dr., 202
Elizabeth, 94, 109
Ellisabeth, 224
Enoch, 48, 49, 110,
150, 153, 178
Felix, 109, 221, 258
Frances, 109
Francis, 110, 155
Hannah, 123
Harriet, 20, 22
John, 94, 109
Lucy, 180
Macaijah, 123
Margaret, 109, 117
Mary, 48, 124
Micaga, 224
Micajah, 99, 135, 182
Nancy, 224

Philip, 188
Reuben, 20, 22, 23,
102, 109, 111,
124, 154, 187,
188, 221, 224, 235
Rewben, 258
Roderick, 109, 124
Samuel, 114, 182,
224, 233
Simon, 47
Thomas, 42, 117,
182
William, 112
Willis, 5, 23, 109, 111
Willis F., 90
TRITAPAUGH
___, 170
TRUSSEL
Charles, 124
TULEY
Joseph, 49, 225
TURBERVILLE
John, 225
TURLEY
Giles, 19
James, 25
TURNER
Amanda, 173
Charles, 27, 96, 135,
165
F., 128
George, 13, 27, 43,
87, 227
Henry S., 10
Mary, 13
Samuel, 121, 173
Sarah, 43
Thomas, 24
Warner, 163
TUSTIN
Isaac, 98
Samuel, 30, 66, 88,
90, 98
TUTT
Ann M., 153
C. P., 37, 193
Charles P., 74, 84,
88, 109, 121, 153,
217
TUTTS
Charles P., 79
TYLER
Edmund, 17, 126
Edmund J., 17

James, 211
John, 17, 152
John W., 33, 247
Nathaniel, 247

UMBAUGH
John, 19
UNDERWOOD
John, 89, 178, 250
Margaret, 67, 89, 178
Samuel, 67, 172,
178, 209
UPDIKE
Rufus, 190, 194
UPP
John, 12, 19, 20, 28,
35, 87, 102
Sarah, 35, 102
URTON
C., 171
Norman, 59, 165
UTTERBACK
Catharine, 48, 117
John, 48, 117

VALLENTINE
Robert, 195
VAN BUSKIRK
John, 246
VANANDER
Elizabeth, 112
John, 112
Thomas, 112
VANBUSKIRK
John, 50
VANCE
David, 75
VANDEVANDER
___, 207
VANDEVANTER
Isaac, 218
VANDEVENTER
___, 161
VANDEVER
___, 125
VANHORN
John, 26, 174, 217
Mary, 105
Sally, 105
Sarah, 174
VANHORNE
Sarah, 217
widow, 149
VANPELT

John, 214
WARD
R. R., 136, 175
WARFORD
Elizabeth, 22
James, 22, 74, 127
John, 74
WARNER
___, 106
George, 197, 254
John, 34
WASHINGTON
Ann, 94
Bushrod, 75, 94
Edward, 42
G., 200
George, 81
John A., 42
Warner, 21, 239
WATERMAN
A. G., 15, 84
Asher, 15, 21
R. G., 218
Waterman and
Campbell, 179, 230
WATERS
Jacob, 75, 94, 256
Levi, 74, 94, 206,
209, 216
Mahlon, 16, 81
Sarah, 206, 216
William, 192
WATKINS
Ann, 203
Bernard, 203
Elender, 203
Louisa, 203
Marks, 69
Sarah Ann, 203
William, 203
WATSON
Joseph, 13
Thomas, 237, 238
WATT
Dewanna, 175
Dewanner, 196, 239,
240
John G., 20, 50, 68,
175, 176, 194,
196, 198, 239, 240
WATTS
John G., 94
R. K., 31
WAUGH

Beverley, 120
WEADEN
Margaret, 69
WEADON
___, 25
Frances, 131
John, 4, 5, 136, 194
Margaret, 5
Richard, 131
William, 131, 194
WEANING
John, 59
WEATHERBY
Jane, 38
Mrs., 254
WEATHERLY
David, 113, 183
Elisabeth A., 183
Jane, 20, 36
John, 20
Mathew, 39, 46
Peter, 183
WEBB
Joseph B., 105
WEEDON
John, 23, 68
WEEKS
B., 244
Burr, 3, 17, 18, 25,
139, 151, 181,
189, 198, 228, 248
James, 29, 218
Thomas, 81, 82
WELLS
Babel, 35
Elizabeth, 229, 233
Lucinda, 50
Troy, 96
Zorababel, 229, 233
Zorobable, 7
WELSH
James, 11, 149
Mary, 11, 149
WENNER
___, 208
Benedick, 159
Benedict, 155
Catherine, 159
Charlott, 158
Daniel, 158
George, 158, 259
John, 42, 155, 158,
201, 234, 246, 253
Jonathan, 159

Joseph, 158, 253
Mary, 159
Sevilla, 155
Solomon, 159, 234
Sybyia, 159
William, 45, 155, 158,
159, 234, 253
WERTS
Conrad, 4
Elizabeth, 4
WERTZ
Adam, 132, 133
Conrad, 133
Peter, 132, 133
William, 161, 206
WEST
Erasmus, 218
Humphrey, 171
John, 63, 165, 206
Polly, 171
Samuel, 206
Thomas, 171
Uree, 171
William, 190
WESTLEY
John, 214
WESTLY
John, 161
WETHERLY
David, 72
WEY
Annah, 41, 80
Thomas H., 29, 56,
80, 102, 255
William H., 41
WHALEY
___, 73, 102, 234
Levi, 21
WHARTON
John, 144
WHEERY
Elizabeth, 116
WHERRY
Silas, 32, 116
WHITACRE
Benjamin, 163
James, 163
John, 184
Joseph, 163
WHITAKER
Alexander, 109
WHITE
___, 92, 105, 206
Ann, 177

B., 112, 181
Beniah, 175
Benjamin, 95
Benniah, 218
Elisabeth, 144, 177
Frances R., 218
Isaac S., 37
James, 27, 175
John, 24, 29, 31, 34,
  35, 39, 44, 53, 55,
  64, 65, 69, 70, 73,
  74, 76, 77, 78, 82,
  86, 92, 95, 97, 98,
  101, 105, 106,
  107, 113, 114,
  121, 122, 123,
  124, 128, 134,
  140, 141, 143,
  144, 147, 151,
  155, 161, 162,
  165, 167, 168,
  169, 173, 178,
  179, 180, 182,
  191, 192, 194,
  198, 200, 205,
  206, 209, 213,
  216, 220, 229,
  230, 235, 237,
  242, 243, 244, 246
Jonah, 179
Josabed, 117
Joseph, 82
Joshua, 196
Josiah, 144
Jozabed, 28, 29, 31,
  52, 64, 68, 95,
  101, 144, 172, 216
Margaret, 29, 52,
  101, 144, 172
Rachael, 144
Robert, 11, 229, 243
Thomas, 25, 34, 140,
  147, 166, 194,
  198, 214, 256
Washington, 144
William, 144, 245
White and Clendening,
  120
WHITING
  Frances, 105
  Frances H., 36
  Francis H., 2
  G. B., 5

George B., 2, 7, 36,
  89, 105
WHITMORE
  George, 169
WICKS
  James, 39
WIGGINTON
  Presley, 203
WILCOXEN
  ___, 45
WILDMAN
  Elener, 118
  Enos, 24, 98, 116,
    126, 147, 187,
    240, 242, 244, 252
  Jane, 176
  John, 118
WILEY
  Hugh, 129
  Jane, 129
WILKERSON
  John, 18
WILKINSON
  ___, 19, 48
  Elisabeth, 137
  Elizabeth, 70, 101,
    129, 136
  Israel, 161, 170, 207
  John, 17, 61, 63, 68,
    94, 186, 187
  Joseph, 70, 101, 136,
    137, 197
  Macha, 161, 170
  Thomas, 191, 227
  William, 6, 40, 96,
    112, 165, 224,
    254, 257
WILLCOXEN
  Reazon, 254
WILLER
  Catharine, 119
  Henry, 119
WILLIAM
  Charles, 129
  Enos, 52
WILLIAMS
  ___, 38
  Abner, 139
  Amelia, 28
  Charles, 27, 28, 111,
    157, 158, 185, 196
  Daniel, 225
  David, 45
  Elisbaeth S., 146

Ellis, 21, 170, 197,
  225
Enos, 27, 28, 157,
  185, 247, 251
Hannah, 27, 28, 185
Henerietta, 224
Israel, 27, 28, 52, 251
J., 10
Jacob, 110, 113
James, 225
John, 2, 17, 18, 24,
  27, 63, 69, 135,
  137, 172, 186,
  187, 225, 247, 255
Levi, 198
Lydia, 2
Martha, 225
Mary, 157, 185, 225
Mr., 148
N. C., 21, 37, 42, 46,
  50, 108, 117, 127,
  202, 208, 215, 223
Notley C., 9, 22, 25,
  42, 43, 45, 57, 70,
  71, 73, 74, 90,
  101, 104, 146,
  148, 172, 187,
  195, 224, 237
Phineas, 27, 251
Presley, 72, 171
Presly, 180
Samuel, 97, 118
Sarah, 158, 198
Sidney, 27
Sidnor, 247, 251
Syddnah, 185
Sydnah, 157
Sydnor, 185
Thomas, 153, 233,
  240
WILLIAMSON
  David, 18
  John, 8
  William, 101
WILLIS
  Carver, 120
WILSON
  ___, 163
  Ebenezer, 59, 85, 97,
    254
  Edward, 16, 77, 197
  Eseph, 60
  Hannah, 59, 85, 254
  Hannah P., 183, 190

Other Books by Patricia B. Duncan:

1850 Fairfax County and Loudoun County, Virginia Slave Schedule

1850 Fauquier County, Virginia Slave Schedule

1860 Loudoun County, Virginia Slave Schedule

Clarke County, Virginia Will Book Abstracts:
Books A-1 (1836-1904) and 1A-3C (1841-1913)

Fauquier County, Virginia Death Register, 1853-1896

Hunterdon County, New Jersey, 1895 State Census, Part I: Alexandria-Junction

Hunterdon County, New Jersey, 1895 State Census, Part II: Kingwood-West Amwell

Genealogical Abstracts from The Lambertville Press, Lambertville, New Jersey:
4 November 1858 (Vol. 1, Number 1) To 30 October 1861 (Vol. 3, Number 155)

Jefferson County, Virginia/West Virginia Death Records, 1853-1880

Jefferson County, West Virginia, Death Records, 1881-1903

Jefferson County, Virginia, 1802-1813 Personal Property Tax Lists

Jefferson County, Virginia, 1814-1824 Personal Property Tax Lists

Jefferson County, Virginia, 1825-1841 Personal Property Tax Lists

1810-1840 Loudoun County, Virginia Federal Population Census Index

1860 Loudoun County, Virginia Federal Population Census Index

1870 Loudoun County, Virginia Federal Population Census Index

Abstracts from Loudoun County, Virginia Guardian Accounts: Books A-H, 1759-1904

Abstracts of Loudoun County, Virginia Register of Free Negroes, 1844-1861

Index to Loudoun County, Virginia Land Deed Books A-Z, 1757-1800

Index to Loudoun County, Virginia Land Deed Books 2A-2M 1800-1810

Index to Loudoun County, Virginia Land Deed Books 2N-2U 1811-1817

Index to Loudoun County, Virginia Land Deed Books 2V-3D 1817-1822

Index to Loudoun County, Virginia Land Deed Books 3E-3M 1822-1826

Loudoun County, Virginia Birth Register 1853-1879

Loudoun County, Virginia Birth Register 1880-1896

Loudoun County, Virginia Clerks Probate Records
Book 1 (1904-1921) and Book 2 (1922-1938)

(With Elizabeth R. Frain) *Loudoun County, Virginia Marriages after 1850,*
Volume 1, 1851-1880

Loudoun County, Virginia, 1800-1810 Personal Property Taxes

Loudoun County, Virginia, 1826-1834, Personal Property Taxes

Loudoun County, Virginia Will Book Abstracts, Books A-Z, Dec. 1757-Jun. 1841

Other Books by Patricia B. Duncan (continued):

Loudoun County, Virginia Will Book Abstracts, Books 2A-3C, Jun. 1841-Dec. 1879 and Superior Court Books A and B, 1810-1888

Loudoun County, Virginia Will Book Index, 1757-1946

Genealogical Abstracts from The Brunswick Herald, *Brunswick, Maryland: Mar. 6 1891-Dec. 28 1894*

Genealogical Abstracts from The Brunswick Herald, *Brunswick, Maryland: Jan. 4 1895-Dec. 30 1898*

Genealogical Abstracts from The Brunswick Herald, *Brunswick, Maryland: Jan. 6 1899-Dec. 26 1902*

Genealogical Abstracts from The Brunswick Herald, *Brunswick, Maryland: Jan. 2 1903-June 29 1906*

Genealogical Abstracts from The Brunswick Herald, *Brunswick, Maryland: July 6 1906-Feb. 25 1910*

CD: *Loudoun County, Virginia Personal Property Tax List 1782-1850*

343484

Made in the USA